SCOTLAND

SALLY COFFEY

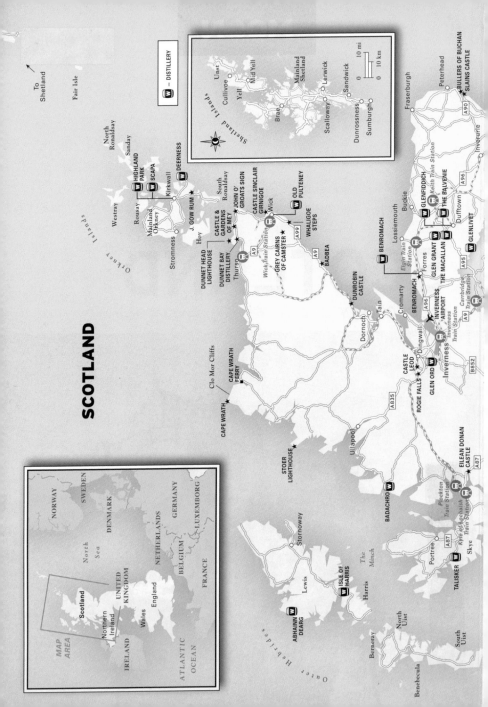

Contents

Although every effort was made to make sure the information in this book was accurate when going to press, research was impacted by the COVID-19 pandemic and things may have changed since the time of writing. Be sure to confirm specific details, like opening hours, closures, and travel guidelines and restrictions, when making your travel plans. For more detailed information, see page 516.

DISCOVER

Scotland

What is it that draws so many people to Scotland, year after year?

There is the kilted-tartan-shortbread view of Scotland, which has been shaped and encouraged by writers from Sir Walter Scott to Diana Gabaldon. There's certainly a poignancy about the place that lies in the fact that its heather-clad hills, glistening lochs, craggy castles, and mighty mountains have been the backdrop to much bloody unrest and rebellion. Those with active imaginations can almost hear the roars of opposing clans on the wind or the cries of warriors hanging in the peat-singed air.

So much has been written about Scotland's obvious charms—her sublime scenery, romantic history and chatty, humorous people, who love to tell a story. All of these are real, and then some.

But to focus only on this romanticized past is to miss the whole point of Scotland, for it's a living, evolving place, not a museum.

Scotland is a land that needs to be experienced, felt, and lived in, not merely admired from the sidelines. For every world-famous tourist attraction, like Edinburgh Castle or Skye's Fairy Pools, there's also the Cairngorms or the Outer

Clockwise from top left: The Royal Mile, Edinburgh; horses in Alladale Reserve; Highland cow; University of Glasgow; White Strand of the Monks, Iona; Ring of Brodgar.

Hebrides, which have all the atmosphere, far fewer people, and lots of room for adventure.

The paradox of Scotland is that it has wide-open spaces, skies that go on forever, and solitude, but when you want it, there is a raucous music session in the pub down the road, too. It's an all-embracing place, where one could never get bored and truly no two experiences are the same (unless you book a generic, whistle-stop tour, in which case, why do you need this guide?).

The essence of Scotland, what makes it really special, underpins our real need to protect it and take a cautious and responsible return to tourism. There really is enough here to see that you don't need to follow the well-trodden trail of top sights.

Scotland is ready to welcome you back, and if you listen to its people and appreciate it for all its variations and endless possibilities, you will receive that famous Scottish welcome most emphatically.

Clockwise from top left: arriving on Iona by boat; Brough of Birsay, Orkney; mussels at the Bosville Hotel in Portree, Skye; Culzean Castle, Ayrshire.

11 TOP
EXPERIENCES

1 Scaling the 822-foot-high (250-m-high) peak of **Arthur's Seat,** a rite of passage for locals and visitors alike that reveals a breathtaking view of Edinburgh (page 54).

2 Driving all or part of the **North Coast 500,** through charming villages and untouched, wild Highland scenery (page 404).

>>>

3 Tasting the heritage, history, and innovation of **Scotch whisky** on **Islay** (page 322) or in **Speyside** (page 180).

<<<

4 Camping out under the stars in **Loch Lomond and the Trossachs National Park** (page 304) or **Galloway Forest Park** (page 275).

>>>

5 Taking in some of Scotland's most iconic **castles,** from sparkling, restored citadels straight out of a fairy tale, to atmospheric and craggy ruined fortresses (page 29).

6 Getting a glimpse into life as it was lived 5,000 years ago at Neolithic sites like the **Calanais Standing Stones** (page 443) or **Skara Brae** (page 487).

>>>

7 Spotting **wildlife in the Cairngorms National Park,** including red squirrels and rutting deer, and reveling in one of the most ambitious rewilding projects in the UK (page 168).

<<<

8 Catching a session at one of the legendary **live music venues in Glasgow,** experiencing Scotland at its most boisterous and welcoming (page 231).

>>>

9 Eating Scottish food at its freshest and most creative in one of **Skye's award-winning restaurants** (page 355).

>>>

10 Teeing off at St. Andrews' **Old Course,** where people have been playing golf, that most Scottish of sports, since the 15th century (page 131).

>>>

11 Bagging **Ben Nevis** (page 337), the tallest of Scotland's Munros, or another of its mountains that rise over 3,000 feet (914 m).

<<<

Planning Your Trip

Where to Go

Edinburgh

Edinburgh, Scotland's handsome capital, is full of history. Explore both the sophisticated 18th-century **New Town** and the crumbling but atmospheric **Old Town,** where medieval wynds (narrow lanes between buildings) will bring you to the **Royal Mile,** a thoroughfare flanked by two of the city's most celebrated attractions: **Edinburgh Castle** and the **Palace of Holyroodhouse.** The latter is overlooked by the volcanic peak of **Arthur's Seat,** which stands in its own windswept hilly park—a small promise of what the Highlands might offer, right here in the city.

Central Scotland

The historic city of **Stirling** is home to what is arguably Scotland's finest castle, and heading a little farther north will bring you to the "Fair City" of **Perth**—Scotland's ancient capital. **Fife** is perhaps best known as being the location of "the home of golf," in the attractive town of **St. Andrews,** but its **East Neuk** seaside villages are one of Scotland's best-kept secrets. And for culture, the rough diamond city of **Dundee** has a few surprises up its sleeve.

The Cairngorms and the North East

For nature lovers, the Cairngorms is one of the most special places in Scotland, home to an enormous number of its most endangered species and the highest concentration of **Munros** in the whole country. Its vastness includes a variety

Stirling Castle

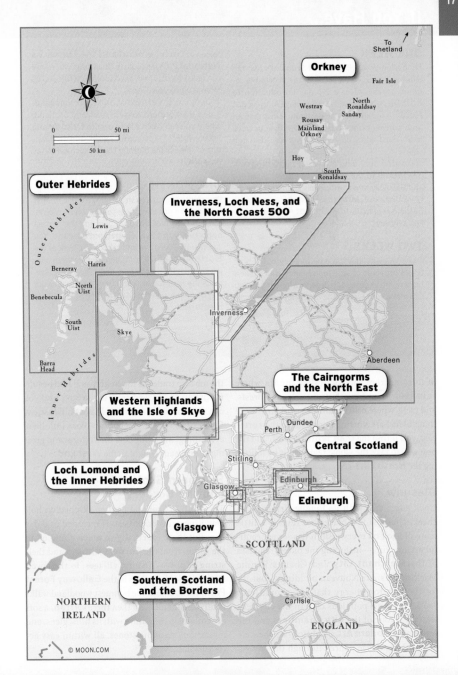

Outer Hebrides

Orkney

To Shetland

Fair Isle

Westray

North Ronaldsay

Sanday

Rousay

Mainland Orkney

Hoy

South Ronaldsay

Inverness, Loch Ness, and the North Coast 500

Outer Hebrides

Lewis

Berneray

Harris

North Uist

Benebecula

South Uist

Barra Head

Inner Hebrides

Skye

Inverness

Aberdeen

The Cairngorms and the North East

Western Highlands and the Isle of Skye

Dundee

Perth

Central Scotland

Stirling

Edinburgh

Loch Lomond and the Inner Hebrides

Glasgow

Edinburgh

Glasgow

SCOTLAND

Southern Scotland and the Borders

Carlisle

NORTHERN IRELAND

ENGLAND

© MOON.COM

0   50 mi

0   50 km

If You Have...

ONE WEEK

Try basing yourself in one of Scotland's two big cities and tacking on some of the accessible regions nearby. After a 2-3-day introduction to **Edinburgh,** spend 2-3 more days in the **East Neuk,** a seaside holiday destination less than an hour's drive north of Edinburgh. Finish your week in **St. Andrews,** home to the world's oldest golf course.

Or, after spending a few days in **Glasgow,** head south to the relatively unvisited Dumfries and Galloway region, hopefully spending a pitch-black night in **Galloway Forest Park,** before heading over to the lovely **Isle of Arran** for a few leisurely days.

TWO WEEKS

A two-week holiday is the perfect amount of time to explore some of Scotland's islands, which take a bit of doing to get to and deserve a longer trip. You can make your way to the Inner Hebrides slowly, taking in **Loch Lomond and the Trossachs National Park** en route to Oban, from where you can reach **Mull.** Then, head south to **Islay** and its famous whisky distilleries.

Or, fly into **Inverness** and take your time heading to the northern coast of mainland Scotland, where you can catch a ferry over to **Orkney** and hole up in a cozy cottage for a week, and then venture to some of the outlying islands, such as Rousay or Sanday.

ONE MONTH

I'm tempted to say you should find a quiet, remote lodging and just stay there for the whole month, but this length of trip does give you the perfect opportunity to travel deeper into Scotland. You can fly into Inverness and take in the bulk of the **North Coast 500,** and then spend a week seeing the **Skye** other visitors don't see. From Skye, catch the ferry to Lewis and Harris and make your way down through the **Outer Hebrides** to Barra over 10 days.

of terrain, from the Arctic-like tundra where **reindeer** roam free, to its moorlands, forests, and glens where other mammals and birds once thought lost are starting to return. To the northeast, you'll find the **Malt Whisky Trail,** and the best way to take the whole region in is by following the **North East 250.**

Glasgow

Cool, edgy, and with its tongue firmly in its cheek, Glasgow is a place that reveals a little more of itself on every visit. It has some beautiful architecture—including the old warehouses of the **Merchant City** and Charles Rennie Mackintosh's Art Nouveau buildings—but it's for the nonstop energy that one should visit Scotland's most populous city. In the city center, take a tour of the **City Chambers** and the **Gallery of Modern Art,** if only to grasp the scale of wealth that once poured through the city via the tobacco trade. To the south you'll find beautiful **green spaces,** whereas in the **East End** you can visit the famous **Barras Market, Glasgow Cathedral,** and the **Necropolis.** For a little bit of everything, including cool thrift stores and great nightlife, head straight to the **West End.**

Southern Scotland and the Borders

The south of Scotland is often skipped on holiday itineraries or, at best, is included as a day trip. But there is actually so much going on in the south, from the **Borders Abbeys** and their string of pretty, historic villages, to the jewel-studded ink-black skies of the **Galloway Forest Park,** with some of the bonniest woodland walks in all of Scotland. And then there's **Arran,** a sort of Scotland in miniature with its hills, glens, and mysterious standing stones, all within easy access of Glasgow.

Loch Lomond and the Inner Hebrides

Dominated by the expansive **Loch Lomond and the Trossachs National Park**—an outdoor playground complete with Scotland's biggest loch, woodland cycling and hiking trails, and many Munros to climb—this region is easily accessible from both Glasgow and Edinburgh. To the west of Loch Lomond, you'll find **Oban**, gateway to the isles of the Inner Hebrides, including **Mull**, from where you can easily take the local ferry over to the spiritual island of **Iona**. You need to travel a little farther south to reach the whisky wonderland of **Islay**; its neighbor **Jura** has a mighty fine distillery to its name too.

Western Highlands and the Isle of Skye

South of Loch Ness, you'll find **Fort William**, the Outdoor Capital of the United Kingdom, where you can go skiing in winter and Munro-bagging at other times. Whatever you do, make sure you travel farther south to visit **Glen Coe**, an extraordinary landscape that will leave you open-mouthed in awe.

The road north to Skye is famously traversed by the **West Highland Rail/Jacobite Steam Train,** and for good reason, the sprawling Isle of Skye is top of most people's Scotland wish list. Photos of the **Fairy Pools, Quiraing,** and the **Old Man of Storr** litter Instagram feeds. To have a more authentic Skye experience, you'd do well to visit some lesser-known spots; the **Cuillin** mountain range is a huge draw for hikers and climbers.

Inverness, Loch Ness, and the North Coast 500

Gateway to the Highlands, Inverness is an attractive city, but most people come here to go somewhere else. For a history lesson, a visit to **Culloden** just east of the city and scene of one of the most brutal battles on Scottish soil, is unforgettable, and whether you believe in its mysterious monster or not, it would feel churlish not to visit **Loch Ness.** For many, though, Inverness is the launchpad for the North Coast 500, an epic driving route that encircles much

driving through Glencoe

Blà Bheinn

Waulkmill Bay, Orkney

of the northwest Highlands, revealing some of Scotland's most stunning scenery en route, from tiny communities to ruined castles, paradisial beaches, and lunar-like landscapes.

Outer Hebrides

For natural beauty and long-held traditions, the long finger of the Outer Hebrides holds an untamed allure. The beaches of **Lewis and Harris** are like something out of a tropical paradise brochure (though not as warm), and Neolithic sites like the **Calanais Standing Stones** rival Stonehenge but without the crowds. There's little tourism infrastructure here, but who needs it? It's a place where the sense of solitude speaks for itself.

Orkney

Scotland's Northern Isles are scattered obliquely off Scotland's northeast coast, as though reaching out to Scandinavia. They are wild, often lonely places, littered with intriguing **standing stones** and lined with **windswept cliffs** where birds congregate in the thousands. **Orkney** is well-groomed and ordered compared to hardy and remote **Shetland,** Scotland's northernmost point.

When to Go

Spring

For **outdoor recreation,** spring (March-May) is best, when the weather is reasonably clement (temperatures average 7°C/45°F to 13°C/55°F, though the term "April showers" refers to the high chance of rain), **wildlife** nest and breed, and the crowds are still thin enough not to scare them away. You'll get good daylight hours for attempting any of the many **Munros** on Skye or in Loch Lomond and the Cairngorms. It's also a good time to visit some of Scotland's most famous sights with fewer other tourists keeping you company.

Summer

Summer (June-August) is when the **festivals hit Edinburgh,** and the best time for dipping your toes into the sea or **loch swimming,** but you'll want to find your own quiet part to appreciate it all without feeling like you're on a merry-go-round with everyone else. Average temperatures in summer range from 15°C (59°F) to 17°C (63 °F) (though can go higher) and though rainfall in western Scotland and the Highlands is almost a certainty throughout the year, it's often dry elsewhere.

Autumn

The **leaves** in autumn (September-November) are something else, a mosaic of golds, yellows, reds and browns, which crunch satisfyingly underfoot. **Cool temperatures**—8°C (46°F) to 14°C (57°F)—give you a good excuse to wrap yourself in a cashmere or lamb's wool blanket and snuggle up after a blustery walk as you listen out for the **rutting deer.** It's also one of the quietest times to visit Scotland.

Winter

Winter (December-February) in Scotland is

loch swimming

cold (the average highest temperature is around 5°C/41°F, but it can be much, much colder) and the winds can be cutting. This is a time of storms, best watched from the window of your holiday home or hotel, of **snow** on the mountains and moors, of **whisky** and fires, and very, very few people to spoil the romance of it all. **Hogmanay** and other holiday traditions help lift the spirits in these months of little daylight.

Know Before You Go

Getting There

Both **Glasgow** and **Edinburgh** are well connected with international flights from the United States, Canada, and Europe, and they are accessible via numerous flights and trains from **London** and other parts of the **United Kingdom.**

FROM ELSEWHERE IN EUROPE

There are numerous options for reaching Scotland from Europe. The cheapest way is by air, on **easyJet** flights from **Berlin** to Edinburgh, for instance, for as little as £35 each way (flight time around 2 hours) and from **Amsterdam** to either Glasgow or Edinburgh for a similar price (flight time 1 hour 40 minutes). For destinations in the Highlands and North East, Inverness and Aberdeen also receive some international flights, so keep a lookout for deals from your point of origin.

However, it's also relatively easy to get to Scotland by train from Europe if you've got the time. **Eurostar trains** from Amsterdam, for example, will get you to London in just over four hours and cost from as little as £40 one way. From London, if you book in advance, you should be able to get a train to Glasgow or Edinburgh for around £35 one way and it will take another 4-5 hours.

FROM NORTH AMERICA

Several major airlines fly from North America to Scotland, including **Virgin Atlantic** and **Delta,** both of which fly direct to Edinburgh from **New York**'s JFK (flight time around 7 hours, from $900 return). **Air Canada** flies from **Toronto** to Glasgow and Edinburgh with a stopover in London Heathrow or France (total travel time 10-12 hours, from $1,000).

FROM NEW ZEALAND, AUSTRALIA, AND SOUTH AFRICA

The main airline flying between Australasia and Scotland is **Emirates,** which has a flight from **Auckland** to Edinburgh via Dubai (total travel time of 30 hours, from NZD 2,250). From Sydney, you can fly with Emirates to Glasgow in 25 hours for around AUD 1,900. For South Africa, **British Airways** has flights from **Johannesburg** to London Heathrow, where you can connect to Scotland (19 hours total travel time, from ZAR 11,250).

Getting Around

Though there are some parts of Scotland that are well connected by public transport, traveling this way can take a good deal of planning, and having your own car still offers the most flexibility. Despite Edinburgh being the capital, **Glasgow** is by far the most well-connected hub, with direct trains and buses to all main towns and cities. If you are traveling from Edinburgh, you will often have to pick up a connection in Glasgow.

PLANE

There are some instances—usually when you're short of time—when you might prefer to fly within Scotland. This is particularly the case for destinations such as the Outer Hebrides and the Northern Isles, which are deserving of trips in themselves and take quite a bit of doing to get to. In these cases, Scottish airline **Loganair** is your friend (www.loganair.co.uk).

TRAIN

Traveling by train in Scotland is quite simple, straightforward, and reasonably affordable. The main train operator is **Scotrail** (www.scotrail.co.uk). There can be delays, especially in bad weather, but it's still preferable to taking a bus. If your destination has a train station nearby I'd always recommend this over taking a bus or coach. There are some train routes in Scotland that are bucket-list routes in themselves for many, including the **West Highland Rail/Jacobite Steam Train** and the **Kyle Line,** which take travelers from Glasgow or Inverness to Skye, respectively.

RENTAL CAR

Car hire in Scotland is well worth it. A lot of places are very hard to get to without your own wheels, and it's a lot cheaper hiring a car than paying for numerous individual tours. Road signs are pretty clear, and on the whole big places are well signposted, but you may want to do a bit of pre-planning if you're staying somewhere small or a bit off the main tourist trail. Be ready for some narrow, single-track roads if you're getting into the countryside and remember that automobiles drive on the left side of the road in Scotland.

BUS

Taking the bus in Scotland is marginally cheaper than taking the train but the main benefit is that there are lots more places (smaller villages, for example) that have bus routes passing through them than have train stations. It's worth bearing in mind that the more remote the place you visit, the fewer local buses there tend to be, so you really will have to plan carefully (or exercise patience) to get around this way. The main bus operators are **Scottish Citylink** (www.citylink.co.uk) and **Stagecoach** (www.stagecoachbus.com). **Traveline** is the best resource for planning your travel by bus in Scotland (www.travelinescotland.com).

FERRY

Many of Scotland's islands are accessible by ferry, including the Inner and Outer Hebrides, the Isle of Skye, and the Northern Islands. Unless you want to take a domestic flight to

get around the islands by ferry

save time to reach some of these destinations, this is a romantic and fairly efficient way to travel, with most ferries offering both passenger and car ferry service. Most ferries are run by **Caledonian MacBrayne** (www.calmac.co.uk).

Passports and Visas

There are few visa restrictions if you are visiting Scotland for no more than six months. If you are an **EU citizen** or come from Switzerland or one of the non-EU member states of the EEA (Norway, Liechtenstein, and Iceland), you do not need a visa. Currently, there is **no visa requirement** for citizens of the **United States, Canada, Australia,** or **New Zealand** who plan to visit Scotland for six or fewer months. Anyone planning to come for more than six months will need to get an entry clearance certificate from the British Embassy in their home country before they travel.

To enter the United Kingdom, travelers from **South Africa** do need a Standard visitor visa (www.gov.uk/standard-visitor-visa), which currently costs £95 and allows stays of up to six months.

You will of course need a **passport** if you are traveling here from outside the United Kingdom, and may also require proof of vaccination and/or a negative COVID test, depending on current pandemic-related restrictions. For the latest advice on travel documents, check the website of the **U.K. Foreign and Commonwealth Office** (www.gov.uk/government/organisations/uk-visas-and-immigration), while for the latest **coronavirus travel advice,** visit www.gov.uk/uk-border-control.

What to Pack

Scotland is quite well facilitated, so you can likely pick up anything you forget at home upon arrival here, but as a general rule, think **layers:** remember that the weather can vary quite a lot here, so having warm clothing to layer on or off (particularly if its waterproof) can be a godsend. For outdoorsy travelers, **comfortable walking shoes** are a must. And don't forget to pack a **European plug adapter** for your electronic devices.

Best of Scotland

You could spend months, years even, traveling Scotland and not run out of places to visit and things to do amid its wide-open landscapes, dramatic coastline, and innumerable islands. But even 10 days can give you a good introduction to the country and its variety, from nature spots to electric cities, stirring castles, haunting heritage sites, and elegant architecture. Consider the below itinerary a very rough sketch; if you have the luxury of time, it's worth spending longer in each spot to truly savor its atmosphere and character or detouring away from some of the well-trodden routes.

Though it's possible to travel much of Scotland by train and bus, for maximum flexibility, you'll want a rental car, especially after leaving the cities of Edinburgh and Glasgow.

Days 1-2: Edinburgh

Start your first day in Edinburgh in the **Old Town.** Of course, you could go to **Edinburgh Castle,** but it would take up a big chunk of your day, so if you're happy to settle for a photo opportunity instead, head down to **Grassmarket** via **Victoria Street,** a gently curved shopping street that is widely believed to be the inspiration behind Diagon Alley in the Harry Potter novels. Climb the steps up to the castle esplanade for a closer look before heading into the **Camera Obscura** for a fun couple of hours. The nearby but hidden away **Jolly Judge** is one of my favorite spots for a low-key lunch along the **Royal Mile,** where you should pop in to see the incredible interior of **St. Giles' Cathedral.** From here, just a few minutes' walk will bring you to the **National Museum of Scotland,** whose halls are filled with fascinating exhibits, and which has panoramic views from the 7th floor roof terrace. Sightseeing done, jump in a cab to **Prestonfield** for a decadent dinner and overnight stay.

On your second day in the city, you'll want to cross over to the graceful New Town. You can

Arthur's Seat, Edinburgh

Jacobite Steam Train crossing the Glenfinnan Viaduct

have breakfast in one of the many good cafés around trendy **Broughton Street,** before pottering along to the **Scottish National Portrait Gallery,** where you can have a history, architecture, and art lesson all in one. Head west a few blocks from here to **Charlotte Square** to admire the neoclassical architecture, then pop into **The Oxford,** the favorite pub of author Ian Rankin's Inspector Rebus, for a pint. Afterward, climb the **Scott Monument** for city views, head to **Stockbridge** for dinner, and finish your night with comedy at **The Stand.**

Day 3: Glasgow

From Edinburgh, it's around an hour by car or train to Glasgow, where if you want to pack as much as possible into your day, you should buy a ticket for the **City Sightseeing** bus and start your tour with a visit to the oldest part of the city at **Glasgow Cathedral** and the **Necropolis** that overlooks it. The bus stops at lots of key sights, but the absolute must-visit is the **Kelvingrove Art Gallery and Museum.** From here, it's just a few minutes' walk to **University of Glasgow,**

where you can join an afternoon tour. For dinner and drinks, walk through Kelvingrove Park to **Dockyard Social,** a lively food market with regular DJ sets and live music.

Day 4: Loch Lomond and Glen Coe

From Glasgow, it's just a half-hour drive to **Loch Lomond and the Trossachs National Park,** home to breathtaking scenery, much of which can be viewed from the main A82 road. En route, stop at **The Village Rest** for warm hospitality and a bite to eat, then pull into the **Falls of Falloch** for a leisurely short woodland stroll to a beautiful waterfall. From here, you drive north out of the park, heading toward **Glen Coe,** an epic valley with numerous steep-sided mountains and myriad waterfalls, where you'll be stopping all the time to take photos. Drive all the way to the village of **Glencoe** for the full edge-of-your-seat driving experience. Visit the **Glencoe War Memorial** and take a few moments to reflect on the massacre of 30 members of Clan MacDonald, who were punished for a perceived slight against the legitimacy of William III and Mary II in the 17th century. For dinner, music, and a bed for the night, head to the warm and hospitable **Clachaig Inn.**

Day 5: Fort William to Skye

Fort William is just a half-hour drive from Glen Coe and is the launchpad for that most mighty of mountains: **Ben Nevis.** If you don't have time to hike the mountain entirely (it requires a full day), you can join one of the excellent walks along the North Face of the mountain with **Wild Roots Highland Guiding,** where you can hear stories about the landscape and its people (bring a packed lunch). Then you'll need to get back on the road if you're going to make Skye by nightfall. It's only an hour by car to **Mallaig,** from where you can catch the ferry to **Skye,** but the scenery is magnificent, and you should allow yourself time and space to appreciate it. Without a doubt the highlight of the journey is **Glenfinnan,** where the train crosses the huge viaduct, and the **Glenfinnan Monument** stands poignantly on the banks of **Loch Shiel.** When you arrive in Mallaig, grab some seafood at **Cornerstone Restaurant** if you need to kill some time before the ferry.

Days 6-7: Isle of Skye

It's almost impossible to squeeze Skye into just two days, so if you really want to visit the Misty Isle, I implore you to try and eke out more time if you can. After breakfast in the hotel, head out on a wildlife tour with **Skyefari,** which will take you to secret corners of the island with an expert guide. Once back at the hotel, you can entertain other guests with tales of otter and eagle sightings over a drink by the fireside, before sitting down for a three-course dinner.

The following morning, pack up and head to the north of the island and drive a circuit of the **Trotternish Peninsula,** where you can park up and trek to the **Old Man of Storr.** Pop into the picturesque harbor town of **Portree** for lunch at one of the many good cafés and restaurants. In the afternoon, check into the **Stein Inn** for the night, before popping next door for dinner at **Loch Bay.**

Old Man of Storr

Plockton Inn

kayaking Loch Ness

Day 8: Skye to Loch Ness

Leaving the island over the **Skye Bridge** to **Kyle of Lochalsh,** it's yet another spectacular drive to reach Loch Ness, detouring slightly to charming **Plockton** for lunch at the **Plockton Inn,** before returning to the A87 to pass by **Eilean Donan** castle. Once you reach **Fort Augustus,** follow the southern shoreline of the loch to check into one of the camping pods at **Loch Ness Shores** and head out for an afternoon kayaking trip in search of Nessie. Back on dry land, take the steep walk up to **Craigdarroch Inn** for dinner, drinks, and a bird's eye view of the loch.

Day 9: Inverness to Royal Deeside

From your campsite at Loch Ness, drive an hour north to the **Culloden Battlefield** and its informative visitor center, for a moving experience. Afterward, have a traditional Scottish lunch at the **Cawdor Tavern,** before driving south into

the **Cairngorms National Park.** You're heading for Royal Deeside, where you can take an afternoon tour of **Balmoral,** the summer home of the British royal family. Have dinner at the **Rothesay Rooms,** housed in the former Old Royal Station, and bed down for the night at **The Fife Arms.**

Day 10: Return to Edinburgh

From here, it's a two-hour drive south to **Stirling,** where you'll want to visit both **Stirling Castle**—one of the most contested fortresses in Scottish history—and the **National Wallace Monument,** the city's two most iconic landmarks. I'd start with the castle, having lunch with a view at the café, before taking the scenic walk to the monument. Then it's time to return to Edinburgh, where you may have an evening flight to catch, or hopefully you can check into the **Edinburgh Grand** for a luxurious last night of your holiday.

Top Five Castles

It's estimated there were once as many as 3,000 castles in Scotland, and though up to half have now disappeared from the landscape, there are still around 1,500 scattered throughout the country, from fairy-tale fortresses that have been beautifully preserved or restored, to craggy ruins that cling to clifftops. Often strategically placed at the head of a loch, on a headland, or perched high above a royal burgh, Scotland's castles were frequently the sites of conflict, built to ward off invaders from England or to act as the stronghold of a ruling clan, and many of the ones that survive still show their battle scars. Often castles were status symbols, with ornamental details that were meant to show off the owners' power and wealth. Castles are almost as synonymous with Scotland as its glens and lochs, and most visits will take in at least one castle, where you can hear dramatic tales of clan battles, illicit liaisons, and ruthless royals, in the very places where history was made.

Eilean Donan Castle

EDINBURGH CASTLE

Seen from almost anywhere you go in the capital, Edinburgh Castle, atop an old volcanic plug, is an idol of Scotland and has defended the nation for centuries. Within its walls are the Honours of Scotland (Scotland's crown jewels), as well as the Stone of Destiny, and Edinburgh's oldest building: St Margaret's Chapel. Even if you don't visit the castle itself, keep an ear out for the One O'clock Gun, which is fired every day except Sundays (page 43).

STIRLING CASTLE

This castle, located between the Highlands and the Lowlands, was once so integral to the swing of power in the country that it was said, "He who holds Stirling, holds Scotland." Though it fell into disrepair for many years, careful restoration has returned some of the interiors to their Renaissance glory (page 111).

DUNNOTTAR CASTLE

Formidable, dramatic, historic—there are many adjectives to describe this ruinous Aberdeenshire castle, where the Honours of Scotland were once hidden away, but none can conjure that feeling you get when you first spy it hanging on precariously atop sheer cliffs above the angry North Sea below (page 158).

ALDOURIE CASTLE

Most visitors to Loch Ness head to Urquhart Castle, a ruin on the western shores that is saturated with tourists in summer, but for a castle visit with more privacy, the exclusive-use Scottish baronial palace of Aldourie on the southern shores is truly spectacular. If you can't stretch to hiring the whole castle, there are also some lovely, quaint cottages to rent within the grounds (page 401).

EILEAN DONAN CASTLE

When you first see this castle on the road to the Skye Bridge, you'll probably feel like you know it, even if you've never been here before, as it's a popular filming location and features regularly on shortbread tins and the like. Much of what you see was re-created in the 20th century, but it doesn't lose any of its atmosphere for it (page 403).

Wildlife and Whisky

This is a great itinerary for those who have already visited Scotland's most famous sights, or who want to explore parts of the country that are often overlooked. The under-visited North East has a mix of cool cities, wild coastline, and genteel countryside. This route offers a snapshot of some of the best things to do in the region, where you may well be surprised at the diversity of wildlife, wealth of castles and other historic sites, and—of course—a venture into the whisky heartland of Scotland: Speyside.

Day 1: Edinburgh

Spend your day in the capital performing a Scottish rite of passage, climbing **Arthur's Seat** for one of the best views of the city. Afterward, you can walk or cycle along the **Water of Leith** to **Dean Village,** a picturesque old milling community. Freshen up at your hotel before heading out for dinner in **Leith,** a destination for Edinburgh's seafood-loving gourmands.

Day 2: Fife

Fife is Edinburgh's well-guarded secret, where many locals come to weekend or take seaside holidays, and it's just an hour's drive north across the Firth of Forth to its most picturesque corner, the **East Neuk.** This string of cute, historic fishing villages, which sit along the **Fife Coastal Path,** are peaceful and interesting, with a sustainable food and drink scene that means you are spoiled for choice. Start your exploration with a stretch of the legs on **Elie's Ruby Bay Beach** and then continue to the village of **Crail;** with its sweet restaurants and shops, it's worthy of an afternoon stop. For dinner and a place to sleep, head inland to the **Peat Inn.**

Day 3: Dundee and Aberdeen

Up early, you shouldn't pass through the old university town of **St. Andrews** without a round of golf on the **Old Course.** Then it's on toward the revitalized industrial town of Dundee, where you should have lunch in **The Newport** restaurant

Dean Village

a dram of Glenfiddich whisky

adult male capercaillie

Glen Grant whisky

before crossing the Tay into the city itself to take at least a brief look around the **Dundee V&A.** Keep heading north along the coast to Aberdeen, another of Scotland's well-kept secrets, where you can have dinner at **Silver Darling** by the harbor, before heading into the center for drinks at one of the city's cool, late-night bars.

Days 4-5: The Speyside Whisky Trail

Squeeze in a few hours in the picturesque **Old Aberdeen** neighborhood before heading north to **Speyside**—Scotland's densest whisky region—about an hour northwest. If you only have a few days to spend here, then you'll probably want to base yourself in **Dufftown** or nearby **Craigellachie.** On your first day, pay a visit to the **Dallas Dhu Distillery,** a museum of all things whisky, and pop into **Speyside Cooperage.** For dinner, check out **Toots at the Train Station** in Rothes.

On your second day, you could visit one or two **distilleries** on your own, but for a more rounded visit, I recommend booking a trip with **Speyside Walking Tours,** run by a pair of locals who have inside knowledge of the industry and provide a gourmet picnic. This is also a great way to get a taste of the **Speyside Way.** Head to the area around Aviemore in the **Cairngorms** before nightfall to find your accommodation without any stress.

Day 6: The Cairngorms

With only one day in the Cairngorms, prioritize seeing some of the national park's wildlife and hearing about its important rewilding work. **Instinct Guides** offers excellent guided tours on which you can expect to see black grouse, capercaillie and red deer, and there is also an option to stay overnight in a tepee. Take the easy hike around **Loch Morlich** with your newfound knowledge of the forest, followed by a hearty dinner at the **Old Bridge Inn.**

Day 7: Return to Edinburgh

If you're up early, get a taste of walking in the Cairngorms with a quick **hike** before your 3-hour drive back to **Edinburgh.** En route, stop for a quick tour of **Scone Palace,** where you can have lunch at the café—after all, you can't visit Scotland without visiting at least one palace.

Island-Hopping the Inner Hebrides

You haven't experienced Scotland until you've visited at least some of its islands, and the Inner Hebrides are some of the most accessible. Below is a suggested route for visiting a couple of the islands if you're time constrained, but if you have more time, I recommend spending longer on the islands to slip into their unique, relaxed pace.

Day 1: Glasgow

To see Glasgow in a day without feeling worn out, hop on two wheels with **Glasgow Bike Tours,** which offers trips that start and end in one of the city's craft breweries and take you past city landmarks in **Glasgow Green** and on the **Clyde Walkway.** Afterward, head out to **BAaD** in the east end for dinner and drinks.

Day 2: Loch Lomond and the Trossachs National Park

Incredibly accessible from Glasgow, Loch Lomond and the Trossachs National Park is an outdoor adventurer's paradise. Hikers who want to bag a Munro can hike **Ben Lomond,** or take a guided kayaking trip with **Loch Lomond Leisure** to ply the waters of Scotland's largest loch. Spend the night in the **Inn on Loch Lomond** and be sure to dine in its very good restaurant, Mr C's.

Days 3-4: Mull, Iona, and Staffa

It's about an hour and a half drive from Loch Lomond to the port town of **Oban,** where you should fill up on some fabulous seafood at the **Oban Seafood Hut** before catching the ferry across to **Craignure on Mull.** Head west toward **Fionnphort,** where you can catch the 10-minute ferry to the **Isle of Iona** and explore the famous **Iona Abbey.** Spend the night on Iona at **St. Columba Hotel.**

On your second day in the Inner Hebrides, head back to Fionnphort for a fresh-caught seafood lunch at **The Creel** before taking a day tour to the **Isle of Staffa,** to see the basalt columns of **Fingal's Cave** and the island's **puffin colony.** After returning to Mull, drive to **Tobermory,** the main town, for the night, where you can have a delicious dinner at **Hebridean Lodge.**

Day 5: Return to Glasgow

En route back to Craignure and the ferry to Glasgow, stop at moody **Duart Castle** before getting on the boat. It's just over 2 hours from Oban to Glasgow, where you can splurge on a meal at **Bar Brett** for the last night of your trip.

Fingal's Cave, Staffa

Best Road Trips

With miles upon miles of open road and big-screen scenery, driving in Scotland is truly memorable. The roads are thrilling, with twists, bends and blind summits that will really test your driving skills, and navigating the many single-track roads takes concentration and anticipation (plus some reading up on the rules of the road). But if you have the stomach for it, you'll be able to reach some of the most remote areas and be left slack-jawed at panoramic views of mountains, glens, and coastline.

THE NORTH COAST 500

515 miles/830 km; 5-7 days; page 404
Encircling the northwest Highlands, this world-famous route offers something for everyone—lush, green countryside, white-sand beaches, castles, traditional villages, and wild, barren lunarscapes. If you don't want to do it all, there are a few smaller sections that will still wow, including the short **Road to Diabaig** in Wester Ross (page 427) and the **Road to Drumbeg** (page 424) farther north.

sheep in the Quiraing

THE NORTH EAST 250

250 miles/402 km; 2-3 days; page 148
A newer, shorter alternative to the NC500, this route, which travels through the northeast Highlands, is a more manageable trip for those with less time, through **whisky country,** taking in Aberdeenshire's castles and rugged North Sea coastline. If you yearn for more excitement, then make sure you include the **Snow Roads** through the **Cairngorms** (page 173), in particular the road down through Glenshee.

TROTTERNISH PENINSULA, SKYE

50 miles/80 km; 3-4 hours; page 357
Skye is an island of huge proportions and other-worldly landscapes, and nowhere is this more evident than on its northernmost peninsula, the Trotternish. Here, in the interior, you will find two of the island's most famous landmarks: the dagger-like **Old Man of Storr** and its neighboring pin-

nacles, and the folded hills of the **Quiraing,** all the result of a dramatic landslip. Skirt the peninsula and you'll see these, as well as some of Skye's more forgotten, atmospheric places, such as **Staffin,** where dinosaurs once roamed.

THE GLEN COE ROAD

30 miles/48 km; 1-2 hours; page 332
Pretty much an essential route for anyone traveling north into the western Highlands from Glasgow, this road, which snakes through Scotland's most scenic valley of Glen Coe, doesn't have a dull moment. There are straight sections of blanket bog before the road ascends, flanked by mighty mountains like the **Three Sisters,** which were carved by glaciers. Countless waterfalls, including the **Meeting of the Three Waters,** continue to cut crevices through their steep sides. You can drive it in less than an hour, but it's unlikely you'll be able to resist pulling over into one of the viewpoints.

Edinburgh

"Edina! Scotia's darling seat! All hail thy palaces and towers," declared Robert Burns in his 18th-century *Address to Edinburgh.*

Today, millions of travelers descend on the medieval city of Edinburgh to see the very same noble buildings that so enraptured Scotland's most celebrated poet. They walk the historic Royal Mile at the center of the city's Old Town, beginning at Edinburgh Castle, perched over the metropolis on its ancient volcanic seat, and follow as it slopes down all the way to the Palace of Holyroodhouse, the Queen's official home in Edinburgh.

On the other side of Princes Street Gardens, the neoclassical "New Town," which is not actually that new, has lots of interesting historical

Highlights

Look for ★ to find recommended sights, activities, dining, and lodging.

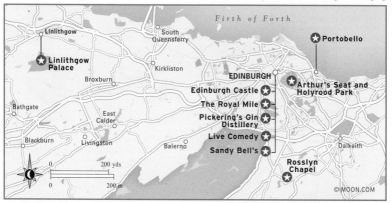

Firth of Forth

Linlithgow
South Queensferry
★ Portobello
★ Linlithgow Palace
Broxburn
Kirkliston
EDINBURGH
★ Edinburgh Castle
★ Arthur's Seat and Holyrood Park
Bathgate
East Calder
★ The Royal Mile
★ Pickering's Gin Distillery
Blackburn
Livingston
Balerno
★ Live Comedy
★ Sandy Bell's
Dalkeith
0   200 yds
0   200 m
★ Rosslyn Chapel
© MOON.COM

★ **Edinburgh Castle:** Perched high above the city, this iconic fortress—the most besieged castle in Britain—has stood to protect the city of Edinburgh for 900 years (page 43).

★ **The Royal Mile:** The epicenter of the Old Town, this thoroughfare is home to some of the city's most historic buildings as well as a network of intriguing closes (residential areas that could be locked up at night to keep undesirables out) that tell another side of the city's story (page 47).

★ **Arthur's Seat and Holyrood Park:** Hike this ancient volcano, the summit of a group of hills to the east of the city center, for panoramic views and a calm retreat from city life (page 54).

★ **Pickering's Gin Distillery:** This tiny distillery in Summerhall, one of the city's coolest cultural spaces, is the place to sample one of the most reputable names in Scotland's gin boom (page 66).

★ **See side-splitting comedy:** Shows at The Stand are legendary, but festival favorites, such as Gilded Balloon, also present laugh-out-loud sets and will hopefully be back with a year-round venue soon (page 69).

★ **Hear traditional music at Sandy Bell's:** Squeeze yourself into this busy bar where there is fantastic folk music every night of the week and a lively, welcoming crowd (page 85).

★ **Portobello:** East of the city center, the seaside suburb of Portobello is a welcome surprise, with grand Georgian villas leading down to golden sands and the sea (page 99).

★ **Linlithgow Palace:** While the interiors of the birthplace of Mary, Queen of Scots, have been ravaged by fire and decay, the medieval walls are remarkably intact (page 100).

★ **Rosslyn Chapel:** Admire the intricate stone masonry of this 15th-century church and decide for yourself if the carvings hide clues from the notoriously secretive Knights Templar (page 102).

Edinburgh Area

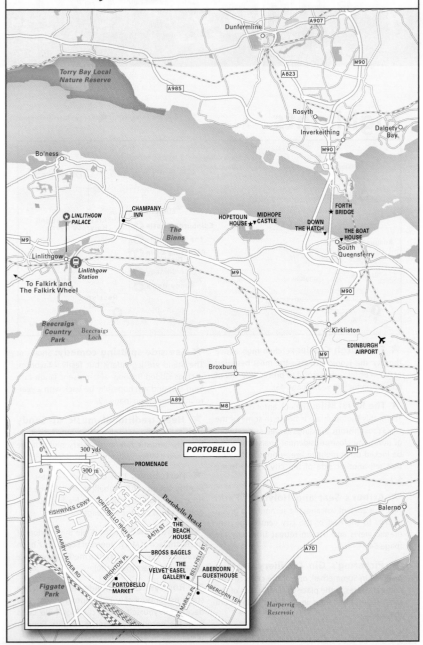

Dunfermline

A907

Torry Bay Local
Nature Reserve

A985

A823

M90

Rosyth

Inverkeithing

Dalgety
Bay

M90

Bo'ness

LINLITHGOW
PALACE

CHAMPANY
INN

HOPETOUN
HOUSE

MIDHOPE
CASTLE

DOWN
THE HATCH

FORTH
BRIDGE

THE BOAT
HOUSE

The
Binns

South
Queensferry

M9

Linlithgow

Linlithgow
Station

To Falkirk and
The Falkirk Wheel

M9

M90

Beecraigs
Country
Park

Beecraigs
Loch

Kirkliston

EDINBURGH
AIRPORT

Broxburn

M9

A89

M8

A71

Balerno

A70

Harperrig
Reservoir

PORTOBELLO

0   300 yds

0   300 m

PROMENADE

FISHWIVES CSWY

PORTOBELLO HIGH ST

BATH ST

Portobello Beach

BELLFIELD ST

THE
BEACH
HOUSE

SIR HARRY LAUDER RD

BROSS BAGELS

THE
VELVET EASEL
GALLERY

ABERCORN
GUESTHOUSE

BRIGHTON PL

PORTOBELLO
MARKET

ST MARK'S PL

ABERCORN TER

Figgate
Park

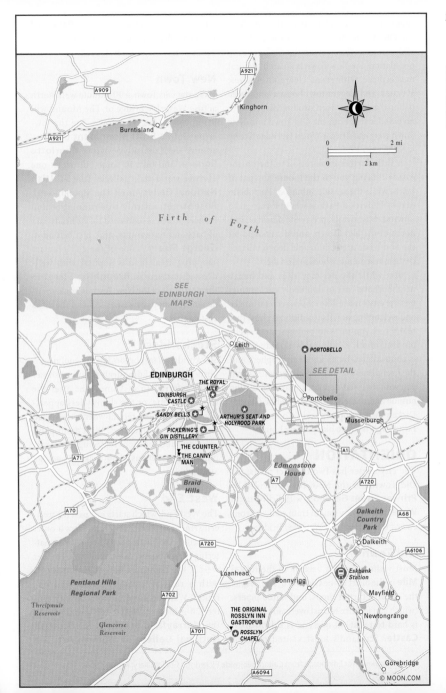

sites that are often a lot quieter than those in the Old Town. Built between the 18th and 19th centuries to cope with the city's growing population, the New Town is an architectural masterpiece, with grand Georgian squares, avenues, and elegant townhouses, and three national galleries within strolling distance. It's no wonder that both the Old Town and New Town were classified a World Heritage Site by UNESCO in 1995.

A little further exploration to the northeast will bring you to the foodie hotspot of Leith, while the seaside suburb of Portobello east of Holyrood Park is where locals go to unwind. Meanwhile, pretty Stockbridge, just north of the New Town, and Bruntsfield on the Southside are fashionable urban villages that embrace a more bohemian vibe.

But, while the heritage sites and buzzy neighborhoods are undoubtedly enchanting, it is the city's maze-like closes, secret tunnels, and welcoming howffs (traditional pubs) that really reel you in. And perhaps most spellbinding of all, Edinburgh's gloomy beauty is contradicted by its jovial atmosphere and the friendliness of its people, who will charm you with their self-deprecating and disarming humor and make you feel much like Charles Dickens, who famously said: "Coming back to Edinburgh is to me like coming home."

ORIENTATION

The city center has two distinct areas: the Old Town and the New Town, divided by **Princes Street Gardens**, with **Edinburgh Waverley**, the city's main train station, at one end of the gardens, on Waverley Bridge.

Old Town

Most visitors make a beeline to the **Royal Mile** in the heart of the Old Town, and despite the crowds, tartan shops, and kilted pipers, (which can feel like tourist overload), this area is hard to resist. At one end is **Edinburgh Castle**, Scotland's most visited paid-for attraction; at the other end is the **Palace of Holyroodhouse**, the official Scottish residence of Her Majesty The Queen.

New Town

From the Old Town, a 10-minute walk north across Waverley Bridge or The Mound will bring you to the New Town. See the towering Gothic **Scott Monument** up close, admire the exquisite design of **Charlotte Square**, and take in some culture at one of three world-class galleries (the **Scottish National Gallery** is on The Mound itself). **Rose Street**, a narrow road running behind Princes Street, is renowned for its heady mix of bars and restaurants, and, just behind it, **George Street** is one of the city's fancier shopping areas, and is popular with well-dressed partygoers. **Broughton Street** in the northeast of the New Town is home to independent shops as well as some of the city's best gay bars.

Stockbridge

Stockbridge is fast becoming the cool neighborhood where Edinburgh natives—sometimes referred to as Dunedians after the city's old name, or the slightly less appealing Edinburghers—retreat when they've had enough of Scottish clichés. With gastropubs, cafés, and antique shops replacing the former junk shops, it retains a laid-back, village-like atmosphere.

West End

The West End, which starts just past the western fringes of Princes Street, offers a quiet oasis from the bustle of city life, with a smattering of boutiques, cafés, and bars. Farther west is the transport hub of **Haymarket**, with a railway station, trams, and bus routes. Walking distance from the city center (20 minutes), West End's proximity to the **Murrayfield Stadium**, the **Scottish National Gallery of Modern Art**, and

---

Previous: view over Edinburgh from Calton Hill; inside Pickering's Gin Distillery; Arthur's Seat.

Dean Village make it a smart choice for those looking for affordable accommodations.

Southside

From Chambers Street south, you are in what is known as Edinburgh's Southside, largely a student area with a string of attractive Victorian villas and tenement buildings. Today, most visitors head to the neighboring districts of Bruntsfield, a low-key area that is home to lots of well-priced restaurants and quirky gift shops.

Leith

A short bus ride northeast of the city center will bring you to the historic Port of Leith where Mary, Queen of Scots, arrived back from her exile in France to stake her claim on the throne. Today it's a foodie destination, with lots of good seafood restaurants and cafés lining the waterfront and trickling out in the roads off the main port. It is also home to the Royal Yacht Britannia.

PLANNING YOUR TIME

Edinburgh isn't huge, and many of the real tourist draws can be explored on foot, including the countless closes and wynds (alleyways just wide enough to allow a horse and cart to wind their way through) that lead off from the Royal Mile and other parts of the Old Town.

Allow a full day to explore the attractions along the Royal Mile properly (more if you are venturing up to Arthur's Seat).

However, tourism is becoming a bit of a problem in the city center, and, as the Royal Mile becomes congested with visitors, locals complain that it has become something of a theme park, particularly during festival season and Hogmanay (New Year's Eve).

A good compromise is to spend a day or two seeing the main sights in and around the Old Town and along or off Princes Street in the New Town before escaping to one of the cooler, less congested neighborhoods for a more authentic taste of Edinburgh life. You may even want to consider visiting out of season, such as in autumn (October and November), when you'll be able to take your time exploring and spend a lot less time queuing.

If you are planning to visit during Hogmanay or the Edinburgh Festivals (most of the month of August), try to book accommodations around six months in advance to secure your top choice. This is particularly important in the wake of the coronavirus, as the cancellation of 2020 events and much smaller festivals in 2021 means people are chomping at the bit to get there.

Popular restaurants such as The Witchery by the Castle need booking in advance, and, if you are planning on doing a tour of The Real Mary King's Close or one of the more popular ghost tours, then it would be prudent to book a couple of weeks ahead, particularly in high season (April-August).

Itinerary Ideas

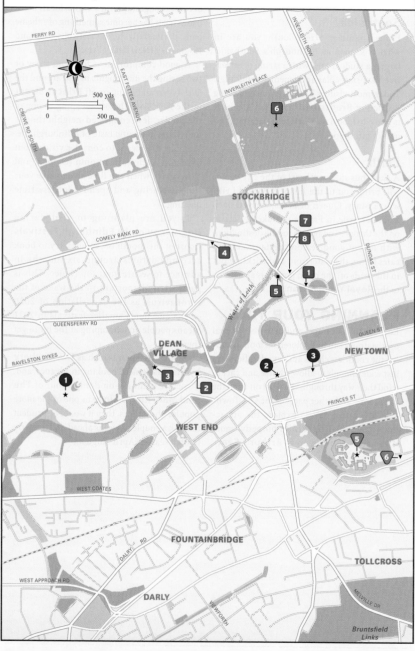

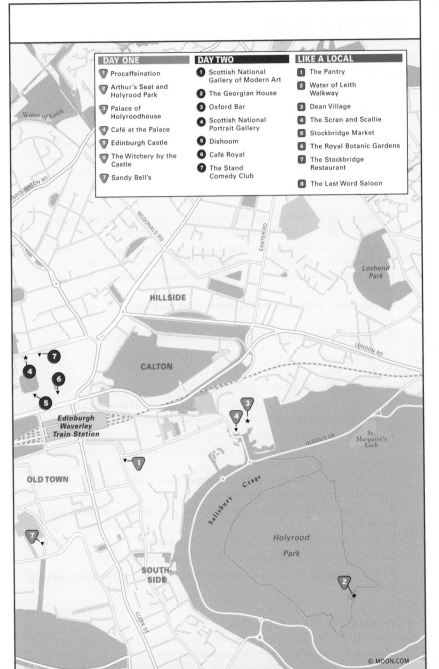

DAY ONE

1. Procaffeination
2. Arthur's Seat and Holyrood Park
3. Palace of Holyroodhouse
4. Café at the Palace
5. Edinburgh Castle
6. The Witchery by the Castle
7. Sandy Bell's

DAY TWO

1. Scottish National Gallery of Modern Art
2. The Georgian House
3. Oxford Bar
4. Scottish National Portrait Gallery
5. Dishoom
6. Café Royal
7. The Stand Comedy Club

LIKE A LOCAL

1. The Pantry
2. Water of Leith Walkway
3. Dean Village
4. The Scran and Scallie
5. Stockbridge Market
6. The Royal Botanic Gardens
7. The Stockbridge Restaurant
8. The Last Word Saloon

© MOON.COM

Itinerary Ideas

DAY 1

Spend your first day taking in the sights of the Royal Mile and Old Town.

1 Stop into **Procaffeination** on St. Mary's Street, off the Royal Mile, for a quick breakfast.

2 Take an early-morning hike up to **Arthur's Seat** in Holyrood Park (weather depending)—first thing is often the quietest time here and you may even have the place to yourself.

3 After your hike, head to the **Palace of Holyroodhouse** at the foot of Holyrood Park to learn about the royal history of Edinburgh, from Mary, Queen of Scots, to Bonnie Prince Charlie.

4 Allow a couple of hours to explore the palace and its grounds fully, and then have lunch or afternoon tea in the **Café at the Palace** in the Mews Courtyard.

5 Enjoy a leisurely stroll past the colorful shop fronts and bustling bars of Victoria Street and Grassmarket on your way to **Edinburgh Castle.** Join one of the free tours to hear tales of bloodshed and bitter rivalries, and to view the famous Honours of Scotland (crown jewels).

6 Have dinner at the legendary **The Witchery by the Castle** on Castlehill (book well ahead).

7 Round off your evening with a live folk session at **Sandy Bell's** pub.

DAY 2

Spend your second day in the New Town, seeing a different side of the city.

1 Start your morning at the **Scottish National Gallery of Modern Art**—home to Scotland's foremost contemporary art collection (allow 1-2 hours).

2 Wander around and admire the crowning glory of New Town: Charlotte Square. Drop in or at least take your photo in front of **the Georgian House,** a perfectly-preserved 18th-century townhouse, now a museum.

3 Stop for lunch and a tipple at the **Oxford Bar,** where Ian Rankin's famous detective Inspector John Rebus regularly goes to mull over his cases.

4 See some of Scotland's most recognizable faces at the **Scottish National Portrait Gallery.**

5 Have a hearty and well-priced Indian meal at **Dishoom.**

6 Pop in for a drink at the ornate Circle Bar in the **Café Royal.**

7 End your night with a riotous introduction to Scottish humor at **The Stand Comedy Club.**

EDINBURGH LIKE A LOCAL

Spend your day in Stockbridge, one of the most fashionable hangouts in the city, much calmer than the frenetic tourist hubs of the Royal Mile and Princes Street.

1 Start your day at **The Pantry** with a waffle or the café's healthier spin on a cooked breakfast: grilled courgettes (zucchini) and sweet potato alongside poached eggs and chorizo.

2 Appetite sated, take the 15-minute walk along the **Water of Leith walkway** to Dean Village.

3 Wander around picturesque **Dean Village,** before returning along the river to Stockbridge.

4 Stop into **The Scran and Scallie** for some excellent and hearty pub grub.

5 Next, it's time for a little shopping, à la Stockbridge: If it's Sunday, pay a visit to **Stockbridge Market.** Alternatively, browse the quirky, bohemian independent retailers or pop into one of the many charity shops, particularly those around Raeburn Place.

6 If the weather is nice, head to the **Royal Botanic Gardens** for a lovely stroll.

7 Finish your day with dinner at **The Stockbridge Restaurant.**

8 Head to **The Last Word Saloon** for a drink or two before calling it a night.

Sights

OLD TOWN
★ Edinburgh Castle

Castlehill; tel. 0131 225 9846; www.edinburghcastle. scot; 9:30am-6pm daily Apr.-Sept., 9:30am-5pm daily Oct.-Mar.; adult £18.50 at gate/£17 in advance, child £11.50 at gate/£10.20 in advance, concessions £15/£13.60

High atop an old craggy volcano, Scotland's most recognizable landmark can be seen from all parts of the city. But you really must pass the castle walls to appreciate this icon of Scottish history, which guards Scotland's crown jewels, and is the location for the daily firing of the One O'clock Gun (except Sunday), a tradition dating back to 1861.

Inside the walls there's a vast complex of historic buildings, interconnected by a series of batteries; give yourself at least two hours to explore it fully.

HISTORY

The volcanic rock on which the castle sits was formed some 340 million years ago and has been home to a hill fort for 2,000 years. Here, embattled kings and queens of Scotland have sought refuge, while marauding forces under the leadership of Edward I, Oliver Cromwell, and Robert the Bruce have fought to snatch the fortress back from enemy hands, making it the most besieged castle in all of Britain.

Over its 900-year history the castle has been a royal palace, an arsenal, a gun foundry, infantry barracks, and even a prison. Today it's still garrisoned, largely for administrative purposes or to deliver the ceremonial pomp for which the castle is known.

EXPLORING THE CASTLE

You can pay for an audio guide (£3.50), which gives useful background on the history and architecture of the castle but is a tad dry. Alternatively, tag along on one of the **free tours,** led by funny and insightful guides, that set off from just inside the Portcullis Gate. They usually run every half hour or so, depending on the time of year, and last 30-45 minutes.

Esplanade: Laid out in 1753 as a place for troops to parade, some 200 years earlier the ground beneath the esplanade was used for darker purposes: Between the 15th and 18th centuries, more than 300 women were burned at the stake here for the crime of witchcraft. A small fountain on the southeastern castle wall, the **Witches' Well,** honors the poor women who were tortured and killed. Today,

Edinburgh

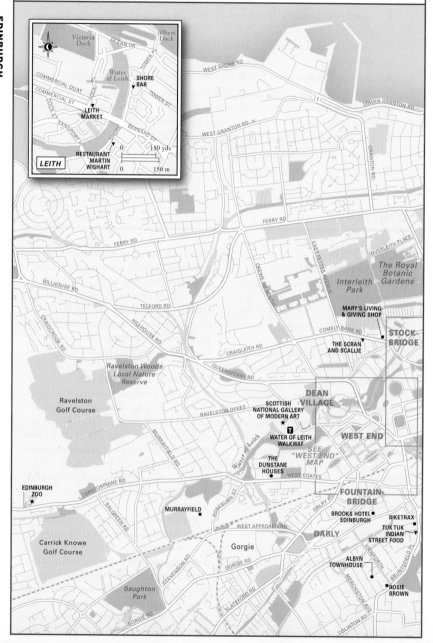

LEITH

- Victoria Dock
- OCEAN DR
- Albert Dock
- WEST SHORE RD
- COMMERCIAL QUAY
- Water of Leith
- SHORE BAR
- COMMERCIAL ST
- DOCK PL
- DOCK ST
- SANDPORT PL
- TOWER PL
- TOWER ST
- LEITH MARKET
- BERNARD ST
- SHORE
- RESTAURANT MARTIN WISHART

0 150 yds
0 150 m

- LOWER GRANTON RD
- WEST GRANTON RD
- GRANTON RD
- FERRY RD
- EAST FETTES AVENUE
- INVERLEITH PLACE
- CREWE RD SOUTH
- Interleith Park
- The Royal Botanic Gardens
- HILLHOUSE RD
- TELFORD RD
- MARY'S LIVING & GIVING SHOP
- COMELY BANK RD
- STOCK-BRIDGE
- CRAIGCROOK RD
- CRAIGLEITH RD
- THE SCRAN AND SCALLIE
- Ravelston Woods Local Nature Reserve
- QUEENSFERRY RD
- HILLHOUSE RD
- Ravelston Golf Course
- DEAN VILLAGE
- RAVELSTON DYKES
- SCOTTISH NATIONAL GALLERY OF MODERN ART
- WEST END
- MURRAYFIELD RD
- Water of Leith
- WATER OF LEITH WALKWAY
- SEE "WEST END" MAP
- THE DUNSTANE HOUSES
- WEST COATES
- EDINBURGH ZOO
- CORSTORPHINE RD
- ROSEBURN ST
- FOUNTAIN-BRIDGE
- DALRY PL
- MURRAYFIELD
- BALGREEN RD
- BROOKS HOTEL EDINBURGH
- BIKETRAX
- WEST APPROACH RD
- DARLY
- TUK TUK INDIAN STREET FOOD
- Carrick Knowe Golf Course
- STEVENSON RD
- Gorgie
- GORGIE RD
- VIEWFORTH
- ALBYN TOWNHOUSE
- MERCHISTON AVE
- BRUNTSFIELD PL
- Saughton Park
- SLATEFORD RD
- ROSIE BROWN
- GORGIE RD
- COLINTON RD

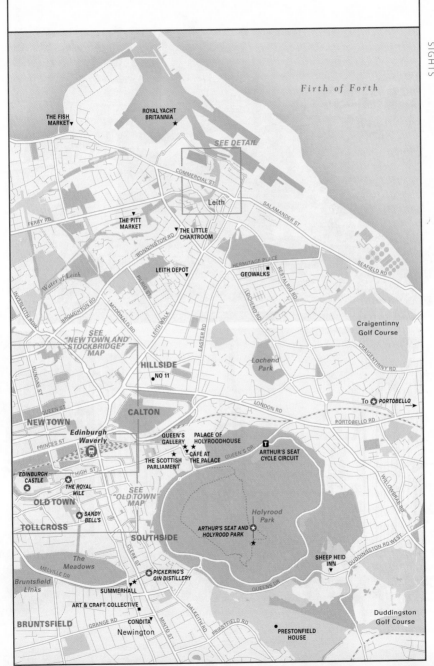

Firth of Forth

THE FISH MARKET ▼

ROYAL YACHT BRITANNIA ★

SEE DETAIL

COMMERCIAL ST

Leith

SALAMANDER ST

FERRY RD

THE PITT MARKET ▼

THE LITTLE CHARTROOM ▼

BONNINGTON RD

HERMITAGE PLACE

SEAFIELD RD

LEITH DEPOT ▲

PILRIG ST

GEOWALKS ■

RESTALRIG RD

Water of Leith

INVERLEITH ROW

BROUGHTON RD

MCDONALD RD

LEITH WALK

EASTER RD

LOCHEND RD

Lochend Park

CRAIGENTINNY RD

Craigentinny Golf Course

SEE 'NEW TOWN AND STOCKBRIDGE' MAP

HILLSIDE
NO 11 ●

CALTON

LONDON RD

To ⓣ **PORTOBELLO** →

PORTOBELLO RD

DUNDAS ST

QUEEN ST

NEW TOWN

Edinburgh Waverly

PRINCES ST

HIGH ST

QUEEN'S GALLERY ★

PALACE OF HOLYROODHOUSE ★

CAFÉ AT THE PALACE ★

THE SCOTTISH PARLIAMENT ★

QUEEN'S DR

🅣

ARTHUR'S SEAT CYCLE CIRCUIT

WILLOWBRAE RD

EDINBURGH CASTLE ✪

THE ROYAL MILE ✪

OLD TOWN

SANDY BELL'S ✪

TOLLCROSS

SEE 'OLD TOWN' MAP

SOUTHSIDE

Holyrood Park

ARTHUR'S SEAT AND HOLYROOD PARK ★

DUDDINGSTON RD WEST

SHEEP HEID INN ▼

The Meadows

MELVILLE DR

CLERK ST

PICKERING'S GIN DISTILLERY ★

Bruntsfield Links

SUMMERHALL ★

QUEENS DR

ART & CRAFT COLLECTIVE ●

BRUNTSFIELD

GRANGE RD

CONDITA ▼

MINTO ST

DALKEITH RD

PRIESTFIELD RD

Newington

PRESTONFIELD HOUSE ●

Duddingston Golf Course

the esplanade is where the Royal Edinburgh Military Tattoo ceremony takes place each August.

Scottish Crown Jewels: Dating from the 15th and 16th centuries, the Scottish crown jewels, or **Honours of Scotland,** comprise a scepter and sword—papal gifts presented to King James IV of Scotland in 1494 and 1507, respectively—and a gold, silver, and gem-encrusted crown, first worn by James V at the coronation of his wife, Mary of Guise in 1540. Three years later the crown and scepter were used for the first time together at the coronation of their daughter, Mary, Queen of Scots, when she was just nine months old. The Honours of Scotland are housed on the first floor of the Royal Palace, to the east of Crown Square, along with the Stone of Destiny, which kings of Scotland stood upon for centuries during their coronation ceremony.

The Honours of Scotland became obsolete following the unification of England and Scotland in 1707, when the Crown Jewels of the United Kingdom—which had been remade in the late 17th century after Oliver Cromwell destroyed the originals—were used in their place.

The Great Hall: With its hammerbeam roof, just across Crown Square from the Royal Palace, the Great Hall is a feat of medieval majesty that once hosted elaborate banquets, but the oldest part of the castle is **St. Margaret's Chapel,** just a short walk away near Foog's Gate. When his forces recaptured the medieval castle in 1314, Robert the Bruce ordered the castle's destruction, but he spared the chapel, perhaps out of reverence to Queen Margaret, mother of David I, for whom the chapel was constructed. Outside the chapel is Mons Meg, a 15th-century bombard (cannon) fired to mark the wedding of Mary, Queen of Scots, and her first husband, the Dauphin of France.

Crown Square: Also worth a visit is the **Scottish National War Memorial,** opposite the Great Hall on the north side of Crown Square. It is an elaborate commemoration of the dead of both World Wars, as well as those who have died on military campaigns since 1945.

Grounds: As you walk around the castle grounds, look for carvings showing the rose and thistle, which celebrate the marriage of King James IV of Scotland (the thistle) and Princess Margaret Tudor of England (the rose—Margaret was Henry VIII's sister) in 1503. The symbols are supposed to signify a reconciliation between their kingdoms, though warfare between the two nations continued.

TIPS

If you want to avoid crowds, try to visit the castle during weekday mornings (9:30am-10am) or later in the afternoon (just before last entry time—always an hour before closing). However, if you do come later in the day, you may find yourself a bit rushed to take everything in.

Whenever you come, book your ticket in advance. This will save you money, as well as time queuing on arrival; at peak times, it can take up to an hour to buy a ticket at the gate.

★ The Royal Mile

Castlehill, Lawnmarket, the High Street, Canongate, and Abbey Strand

This mile-long thoroughfare, made up of a series of streets that lead on to one another, runs west to east from **Edinburgh Castle** to the **Palace of Holyroodhouse;** strictly speaking, it is a Scots mile, which is slightly longer than an English mile (by around 107 yards/98 m).

It's easy to tour the Royal Mile on your own with a guidebook in hand. You can do the route from the castle to the palace or vice versa. Here I have chosen the former option. It's an easy enough walk that should take no more than 25 minutes, but allow one to two hours if you want to stop by some of the attractions en route or pop into the shops.

1: Edinburgh Castle from Grassmarket
2: The Royal Mile

Old Town

NEW TOWN

GEORGE ST

ROSE ST N LN
HANOVER ST
ROSE ST

ROSE ST N LN
ROSE ST S LN
FREDERICK ST

ROSE ST
ROSE ST S LN

ROSE ST S LN

S ST DAVID ST

SCOTT
MONUMENT ★

PRINCES ST

ROYAL
SCOTTISH
ACADEMY
★

East
Princes Street
Gardens

PRINCES ST

SCOTTISH
NATIONAL
GALLERY
★

West
Princes Street
Gardens

THE MOUND

MARKET ST

GLADSTONE'S
LAND

THE NATIONAL TRUST ●
GLADSTONE'S LAND
APARTMENTS

WRITERS' ★
MUSEUM ★

Princes Street
Gardens

MOUND PL

EDINBURGH'S
CAMERA
OBSCURA
★

JOLLY ▼
JUDGE

BRODIE'S ★
CLOSE

EDINBURGH
CASTLE
✪

Esplanade

CASTLEHILL

SCOTCH ★
WHISKY
EXPERIENCE

▼ THE WITCHERY
BY THE CASTLE

VICTORIA ST

JOHNSTON TERRACE

THE GRAIN
STORE

▼ BOW
BAR

EDINBURGH
FARMERS'
■ MARKET

CASTLE TERRACE

JOHNSTON TERRACE

■ CASTLE
ROCK

CASTLE TERRACE

GRANNY'S
GREEN
STEPS

KING'S STABLES RD

EDINBURGH ■
LITERARY
PUB TOUR

Grassmarket Square

GRASSMARKET

MR WOOD'S ■
FOSSILS

LADY LAWSON ST

KING'S STABLES LANE

GREYFRIARS
KIRKYARD
★

HERIOT PL

TIMBERYARD ▼

WEST PORT

■ ARMCHAIR
BOOKS

KEIR STREET

LADY LAWSON ST

LAURISTON ST

LAURISTON PL

☾

0   100 yds

0   100 m

LAURISTON PL

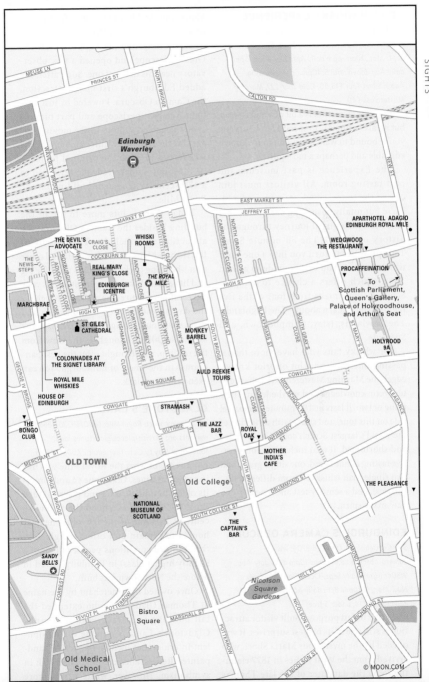

MEUSE LN

PRINCES ST

NORTH BRIDGE

CALTON RD

WAVERLEY BRIDGE

Edinburgh Waverley

NEW ST

EAST MARKET ST

JEFFREY ST

MARKET ST

FLESHMARKET CLOSE

CARRUBBER'S CLOSE

NORTH GRAY'S CLOSE

APARTHOTEL ADAGIO
EDINBURGH ROYAL MILE

CRAIG'S CLOSE

THE DEVIL'S ADVOCATE

WHISKI ROOMS

COCKBURN ST

WEDGWOOD
THE RESTAURANT

THE NEWS STEPS

ROXBURGH'S CLOSE

ADVOCATE'S CLOSE

BYRES CLOSE

ANCHOR CLOSE

REAL MARY KING'S CLOSE

EDINBURGH ICENTRE

THE ROYAL MILE

PROCAFFEINATION

HIGH ST

To
Scottish Parliament,
Queen's Gallery,
Palace of Holyroodhouse,
and Arthur's Seat

ST MARY'S ST

MARCHBRAE

HIGH ST

OLD FISHMARKET CLOSE

BORTHWICK'S CLOSE

OLD ASSEMBLY CLOSE

BELL'S WYND

STEVENLAW'S CLOSE

NIDDRY ST

BLACKFRIARS ST

SOUTH GRAY'S CLOSE

HOLYROOD
9A

ST GILES' CATHEDRAL

MONKEY BARREL

BLAIR ST

SOUTH BRIDGE

COLONNADES AT THE SIGNET LIBRARY

ROYAL MILE WHISKIES

TRON SQUARE

AULD REEKIE TOURS

COWGATE

GEORGE IV BRIDGE

HOUSE OF EDINBURGH

COWGATE

STRAMASH

GUTHRIE

THE JAZZ BAR

ROBERTSON'S CLOSE

HIGH SCHOOL WYND

PLEASANCE

THE BONGO CLUB

MERCHANT ST

ROYAL OAK

INFIRMARY ST

MOTHER INDIA'S CAFE

OLD TOWN

GEORGE IV BRIDGE

CHAMBERS ST

WEST COLLEGE ST

Old College

SOUTH BRIDGE

THE PLEASANCE

DRUMMOND ST

NATIONAL MUSEUM OF SCOTLAND

SOUTH COLLEGE ST

THE CAPTAIN'S BAR

RICHMOND PLACE

SANDY BELL'S

BRISTO PL

FORREST RD

HILL PL

W RICHMOND ST

TEVIOT PL

POTTERROW

MARSHALL ST

Bistro Square

Nicolson Square Gardens

NICOLSON ST

Old Medical School

W NICOLSON ST

POTTERROW

© MOON.COM

SCOTCH WHISKY EXPERIENCE

354 Castlehill; tel. 0131 220 0441; www.
scotchwhiskyexperience.co.uk; 10am-5pm daily
Sept.-Mar., 10am-6pm daily Apr.-July, 10am-5pm
daily Aug. (open until 5:40pm on weekends in
Aug.); Silver Tour £15.50, Gold Tour £27, Morning
Masterclass £40

This visitor attraction is a bit of a tourist trap, but it's also a fun way to spend a few hours and you're bound to walk away a bit more knowledgeable and perhaps a tad squiffy.

The Experience is part museum and part tasting room. All visitors must join one of the tours, which start aboard a bizarre but totally absorbing barrel ride that takes you on a visual journey through the history of Scotch. The 50-minute Silver Tour promises to turn you into a one-hour whisky expert. You can upgrade to a Gold Tour, which offers a chance to compare Scottish single malts from four of the five regions you'll learn about—The Highlands, The Lowlands, Islay, Campbeltown, and Speyside.

For whisky fans who have more than a passing interest (and a bit of prior knowledge), the Morning Masterclass is a chance to test your knowledge and maybe learn a new thing or two. It lasts just 90 minutes (no barrel ride on this tour) and starts with a viewing of the world's largest Scotch collection over tea and shortbread. It also includes a comparative tasting of one blend, one single grain, and two single malt whiskies (from different distilleries), and a sensory test and a nosing of a new-make spirit.

EDINBURGH'S CAMERA OBSCURA

549 Castlehill; tel. 0131 226 3709; www.
camera-obscura.co.uk; 9am-10pm daily July-Aug.,
9:30am-8pm daily Sept.-Oct., 10am-7pm daily
Nov.-Mar., 9:30am-8pm daily Apr.-Jun.; adult £18,
child (5-15) £14, under 5 free

The city's oldest purpose-built visitor attraction is still one of its biggest surprises. It was opened by the mysterious Maria Short, who arrived from the West Indies in 1827 claiming to be the daughter of the late Thomas Short, who had built the city's first public observatory on Calton Hill.

Maria inherited her supposed father's Great Telescope and opened a new observatory near his defunct one. Soon after, she added Edinburgh's first major attraction, the Camera Obscura. Powered by just daylight, the part periscope and part pinhole camera enabled visitors to see moving images for the first time. Unfortunately, Maria was forced to close the original building in 1849, but, undeterred, she relocated to a 17th-century tenement building on the Royal Mile.

Today there is lots more to see in the building besides the Camera Obscura; the attraction also includes **The World of Illusions** with its maze of mirrors and other mind-bending tricks, which is a must for big and little kids. What I love most is that your ticket allows you to come and go throughout the day, so you can pop out for lunch and snacks without having to rush. Perhaps the biggest highlight, though, is the view from the rooftop, which might offer the best panoramas in the whole of Edinburgh. You can even visit after dark.

GLADSTONE'S LAND

477B Lawnmarket, Royal Mile; tel. 0131 226 5856;
www.nts.org.uk/visit/places/gladstones-land;
10am-3pm May to Oct.; tour adult £7.50, child £5

For a sense of what the Royal Mile was like in medieval times, Gladstone's Land, one of its oldest buildings, is a good place to start. Built in 1550 and extended the following century, it is one of the few old tenement houses to remain and offers insight into the cramped conditions people (albeit of a slightly higher class) in Edinburgh lived in before the New Town was built.

Once owned by a merchant by the name of Thomas Gladstone, who extended the tall building to attract wealthy tenants, Gladstone's Land is notable for its opulent interiors that include incredible hand-painted Renaissance ceiling panels rich in symbolism. However, while it was more luxurious than most, the property was still subject to the same limitations of 16th- and 17th-century society: lack of running water, open fires for heat, and glassless windows.

Between 12pm and 4pm every day, handlers set up outside Gladstone's Land with birds of prey that you can hold for a donation (£4). Entry is by guided or self-guided tour only (about one hour) and must be booked in advance, either by phone or at the venue.

REAL MARY KING'S CLOSE

2 Warriston's Close, off the Royal Mile; tel. 0131 225 0672; www.realmarykingsclose.com; 10am-9pm daily Apr.-Oct., 9am-5:30pm Mon.-Thurs., 9:30am-9pm Fri.-Sat., 9:30am-6:30pm Sun. Nov., 10am-5pm Sun.-Thurs., 10am-9pm Fri.-Sat. Dec.-Mar.; adult £18.95, child £12.45, family £54

This labyrinth of medieval underground streets and homes tells the stories of real 17th-century residents, including Mary King, a local merchant burgess.

What remains of the close stays true to its origins. The narrow lanes are much as they were when they were surrounded by tenement buildings as the city's population swelled in the 17th century.

Prior to Mary King's time, Mary, Queen of Scots, is said to have spent a night in **Stuart's Close,** at the top of the warren of lanes, in 1567 following her abdication. In 1644 the close was sealed off to prevent the spread of the plague. However, it was a decision to build the **Royal Exchange** over the top of the close, thus effectively turning it into a perfectly preserved ghost town, that led to some of its more enduring unsettling tales.

A one-hour tour with a costumed guide is mandatory with visits. Your guide will dispel some myths, while hamming up some of the spooky tales, including the chilling story of Annie, a young girl who it is said was left to die by her parents when the plague took hold. In summer, book tours a week or two in advance; walk-ups may be available in quieter winter months.

ST. GILES' CATHEDRAL

High Street, Royal Mile; tel. 0131 226 0674; www.stgilescathedral.org.uk; 9am-7pm Mon.-Fri., 9am-5pm Sat., 1pm-5pm Sun. Apr.-Oct., 9am-5pm Mon.-Sat., 1pm-5pm Sun. Nov.-Mar.; free (donations encouraged), £2 fee for photos

The unusual steeple of this cathedral can be seen from across the city. While there may have been a church here as early as 1124, much of the interior you see dates from the 14th century, and it was largely restored in the 19th century.

The stained glass is stunning, but the highlight is the **Thistle Chapel**—home to the Order of the Thistle, the highest order of chivalry in Scotland. Completed in 1911, it features elaborate carvings, stalls for each of the 16 knights, and an ornate stone vaulted ceiling.

Near the west door of St. Giles' Cathedral is a heart-shaped mosaic set in the pavement, known as the **Heart of Midlothian,** which marks the site of the former 15th-century tolbooth building, where executions and torture took place until the building was demolished in the early 19th century. It was immortalized with the publication of Sir Walter Scott's *The Heart of Midlothian,* which tells the tale of a woman desperately trying to get a pardon for a condemned prisoner.

One strange tradition long adhered to is that of spitting on the heart, supposed to bring good luck. Taking part in this tradition in post-COVID times is probably not recommended.

Palace of Holyroodhouse

Canongate, Royal Mile; tel. 0303 123 7306; www.royalcollection.org.uk/visit/palace-of-holyroodhouse; 9:30am-6pm Thurs.-Mon. Apr.-Oct., 9:30am-4:30pm Thurs.-Mon. Nov.-Mar.; adult £16.50, under 17 £9.50, under 5 free, family £42.50

The official residence of Her Majesty The Queen in Edinburgh, the Palace of Holyroodhouse has been the principal home of the kings and queens of Scotland since the 16th century. What you see today is largely

the result of a major overhaul ordered by King Charles II in the 17th century. Though he never visited the palace, Charles used it to show the might of the Royal Family at a time when there was a power struggle between the church in Scotland and the Crown. Its classical style was later borrowed by much of the nobility in their houses and palaces around Scotland.

In the forecourt, during the Ceremony of the Keys, the Queen is welcomed into the city of Edinburgh each year. The spectacle occurs during Holyrood Week (usually late June or early July).

VISITING THE PALACE

The quadrangle you see as you first step beyond the castle walls is a great place to view the architectural style, with Doric columns on the ground level, the slightly more decorative Ionic on the floor above, and finally the Corinthian columns on top.

A free audio guide will take you through the other rooms in the palace. The first room you reach at the top of the staircase is the **Royal Dining Room,** where the Queen and the Royal Family dine when they are in residence. Charles II had the state apartments laid out to get progressively more opulent as you approach the **King's Bedchamber,** a style copied from the Palace of Versailles. The paintings and tapestries flatter the king by associating him with great classical heroes.

The **Great Gallery**—where the walls are lined with the portraits of the kings and queens of Scotland, all commissioned by Charles II—is a particular highlight. When Bonnie Prince Charlie overtook Holyroodhouse for six weeks in 1745, he reputedly held lavish balls here, buoyed by his triumphant return to the royal palace of his Stuart ancestors.

1: St. Giles' is home to the Order of the Thistle.
2: Greyfriars Bobby outside Greyfriars Kirkyard
3: a plaque commemorating Mary, Queen of Scots's, stay at Mary King's Close 4: the Palace of Holyroodhouse

The **bedroom of Mary, Queen of Scots,** is accessed via a narrow winding staircase in the northwest tower toward the end of the tour. Mary grew up around great Renaissance opulence—a style she tried to re-create here in Holyroodhouse, as evidenced in her lavish bedchamber, complete with decorative oak ceiling and painted frieze. Mary, who was almost 6 feet (1.8 m) tall, must have found the low doorway a struggle.

Once you have finished the audio tour inside, you can explore the ruins of **Holyrood Abbey** during palace opening hours and walk around the palace gardens for beautiful views of Holyrood Park and Arthur's Seat. All that's left of the original abbey, founded by King David I, is the east processional doorway. What you see today are the remains of a medieval Gothic abbey church built in its place; nevertheless, there is an eerie romance about the place.

Queen's Gallery

Canongate; tel. 0303 123 7306; www.royalcollection. org.uk/visit/the-queens-gallery-palace-of-holyroodhouse; 9:30am-6pm Thurs.-Mon. Apr.-Oct., 9:30am-4:30pm Thurs.-Mon. Nov.-Mar.; adult £7.80, under 17 £3.90, under 5 free, family £19.50, combined tickets with the palace adult £21.90, child £12, family £55.80

Located right next to the Palace of Holyroodhouse and featuring some incredible paintings from the Royal Collection, this gallery hosts a series of rolling exhibitions. An hour-long multimedia guide will point out the biggest attractions, and you can combine your visit with the Palace of Holyroodhouse for a reduced rate. Last admission is an hour before closing.

The Scottish Parliament

Horse Wynd, Canongate; tel. 0131 348 5200; www. parliament.scot/visitandlearn; 10am-5pm Mon.-Sat.; free

Opened in 2004 following Scotland's devolution some seven years earlier—in which the U.K. government transferred powers to the Scottish Parliament to allow it to legislate on day-to-day matters that affect Scottish life—this is where Scotland's laws are made and debated.

At the foot of the Royal Mile, opposite the Palace of Holyroodhouse, the building, or rather complex of buildings, was completed three years behind schedule and massively over budget. Nevertheless, the unique design—a mix of steel, oak, and granite with a turf roof, and solar panels to blend in with the surrounding landscape—has been embraced, or at least accepted by residents.

Guided tours are free and are a good way of gaining insight into how the Scottish Parliament works. You can also book a seat in the public gallery of the **Debating Chamber** (Tues.-Thurs.). There is no need to book ahead to go to the public areas, but for guided tours booking opens three months before and to sit in on debates you can book up to a week in advance. On-the-day tickets are sometimes available but not guaranteed, and don't forget to check dates when Parliament is not sitting, such as the summer holidays from late June to early September. Last entry is at 4:30pm.

★ Arthur's Seat and Holyrood Park

Queen's Drive; www.walkhighlands.co.uk/lothian/ arthurs-seat.shtml

The hill known as Arthur's Seat was left by a volcanic eruption 350 million years ago, and looms 822 feet (251 m) above sea level in Holyrood Park. It was once the site of one of four hill forts that date back 2,000 years. Today, ascending it is a rite of passage: It's an Edinburgh tradition to climb Arthur's Seat on the first day of May and wash your face in the morning dew.

The park is just a few minutes' stroll from the eastern end of the Royal Mile near the Palace of Holyroodhouse, and the route follows a **well-marked walkway** from Queen's Drive (use the path that bears left), taking you up behind Salisbury Crags via a grassy path. As it climbs up and to the east, you'll get a good view of the summit. Near the end of the escarpment, take the muddy path just to your left and bear right to join the incoming path; then cross over to a path of steps that zigzag up. This section is steep but not too long, and from the path curves round the hill before bearing left and starting the final rocky

Arthur's Seat

climb to the summit. In total, you'll cover a distance of 3 miles (4.75 km), and it should take you 2-2.5 hours to reach the summit and come back down on a different path to the east, where there is a metal chain to help you in your descent.

You are exposed here, so be sure to dress appropriately: sunblock is advisable in summer, and good walking shoes plus wind protection are recommended at all times. If you don't want to walk to Arthur's Seat on your own, then join a tour accompanied by a geologist with Geowalks (see Sports and Recreation, page 72).

Some say Arthur's Seat looks like a reclining lion, hence its nickname: The Lion. There is also some debate over where its actual name originated. Contrary to what many assume, its moniker has nothing to do with the legendary King Arthur and is more likely a corruption of Àrd-na-Said, "Height of Arrows," which over time has evolved into "Arthur's Seat."

On the way back down, you will pass St Margaret's Loch in the northeast of the park, which affords wonderful views of the ruins of the 15th-century **St. Anthony's Chapel** above.

National Museum of Scotland

Chambers Street; tel. 0300 123 6789; www.nms. ac.uk; 10am-5pm daily; free

A huge museum of national and international significance, the most visited overall attraction in Edinburgh is set across seven floors and is more than worthy of a couple of hours of your time.

Half of the museum, housed in a grand Victorian building, is very much geared toward younger people and families, with hanging planes and hands-on exhibits, while the other half shows a more serious side and will take you through the history of Scotland. Popular exhibits include the famous Dolly the Sheep, the Lewis Chessmen, and a T. rex skeleton cast. It's also here that you will find the rather macabre miniature coffins discovered in a cave on the northeast slopes of Arthur's Seat by a group of schoolboys in

1836, which are so small you could hold several in one hand. The eight surviving coffins (there were originally 17) are carved of wood and have remained a mystery. Were they related to witchcraft? Were they some form of surrogate burial for people who died abroad or at sea? Or maybe they served as an eerie memorial to some of the people killed by graverobbers and murderers Burke and Hare, who were convicted shortly before it is thought these coffins were made.

Avoid visiting the museum during school holidays, when it can get stiflingly busy. If you want to visit the rooftop terrace, enter via the tower entrance and take the lift or stairs to the seventh floor. It's a nice space with a different view over the city. Prior to the pandemic, free daily volunteer-led tours set off from the entrance hall at 11am, 1pm, and 3pm, and hopefully they will restart soon. Check the website for updates.

Greyfriars Kirkyard

Candlemaker Row; www.greyfriarskirk.com; kirkyard always open, kirk open 10:30am-4pm Mon.-Fri., 11am-2pm Sat. Apr.-Oct.

This churchyard, where burials have been taking place since the late 16th century, is associated with the dark period in the late 17th century when hundreds of Covenanters (supporters of the Presbyterian church) were caged here in a makeshift prison during the notorious "Killing Time."

In recent years its rows of aging headstones and weathered mausoleums with their faded epitaphs have been more associated with a certain J. K. Rowling, who is said to have taken inspiration from here for many of the characters in her Harry Potter tales. Volunteer-run tours are sometimes available for a small fee (check the website) at the guide's discretion, and though they won't take you to the grave of the "real" Voldemort, Thomas Riddell Esq., they may give you a nudge in the right direction; otherwise, look for one of the graves surrounded by other tourists.

Probably most famous of all is the grave of **Greyfriars Bobby,** a Skye terrier whose

The Haunted City

It's pretty much impossible to walk around Edinburgh without seeing at least one flyer promising a supernatural experience. Though many of the tours are predictably gimmicky, the city's winding, brooding passages, together with its very real bloody history, make it a ripe backdrop for spooky tales.

EDINBURGH CASTLE

There have been many supposed sightings of a ghost dog, which many presume to be the famous Greyfriars Dog, in Edinburgh Castle's dog cemetery (a dedicated resting place for soldiers' loyal canine friends). There have also been numerous reports of a headless drummer boy, who if seen is supposed to be an ominous sign that the castle will soon come under attack.

The most eerie of all the castle's spirits, though, is that of the ghost piper. The story goes that a boy was instructed to play the bagpipes as he descended into the tunnels below the castle to see where they led. He played loudly as he went underground, but eventually the bagpipes stopped, and the boy was never seen again. To this day, visitors report hearing the muffled sound of bagpipes beneath Edinburgh Castle.

EDINBURGH VAULTS

The Edinburgh Vaults are a series of underground chambers found in the 19 arches of South Bridge just off the Royal Mile. Once home to 18th-century taverns, cobblers, and other businesses, it later became a crime-ridden slum. It is even claimed that notorious 19th-century serial killers

loyalty made him one of Edinburgh's beloved characters. According to local legend, when Bobby's owner died in the 19th century, the faithful dog guarded his grave until his own death 14 years later. More romanticized versions of the story tell how the dog would hear the firing of the One O'clock gun each day and come running back to Greyfriars, where he would stay for the rest of the day. There is a statue dedicated to the dog outside the entrance to the graveyard, by the pub that bears his name, and as you enter the churchyard you can see his little grave.

Writers' Museum

Lady Stair's Close, Lawnmarket; tel. 0131 529 4901; www.edinburghmuseums.org.uk; 10am-5pm Weds.-Sat., 12pm-5pm Sun.; free

This small museum tucked into a close just off Lawnmarket pays homage to three of Scotland's most celebrated writers: Robert Burns, Robert Louis Stevenson, and Sir Walter Scott, and goes some way to explain why Edinburgh was granted City of Literature status by UNESCO. Exhibits include first editions of Walter Scott's *Waverley* (from which Edinburgh's train station takes its name) and Robert Louis Stevenson's *A Child's Garden of Verses*.

Poignantly, there is even a cast of Burns's skull (one of only three made), plus the national poet's writing desk and his manuscript of "Scots Wha Hae" (also known as "Robert Bruce's Address to His Troops at Bannockburn").

PRINCES STREET GARDENS

These lovely gardens in the shadow of the castle, which effectively divide the Old Town from the New Town, are a popular place for locals and visitors to stroll. The gardens also ordinarily host many events during the year, from concerts in summer to an annual Christmas extravaganza.

The gardens gradually start to close about an hour before full closing at sunset.

Scott Monument

Princes Street Gardens; 7am to sunset daily (monument standard hours 10am-3:30pm, may

Burke and Hare came here to hide the bodies of their victims, though there is no proof. Today, visitors who take ghost tours here have reported receiving mysterious scratches and bruises as well as seeing a strange figure called The Watcher.

MARY KING'S CLOSE

In the hidden streets of Mary King's Close, a subterranean community walled up to prevent the spread of the plague, some people have reported being grabbed by the tiny hand of Wee Annie—a little girl with the plague said to have been deserted by her parents and sealed up underground for ever more.

BRODIE'S CLOSE

And finally, does the ghost of the real-life Jekyll and Hyde haunt Brodie's Close?

William Brodie (or Deacon Brodie) was an affluent and respected Edinburgh cabinet maker who is said to have inspired the title character in Robert Louis Stevenson's Gothic novella *Strange Case of Dr. Jekyll and Mr. Hyde*. A peer of Robert Burns, by day Brodie mingled with the city's gentry, but by night he is said to have used his skills as the city's leading locksmith to break into people's homes and rob them, presumably to fund his secret life of gambling and philandering. Brodie was hanged for his crimes in the Old Tolbooth in 1788. He supposedly can still be seen walking around Brodie's Close, just off the Royal Mile, carrying a lantern.

---

be extended when the monument reopens post pandemic); £5 to climb, cash only

The gargantuan monument to Sir Walter Scott, which stands proud over the gardens, is one of the largest monuments in the world to a writer and gives some indication of just how much he is revered here. The monument is adorned with 64 figures representing characters from Scott's much-loved books. You can actually climb the 287 steps to the top of the 200-foot (61 m) monument for a view of the city's skyline, but be warned, the spiral staircase can be unforgiving.

Scottish National Gallery and Royal Scottish Academy

The Mound; tel. 0131 624 6200; www. nationalgalleries.org/visit/scottish-national-gallery; Scottish National Gallery 10am-5pm daily, Royal Scottish Academy 10am-5pm Weds.-Sat., 12pm-5pm Sun.; free

Located on The Mound, a man-made hill that overlooks Princes Street Gardens between the Old Town and New Town, the Scottish National Gallery is one of the three main art galleries in Edinburgh and is home to world-class works by Renaissance artists, including Raphael and Titian; the Impressionists; and British landscape artists such as Turner. It's also a great introduction to the history of Scottish art, with pieces by Ramsay, Wilkie, McTaggart, and Raeburn. *The Skating Minister,* arguably Raeburn's most famous painting, depicts the Reverend Robert Walker, minister of Canongate Kirk, ice skating on Duddingston Loch and has become something of a symbol of Scotland. The contrast of Walker's stern outfit with the wild landscape beyond is mesmerizing, and many Scots find a great deal of humor in it: it's been parodied many times and it's even said that Walker's outline inspired the shape of the windows in one of the Scottish Parliament's buildings. Unfortunately, all the pieces outlined in the gallery's highlight tour are by white men, and pretty much all by men of a certain status too. One contemporary piece on display that feels more relatable is a portrait of singer-songwriter Horse McDonald by Roxana Halls.

The Scottish National Gallery is linked

New Town and Stockbridge

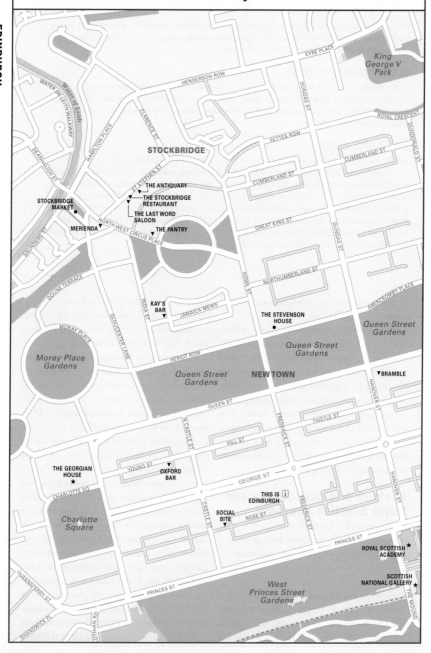

EYRE PLACE

King George V Park

HENDERSON ROW

ROYAL CRESCENT

WATER OF LEITH WALKWAY

Water of Leith

HAMILTON PLACE

CLARENCE ST

DUNDAS ST

DUNDONALD ST

FETTES ROW

STOCKBRIDGE

CUMBERLAND ST

CUMBERLAND ST

DEANHAUGH ST

ST STEPHEN ST

THE ANTIQUARY

THE STOCKBRIDGE RESTAURANT

STOCKBRIDGE MARKET

THE LAST WORD SALOON

NORTH WEST CIRCUS PLACE

GREAT KING ST

DUNDAS ST

SAUNDERS ST

MERIENDA

THE PANTRY

NORTHUMBERLAND ST

HOWE ST

DOUNE TERRACE

GLOUCESTER LANE

INDIA ST

KAY'S BAR

JAMAICA MEWS

THE STEVENSON HOUSE

ABERCROMBY PLACE

Queen Street Gardens

MORAY PLACE

HERIOT ROW

Queen Street Gardens

Moray Place Gardens

Queen Street Gardens

NEW TOWN

BRAMBLE

HANOVER ST

QUEEN ST

N CASTLE ST

HILL ST

THISTLE ST

FREDERICK ST

YOUNG ST

OXFORD BAR

GEORGE ST

HANOVER ST

THE GEORGIAN HOUSE ★

CHARLOTTE SQ

CASTLE ST

THIS IS ⓘ EDINBURGH

SOCIAL BITE

ROSE ST

FREDERICK ST

Charlotte Square

PRINCES ST

PRINCES ST

ROYAL SCOTTISH ★ ACADEMY

QUEENSFERRY ST

SCOTTISH ★ NATIONAL GALLERY

West Princes Street Gardens

THE MOUND

SHANDWICK PL

LOTHIAN RD

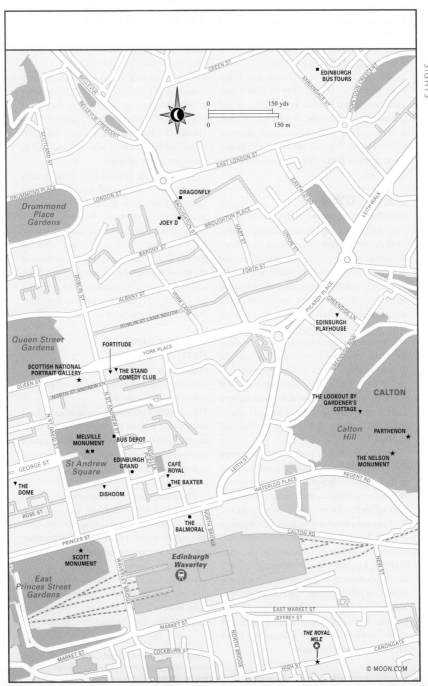

EDINBURGH BUS TOURS

GREEN ST

ANNANDALE ST

HOPETOUN CRESCENT

BELLEVUE

BELLEVUE CRESCENT

SCOTLAND ST

EAST LONDON ST

0   150 yds

0   150 m

DRUMMOND PLACE

LONDON ST

GAYFIELD SQ

LEITH WALK

DRAGONFLY

Drummond Place Gardens

JOEY D

BROUGHTON PLACE

BROUGHTON ST

HART ST

UNION ST

DUBLIN ST

BARONY ST

FORTH ST

ALBANY ST

YORK LANE

PICARDY PLACE

GREENSIDE LN

DUBLIN ST LANE SOUTH

Queen Street Gardens

FORTITUDE

YORK PLACE

EDINBURGH PLAYHOUSE

GREENSIDE ROW

SCOTTISH NATIONAL PORTRAIT GALLERY

THE STAND COMEDY CLUB

QUEEN ST

NORTH ST ANDREW LN

N ST ANDREW ST

THE LOOKOUT BY GARDENER'S COTTAGE

CALTON

N ST DAVID ST

Calton Hill

PARTHENON

MELVILLE MONUMENT

BUS DEPOT

REGISTER PLACE

THE NELSON MONUMENT

GEORGE ST

St Andrew Square

EDINBURGH GRAND

CAFÉ ROYAL

LEITH ST

REGENT RD

THE DOME

DISHOOM

THE BAXTER

WATERLOO PLACE

ROSE ST

CALTON RD

PRINCES ST

THE BALMORAL

NORTH BRIDGE

NEW ST

SCOTT MONUMENT

WAVERLEY BRIDGE

Edinburgh Waverley

East Princes Street Gardens

EAST MARKET ST

JEFFREY ST

MARKET ST

THE ROYAL MILE

CANONGATE

MARKET ST

COCKBURN ST

NORTH BRIDGE

HIGH ST

© MOON.COM

by an underground walkway with the Royal Scottish Academy. Both buildings were the work of William Playfair, the renowned architect behind many of the city's finest buildings. A major renovation, which has been partially completed to include a new entrance in East Princes Street Gardens and the addition of the excellent Contini café, will eventually shift focus to the galleries' collections of Scottish art. Though general admission is free, there is a fee for some exhibitions.

NEW TOWN

Charlotte Square, a dignified 18th-century plaza to the west of George Street in the New Town, puts London's Grosvenor Square to shame. The swan song of revered Scottish architect Robert Adam, who died a year after building began, the palace-fronted edifices of the north and south side of the square mirror each other, and, together with the statuesque sphinxes that guard the pyramid-shaped roofs, lend a resplendent air. You can almost picture leading figures of the Scottish Enlightenment, who set up home in the New Town, going about their business—gentlemen in their skirted knee-length coats, breeches, and silk stockings, and ladies in their corsets and hooped dresses.

Just under a mile to the east of George Street, **St. Andrew Square,** once the blueprint for Charlotte Square, is now the hub of the business district, with some contemporary office blocks and bars and restaurants. The square's most prominent landmark is the 140-foot (43-m) **Melville Monument,** in memory of Henry Dundas, 1st Viscount Melville, a member of parliament (MP) until his impeachment in 1806 on the grounds of a misuse of public funds. The monument was vandalized during the Black Lives Matter protests during 2020 and debate rumbles on about wording on a new plaque that links Melville to the slave trade.

The Georgian House

7 Charlotte Square; tel. 0131 225 2160; www.nts.org. uk/visit/places/georgian-house; 10am-4pm Apr.-Oct.; adult £10, concessions £8, family £19.50

Taking pride of place in the exquisite surroundings of Charlotte Square is this museum of living history, right next door to the official residence of Scotland's First Minister, **Bute House** (5 Charlotte Square). Step across its threshold for a taste of what life was like in 18th-century Edinburgh.

The striking townhouse, designed by Robert Adam, suggested wealth and good taste to those who lived here during the Scottish Enlightenment. Today it has been restored with period furniture, paintings, and silverware, as well as a glimpse into what life was like "below stairs" for the servants of the house. Kids (and more imaginative adults) will love dressing up in some of the costumes left out for this purpose—you can even tour the house in character if you like.

Scottish National Portrait Gallery

1 Queen Street; tel. 0131 624 6200; www. nationalgalleries.org/visit/scottish-national-portrait-gallery; 10am-5pm daily; free

This collection of paintings of Scotland's great and good is housed in one of the city's most magnificent buildings—a neo-Gothic palace built of red sandstone, which, when it opened in 1889, became the world's first purpose-built portrait gallery.

The initial collection, bequeathed by David Erskine, 11th Earl of Buchan, who collected portraits of famous Scots in the late 18th century, has been added to over the years by other gifts and the commissioning of portraits of contemporary Scots.

It's a chance to look upon the faces of the men and women who have shaped Scotland, from Bonnie Prince Charlie to the woman who folklore says helped him escape the

1: inside the National Portrait Gallery **2:** Scott Monument **3:** view from the Nelson Monument of the Parthenon

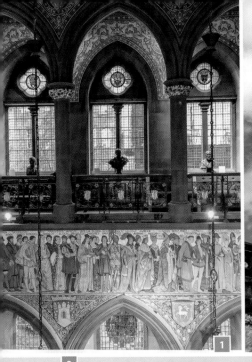

clutches of British forces, Flora Macdonald, and from Robert Louis Stevenson to Sir Walter Scott. The building's architect, Sir Robert Rowand Anderson, employed by philanthropist John Ritchie Findlay, owner of the *Scotsman* newspaper, designed it as a shrine to the nation's heroes and heroines, hence the elaborate friezes, sculptures, and murals.

Look up as you enter to see the faces of William Wallace and Robert Burns peering down at you. And don't miss the Great Hall where a painted frieze charts some of the most significant figures in Scottish history in reverse order. The building, which includes 17 gallery spaces across three floors, is also home to the National Photography Collection. Allow at least two to three hours to appreciate it fully. Though admission is free, there is a fee for some exhibits.

The Nelson Monument

32 Calton Hill; tel. 0131 556 2716; www. edinburghmuseums.org.uk/venue/nelson-monument; 10am-4pm Mon.-Sat. (open until 7pm in summer); £6 to climb the tower

This memorial to Admiral Horatio Nelson, completed in 1808, offers some of the best views in the city. Commanding a prime position atop **Calton Hill,** it commemorates Nelson's victory against the Spanish and French at the Battle of Trafalgar, in which the British naval hero was fatally wounded.

It stands at the highest point of Calton Hill, 561 feet (171 m) above sea level, and is said to resemble an upturned telescope, although the castellated design may have been added to fit in with some of the surrounding prisons in the area at the time.

A **free museum** on the ground floor is worth checking out to see the scale model of Nelson's ship *HMS Victory*, a piece of timber of the original ship, and a large time ball, which is lowered when the One O'clock gun is fired each day. I recommend paying the £6 to climb the 143 steps to the **viewing gallery** too.

Also on Calton Hill is the unfinished

Parthenon, which was envisioned as a national monument to those who lost their lives in the Napoleonic Wars. However, despite support from the likes of Sir Walter Scott, the project ran out of funds, a stark reminder of the city's occasional folly.

WEST END

Though this area, just west of Princes Street, is largely a commercial district, there's a lot of history here, too: A short walk amid its neatly compact streets will bring you past the home of leading suffragette Elsie Inglis (8 Walker Street), while at 2 Melville Crescent there is a plaque commemorating former resident Joseph Bell, the physician who inspired Arthur Conan Doyle's famous detective, Sherlock Holmes.

St. Mary's Cathedral

Palmerston Place; tel. 0131 225 6293; www.cathedral. net; opening times vary

Built by Sir George Gilbert Scott (most famous for his masterpiece the Midland Grand Hotel at London's St. Pancras Station), this cathedral is an astonishing example of Gothic revival architecture, with a soaring central spire (plus two smaller ones by its western entrance added later), numerous lancet windows, and giant pointed arches adding drama along its nave.

But while the building is stunning, the Charles I Chapel is sadly underwhelming, with a few random bits of memorabilia related to the monarch that look as though they have been gathering dust. It is worth a peek in here, though, if only to see the family pew of Sir Walter Scott.

Scottish National Gallery of Modern Art

75 Belford Road; tel. 0131 624 6200; www. nationalgalleries.org/visit/scottish-national-gallery-modern-art; 10am-5pm daily; free

This exciting gallery set across two handsome buildings is a must-see for modern and contemporary art lovers. It's set back from the

West End

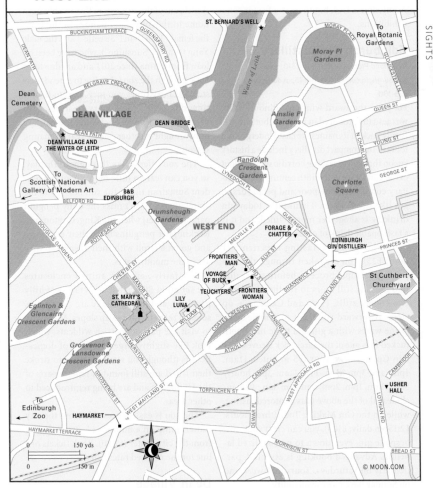

Water of Leith in a peaceful location amid a pretty sculpture park.

In front of the first building, neoclassical Modern One, you can admire the landscaped lawn of postmodernist Charles Jencks. Inside Modern One are two unnerving early pieces by Francis Bacon (*Figure Study II* depicts a deformed screaming character emerging from beneath an umbrella), alongside some of the artist's later works and a good selection of abstract art. Though born in England,

Joan Eardley was known for her portraits of Glasgow street kids and coastal landscapes in and around the Aberdeenshire fishing village of Catterline, and there are several of her pieces in Modern One.

Head to Modern Two, housed in the former Dean Gallery, across Belford Road, to view the impressive collection of Dada and surrealist art and to see a re-creation of the studio of Scottish artist Eduardo Paolozzi.

An hour in each gallery should be enough

time to admire the main pieces. If you're short of time, make Modern One your priority. Admission is free, but there is a fee for some exhibitions.

Edinburgh Gin Distillery

1a Rutland Place; tel. 0131 656 2810; www. edinburghgin.com; 9:45am-4:45pm daily; tours £25-100

For years the award-winning Edinburgh Gin was actually produced in England, but now it is firmly back in its namesake city. Underground tours of the compact distillery include a history lesson that will reveal the horrific social fallout of the Gin Craze of the 18th century when sanitary conditions were poor and people drank gin like it was water. Thankfully, today gin drinking is altogether more refined, and it is a fashionable drink of choice.

On the Distillery Tasting Experience (1 hour; £25), you are taken through the surprisingly simple process, before squeezing into the tiny still room to see the distillery's two copper stills, Flora and Caledonia, up close. Afterward you'll get to sample some of the wares with a gin and tonic in a booth tucked into one of the bare-brick alcoves. The Gin Connoisseur Tour (75 minutes; 11am, 1pm, and 3pm Mon.-Fri., 11am-3pm hourly Sat., 11am, 1pm, 2pm, and 3pm Sun.; £25) includes all of the above plus a tutored tasting, while on the Gin Making Tour (three hours; 12:15pm daily; £100), you can craft your own bespoke gin, even down to personalized labeling. Advanced booking is essential, particularly on Saturdays. Tours mid-week and on Sunday have more availability.

After dark, when the distillery is closed for the day, the venue turns into Heads & Tales, a speakeasy-style gin bar. Edinburgh Gin also now has a second distillery in the Biscuit Factory in Leith (4-6 Anderson Place), though tours are not yet available.

Edinburgh Zoo

134 Corstorphine Road; tel. 0131 334 9171; www. edinburghzoo.org.uk; 10am-6pm daily Apr.-Sept., 10am-5pm daily Oct. and Mar., 10am-4pm daily
Nov.-Feb., last entry one hour before closing; adult £19.95, child £11.35, under 3 free, concessions £18.10

A little out of the city center, this zoo has been home to the only giant pandas in the U.K., the female Tian Tian ("Sweetie") and the male Yang Guang ("Sunshine"), who have been on loan from China since 2011 and are due to go back (though the zoo is hoping to extend their stay). At busy times you may need to book a time slot to view the solitary creatures, each of which has its own enclosure; the pair are only brought together once a year in mating season.

The zoo offers talks throughout the day, so you can learn a little more about the resident Sumatran tigers, the sun bears, and the chimpanzees. Don't miss the daily penguin parade (2:15pm) when the King, Gentoo, and Rockhopper penguins leave their enclosure and go on a stroll with their keeper—if they are in the mood, that is.

The fairly generous animal enclosures are set amid 80 acres (32 hectares) of hilly parkland, and, though there are clear paths, some of them involve steep slopes. Make sure to visit the pair of Scottish wildcats, which look like slightly larger versions of domestic cats (though you wouldn't want to stroke them), and are still found in remote parts of the Highlands and are being reintroduced to other areas.

The zoo is easily accessible from the city center; jump on a number 12, 26, or 31 bus from the city center (£1.80). Book tickets online for the reduced rates listed.

Dean Village

Dean Path, Edinburgh EH4 3AY

Edinburgh's secret water mill village looks more like it belongs in Amsterdam than Scotland. Just a 10-minute walk from the West End (20 minutes from Princes Street), it's the remains of a former thriving milling community, and mill stones and plaques

1: Scottish National Gallery of Modern Art
2: St. Bernard's Well along the Water of Leith
3: Dean Village

decorated with bread and pies can still be found throughout the village.

In modern times the conservation area has been sensitively regenerated, and the old granaries are now home to offices and luxury flats—a calm sanctuary from city life. From here, it's a lovely walk along the Water of Leith into Stockbridge, via **St. Bernard's Well**—a well once said to have healing waters that is marked in a typically showy fashion with a pillared dome around a marble statue of Hygieia, the Roman and Greek Goddess of Health.

From street level, most visitors reach the village via Bells Brae, a small road that leads under the Thomas Telford-designed **Dean Bridge** and on to Dean Path (bus 37 or 113 will take you to Drumsheugh Place, from where it's just a five-minute walk). However, far more romantic is to arrive along the Water of Leith, a river that flows through the city, either from Stockbridge or the path that leads down to the river from Belford Road, just before the entrance to the Scottish National Gallery of Modern Art.

Royal Botanic Gardens

Arboretum Place; tel. 0131 248 2909; www.rbge.org. uk; 10am-6pm daily Mar.-Sept., 10am-5pm daily Feb. and Oct., 10am-4pm daily Nov.-Jan.

This huge green space, which dates from 1670, is the perfect place to while away a leisurely Sunday afternoon and is just a short walk from the shops and restaurants of Stockbridge. Entrance to the garden, which includes 70 acres (28 hectares) of grounds, is free. There is normally a charge to enter the glasshouses, but these are closed for the foreseeable future while restoration work takes place to secure the future of the thousands of exotic plants within.

SOUTHSIDE
★ Pickering's Gin Distillery

1 Summerhall; tel. 0131 290 2124; www.pickeringsgin. com; office open 9am-5pm Mon.-Fri., tours Thurs.-Sun.; tours £15

In 2013, Pickering's became Edinburgh's first exclusive gin distillery to open in the city for 150 years. But that's beside the point. What makes Pickering's stand out—apart from its award-winning handcrafted gins—is its location in the very cool **Summerhall arts venue,** which becomes a fashionable hub come festival season. Interestingly, the distillery is also located on the site of an old animal hospital, but don't let that put you off.

Everything is done on site, from the distilling right through to the bottling and shipping,

the Royal Dick bar at Pickering's Gin Distillery

and this personal service shows. Though you should really book tours in advance, staff will accommodate walk-ins when they are able to, and you can usually pop in for a chat or to buy a bottle.

Tours (allow 1.5 hours) begin in the buzzing Royal Dick bar (open to visitors outside tour times, too), where you'll be met by a super helpful and enthusiastic member of staff who will have story upon story to tell you. There are usually one to two tours a day, but times vary. First things first—you'll be handed a gin and tonic to sip on as you're taken through to the miniscule distillery where you can see the two copper stills, Emily and Gertrude (named after the grandmothers of co-founders Marcus Pickering and Matt Gammell). You'll also see the bottling room before being taken back to the bar for some more tasting.

During Edinburgh Festivals, book ahead; Summerhall is a very popular venue.

LEITH
Royal Yacht Britannia
Ocean Drive; tel. 0131 555 5566; www. royalyachtbritannia.co.uk; 10am-3:30pm daily Jan.-Mar. and Oct.-Dec., 9:30am-4:30pm daily Apr.-Sept.; adult £17, child £8.75, under 5 free, family £47

Step aboard the Royal Yacht Britannia, one of Scotland's most popular attractions, for a glimpse into what life was like for Her Majesty The Queen and her family on their annual holiday around Scotland's Western Isles— the Queen once labeled it the one place in which she could truly relax. Its lavish decks and staterooms have also accommodated and entertained world leaders, including Nelson Mandela, Rajiv Gandhi, and Ronald Reagan. Highlights of a tour include seeing the bedroom Her Majesty once slept in and taking afternoon tea in the Royal Deck Tea Room.

Royalists will love peeking into the Royal Family's private lives, but for everyone else it may feel a bit sycophantic. Steer clear on wet days, which will spoil your enjoyment of the deck areas. The Royal Deck tearoom is a good place to warm up with a cuppa, but it can get busy.

To get here from the city center, you can take one of three buses: the 11, 22, or Skylink 200. Tickets cost £1.80 each way (£4.50 for Skylink) and can be bought on board with the correct change. Alternatively, you can get a Majestic Tour bus from Waverley Bridge (£16 per adult), which costs more but includes onboard commentary throughout the hour-long journey, a tour of the city, and 10 percent off Royal Britannia entry. Somewhat surprisingly, the Royal Yacht is accessed through a modern shopping mall, which slightly dampens the experience.

Performing Arts and Entertainment

CONCERT HALLS AND EVENT VENUES
USHER HALL
Lothian Road; tel. 0131 228 1155; www.usherhall. co.uk; lunchtime concerts £4, price varies for other events

First opening in 1914, today Scotland's premier concert hall, renowned for its acoustics, is housed in an Edwardian-modern hybrid building in the West End. It has been the main venue for the Edinburgh International Festival since 1947 and is used in Freedom of the City ceremonies. It also hosts visiting orchestras as well as respected world music, jazz, and blues musicians. The opulent **Usher Hall Organ,** covered in Spanish mahogany, takes center stage, and a lunchtime concert by city organist John Kitchen is not to be missed once it starts running again. Book in advance, as often there is a huge queue on the day.

SUMMERHALL

Summerhall Place; tel. 0131 560 1580; www. summerhall.co.uk; 9am-11pm Mon.-Thurs., 9am-1am Fri., 9:30am-1am Sat., 11am-11pm Sun.

One of the coolest places to hang out both during the Edinburgh Festivals and at other times of the year, this multi-arts complex is a go-to place for the city's hungry culture vultures looking for intimate events (none of the spaces are huge). It's set on the site of the old Royal Dick Veterinary College, and you'll see many artifacts from the building's former function on display. Shows here consistently attract critical acclaim and are held across several venues, including outside areas such as **The Terrace and the Roundabout** (particularly popular during the festival) and inside venues like **The Dissection Room**—home to the popular live music lineup of Nothing Ever Happens Here—which showcases new bands as well as established artists. There is also a regular Ceilidh night every Tuesday from 8pm.

THE PLEASANCE

60 Pleasance Courtyard; tel. 0131 556 1513; www. pleasance.co.uk

One of the most revered venues during festival season, The Pleasance is situated on the eastern fringes of the city near Holyrood Park and attracts international performers of repute. Throughout August the cobbled courtyard between the two main buildings becomes a huge beer garden for people attending one of the performances as they wander in and out of the main venues of **The Pleasance Bar** and the **Cabaret Bar,** which accommodate 320 and 164 people, respectively. More popular shows can also be hosted in the 750-seater **Pleasance Grand,** and there is a kidzone for little ones. It's so well catered for that many people set up here for the day and don't venture elsewhere.

Outside festival season, there are comedy and music events throughout the year, and the Edinburgh Festival previews in July are always worth a visit.

THEATER
EDINBURGH PLAYHOUSE

18-22 Greenside Lane; tel. 0844 871 3014; www. atgtickets.com/venues/edinburgh-playhouse

This former movie theater, modeled on New York's Roxy Cinema, hosts touring musicals and concerts at a snip of the London prices. Its authentic art deco facade gives it a vintage feel, but bar prices feel anything but old-fashioned, with drinks starting at around £4.50 for a can of beer.

The Pleasance

★ COMEDY

Edinburgh has something of a reputation to live up to when it comes to comedy: In 1960, a late-night revue called *Beyond the Fringe* at the Lyceum Theatre, starring Peter Cook, Dudley Moore, Alan Bennett, and Jonathan Miller, was so groundbreaking that many consider it as the forerunner of what was soon known as the "British satire boom." Much later, in 1981, the Perrier Comedy Awards became the first embodiment of the Edinburgh Comedy Awards, and ever since, comedians have been falling over themselves here to make audiences fall out of their seats.

In addition to the clubs featured below, Gilded Balloon (gildedballoon.co.uk) is a festival favorite, with pop-ups throughout the city. Though it was forced to close its permanent Rose Street venue in 2020, it does hope to open another year-round venue soon.

Freebie magazines *The List* and *Skinny*, available in pubs and cafés around the city, are useful for finding out what's on; www.timeout.com/edinburgh provides up-to-date reviews and gig listings.

THE STAND COMEDY CLUB

York Place; tel. 0131 558 7272; www.thestand. co.uk; 7:30pm-12am Mon.-Weds., 7pm-12am Thurs., 6pm-12am Fri.-Sat., 12:30pm-3:30pm and 7:30pm-12am Sun., box office 10am-7pm Mon.-Fri. and 12pm-7pm Sat.; tickets £3-15

With venues in Glasgow and Newcastle, The Stand is the undisputed king of Edinburgh's comedy scene. There's comedy every night of the week, but tickets, particularly for the much-lauded Saturday night show, do sell out, so book a few days before to avoid disappointment. Many big touring acts perform here, but with £3 tickets on Monday for The Stand's infamous Red Raw night of new talent and a free improv show on Sunday afternoons, it really won't break the bank.

MONKEY BARREL COMEDY

9-11 Blair Street; tel. 0131 460 8421; www. monkeybarrelcomedy.com; 7pm-11pm Mon.-Fri., 4pm-11pm Sat., 4:30pm-11pm Sun.; tickets from £8

Just off the Royal Mile, this relatively new but respected venue is where you'll find many comedians between shows watching some of their peers. It's small, with bare brick walls and the teeniest of bars, but the atmosphere is electric—as long as you don't mind running the risk of being picked on.

Festivals and Events

For the month of August, the whole of Edinburgh is taken over by festival fever as five major cultural events take place concurrently, more than doubling the number of visitors to the city. It's not for the fainthearted, but it's when Edinburgh is at its best—a vibrant celebration of music, comedy, performance, and literature. The only other time of year that can perhaps live up to festival time in terms of liveliness is the annual New Year's celebration of Hogmanay.

AUGUST

EDINBURGH FRINGE FESTIVAL

Various locations; tel. 0131 226 0026; www.edfringe. com; August; ticket prices vary

When people talk about the Edinburgh Festival, they're usually referring to the Edinburgh Fringe Festival. What began as a slight act of rebellion by a small number of theater groups has now grown into the largest arts festival in the world—thousands of performances take place across hundreds of venues each year. Pretty much anyone can perform, meaning that the quality ranges massively, but that's part of the fun. There

Navigating the Edinburgh Festival

Edinburgh is a lively, fun city year-round, but it really comes into its own each August, when hundreds of thousands of people arrive for the giant extravaganza that is the Edinburgh Festival. The pandemic has meant things were more subdued in 2021, but I suspect this is just a short-term change—people are itching for the festival to return.

Usually held over 25 days, the world's largest arts festival takes place in every corner of the city, in arts houses, theaters, comedy clubs, and pubs. **Princes Street Gardens** becomes an outdoor concert space, and huge temporary structures are erected across Edinburgh to house the seemingly endless stream of comedians, musicians, acrobats, and artists. Events go from the morning until 5am, with just a short closure before it all starts again—it's the only way to fit in all 50,000 performances. Allow at least two days to have an enjoyable festival experience (three to five days is better).

Though it's known collectively as the Edinburgh Festival, it is made up of several festivals that run at the same time—most significantly, the **Edinburgh International Festival,** which features a program of dance, opera, music, and theater; and the **Edinburgh Festival Fringe,** which began as an unofficial sideshow to the Edinburgh International Festival but is now a legendary festival in its own right. Also running at the same time are the **Royal Edinburgh Military Tattoo,** the **Edinburgh Art Festival,** and the **Edinburgh International Book Festival.** It's hard to know where one festival begins and the other ends.

TICKETS

Many of the events are free, but some are ticketed. It can be hard to decide what to see, and some shows will be better than others. It's best to choose two to three shows to pre-book, leaving a bit of time in your schedule to fit in an unexpected visit to the best new thing that your new pal at the bar just told you about.

To learn about what's on, grab a copy of the official **Fringe Programme** (www.edfringe. com), released online each June. It's also worth following the festival's social media channels throughout August for last-minute changes and surprise appearances. The *Scotsman* news-

is everything from comedy to music, cabaret, and dance. You do need to book tickets for more well-known acts or hyped-up performances (from a few quid for relative unknowns to around £25-30 for big acts), but for a lot of performances you can just turn up, and some events may be free.

EDINBURGH INTERNATIONAL FESTIVAL

Various locations; tel. 0131 473 2000; www.eif.co.uk; August; ticket prices vary

The more mature sibling of the Fringe, this showcase of music, dance, and spoken word leans heavily toward the classical side of things and is often deemed a lot more serious than its Fringe sister. Nevertheless, quality is assured as—unlike the Fringe Festival where anyone can apply for a slot—here top-class

musicians, dancers, and visual artists are invited to perform. As it runs at the same time as the Fringe, there's no reason you can't do a little bit of both. Some events may be free.

EDINBURGH MILITARY TATTOO

Castle Esplanade; 9pm Mon.-Fri. and 7:30pm Sat. August; from £25

Each evening throughout festival season, this showcase of military pomp and ceremony takes place in front of the backlit Edinburgh Castle and is watched live by more than 200,000 people. Tightly choreographed routines are performed against a sea of pageantry and accompanied by the rousing battle tunes of Scotland's regiments played by the Massed Pipes and Drums and the Massed Military Bands. The pinnacle of the evening is when the lone piper plays his sorrowful lament

paper does a good hour-by-hour listing of what's on, local freebie magazine *The List* publishes weekly during the festival (it's normally every other month), and reviews in the *Edinburgh Evening News* are really useful.

In an attempt to combat the lack of diversity at the Edinburgh Festival, in 2018, **Fringe of Colour,** a public database listing all shows featuring people of color at the festival was launched by Jessica Brough. The database aims to promote awareness of these shows (particularly those where 50 percent of performers are people of color). Brough also wants to attract a more diverse audience, and, to this end, the project offers 50 percent or more off ticket prices for certain shows for people of color under 25 (www.fringeofcolour.co.uk).

ACCOMMODATIONS

Accommodations fill up fast around the festival, so if you want a good choice of places to stay without having to remortgage your house, you should book around six months in advance.

The **Festival Partnership** (edinburghfestival.net), a letting agent focused on finding accommodation in the city in August, has lots of private apartments to rent, but you would be looking at paying upward of £750 per week for a studio apartment. The **Edinburgh International Festival's website** (www.eif.co.uk) has suggestions of places to stay, from premium hotels to much more affordable self-catering or Airbnb options.

One alternative is a room in the University of Edinburgh's **Pollock Halls** (www.book.accom. ed.ac.uk), where you can get a basic en suite with buffet breakfast for £490 per week (less for a shared bathroom). Perhaps the best value for money, **Edinburgh Festival Camping** (Hallyards Road, Ingliston; tel. 0131 564 1405; https://edinburghfestivalcamping.com) has pitches plus bell tents for hire (from £16pp each night in your own tent, £38pn for two in a motorhome/campervan pitch, and £43pn for two in a pre-pitched tent). The campsite is serviced by buses until 11:50pm (£1.80 or £2.80 each way, depending on the bus), after which you can try two late-night buses at 1:30am or 3am. Or you can get an Uber for around £25 if you want to stay out and head back to your campsite when you choose (probably more likely).

from the castle walls, which is then followed by a chorus of "Auld Lang Syne," a riotous fireworks display, and a military flyby. It's rare to witness such a scene of unapologetic patriotism.

Tickets start at £25, but you will be positioned right at the back. There is a much wider choice of seats if you are willing to pay up to £60, while £80 will get you near the front, £150 will get you Premier Seats, and for a place in the Royal Gallery you'll need to fork out upward of £300 per ticket. Some Saturdays there is a second performance at 10:30pm.

EDINBURGH ART FESTIVAL

Various venues; tel. 0131 226 6558; www. edinburghartfestival.com; prices vary for special exhibitions

Since 2004 this festival, which usually kicks off just prior to the other festivals, has been providing some visual arts amid the forest of stand-up comics and avant-garde theatrics. Set across various galleries throughout the city, including the Dovecot Studios and the City Art Centre, as well as incorporating some site-specific work in pop-ups designed with the festival in mind, it covers everything from photography to painting and textiles. Many events are free.

EDINBURGH INTERNATIONAL BOOK FESTIVAL

Charlotte Square; tel. 0345 373 5888; www. edbookfest.co.uk; many events free

This literary event used to be set across a mini tented village in the center of Charlotte Square, but in 2021 it moved to Edinburgh College of Art, so it remains to be seen where future events will be held. Nevertheless, for two weeks in the middle of August, this festival celebrates the printed word and beyond, with talks from novelists, comic-book creators, illustrators, biographers, and more. There are over 900 events, ranging from sessions to get young readers interested in books to creative writing workshops and discussions on everything from characterization to reporting ethics. Hopefully, slightly naughtier events for bookish minds, such as the night **Unbound literary cabaret,** will also return.

DECEMBER
HOGMANAY

Various locations; tel. 0131 510 0395; www. edinburghshogmanay.com; street party tickets from £31, concert in the Gardens from £65, other prices vary

During Hogmanay, one of the greatest New Year's celebrations in the world, the streets of Edinburgh once came alive with festivities, and I've no doubt the jubilation will soon be back. Central to proceedings has always been the huge street party, plus there is a Ceilidh under the castle, a concert in Princes Street Gardens, and an incredible fireworks display. Tickets sell out fast and so do hotels, so book well in advance.

For a long time an evocative torch procession, inspired by Viking tradition, has taken place down the Royal Mile to Holyrood Park, where guests have been able to pay a little extra for the chance to join in with their own torch rather than remain mere bystanders. There's yet to be an overriding Hogmanay ticket to get you access to everything, but a ticket for the Concert in the Gardens generally gives you access to the street party where you'll be able to view the fireworks. Don't forget, Hogmanay celebrations carry on to New Year's Day (January 2 is a national holiday).

JUNE/JULY
CEREMONY OF THE KEYS

Palace of Holyroodhouse; June/July; free

Each summer Her Majesty The Queen takes up residence in the Palace of Holyroodhouse during what is known as Holyrood Week (or Royal Week). Ancient tradition dictates that, before she does so, she must be handed the keys on the forecourt of the palace by the Lord Provost in the Ceremony of the Keys. Then she hands them back—a symbolic gesture that shows she is entrusting the keys into the hands of elected officials. During the ceremony, the national anthem is played, and a 21-gun royal salute rings out from Edinburgh Castle at the other end of the Royal Mile.

Sports and Recreation

Edinburgh has lots of green spaces in which to kick back and take in the views or to recover from the night before. With cycle routes, waterways, and its own nature park in the form of Holyrood Park, the city also offers opportunity for adventure.

TOURS
BLACK HISTORY WALKS EDINBURGH

Melville Monument, St. Andrew Square; tel. 07429 540 849; www.facebook.com/blackhistoryedinburgh; 2pm Weds., 10am Sat.-Sun., check ahead

Finally, a tour of Edinburgh that tells the city's story through the eyes of people of color, by bringing to life the city's residents and visitors of African and Caribbean descent from the 16th century onward, with a focus on Edinburgh's part in the transatlantic slave trade. Tours last two hours and are run by Lisa Williams, founder of the Edinburgh Caribbean Association, who will offer discounts at her discretion to people who cannot afford the full cost.

EDINBURGH LITERARY PUB TOUR

*18-20 Grassmarket; tel. 0131 226 6665; www.
edinburghliterarypubtour.co.uk; 7:30pm daily
May-Sept., 7:30pm Thurs.-Sun. Apr. and Oct., 7:30pm
Fri. and Sun. Jan.-Mar., 7:30pm Fri. Nov.-Dec.; £16 or
£14 in advance online*

This lively two-hour tour, which starts inside
the Beehive Inn in Grassmarket, is as much
a pub tour as it is a literary one. Told by two
actors—one playing a bohemian, one an intellectual—who take visitors in and out of
some of the city's oldest taverns, or howffs,
their stories give invaluable insight into the
writing habits of some of Scotland's literary
greats.

AULD REEKIE TOURS

*45 Niddry Street; tel. 0131 557 4700; www.
auldreekietours.com; from £14*

Want to scare yourself witless? These ghost
tours take place at some of the spookiest locations across the city, the Edinburgh Vaults
(sometimes called the Niddry Street Vaults).
The original Vaults Tour (about one hour)
burrows beneath South Bridge Street where
your guide will regale you with horrid tales
of life in the slums and even bring you to an
underground witches' temple.

EDINBURGH BUS TOURS

*Waverley Bridge; tel. 0131 220 0770; www.
edinburghtour.com; Edinburgh Tour adult £8,
under 15 free, Royal Edinburgh Ticket adult £59,
concessions £52, child £32, under 5 free*

While it's by no means the cheapest way of
traveling around the city, if time is short,
then hopping on or off one of these bus
tours with a knowledgeable guide can be
a great way to cram in as many sights as
possible. The Edinburgh Tour takes in
many of the main sights of the Old Town
and New Town, and you can jump on and
off at your leisure throughout the day; the
Royal Edinburgh Ticket allows unlimited
travel aboard three bus routes over two
days, plus entry to Edinburgh Castle, the
Royal Yacht Britannia, and the Palace of
Holyroodhouse.

GEOWALKS

*23 Summerfield Place; tel. 0131 555 5488; www.
geowalks.co.uk/iarthur.html; £25 for a two-hour tour*

Join this tour of Arthur's Seat with Geowalks,
accompanied by a geologist. Setting off from
Canongate, you can opt to do it on your own
or in a group (the more people, the cheaper it
will be). Choose between a two-hour hike to
Arthur's Seat or a gentle circular walk around
Salisbury Crags for views of Edinburgh's most
famous peak.

PARKS
THE MEADOWS

Melville Drive

This park, just south of the Old Town,
marks the boundary with the Southside and
hosts many community events and festivals
throughout spring and summer. It's got a
small café and is home to the largest play area
in the city. It's a good place to catch some rays
when the sun does have its hat on, all while
taking in views of Arthur's Seat.

INTERLEITH PARK

Arboretum Road

This is where Stockbridge locals come to walk
on Sunday or laze about on warm afternoons.
It also offers nice views of Edinburgh Castle,
so it's a good place to watch the New Year's
fireworks. There are several lakes to walk by,
and the sundial garden is a lovely spot for a
picnic.

HIKING AND CYCLING
WATER OF LEITH WALKWAY

Distance: *1.2 miles (1.9 km)*
Walking/Cycling Time: *25 minutes/15 minutes*
Trailhead: *Scottish National Gallery of Modern
Art*
Information and Services: *www.waterofleith.
org.uk*

The Water of Leith is a river that runs through
Edinburgh, and this pedestrian pathway runs
gently alongside much of it, occasionally leading up and onto the road before coming back
down to the river's side. Though the water-
way actually runs all the way from Balerno,

southwest of the city, to Leith in the east, this walk starts just outside the **Scottish National Gallery of Modern Art** and leads to Stockbridge, passing through Dean Village en route.

From the gallery, you descend some steps from Bedford Road, onto the river path, and from here follow signs toward **Stockbridge,** where on Sunday you will find a bustling craft and food market (10am-5pm).

If you're feeling particularly energetic, you could follow the Water of Leith all the way to Leith itself (a further 3 miles/5 km from Stockbridge), where there are plenty of lunchtime spots along the Shore.

ARTHUR'S SEAT CYCLE CIRCUIT
Distance: *3.3 miles (5.3 km)*
Cycling Time: *30-40 minutes*
Trailhead: *Queen's Drive, St Margaret's Loch*
Information and Services: *www.strava.com/routes/4271906*

Circling Edinburgh's most famous crag, Arthur's Seat, this cycle route is fairly strenuous, but you'll be rewarded with breathtaking views across Holyrood Park and the Firth of Forth. Starting at St. Margaret's Loch, the route follows Queen's Drive, which loops around the park, with the long-extinct volcano in the middle, before bringing you back to your start point. Be aware that the road is open to traffic, except on Sunday, and the path that runs alongside it is also used by walkers.

Leaving St. Margaret's Loch (with the loch on your right-hand side), you'll ascend over the next mile to Dunsapie Loch. This is the toughest part of the route. Once you reach Dunsapie, there is a flat stretch where you can enjoy the views. Keep following Queen's Drive up a slight incline for views over Edinburgh's Old Town, and then it's the fun bit: downhill all the way to the Palace of Holyroodhouse and back to where you started. In total, the route is about 3 miles (5 km) and should take 30-40 minutes.

BIKETRAX
11 Lochrin Place; tel. 0131 228 6633; www.biketrax. co.uk; from £20 per day

While cycling in the city center can be tricky, getting on two wheels can be great for a little off-road exploration, including around Arthur's Seat and along the banks of the Union Canal. The rental office for this hire company is based in Tollcross in Southside (toward Bruntsfield).

RUGBY

MURRAYFIELD
Roseburn Street; tel. 0131 346 5160; ticket.centre@ sru.org.uk; www.scottishrugby.org; match prices vary; tours 11am Mon.-Sat., extra tour 2:30pm Thurs. and Fri.; adult £12, child £7, under 5 free

Though many sports fans who come to Scotland think of golf, the sport Edinburgh is probably most associated with is rugby. To the west of the city center, this sports stadium is the largest of its kind in Scotland and the home of Scotland's Rugby Union. Tickets to matches can be booked through Scottish Rugby, and those for more popular matches are released in batches over a few months.

Watching a rugby match here is a must for any fan—the stands are famed for their high-spirited fans and good-humored banter. Lots of spectators bring children, and there is food and drink available (burgers and hot dogs, etc.), or you can bring a small amount of food (no large hampers) or sealed bottles of water or soft drinks.

If you can't make a match, tours of the stadium allow you to see the Calcutta Cup, the trophy awarded to the winning team when England and Scotland play each other in February or March each year (at least until England wins it back), and visit the players' locker room before walking through the tunnel right up to the pitch. Tours should be booked in advance.

Shopping

From boutique outlets to designer shops, high-street brands, and the ubiquitous tartan and whisky stores, Edinburgh has no shortage of places to spend your vacation money.

OLD TOWN

The Old Town is the obvious place to shop for souvenirs and specialty Scottish gifts and produce. While the wares in some of the shops on the **Royal Mile** are overpriced and of questionable quality, there are still some reputable places to buy authentic items. Just a few minutes' walk from the castle end of the Royal Mile, **Grassmarket** and the higgledy-piggledy shops of nearby **Victoria Street** (one of the places that inspired J. K. Rowling's Diagon Alley) are filled with independent and specialist proprietors of a slightly higher caliber than Scottish-themed gift shops elsewhere.

Clothing
MARCHBRAE

375 High Street; tel. 0131 226 3997; https:// marchbrae.com; 10am-7pm daily

This shop matches traditional Scottish fabrics and designs with practical clothing that will actually come in handy should you venture to the Highlands. Choose from quilted Barbour jackets perfect for keeping the Scottish chill off, fitted tweed jackets, and cozy tartan slippers.

HOUSE OF EDINBURGH

2 St. Giles Street; tel. 0131 225 5178; 10am-6pm daily

House of Edinburgh offers a good selection of lambswool tartan scarves, alongside kilts, cashmere jumpers, and cardigans, and quality is higher than what you'll find in some Royal Mile shops. Rows of color-coded men's and women's sweaters make for a pleasurable browsing experience.

Whisky
WHISKI SHOP

4-7 North Bank Street; tel. 0131 225 1532; www. whiskirooms.co.uk; 10am-7pm daily

This shop, which also has a good restaurant and offers **whisky tastings** (must be booked in advance; from £25; a more serious and grown-up alternative to the Scotch Whisky Experience), has more than 500 whiskies on offer. If you know what you want, they should have it here. If you don't, the knowledgeable staff will be able to talk you through some choice buys. If you don't want to carry your purchases home with you, you can order online as the shop ships worldwide.

ROYAL MILE WHISKIES

379 High Street; tel. 0131 524 9380; www. royalmilewhiskies.com; 10am-6pm daily

This renowned whisky merchant is a good place to pick up a bottle of your favorite tipple. Its interior is a little more old-school than others in the area, with row upon row of wooden shelves crammed with whiskies, and attentive staff to help guide your choice of single malts from well-established distilleries and smaller scale producers. There's also a good international selection. Plus, they ship worldwide if you haven't space to cart it home.

Gifts
MR WOOD'S FOSSILS

53-59 Cowgatehead; tel. 0131 220 1344; www. mrwoodsfossils.co.uk; 10am-5:30pm daily

This unique treasure trove began by selling the collections of renowned fossil hunter Stan Wood, who died in 2012. Self-taught Wood is known for discovering the *Westlothiana lizziae*—"Lizzie"—thought at the time to be the oldest reptile ever discovered, now on display in the National Museum of Scotland. Alongside fossils, minerals, and meteorites, there's also jewelry featuring the likes of ammonite spirals or even 500-million-year-old trilobites. Minerals start from as little as £2.50, while a meteorite pendant (some dating back billions of years) are priced from just £85.

Books
ARMCHAIR BOOKS

72-74 West Port; tel. 0131 229 5927; www. armchairbooks.co.uk; 12:30pm-5:30pm Sun.-Thurs., 10am-6:30pm Fri.-Sat.

Located just above Grassmarket, this secondhand bookstore is a book lover's dream. Take your time searching the dusty shelves for unexpected finds, which are "very nearly" alphabetized.

NEW TOWN

You'll find high-street favorites such as Urban Outfitters on **Princes Street,** parallel to **George Street,** home to more upmarket and chic clothing stores, such as Hobbs and LK Bennett. **Broughton Street,** a little northeast of George Street, is a hot spot for trendy independents.

Clothing
JOEY D

54 Broughton Street; tel. 0131 557 6672; 10:30am-6pm daily

For couture clothing with a distinct Scottish edge, Joey D specializes in cutting-edge fashion (for men and women) using old cast-offs of tweed, tartan, and army-wear. The end results have quite a punk feel, and Joey himself is quite a character. Don't be put off by the slightly dingy workshop; anyone is welcome to browse the shop and Joey is usually around, working on his next project.

Gifts
DRAGONFLY

111a Broughton Street; tel. 0131 629 4246; www. thedragonflygifts.co.uk; 10am-6pm Mon.-Sat., 11am-4pm Sun.

For a bit of gift-buying inspiration, visit this original little shop. There are quaint tea sets,

local artworks, retro and vintage clothing for kids and adults, and well-priced jewelry.

STOCKBRIDGE

This neighborhood is home to a variety of quirky, bohemian independent retailers and charity shops, particularly around **Raeburn Place.** On Sunday, it's almost compulsory to pop along to **Stockbridge Market** and browse the artisan stalls for gifts or nibbles.

Markets
STOCKBRIDGE MARKET

1 Saunders Street; tel. 0131 261 6181; www. stockbridgemarket.com; 10am-5pm Sun.

This popular outdoor Sunday food and craft market isn't huge, but it's always bustling—a good place to pick up organic goods or unusual gifts, such as framed prints of Scottish wildlife and handmade tweed bags, from small independent traders. It's a good, cheap lunchtime spot too. **Harajuku Kitchen** serves good Japanese street food, while the health conscious will want to stop by the **Edinburgh Fermentarium** stall for some Stoatin' Sauerkraut (including turmeric root and Himalayan salt) or the Braw Slaw—its version of coleslaw that includes beetroot, apple, cabbage, and star anise.

Clothing
MARY'S LIVING & GIVING SHOP

34a Raeburn Place; tel. 0131 315 2856; www. facebook.com/mlgstockbridge; 10am-5pm Mon.-Sat., 12pm-4pm Sun.

Stockbridge is overflowing with good secondhand shops, but this is perhaps the best when it comes to kitting yourself out. Part of fashion and retail expert Mary Portas's brainwave of transforming the high street by turning charity shops into places people actually want to go to, it feels more vintage boutique (think London's King's Road, circa 1969) than jumble sale, and the quality of clothing (particularly women's) is high, even though the prices are not.

WEST END
Clothing
FRONTIERS MAN

18 Stafford Street; tel. 0131 538 3546; www.
frontiers-man.com; 10:30am-5:30pm Mon.-Fri.,
10am-6pm Sat., 12pm-4pm Sun.

The nearby **Frontiers Woman** (16b Stafford Street) has been a favorite West End shop for years, and a couple of years ago they opened this second shop. Both sell luxurious clothes from smaller labels. The ethos is individual style with a little flair, so bright colors and vibrant prints feature heavily. The lambswool hats and scarves made here in Scotland are particularly lovely.

Jewelry
LILY LUNA

43 William Street; tel. 0131 467 8245; www.lilyluna.
co.uk; 10am-5:30pm Mon.-Sat.

This jewelry shop is a great little find. Pieces are all handmade and sourced from across the world, and fairly priced, too. You can find ethical pieces from Ethiopia alongside delicate necklaces and rings made with unusual geometric designs, and they are pretty much all gorgeous.

SOUTHSIDE

A 20-minute walk south from Grassmarket (or a ride on the no. 42 bus from outside the Scottish National Gallery) will bring you to **Bruntsfield,** an affluent neighborhood known for its unique shops, especially when it comes to food and drink, while other gems can be found just south of the Meadows.

Jewelry
ROSIE BROWN

148 Bruntsfield Place; tel. 0131 228 9269; www.
rosiebrownjewellery.com; 10am-5:30pm Mon.-Sat.,
11am-5pm Sun.

The lovely pieces in this shop are designed by owner Rosie herself and made in the shop's workshop by experienced jewelers. The range is very feminine and classic, with links featuring motifs such as butterflies and raindrops around pearl bracelets, and silver and gold bangles and chains. The small shop is genteel with a calm ambience, and each piece is hallmarked and presented in a gift box wrapped in ribbon, which will make the receiver of your gift feel very special indeed.

Handicrafts
ART & CRAFT COLLECTIVE

93 Causewayside; tel. 0131 629 9123; www.
artcraftcollective.co.uk; 11am-5pm Thurs.-Sat.,
11am-4pm Sun.-Weds.

This gallery and gift shop, a little farther south of Summerhall, is a great place to pick up beautiful handmade gifts and support local artists at the same time. There are regularly rolling exhibitions showcasing the work of local artists, and the place is crammed with affordable pieces to buy, from ceramics to prints to jewelry and clothes.

Food

In 2021 there were four Michelin-starred restaurants in the city, meaning food in Edinburgh is serious business. There are good restaurants in pretty much every corner of the city. Around the Old Town fine-dining restaurants make the most of the splendid views and the city's heritage, while a slightly more glamorous crowd can be seen in the dining rooms of the New Town. The port district of Leith is understandably the go-to place for fresh seafood, while Stockbridge is becoming a foodie destination of note. Meanwhile, in the Southside, the village-style vibe creates the perfect setting for an array of relaxed cafés and ethical coffee shops.

If you want to sample traditional Scottish

fare, then **haggis** is the first dish you'll want to try. Most of the restaurants in the city will have some variation of this dish of sheep liver, lungs, and heart minced with lots of spices, onion, suet, and oatmeal, and, if it doesn't appear with your cooked breakfast, then to my mind you're within your rights to send the breakfast back (the same applies if there is no black pudding or tattie scones). If sheep entrails don't sound appealing, then vegetarian alternatives are available, which are also spicy and flavorsome. The common accompaniment to haggis is **neeps and tatties** (swede, or rutabaga, and potato), usually mashed together.

If you see it on a menu, you'd be a fool not to try **Scottish wild salmon** (ideally smoked) and if you like game, you might want to try **roasted grouse** (particularly when shooting season starts after the Glorious 12th, or August 12). Generally, what the best restaurants in Edinburgh have gotten very good at is serving up locally sourced and seasonal produce, often coming from the Borders or Fife, so try to stick to those places. It's also worth noting that most restaurants reduced opening hours after opening post-lockdown, but I would expect those opening times to start creeping up soon.

OLD TOWN
Traditional Fare
★ THE GRAIN STORE

30 Victoria Street; tel. 0131 225 7635; www. grainstore-restaurant.co.uk; 12pm-4pm and 5:30pm-10:30pm Thurs.-Sat., 12:30pm-4pm Sun.; entrées £14

Set beneath the stone archways of the original storerooms high above Victoria Street's shops, this intimate candlelit restaurant is a lovely setting for sampling Scottish produce with a creative edge. Absolutely everything is made on site—from the pasta to the freshly baked bread—and dishes include home-smoked Orkney salmon and a good selection of game, including pigeon and partridge. It's not cheap, but food this good does come at a price.

Modern Scottish
★ WEDGWOOD THE RESTAURANT

267 Canongate; tel. 0131 558 8737; www. wedgwoodtherestaurant.co.uk; 12pm-4pm and 5pm-10:30pm Weds.-Sun., last booking around 1 hour 30 minutes before closing; entrées £9.95

Though the food at this husband-and-wife-run restaurant is definitely of fine-dining quality, the service is anything but sniffy. The set lunch menus offer the best value, but for a real taste of what they are capable of, try the Wee Tour of Scotland tasting menu (£60). It's Scottish food, no doubt about it, but with international influences: the Scottish scallops come with a cauliflower korma with pistachio and peanut crust, while the Highland venison with West Calder black pudding has the surprise addition of smoked paprika. Add a wine pairing for an extra £35.

Fine Dining
THE WITCHERY BY THE CASTLE

352 Castlehill, Royal Mile; tel. 0131 225 5613; www. thewitchery.com; 12pm-10:30pm daily, afternoon tea 3pm-4pm Mon.-Fri.; entrees £10

The Witchery's rich baroque dining room is one of the most romantic places to dine in the city, and the restaurant's Angus beef steak tartare is the stuff of legend. On warm nights, **The Secret Garden** is a lovely little enclave hidden in a historic courtyard with its own terrace. Whenever you come, you will inevitably see well-dressed locals and travelers splashing out and tucking into fresh seafood platters and rich dishes of game, beef, lamb, or fish, all served in the most theatrical of settings.

Indian
MOTHER INDIA'S CAFÉ

3-5 Infirmary Street; tel. 0131 524 9801; www. motherindia.co.uk; 12pm-10pm daily; dishes £5.75

Serving tapas-style Indian food, this is a very wallet-friendly option that is popular among the student population. Service is swift yet friendly, and dishes are well-sized—4-6 dishes are usually plenty for two people, meaning you could have a tasty meal for under £15 a head.

Afternoon Tea
COLONNADES AT THE SIGNET LIBRARY

Signet Library, Parliament Square; tel. 0131 226 1064; www.thesignetlibrary.co.uk/colonnades; 11am-4:30pm Weds.-Sun.; afternoon tea £45 per person

Perhaps the grandest place in the city for afternoon tea, this 19th-century building has been restored in all its glory, complete with fluted Corinthian columns and neoclassical balustrades. The food is of the utmost quality, provided by one of Her Majesty The Queen's very own caterers (and it should be at this price). Afternoon tea is served on silver trays and starts with a selection of savories (ham, pea and truffle pie, and tomato chutney finger sandwiches), followed by sweets (such as a rosewater Battenberg cake and a strawberry and basil tart), plus freshly made scones with the obligatory clotted cream and jam.

Local Produce
TIMBERYARD

10 Lady Lawson Street; tel. 0131 221 1222; www.timberyard.co; 3pm-11pm Thurs., 12pm-11pm Fri.-Sun.; entrées £10

This ethical restaurant is one of the most inventive in Edinburgh. All the wine is organic, edible herbs and flowers grown in the restaurant's raised beds feature heavily on the menu, and everything else is sourced from artisan growers and producers. Tasting menus include a pescatarian option, and the setting in a former warehouse has a very cool ambience. Seasonal options change all the time, but you can expect to see a good selection of seafood dishes (scallops with apple and parsley, for example) alongside the likes of sweetbreads and lamb or beef options.

Light Bites
PROCAFFEINATION

4 St Mary's Street; tel. 07480 641 806; 10am-6pm daily; coffee £2.60, pastry £2.45

If you're heading down to the palace along the Royal Mile, take a right onto St. Mary's Street and you'll find this small café, which does barista-style coffee, homemade pastries, and yummy smoothies. The interior has a stripped-back bohemian feel, and with only three tables, most people take away, but there's always a nice buzz about the place even as you're waiting in line.

CAFÉ AT THE PALACE

Palace of Holyroodhouse; tel. 0131 652 3685; www.rct.uk/visit/palace-of-holyroodhouse/cafe-at-the-palace; 12pm-4pm Thurs.-Mon. Apr.-Oct., 12pm-3pm Thurs.-Mon. Nov.-Mar.; afternoon tea £21 per person

End your visit to the Palace of Holyroodhouse with lunch or afternoon tea here. Lunch options include soups, sandwiches, and one or two hot options. You can eat outside at tables in the historic mews or retreat to the pleasant back room. The latter is best for afternoon tea, and at £21 (£30 with a glass of champagne) it's a fair bit cheaper than the offering at Colonnades.

NEW TOWN
Contemporary
THE LITTLE CHARTROOM

14 Bonnington Road; tel. 0131 556 6600; www.thelittlechartroom.com; 5pm-11pm Thurs.-Fri., 12pm-4:30pm (last seating 2pm) and 5:30pm-11pm Sat., 12pm-4:30pm and 6pm-11pm Sun.; entrees £12.50

Recently moved into a new, larger venue, this is a very special place to savor chef Roberta Hall's take on modern French-British-style cooking. The menu is small and rightly so; you wouldn't expect a wide range of choice at your friend's house, so why here? Trust in Roberta's flair and expertise. Her husband, Shaun McCarron, is front of house. Last dinner seatings are 8:15pm and the couple are also opening a new restaurant in Little Chartroom's former home in Albert Place.

Local Produce
★ THE LOOKOUT BY GARDENER'S COTTAGE

Calton Hill; tel. 01875 870 884; www. thelookoutedinburgh.co; 10am-10pm Sat.-Sun., 12pm-10pm Thurs.-Fri.; entrees £10

This new restaurant, a partnership between the well-established nearby Gardener's Cottage restaurant and the Collective, who helped turn the nearby City Observatory into a cool new art space, is part of the reason Calton Hill is becoming the new place to be. Floor-to-ceiling windows and its position on a cantilever suspended over Calton Hill's northwest slope ensure excellent views, while the strictly seasonal menu will leave you feeling good from the inside out.

Coffee
★ FORTITUDE

3C York Place; tel. 0131 557 3063; www. fortitudecoffee.com; 9am-1pm and 1:30pm-4pm daily; entrees £7.95

Edinburgh's coffee game is strong and this coffee shop (and its sister coffee/cycle shop at 66 Hamilton Place, Stockbridge), right by the Scottish National Portrait Gallery, is so renowned for its specialty roasts that it even has its own merchandise. Like many coffee shops, it's small—though they manage to squeeze quite a few people in—and the clean, minimalist interiors are instantly relaxing. Just as well, as you may have to wait—each coffee is ground to order.

Steak
THE DOME

14 George Street; tel. 0131 624 8624; www. thedomeedinburgh.com/grillroom; 12pm-late daily; entrées £8.50

Once the Commercial Bank of Scotland head-quarters, this is now a favored lunch spot where you can dine under the spectacular glass dome that gives the building its name, in the **Grill Room.** The set menu is well priced, though a bit uninspiring; the à la carte menu is more exciting and includes ribeye steak or an option for Angus venison fillet. Afternoon tea (£22) is served in the opulent **Georgian Tea Room** (all crisp linen, cushioned ebony chairs, and chandeliers).

Indian
DISHOOM

3a St. Andrew Square; tel. 0131 222 8975; www. dishoom.com/edinburgh; 8am-11pm Mon.-Thurs., 8am-12am Fri., 9am-12am Sat., 9am-11pm Sun.; dishes £5.50

The first restaurant outside London for this much-lauded chain, Dishoom pays homage to the Irani cafés of Bombay and is utterly sublime. Grab a morning bacon naan roll or pop in for dinner to try the house black daal, which is cooked for over 24 hours. Dishes are well-priced and memorable.

Light Bites
SOCIAL BITE

131 Rose Street; tel. 0131 220 8206; https:// social-bite.co.uk; 7am-3pm Mon.-Fri., 8am-4pm Sat.; breakfast bagels £2.50

This sandwich shop (one of four and counting in the city) is part of an ambitious plan: to end homelessness in Scotland. Social Bite donates 100 percent of its profits to charity. Plus, it uses a pay-it-forward scheme whereby customers are able to buy a meal for an un-sheltered person who can come in to claim a free meal in the same way that a paying cus-tomer would, thereby removing some of the stigma. The breakfast bagels are outstanding value and pretty tasty, too. There is also now a Social Bite restaurant nearby, Vesta Bar & Kitchen (7-8 Queensferry Street), which closes for two hours every Monday to serve two-course meals to unsheltered people.

STOCKBRIDGE
Modern Scottish
★ THE SCRAN AND SCALLIE

1 Comely Bank Road; tel. 0131 332 6281; https:// scranandscallie.com; 12pm-10:30pm daily, last orders 9pm; entrées £9.50

This is a gastropub in the real sense of the word—simple pub grub (or scran as the Scottish like to say) cooked very well. The

Sunday roasts are renowned (book at least a few days in advance). Other highlights include the Highland burger and chips and The Scran and Scallie fish pie. It has a relaxed atmosphere and families are well looked after, with a living room with a sofa and TV if the kids get fidgety. Chef Tom Kitchin has also recently opened a bistro-style restaurant, Southside Scran, in Bruntsfield.

Small Plates
MERIENDA

30 North West Circus Place; tel. 0131 220 2020; https://eat-merienda.com; 12pm-2:30pm and 5:45pm-9:30pm Weds.-Sat., 12pm-8:30pm Sun.; plates £7

This restaurant, which serves up tapas-style plates of Scottish produce and seafood platters, was recently awarded a Michelin Bib Gourmand for serving quality food at good value. However, "good value" is a relative term as you'll need at least four or five dishes per person. Yet to reopen post pandemic, locals are hoping owners Campbell and Giselle will soon be back to doing what they do best; in the meantime, they will be running Eddie's Seafood Market in Marchmont (where their seafood platters may make the occasional appearance).

Fine Dining
★ THE STOCKBRIDGE RESTAURANT

54 St. Stephen Street; tel. 0131 226 6766; www. thestockbridgerestaurant.co.uk; 7pm-9:30pm Mon.-Fri., 12:30pm-2pm and 7pm-9:30pm Sat.-Sun.; entrées £9.45

This high-spirited neighborhood restaurant is everything a good local should be: welcoming you in with good food, wine, and company. The basement restaurant has a slight Gothic feel, with bare black walls, a fireplace overflowing with melted wax, and the soft glow of candlelight.

Established in 2004, it's run by couple Jason and Jane (he's the chef, she manages the front of the house), who have built up strong relationships with Scottish suppliers, including

Danny of Neptune's Larder. Meat dishes include rump steak with wild mushrooms, sauteed potatoes, and jus, and all meat comes from the local Gilmore butchers.

Brunch
★ THE PANTRY

1 North West Circus Parade; tel. 0131 629 0206; www.thepantryedinburgh.co.uk; 9am-4pm daily (last orders 3:30pm); cooked breakfasts from £8.75

This is the go-to place for residents of Stockbridge looking for breakfast or brunch on the weekends. With white tiles behind the counter, colorful artworks on the wall, and a variety of mid-century tables and chairs to sit upon, it has a cool, retro feel. House favorites include the Sunshine on Stockbridge brunch (£9.50)—a vegetarian cooked breakfast with sweet potato and grilled courgette, but the waffles and the millennial favorite of smashed avocado on sourdough are also tempting.

WEST END
Local Produce
★ FORAGE & CHATTER

1a Alva Street; tel. 0131 225 4599; www. forageandchatter.com; 12pm-2:30pm and 5:30pm-11pm Tues.-Sat.; entrées £8

This intimate basement restaurant has such a good reputation that you'd be lucky to get a table on a weekend. With bare-brick walls and low lighting, dishes such as aged beef sirloin and ox tongue with wild leeks are a delight. It feels very much like you've stumbled upon the real Edinburgh.

SOUTHSIDE
Fine Dining
★ CONDITA

15 Salisbury Place; tel. 0131 667 5777; www.condita. co.uk; dinner 7pm Tues.-Sun; £110 for eight courses

Edinburgh's newest receiver of a Michelin star, this is not the place for people who are on a tight budget, nor for those who like a little say in what they will be eating. That said, the eight-course set menu is a surprise and changes regularly so it's hard to give an idea of what it's like, except to say dishes are the result

Food Markets

With so many good independent food and drink shops in Edinburgh, several food markets now cater to people who want to buy food from small-scale producers.

STOCKBRIDGE MARKET

1 Saunders Street; tel. 0131 261 6181; www.stockbridgemarket.com; 10am-5pm Sun.

Held every Sunday in the cool neighborhood of Stockbridge with a discerning crowd, the food produce here is of good quality (though there's more than food; page 76).

LEITH MARKET

Dock Place; tel. 0131 261 6181; www.stockbridgemarket.com/leith.html; 10am-4pm Sat.

This is a great place to sample some Scottish produce, and there's a Vegan Quarter on the first Saturday of the month.

THE PITT MARKET

125-137 Pitt Street; tel. 07534 157 477; www.thepitt.co.uk; 6pm-10pm Fri., 12pm-10pm Sat., 12pm-8pm Sun.; £2 entry

For something a little edgier, this street food market, held on a tucked-away street in Leith every weekend, is a great place to chill out, soak up the local vibe, and enjoy freshly cooked food and live music.

EDINBURGH FARMERS' MARKET

Castle Terrace; tel. 0131 220 8580; www.edinburghfarmersmarket.co.uk; 9am-2pm Sat.

Peruse some of the finest produce from Scotland's natural larder at Edinburgh Farmers' Market, held just below the castle on Castle Terrace. There's a casual vibe about the place with lots of time to pick the brains of stallholders, most of whom grow or raise what they sell themselves. Stallholders from across Scotland include Arbroath Fisheries from Angus; Arran Cheese, based in the Firth of Clyde; and Seriously Good Venison, which sells meat raised on its farm less than 50 miles (80 km) away in Fife.

of technical wizardry and include only the most seasonal of ingredients. It's a real event meal, with champagne and nibbles to begin, followed by the eight courses, and malt whiskies and coffee to finish. Don't plan on going anywhere else afterward, except home to bed.

Indian
TUK TUK INDIAN STREET FOOD

1 Leven Street; tel. 0131 228 3322; https:// tuktukonline.com; 12pm-10pm daily; plates £5

Dishes here taste straight out of a market in Mumbai; you'd be hard-pushed to get tastier comfort food for less. The curries are particularly well-priced, and the gulab jamun (warm milk dumplings served with pistachio and cardamom syrup and ice cream) are every bit as delicious as they sound.

Coffee
★ THE COUNTER

Various locations; www.instagram.com/thecountered; 7:30am-3pm daily; coffee from £2

This small chain of coffee shops makes a great flat white (double espresso with steamed milk) and includes several locations housed in old police boxes—one in Argyle Place, one by Usher Hall, and one in Tollcross—plus a new canal boat coffee shop on the Union Canal.

LEITH
Fine Dining
RESTAURANT MARTIN WISHART

54 Shore; tel. 0131 553 3557; https:// restaurantmartinwishart.co.uk; lunch 12pm-1:30pm Tues.-Sat., dinner 7pm-9pm Tues.-Thurs. and

6:30pm-9:30pm Fri.-Sat.; lunch menu £42.50 for three courses, six-course tasting menu £110-85

One of many fine restaurants lining Leith's Shore, this is one of the best—as proven by its Michelin Star—and its elegant dining room with spotless white tablecloths and glinting glasses makes you feel that you're in for a special meal. Its three-course lunch menu isn't the cheapest, but with langoustine ravioli or tartare of rose veal, it is more adventurous than most. The tasting menus are what Wishart is really known for, and the six-course menu also has a slightly cheaper vegetarian option. There is no lunch menu available on Saturday.

Seafood
THE FISH MARKET

23A Pier Place, Newhaven; tel. 0131 552 8262; www. thefishmarketnewhaven.co.uk; 11am-10pm daily; coffee from £2.20

Fish and chips can be hit and miss in Edinburgh, but here, where the fish comes virtually from the boat to the table, it's as good as you will find. It shouldn't really be much of a surprise—fishing has been at the heart of the Newhaven community for 500 years. The dining room has a modern feel with nods to its heritage, including vintage green tiles. All fish is sustainably sourced, and choices include lobster, crab, or lemon sole goujons. For me, it's all about the battered haddock and chips with mushy peas. Delicious.

Nightlife

There is no end of pubs or howffs (an old Scottish word for a pub) in the city, from traditional taverns to cool cocktail bars, and good music can be heard every night of the week (something that has been sorely missed through the pandemic).

It's thought that one of the reasons the 18th-century Scottish Enlightenment took off here is due to the large number of pubs where inquisitive minds could share ideas. True or not, it's certainly accurate to say that many of the historic pubs have changed little for centuries.

Be prepared to share a table, particularly if there's music playing—with few tables, if everyone sat on their own, there would be a lot of people standing (do ask first if you're going to join someone else). Standard pub opening hours are 11am-11pm (12pm-10:30pm on Sundays), but most pubs and bars have licenses to stay open to 12am or 1am, particularly on Friday and Saturday. Numerous clubs and music venues are open even later, especially during the Edinburgh Festival.

Expect to pay around £4-4.50 for a pint in Edinburgh, slightly less if you are drinking hand-pumped ales and considerably more if you go for one of the growing number of craft beers. Cocktails range from around £7-10. Whiskies usually come in 25ml measures (though some pubs serve 35ml) and usually cost around £3 for a blended whisky and around £4 for a single malt. The more aged the whisky the more you will pay, so stick to 10-15-year-old whiskies.

NIGHTLIFE DISTRICTS

You can listen to folk music for free in many city center pubs in and around the **Grassmarket.** If you're looking to bar hop, on **Rose Street** in the New Town, which runs parallel with Princes Street, there's a pub every few yards for almost a mile. **Lothian Road,** which runs from the West End down to the Southside, has a similarly high concentration of bars, but it can get a bit unruly late at night.

OLD TOWN
Bars
THE DEVIL'S ADVOCATE

9 Advocate's Close; tel. 0131 225 4465; https://
devilsadvocateedinburgh.co.uk; 12pm-12am daily;
cocktails £8-10, bottles of wine from £22

If you're looking for a smarter alternative to some of the Old Town's more historic pubs, then this bar is a good bet. With a cool industrial feel, the venue was once a Victorian pump house, but today it's known for its broad whisky collection (around 400 malts and blends), plus seasonal cocktails and a curated wine list. The best tables are on the mezzanine level, where food is also served, and there's a good outside terrace.

HOLYROOD 9A

9a Holyrood Road; tel. 0131 556 5044; www.
theholyrood.co.uk; 12pm-12am Sun.-Thurs., 12pm-1am
Fri.-Sat.; cocktails £9.25, bottles of wine from £19.50

This upmarket joint at the eastern end of the Royal Mile serves a good cocktail, from firm favorites (old fashioned and whisky sour) to the delectable Edinburgh Royale, which includes Edinburgh Gin Liqueur topped with prosecco. It also has a good line of craft beer (over 20 beers on tap) and is renowned for its tasty burgers, which go down extremely well after a trek up to Arthur's Seat.

Pubs
★ BOW BAR

80 West Bow; tel. 0131 226 7667; www.thebowbar.
co.uk; 12pm-12am Tues.-Weds., 12pm-1am Thurs.-Sun.,
12pm-11pm Mon.; from £4 a pint, whiskies from £4.50

Set amid the elegant facades of Victoria Street is this small, grown-up pub, all wood paneling with old pub signs. There are no gimmicks, just good beer, lots of whiskies, and a friendly welcome. Take a seat and let the gentle hum of chatter wash over you. A selection of tasty pies is on offer (pheasant and pancetta, Moroccan lamb, etc.) at £3.50-4.50 a piece.

JOLLY JUDGE

7 James Court, Lawnmarket, Royal Mile; www.
jollyjudge.co.uk; tel. 0131 225 2669; 12pm-9pm
Mon.-Thurs., 12pm-10pm Fri.-Sat., 2pm-8pm Sun.;
from £4 a pint, whiskies from £4

Tucked away on a close at the bottom of Castlehill, Jolly Judge is friendly, warm, and snug. Though some savvy tourists find their way here, it's mostly filled with locals who pop in for a pint of ale or one of the simple but delicious toasties or bowls of soup (served until 3pm). When the fire is lit, there are few places better to be perched than around a table here under its low beams, where the calm air is at odds with the hectic throb of tourists just yards away.

Traditional Music Pubs
★ SANDY BELL'S

25 Forrest Road; tel. 0131 225 2751; www.sandybells.
co.uk; 12pm-12am Mon.-Sat., 12:30pm-12am Sun.;
from £4 per pint, whiskies from £4 (35ml measures)

This is the most renowned spot in the city for traditional folk music sessions and is a great place to hear locals and tourists mingle happily, while those who want to hear the music properly have to squeeze themselves into the space at the back of the pub by the seated musicians. It's not a large pub—essentially just one longish room with a snug at the end, the bar to one side, and small tables with wooden stools placed where there's room.

Music sessions have been held in this former grocery store since the 1940s, with the focus on Scottish and Irish folk music. Nightly evening sessions include fiddles, guitars, flutes, and "mouthies" (harmonicas) from 9:30pm, and there are afternoon sessions on Saturday and Sunday at 2pm and 4pm, respectively. Throughout August music all day every day coincides with the Edinburgh Festival. Locals embrace the in-the-know tourists who find themselves here, and the atmosphere is amiable and loud. Table sharing is the norm, so find a seat or cram into a free space and let the music carry you away.

★ ROYAL OAK

1 Infirmary Street; tel. 0131 557 2976; www.
royal-oak-folk.com; 1pm-3am Mon.-Fri., 12pm-3am
Sat.-Sun.; from £4.35 per pint, whiskies from £3.80

Renowned for its folk music, this stripped-back late-night pub is where many musicians end the night. There's music every night of the week, and if you arrive with a guitar or a song to sing, you will be invited into the fold. Otherwise, just be prepared to share your table in either the cramped bar downstairs or the slightly bigger bar upstairs, where it is often standing room only. During the Edinburgh Festival, you may need to book a ticket through the Fringe Festival website, though you can usually do this on short notice. That said, you'll rarely be turned away for a late-night drink.

★ THE CAPTAIN'S BAR

4 South College Street; tel. 07493 555 702; https://captainsedinburgh.webs.com; 2pm-7pm Thurs. and Sun., 2pm-10pm Fri., 1pm-10pm Sat.; beer from £4 a pint, whiskies from £4

A tiny pub with a big heart, this is one of the best places to catch an afternoon music session on the weekend. It's pretty informal, but it usually kicks off around 3pm and goes on until 6-ish. There are a few regular musicians who turn up to keep proceedings ticking along but anyone can join in, and while the emphasis is on folk music, contemporary songs are welcome too. A highlight is when the bar man leaves his regular spot behind the bar, picks up his fiddle, and joins in the music. There used to also be sessions on Tuesday and Wednesday afternoons, and they may be reinstated at some point.

Other Live Music
★ THE JAZZ BAR

1 Chambers Street; tel. 0131 220 4298; www.thejazzbar.co.uk; 5pm-3am daily (open at 1:30pm and 2pm on Sat. and Sun. if there is an afternoon gig); tickets from £4, from £4.50 a pint, bottle of wine £18-22

If you've had your fill of folk music, this cool local favorite just off South Bridge is a great place to finish your night. It's the brainchild of Edinburgh musician Bill Kyle, who has worked tirelessly to build up its reputation as a happening and unpretentious music space.

There is always something to listen to, and while much of it is jazz, there is also blues, roots, acoustic, funk, and soul. Some events, particularly daytime gigs, are free and the quality of bands is exceptional.

STRAMASH

207 Cowgate; tel. 0131 623 4353; www.oldtownpubco.com/our-bars/stramash-live-music-bar-edinburgh; 5pm-3am Mon.-Thurs., 1pm-3am Fri.-Sun.

Even on a weeknight, this place is heaving with live music all the way through until 3am. You might hear anything from ironic cover bands to hip-hop acts and rock 'n' roll. Housed in a former church, the high ceilings provide excellent acoustics, which can be enjoyed on the first-floor mezzanine, or you can join everyone down below on the dancefloor.

Nightclubs
THE BONGO CLUB

66 Cowgate; tel. 0131 558 8844; www.thebongoclub.co.uk; 11pm-3am daily; ticket prices vary, from £2.50 a beer

Run by a local arts charity, which saved this Edinburgh institution from closure in 2012, The Bongo Club attracts some of the hottest DJs around. With drinks starting at just over £1 a shot, Midnight Bass on Tuesday nights is a student favorite. Playing a mix of drum and bass, jungle and grime, this venue attracts clubgoers dressed down in streetwear ready to rinse out.

NEW TOWN
Bars
★ CAFÉ ROYAL

19 West Register Street; tel. 0131 556 1884; www.caferoyaledinburgh.com; 11am-11pm Sun.-Weds., 11am-12am Thurs., 11am-1am Fri.-Sat.; pints from £4.35, bottle of wine from £20

Just try to find a more salubrious drinking venue in Edinburgh, why don't you? With its high ceilings, Victorian plasterwork, stained-glass windows, and famed circular bar, Café

1: Café Royal 2: fish and chips at the Fish Market 3: Blueswater take to the stage at the Jazz Bar. 4: Play the Hoop of Destiny at Teuchters.

Royal is a great place for a pre-dinner glass of champagne or even a whisky digestif. You may struggle to get a seat, and if you do, be prepared to share. The Parisian-style **oyster bar** upstairs was famously used in the dining scene in Oscar-winning film *Chariots of Fire* and has changed little over the years.

BRAMBLE

16A Queen Street; tel. 0131 226 6343; www. bramblebar.co.uk; 4pm-1am Weds.-Sun.; cocktails from £9, wine from £21 a bottle

Not only does this decadent bar serve smashing cocktails in a cool subterranean venue, but it has a rolling lineup of cool DJs too. It's classier than a lot of modern joints as well—grab a seat in a high-backed leather armchair and leaf through a book-bound menu to select your drink.

Pubs
★ KAY'S BAR

39 Jamaica Street; tel. 0131 225 1858; www.kaysbar. co.uk; 11am-12pm Mon.-Thurs., 11am-1am Fri.-Sat., 12:30pm-11pm Sun.; pints from £3.50, wine from £14 a bottle

This fantastic locals' bar is set on a pleasant mews, a short walk from Charlotte Square. While it has an impressive whisky collection (including rare bottlings), it's widely considered Edinburgh's premier cask ale house, with seven guest ales on tap. The pub was actually a reputable wine merchant during the Victorian era, and many of the features from its Victorian heyday remain, including signage around the frieze, cast-iron pillars, and old barrels. It also offers exceptionally good-value lunches such as haggis with neeps and tatties, or Scotch pie with chips and beans for just £4.50.

★ OXFORD BAR

8 Young Street; tel. 0131 539 7119; www.oxfordbar. co.uk; 12pm-12am Mon.-Thurs., 11am-1am Fri.-Sat., 12:30pm-11pm Sun.; pints from £3.50

"The Ox," just off Charlotte Square, is one of those places you always hope to find but assume have been confined to the memory bank. The back room, with its framed pictures, wooden seats built into the wall, and a fire lazily simmering, is the perfect place to have a pint, do the crossword, or exchange stories with your neighbor. For a bit more life, sidle into the bar near the entrance and wait for a local to bring you into their conversation. It will happen. And yes, this is the bar where Inspector Rebus, the fictional character in Ian Rankin's detective novels, likes to come.

STOCKBRIDGE
Bars
THE ANTIQUARY

72-78 St. Stephen Street; tel. 0131 225 2858; www. theantiquarybar.co.uk; 4pm-10:30pm Mon.-Tues., 12pm-10:30pm Weds.-Fri., 11am-10:30pm Sat.-Sun.; beer from £4 a pint, whiskies from £3.50

This basement bar in the hip neighborhood of Stockbridge is all wooden floors and wood-paneled walls. The bar takes its name from the book of the same name by Sir Walter Scott. The remains of a 19th-century bakery can be found at the back of the bar, which is also said to have its own resident ghost in the shape of a female baker. There is a good folk session on Thursday at 8:30pm.

★ THE LAST WORD SALOON

44 St. Stephen Street; tel. 0131 225 9009; www. lastwordsaloon.com; 4pm-12am Thurs.-Sun.; cocktails from £8, wine from £16 a bottle

Everyone in Stockbridge knows that if you want good cocktails, this is where you come. It's a bit on the grungy side compared to some, but who said cocktails were only for the glamour set? Music plays at a good level in the dark basement bar, and you can buy a measure of the bar's "break even bottle" for the price they paid for it if you fancy trying a more expensive whisky than the norm. I also recommend some of the quirkier single-pour drinks, such as the Great King Street Glasgow Blend Whisky, which comes with cream soda. Yum.

WEST END
Bars
VOYAGE OF BUCK

29-31 William Street; tel. 0131 225 5748; www.
thevoyageofbuckedinburgh.co.uk; 10am-12am
Sun.-Weds., 10am-1am Thurs.-Sat.; cocktails £9-11

This bar, which opened in 2017 in the smart
West End, could so easily be dismissed as too
gimmicky—it is all centered around the idea
of a fictional Victorian philanthropist, after
all. But somehow it works. The cocktail menu
is inspired by "Buck's" supposed travels. The
reasonably priced cocktails are served with
finesse, and the low-lit, classy bar with cozy
booths is reminiscent of a train station café
circa 1920.

Whisky Bars
★ TEUCHTERS

26 William Street; tel. 0131 225 2973; https://
teuchtersbar.co.uk/teuchters-west-end-bar;
12pm-11pm Sun.-Weds., 12pm-12am Thurs.-Sat.; from
£4.25 a pint, whiskies from £4, whisky flights from
£11.75

While some people come to Teuchters for
dinner in the downstairs restaurant, which
serves Scottish dishes, the whisky bar upstairs is where the fun is really to be had.
Pivotal to festivities is the Hoop of Destiny
game: for £4 you get three goes at throwing
a hoop over one of the many whiskies on display, and you win whichever one you land. If
you don't land a single malt, don't fret, you'll
still be rewarded with a glass of Sheep Dip—a
good local blended whisky.

SOUTHSIDE
Pubs
SHEEP HEID INN

43-45 The Causeway; tel. 0131 661 7974; www.
thesheepheidedinburgh.co.uk; 12pm-11pm Mon.-Sat.,
12pm-10:30pm Sun.; beer from £4 a pint, wine from
£16 a bottle, cocktails £9

Possibly dating from the 14th century, the
Sheep Heid is one of the city's oldest surviving pubs. Once visited by King James VI (I
of England) and his mother, Mary, Queen
of Scots, who reputedly played skittles here,

today it is a cozy gastropub with plentiful
memorabilia on its walls, a good selection of
real ales, and even a Victorian bowling alley,
which is fully utilized.

THE CANNY MAN'S

237 Morningside Road; tel. 0131 447 1484; www.
cannymans.co.uk; 11am-11pm Sun.-Weds., 11am-12am
Thurs. and Sat., 11am-1am Fri.; whiskies from £6 (35ml
measure), wine from £13.50 per carafe

This Morningside pub, in the same family for
generations, is a local favorite, though its reputation for serving up the best bloody Mary in
town ensures a steady stream of tourists too.
There are two bars: the main bar, where you'll
find most of the tourists, and the back bar,
where locals hide away. The décor is eclectic,
with floral curtains, red velvet bench seats,
and walls chockablock with memorabilia. Free
snacks are served with drinks, and there's a
free buffet 5pm-6pm Monday-Thursday.

LEITH
Pubs
SHORE BAR

1 Shore; tel. 0131 553 5080; www.fishersrestaurants.
co.uk/shore-bar-and-restaurant; 12pm-late
Mon.-Sat., 12:30pm-late Sun.; entrées £9

An adjunct to the seafood restaurant Fishers,
this waterside bar and restaurant is a good
place to stretch out a leisurely Sunday lunch
accompanied by some jazz (there's also live
jazz music on Tuesday and Thursday evenings). Wood paneling and smart banquette
seating give the place something of a Parisian
air.

Live Music
★ LEITH DEPOT

138-140 Leith Walk; tel. 0131 555 4738; https://
leithdepot.com; 12pm-12am Mon.-Weds., 12pm-1am
Thurs.-Sat., 12pm-12am Sun.; cocktails £7.50, pints
from £4

This independent bar, about halfway down
Leith Walk, is one of the leading forces in
the gradual gentrification of this formerly
down-at-heel suburb. Downstairs, the airy
bar space with wooden floorboards and the

menu scrawled on chalkboards, has a laid-back, welcoming feel, while upstairs in the cozy gig room there's a regular schedule of live music. They also cater well to vegetarians and pescatarians (I even spied vegan whisky on the menu).

Accommodations

If you are only here for one or two days, then it makes sense to stay in the **Old Town** in order to see the main sights. For trips of a few days or more, the **New Town** with its classic Georgian properties is a good option, while **West End** accommodations are still within reasonable walking distance of the Royal Mile, and they provide a little respite from the tourists and a better value. For a hip crowd, independent shops, and chill café culture, you can't beat **Stockbridge.**

OLD TOWN
Under £100
CASTLE ROCK HOSTEL

15 Johnstone Terrace; tel. 0131 225 9666; www. castlerockedinburgh.com; £13 dorm, £55 d
Situated beneath the castle at the bottom of Castle Wynd North steps, this hostel is a great base for solo travelers to Edinburgh. Staff organize pub crawls and ceilidhs for guests. The posh lounge with its free book exchange (and piano) and the groove lounge are great places to make new friends over a free tea or coffee. Accommodation is in dorms or double and triple rooms.

£100-200
APARTHOTEL ADAGIO EDINBURGH ROYAL MILE

231 Canongate, Royal Mile; tel. 0131 322 8299; www. adagio-city.com/gb/hotel-9289-aparthotel-adagio-edinburgh-royal-mile/index.shtml; £92 studio for 2, £140 4-person apartment
At the lower end of the Royal Mile, toward the palace, these compact apartments with their own kitchenettes offer good value for money and are great for families. Downstairs there are all the facilities you would expect of a hotel: a reception, drinks and snacks to buy, and a very good help-yourself breakfast (kids love the yummy donuts) each morning, plus a lounge area with books and games and plenty to keep little ones entertained. Families can book an apartment for four, with sliding doors to separate the kids' sleeping area from the adults.

★ THE NATIONAL TRUST GLADSTONE'S LAND APARTMENTS

477B Lawnmarket, Royal Mile; tel. 0131 226 5856; www.nts.org.uk//holiday-accommodation; from £130 per night for a one-bed apartment
In one of the Royal Mile's oldest tenement buildings, these small apartments (recently restored) with self-catering kitchens feel like secret hideaways. In truth, they're not that secret, and they book up fast—not surprising since they do offer a good value for a cozy retreat in the Old Town. The steep turnpike staircase is not accessible for people with disabilities, and there is a three-night minimum stay.

Over £200
★ THE WITCHERY BY THE CASTLE

352 Castlehill, Royal Mile; tel. 0131 225 5613; www. thewitchery.com; suites from £395
The nine suites in this enviably located hotel, at the top of the Royal Mile by the castle, are famously indulgent. Choose between the fairytale romance of The Turret, with its oak-paneled bathroom and tapestry-lined entrance, and the rich furnishings of the seductively Gothic Vestry, with its silk walls and organ-piped headboard. Guests are greeted with a bottle of champagne on arrival and can opt for a breakfast hamper in the room or start their day by dining in the **Witchery Dining**

Room. It's not cheap, but you are unlikely to stay anywhere quite like this ever again.

NEW TOWN
Under £100
★ THE BAXTER

5 West Register Street; tel. 0131 503 1001; www. thebaxter.eu; dorm beds from £26

This hostel is more boutique than many. Its classy lounge area—with a cool day bed, modern kitchen, fake fur throws, and Sonos sound system—definitely feels more hipster than hippie. Even the dorms with their custom-built beds, personal night lights, power sockets, and French-style tiled bathrooms have an air of sophistication, and breakfast is included. This is hosteling for millennials and Generation Z, who expect more, so much more.

£100-200
THE STEVENSON HOUSE

17A Heriot Row; tel. 0131 556 1896; www. stevenson-house.com; £115 twin, £135 d

Once the home of Robert Louis Stevenson, this heritage building is still a family home that operates as a B&B year-round. The two rooms (a double and a twin) are like a time warp. In the double, there is a resplendent four-poster bed and William Morris wallpaper, while the twin is dressed like a Georgian boarding room. Breakfast is included and comes with homemade bread and jam.

NO 11

11 Brunswick Street; tel. 0131 557 6910; www.11brunswickst.co.uk; £155 d

This is a sly choice for those looking for luxury accommodation at a snippet of the price as there are often good deals to be had (particularly in low season). Once the Black Watch Regimental Club (the private club of the oldest Highland regiment), the building was originally commissioned by William Playfair and completed in 1822. Today, it is a small, refined hotel that makes the most of its former grandeur, including its cupola, which lords over the sweeping staircase. Georgian suites with

daring dark walls include four-poster beds, freestanding baths, and floor-to-ceiling windows.

Over £200
★ EDINBURGH GRAND

42 St. Andrew Square; tel. 0131 230 0570; www. chevalcollection.com/edinburgh; £285 d

In a former bank, these 50 serviced apartments take the building's 1920s heyday and infuse period features with modern technology, such as intelligent heating, Bose sound systems, drench showers (which you won't want to leave), and designer furniture. For out-and-out luxury, the two-bed grand apartments are pretty hard to beat, but even the Capital Studio Apartments are perfectly formed. Breakfast is served upstairs in the time capsule that is the Register Club, also a nice spot for an aperitif or a game of table tennis in the secret games room.

THE BALMORAL

1 Princes Street; tel. 0131 556 2414; www. roccofortehotels.com/hotels-and-resorts/the-balmoral-hotel; £510 d

Standing at Edinburgh's most prestigious address, this grand dame of a hotel is a prominent feature of the city's skyline. Inside, you can dine in the Michelin-starred **Number One** restaurant, relax in the spa, or simply soak up the timeless glamour of one of the 168 bedrooms, each individually designed by Olga Polizzi with definite nods to the hotel's Scottish heritage.

WEST END
£100-200
B+B EDINBURGH

3 Rothesay Terrace; tel. 0131 225 5084; www. bb-edinburgh.com; £110 d

This private B&B with fully licensed bar in a listed building is just a few minutes from Princes Street. The contemporary rooms are immaculate, and a full Scottish breakfast (which is included and comes with haggis and square Lorne sausages) is served in the ground-floor breakfast room. The website might look a bit cheap, but don't let that put you off—the guest bar and library with open fire, guest laptop, and daily newspapers more than make up for it.

Over £200
★ THE DUNSTANE HOUSES

4 West Coates; tel. 0131 337 6169; https:// thedunstane.com; £204 d

Despite being set across two period properties on either side of a main road, this sophisticated hotel is a quiet haven. Rooms have Nespresso machines, huge flat-screen TVs, and Roberts radios, and those at the front are even equipped with telescopes. Downstairs in the main building, you can order from the brasserie-style menu in the *Mad Men*-esque **Ba' Bar,** with its velvet wingback chairs, until 9:30pm. There are books to borrow, framed prints on the wall, and everything about it is achingly chic.

SOUTHSIDE
Under £100
BROOKS HOTEL EDINBURGH

70-72 Grove Street; tel. 0131 228 2323; www. brooksedinburgh.com; £99 d

This charming B&B that lies halfway between Haymarket and Southside features peculiar interiors, where stag heads meet contemporary artwork and vintage furniture abounds. Rooms are fresh and clean, while the lounge, honesty bar, and pretty courtyard make it all more boutique than budget.

£100-200
ALBYN TOWNHOUSE

16 Hartington Gardens; tel. 0131 229 6459; https:// albyntownhouse.co.uk; £149 d

At this Victorian listed property, formerly St. Oswald's Church Manse, the bright and bold rooms are set across three floors. You can expect a warm welcome as well as a comfy room and a hearty breakfast to set you up for the day in this family-run establishment, and you'll need it because Lydie and David will arm you with lots of insider knowledge to help you make the most of your time. Book well ahead and you could even get a double in spring or autumn for just £55.

Over £200
PRESTONFIELD HOUSE

Priestfield Road, EH16 5UT; tel. 0131 225 7800; www. prestonfield.com; £375 d

Shy and retiring it is not, but the sister hotel to the Royal Mile's Witchery was never going to be, was it? From the outside, it is an elegant

Prestonfield House

country house hotel, with peacocks on the lawn, staggering views of Arthur's Seat, and a calm, genteel setting that feels far removed from the city's bustle (though only a 10-minute cab ride away). Inside, though, it is all heavy red velvet curtains, huge tapestries on the wall, antique chairs, and beds so high you need a step up onto them. The decadent, rich atmosphere continues in the dining rooms and drawing room, which are ostentatious for sure, but never knowingly conventional.

Information and Services

TOURIST INFORMATION

As of 2019, the main tourist office, **Edinburgh iCentre** (249 High Street; tel. 0131 473 3868; 9am-5pm Mon.-Sat., 10am-5pm Sun., open later in summer), has moved to the Royal Mile. It's a good place to pick up lots of free leaflets and maps of the city, as well as tickets for many of Edinburgh's attractions, including tours and the Royal Edinburgh Ticket. There is also an outlet at the airport.

This is Edinburgh (tel. 0131 473 3666; https://edinburgh.org) is the official guide to the capital and is a particularly useful reference for events taking place across the city.

The **Royal Edinburgh Ticket** (adult £59, child £32) allows unlimited travel on three Edinburgh Bus Tour routes for two days, plus entry to Edinburgh Castle, the Royal Yacht Britannia, and the Palace of Holyroodhouse. Buy it at Edinburgh iCentre or from Edinburgh Bus Tours (tel. 0131 220 0770; https://edinburghtour.com). Including the bus tours (£15 each), this does work out cheaper.

Getting There

BY AIR

Edinburgh Airport (EDI; www.edinburghairport.com) is located 8 miles (12 km) west of the city. Most overseas visitors to Edinburgh come into London first, but Edinburgh Airport does have direct international flights from a number of U.S. cities, including New York and Chicago **(United Airlines).** It may also be possible to fly to Edinburgh via Paris or Amsterdam, and **Icelandair** runs routes via Iceland from Boston, Minneapolis, and Chicago to Glasgow, just a short train ride from Edinburgh.

From London, several budget airlines, including **easyJet** and **Ryanair,** offer many daily flights from each of London's airports. Flight time is just over an hour, and, if you fly on a weekday outside school holidays, you can pick up a brilliant bargain.

Airport Transportation

Public transport options from the airport to city (www.edinburghairport.com/transportlinks) include a tram or the bus. The tram has only been operating for a short while but is hugely popular with locals. Transport links are all fairly well-signposted, and staff are only too happy to direct you.

TRAM

The trams are a two-minute walk out of the airport's main entrance. At £9 for an open return, trams are slightly more expensive than buses, but they are also less crowded and a bit quicker, and you are not at the mercy of city center traffic. The trams run all the way from the airport to York Place in the east end of the city, stopping at Haymarket and Princes Street en route. Another benefit of the tram compared with the train is that it stops at a greater number of stations in town.

BUS

Airlink 100 buses that go directly to the city center wait right outside the main entrance to the airport and are a smidgen cheaper than the tram (£4.50 single, £7.50 return). They are incredibly reliable, making the roughly 30-minute journey into the city center every 10 minutes between 4:30am and 12:35am, and then every 30 minutes or so until they start again fully for the day. Similarly, **Skylink 200** buses (also £4.50 each way, £7.50 for an open return) go from the airport to Leith via north Edinburgh (from 4:10am-12am every 30 minutes, journey time 40 minutes).

TAXI

You'll find taxis on the ground floor of the multistory car park opposite the main terminal. **City Cabs** is the official taxi provider and does not need to be booked. The cabs seat four to five people with a reasonable amount of luggage, and take an average of 25 minutes to the city center (£20-30).

BY TRAIN

Edinburgh Waverley (Princes Street; www.networkrail.co.uk/stations/edinburgh-waverley) on Waverley Bridge, which overlooks Princes Street Gardens, is the city's main station and is the departure and arrival station for trains from London and Glasgow, among other destinations.

Flying may be quicker (and sometimes cheaper), but traveling by train is virtually stress-free. **London North Eastern Railway** (www.lner.co.uk) provides high-speed trains between London and Edinburgh, which take about 4.5 hours and cost anywhere from £40-80 for a single. The earlier you can book your ticket, the better in terms of price. There is also a new service with **Lumo** (www.lumo.co.uk), which started up in late 2021, which has a similar journey time but sometimes has cheaper prices.

Perhaps the most romantic way to travel is on the **Caledonian Sleeper train** (tel. 0330 060 0500; www.sleeper.scot), which departs London's Euston at night (except Saturday) with just enough time for a spot of dinner in the Club Car before you bed down for the night in your cabin. Tickets cost from £45 for a standard seat (one way) to upwards of £125 each way for a cabin.

It's also really easy to travel between Edinburgh and Glasgow by train. Edinburgh Waverley has several trains an hour from Glasgow Queen Street (50 minutes, from £13 return).

BY CAR

If you're driving from **London** (400 miles/644 km), you need to allow a good eight to nine hours. It's best to split your journey into two days, perhaps stopping at the Lake District (260 miles/418 km from London) or the Yorkshire Dales (230 miles/143 km from London). Your route will very much depend on your starting point in London, but the main options include taking the M1 and then joining the A1 (M), which takes you close to Leeds, in Yorkshire, or following the M40 past Oxford before taking the M6 up through the Lake District and then joining the A702. From **Glasgow** (47 miles/76 km; from one hour, depending on traffic), it's quickest to take the M8 and then the A71 into Edinburgh.

Getting Around

ON FOOT

By far the most enjoyable way to explore the city is on foot, to discover the city's secret passageways and hidden corners. It's a great way to get your bearings too, particularly in the New Town, which is laid out neatly with parallel streets.

BY BUS

The main bus provider in Edinburgh is **Lothian.** The main **bus depot** is just north of St. Andrew Square, and the vast majority of buses run along Princes Street. Prices are £1.80 for a single or £4.40 for a day ticket. A NIGHTticket, which covers travel on buses from 12am to 4:30am, is £3. You can pay in exact change on the bus (feed through the slot at the top of the ticket machine or the bus driver will just stare at you blankly), or you can download the **Transport for Edinburgh** app (https://tfeapp.com) and buy your tickets in advance, though you must make a minimum purchase of £10.

Lothian runs 50 routes in and around the city, including the Airlink and Skylink buses from the airport, and the nos. 43 and X43 buses to South Queensferry. To get to the port district of Leith (15 minutes), you can take the no. 22 or no. 300 buses.

BY TAXI

Taxis are in abundance. Hail a black cab from the street or go to one of the designated taxi ranks (such as the one outside Waverley Station). There are three main black cab firms in Edinburgh: **City Cabs, Central Taxis,** and **ComCabs.** They are all metered with their prices regulated by the council. Step-in charges start at £2.60 for two people (rising to £4.60 at peak times with a small surcharge for additional people). You can prebook these cabs for a small fee, but it's rarely necessary.

Average taxi journeys from the New Town to the Old Town cost around £5, while travelers from Princes Street to Leith can expect to pay around £10. There are private mini cabs too, and, though these are occasionally cheaper, they are nowhere near as reliable.

Around Edinburgh

Escaping the hustle of Edinburgh is easy. To the east of the capital is the seaside suburb of **Portobello,** where on sunny days (or at least ones when it's not raining too much), locals make the most of the beach cafés and ice cream parlors and saunter over its golden sands.

The harbor town of **South Queensferry,** a 15-minute train ride north of Edinburgh, has seen a resurgence due to the opening of the new Queensferry Crossing in 2017, with incredible views of the famous Forth Bridge, plus the area's starring role in the *Outlander* TV series.

Alternatively, you can visit the haunting ruins of Linlithgow Palace, the birthplace of Mary, Queen of Scots, or venture to the enigmatic 15th-century Rosslyn Chapel to the south of the city, made famous in the *Da Vinci Code* films and home to innumerable mysterious stone carvings.

SOUTH QUEENSFERRY

A little less self-aware than Portobello, Queensferry is turning into a charming little weekend spot, with a terrace of colorful houses, front-seat views of the Forth Bridge, and a nice collection of shops and restaurants on the narrow high street that runs just behind the waterfront.

Day Trips from Edinburgh

Destination	Travel Time	Why Go?
Linlithgow Palace (page 100)	20 minutes by train	The ruins of the birthplace of Mary, Queen of Scots, are some of the most haunting in Scotland.
South Queensferry (page 95)	15 minutes by train, plus 15-minute walk	See stately centuries-old homes alongside the spectacular 19th-century Forth Bridge.
Portobello (page 99)	30 minutes by bus	Whenever the weather allows, locals head to this beachside suburb to lay out on the sand.
Rosslyn Chapel (page 102)	1 hour by bus	The exquisite masonry of this chapel may contain clues to a mysterious connection to the Knights Templar.
Stirling (page 110)	1 hour by train	With its grand castle and cobbled streets, Stirling is like Edinburgh in miniature.
Dunfermline (page 121)	1 hour by train	The dramatic Romanesque ruins of Dunfermline Abbey and Palace are covered in greenery and surrounded by a lush park.
Perth (page 138)	1.25 hours by train	Scotland's "Fair City," with a few good museums and galleries, is a great launchpad to beautiful Perthshire.
Melrose (page 253)	1 hour by train, plus 20-30-minute walk	The charming town of Melrose, its eponymous abbey, and the home of Sir Walter Scott make for an idyllic day or two.
Dundee (page 134)	1.5 hours by train	Walk along Dundee's revitalized waterfront, with its crown jewel, the V&A Dundee museum.

The success of the TV series *Outlander* has also brought a new generation of visitors who come to follow in the footsteps of Jamie and Claire, as several of the scenes were shot right here.

Sights
FORTH BRIDGE

Spanning the Firth of Forth and connecting Edinburgh with Fife, the Forth Bridge (sometimes called the Forth Rail Bridge to distinguish it from the Forth Road Bridge) is a true icon of Scotland.

Work on the triple cantilever bridge, which includes an unbelievable 6.5 million rivets, began in 1882 but befell many tragedies before its completion in 1890, with 78 workers (possibly more) dying during the build. It was celebrated as the world's foremost steel structure when it opened in 1890, and it was designated a UNESCO World Heritage Site in 2015.

It's well worth getting the bus over the old Forth Road Bridge or driving yourself over the new Queensferry Crossing, which opened in August 2017, to see the Forth Bridge in all its glory. The Queensferry Crossing supports the ailing Forth Road Bridge, which was struggling with the weight of traffic and is now reserved for public transport. The new bridge is a vital upgrade to the cross-Forth transport links and has opened up more of Fife and Aberdeenshire to Edinburgh.

If traveling by bus, take the bus from Queensferry Street, just two minutes from Princes Street, over the Queensferry Crossing to the Ferrytoll Park and Ride. Several buses do this route (nos. X54, X55, X56, X58, X59, X60). They are run by **Stagecoach** and cost £5 each way or £9 return; tickets can be purchased on board. The Queensferry Crossing is not open to pedestrians or cyclists, but the Forth Road Bridge is.

The best places to get views of the Forth Rail Bridge from South Queensferry are from one of the restaurants, such as **The Boat House,** on the waterfront.

HOPETOUN HOUSE

Queensferry, EH30 9RW; tel. 0131 331 2451; https://hopetoun.co.uk; 11am-5pm Fri.-Mon. (last entry 4pm); adult £11.50, child £6, family £30

One of Scotland's grandest stately homes, this 17th-century palace has been home to the Hope family for generations. Designed by William Bruce, the house was later extended in the 18th century by William Adam, who added the huge colonnades and the north and south pavilions. Its interiors were completed by his sons, Robert Adam and John Adam, following his death.

So spectacular was the finished house that King George IV visited here at the end of his state visit to Scotland in 1822, which was the first time an English monarch had visited Scotland in 200 years. Recently, people have come to Hopetoun for an altogether different reason—to see some of the locations that appeared in the TV series *Outlander*.

In the first season, scenes set in the Duke of Sandringham's house were filmed in the house's resplendent **Red Drawing Room.**

Forth Bridge, South Queensferry

Elsewhere, the **Sea Trail** and **West Lawn** were settings for a duel between the Duke and the head of the MacDonald Clan.

MIDHOPE CASTLE

Accessed via the Hopetoun House entrance; https:// hopetoun.co.uk/estate/outlander-at-hopetoun; car permit £10, £4 per person

For years this 16th-century tower house in the hamlet of Abercorn on the Hopetoun estate was out of bounds to tourists. However, with the success of TV's *Outlander,* in which the castle doubles as Lallybroch, Jamie's family home, visitor interest shot up. Owners have relented to pressure from *Outlander* fans and now charge a small fee to cover security costs, and tickets can now be booked online (don't turn up without one). Because it is located on a private part of the estate, the house is only accessible by car, though the final section is on foot. Please note, you will only be able to see the exterior of the property.

Recreation

JOHN MUIR WAY TO LINLITHGOW

Distance: *14 miles (22.4 km)*
Walking Time: *6 hours*
Cycling Time: *3 hours*
Trailhead: *Jubilee Clock Tower, South Queensferry*
Information and Maps: *https://johnmuirway. org/route/linlithgow-south-queensferry*

This long-distance walking path named after the famous naturalist John Muir stretches from coast to coast across the central belt of Scotland, from Muir's birthplace in Dunbar, East Lothian, all the way to Helensburgh. Known as the Father of the National Parks, John Muir emigrated to America at age 10, yet he never forgot his early years in Scotland.

The route passes attractions including **Linlithgow Palace** and the **Falkirk Wheel.** You can join the walk at South Queensferry. For Linlithgow, head west out of South Queensferry along Hopetoun Road before bearing slightly right on to Farquar Terrace and following this on to Society Road (the route in the link assumes you leave Linlithgow and do the walk the other way around). From South Queensferry, it's 14 miles (23 km) to Linlithgow, along mainly quiet roads and tracks through rural countryside. It will take you past **Hopetoun House** before reaching the famous town of **Linlithgow.**

Food

THE BOAT HOUSE

22 High Street, South Queensferry; tel. 0131 331 5429; https://theboathouse.online; 12pm-8:30pm Mon.-Sat., 12:30pm-8pm Sun.; entrées £6.75

The views of the **Forth Bridge** from this lower-deck restaurant are lovely, but the fish and chips are pretty good too. It's hard to argue with delicious homemade tartar sauce and a golden crispy batter.

DOWN THE HATCH

Port Edgar Marina, South Queensferry; tel. 0131 331 1387; www.downthehatchcafe.com; 8:30am-5pm daily; Hatch Burger £8.25, sandwiches £9

This café-diner provides North American-influenced food featuring locally sourced ingredients. The coffee comes from Forth Coffee Roasters, and the portions are huge—try the popular Hatch Burger with an Angus beef patty, topped with bacon, cheese, onion, and pickles. A great find for North Americans—particularly Canadians—who are feeling a little homesick.

Getting There and Around

Trains depart Edinburgh's **Waverley Station** around every 15 minutes for Dalmeny (15 minutes, from £4.90 return), the nearest station to South Queensferry. From Dalmeny, it's about a 15-minute walk to South Queensferry, or you can take the no. 43 Lothian bus (every 20 minutes Mon.-Sat., every 30 minutes Sun., £1.80) from the station and get off at Stonycroft Road less than 10 minutes later. Alternatively, you can get the no. 43 bus all the way to South Queensferry from St. Andrew Square (40 minutes; £1.80 each way or £4.40 for a day ticket). Buses run every half an hour.

Driving takes about a half hour from the city center, on the A90 and then B924 (9.5 miles/15 km).

★ PORTOBELLO

This seaside suburb, known affectionately as "Porty," is home to street after street of stunning period properties in a mix of styles—from double-fronted houses with upper gabled windows to huge Georgian properties on **Pittville Street,** which leads down to the beach. There is a smattering of artisan shops, cafés, and ice cream parlors on the main road, too.

Sights
PORTOBELLO BEACH

This huge sweep of sand is the perfect place to wear out the kids. In summer and basically any time when it's not bucketing down, locals come here to chill out, walk the dog, and let the kids run wild. Some mad people even swim in the icy waters. There's something pretty cool about walking along a sandy beach with blue skies overhead and snow-capped mountains in the distance. Well, no one said it would be warm. There's tons of space, so it never feels too busy.

Recreation
PROMENADE

Distance: 2 miles (3.2 km)
Walking Time: 40 minutes
Trailhead: Portobello Promenade View, Joppa
Information and Maps: https://getoutside. ordnancesurvey.co.uk/local/portobello-city-of-edinburgh

Walk off the whisky from the night before with a brisk wander along the promenade. It's a great people-watching spot with lots of places to stop for refreshment en route, including the cute **Little Green Van,** usually parked on the promenade at the end of Pittville Street, that serves coffee and ice cream. The promenade runs alongside the seafront for the whole of the beach's 2 miles (3.2 km) and is pedestrian only (plus cycles). There are lots of play areas running off it too,

as well as an old arcade. You can use a map if you like, but really all you need to do is to start walking with the beach on your right and follow the promenade.

Shopping
THE VELVET EASEL GALLERY

298 Portobello High Street; tel. 07813 916 684; https://velveteasel.co.uk; 10am-5pm Thurs.-Sat. and 12pm-5pm Sun.

This contemporary gallery specializes in modern pieces by both Scottish and international artists and prides itself on championing new artists. Browse the paintings, ceramics, jewelry, and sculptures on show, or buy a print or postcard to take home.

PORTOBELLO MARKET

Brighton Park; www.pedal-porty.org.uk/food/portobello-market; 9:30am-1:30pm first Sat. of every month except January

Portobello Market, in Brighton Park, is just a five-minute walk from the main strip. More than 20 traders sell the best of local produce, including organic fruit, fish, and meat, along with local crafts.

Food
THE BEACH HOUSE

57 Bath Street; tel. 0131 657 2636; www. thebeachhousecafe.co.uk; 8am-10pm daily; light bites £7.50

Perfectly positioned by the beach, this is a great spot to stop for a gelato, a light lunch, or even a gin and tonic—go for the Seaside from Edinburgh Gin, which has ground ivy and bladderwrack seaweed among its botanicals.

BROSS BAGELS

177 Portobello High Street; tel. 0131 629 1860; 9am-4pm daily; bagels £6.50

If you like bagels, you'll like this place, which opened up in 2017 and has become part of the fabric of Portobello since. It's run by a Montreal native, and the bagels are tasty and come brimming with toppings, from your standard pastrami, to vegan Pastramheat and the downright absurd option of haggis. It's proved so popular there are also now shops in Leith, Stockbridge, and Bruntsfield.

Accommodations
ABERCORN GUESTHOUSE
1 Abercorn Terrace; tel. 0131 669 6139; www. abercornguesthouse.com; £100 d
This charming property near the beach has gorgeous wooden shutters, a large walled garden, and open fires. Rates start at just £60 out of season—somehow that includes breakfast.

Getting There and Around
There's a direct train from Edinburgh Waverley to Brunstane Station (7 minutes), which is about a 15-minute walk away from Portobello beach. Trains run every half an hour (seven minutes; £2.90 each way). Taxis from the city center take just 10 minutes and cost around £10, but the best way to get there is to jump on the no. 26 bus from Princes Street (about every 20-30 minutes), which will take you all the way to Portobello High Street (30 minutes; £1.80 each way).

To get here by car (4 miles/6 km; 15 minutes), head east along Queen's Drive, which runs through Holyrood Park, turn right onto the A1140, and follow all the way to Portobello High Street.

★ LINLITHGOW PALACE
Kirkgate, Linlithgow; tel. 01506 842 896; www. historicenvironment.scot/visit-a-place/places/ linlithgow-palace; 9:30am-5:30pm Apr.-late Sept., 10am-4pm Oct.-late Mar., last entry 45 minutes before closing; adult £7.20, child £4.30, under 5 free
The haunting ruins of Linlithgow Palace—the birthplace of Mary, Queen of Scots, and her father, James V—are arguably the most outstanding of all of Scotland's medieval palaces. The exterior has remained much as it was in the 15th century, though its once grand halls have been ravaged by fire and time.

History
Built to replace an earlier structure devastated by fire in 1424 by King James I of Scotland, this was a chance for the Royal Family to show off their wealth and power. Linlithgow's location was both beautiful and easy to defend, and it was developed by successive monarchs over the next 200 years until it became the quadrangular palace around a central courtyard that you see today.

Sadly, the house fell out of royal favor in the late 16th century, and by 1600 it was in decline, with the north range collapsing in 1607. James VI attempted to restore it, but it never returned to the same level of prestige. When Charles I spent one night here in 1633, he became the last reigning monarch to sleep in the palace. Oliver Cromwell and his roundheads lodged at the palace in 1650. In 1745 the Young Pretender, Bonnie Prince Charlie, stopped at Linlithgow en route to Edinburgh to claim the crown of Scotland for the Stuart dynasty. It then suffered a devastating fire in 1746.

Since the early 19th century the castle has been actively preserved, and today it is looked after by Historic Environment Scotland and is open to visitors year-round.

Visiting the Palace
The flamboyant fountain in the courtyard was commissioned by King James V (father of Mary, Queen of Scots) around 1538. It is decorated with sculptures, including a drummer, a man holding a scroll, and a mermaid, a nod to James's role as a patron of the arts. Though staff dismiss the rumors, it's been said that the fountain once flowed with red wine to celebrate Bonnie Prince Charlie.

Inside, Linlithgow Palace is a bit spooky, with lots of hidden rooms, low passages, and turnpike staircases that climb up towers. You may find yourself alone in some of the rooms, with the faces of unicorns and ancient angels staring down at you. **The Great Hall,** originally added by James I but later remodeled, still dominates the layout. Magnificent medieval banquets took place in this once ostentatious room, where the walls are now bare.

1: Rosslyn Chapel 2: Portobello Beach 3: Linlithgow Palace

At the very top of the palace is **Queen Margaret's Bower,** a tiny room often linked to the wife of King James IV that boasts far-reaching views across the surrounding countryside. Popular myth says that this is where the queen sat in the autumn of 1513, waiting in vain for her husband, who was slain at the Battle of Flodden, to return.

Food and Accommodations
THE FOUR MARYS

65-67 High Street, Linlithgow; tel. 01506 842 171; www.fourmarys-linlithgow.co.uk; 12pm-9pm daily; entrées £5.80

This stone-walled inn by Linlithgow Cross, a short walk from the castle, is named after the four ladies in waiting who were sent with Mary, Queen of Scots, to France. Inside you'll find low ceilings, tartan carpet, and plenty of pub grub at good prices, including tasty burgers and staples such as steak and chips. There are meal deals Sunday to Thursday.

CHAMPANY INN

Linlithgow, EH49 7LU; tel. 01506 834 532; www.champany.com; £119 d

This cozy inn within converted farm buildings is as traditional as they come, though the decor is a little dated and the floorboards a little creaky. Rooms are spacious and feature tartan bedspreads and curtains. In truth, Champany Inn is more of a restaurant with rooms than a typical inn.

The slightly chintzy **restaurant** (12pm-10pm Mon.-Sat., 12:30pm-10pm Sun.; entrées £8.35), where carpets are patterned with the hotel's logo and there are fruit bowls on the table, serves good food; try the house specialty of hot-smoked salmon or one of the very good chophouse-style burgers.

Getting There and Around

There are about four trains an hour from **Edinburgh Waverley** to Linlithgow (20 minutes; £5.90 each way). The station is centrally located in the town, and it's a five-minute walk to the palace. To drive here (20 miles/32 km; 30 minutes), follow the M8 west out of the city to join the M9 after 20 minutes. Take Exit 3 off the M9 and take the A803 to Linlithgow.

★ ROSSLYN CHAPEL

Chapel Loan, Roslin; tel. 0131 440 2159; www.rosslynchapel.com; 9:30am-5pm Mon.-Sat Jan.-May, 9:30am-6pm Mon.-Sat. June-Aug., 9:30am-5pm Mon.-Sat. Sept.-Dec., 12pm-4:45pm Sun. year-round; adults £9.50, concessions £7.50, under 18 (with adult) free

This beautiful 15th-century chapel, known for its elaborate masonry, has seen visitor numbers soar since its appearance in the *Da Vinci Code* films, but it has been wowing visitors for centuries. Regular talks take place within the chapel (10am, 11am, 12:15pm, 2pm, 3pm, and 4pm Mon.-Sat.; 1pm, 2pm, and 3pm Sun.) to explain the significance of the many stone carvings around the church.

History

Rosslyn Chapel was founded in 1446 by William Sinclair, 1st Earl of Caithness, who saw it as his way into heaven. Originally intending to build a "Bible in stone," Sinclair wanted a place of worship of cathedral proportions, but sadly work stalled following his death.

By the 1590s, following the Scottish Reformation, the Sinclair family was forced to abandon the chapel. In the 1650s Oliver Cromwell's army used it as a stable, and by the 1850s it was so overrun with foliage that it became known as the garden chapel. In 1862, Queen Victoria fell in love with Rosslyn and ordered its repair, and it opened as a Scottish episcopal place of worship.

Since the late 1980s, there has been speculation that the chapel was in some way connected to the Knights Templar and the Holy Grail. These theories and the excitement around them reached fever pitch following the filming of the *Da Vinci Code* here in 2006, and now conspiracy theorists as well as fans of Dan Brown's book and the subsequent film come in droves.

Visiting the Chapel

In the chapel, incredible carvings depict scenes of the crucifixion and resurrection alongside symbols of fertility and the natural world, including the famous green men: dozens of faces carved into the stone that have foliage coming out of their mouths. There even appear to be what look like sheaths of maize and corn, which are native to North America, giving some weight to a wild theory that founder William Sinclair's grandfather actually made it to the Americas before Columbus.

There is much debate over what each of the carvings mean. Do they tell just a biblical story, or do they reference the Sinclair family's Norse heritage? Or maybe, just maybe, they are secret messages from the Knights Templar.

The chapel contains a good visitors center with a café, gift shop, and free leaflets, giving an overview of the chapel and its highlights in a number of languages.

Food

THE ORIGINAL ROSSLYN INN GASTROPUB

2-4 Main Street; tel. 0131 440 2384; http://theoriginalrosslyninn.co.uk/gastropub; 12pm-3pm and 5pm-11pm Mon.-Fri., 12pm-11pm Sat. and Sun.; entrées £5.95

This is a good lunch or dinner spot before getting the bus back to Edinburgh. All produce is locally sourced; the fish comes from Clark Brothers of Musselburgh, while the Scottish beef is supplied by local master butcher John from J Gilmour. There are light bites for lunch (sandwiches and soup of the day), or, if you're famished, try the haggis clapshot.

Getting There and Around

The village of Roslin and Rosslyn Chapel are just 7 miles (11.2 km) south of Edinburgh, an easy day trip. The no. 37 bus (make sure it says Penicuik/Deanburn on the front) from Edinburgh leaves from Princes Street or North Bridge (45 minutes-1 hour; £1.80 each way). It drops you just outside the Original Rosslyn Inn Gastropub from where it is just a short walk down a lane to the chapel. There are only two buses an hour, so check times before you set off.

It is possible to reach Rosslyn via the newest train route in Britain, the **Borders Railway,** if you want to combine your visit with one to the Borders Abbeys. Trains from Edinburgh Waverley leave for Eskbank every half hour (18 minutes; £5each way). From Eskbank, take the **East Coast Bus** service no. 140 from the main road to Roslin (every half hour with a journey time of 30 minutes, just £1.80 each way), or take a short taxi ride from here with **Dalkeith Taxis** (tel. 0800 625 0362) or the **Midlothian Taxi Hire Company** (tel. 0131 440 2985), which would cost around £12.

There are also lots of tour companies that travel here, including **Rabbie's** (tel. 0131 226 3133; www.rabbies.com), **Highland Experience** (tel. 0131 226 1414; www.highlandexperience.com), and **Go Scotland** (tel. 0131 258 3306; www.goscotlandtours.com), but it is very easy to do independently.

Roslin is just a half-hour drive south of Edinburgh (8 miles/12.9 km) via the A701. There will be brown tourist signposts as you approach the village, and there is free parking at the chapel.

Central Scotland

This region, lying north of Edinburgh, northeast of Glasgow, and edging up to just beneath the Highlands, is considered the heart of Scotland and should not be bypassed or rushed through as you venture to more headline-grabbing destinations. For a start, there's the history. Stirling Castle, a mighty fortress overlooking Scotland's historic city, was once the domain of many of Scotland's most notorious kings and queens—Mary, Queen of Scots, was even crowned here at just nine months old—while Scone Palace, just outside Perth, was the ancient coronation site of Scotland's kings for centuries.

For a true feat of engineering, see the world's only rotating boat-lift, the Falkirk Wheel, or cross the Firth of Forth from Edinburgh to discover Fife's impeccably preserved old fishing ports, such as

Highlights

Look for ★ to find recommended sights, activities, dining, and lodging.

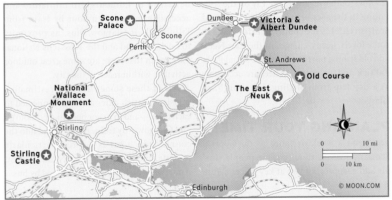

★ **Stirling Castle:** History permeates this medieval royal court, which played a pivotal role in the Wars of Independence (page 111).

★ **National Wallace Monument:** This dramatic monument to one of Scotland's national heroes towers over Stirling, offering a magnificent view of the surrounding countryside (page 115).

★ **The East Neuk:** This quiet corner of Fife is home to cute fishing villages, delicious fish and chips, and cozy pubs and inns (page 124).

★ **Old Course:** The birthplace of golf is a mecca for lovers of the sport, especially the famous Old Course (page 131).

★ **Victoria & Albert Dundee:** The centerpiece of Dundee's cultural reawakening is a startling addition to the city's skyline (page 135).

★ **Scone Palace:** This grand estate was once the coronation site of Scotland's kings, from Macbeth to Robert the Bruce (page 139).

17th-century Culross, a favored filming location for *Outlander*. Head farther east to the quaint villages of the East Neuk, where you can eat mouth-watering seafood or take a boat trip out to the wildlife sanctuary of the Isle of May. In St. Andrews, farther north, you can tee-off at one of the oldest golf courses in the world. Meanwhile, Dundee is a city on the rise, chosen as the location for the first Victoria & Albert museum outside London.

ORIENTATION

Central Scotland is a relatively compact area north of Glasgow and Edinburgh, and east of Loch Lomond and the Trossachs National Park. If you look at it on a map, the "fair" city of **Perth** is pretty much in the center, with **Stirling** a quick 34 miles (55 km) southwest on the A9, **Dundee** another 22 miles (35 km) east on the A90, and **St. Andrews** 14 miles (23 km) south over the River Tay on the A91. Filling in the area between these less visited Scottish cities is the county of **Fife,** home to some lovely sleepy villages in the East Neuk and old fishing ports on the Fife Coastal Path. **Falkirk** and its famous Wheel are accessible as a day trip from Stirling, Edinburgh, or Glasgow.

PLANNING YOUR TIME

You need a week or more to do Central Scotland justice, though some people simply add a stop-off or two at key places before heading north to Inverness and beyond when traveling from Edinburgh or Glasgow. To encourage visitors to linger more, a new driving route, the **Heart 200** (https://heart200.scot), suggests a circular route that connects Loch Lomond and the Trossachs National Park with the historic cities of Perth and Stirling, lots of pretty villages along the River Tay, and the mighty Cairngorms National Park in the north, with optional detours to some lesser-known places of outstanding beauty.

Perth is an excellent base for visiting Scone Palace and the city of Dundee, and it is a gateway to the Highlands. You wouldn't be disappointed spending a week here, taking day trips to mix it up. Fife is a real underplayed corner of Scotland that is incredibly accessible to Edinburgh, and the East Neuk is easily combined with a trip to St. Andrews. But don't, whatever you do, forget Stirling, often described as Edinburgh in miniature and accessible in under an hour by train from Edinburgh or Glasgow. Plus, its proximity to Loch Lomond and the Trossachs National Park mean that there are some great outdoor activities within reach of the city.

All of these somewhat underestimated, midsize Scottish cities are well-connected to each other—and to major hubs like Edinburgh and Glasgow—by train. But to travel into the countryside, a car is helpful, particularly for Fife, including the East Neuk, and St. Andrews, which are only connected by bus.

Previous: Stirling Castle; National Wallace Monument; The Old Course at St. Andrews.
Opposite: 1: Glamis Castle **2:** food festival in Crail **3:** a canon at Stirling Castle.

Central Scotland

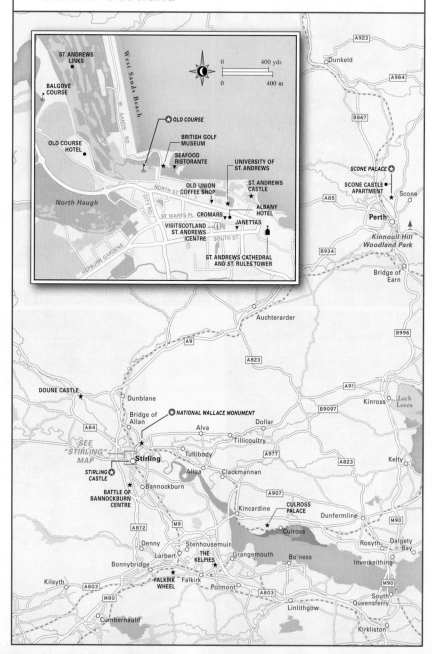

ST. ANDREWS LINKS

BALGOVE COURSE

West Sands Beach

W. SANDS RD.

OLD COURSE

BRITISH GOLF MUSEUM

OLD COURSE HOTEL

SEAFOOD RISTORANTE

UNIVERSITY OF ST. ANDREWS

North Haugh

NORTH ST.

CITY RD.

OLD UNION COFFEE SHOP

ST. ANDREWS CASTLE

ST MARYS PL.

CROMARS

ALBANY HOTEL

JANETTAS

VISITSCOTLAND ST. ANDREWS iCENTRE

SOUTH ST.

HEPBURN GARDENS

ST. ANDREWS CATHEDRAL AND ST. RULES TOWER

0   400 yds
0   400 m

A923

Dunkeld

A984

B867

SCONE PALACE

SCONE CASTLE APARTMENT

Scone

A85

Perth

B934

Kinnoull Hill Woodland Park

Bridge of Earn

Auchterarder

A9

B996

A823

DOUNE CASTLE

A91

Dunblane

NATIONAL WALLACE MONUMENT

Kinross

Loch Leven

A84

Bridge of Allan

Alva

Dollar

B9097

SEE "STIRLING" MAP

Tillicoultry

Stirling

Tullibody

A977

A823

Kelty

STIRLING CASTLE

Alloa

Clackmannan

BATTLE OF BANNOCKBURN CENTRE

Bannockburn

A907

Kincardine

CULROSS PALACE

Dunfermline

M90

Culross

A872

M9

Rosyth

Dalgety Bay

Denny

Stenhousemuir

Grangemouth

Bo'ness

Inverkeithing

Larbert

THE KELPIES

Bonnybridge

Kilsyth

A803

FALKIRK WHEEL

Falkirk

Polmont

A803

M90

South Queensferry

M80

Linlithgow

Cumbernauld

Kirkliston

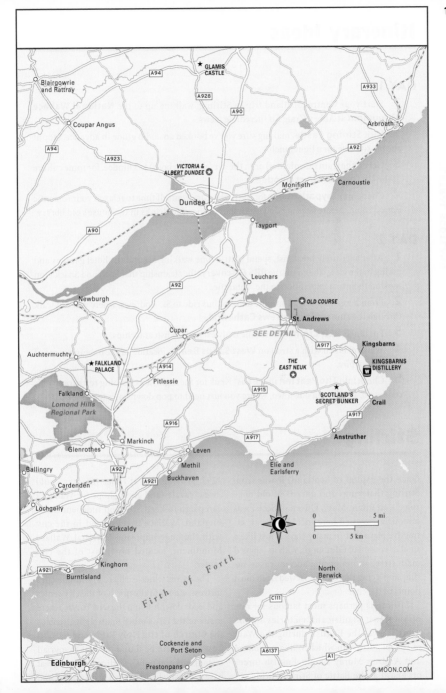

Itinerary Ideas

DAY 1

1 Start your Central Scotland trip in Stirling, walking up to the **National Wallace Monument** at Abbey Craig for incredible views.

2 Visit **Stirling Castle,** making sure you've booked an audio guide in advance. Stop at the on-site café for a light lunch.

3 Get on the train (55 minutes) or in the car (about an hour) to Dundee, for some culture at the **Victoria & Albert Dundee.**

4 Check into **Taypark House** for the night. Give yourself time to relax in your romantic period room, before heading downstairs for dinner and drinks in the house's old library.

DAY 2

1 After a leisurely breakfast, spend a little time walking around the hotel gardens and taking in the view. Then visit the **RRS *Discovery,*** the steamship that Scott and Shackleton took on their first expedition to the Antarctic.

2 From here, it's just a 30-minute drive or bus ride to St. Andrews, where you can walk through the ruins of **St. Andrews Cathedral.**

3 For lunch, visit **Cromars** for some truly exemplary fish and chips.

4 Walk off lunch with a stroll on **West Sands Beach,** location of the opening scene of *Chariots of Fire.*

5 Check into **The Peat Inn** in the East Neuk for the night, a welcoming restaurant with rooms a few miles outside town, where you just need to pop downstairs for dinner.

Stirling

Once the capital of Scotland, it was from Stirling that kings and queens of old once ruled—an infant Mary, Queen of Scots, was famously crowned here in 1543. It's an attractive place that in many ways is just like a smaller version of Edinburgh, with its cobbled main street and imposing ancient castle sitting atop a crag that can be viewed from most points of the city.

Stirling is perhaps most famous for one of the most significant victories of the Scottish over the English during the Wars of Independence, in which William Wallace and Andrew Moray caught English forces off guard at the Battle of Stirling Bridge in 1297, proving that at times infantry could defeat cavalry and giving hope for Wallace's campaign to keep Scotland independent of England. Wallace is celebrated in the city with the huge imposing National Wallace Monument, located northeast of the city center.

The castle, which easily rivals Edinburgh's fortress, stands at the north of the city center and leads downhill into the **Old Town,** where many of the city's other main sights, such as the **Church of the Holy Rude** and the **Old Town Jail,** can be found (as well as myriad restaurants and pubs). Stirling is also a great base from which to explore Loch Lomond and the Trossachs National Park to the west, and it is very easily accessible from both Edinburgh and Glasgow.

SIGHTS
★ Stirling Castle

Castle Esplanade, Stirling; tel. 01786 450 000; www. stirlingcastle.scot; 9:30am-6pm late Mar.-Sept., 9:30am-5pm Oct.-Mar.; adult £15, child £9, concessions £12

While Edinburgh Castle may hold the crown of Scotland's most-visited stronghold, few can visit the 16th-century Stirling Castle from where Renaissance monarchs ruled and not be wowed by the ostentatious interiors of its palace or stirred by its tales of heroics and royal rivalries. It was to this castle that a young Mary, Queen of Scots, was taken as a young child; indeed, special slits were carved into the battlements to enable the toddling queen to look out over her realm.

The present building dates from the 16th century, but a castle has stood here since at least 1107, when we see the first written record of it during the reign of Alexander I. Soon after, the castle was given to King Henry II by William the Lion to meet the demands of his ransom, and so began a lengthy tug-of-war between the Scottish and English for control of the castle, which reached its peak during the Wars of Independence. It was once said that, if you held Stirling, you controlled Scotland. Famously, William Wallace and Andrew Moray executed a magnificent defeat of English forces during the Battle of Stirling Bridge.

On first appearances the castle is not unlike Edinburgh's, surrounded as it is on three sides by steep cliffs, but look closer and it is prettier, grander even, with a pair of rounded towers marking the main entry. Inside, the Royal Palace's suite of six rooms, restored to how they would have looked during the reign of King James V in the mid-16th century (the height of its role as a Renaissance palace), are typically grand and decorated with flashes of rich color. Don't miss the Stirling Heads—3.2-foot-wide (1-m-wide) 16th-century carved oak medallions featuring the images of monarchs, gods, classical figures, and nobles that once hung on the ceiling in the chamber where the king received guests—or the re-creations of the incredibly detailed Hunt of the Unicorn tapestries (the originals are on display in New York), the likes of which would have hung in the castle in the 16th century.

Meanwhile, in the Great Hall, the largest ever built in Scotland, you can see the

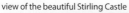

view of the beautiful Stirling Castle

Itinerary Ideas

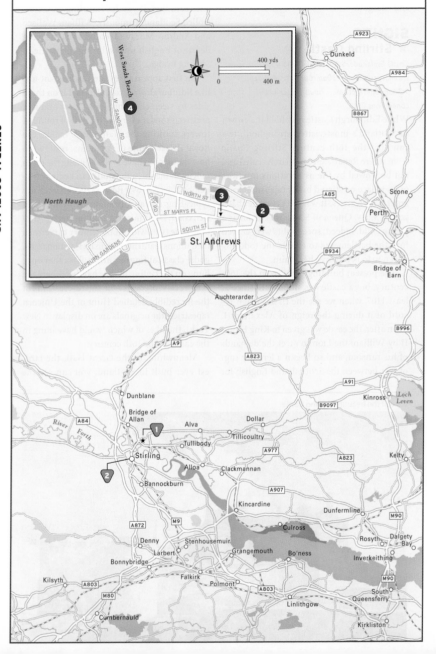

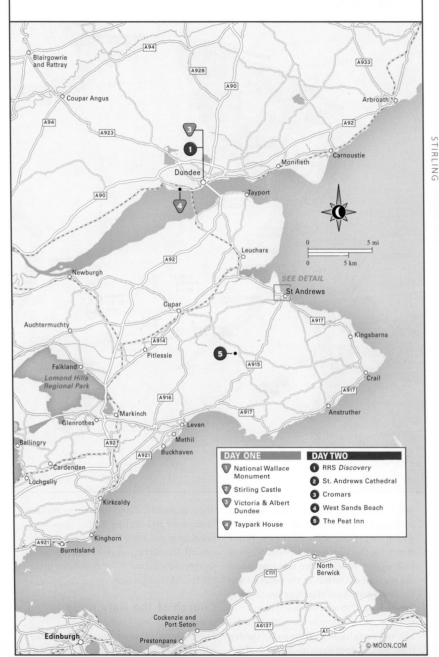

Blairgowrie and Rattray
A94
A928
A90
Coupar Angus
A94
A923
Arbroath
A92
Carnoustie
3
1
Monifieth
Dundee
Tayport
4
A90
Leuchars
A92
SEE DETAIL
Newburgh
St Andrews
Cupar
A917
Kingsbarns
Auchtermuchty
A914
Pitlessie
5
A915
Crail
Falkland
A917
Lomond Hills Regional Park
A916
Glenrothes
Markinch
A917
Leven
Anstruther
Ballingry
A92
Methil
A921
Buckhaven
Cardenden
Lochgelly
Kirkcaldy
Kinghorn
A921
Burntisland
North Berwick
C111
Cockenzie and Port Seton
A6137
A1
Edinburgh
Prestonpans

0   5 mi
0   5 km

DAY ONE
1 National Wallace Monument
2 Stirling Castle
3 Victoria & Albert Dundee
4 Taypark House

DAY TWO
1 RRS *Discovery*
2 St. Andrews Cathedral
3 Cromars
4 West Sands Beach
5 The Peat Inn

© MOON.COM

Stirling

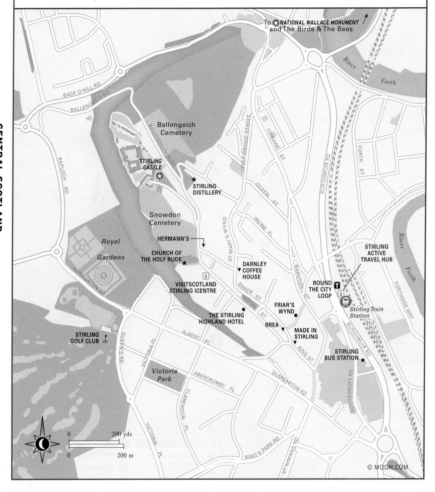

To **NATIONAL WALLACE MONUMENT**
and The Birds & The Bees

River Forth

BACK O'HILL RD

BALLENGEICH RD

BALLENGEICH PASS

Ballengeich
Cemetery

STIRLING
CASTLE

★ STIRLING
DISTILLERY

Snowdon
Cemetery

RAPLOCH RD

Royal
Gardens

HERMANN'S

CHURCH OF
THE HOLY RUDE ★

DUMBARTON RD

VISITSCOTLAND
STIRLING ICENTRE

THE STIRLING
HIGHLAND HOTEL

STIRLING
GOLF CLUB

QUEEN'S RD

VICTORIA PL

ALBERT PL

Victoria
Park

ABERCROMBY PL

CLARENDON PL

VICTORIA PL

UPPER BRIDGE STREET

COWANE ST

QUEEN ST

IRVINE PL

ST MARY'S WYND

DARNLEY
COFFEE
HOUSE

BAKER ST

SPITTAL ST

FRIAR'S
WYND

BREA

BARNTON ST

MADE IN
STIRLING

KING ST

DUMBARTON RD

ABERCROMBY PL

KING'S PARK RD

ST NINIANS RD

BURGHMUIR RD

FORTH ST

River Forth

STIRLING
ACTIVE
TRAVEL HUB

ROUND
THE CITY
LOOP

Stirling Train
Station

FORTHSIDE WAY

STIRLING
BUS STATION

BURGHMUIR RD

GOOSECROFT RD

0   200 yds
0   200 m

© MOON.COM

gallery where minstrels and trumpeters once performed at famously lavish feasts below—during the baptism of James VI's son, Prince Henry, the fish course was reportedly served from a giant model wooden ship from which cannons fired. Outside in the peaceful and discrete Queen Anne's Gardens you can sit in the shade of a 200-year-old beech tree.

Many visitors come to the castle on a day trip, so it's much quieter at the end of the day, from around 4pm onward. There is also a discount available if you visit both the Wallace Monument and Stirling Castle; show your ticket from one attraction to receive 10 percent off. It's more expensive to visit the castle, so, if you're wise, you'll buy your ticket to the Wallace Monument first.

Church of the Holy Rude

St John Street, Stirling; www.holyrude.org

This is the second oldest building in Stirling (after the castle), with the church founded in the 12th century (though the current building dates from the 15th century). Surely the most significant moment in the church's history was when King James VI was crowned here in 1567. The sermon was performed by none other than the pious John Knox, who had campaigned for the overthrow of the king's mother, Mary, Queen of Scots. James VI was just one year old at the time of his coronation. From its elevated position just downhill of the castle, at the top of the Old Town, the medieval church can be seen from throughout much of the city, but other than that, it looks like a fairly modest parish church and it still serves that purpose today. Inside, there is an impressive hammer-beam roof and some stunning stained glass. It's a good stop-off on your way up to the castle.

Old Town Jail

St John Street; tel. 01786 464 640; https://oldtownjail.co.uk; 10:15am-5:15pm every half hour daily July-Sept.; adult £6.50, child and concessions £4.50, under 5 free

If you like your history played out for you in a dramatic fashion, then these performance tours of what was once labeled the "worst prison in Britain" should amuse you. Taking place over the summer months each year, the tours are a harmless foray into social history. While the performers ham up certain aspects (horrible histories and horrific and gory punishments), these dramatizations are undeniably entertaining. You'll be given a 25-minute tour and can then explore the cells and visit the observation tower for amazing views of the city, which should take another half an hour or so.

Stirling Distillery

The Old Smiddy, Lower Castlehill; tel. 01786 596 496; https://stirlinggin.co.uk; 10am-6pm daily; Classic Tour £10 (1 hour); Old Smiddy Gin School £90 (2 hours)

Housed in a restored 19th-century building at the foot of the castle, this gin distillery, which only opened its doors in summer 2019, produces a base gin using Stirling nettles,

alongside angelica, juniper and basil, lemon and orange peel. Husband-and-wife team June and Cameron McCann began making Stirling gin almost four years before finding a permanent home in the Old Smiddy, a beautiful Victorian stone building on an even older historic site—King James V is thought to have kept his horses here in the 16th century.

As a nice touch, kids and dogs are welcome for free—youngsters will be given a free mocktail, and dogs a bowl of water. For adults, all tours start with a cocktail and end with a lesson in mixing (and tasting) the perfect G&T, making it excellent value. On the Old Smiddy Gin School experience you will be given your own mini still and shown how to make gin.

★ National Wallace Monument

Abbey Craig, Hillfoots Road, Stirling; tel. 01786 472 140; www.nationalwallacemonument.com; 10am-4pm Nov.-Feb., 10am-5pm Mar., 9:30am-5pm Apr.-June and Sept.-Oct., 9:30am-6pm July-Aug.; adult £10.50, child £6.50

Towering over the city is this lasting tribute to one of the most celebrated figures in Scottish history, William Wallace. Though Mel Gibson's portrayal may have romanticized the story somewhat, most Scots do still hail Wallace as a hero, not least for his role in the infamous Battle of Stirling Bridge, where bravery and a bit of luck saw rival Highland clans, united in their bid for freedom, win out against the English. The monument, which stands atop an old crag where William Wallace camped out before the battle with his army, was built in 1861 when the Highland Revival was in full swing—it's one of 20 or more Wallace monuments around Scotland.

Visitors to the monument often get here via the **Wallace Way,** a woodcarving trail that starts at the car park at the ticket office and continues up to Abbey Craig and the monument (15-20 minutes), though there is a free shuttle bus too. No expense was spared in the building of the monument, which stands 220 feet (67 m) high and is an example of Gothic grandeur, with a typical tower house topped with an elaborate crown spire and a proud statue of Wallace beneath a crown, brandishing his sword victoriously.

If you just want to admire the monument from outside, there is no need to pay, but you would be missing out on fabulous views and the many treasures inside. Climbing the 246 spiral steps (which are very narrow and steep) is no easy feat, but you can stop at each of the three galleries to break the journey up. In the **Hall of Arms,** on the first floor, you can learn about the Battle of Stirling Bridge, while in the **Hall of Heroes** on the next floor up, you can see Wallace's sword, protected by a glass case, as well as the busts of other Scottish heroes, including Robert Burns and King Robert the Bruce. In 2019 (finally) the first busts of female figureheads were added, including Mary Slessor, a missionary; Elsie Inglis, a highly respected and pioneering doctor; and Maggie Keswick Jencks, who, as she fought her own terminal cancer, devised a new approach to end-of-life cancer care.

At the **Royal Chamber** on the next floor up, you can learn about the construction of the monument (and there are some hands-on activities for kids), but you'll be eager to keep going to the pinnacle of **The Crown.** Stepping outside is a slightly dizzying experience, but,

if you can handle it, you can see all the way to Ben Lomond and the Trossachs in the west, and to the Pentland Hills to the east. If you can't manage the stairs, the **Keeper's Lodge** on the ground floor is a nice spot to rest or have a coffee.

The National Wallace Monument is a 1.5-mile (2.4 km) trek to the northeast of the city over the "new" Stirling Bridge. If you don't fancy the walk, the no. 52 bus from opposite Stirling Bus Station will take you there, or in summer the 1314 hop-on, hop-off bus (£4.90 per adult per day) connects the castle with the monument.

SPORTS AND RECREATION
Golf
STIRLING GOLF CLUB

Queen's Road, Stirling; tel. 01786 464 098; www. stirlinggolfclub.com; 8am-5pm daily; green fees from £20

Located in the shadow of Stirling Castle, this 18-hole course certainly gets top marks for scenery. It's also one of Scotland's oldest and is kept in excellent condition. Staff are friendly and unstuffy, offering a good all-round experience. Make time for a traditional Scottish lunch in the clubhouse.

National Wallace Monument, Stirling

Cycling

Stirling is a compact city that is easy to get around on two wheels. The simplest way is to hire one of the **Nextbikes** (tel. 020 8166 9851; https://nextbike.co.uk; £1 per half hour or £10 per day) situated throughout the city. You'll need to download the Nextbike app and follow the instructions (there will be instructions at the terminal too), after which you'll be given a code to unlock a bike. Once you've had enough cycling for the day, just return it to one of the designated docks and lock the bike up again.

Stirling Active Travel Hub (Stirling Train Station; tel. 01786 474 160) is the go-to place for cycling queries in and around Stirling. with routes that circle the castle or even head out of the city to places like the Battle of Bannockburn Visitor Centre.

ROUND THE CITY LOOP

Distance: *10.6 miles (16.8 km)*
Time: *2 hours*
Trailhead: *Stirling Active Travel Hub (by the train station)*
Information and Maps: *www.stirlingactivetravelhub.org/services/route-planning/destination-stirling*

Covering just over 10 miles (16 km), this circular route will bring you round the whole of the city, taking in major sights like Stirling Castle and the Wallace Monument along quiet roads and cycling routes. There are two steep (though short) hills to conquer, but no one will think any less of you if you need to jump off and push for a bit.

FOOD

MADE IN STIRLING

44 King Street; www.neighbourfood.co.uk/markets/stirling/8; collections weekly

If you are staying in a self-catering property in or around Stirling then this one-stop shop with over 36 local producers is a wonderful place to stock up the fridge and cupboards. You can order creamy hand-made fudge from Clantastic, fresh bread from Wild Hearth Bakery, and fully traceable venison from Highlander Ridge Larder. To order, you go to the website, choose what you want, and when it comes to collection time (done weekly, so check the dates ahead of travel), you can pick up your produce and meet some of the farmers and makers in person. You can usually get a few extra tastings for free too.

DARNLEY COFFEE HOUSE

18 Bow Street; tel. 01786 474 468; www.facebook.com/DarnleyCoffeeHouse; 11am-4pm daily; coffee £2.20, cakes £2.20

Just a few minutes' walk from the castle in an old stone building, this place serves delicious soups and sandwiches (with crisps on the side), and daily specials such as Parma ham and mozzarella and nectarine salad, in addition to good coffee and well-priced cakes. The homemade coleslaw is also delicious.

HERMANN'S

Mar Place House, 58 Broad Street; tel. 01786 450 632; www.hermanns-restaurant.co.uk; lunch 12pm-2pm, dinner from 6pm; entrées £5.90

Fusing Scottish ingredients with his Austrian hankering for schnitzel and strudel, chef and owner Hermann Aschaber seems to have hit a winning formula, which has proved pretty much impossible to top in over two decades. Try the pan-fried veal or the excellent-value set dinner menu. This is fine dining with affable and trouble-free service.

THE BIRDS & THE BEES

Easter Cornton Road, Causewayhead; tel. 01786 473 663; www.thebirdsandthebees-stirling.com; lunch 12pm-2:30pm daily, dinner 5pm-11pm Mon.-Fri., food served 12pm-10pm Sat.-Sun.; entrées £5.90

In an old farm stead, this slightly grown-up take on pub grub—there's slow roast pork ribs and the fish and chips come with crushed minted peas rather than mushy—is a local hit worth heading a little out of town for, and it's relatively handy for visitors to the National Wallace Monument. In winter, cozy up by the fire in the bar, or in summer eat on the pretty garden terrace.

BREA

5 Baker Street; tel. 01786 446 277; www.brea-stirling. co.uk; 12pm-9pm Mon.-Thurs. and Sun., 12pm-10pm Fri.-Sat.; entrées £6.95

Just a five-minute walk from the Holy Rude church, this is a great place for a leisurely lunch once you've taken in the historic sights, or a more extravagant meal with wine pairing come evening time. Using Scottish ingredients—seafood comes from the west coast—it serves a good choice of meat and fish dishes, plus there's a full vegan menu too.

ACCOMMODATIONS

MUNRO GUEST HOUSE

14 Princes Street; tel. 01786 472 685, www. munroguesthouse.co.uk; £75 d

A good budget option on a road lined with period houses between the train station and the Old Town, this guest house has just five rooms—one of which is a family suite—and owner Richard goes out of his way to make you feel at home. Rooms are spotless, breakfasts are good, and there is a colorful and comfortable lounge for when you want a bit of a break from your room.

THE STIRLING HIGHLAND HOTEL

Spittal Street; tel. 01786 272 727; www. thecairncollection.co.uk/hotels/the-stirling-highland; £146 d

Part of the Cairn Collection of luxury hotels, this hotel is housed in a smart Victorian building on the site of a former convent founded by King James IV. Rooms are immaculate if a little soulless, but guests can make use of the well-equipped spa, gorgeously refined social areas, and even an old observatory, a relic from the building's former guise as a school.

FRIARS WYND

17 Friars Street; tel. 01786 447 501 or 07858 136 818; www.friarswynd.co.uk; £179 d

At the foot of castle hill and just a couple of minutes' walk from the train station, this boutique hotel in a renovated Victorian townhouse is a great find. The classically styled rooms have comfy beds, modern en suites, and period features—some even have window seats—and there's an intimate wine bar and restaurant downstairs.

INFORMATION AND SERVICES

The VisitScotland iCentre for Stirling is in the **Old Town Jail** (tel. 01786 475 019; www. visitscotland.com/info/services/stirling-icentre-p332521). The **Your Stirling** website (www.yourstirling.com) is a useful starting point with lots of ideas to help you shape your itinerary, also offering the **Stirling City Pass** (July-Sept. only; adult £27, child £17), which gives you entry to the town's major attractions, complete with audio guides and lots of other local discounts. You'll also be given a guidebook and map to help you navigate the city. Buy the pass online at or at the Old Town Jail.

GETTING THERE

Stirling is easily accessible to both Glasgow and Edinburgh; you can get here from either city in under an hour.

By Car

From Glasgow, it's just 26 miles (42 km; 30 minutes) to Stirling, along the M8, M80, and then A872. From Edinburgh it's 36 miles (57 km; 50 minutes); take the A90, M9, and then the A872. From Perth, it's a 37-mile (60-km) drive southwest via the A9 to Stirling (about 45 minutes), while from Callander in Loch Lomond it's a 23-mile (37-km) drive southeast along the A84 (just under an hour).

By Train

If traveling by train, **ScotRail** has regular connections from Glasgow (3 trains an hour, 27 minutes; £8.30 one-way) and Edinburgh (every half-hour, 50 minutes; £9.10 one-way). **Stirling Train Station** is located on Goosecroft Road, just a two-minute walk from the modern city center. To walk to the Old Town from the train station, go straight across the roundabout in front of the station onto Station Road, turn right onto Murray Place, turn left down Friars Street, and right onto Baker Street. Then take the first left onto Bank Street and turn right onto John Street, where you will find the Old Town Jail. It's just under 10 minutes all together.

GETTING AROUND

The Old Town and Stirling Castle are both a bit of a walk from the modern city, but chances are it's in these more historic areas that you'll want to spend most of your time. Parking does fill up at the castle quickly in summer, and there is still a nice (but uphill) walk to the castle. If it's busy, use one of the city's **Park and Ride** bus services (https://stirling.gov.uk/roads-transport-streets/parking-zones-permits/park-ride/), which will transport you to the castle and other main attractions. There are three Park and Ride car parks, which are well signposted as you drive into the city. The best one is probably **Springkerse Retail Park** to the east of the city center as buses from this location are slightly more regular (every 12 minutes), but there isn't much difference between them all otherwise. Parking is free, but you'll need to pay £1.20 for an adult return on the bus, or 60p for a child return. Travel time is about 15 minutes, traffic depending.

From the **bus station** (Goosecroft Road), which is adjacent to the train station, you can take the no. 52 bus to the Wallace Monument with **First Bus** (www.firstbus.co.uk); 12 minutes; £1.60 one-way, 80p child). In summer, the no. 1314 hop-on, hop-off bus goes from the castle to the National Wallace Monument (£2.50 one-way, £1.30 child, or £4.50 for a day ticket, £2.30 child's day ticket).

There are also taxi ranks at the train station; expect to pay £4-5 for a ride from the train station to the castle.

AROUND STIRLING

Battle of Bannockburn Centre

Glasgow Road, Whins of Milton; tel. 01786 812 664; www.battleofbannockburn.com; 10am-5:30pm daily Mar.-Oct., 10am-5pm daily Nov.-Mar.; adult £11.50, child and concessions £8.50, family £30.50

Learn more about this landmark victory for the Scottish during the first Wars of Independence at this 3D interactive experience, just 2 miles (3 km) outside Stirling. At the Battle of Bannockburn, Robert the Bruce defeated the forces of the English King Edward II. The village of Whins of Milton, near the famous battle site, is just an eight-minute drive from Stirling, or you can get the no. 54A or no. 909 bus from Stirling Bus Station, which will get you there in minutes.

Doune Castle

Castle Hill, Doune; www.historicenvironment.scot/visit-a-place/places/doune-castle; 9:30am-5:30pm Apr.-Sept., 10am-4pm Oct.-Mar.; adult £6, child £3.60

This medieval stronghold 8 miles (13 km) outside Stirling has one of the best surviving great halls in Scotland, plus an impressive 100-foot-high (30.5 m) gatehouse. The castle was built in the 14th century for the Duke of Albany and has changed very little since.

Its atmospheric timeworn walls have led to it being featured on both the big and small screen. First, it starred in the cult classic *Monty Python and the Holy Grail* in the 1970s (the audio guide is even narrated by Terry Jones of Monty Python fame). More recently, it has appeared in both the pilot of *Game of Thrones* as Winterfell and in *Outlander* as Castle Leoch.

Once through the large gatehouse, you'll find another slightly smaller tower, and a large courtyard enclosed by a high curtain wall. Explore cobbled tunnels, a cellar, and spiral staircases connecting the floors. The **Lord's Hall** (or Great Hall), with its double fireplace, carved oak screen, and musicians' gallery, is where lavish feasts would have taken place; in the kitchen, you can find out about the preparation that went into such boastful banquets. Doune Castle is a 20-minute drive north of Stirling, mostly on the A84 before turning off on the A820 at Doune.

The Falkirk Wheel

Lime Road; www.scottishcanals.co.uk/falkirk-wheel; 1-hour boat trip adult £13.50, child £7.50, under 5 free; 1 hour

Pretty much halfway between Edinburgh and Glasgow and only 30 minutes south of Stirling, Falkirk played an important role in Scotland's Industrial Revolution, a vital transport link between many of Scotland's major cities. Its world-famous boat lift is a feat of engineering that connects the Forth and Clyde, and the Union canals, and it is the only rotating boat lift in the world. It attracts crowds of tourists who come to marvel at its mechanical workings, which demonstrate how Scotland has long been at the forefront of industrial technologies. There is a **café** where you can sit and watch the boats go up and down, or you can book a boat trip, which includes a rotation on the wheel before cruising down to the Union Canal and back.

Falkirk Wheel

KELPIES

The Helix, Falkirk; tel. 1324 590 600; www.thehelix.co.uk; 9:30am-5pm daily; adult £7.50, concessions £6.50, child free

Nearby is Falkirk's newest tourist attraction, the Kelpies, a giant pair of 100-foot-high (30-m) horse heads that are both a piece of art and a demonstration of Scotland's engineering prowess. Step inside the Kelpies on a 30-minute tour (30 minutes, 20 minutes in winter), which will explain artist Andy Scott's vision.

INFORMATION AND SERVICES

The best resource for information on the Falkirk area is **Visit Falkirk** (www.visitfalkirk.com), which includes links to tips on accommodation and places to eat. The site is frequently updated to show which businesses are operating, and which ones have limited capacity—very useful in these post-COVID times.

GETTING THERE

From **Stirling,** Falkirk is just 30 minutes away, a 12-mile (19-km) drive. Make your way to the A9 south from Stirling until you reach a roundabout that will take you to Falkirk. From **Edinburgh,** take the M9 toward Stirling until Junction 5 (26 miles/42 km, 50 minutes). From **Glasgow,** take the M80 toward Stirling, exit at Junction 5 onto the M876, and follow signs for Falkirk (26 miles/42 km; 40 minutes).

Falkirk is well served by local transport. Scotrail runs trains from Stirling to Camelon Station in Falkirk, a 12-minute ride (£4.90 single). The train station is a 1.5-mile (2.4-km; 30-minute) walk northeast of the Falkirk Wheel. From Edinburgh, the X38 bus with First Scotland East will get you here in 1 hour 30 minutes (£6.30 single/£10.70 return), or you can get the train from Edinburgh Waverley to Falkirk Grahamston (1 hour 15 minutes; £7.20 single/£10.10 return). From Glasgow Queen Street, the train is definitely the best option, taking as little as 30 minutes (£8.70 single/£11.30 adult).

Fife

In east Scotland, just across the Firth of Forth from Edinburgh, Fife is a rural region where farming and fishing are still a major employer—a fact that has been seized upon by many canny tourism providers in recent years to create an exciting food and drink scene. Seasonal produce keeps guests coming back for more, including a couple of contenders for the best fish and chips in Scotland.

Follow the coastline to the towns and villages of the East Neuk; in Scottish, *neuk* means corner or "nook," and that is exactly what you will find here: a hidden corner. Aside from cute shop fronts, fish fresh from the boat, and the gentle murmur of waves kissing the shore, there are also over 300 miles (482 km) of cycleways that lead through a network of forest trails for gentle escapism. Plus, in southwest Fife, you'll find the 16th-century conservation area of Culross, which for many years was little more than a sleepy backwater but which has been placed firmly on the tourist trail due to its starring role in TV's *Outlander*.

Covering the area between Edinburgh and the beautiful town of St. Andrews, Fife's miles and miles of countryside and coast offer no fewer than 15 award-winning beaches, and this region is regularly voted the best for outdoors enthusiasts. Visit the **Welcome to Fife** website (www.welcometofife.com) to get a better understanding of the region; it even has a useful trip planner. Fife is actually pretty accessible by bus and train, though you won't want to rely on either too much once you're here, making it a good option if you're planning a big walk or you think you will base yourself in one location for your visit.

DUNFERMLINE ABBEY AND PALACE

St. Margaret's Street, Dunfermline; tel. 01383 739 026; www.historicenvironment.scot/visit-a-place/ places/dunfermline-abbey-and-palace; 10am-4pm Tues.-Sat. Apr.-Sept., 10am-4pm Sat.-Weds. Oct.-Mar.; free

Once a place of worship among Scotland's most powerful people, this priory, made an abbey by King David I in the 12th century, became the burial place of some of the most powerful and famous people in Scottish history, including David I himself; his mother, St. Margaret; and Robert the Bruce.

Located in the center of Scotland's ancient capital, Dunfermline, what remains of the abbey is a beautiful example of Romanesque architecture, with its huge nave—the caved-in roof, walls standing alone in some places, and greenery growing over the stones—taking center stage. The 19th-century abbey church (tel. 1383 723005l; https://dunfermlineabbey. com/wwp; 10am-4:30pm Mon.-Sat., 2pm-4:30pm Sun. Apr.-Oct.; free) is still a working church. The adjoining palace, built as a personal residence of King James VI's queen, Anne of Denmark, was also the birthplace of their son, King Charles I—the last king to be born in Scotland, and will incur a fee when it eventually reopens.

The Abbey backs up to **Pittencrieff Park** (Pittencrief Street; tel. 3451 550 000; www. fife.gov.uk/kb/docs/articles/community-life2/ parks,-allotments,-core-paths/pittencrieff-park; open 24/7; free), a 76-acre green space dotted with monuments to famous Scots, including "richest man in the world" Andrew Carnegie, who was born in Dunfermline. Pretty Dunfermline itself is worth a stopover anyway, particularly if you're crossing the Forth Bridge from Edinburgh, as it's virtually the first place you come to.

Food and Accommodations
★ JACK O'BRYANS

5 Chalmers Street, Dunfermline; tel. 01383 324720; www.jackobryans.com; brunch 10am-3pm daily, a la carte from 5pm daily; entrées £8

Having only opened in early 2019, this

restaurant is as far removed as possible from the Irish pub that the name suggests and has already accrued a devoted following. Some of those loyal customers have followed the team from Edinburgh, where they used to run the popular Iberian-style Black Pig & Oyster restaurant. Here, though, it's all about high-quality Scottish dishes and it's very much a family affair, with the kitchen run by Bryan Coghill and his son Jack, and front of house looked after by Bryan's wife, Michelle; his daughter, Yasmine; and Jack's girlfriend, Sarah. This is a friendly place with the kind of food that will make you want to come back.

GARVOCK HOUSE HOTEL

St John's Drive, Dunfermline; tel. 01383 621 067; www.garvock.co.uk; £87 d; dinner meals 6pm-9pm; entrées £9.60

Rooms in this 200-year-old hotel, which overlooks Dunfermline, come with big windows, comfy beds dressed in rich fabrics, and big, luxury bathrooms. Guests can get their day off to a good start with a full Scottish breakfast, before taking a calming walk in the peaceful gardens. At the on-site restaurant, freshly pressed linen tablecloths and candlelight create a formal yet intimate environment.

Getting There

From Edinburgh it's just a 40-minute drive out of the capital to Dunfermline, following the A90, which turns into the M90 as you cross the Queensferry Bridge across the Forth of Firth, turning off for the A823 at Exit 2 (18 miles/29 km). From Glasgow, it's just over an hour by car to Dunfermline: follow the M80 northeast out of the city, before joining the M876 at Falkirk and then the A985 past Culross and Crombie before taking the A823 into Dunfermline (42 miles/68 km).

By train, Dunfermline is just over half an hour from Edinburgh (£6 single, £5.50 day return—restricted to certain times). The train station in Dunfermline is centrally located, a 15-minute (0.5-mile/0.8-km) walk from the Abbey. From Glasgow, the Stagecoach X24 bus (www.stagecoachbus.com/ regional-help-and-contact/east-scotland) from Buchanan Bus Station will get you to Dunfermline in 1 hour 10 minutes (£12 single, £19.50 return).

CULROSS

Fife KY12 8JH; tel. 01383 880 359; www.nts.org.uk/ visit/places/culross; palace 10am-5pm Apr.-Oct.; adult £10.50, concessions £7.50

Culross was just a picturesque 16th-century Scottish village off the tourist radar, until the village's role in *Outlander* led to a steady stream of coach tours stopping off for visitors to snap photos of the cobbled streets and huddled houses.

Wandering around this charming town is about as close to stepping back into the 16th century as possible, with whitewashed, red-tiled buildings such as the **Town House** (Orchard Grove, 9 Back Causeway, Balgownie W; www.visitscotland.com/info/see-do/ culross-palace-townhouse-study-p250721), where witches were tried and held while awaiting execution. The nearby ochre colored **Culross Palace** (Blair Castle; tel. 1383 880 359; www.nts.org.uk), built by wealthy coal merchant George Bruce in the late 16th century, is in fact not a palace but a grand and impressive house. You can explore the small rooms and connecting passageways, with wonderful painted ceilings, pine paneling, antique furniture and curios. The garden is planted with grasses, herbs, and vegetables of the period.

Stroll up a cobbled alleyway known as **Back Causeway,** complete with a raised central aisle formerly used by noblemen to separate them from the "commoners." This leads up behind the Town House to the **Study** (The Cross, Tanhouse Brae; tel. 131 458 0200; www.nts.org.uk/Property/Royal-Burgh-of-Culross/), built in 1610, taking its name from the small room at the top of its tower.

Hiking
FIFE COASTAL PATH
Distance: 93 miles (150 km)
Time: 7-10 days

Trailhead: *Kincardine (west of Culross) or Tayport (southeast of Dundee)*

Information and Maps: *https://fifecoastandcountrysidetrust.co.uk/walks/fife-coastal-path*

Stretching all the way from Kincardine in the southwest to Tayport in the northeast, the Fife Coastal Path is the longest continuous walk in the whole of Scotland. You can follow the path as it wends through pretty fishing villages, along rugged coastline, and via wildlife reserves and wide sandy beaches. It is well-marked and can be attempted in one giant slog (over many days, of course) or broken down into smaller sections, such as an exploration of the **East Neuk,** from Elie to Crail (3 miles/5 km). As you walk, if you are very, very lucky you may be able to spot a white-tailed eagle, the UK's largest bird of prey. A concerted reintroduction program over the past few decades has seen white-tailed eagles (also known as sea eagles), which were once hunted to extinction, reintroduced to Scottish shores.

Food and Accommodations
RED LION

Low Causeway, Culross; tel. 01383 880 225; https://redlionculross.co.uk; 12pm-9pm daily; entrées £5.75

This traditional inn in Culross is the obvious place for lunch or dinner when visiting the heritage village, though it is justifiably popular, so book ahead. It's a snug, jovial type of place, with beams, and a mix of wood-paneled and stone walls. You can just pop in for a drink if you like, but if that is all you want, try to avoid lunchtime, when people come to tuck into the big portions of pub meals.

SAORSA HOUSE

Low Causeway, Culross; tel. 01383 882 729 or 07845 693 938; https://saorsa-house-bb.business.site; £65 d

A small B&B just outside Culross, Saorsa House has simple and clean rooms and a good breakfast at decent prices. Guests can also join in workshops by local craftspeople with the chance to buy goods direct from the makers. Walkers are welcomed.

Getting There

Culross is about an hour (25 miles/40 km) from Edinburgh on the A90, across the Queensferry Bridge, and west on the A985. From Glasgow, Culross is under an hour (30 miles/48 km) away, on the M867 to the A985. If you want to tack Culross onto a visit to Dunfermline Abbey, they are only about 20 minutes (8 miles/13 km) apart, on the A994 and A958.

FALKLAND PALACE

Near Cupar, KY15 7BY; tel. 01337 857397; www.nts.org.uk/visit/places/falkland-palace; 11am-5pm Apr.-Oct.; adult £5, concessions £4

The playground of the Stuart kings and queens—Falkland was a favorite hideaway of Mary, Queen of Scots—this Renaissance palace was imagined by James IV and then his son James V (Mary's father) as their answer to the opulent chateaus of their cousins in France. Mary spent a lot of time at this country retreat when she returned from France to reclaim the throne, hunting for stags and boar and practicing falconry. She would have also played tennis on what is the oldest surviving tennis court in the world.

Though the palace and its grounds fell into disrepair in the 17th century, it was thankfully saved and restored in the 19th century by the 3rd Marquess of Bute. Today you can wander amid rooms rich in detail, from wood paneling to hand-painted ceilings and huge tapestries, giving some idea of what it would have looked like in its Stuart heyday.

Food
PITLESSIE VILLAGE INN & PANTRY

Cupar Road, Pitlessie; tel. 01337 830 595; www.pitlessievillageinn.com; 5pm-10pm Mon.-Tues., 12pm-3pm and 5pm-10pm Weds., 12pm-11pm Fri.-Sat., 12pm-10pm Sun.; entrées £5.95

This recently refurbished pub in the village of Pitlessie, just a few miles from Falkland Palace, serves pub grub with a Scottish twist (think haggis pakora and black pudding fritters), as well as pub classics such as pies, steaks, and burgers. For the really hungry, there's also a good selection of High Teas (not to be confused with afternoon tea)—main courses such as fish and chips that also come with a side order of toast, tea, and cakes.

Getting There

In Central Fife, getting closer to St. Andrews and Perth, Falkland Palace is about an hour north of Edinburgh via the Queensferry Bridge, M90, and A91, a 40-mile (64-km) drive. From Glasgow, it's about 1 hour 15 minutes (56 miles/90 km), on the M80, M876, and A977. From Dunfermline, it's a 35-minute (24-mile/39-km) drive northwest on the M90 and A91.

★ EAST NEUK

This little chain of small ports in the southeast corner of Fife is a tucked away secret for locals, weekenders from Edinburgh, and in-the-know travelers. Home to sweet villages with colorful houses, postcard-worthy harbors, glorious beaches, and abundant wildlife along the Fife Coastal Path, it's an easy way to get off the beaten track without traveling too far—especially considering none of the towns is more than 30 minutes from St. Andrews.

In the west, the cute little nook of Earlsferry and Elie (more commonly known as simply **Elie**) on Fife's southeast coastline is the entry point into these villages, which stretch east as far as **Kingsbarns**, just over a 20-minute drive along the coast or picturesque inland roads. In between are **Anstruther,** the largest of the East Neuk fishing villages, and **Crail** with its beautiful harbor. Another reason to come is to take a boat to the Isle of May from May to September, when you're almost guaranteed to see seals and puffins.

Be warned—the East Neuk is the kind of place that makes you wonder why you don't just pull up stakes and head to the coast for good. The more you see, the more you will want to come back.

Sights

SCOTTISH FISHERIES MUSEUM

St Ayles, Harbourhead, Anstruther; tel. 01333 310 628; www.scotfishmuseum.org; 10am-3pm Weds.-Sun.; adults £9, concessions £7

The fishing industry has played a huge role in the lives of many Scottish people, particularly in this little string of villages, and so this museum, set across several old whitewashed buildings by Anstruther's harbor, goes some way to tell the story of fishing in Scotland. From black and white photos of families baiting lines together, to paintings by the likes of Telfer Thomson and John McGhie, to historic boats, this museum is a great place to learn of the resilience of the workers and families who have weathered many storms to eke out a living from the sea as well as celebrate the customs, traditions, and superstitions linked to the industry. Fishing remains one of the most dangerous occupations in Scotland and this is felt keenly in the Memorial Room, where a book lists names of fishermen lost to the sea pre-1945 and plaques remember those lost since.

CRAIL HARBOUR

Shore Gate, Crail

In Crail, all roads lead down to the harbor, not literally, but with the village gently sloping down to the shorefront it certainly feels like it. There are benches to enjoy the view, or you can sit with your legs dangling over the slipway as you watch the boats come and go. For better views, a walkway leads from the top of the slipway to some of the bigger houses overlooking the beach.

SCOTLAND'S SECRET BUNKER

Crown buildings, Troywood; tel. 01333 310 301; https://secretbunker.co.uk; 10am-5pm daily; adult £12.95, child £8.95, concessions £11.95, under 3 free

For 50 years, an unprepossessing farmhouse hid a big secret, and now you can step inside it. This house was once an underground nuclear command center that formed the nucleus for the Scottish government's Cold War activity.

Built in 1951 and operational until 1993, today the bunker is open as a museum, with two cinemas, a nuclear operations room, an RAF control center and Royal Observer Corps, dormitories, and a 1950s-style café. It's pretty cool to be able to step 100 feet (30 m) below ground and see where central government and military commanders would have run the country from after a nuclear attack.

KINGSBARNS DISTILLERY

East Newhall Farm, Kingsbarns; tel. 01333 451 300; www.kingsbarnsdistillery.com; 10am-5pm daily; standard tour adult £12, child 8-17 £4

This relatively new distillery only opened its doors in 2014 as part of a major project to restore a 19th-century farm. Many visitors admire the turreted tower of the building, once the doocot (dovecot) that would have supplied the laird with his meat and eggs.

Today, it's a modern distillery that's built up quite a reputation. The one-hour standard tour includes a tasting of both the distillery's new-make spirit and a dram of its award-winning single malt "Dream to Dram." The price also includes a £2 off voucher in the shop against a bottle of whisky or local Darnley's Gin, which is also distilled here.

Beaches
ELIE RUBY BAY BEACH

Wadeslea Road

This crescent of beach backed by dunes just east of Elie provides sheltered swimming as well as lots of rock pools to survey at low tide, when you might find limpets, barnacles, and sea anemones, as well as hiding crabs. It's also a fabulous bird-watching spot as the rich marine harvest attracts curlew, redshank, and eider ducks. If you look up from the beach, you can see a ruined tower named as **Lady's Tower,** built in 1770 for Lady Janet Anstruther. According to the Elie and Earlsferry History Society, Lady Anstruther used the tower as a viewpoint to sit and recover following a session of seabathing.

Walks
EAST NEUK COASTAL WALK

Distance: *10 miles (16 km)*
Time: *3 hours 15 minutes*
Trailhead: *Elie and Earlsferry*
Information and Maps: *https:// fifecoastandcountrysidetrust.co.uk/walks/ fife-coastal-path*

The Fife Coastal Path connects all the villages of the East Neuk, so you can walk it fairly easily: it's just over 10 miles (16 km) between Elie and Crail, passing St Monans, Pittenweem, and Anstruther along the way.

Cruises and Water Sports
CRUISE TO THE ISLE OF MAY

Middle Pier, Anstruther; tel. 07473 631 671; www. isleofmayboattrips.co.uk; Easter-Sept.; 4- to 4.5-hour excursion adult £40, child £30

On the northeast edge of the Firth of Forth, the Isle of May is a National Nature Reserve. Seals flounder on its rocky shoreline and thousands of seabirds cram themselves onto the jagged cliffs. These trips, aboard an open rigid inflatable boat (tie your hair back and wear a hat), are fun and exhilarating, and allow for around three hours to explore the island on foot before heading back to the mainland. May-July is best to see the nesting seabirds, including loveable and brightly-beaked puffins. There is also a slightly more sedate **ferry** (www.isleofmayferry.com; adult £34, child £17) over to the isles with a good number of covered seats if you don't fancy getting wet.

EAST NEUK OUTDOORS

Cellardyke Park, Cellardyke, Anstruther; tel. 01333 310 370; https://eastneukoutdoors.co.uk; half-day kayaking adult £50, child £40, sea kayaking taster (over 13 only) £40 for 2 hours

If you want to flex your adventurous muscles, then this activity center, based in the well-preserved fishing village of Cellardyke, near Anstruther, is the place to do it. A tidal pool, once used as a swimming pool for Victorians, is now a great place for novices to try kayaking in a safe environment. The center also offers a sea kayaking taster session for something a little more difficult. Other activities include stand-up paddle boarding, bushcraft, and fire making. There is a 10 percent discount for groups of more than three.

Shopping
CRAIL POTTERY

75 Nethergate, Crail; tel. 01333 451 212; www. crailpottery.com; 9am-5pm Mon.-Fri., 10am-5pm Sat.-Sun

This family-run business tucked away in one of the lanes that runs from the center of Crail to the harbor produces gorgeous ceramics, pottery, and earthenware in a range of style and colors. All the pieces are hand thrown and are decorated, glazed, and fired right in the workshops owned by the Grieve family. It's worth ducking in to have a look at some of the pieces on display in the pretty courtyard, or venture up the stairs to the small shop above and you might come away armed with a beautiful and unique piece.

Food
★ THE LOBSTER HUT

34 Shoregate, Crail; tel. 01333 450 476; www. facebook.com/reillyshellfish; 12pm-4pm Tues.-Sun. in summer, other months weekends only; crab roll £2.50

And now for one of my favorite finds ever. At this little shed at Crail harbor you can get a lobster (£5) or crab (£2.50) roll, which comes in white flour bap with lots of butter, mixed with pink sauce. The food is so simple yet delicious, and a bargain of a lunch. The rolls are best eaten on one of the benches overlooking the harbor or with your legs dangling over the water on the slipway.

THE CHEESY TOAST SHACK

Kingbarns Beach, Kingsbarns; tel. 07792 910 507; www.facebook.com/thecheesytoastshack; 10am-4pm Weds.-Mon.; toasties £4

Come rain or shine, these fully loaded toasted cheese sandwiches are available on Kingsbarns beach from a little wooden hut. Carb-heavy but oh so tasty, belt-busting fillings include mac and cheese or red leicester

and chorizo. They also have a second outlet on St. Andrews' East Sands that is open seven days a week. This is the perfect accompaniment for a windy beach walk.

THE PAVILION ELIE

Golf Club Lane, Elie; tel. 01333 331 132; www. thepavilionelie.co.uk; open in daytime year-round plus evenings in summer; entrées £5.50

It might not look like much from outside, but this old green pavilion right next to a golf course serves up a mean seafood platter and is something of a hub of the community, with regular local events hosted here and all the produce coming from local suppliers. During the day it's a good spot for coffee, cake, sandwiches, or an ice cream sundae, but the main meals, particularly the seafood, is what makes it really stand out, either for lunch or in summer when the café does a dinner service.

ANSTRUTHER FISH BAR

42-44 Shore Street, Anstruther; tel. 01333 310 518; www.anstrutherfishbar.co.uk; 12pm-9pm daily in summer, winter hours vary; fish and chips £6.30

Claiming to be the "best fish and chips in Britain" is quite bold, but Anstruther Fish Bar has won enough accolades to warrant it. Best or not, it really is very good and it's little wonder, since owners Robert and Alison Smith both come from a long line of fishermen. The quality of the hand-filleted fish and other seafood is high, with only the best selected from market every day. Of course, the traditional battered haddock with "secret recipe" light batter has to be tried, but you can also choose from lemon sole in batter (or breadcrumbs), dressed crab, and prawns in breadcrumbs. It's also always worth checking the specials board for in-season lobster and smoked haddock from the company's own smokehouse. You can, of course, take it away, but if you dine in you will get bread and butter alongside your fish supper, as well as a pot of tea, which is altogether much more civilized.

1: beach in Elie 2: Anstruther Fish Bar 3: The Ship Inn 4: terrace at The Ship Inn

★ **THE SHIP INN**

The Toft, Elie; tel. 01333 330246; www.shipinn.scot;
bar food 12pm-8pm daily, £8.95 entrées

The main food spot in Elie, the Ship Inn has unrivaled views over the beach from its terraced garden, while inside it's the kind of place you always hope to find to hide away from the wind and rain so prevalent in Scotland. The bar has an open fire, plus a couple of wood-burning stoves to warm up by, a good selection of local ales and a short but good bar menu—local haddock with chips or warming dishes like cullen skink. The slightly more formal and brighter nautical-style restaurant serves 100 percent fresh Scottish fish and meat, from pub favorites (try the Fife burger) to shellfish, but it fills up quickly so book ahead. If you want to sit outside (and in summer you really should), you'll just have to get here early, as it's first-come, first-served.

They also have six pretty rooms (£180 d), with blue wood paneling on the walls and white wooden shutters on the windows. All rooms come with Nespresso machines, carefully selected fine teas, crisp Egyptian cotton linen, and fluffy large towels.

Accommodations
MURRAY LIBRARY HOSTEL

Murray Building, 7 Shore Street, Anstruther; tel.
01333 311 123; www.murraylibraryhostel.com; £53
private double

This hostel, in a red sandstone building that was once a library, offers glorious harbor views from every room, private rooms for 1 or 2 guests, plus family rooms for up to four guests. Dorms offer bunks for four to eight guests, and the bedding is snuggly for a hostel. The shared kitchen and lounge are bright and welcoming—a lot more appealing than those in many hostels, and there is free tea and coffee, which is a nice touch. This hostel is a clean and friendly base on your East Neuk travels.

KINGSBARN INN

5 Main Street, Kingsbarns; tel. 01334 880 778; www.
theinnatkingsbarns.co.uk; 10am-4pm, closed Tues.;
£135 d, 2-night minimum stay

Set in an attractive 18th-century coaching inn, this six-bed hotel is a nice surprise. Rooms are clean and comfortable, and the bar and on-site restaurant, the Scranhoose, are a good addition. Another big selling point is the friendly and knowledgeable hosts Maxx and Anette. Annette is a great cook and gets the meat and poultry for her breakfasts and dinners locally.

THE PEAT INN

Near St. Andrews; tel. 01334 840 206; www.
thepeatinn.co.uk; £240 d

It's not cheap, but this restaurant with rooms, just a few miles outside St. Andrews (well-placed for the East Neuk, too), has the ideal balance of cozy interiors with modern flourishes. The eight bedrooms are dressed in fine Scottish fabrics, and you have every home comfort you need, including Nespresso machines and luxurious Noble Isle toiletries, while the Michelin-starred restaurant downstairs produces contemporary Scottish cooking in a relaxed setting.

PUFFIN COTTAGE

Nethergate, Crail; tel. 0345 498 6900; www.
cottages.com/cottages/puffin-cottage-s62; £1,085
per week, sleeps 5

This charming stone holiday cottage is only a few minutes' walk from the pretty harbor. Adjoining another property, it was originally a fisherman's cottage but is now tastefully furnished to make a cozy holiday home. Weekly prices can be as low as £450 in low season, making it a good-value option for visitors who would like to stay in the area for a while.

Getting There and Around

From Edinburgh to the East Neuk, it's 1 hour 20 minutes, crossing over the Queensferry Bridge on the M90 and then taking Exit 2A east onto the A92 before joining the A915 and then the A917 that connects the villages (46 miles/74 km). For the East Neuk (1 hour 45 minutes), the best route from Glasgow is to take the M8 toward Edinburgh before joining the M90 to cross the bridge (78 miles/126 km).

From St. Andrews, the easternmost of the East Neuk villages, Kingsbarns, is only 15 minutes (7 miles/11 km) to the south.

If you're short of time, a car will make getting around easier, but there are other options. The **Fife Coastal Path** connects all the villages of the East Neuk, so you can walk it fairly easily. Local buses also serve this stretch of coastline; for instance, the hourly no. 95 with Stagecoach will take you from Elie to Crail in just 32 minutes (www.stagecoachbus.com; £4.50 single). You can buy a paper ticket on the bus, or book through the Stagecoach Bus app.

St. Andrews

One of Scotland's oldest settlements, St. Andrews is a university town of note, with intricate medieval architecture that could make England's Oxford blush. While the university is a big draw to visitors, most people come here to pay homage to its position as the home of golf, and playing a round on the Old Course is a must for any golf fan. However, there's lots more to discover besides: walk the expansive sands of the beach that starred in the opening scenes of Hollywood's *Chariots of Fire,* and around town you'll uncover old ruins, historic sites, and myriad old lanes and quadrants little changed in centuries.

SIGHTS
University of St. Andrews
College Gate, St. Andrews

The ancient university, founded in 1413, also known for being where the Duke and Duchess of Cambridge courted, has had a complex history. It was partially demolished during the Scottish Reformation, and when Samuel Johnson visited on his epic trip in 1773, he lamented its appearance, writing: "to see it pining in decay and struggling for life, fills the mind with mournful images and ineffectual wishes."

Since then, many of the buildings have been rebuilt or restored, but you can still see some of the crumbling remains of the old university buildings as well as many of its old quadrangles, dotted throughout the town, many of which have pretty floral displays and benches where you are free to sit. The biggest concentration of university buildings is along the town's northern coastline, between North Street and the Scores. The **Wardlaw Museum** (7 The Scores; tel. 1334 461 660; www.st-andrews.ac.uk/museums; 11am-7pm Mon.-Fri., 10am-5pm Sat.-Sun.; free) gives a good overview of the history of the university and has a beautiful view of the sea, while campus church **St. Salvators Chapel** (North Street; tel. 1334 476 161; www.st-andrews.ac.uk/about/history/st-salvators) is a rare example of late medieval architecture.

St. Andrews Castle
The Scores; tel. 1334 477 196; www.historicenvironment.scot/visit-a-place/places/st-andrews-castle; 10am-4pm daily; adults £6, children £3.50, joint tickets to cathedral £9 adults, £5.40 children

Romantically situated on the coastline, the ruins of this 13th-century castle are dramatic and moody, and though not much remains intact, there are some wonderful stories here, which you can learn more about at the visitors center. For example, it's still possible to walk along siege tunnels dug here in the 16th century by Catholic forces trying to take the castle back from Protestant reformers. After wandering around the ruins for a half-hour or so, you can stroll down to the **Castle Sands** for a view of the impressive, still-standing facade from a different angle.

St. Andrews Cathedral and St. Rules Tower
The Pends; tel. 1334 472 563; www.historicenvironment.scot/visit-a-place/places/

st-andrews-cathedral; 9:30am-5:30pm daily Apr.-Sept., open til 8pm Tues. and Thurs in July; 10am-4pm daily Oct. to Mar.; adult £5, child £3, under 5 free

One of the city's most prominent landmarks, the remains of St. Andrews Cathedral, founded in the 12th century and once the headquarters of the medieval Scottish church, are some of Scotland's finest ruins. Pillaged during the Reformation, the front and back walls of the cathedral still stand, tall and alone, with grass interrupted by former foundations and ancient gravestones. A photographer's dream, the site is perhaps more evocative than it would be if it were still intact, with lots of informative signage throughout. It's free to wander among the ruins, but a fee applies to the museum, which houses some interesting artifacts from the cathedral's history, and St. Rule's Tower. The one thing you should do here if you visit is to climb the steep, narrow, and winding steps to the top of the tower for far-reaching views across the town and the rest of Fife.

British Golf Museum

St. Andrews Bruce Embankment; tel. 1334 460 046; www.britishgolfmuseum.co.uk; 9:30am-5pm Mon.-Sat., 10am-5pm Sun.; adult £8.50, concessions £5

This museum is located next to the Old Course, and if you're a golf fan then a visit here is a no-brainer. There are more than 16,000 items to view, including artifacts from the 17th century to the present day, and exhibits present a comprehensive history of golf in Scotland.

BEACHES

WEST SANDS BEACH

West of the Old Course; www.visitscotland.com/info/towns-villages/st-andrews-west-sands-p315881

Just in front of the Old Links course lies the huge stretch of sandy beach known as West Sands, made famous as the location for the opening sequence from the film *Chariots of Fire*. Wide and rarely crowded, the picturesque skyline of St. Andrews makes for a good background at this beach, which stretches for almost 2 miles (3 km). Lifeguards are on duty in summer.

GOLF

★ Old Course

St. Andrews Links; tel. 1334 466 718; www.standrews.com/Play/Courses/Old-Course

Nothing short of a mecca for golf fans, the highlight of any visit to St. Andrews is teeing off and playing a round on the famous course yourself. For golf fans there is nothing quite like playing the same course where great champions have swiped and hammered balls home for over 600 years—including Seve Ballesteros's blistering win at the Open Championship here in 1984—and seeing how you fare against legendary obstacles such as Hell Bunker or the Swilcan Bridge. If you have a maximum handicap of 36, you can enter a ballot system a couple of days before you hope to play to see if you are lucky enough to win a slot. It is also possible to book an advanced tee time, but these do book up quickly and with a huge backlog of rescheduled tee times from 2020, it's likely this will be even harder for the next couple of years. You may have better luck trying to book a winter package, when people are less likely to visit.

If you don't secure a place there are lots of other links courses in St. Andrews where you can book in advance. There are six Links courses (old Scottish courses that were set on rising ground or ridges) in the city itself, all of which are described at www.standrews.com/Play/Courses. Or you can turn up on the day at the nine-hole **Balgove Course** (Old Guardbridge Road; tel. 1334 466 666; www.standrews.com/Play/Courses/Balgove-Course; 7am-9pm daily; £8-15). Set in and around the Old Course, **St. Andrews Links**

1: St. Andrews Castle 2: Old Course

The Scottish Golf Legacy

The Scots are widely celebrated for having introduced the US to the game of golf, though the jury is out over who actually invented the sport, with early forms of the game played in the Netherlands, and some academics even suggest it could be an evolution of a game invented by China's Ming Dynasty. Regardless of who invented it, it has been played in St. Andrews since at least the 1400s, and Scotland's influence on the rest of the world (particularly the USA) following the growth of tourism here in the Victorian era has led to the sport's worldwide success.

HISTORY

Things have gotten a bit more sophisticated since games were first played on a simple track overgrown with bushes and heather at St. Andrews Links course, but the game itself has changed relatively little. That's not to say the evolution has been completely smooth; in medieval times, King James II of Scotland actually banned the game on the grounds that is was distracting young men from their archery practice. The ban was only lifted when King James IV—a keen golfer himself—came to the throne. Interestingly, the Old Course was once 22 holes, and it was only when players complained that the first four holes and the last two holes were too short that four holes were removed and the standard of 18 holes began.

PLAYING GOLF IN SCOTLAND

Golf fans the world over make the pilgrimage each year to St. Andrews, which now has six Links courses. So far it has hosted 29 Opens; that number will reach 30 in 2022 when it will host the 150th Open Championship. But there are many other great golf courses across Scotland; below are just a few.

- **Stirling Golf Club:** Take a swing in the shadow of Stirling Castle at this popular and scenic course (page 116).

- **Royal Dornoch Golf Course:** On the popular North Coast 500 route, this is one of the more approachable of Scotland's "must-play" golf courses (page 406).

- **Fort William Golf Club:** Brand-spanking-new in comparison to St. Andrew's Old Course (it was founded in 1976), this course offers a wonderful view of Ben Nevis (page 339).

(8 The Links; tel. 01334 466 666; www.standrews.com/shop; 9am-5pm daily) is a collection of four outlets where you can buy official golfing merchandise, including the unique St. Andrews tartan. And you can always photograph the 18th hole of the Old Course from over the low fence by the roadside.

FOOD

OLD UNION COFFEE SHOP

79 North Street; tel. 01334 46 2700; 8.30am-5.30pm mon.-Fri., 9am-5.30pm Sat.

If you're taking a meander through the university quadrants or visiting St. Salvador's Chapel, then stop off at this good-value café for a coffee or snack. All proceeds go toward supporting the university's Students'

Association. It's a handy pitstop if you are in a rush and want to grab a takeaway sandwich between sightseeing trips.

JANNETTAS

31 South Street; tel. 01334 473 285; https://jannettas. co.uk; 9am-10pm Mon.-Sat., 10am-10pm Sun.; one-scoop sundae from £3.60

Everyone in St. Andrews knows that when you want an ice cream, you go to Jannettas. The fourth-generation family-run business has been serving up a colorful and delicious variety of ice cream since 1908. The 54 flavors include the litmus test that is vanilla, alongside more adventurous pairings such as orange and mascarpone. It seems that whenever you pass the shop there's a queue, but the wait is never too long. There is also a bright café, with a bit of a 1950s vibe, that serves huge sundaes you'll need to sit down for.

CROMARS

1 Union Street; tel. 1334 475 555; https://cromars.
co.uk; 11:30am-10pm daily; entrées £7.50
The smell of this delicious fish and chip shop wafts down the street, luring even those not drawn by its reputation. It's certainly not the cheapest but boy is it good—try the charred prawns or seared scallops to start. This is definitely not your average fish and chip shop.

SEAFOOD RISTORANTE

Bruce Embankment; tel. 01334 479475; www.
theseafoodrestaurant.com; Mon.-Sat. 12pm-9:30pm;
Sun. 12:30pm-9:30pm; entrées £8.50
When you walk along the seafront in St. Andrews and see the amazing glass building that juts into the sea, it's not someone's Grand Designs home but rather a very well-placed seafood restaurant. Dishes include hand-dived Ardnamurchan scallops and Scottish west coast langoustines, though it's very much the location you come here for.

ACCOMMODATIONS
ALBANY HOTEL

56 North Street; tel. 1334 477 737; www.
albanyhotelstandrews.co.uk; £112 d
This three-star hotel in a Georgian townhouse conversion is centrally located and informal, with everything you'd expect from a mid-range hotel. It's family-run, does a good breakfast, and all the doubles have views over the private walled garden.

OLD COURSE HOTEL

Old Station Road; tel. 1334 474 371; www.
oldcoursehotel.co.uk; £350 d
The obvious choice for golfers, this five-star hotel stands back from the Old Course like a referee, always there but never intrusive. Many of the 144 rooms come with views over the golf course. No expense is spared in the suites, which boast silk wallpaper and velvet furniture. The hotel also has a luxury spa, rooftop hot tub, and a good restaurant that also serves afternoon tea.

INFORMATION AND SERVICES
The only **VisitScotland iCentre** in Fife is in St. Andrews (70 Market Street, St. Andrews, tel. 01334 472 021; www.visitscotland.com/info/services/st-andrews-icentre-p333231), where you can equip yourself with local maps and information.

GETTING THERE
St. Andrews is a drive of 1 hour 25 minutes in total from Edinburgh (52 miles/84 km; take the M90, A92, A915, A916, B939). From Glasgow, it's just over 1.5 hours, a 73-mile (117-km) drive on the M80 to the M876 to the A976 to the A91. From Stirling, St. Andrews is also about 1.5 hours away, a 52-mile (84-km) drive east across Fife, mostly on the A91. Finally, from Dundee, St. Andrews is only half an hour away, a 14-mile (23-km) drive south on the A92 and A91.

St. Andrews does not have a train station, so by public transport, the best way to reach St. Andrews from Edinburgh is to take the train to Leuchars and then transfer to the Stagecoach no. 99 bus (https://scotrail.com, www.stagecoachbus.com/regional-help-and-contact/east-scotland; 1 hour 25 minutes; £9 single). Or, from Glasgow, you should take the train to Dundee and then get the no. 99 bus going south (2 hours 20 minutes; £9 single). Once in St. Andrews, it's easy enough to get everywhere on foot.

Dundee

It is said Dundee is famous for the three Js: jute, jam, and journalism. Once playing an important role in world's jute trade, in the 19th century Dundee also made its money from whaling and shipbuilding, though from the early 20th century onward the demise of all three industries saw the city's fortunes decline. Since then, Dundee has worked hard to shake off its post-industrial despair and it's finally working. In 2014 Dundee was named the UK's first UNESCO City of Design, and a major investment into its shorefront, which looks onto the River Tay, with the new V&A museum at its fore, has given it seriously impressive credentials. The V&A is part of a £1 billion regeneration of the city that includes lots of new hotels and restaurants to accommodate the new influx of visitors.

Dundee is a midsize city, with a population of around 150,000, but its waterfront and city center are fairly walkable, with trains arriving right next to the V&A Dundee on the River Tay. West of the city center is an area known as Westport, characterized by the University of Dundee and a concentration of bars and restaurants. Even farther west (approximately 1 mile/1.6 km from the V&A), the West End is a bit more affluent, with various green spaces and grand houses. Finally, Broughty Ferry is 15 minutes by bus from the city center to the east, but it's worth the trip—the quaint seaside suburb makes for a good afternoon expedition.

SIGHTS

As you walk through Dundee, look for the **Street Art Trail** (various locations; www. openclosedundee.co.uk; free, download map or pay £1 for one at the V&A or McManus), with colorful works of street art, created by local artists, which have been brightening up the place for the last few years. As you can imagine, it's constantly evolving, with new legal works of graffiti being added to the city's canvas all the time. Open/Close provides maps of two trails with more than 40 artworks, including the City Centre Trail and the Stobswell Trail, an area just a 10-minute walk northeast of the city center, where many of the jute mills and factories used to operate.

Victoria & Albert museum and the *RRS Discovery*

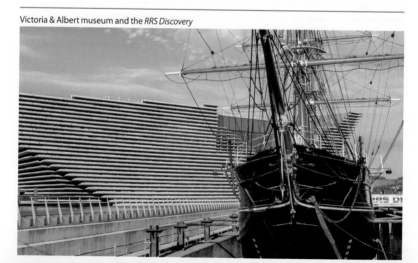

★ Victoria & Albert Dundee

*1 Riverside Esplanade; tel. 01382 411 611; www.vam.
ac.uk/dundee; 10am-5pm Thurs.-Mon.; free, charges
for some exhibitions*

Like a beacon of creativity on Dundee's shore-front since it opened in 2018, the V&A has played no small part in the city's reinvention as a cultural destination of note. Depending on whom you ask, Japanese architect Kengo Kuma's building design of layered concrete slabs that jut over the water's edge resembles either a permanently docked ship or the jagged cliff edges of Scotland's northeast coast. Whatever the effect on you, there's no doubting it's a striking design.

Inside, the museum, which is free for all (though there are charges for touring exhibitions, often transferring from London), includes a reassembly of Charles Rennie Mackintosh's 1907 Oak Room, a dark-stained wooden interior with huge double-height ceiling and the designer's signature colored glass panels, which once stood in Glasgow's Ingram Street tearooms. The oldest item in the collection is an illuminated 15th-century prayer book, and there are other historic artifacts, such as a pair of Jacobite pistols. Recent major exhibitions include the Mary Quant exhibition, which showed how the designer helped define the Swinging Sixties look.

RRS Discovery

*Discovery Point, Riverside Drive; tel. 01382 309 060;
www.rrsdiscovery.co.uk; 10am-4.30pm Mon.-Sat.,
11am-4.30pm Sun.; adult £11.50, concessions £8.95,
child £6.40, family £32*

Right next door to the V&A is the *RRS Discovery,* the 1901 wooden steamship used by Captain Scott and Ernest Shackleton for their first expedition to the Antarctic (not to be confused with Scott's later ill-fated expedition). The ship was built right here in Dundee. Visitors can come on board and creep below decks for a taste of what life at sea must have been like for the two explorers and the rest of the crew. You can even see Scott's rifle and pistol.

The McManus

*Albert Square; tel. 01382 307 200; www.mcmanus.
co.uk; 10am-5pm Tues.-Sat.; free though some
exhibitions may charge*

Dundee is more than its waterfront, and a 10-minute walk through the city to this staple of its cultural landscape is worth an hour or two of your time. In this Victorian gothic revival building, the city's history is charted, albeit in a slightly old-fashioned higgledy-piggledy way (which I think adds to the charm). Aside from objects used to soften the coarse fiber in the jute mills, there are also portraits by some reputable Scottish painters, such as Henry Raeburn, and one of the city's long-term big employers DC Thomson—publishers of *The Beano* and *The Dandy* among others—is celebrated, particularly in the gift shop. The DC Thomson building, also on Albert Square, sometimes offers guided tours.

SPORTS AND RECREATION
PIRATE BOATS LTD

*Castle Approach, Broughty Ferry; tel. 07931 231 054;
www.pirateboatsltd.com; 10am-4pm daily Apr.-Nov.;
adult £24, child £18, 1 hour*

Hold onto you hats and dress up warm on these fast RIB rides on the Tay as you go in search of the resident bottlenose dolphins or whizz down to see the V&A from a unique angle, where its pointed concrete corners hang over the water. The boat trips embark from Broughty Ferry, a little seaside suburb just a short drive or 15-minute bus ride outside Dundee (no. 73 or 73A from Stagecoach; 18 minutes; £2 single).

FOOD AND BARS
GALLERY 48

*48 Westport, Dundee; tel. 01382 225 666; http://
gallery48.co.uk; 12pm-10pm daily; plates from £4.50*

In the popular Westport part of the city, where there's no shortage of bars and restaurants, this place still stands out. Part art gallery, part Spanish tapas bar with tasty small plates such as salted cod fritters and goat cheese fig and honey salad, it's a cool place to eat as little or as much as you like while perusing new art between nibbles. There's also a good selection of Spanish wines and gin.

VISOCCHI'S

40 Gray Street, Broughty Ferry; tel. 01382 779 297; https://visocchis.com; 11am-9pm daily; cappuccino from £2.10, ice cream from £2.50, pizza from £9.50

This authentically retro Italian café sells the best ice cream and coffee in the area, hands down (though it is a little out of town in Broughty Ferry) and has been doing so since the 1950s. You can get something to take away or, for a full Italian experience, sit down in the old-style ristorante and fill up on homemade pizza and pasta dishes.

THE NEWPORT

1 High Street, Newport-on-Tay; tel. 01382 541 449; www.thenewportrestaurant.co.uk; 12pm-2:30pm and 6pm-9pm Thurs.-Sat., 12pm-3.30pm Sun.; set menus from £32

Head over the River Tay to The Newport, the fine-dining restaurant run by local celebrity Jamie Scott (former Masterchef Professionals winner). Jamie's set menus and tasting menus are inventive and use only the freshest seasonal ingredients, so menus change regularly. However, it's for the stunning views and amazing sunsets through the floor-to-ceiling windows that most people come to this side of the river. There are also a few rooms (from £140 d) if you'd like to stay over.

THE SPEEDWELL

165-167 Perth Road; tel. 01382 667 783; http:// speedwell-bar.co.uk; 11am-12am daily; pints from £3.50, whiskies from £3.20

This Edwardian bar in Dundee's West End is otherwise known as "Mennies" after a long-time former landlady. It's the place to come for a proper pint or a whisky and to mingle with locals, and the original interior, with gleaming mahogany, etched glass and a separate bar with two lounges is something to behold. The Speedwell is one of a dying breed of pubs, I'm afraid, so get here while you can.

DRAFFENS

Coutties Wynd; 5pm-12am Mon.-Thurs. and Sun., 5pm-1am Fri., 12pm-1am Sat.

Now, if I told you exactly where this '20s-style speakeasy is then it would be cheating a little bit, wouldn't it? What I will say, is that if you walk down Couttie's Wynd after dark (it can be a little disconcerting, admittedly), and listen for music at a few doorways and give a couple a nudge, then you may just stumble upon this really cute cocktail bar, where there is always fantastic music (jazz, jive, etc.) being played and the drinks are flowing until the early hours. Clue: Draffens used to be a department store, so look for a delivery doorway.

ACCOMMODATIONS

APEX CITY QUAY HOTEL DUNDEE

1 West Victoria Dock Road; tel. 01382 202 404; www. apexhotels.co.uk/apex-city-quay-hotel-spa; £89 d

If you are looking for a central place to stay with well-priced but simple and clean rooms, then this is it—the V&A is just a couple of minutes away. There's a glamorous restaurant and bar area that leads from the lobby downstairs (you'll have breakfast here even if you choose not to have dinner) and a really nice on-site spa, too. The bedrooms and bathrooms are very large for the price.

TAYPARK HOUSE

484 Perth Road, Tel. 01382 643 777; www. tayparkhouse.co.uk; £150 d

This boutique hotel within a baronial style grand house is located in Dundee's West End. There are large suites with rolltop baths in the main house, plus a selection of more modest but still very lovely superior and standard rooms. There's also a garden annex where each room has either a river view or its own terrace, and each room comes with nice period features, such as exposed beams or stone walls, and a comfy tartan armchair to sit and read in. There's a good restaurant and gin bar in the main house, and the gardens are a real joy. If you're game for a laugh, the house also offers afternoon tea tuk tuk tours around the city—don't worry, you have the afternoon tea when safely back at the hotel, not on the road.

INFORMATION AND SERVICES

To help plan your Dundee itinerary, visit the **VisitScotland iCentre** (16 City Square; tel. 01382 527 527; 10am-3pm Tues.-Sat.), or head to www.dundee.com, which offers suggested city guides, and can keep you up to date with openings and closures post-COVID.

GETTING THERE AND AROUND

Dundee can largely be explored on foot, as it's a pretty compact city. If you'd rather save your feet, then flag down a taxi with its orange light on, or book one through Dundee Taxis (https://dundeecitytaxis.com). Meanwhile, local buses are largely run by Stagecoach, which runs the no. 73 and 73A to Broughty Ferry (18 minutes; £2 single), plus the 77 to Newport-on-Tay for the excellent Newport restaurant (9 minutes; £2 single).

By Car

Dundee is roughly equidistant between two international airports: Aberdeen and Edinburgh. From the former, it's about 1 hour 20 minutes by car, mainly down the A90 (68 miles/109 km) while from Edinburgh Airport, it's about 10 minutes quicker, following the A92 once over the Queensferry Crossing (53 miles/85 km). From Perth, it's just a 40-minute drive east to Dundee along the A90 (23 miles/37 km); from St. Andrews, its 30 minutes (14 miles/23 km) north on the A91 and A92.

By Train

Dundee can be reached by train in 1 hour 20 minutes from Edinburgh (£20 single/£29.40 off peak return) and in just under 2 hours from Aberdeen (£22.20 single, £32.20 off-peak return). The train from Perth takes just 20 minutes (£8.80 single/£9 off-peak return). **Dundee Train Station** (S. Union St.; www. scotrail.co.uk/plan-your-journey/stations-and-facilities/dee) is conveniently located right on the waterfront, just steps away from the RRS *Discovery* and V&A Dundee.

By Air

If you're coming from London, I suggest flying to **Dundee Airport** (Riverside Dr; tel. 1382 662 200; www.hial.co.uk/dundee-airport) with Loganair (www.loganair.co.uk; 1 hour 45 minutes; £70 each way). The level of

Glamis Castle

service is personable for a budget airline (easy-Jet and Ryanair could learn a thing or two), and it puts you much closer to the attractions of the Cairngorms and the Highlands.

AROUND DUNDEE
Glamis Castle

Angus, DD8 1RJ; tel. 01307 840 393; www. glamis-castle.co.uk; 10am-5pm daily; adult £15.50, child £10, family £50, concessions £12

This castle (pronounced "glarms"), just 13 miles (21 mi) north of Dundee, is every bit as beautiful as Balmoral in the Cairngorms, in my opinion (though Balmoral's location is pretty hard to beat). The bonus here is that you can enter a lot more of it—though not all,

as it's still home to the Earl of Strathmore and Kinghorne and his family.

Like Balmoral, it also has strong royal links: it was the childhood home of the Queen Mother and the birthplace of Princess Margaret. Its history goes way back before these "modern" royals, though, to the likes of Mary, Queen of Scots, King James V, and Bonnie Prince Charlie. William Shakespeare is even said to have taken the castle as inspiration for Macbeth. Inside, the house is as grand as you'd expect, and the best way to view it is on a guided tour, where staff can reveal some of the secrets of past residents. From Dundee, Glamis is less than 30 minutes (13 miles/21 km) away via the A90 and A928.

Perth

Known as the "Fair City" for its handsome location on the banks of the River Tay, the city of Perth, just 35 miles (56 km) northeast of Stirling, is one of Scotland's most attractive centers. There are many culturally significant buildings to discover in and around the city, plus it's a good base for exploring the northern part of Loch Lomond and the Trossachs National Park.

It was near Perth that Kenneth MacAlpin united two separate kingdoms to become the first King of Scots. The city's location near Scone Palace, where Scotland's kings were crowned for centuries, led to it being the effective ancient capital of Scotland. It could have become the modern-day capital were it not for the 1437 murder of King James I at the old Blackfriars monastery (destroyed during the Scottish Reformation). The city was thrice occupied by Jacobites during the various uprisings, but nevertheless it went on to become a center of major industries such as linen and whisky in the 18th century. Despite its continued prosperity, it has actually been downgraded to status of "former city," though locals refuse

to accept it (road signs still declare it the "City of Perth").

Its compact city center on the west bank of the River Tay is flanked by two areas of greenery: the larger **North Inch** (1 Barossa Pl.; open 24/7; free), where the gory Battle of the Clans (a deadly battle that seemed staged for the entertainment of King Robert III and his cronies) took place in 1396, and **South Inch** (tel. 1738 475 000; www.pkc.gov.uk/article/15316/The-South-Inch-Perth; open 24/7; free), which also has a murky history as witch trials took place here in the 17th century. Thankfully, today you're more likely to see locals walking their dogs, picnicking, or jogging in the two parks.

With streets of elegant houses and grand Victorian buildings, the modern city of Perth is a very appealing place to wander, and it is home to fantastic restaurants, good shopping, and a few very well-regarded museums and galleries. Its location, just 14 miles (22.5 km) south of Dunkeld (which once guarded one of the main passes between the Highlands and Lowlands), also leads many people to refer to it as the "Gateway to the Highlands."

SIGHTS

Perth Museum and Art Gallery

*78 George Street, Perth; tel. 01738 632 488; www.
culturepk.org.uk/museums-and-galleries/perth-
museum-and-art-gallery; 10am-5pm Tues.-Sun.; free*

This great gallery is housed in a resplendent neoclassical building with an exciting program of rolling exhibits. The gallery is just one small part of one of the oldest museums in Scotland, and among its highlights is a cast of the biggest salmon caught in Britain—a whopping 64-pound (29 kg) fish caught in the River Tay by one Georgina Ballantine, still revered by anglers across Britain.

Fergusson Gallery

*Marshall Place; tel. 01738 783 425; www.culturepk.
org.uk/museums-and-galleries/the-fergusson-gallery;
10am-5pm Tues.-Sat., 12pm-4:30pm Sun.; free*

This gallery in the city's former waterworks is dedicated to the work of Scottish colorist J. D. Fergusson (although he was Edinburgh-born, he had many ties to Perthshire), and his lifelong partner, Margaret Morris, herself a pioneer of modern dance. Visitors can view thousands of pieces of work by prolific Fergusson, as well as many personal items, and the many costumes and artworks of Morris.

Black Watch Castle and Museum

*Balhousie Castle, Hay Street; tel. 01738 638 152;
www.theblackwatch.co.uk; 9:30am-4:30pm daily
Apr.-Oct., 10am-4pm daily Nov.-Mar.; adult £8, child
£3.50, under 5 free, family £19, guided tour adult
£12.50, child £7.50*

Home to the most legendary of Scotland's Regiments, this museum and castle, adjacent to North Inch, is recommended for anyone with even the smallest interest in military history or Highland culture. Inside the museum, you can peruse diaries, weapons, and photographs of the regiment from the 18th century right up to the present day and hear the story of the Black Watch regiment.

The Black Watch regiment began life way back in 1725 when members of Highland clans loyal to the crown formed companies to keep watch for crime in the wake of the Jacobite Rising of 1715. Later, these companies formed a regiment that became renowned for its ferocity, and the distinct tartan of black and green is now one of Scotland's most recognizable. Located inside the baronial Balhousie Castle, the museum isn't huge, so you should probably allow an hour and a half, though there is also a café and gift shop on-site. Guided tours, which take place at 11am and 2pm daily, are informative and give detailed analysis of the exhibits as well as personal stories of some of the members of the regiment. Book in advance.

★ Scone Palace

*Perth PH2 6BD; tel. 01738 552 300; https://
scone-palace.co.uk; 9:30am-5pm May-Sept.,
10am-4pm Mar.-Apr. and Oct.; adult £12, child
£8.50, family £40*

Just 2.5 miles (4 km) north of the city center, this stately home, once the location for the crowning of Scotland's kings, is a must-see on any visit to Perth. Both Macbeth and Robert the Bruce were crowned on the famous Stone of Destiny (now kept in Edinburgh Castle), which stood here until the 17th century. Scone Abbey was attacked by a mob following an anti-Catholic sermon by John Knox, but it continued to function on some level for 90 years or so. The palace as it stands, originally built in the 16th century but restored in the 19th century, has been the grand, stately family seat of the Earls of Mansfield for almost four centuries.

Aside from the sense of history in terms of the famous Scottish figures who walked its grounds, it's worth a day trip here for the stunning gardens and the splendid state rooms, which are some of the best in Scotland and are home to fine porcelains, rare ivories, antiques, and paintings. It's like a history lesson in British period furniture too, with pieces by Chippendale and Robert Adams proudly on display. Ticket holders can explore the house and grounds at their leisure, and stewards are on hand to answer any questions you might have.

Outside, **Moot Hill,** where you will find a small Presbyterian chapel, is the site of the historic coronations, and a replica of the famous Stone of Destiny sits in front of the chapel. There are beautiful walks through the grounds, including through the **Pinetum,** where you will find giant redwoods, noble firs, and conifers, and to the **Murray Star Maze,** planted with a mix of copper and green beech trees to resemble the tartan of the Earls of Mansfield. Though the palace is only open March-October, there is free admission to the grounds, maze, café, and children's playground Friday-Sunday in February, March, November, and some days in December.

SPORTS AND RECREATION

Hiking

KINNOULL HILL WOODLAND PARK
Hiking Distance: 4 miles (6.5 km)
Hiking Time: 2-3 hours
Trailhead: Perth city center
Information and maps: www.kinnoull.org.uk

This woodland park just 2 miles (3.2 km) east of the city has miles of nature trails to choose from and gives a little taste of what rural Perthshire has to offer. Look for the wooden animal sculptures as you go, because they show some of the very real wildlife you may be able to spot, including roe deer and red squirrels. If you have time, climb one of the five hills—Corsiehill, Deuchny Hill, Barn Hill, Binn Hill, or the park's namesake of Kinnoull Hill, which offers glorious views across the River Tay and countryside.

Walks that set off from Perth's city center initially follow the River Tay before reaching woodland rich with native trees and mushrooms, toads, and insects. There's a folly atop Kinnoull Hill, but stay clear of the edge of the cliff, which is steep.

FOOD

HINTERLAND

10 St. Johns Place; www.hinterlandcoffee.co.uk; 9am-5pm Mon.-Sat., 11am-5pm Sun.; coffee £2.75

This independent coffee shop in the center of Perth serves its own roasted coffee alongside some carefully selected teas. The shop's handcrafted coffee blends two Arabica beans and then uses a traditional drum method to roast them until they are the color of dark chocolate—try it in a mocha or good old americano.

★ NORTH PORT RESTAURANT

8 North Port; tel. 01738 580 867; www.thenorthport. co.uk; lunch 12pm-2:30pm Tues.-Sat., dinner 5pm-late Tues.-Sat.; entrées £7.45

Located on a lovely cobbled street just behind the Perth Museum & Art Gallery, this small restaurant has attracted a big following since opening in 2011. From the tasty homemade bread to an impressive menu that features local-ish ingredients such as pork fillet served with Isle of Skye langoustine or Scrabster plaice, it rarely disappoints. The low-slung ceilings and intimate atmosphere simply round things off for happy diners.

DEAN'S AT LET'S EATS

77-79 Kinnoull Street; tel. 01738 643 377; www. letseatperth.co.uk; 12pm-6pm Sun., 12pm-2:30pm Weds.-Sat., dinner 6pm-8:30pm Weds.-Thurs. and 6pm-9pm Fri.-Sat.; entrées £7.95

This establishment has a contemporary and suave interior with high-back dining benches covered in lush red velvet, but it's not all about looks here—the food is pretty good too. The modern Scottish cuisine uses seasonal produce: choose from pink roast rump of lamb or seared and blackened Atlantic cod, and don't miss the restaurant's signature Black Forest Baked Alaska for afters.

63 TAY STREET

63 Tay Street; tel. 01738 441 451; www.63taystreet. com; lunch 12pm-1:45pm Thurs.-Sat., dinner

---

1: Perth **2:** Scone Palace **3:** Kinnoull Hill Woodland Park

5:45pm-8:45pm Tues.-Fri. and 6:30pm-8:45pm Sat.; entrées £9.50

For many years this was the place for fine food in Perth, but a slew of new competitors means it's had to stay on point and it has obliged fully. There's an extensive wine list, and good hearty food, such as roast quail with butterbean stew, keeps people coming back.

ACCOMMODATIONS

THE SALUTATION

34 South Street; tel. 01738 630 066; www.strathmorehotels-thesalutation.com; £85 d

Perth's oldest hotel—in fact, maybe Scotland's oldest—is another of those places where the folk hero Bonnie Prince Charlie is said to have stayed. The gray and white façade is incredibly grand, with a huge arched window, and, though the inside it is a little corporate, it nevertheless is a good standard of a hotel, well priced, and well placed in the city center.

THE TOWNHOUSE

17 Marshall Place; tel. 01738 446 179; https://thetownhouseperth.co.uk; £140 d

This elegant boutique hotel is located within a Georgian terraced property. The rooms here are pleasingly traditional, with Queen Anne chairs, antique wardrobes, and crisp bed sheets, but with modern en suites, good Wi-Fi, and TVs. Overlooking South Inch Park, the hotel is close enough to bars and restaurants but just far enough away to feel like a peaceful sanctuary.

★ SCONE CASTLE APARTMENT

Balvaird Wing, Scone Palace; tel. 01738 552 300; www.airbnb.co.uk/rooms/5908470; £500 per night, sleeps six, 2-night minimum

If you are traveling with friends, then this grand five-star apartment looks very tempting indeed. Located in the west wing of the palace, with unbeatable views of the parkland, it is like your own mini royal retreat. It's just a 10-minute taxi ride from here to Perth city, too, to see the rest of the sights.

INFORMATION AND SERVICES

Open year-round, the **VisitScotland Perth iCentre** (45 High Street; tel. 01738 450 600; www.visitscotland.com/info/services/perth-icentre-p234431; 9:30am-5pm Mon.-Sat. and 11am-4pm Sun. in summer, 9:30am-4:30pm Mon.-Sat. and 11am-4pm Sun. in winter) is a good starting point for local leaflets and itineraries. There's also lots of advice on places to stay and visit on the **City of Perth website** (www.perthcity.co.uk).

GETTING THERE

Perched in the heart of central Scotland, Perth is pretty easy to get to from anywhere in the UK. Indeed, as much as 90 percent of Scotland's population lives within 90 miles (144.8 km) of the city.

By Car

It's just an hour's drive here from Glasgow Airport (67 mi/108km along the M80 and the A9), while both Edinburgh (M90, 41 miles/66 km; 50 minutes) and Dundee airports (A90, 20 miles/12 km; 30 minutes) are under an hour away. Aberdeen Airport is 92 miles (150 km; 2 hours) away. From Stirling, Perth is 45 minutes away by car (34 miles/55 km); from Dundee, it's a 35-minute drive (22 miles/35 km).

By Train

ScotRail (www.scotrail.co.uk) runs services from Edinburgh (1 hour 15 minutes, 2 per hour; £17.10 one-way) and Glasgow (1 hour, 2 per hour; £17.10 one-way) to **Perth Train Station** (Leonard St.), and the **Caledonian Sleeper** (www.sleeper.scot) train from London also stops here once a day (8.5 hours; from £50 one-way). ScotRail also runs direct trains from Stirling to Perth that take 35 minutes (2 per hour; £8.30 one-way). The station is located just west of the South Inch park.

The Cairngorms and the North East

Scotland's North East gets a bad press, or rather, it gets very little press at all, and frankly, it's baffling. It's a huge region that has it all: whisky, wildlife, long, empty beaches, mountains and sea, rumbling rivers, and more castles than any other part of Scotland.

The Cairngorms alone is reason enough to visit. The largest national park in the UK is a place where Highland hills meet tundra and moorlands meet lochs. Here, wildlife thrives, helped in no small part by a conscious rewilding program designed to encourage native species to return by turning back the clock of human interference. It's a place of natural beauty, of hikes and unexpected encounters, be they with reindeer or with a rare sighting of a capercaillie or even a Scottish wildcat.

On the eastern fringes of the park, Royal Deeside is home to one of

Highlights

Look for ★ to find recommended sights, activities, dining, and lodging.

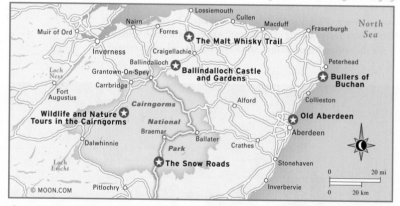

Lossiemouth
Cullen
Macduff
Fraserburgh
North Sea
Nairn
Muir of Ord
Forres
★ **The Malt Whisky Trail**
Inverness
Craigellachie
Peterhead
Ballindalloch
★ **Ballindalloch Castle and Gardens**
Loch Ness
Grantown-On-Spey
Carrbridge
Fort Augustus
Cairngorms
Alford
Collieston
★ **Bullers of Buchan**
Wildlife and Nature Tours in the Cairngorms ★
National
★ **Old Aberdeen**
Braemar
Aberdeen
Dalwhinnie
Park
Ballater
Crathes
Loch Ericht
★ **The Snow Roads**
Stonehaven
© MOON.COM
Pitlochry
Inverbervie

0   20 mi
0   20 km

★ **Old Aberdeen:** Amid the cobbled lanes of this medieval neighborhood, you'll find atmospheric 14th- and 15th-century buildings (page 149).

★ **Bullers of Buchan:** A testament to nature's force, the cliffs around this collapsed sea cave are home to thousands of seabirds (page 161).

★ **Wildlife and Nature Tours in the Cairngorms:** See firsthand the impact important conservation projects are having on the national park (page 166).

★ **The Snow Roads:** This secret route from Perthshire to Deeside and beyond takes you high into the hills (page 173).

★ **Malt Whisky Trail:** With a higher density of single malt distilleries than anywhere in the world, this is the place to try Scotch whisky (page 182).

★ **Ballindalloch Castle and Gardens:** For beautiful gardens and a historic house with a story, this stately home is a good alternative to Balmoral (page 185).

the largest areas of ancient Caledonian pine in all of Scotland. Ballochbuie Forest was bought by Queen Victoria in 1878 to protect it from being felled. Perhaps Victoria was before her time and saw the importance of preserving natural landscapes and habitats—more likely she just wanted to preserve the view from Balmoral Castle. To the north of the park, Grantown-on-Spey, on the banks of the River Spey, gives way to another pastoral region, one with an unusually high density of whisky distilleries: Speyside. Meanwhile, to the far east of the park is one of Scotland's most underrated cities, Aberdeen. A short drive brings you to some of the most wild and beautiful coast in the UK.

The North East may have a reputation of being bleak and dreary with its end-of-the-world location, but the reality is far from it. There's a rugged realism to the region, where farming and fishing have been vital industries for centuries. With tourism ventures such as the North East 250 route aiming to open it up to more people, it's only a matter of time before everyone finds out about it.

ORIENTATION

The **Cairngorms** can be accessed via three main routes: from Inverness in the north, Aberdeen to the east, and from Perthshire to the south. From Inverness, it's just a 45-minute drive to either **Aviemore** (best for Cairngorm Mountain and general hiking) or to **Grantown-on-Spey,** from where you can explore both the Cairngorms National Park and the distilleries of **Moray Speyside.**

Approaching the Cairngorms from Perthshire in the south, you can either continue up the **A9,** past Blair Atholl to Dalwhinnie, which will take you to the western side of the park and on to Aviemore, or take the far more scenic **Glenshee road,** which forms part of the **Snow Roads** route. This 90-mile (145-km) route, which sets off from Blairgowrie, just a few miles north of Perth, weaves and wends as it ascends and descends the highest public roads in Britain through Royal Deeside, all the way to Grantown-on-Spey.

For travelers wishing to explore rural Aberdeenshire and the Aberdeenshire coast before heading to Speyside or the Cairngorms, **Aberdeen** is the obvious launchpad. From here, as you head north and west, there are some nice coastal villages to pop into along the coast before you drop down into Speyside and then farther into the Cairngorms.

PLANNING YOUR TIME

Ideally, you'd have a couple of weeks to explore the North East—a week or so in **The Cairngorms** and **Royal Deeside,** and another to go whisky-tasting in **Speyside** and explore the Aberdeenshire coastline, with at least one night in the city of **Aberdeen** itself.

The **North East 250** (www.northeast250. com), a 250-mile (400-km) driving route through the region, is gaining momentum as a tourist route. As this region is vast, a car does make life easier, but it is possible to travel by public transport, with train stations in major towns and good local bus services. Certain areas lend themselves well to car-free travel, too—in Royal Deeside and Speyside, for instance, cycle routes are good, and there is lots of excellent hiking in the Cairngorms.

The weather in Aberdeenshire is known to be windy and sometimes wet. It may not have quite the level of rainfall as places like Glasgow, but when it rains here, it really rains. Aberdeenshire's exposed North Sea coastline means its beaches are more suited to windswept walks than bucket and spade holidays, but they are far quieter because of it.

The Cairngorms and the North East

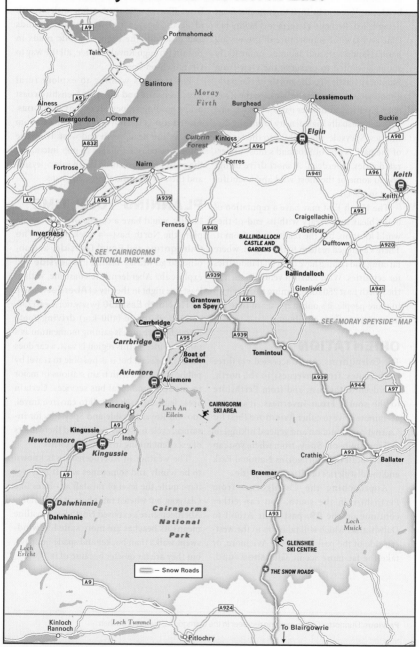

Portmahomack

Tain

Balintore

A9

Alness

Invergordon   Cromarty

A832

Fortrose

Nairn

Inverness

A9

A96

Ferness

A9

Moray Firth

Burghead

Lossiemouth

Buckie

Culbin Forest

Kinloss

Elgin

A96

Forres

A941

A96   Keith

Keith

A939

A940

Craigellachie

Aberlour

Dufftown

A920

BALLINDALLOCH CASTLE AND GARDENS

Ballindalloch

Glenlivet

A941

SEE "CAIRNGORMS NATIONAL PARK" MAP

A939

Grantown on Spey

A95

SEE "MORAY SPEYSIDE" MAP

A9

Carrbridge

Carrbridge

A95

A939

Tomintoul

A939

A944

A97

Boat of Garden

Aviemore

Aviemore

Kincraig

Loch An Eilein

CAIRNGORM SKI AREA

Kingussie

A9

Newtonmore

Insh

Kingussie

Crathie

A93   Ballater

Braemar

A9

Dalwhinnie

Dalwhinnie

Cairngorms National Park

A93

Loch Muick

Loch Ericht

— Snow Roads

GLENSHEE SKI CENTRE

THE SNOW ROADS

A9

A924

Kinloch Rannoch

Loch Tummel

Pitlochry

To Blairgowrie

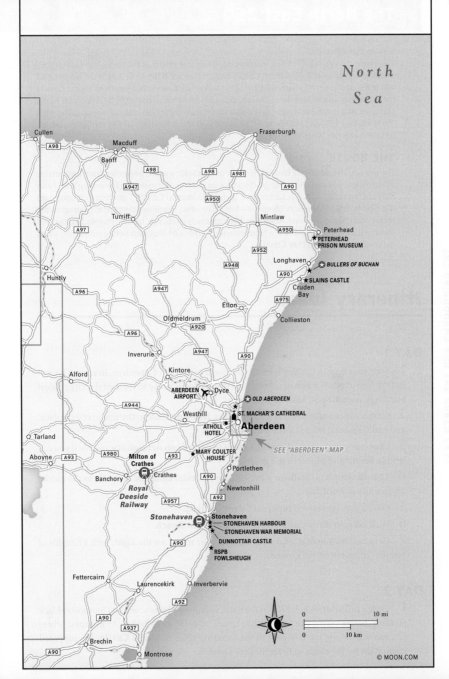

North Sea

Cullen
A98
Macduff
Banff
A98
A98
A981
A947
A950
A90
Fraserburgh
Turriff
A950
A97
A948
Mintlaw
Peterhead
★ PETERHEAD PRISON MUSEUM
A952
Longhaven
Huntly
A96
A947
⚙ BULLERS OF BUCHAN
A90
★ SLAINS CASTLE
Cruden Bay
Ellon
A975
Oldmeldrum
A920
Collieston
A96
A947
A90
Inverurie
Alford
A944
Kintore
ABERDEEN AIRPORT ✈ Dyce
⚙ OLD ABERDEEN
ST. MACHAR'S CATHEDRAL
Westhill
ATHOLL HOTEL
Aberdeen
Tarland
A93
A980
A93
MARY COULTER HOUSE
SEE "ABERDEEN" MAP
Aboyne
Milton of Crathes
Portlethen
Banchory
Crathes
A90
Royal Deeside Railway
Newtonhill
A957
A92
Stonehaven
Stonehaven
STONEHAVEN HARBOUR
★ STONEHAVEN WAR MEMORIAL
DUNNOTTAR CASTLE
A90
★ RSPB FOWLSHEUGH
Fettercairn
Laurencekirk
Inverbervie
A92
A90
A937
Brechin
A90
Montrose

0   10 mi
0   10 km

© MOON.COM

The North East 250

www.northeast250.com

This route, the brainchild of Guy Macpherson-Grant (the owner of the under-the-radar stately home and gardens of Ballindalloch Castle), hasn't taken off in the same way as the North Coast 500 in the northwest Highlands did, perhaps because of dreary preconceptions visitors have of the North East and of Aberdeen. There is also a fair bit of motorway-style driving on the route, along the east coast, but if you can see past that (follow the tourist route where possible), then the North East 250 has a little bit of all the best things about Scotland: whisky distilleries, castles, beautiful beaches, and mountain passes.

THE ROUTE

The journey should ideally be broken down over at least a week. Beginning from just outside **Aberdeen,** you can choose to go clockwise or counterclockwise. Clockwise, you'd first visit **Royal Deeside** and famous attractions such as **Balmoral Castle**—perhaps detouring onto the **Snow Roads** through Glenshee—before heading north to **Speyside,** then up to the Moray coast, along the north Aberdeenshire coast to Fraserburgh, before returning via the wild east coast, where you can see the extraordinary **Bullers of Buchan** before continuing south to the cliff-top **Dunnottar Castle.**

Itinerary Ideas

DAY 1

1 Start your time in the North East in the north of the city of Aberdeen, in an area known as **Old Aberdeen**—a web of cobblestone streets that is home to some of the city's oldest buildings, including St. Machar's Cathedral.

2 Grab a coffee and brunch at **Foodstory,** a zero-waste café in the university complex, and make a mental note of any events coming up.

3 Continue your day of culture with a visit to **Aberdeen Art Gallery** and see if you can spy the Renoir and Monet in the galleries.

4 Take the half-hour walk (or a five-minute taxi ride) along the quayside to the quirky community of **Footdee.**

5 Have a slap-up seafood supper at **Silver Darling.**

6 Walk off your dinner with a stroll on **Aberdeen Beach.**

7 Get a taxi back to **Mary Coulter House,** your refuge for the night, with a Knights of Templar cemetery on the grounds.

DAY 2

1 Have a full Scottish breakfast in the hotel, including a tattie scone and Stornoway black pudding, before taking the A90 north to Cruden Bay (37 miles/60 km; 45 minutes), where you can walk along the cliff path to the haunting ruins of **Slains Castle,** the supposed inspiration for the castle in Bram Stoker's *Dracula.*

2 From Slains Castle, continue along the coast path to **Bullers of Buchan,** a collapsed sea cave set amid dramatic coastal scenery, where you can see puffins perched on cliff edges.

3 Head inland to **Glenfiddich** for an afternoon tour of this iconic distillery, where you can grab a late lunch at the Robbie Dhu Terrace.

4 Drive south (50 miles/80 km; 1 hour 10 minutes) deep into the Cairngorms, for a stay in the farmhouse at **Killiehuntly,** where supper will be served in the dining room.

DAY 3

1 Have a hearty cooked breakfast at the farmhouse before setting off for your hill trip to see the **Cairngorm Reindeer.**

2 After spending a couple of hours in the hills, stop into Glenmore Visitor Centre for a delicious deep-filled sandwich with salad and crisps at the excellent **Cobbs Café.**

3 From the visitor center, you can join the **Loch Morlich Circuit,** walking through forest and along the loch's sandy beach, to work off your lunch.

4 If you have a car, you really should experience **the Snow Roads** route—at least some of it. From Glenmore, the easiest section to access is from Grantown-on-Spey through Tomintoul, Ballater, and Braemar.

5 Check into the impeccably designed five-star art-gallery hotel **The Fife Arms.** You'll probably only come here once, so splash out on dinner in the Clunie Dining Room and resolve to complete the most thrilling section of the Snow Roads in the morning.

Aberdeen

I've leafed through other guidebooks and travel articles, and it's struck me that Aberdeen is often described in economic or industrial terms (it became rich off the North Sea Oil industry, which has been wobbly in recent years), making it seem, well, quite boring. However, it's anything but. Known as the Granite City due to the widespread use of granite in its historic buildings, Aberdeen has a lot more going for it than locals would have you believe.

Aberdeen is a built-up but attractive city. There's a lot of grey, it's true, but the grey seems to glisten after it rains, and there's a vitality about the place, as evidenced in the art that colors its streets and the cool bars and music venues that liven up its nights. The city is also grand in places—Old Aberdeen could be mistaken for Oxford from some angles—and the signs of industry around the harbor and elsewhere, however flailing, help tell the city's story.

There are lots of things to see and do in Aberdeen—I've barely scratched the surface here—but hopefully it's enough to persuade you to give this vastly underrated city a chance.

SIGHTS
★ Old Aberdeen

One of the hidden cards up Aberdeen's sleeve is undoubtedly the Old Aberdeen quarter, where a web of cobbled lanes and streets connect around some of the city's best preserved and oldest buildings.

ST. MACHAR'S CATHEDRAL

The Chanonry; tel. 01224 485 988; www.stmachar.com; 10am-4pm daily; free

The building that attracts most attention in this area is the cathedral, which probably stands on the site of a much older place of worship, established by St. Machar, a disciple of St. Columba around AD 580. By the

Itinerary Ideas

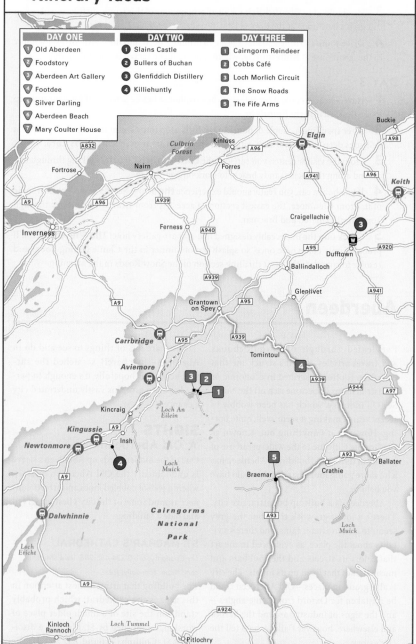

DAY ONE
1. Old Aberdeen
2. Foodstory
3. Aberdeen Art Gallery
4. Footdee
5. Silver Darling
6. Aberdeen Beach
7. Mary Coulter House

DAY TWO
1. Slains Castle
2. Bullers of Buchan
3. Glenfiddich Distillery
4. Killiehuntly

DAY THREE
1. Cairngorm Reindeer
2. Cobbs Café
3. Loch Morlich Circuit
4. The Snow Roads
5. The Fife Arms

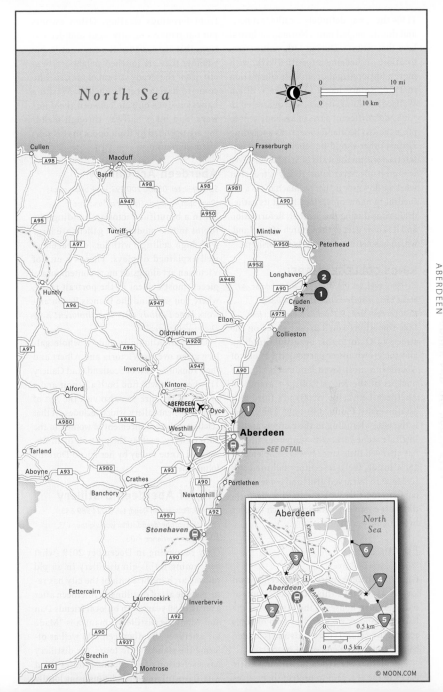

North Sea

Cullen
A98
Macduff
Banff
A98
A947
A98
A981
A95
A950
Turriff
Mintlaw
A97
A952
Longhaven
A948
A90
A96
Huntly
A947
Cruden Bay
A96
Ellon
A975
Oldmeldrum
Collieston
A920
A97
A96
Inverurie
A947
A90
Alford
Kintore
ABERDEEN AIRPORT
Dyce
A980
A944
Aberdeen
Westhill
SEE DETAIL
Tarland
Aboyne
A93
A980
A93
Crathes
Portlethen
Banchory
Newtonhill
A957
A92
Stonehaven
A90
Fettercairn
Laurencekirk
Inverbervie
A90
A92
A937
Brechin
A90
Montrose

Fraserburgh
A90
Peterhead

0   10 mi
0   10 km

Aberdeen
North Sea
KING ST
MARKET ST
Aberdeen

0   0.5 km
0   0.5 km

© MOON.COM

1130s there was definitely a cathedral here, and this developed into a Norman cathedral later that century. During 13th-century restorations, it became a fortified kirk, with more additions right up until its completion in 1530. Rumor has it that after William Wallace was hung, drawn, and quartered in 1305, with different parts of his body sent to places across Scotland to serve as a warning against other would-be rebels, his arm was interred within the walls of St. Machar's. We will probably never know if this is true, but what we do know is that St. Machar's is a cathedral in name only, since it lost its cathedral status during the Scottish Reformation and it is now part of the Church of Scotland, which has neither cathedrals nor bishops.

KINGS COLLEGE CHAPEL

25 High Street; tel. 01224 272 137; www.abdn.ac.uk/about/campus/kings-college-chapel-380.php; 10:30am-5pm Mon., 9:30am-5pm Tues.-Fri.; free

Like something you'd expect to see on the streets of Oxford, this beautiful building, and the crown tower particularly, is one of Aberdeen's most loved landmarks. It's the nucleus of the Kings College Campus of Aberdeen University, Scotland's third oldest university, founded in 1490. The chapel is the oldest building in the campus and its intricate stonework, with numerous finials, has changed little since it was completed in 1509. Inside, the 16th-century tall rood oak screen with its carved grills and confessional cubicles, together with the choir stalls, form the most complete medieval church interior in Scotland.

Footdee

Footdee; open 24/7; free

One of Aberdeen's quirkiest corners, known locally as "Fittie," this little collection of old fishermen houses at the east end of the harbor connects via a grid pattern of lanes around two central courtyards and is hidden behind the eastern end of the beach.

The homes are cute and all have their backs to the sea, as if to protect themselves

from ferocious weather. Often owners put out trinkets or silly signs and decorations that are designed to raise a smile, but whether they are for their neighbors' benefit or for the steady stream of tourists who come to have a peek is unclear. Washing hangs on lines outside between the doorways, and bikes halfway through mending are upended by front doors in this safe, warm community.

Aberdeen Art Gallery

Schoolhill; tel. 03000 200 293; www.aagm.co.uk; 10am-5pm Mon.-Fri., 11am-4pm Sun.; free

Set in a beautiful Victorian building, the rooms in this modern art gallery are large with high ceilings, with lots of space and well-explained displays. There's a mix of Victorian art alongside more contemporary pieces, most evident in the portrait room, where you will find the Francis Bacon artwork *Pope I (Study after Pope Innocent X by Diego Velázquez)*.

Other highlights include a whole gallery given over to Victoria and Albert and their romantic view of Scotland, and Gallery 11, where you will find both a Renoir and a Monet. Make sure you also visit the Art of Empowerment gallery, which includes art that celebrates the advancement of women in the 20th century, such as the portrait of an unabashed Anne Finlay by her friend Dorothy Johnstone.

City of Aberdeen Distillery

Arch 10, Palmerston Road; tel. 01224 589 645; https://cityofaberdeendistillery.co.uk; tour £13, 3-hour gin experience £105

Only reopening in December 2019 (what bad timing!), this gin distillery in an old railway arch in the south of the city has returned the art of distilling to Aberdeen after a break of 80 years. Run by local friends Dan and Alan, the distillery's mantra is "Made for Aberdeen, by Aberdeen." As well as offering the standard gin tours, the distillery has a selection of demijohns (bottles filled with flavorful single-batch gins using locally

Aberdeen

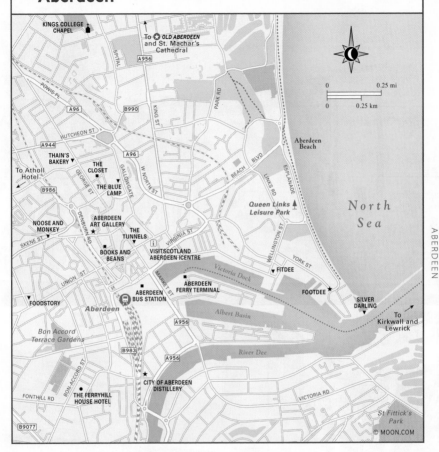

sourced fruit) to try, and a gin school experience, where you can learn how to distil your own gin.

SPORTS AND RECREATION
Beaches
ABERDEEN BEACH
Aberdeen; open 24/7; free

Just a short walk from the city center are the golden sands of Aberdeen's beach, which stretch south to Footdee, with a wide path along the esplanade for cycling and walking. By the **Queen Links Leisure Park** (Links Rd.; tel. 0207 747 2394; www.queenslinka-berdeen.co.uk; 9am-11pm daily) there are some rides at Codona's Amusement Park (Beach Boulevard; tel. 1224 595 910; www. codonas.com; 10am-10pm daily; wristbands £20.99 adult, £14.99 child), as well as some fairly uninspiring chain restaurants and fast-food joints. Head a little farther north to find some much better food trucks and stands.

Tours
HIDDEN ABERDEEN CITY & SHIRE

Various locations; tel. 07572 582 198; www.
hiddenaberdeentours.co.uk; adult £15, concessions
£10

This company, which works as a research resource, also offers tours, which must be booked in advance (the more in advance the better), and usually last about two hours. Taking one is an excellent way to learn more about the city's past.

SHOPPING
THE CLOSET

31 Jopp's Lane; tel. 01224 625 450; http://
closetvintageabdn.com; 9:30am-5pm Weds.-Sat.

Many shops call themselves vintage these days, but this one, which opened in 1980, is the real deal. Current owner Elaine Colville-Arthur is passionate about selling sustainable used clothing. Elaine sources most of her pieces from individuals living nearby; many items date from the 1930s and 1940s and are in good condition, as well as being well-priced. It's like a grown-up dressing up box.

BOOKS AND BEANS

22 Belmont Street; tel. 01224 646 438; www.
booksandbeans.co.uk; 10am-4pm daily

Though it has a good Fairtrade café attached, it's for the vast array of second-hand books that most people come here. It has a little of the library canteen about it, and to experience it the right way, you should come and buy a book or two and then grab a table for a coffee and a toastie while you get lost in your new purchases.

FOOD
THAIN'S BAKERY

341 George Street; tel. 01224 638 698; www.thains.
com; 2am-6pm Mon.-Weds., 2am-11pm Thurs.,
2am-10am Fri.-Sun.; pies from £2.30

The post-pub crowd can't get enough of the late-night pies in this bakery. Among must-try pastries are the macaroni pies, stovies (stews), and the veggie rowies: savory rolls with a buttery flavor—sometimes called butteries—that were supposedly created in Aberdeen to provide sustenance for fishermen at sea.

★ FOODSTORY

13-15 Thistle Street; https://foodstorycafe.co.uk;
8am-9pm Mon.-Thurs., 8am-10pm Fri., 9am-9pm Sat.,
11am-3pm Sun.; lunch from £6

So much more than a café, this is like a manifesto for modern living. With a vegetarian/plant-based menu, the food is wholesome yet feel-good with dishes such as portobello mushrooms crusted with roasted chickpeas and tahini. But that's just one part of the story: set up through crowdfunding in 2013, it's a place where community counts. The decor is a little hodgepodge (most of it was donated or rebuilt from salvaged bits), which only makes it feel even more welcoming, and the space is used for all sorts—yoga and meditation, arts and crafts workshops, reggae nights and gigs. Come here to experience Aberdeen's creative and inclusive side.

★ SILVER DARLING

Pocra Quay; tel. 01224 576 229; www.
thesilverdarling.co.uk; lunch 12pm-2pm Mon.-Thurs.
and 12pm-3pm Fri., dinner 5:30pm-8:30pm Mon.-Fri.,
all-day menu 12pm-9:30pm Sat., 12pm-8pm Sun.;
entrées £8

This restaurant, right by the edge of the harbor, just beyond Footdee, is a highlight of the Aberdeen dining scene. Large windows look out over the water and it's not uncommon to see an oil tanker coming past. It's pretty but in an industrial way. The menu is good, with catches of the day—occasionally lobster—and some meat alternatives. The wine list is also very good.

1: St. Machar's Cathedral **2:** Footdee

BARS AND NIGHTLIFE

THE TUNNELS

Carnegie's Brae; tel. 01224 619 930; www.facebook.com/tunnelsaberdeen; times vary; tickets from £6

When live entertainment returns to Aberdeen, this duo of rough-and-ready subterranean passageways is one of the best places to listen to bands, and watch comedy and other avant-garde and risqué shows, plus rave to some excellent electronic music.

★ THE BLUE LAMP

Gallowgate; tel. 01224 647 472; www.jazzatthebluelamp.com; 7:30pm-late; tickets from £15

This small, candle-lit venue is best known for its jazz output, but also hosts folk bands, rock'n'roll nights, and a variety of Americana and Bluegrass musicians. This place is for serious music lovers who like to sip on a cocktail or premium beer and wine as they listen in.

FITDEE

18 Wellington Street; tel. 01224 582 911; www.facebook.com/fittiebar1821; 11am-12am Mon.-Sat., 12pm-11pm Sun.; £3.80 pint

This small traditional pub, with friendly staff and a good bunch of locals and dock workers (you might get a second look if you walk in with an out-of-town accent) is a decent spot for a pint. Food is served and, though it's nothing fancy, it's pretty good.

ACCOMMODATIONS

THE FERRYHILL HOUSE HOTEL

421 Great Western Road; tel. 01224 317 186; www.ferryhillhousehotel.co.uk; £50 d

With just nine rooms, all comfortably furnished, the Ferryhill, close to the gin distillery, is a really good budget option. Its double-bay fronted exterior (dating from 1900) is very attractive, and the bar—with its wood-paneling, leather seating, and open fire—has recently been refurbished. The restaurant is decent, with homecooked comfort food, and there's a beer garden outside.

★ ATHOLL HOTEL

54 King's Gate; tel. 01224 323 505; https://atholl-aberdeen.co.uk; from £80 d

With just 34 bedrooms, this smart Victorian hotel, with its stepped gables, turrets, and beautiful Gothic revival windows, offers a bit of stately home grandeur, but it's still (just about) within walking distance of many of the city's main attractions. Rooms are a little on the old-fashioned side, with airport-style carpets and pine cupboards, but at this price, don't let that worry you.

★ MARY COULTER HOUSE

South Deeside Road; tel. 01224 732 124; https://maryculterhouse.com; £90 d

If you want to stay in a house with history, this property, originally founded by the Knights Templar in 1227, has been recently updated. Though the only part of the house remaining from the Knights of Templar time are the vaults and the churchyard outside, much of it is still very old, with the Great Hall dating from 1460. Despite this, it doesn't have a dusty museum feel, and the 40 bedrooms strike just the right chord with their contemporary Scottish interiors mixed with the odd piece of antique furniture. Bathrooms are luxurious—some even have baths overlooking the River Dee passing by below—with Molton Brown toiletries. Staff are attentive and chatty, and the setting, about a 15-minute drive from the city center, is beautiful.

INFORMATION AND SERVICES

Rebranded as "Majestic Aberdeenshire," to reflect its many castle attractions and big, open landscapes, **Visit Aberdeenshire** (www.visitabdn.com) is the main tourist board for Aberdeen and the wider region, and has lots of useful information on getting here, places to stay, and inspiring itineraries. The **VisitScotland Aberdeen iCentre** (23 Union Street; tel. 01224 269 180; www.visitscotland.com/info/services/aberdeen-icentre-p332241; 9:30am-5pm Mon.-Sat. and 11am-4pm Sun.) is centrally located and a good place for maps, discounts, and up-to-date information.

At the time of writing, the **Northern HighLights pass** (https://northernhighlightspass.co.uk) was just being launched, offering discounts across a range of attractions in Scotland's North East.

GETTING THERE

If Aberdeen is your first port of call in Scotland, then you will probably arrive either by Caledonian Sleeper train from London, or by plane into the city's airport. For those traveling from other parts of Scotland, the most obvious routes are from Glasgow, Edinburgh, and Inverness, all of which offer good rail services within reasonable driving distance.

By Air

Aberdeen Airport (www.aberdeenairport. com) has regular flights from many European destinations, including Dublin, Paris, Amsterdam, and Copenhagen. Domestic flights arrive each day from London Gatwick, Heathrow, and Luton, as well as Birmingham, Belfast, and Bristol. You can also fly direct to Aberdeen from Sumburgh Airport on Shetland Mainland with Logan Air (www. loganair.co.uk; 1 hour; from £80 each way).

From Aberdeen Airport, there is a bus stop just outside the main terminal, well-signposted from inside the terminal building. Stagecoach runs the 727 service into the city center, which takes around 30 minutes (every 20-30 minutes, fewer at night/very early in the morning). Tickets can be bought on the bus (£3.50 single/£6.30 return). First Bus (www. firstbus.co.uk/aberdeen) also runs a bus, but this has been less regular due to the pandemic and doesn't always go direct, so check before boarding. There are also official Aberdeen Airport taxis from outside the terminal building (turn left when you come out) that should ideally be booked in advance (01224 725 725; www.aberdeenairport.com/transport-and-directions/taxis). Fares cost £15-20 to the city center, depending on traffic. If you are hiring a car from the airport, you'll pick it up to the left of the terminal building via the covered walkway (www.aberdeenairport.com/plan-and-book-your-trip/book-your-trip/car-hire), and it's just 7 miles (11 km) along the A96 to the city center, with a journey time of around 20 minutes.

By Car

Aberdeen is around a 3-hour drive from Inverness, with the most direct route along the A96 (104 miles/167 km). From Glasgow, you'll largely be following the A90 northeast; though you're covering a bigger distance, it's a faster road, so it will take about the same time (3 hours; 145 miles/233 km) as traveling from Inverness. From Edinburgh, cross over the Forth Bridge on the M90, joining the A90 east at Perth, and you'll arrive in Aberdeen in around 2.5 hours (127 miles/204 km). From Dundee, head northeast along the A90 to Aberdeen (1.5 hours; 65 miles/ 105 km).

By Train and Bus

Aberdeen Train Station on Guild Street is well-serviced by other stations. There are several trains per day from Inverness (2 hours 20 minutes; £32.10 single), Glasgow Queen Street (2 hours 45 minutes; £45 single), and Edinburgh (2 hours 30 minutes; from £24 single); and this is the best mode of public transport on which to travel between major cities.

To connect to smaller places by public transport, you'll have to rely on the bus; most set off from the **Aberdeen Bus Station** on Union Street. Stagecoach bus no. 201 is great for connecting to Aberdeen from Royal Deeside (2 hours; single £11, return £19.80).

By Ferry

Aberdeen Ferry Terminal Building (Ferry Terminal Building, Jamieson's Quay; tel. 8001 114 422; www.northlinkferries.co.uk) is also a main jumping off point to the Northern Isles of Orkney and Shetland (page 470). You'll find the ferry terminal just south of city center and the Aberdeen Art Gallery, just a half-mile walk (0.8 km; 10 minutes) from the train station.

GETTING AROUND

Exploring Aberdeen on foot is a great way to see the Granite City in all her silvery-grey glory. The city center is compact—most of the restaurants, bars, and hotels lead off from **Union Street,** the city's beating heart. Heading north of Union Street, **Old Aberdeen** is less than 50 minutes away on foot. Even **Footdee,** which feels like a very different place to the city center, is less than a half-hour walk from Union Street. Of course, if you don't want to walk these kinds of distances, it's relatively easy to get round by bus, and taxis are reasonably priced.

By Bus

First Bus (www.firstbus.co.uk/aberdeen) runs a good network of buses throughout the city, which can be good on days when you want to fit a lot in. On its website you'll find a good map pinpointing where the bus stops are, as well as a journey planner to help you work out the best routes. Single tickets cost £1.70, or if you're planning to use the buses a fair bit, ask for a FirstDay ticket, which gives you unlimited travel for £4.20, or even a FirstWeek, with unlimited travel for a whole week.

Taxis

If you're traveling late at night or staying a little out of town, you'll want to familiarize yourself with the local taxis. The two main firms are **Aberdeen Taxis** (01224 200 200) and **Rainbow Taxis** (01224 878 787). Fares are fixed, so it should cost the same whoever you go with. In normal hours, there is an initial fee of £2.40 (rising to £3.40 at night) and then it's £1.21 per km. From 8pm-12am is the busiest time to get a taxi, with people coming into and leaving the city, so be prepared to wait.

STONEHAVEN

Stonehaven is an attractive harbor town with some nice cafés and pubs overlooking the water. As you drive to Stonehaven from Dunnottar, you can't miss the large coliseum-style structure on a hill to your right; this is Stonehaven War Memorial. Stonehaven Harbor is still very much a working port, and taking a post-lunch walk on the harbor beach is a nice way to spend an afternoon.

Sights

DUNNOTTAR CASTLE

Stonehaven; tel. 01569 766 320; www. dunnottarcastle.co.uk; 9:30am-5:30pm daily; adult £8, child £4, under 5 free

This castle, perched dramatically on a rocky headland that juts out into the North Sea, is one of Scotland's most photographed. You don't need to pay to walk down to it or to view it from outside (and parking is free), but tickets must be purchased if you want to step inside the ruined castle walls. Once considered an impregnable fortress, Dunnottar has certainly had to prove her prowess throughout history, not least when the Honours of Scotland were taken here in the 17th century to keep them away from Oliver Cromwell's army (the Puritan destroyed the English equivalent, the Crown Jewels, when he got his hands on them). Once the seat of the Earl Marischal, when the last earl was forced to forfeit his lands after taking part in the Jacobite Rising of 1715, the castle fell into ruin. There is a food truck by the car park, where you can grab a coffee before walking down the wide path to the castle, for excellent views of the castle. From Aberdeen, the castle is 18 miles (29 km; 25 minutes) south of the city; you can also take the train to Stonehaven and walk or take a taxi from there (2.5 miles/4 km).

RSPB FOWLSHEUGH

Crawton; tel. 01346 532 017; www.rspb.org.uk/ reserves-and-events/reserves-a-z/fowlsheugh; open 24/7; free

In spring and summer, the Aberdeenshire coastline is alive with breeding seabirds such as fulmars, guillemots, razorbills, kittiwakes, and puffins, and this reserve is home to the largest mainland seabird colony in the east of

Scotland. The reserve is set along a cliff-top walk through grassland peppered with colorful wildflowers. If you walk to the end of the trail, there is a little shelter well-positioned for watching the birds on their breeding ledges. From Aberdeen, it's just under 20 miles (32 km) south along the A92, passing Stonehaven and Dunnottar Castle. If you are traveling without a car, the no. 107 bus from Stonehaven will drop you off at the end of the Crawton Road (you need to request it), and from here it's a mile's (1.6-km) walk to the reserve.

Information and Services

A community initiative, the Stunning Stonehaven (www.stunningstonehaven. co.uk) website and app are actually really useful, with lots of hyper local info on events, attractions, and places to eat that are probably missed by the people at Visit Aberdeenshire.

Getting There and Around

From Aberdeen, Stonehaven is 14.5 miles (23 km) south following the A92 out of the city. This fishing town has a train station, and can be reached from Aberdeen in just 15 minutes (single £5.90, return £6.90).

NORTH OF ABERDEEN
Slains Castle

A975, Cruden Bay; https://canmore.org.uk/site/21149/ slains-castle; open 24/7; free

Gothic, foreboding, and lonesome, the ruin of Slains Castle (sometimes called New Slains Castle, as there was another, older, Slains Castle on this stretch of coastline) looks creepy on the south-facing cliffs just east of Cruden Bay. Dating from the 16th century, the castle would have looked somewhat less unkempt than it does today when Bram Stoker visited Cruden Bay in the 19th century, as it wasn't until 1925 that the roof was removed by its then-owner in a bid to avoid taxes (it soon fell into disrepair). Bram Stoker's visit coincided with him beginning to write his unnerving novel Dracula, so it's assumed that he drew inspiration for the

Count's castle from Slains, a theory that's supported by the fact the castle had an octogen hall (as Dracula's did).

The castle is best reached via the coastal path from Cruden Bay (there's a 2.5-mile/4-km loop from Cruden Bay, which you can start just to the left of the beach) that has windswept sea views, but take care as you approach since the cliffs fall away suddenly in places. The sound of the crashing waves is a warning that you really don't want to fall here. To reach Cruden Bay from Aberdeen, take the A90 north out of the city (27 miles/43 km; journey time 40 minutes).

From Aberdeen, it's a 45-minute drive north along the A90 (28 miles/45 km). Heading north of Aberdeen, the Stagecoach no. X63 bus will take you to Bullers of Buchan in around an hour, Cruden Bay in just over an hour (single £7.50, return £13.50 for both destinations), and Peterhead in 1 hour 15 minutes (single £8, return £14.40).

Peterhead Prison Museum

Admiralty Gateway, Peterhead; tel. 01779 581 060; https://peterheadprisonmuseum.com; 10am-6pm daily Apr.-Oct., 10am-4pm daily; adult £10, child £5.50

One of the strangest tourism experiences I've ever had is this audio guide tour through Scotland's "toughest jail," which incarcerated men from 1888 to 2013. As you walk through the cell blocks, you can see cells as they would have been at times throughout the prison's history, from the very cramped and basic boxes of the Victorian era, when it was a convict prison (for prisoners sentenced to hard labor), progressing to larger cells with more humane conditions. Being inside the prison is a moving and quite suffocating experience, made all the more poignant by the fact the modern-day HMP Grampian, which replaced it, is just next door. It makes for grim viewing, and listening at times, too. You can visit the laundry and toilet blocks while listening to accounts of conditions and events from former prison officers. For me, the most

disturbing part was standing in the separate block where in later years sex offenders were held.

★ Bullers of Buchan

Peterhead; open 24/7; free

This sunken sea cave, just a little north of Cruden Bay, is a huge bowl carved into the coastline by the relentless force of the sea and wind. It's a dramatic sight and easily reached from the free car park as you follow a pathway past some cottages and steer left along a well-trodden wide grassy path. Stay well back from the edge as you approach, and you can see waves push through an archway at the far side of the cave. Walk round to that side of the cave, and from spring to summer you will see thousands of seabirds clamoring for space on the cliff ledges before setting off for their next chance of a feed.

For a quieter bird-watching experience—at least in terms of people—walk back toward the car park and take the thin cliff ledge to the left as you near the cottages and follow it round to the other side of the chasm. You will then join the path to the pink-sandstone granite cliffs of Longhaven Nature Reserve, home to even more bird traffic. As long as you watch your footing, you can find a spot to sit and observe (and listen) as kittiwakes, guillemots, razorbills, and puffins soar and swoop between the cliffs and sea. It's a wonderful place—be warned, you may spend longer here than planned.

From Aberdeen, it's a 45-minute drive north along the A90 (28 miles/45 km). Heading north of Aberdeen, the Stagecoach no. X63 bus will take you to Bullers of Buchan in around an hour, and Cruden Bay in just over an hour (single £7.50, return £13.50 for both destinations), and Peterhead in 1 hour 15 minutes (single £8, return £14.40).

Cairngorms National Park

The Cairngorms national park is the UK's largest, covering 1,748 square miles (4,528 sq km). It's home to huge chunks of Caledonian forests, and streams and lochs gushing with crystal-clear water. It is also here that you will find Scotland's coldest and most unforgiving plateau, where a tundra climate, similar to that of Scandinavia, means that creatures such as mountain hares, ptarmigan, and reindeer have had to adapt to survive the harsh winters (even in summer snow is regularly sighted).

In its wild innumerable acres, you will find five of Scotland's six highest mountains, among a total of 55 Munros. It's also an area of supreme biodiversity, home to 25 percent of the UK's most threatened wildlife species, including the elusive Scottish wildcat (it's said if they don't survive in the Cairngorms, they will become extinct), red squirrels, and

the dangerously rare capercaillie, the largest grouse in the world—80 percent of the remainder of the species lives in one small area of this park.

The Cairngorms are popular with people looking for nature escapes, with plenty of opportunities for walking, cycling, mindfulness, and seeing wildlife and plant life return to its natural state. With three ski resorts to choose from—Cairngorm Mountain, the Lecht 2090, and Glenshee—it's also a great winter sports destination, alongside myriad other adventure activities.

VISITING THE PARK

There are no gates or entry fees to the Cairngorms—it's an area where people are free to roam, protected and recognized as an important place of national heritage. The park can be entered from numerous points, with the main A9 road providing a C-shaped route through the west of the park, passing through

1: Dunnottar Castle **2:** Stonehaven Harbour
3: Bullers of Buchan

Cairngorms National Park

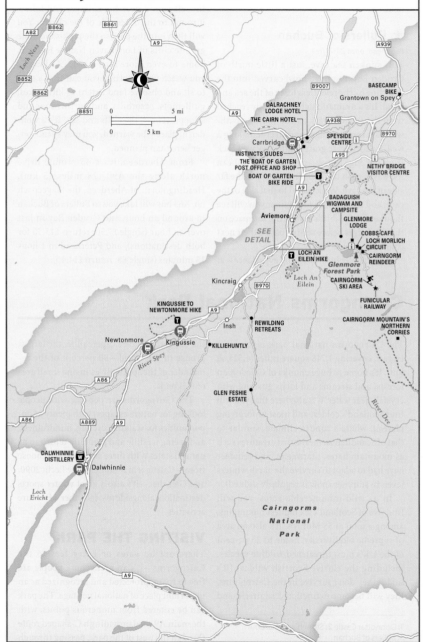

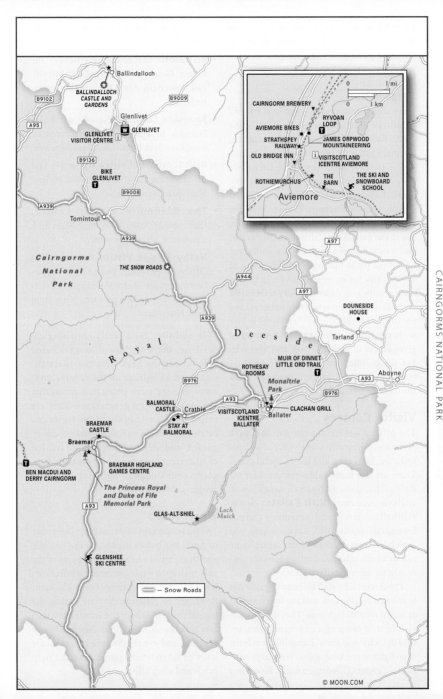

© MOON.COM

Blair Atholl in the far south, Aviemore and Boat of Garten; and the Snow Roads of Glenshee passing through Braemar, Ballater and Grantown-on-Spey.

Orientation

The Cairngorms is huge—you could spend months here and still not see it all. Without a doubt, **Aviemore** in the west is the main hub, a popular gathering place for walkers, cyclists, and activity-hungry travelers. Glenmore Forest Park (Glenmore; tel. 0300 676 100; https://forestryandland.gov.scot/visit/forest-parks/glenmore-forest-park; open 24 hours; free), renowned for its Caledonian pinewoods, sits at the foot of the Cairngorm Mountains and is a good place to embark on a walk along one of the paths that make up a network of forest trails, before or after a visit to the funicular railway in Aviemore. **Royal Deeside** to the east is where you will find Balmoral and the landscapes that Queen Victoria fell in love with, and in the north **Grantown-on-Spey** gives access to both the park and Speyside. For the middle, you'll just have to put on your walking boots, as there aren't any roads through the mountains.

Visitor Centres

The official website for the national park (www.visitcairngorms.com) is packed with inspiration, local info, and lots of useful maps. There are also some online resources for individual locations, such as Aviemore's (www.visitaviemore.com), **Visit Ballater** (www.visitballater.com), and Braemar's (http://braemarscotland.co.uk). But once here, you can't beat stopping into a visitor center, some run by VisitScotland and others run independently, for more specific advice.

The centers have staff on hand to guide you to the best cycling and walking trails, as well as recent wildlife sightings. They can also advise on wild camping and general rules, including why you should absolutely refrain from lighting any kind of fire. With large remnants of ancient Caledonian forest, forest fires

here can be devastating to the native trees and wildlife. The key visitor centers are:

- **VisitScotland iCentre Aviemore:** 7 The Parade, Grampian Road; tel. 01479 810 930; 9am-5pm daily Apr.-Oct., check for winter hours

- **Speyside Centre:** Skye of Curr Road, Dulnain Bridge; https://speysidecentre.com; 9am-5pm Mon.-Sat., 10am-5pm Sun.

- **VisitScotland iCentre Ballater:** Old Royal Station; tel. 01339 755 306; 9:30-5pm Mon.-Sat., 10am-5pm Sun.

- **The Glenmore Visitor Centre:** Glenmore; tel. 0300 067 6100; 9:30am-5pm summer, 9:30am-4pm winter

- **Nethy Bridge Visitor Centre:** Post Office; https://nethybridge.com/visitor-centre/explore-abernethy/ranger-service; 9:30am-5pm daily Apr.-Oct., 10am-4pm daily Nov.-Mar.

In addition, for a really enriching experience, there are lots of rangers based throughout the park who can share insights and knowledge on the natural landscape and the work going into protecting the park for future generations. They are employed by a mix of charitable trusts and estates and often run Landrover tours or guided wildlife expeditions. For a full list of all current rangers, go to www.visitcairngorms.com/things-to-do/nature-wildlife/ranger-guided-walks.

When to Go

The ski season typically runs from December to April, but it does depend on the weather, and though you can visit other parts of the park in deepest winter, attempting hill climbs is not advisable at this time of year. The Snow Roads are so called as they are among the highest roads in Britain and snow can be seen here year-round, so in winter they may be impassable, and even if they are not, real care must be taken when approaching the tight bends and steep hills.

AVIEMORE AND THE WESTERN CAIRNGORMS

The region known as Badenoch and Strathspey encompasses the west of the Cairngorms, all the way to Grantown-on-Spey, and includes the towns and villages in the west of the park, including Aviemore. No matter what the time of year, you'll see eager hikers, cyclists, and adventure sports enthusiasts in Aviemore, dressed to the hilt in walking boots, Lycra, and waterproofs and equipped with all the necessary poles, maps, and books for exploration from this main gateway town.

A thriving ski resort in the 1960s, Aviemore may not be the prettiest of towns, but it is certainly functional, with lots of places to stay, refuel, and pick up essentials, and there is generally a lively buzz about the place. From here, it's easy to reach Cairngorm Mountain Resort—where you'll find the funicular railway—as well as the famous reindeer herd and the road to Rothiemurchus, a region rich in wildlife and history.

North of Aviemore is Boat of Garten, a small village in an area of outstanding beauty, where the Strathspey railway stops off. Boat of Garten has a golf course designed by the legendary golf architect James Braid, and a popular osprey breeding place in Loch Garten (April-August). South of Aviemore, along the A9 road, are Kingussie, Newtonmore, and Dalwhinnie, other historic towns and villages where you could quite happily base yourself.

Sights
STRATHSPEY RAILWAY

Platform 3 Aviemore Station, Aviemore; tel. 01479 810 725; www.strathspeyrailway.co.uk; adult £16.75, child £8.40, under 5 free (return travel only), first-class from £58.50 for two; afternoon tea service adult £35.25, child £15.75

Days out don't get much more nostalgic than a ride on a vintage steam railway, and this one goes along a restored 10-mile (16 km) section of the old Highland Railway line, following the route of the Speyside Way to Broomhill and back, stopping at Boat of Garten en route.

The cheapest tickets include a seat on a communal carriage, but by upgrading to first-class, you can have a private compartment to yourself. The trips last 1 hour 45 minutes, and add-ons such as afternoon tea can be booked in advance for a really special journey.

ROTHIEMURCHUS

By Aviemore; https://rothiemurchus.net; open 24/7; free

This huge estate, owned and managed by the same family for generations, is like a park within the park. Rich with ancient Caledonian forest, it's a place where wildlife thrives and it's not uncommon to come across wandering Highland cattle, red squirrels, or even deer as you follow one of its many walks. There are also lots of other activities that can be arranged through the estate office, including quad bike adventures, ranger-led tours, Segway hire, and pony trekking.

LOCH AN EILEIN

Rothiemurchus by Aviemore; https://rothiemurchus.net/visit/loch-an-eilein; free

A place of natural beauty, this loch with a ruined castle on an island in the middle, is a popular picnic and paddling (or even swimming) spot on the Rothiemurchus estate. From the car park (£4.50), it's just a short walk to the loch, which is surrounded by ancient pine forest. The car park attendant can advise on the best places to swim and on the walking loop around the loch, as well as where you might be able to spot red squirrels, osprey, and other wildlife. Before you arrive, pop into the Estate Farm Shop & Deli (10am-4pm daily) for picnic supplies, where the emphasis is on low food miles and ethical farming.

FUNICULAR RAILWAY

Cairngorm Mountain Resort, Aviemore; tel. 01479 861 261; www.cairngormmountain.org; 9:30am-4:30pm daily

Having been closed since 2018, with new funding announced for repairs, this mountain railway will soon reopen (winter 2022) and is a must-visit for those without the time or agility for a big walk. The only funicular railway in the whole of Scotland, it takes you 3,500 feet (1,070 m) above sea level and feels a little as though you are on a toy train as you power up the mountain through clouds, dwarfed by the huge expanse of space around you. Once at the top, you can send postcards from the highest post office in the British Isles.

DALWHINNIE DISTILLERY

General Wade's Military Road, Dalwhinnie; tel. 01540 672 219; www.malts.com/en-row/distilleries/ dalwhinnie; 10am-5pm daily; whisky and chocolate masterclass £10.50

Around halfway south along the A9 road between Aviemore and Blair Atholl, this distillery is the highest in Scotland. Its name comes from the Gaelic for "meeting place," due to its unique position at the crossroads of old drove roads between mountains. As well as producing a number of "gentle spirit" single malts (the 15-year-old is its signature malt), it also doubles as a meteorological station, with readings taken every day. The whisky and chocolate pairing masterclass, which includes four whisky tastings with individual chocolate pairings, is good value, and for an extra fee you can also take a shuttlebus service to and from Aviemore.

★ Wildlife and Nature Tours
CAIRNGORM REINDEER

Glenmore, Aviemore; tel. 1479 861 228; www. cairngormreindeer.co.uk; hill trips 11am daily year-round, plus 2:30pm May-Sept. and 3:30pm Mon.-Fri. July-Aug.

In 1952 reindeer were reintroduced to the mountains of the Cairngorms, where they were once native. Since then, they have thrived, and they are now the only wild reindeer in Britain. On this hill trip you follow a 20-30-minute walk (each way) onto the lower slopes of the Cairngorms, where you can walk amid the wandering reindeer and even hand feed them—you'll never forget the feeling of their wet noses snuffling for food. If you are traveling by car, park in the layby on the main

road to collect your tickets and then you'll be instructed where to drive to start the hill walk. If you are traveling on public transport, the no. 31 bus from Aviemore can drop you in Glenmore and once you've collected your ticket, you'll need to walk a mile uphill to the start of the trek. Staff will direct you, and they rent out walking boots if you don't have appropriate footwear for walking in the park.

INSTINCT GUIDES

16 Crannich Park, Carrbridge; tel. 7944 280 986; www.instinctguides.com; adult £140, child 12-16 £55, lek £120 pp

Collecting guests from their accommodation in and around Aviemore, these bespoke trips, which last around six hours, set out into the hills and moors, past lochs, rivers, and burns, and through native pine forest in a 4x4. With exclusive access to tracks and trails, guides hope to show you eagles, ospreys, capercaillie, deer and more, while teaching you about conservation in the process. As well as general day trips, the company has a private lek with a hide for observing black grouse—one of the big success stories of rewilding in the Cairngorms—and it also has a 10-person tepee, which can be utilized for overnight outdoor adventures on request.

REWILDING RETREATS

Ballintean Mountain Lodge, Glenfeshie Estate; tel. 01540 580 015; www.wildernessscotland.com/ adventure-holidays/wildlife/big-picture; several tours a year; from £1,395

On these immersive six-night retreats, you will stay on a beautiful rewilding reserve and learn about the work going into regenerating the Glen Feshie landscape—and, more importantly, why. You'll hear discussions from experts in the field and spend your days and nights searching for wildlife, in the Cairngorms and sometimes farther afield. Think beavers, red squirrels, golden eagles, mountain hares, and red deer. With the price

---

1: hiking in the Cairngorms **2:** trail in Cairngorms National Park **3:** reindeer

Cairngorms Rewilding

Across Scotland, there have been rallying calls to take a serious stance about protecting its natural settings over recent years. In June 2021, charity **Rewilding Britain** put out a statement saying that our national parks are not "fit for purpose" to tackle the nature and climate crises we face and that wilder parks should be created with stronger powers to expand efforts to seriously tackle the issues of biodiversity and climate breakdown.

This follows on from calls in March 2021 from **The Scottish Rewilding Alliance,** a coalition of over 20 organizations, for Scotland's ministers to support a motion, lodged at Holyrood, that would ultimately lead to Scotland becoming the world's first rewilding nation. It wants the Scottish Government to commit to rewilding 30 percent of Scotland's land and sea by 2030, as well as some of Scotland's towns and cities.

While we're still a way off from that, change is certainly afoot, and Scotland is leading the way across the UK when it comes to returning its land to how nature intended. **Cairngorms Connect,** for instance, is the UK's largest landscape-scale restoration project and asks estate managers, landowners, and other organizations from across the national park to commit to a bold 200-year project to enhance habitats, species, and ecological processes across a vast 150,000-acre (60,000-hectare) area.

Estates involved in the project include the **Glen Feshie Estate** (www.glenfeshie.scot), an area of 45,000 acres (18,000 hectares), whose glens and ancient Caledonian forest are open to walkers and cyclists at all times, and which can already congratulate itself for undertaking one of the most spectacular woodland regeneration projects in Scotland—one that experts say will be hard to reverse. It is possible to stay on the estate in either the Glen Feshie lodge or one of its cottages, and by doing so you can help to contribute to the long-term restoration work.

For a more hands-on stay, **Rewilding Escapes** (www.scotlandbigpicture.com/rewilding-escapes/retreat/wilderness-weekend) runs weekends where guests go on wildlife expeditions and are talked through the ongoing conservation work of Cairngorms Connect by expert guides and rangers. James Shooter, a guide on Rewilding Escapes, says, "After many years of decline, the last remnants of the Caledonian Forest are beginning to recover. The gnarled granny pines, some centuries-old, are now surrounded by new life as saplings begin to erupt from the undergrowth and spread."

including all accommodation, guides, and meals, it is a pretty good value.

CAIRNGORM MOUNTAIN'S NORTHERN CORRIES

Day Lodge, Cairngorm Mountain Resort; tel. 01479 861 261; www.cairngormmountain.co.uk/mountain-activities/guided-walks/ranger-guided-walks; 10:15am Thurs. May-Oct.; adult £10, child £5

These guided walks, which last approximately five hours, are an absolute bargain. Prebook to meet your guide outside Day Lodge in the Cairngorm Mountain resort for a departure onto the mountain. You'll walk right into Coire an t-Sneachda, a huge corrie surrounded by jagged cliffs that is popular with rock and ice-climbers. Your guide will tell you about the landscape, its history, and its inhabitants as you go. It's almost impossible not to see any wildlife, including ptarmigan and mountain hare, and you will return to the ski center car park via the Fiacaill a' Choire Chais mountain summit. Packed lunches can also be pre-ordered for an extra fee, and there is a much easier and shorter guided walk for those who just want an introduction to the mountain.

JAMES ORPWOOD MOUNTAINEERING

Aviemore; tel. 07887 622 470; www. jamesorpwoodmountaineering.co.uk; group hikes from £80 pp per day, private hikes for two from £160, from £80 for a family hike

If you have come to the Cairngorms for a lot of hiking, then I recommend taking a guided walk with someone like James Orpwood Mountaineering. Unless you are a serious hiker, the hills and weather can be unpredictable and challenging, and a guided hike will not only help build your confidence and equip you with the skills needed, but also open your eyes to the landscapes you see. James offers tours either in summer or winter—though you will need at least some experience for the latter—and can plan either a family-friendly half-day walk around lochs and glens, or a more challenging adventure to help you conquer a Munro or tackle the mountain plateau and find secret corries.

Hiking
LOCH AN EILEIN HIKE
Hiking Distance: *4 miles (7 km)*
Hiking Time: *2 hours*
Trailhead: *Loch an Eilein Car Park*
Information and Maps: *Pick up an Explorer Map, which includes the route, at the Rothiemurchus Centre and at Loch an Eilein itself*

Starting at the car park for the loch—there's a signpost at the far end—this circular walk is popular with visitors as it's pretty easy and not time-consuming. Take the path that follows the shoreline to the left and then you will cross a small bridge before entering the forest. There are a few possible extensions to the route, but if you want to stick to the loch loop, keep right, and eventually you will come out loch-side with great views of the castle on the island. Though there are no long or steep gradients, you will still want to wear proper walking boots as it can get muddy or icy underfoot.

LOCH MORLICH CIRCUIT
Hiking Distance: *3.6 miles (5.8 km)*
Hiking Time: *2 hours*
Trailhead: *Glenmore Visitor Centre*
Information and Maps: *https://scotland. forestry.gov.uk/forest-parks/glenmore-forest-park, or local visitor centers*

Most people start this walk in the verdant **Glenmore Forest Park** at the Glenmore Forest Visitor Centre, where you can pick up maps. It also has a very family-friendly café attached to it. If you are short of time or don't fancy too much exertion, you could simply cross the road to Loch Morlich beach—a beautiful pine-fringed beach renowned for its naturally clear waters—and circle it before heading back to the café for ice cream. The path is mainly wide, smooth, and flat with gravel underfoot, though it may be muddy in places.

KINGUSSIE TO NEWTONMORE
Hiking Distance: *7 miles (11 km)*
Hiking Time: *2.5-3.5 hours*
Trailhead: *Ardvonie Car Park, Kingussie*
Information and Maps: *www.walkhighlands. co.uk/cairngorms/loch-gynack.shtml*

For some superb scenery, follow the new path out of Kingussie to Newtonmore, crossing the Gynack Burn before passing by Loch Gynack. The route follows a mix of muddy paths and tracks. At Newtonmore you may choose to continue onto the Scottish Wildcat Trail (a map can be bought for £4 at The Wildcat Centre in Newtonmore), where 132 wildcat models are hidden around the village and the neighboring countryside as part of an unusual treasure hunt, aimed to raise awareness of the importance of regenerating native woodland.

Cycling
AVIEMORE BIKES
5a Myrtlefield Shopping Centre, Aviemore; tel. 1479 810 478; www.aviemorebikes.co.uk; 10am-5pm Mon.-Sat.; from £20 for a half day and £25 for a full day, electric bikes from £40 for a half day and £50 for a full day, trail maps available from £2.50

There are all types of bikes for hire at this shop, also known as Mikes Bikes: electric mountain bikes, endurance road bikes, and premium mountain bikes for off-road cycling. Plus, the shop is just a five-minute cycle from the trails of Rothiemurchus, so even beginners can be on the road in no time. All staff are experienced cyclists and can advise on local routes. Make sure to prebook.

BOAT OF GARTEN BIKE RIDE

Cycling Distance: *7 miles (11 km) round-trip*
Cycling Time: *40 minutes*
Trailhead: *Community Hall, Boat of Garten*
Information and Maps: *https://cairngorms. co.uk/wp-content/uploads/2019/02/CycleRouteCard-BoatofGarten.pdf*

This is an easy family-friendly bike ride, on flat trails and roads, that is suitable for beginners or occasional cyclists. The route takes you through the village of Boat of Garten, up over the Spey, to the RSPB Abernethy National Nature Reserve and its Osprey Centre and back. Along the way you'll pass granny pines—trees with thick trunks that are hundreds of years old—and get tremendous views of Loch Garten. From April to August you may even spy nesting capercaille.

RYVOAN LOOP

Cycling Distance: *25 miles (40 km) round-trip*
Cycling Time: *2-4 hours for the loop*
Trailhead: *High Street, Aviemore*
Information and Maps: *www.aviemorebikes. co.uk/3-top-intermediate-rides-from-aviemore*

A bit more of a challenge, largely due to distance, this intermediate route sets off from right outside Aviemore Bikes. Simply follow along the the high street, dip under the railway bridge, and then follow the cycle path to Rothiemurchus. Once here, there are some easy trails through the forest that will bring you to, first, Loch Morlich, and then past Glenmore Lodge and up to An Lochan Uaine, which locals call the Green Loch for reasons that will become obvious. From here, the route continues to Ryvoan Bothy at the foot of Meal a' Buichalle—where you can stop and catch your breath—and then through Abernethy Forest to Forest Lodge from where you can return to Aviemore via the Speyside Way.

Adventure Sports
GLENMORE LODGE

Aviemore; tel. 01479 861 256; www.glenmorelodge. org.uk; two-day adventures from £235

Glenmore Lodge is the national outdoor training center and there is so much going on here that it's worth checking if any of the courses appeal. They offer short 1-2-day courses on everything, from orienteering to women-only events that aim to empower. There is also some basic B&B accommodation in the lodge, and it's perfectly placed in the middle of the park, surrounded by hills and forests and no end of trails for running, walking, and cycling.

Skiing
THE SKI AND SNOWBOARD SCHOOL

Coylumbridge Hotel, Aviemore; tel. 01479 811 066; www.schoolofsnowsports.co.uk; 8am-5pm Mon.-Fri.; from £40 pp in a group session

If you haven't skied or tried snow sports, or are just a little rusty, then this place could be just what you need. They run ski lessons for everyone, from complete beginners to people who just need to refresh their skills, and they hire out ski equipment, so you could be hitting the slopes on your own in no time.

CAIRNGORM SKI AREA

Aviemore; tel. 01479 861 261; www. cairngormmountain.co.uk; day passes adult £30, child £18.50, under 5 free, gear from £30 per day adult for skis, boots and poles, child gear £25

If you're itching to ski or board Britain's sixth highest mountain, and you feel ready, then there are lots of choices here, from easy green runs, through intermediate blue runs, all the way to the tricky red and black runs.

Rental gear can be booked up to 48 hours in advance; for morning collections, head to Level 3 of the Day Lodge. I've been told of plans to open a Ski Hire Bothy at Inverdruie on the ski road between Aviemore and Coylumbridge where guests can pick up their equipment the night before so they can be first on the slopes in the morning, so it's worth inquiring about this. Beginners may be asked to book lessons before hiring equipment.

There is a car park, but it gets very busy, so if you can, jump on the bus at Aviemore, which will bring you right to the door of the ski center in around 20 minutes. It's always a good idea to keep an eye on the website's mountain report for the latest weather.

Food and Bars
THE BOAT OF GARTEN
POST OFFICE AND SHOP
Deshar Road, Boat of Garten; tel. 01479 831 527; 7am-6pm Mon.-Sat., 9am-2pm Sun.

Just 6 miles (10 km) northeast of Aviemore on the Speyside Way, this local lifeline is renowned as the friendliest shop in the Cairngorms. If you're heading out for the day, stop off here to pick up some freshly baked goods and coffee, or to send that postcard.

COBBS CAFÉ
Glenmore Forest Visitor Centre; tel. 01479 861 700; 9:30am-3:30pm Mon.-Fri., 9:30am-4pm Sat.-Sun.; coffee £2.60, sandwiches £6.25

Visitor center cafés are usually pretty bad, but not so here. With lots of tables, great staff, and a family-friendly menu, it's a really good choice for brunch or lunch. Baked potatoes, sandwiches, and croissants all come filled to the brim, with a generous helping of salad and crisps on the side.

THE BARN
Rothiemurchus; tel. 01479 812 345; https:// rothiemurchus.net/visit/food-drink; 10am-4pm daily; mains £6.50

This stripped-down café has a very earthy vibe. They take food provenance very seriously—most of the produce is grown or reared on the Rothiemurchus estate before ending up on your plate via homemade burgers, stews, pies, and soups. If you're after something a little lighter, the coffee and baking are good too, and they do amazing hot chocolates. Don't leave without checking out the nearby Estate Farm Shop & Deli, too.

★ OLD BRIDGE INN
Dalfaber Road, Aviemore; tel. 01479 811 137; www.oldbridgeinn.co.uk; 12pm-2:30pm and 5:30pm-8:30pm daily, hours may be reduced at quieter times; entrées £8

In an old, converted cottage, the pub side of this place is always awash with travelers exchanging tales of their day's activities, while the restaurant side is a slightly calmer candle-lit affair (though mud-splattered boots are welcome). The Old Bridge burger usually hits the spot, or there's normally at least one steak, fish, and vegan option. The inn also runs a bunkhouse next door. Pre-pandemic they had regular live music and DJ nights, so here's hoping it will return.

CAIRNGORM BREWERY
Dalfaber Industrial Estate, Aviemore; tel. 01479 812 222; 10am-5:30pm Mon.-Sat.

For a local tipple, this craft brewery, which opened for business in 2001, is walking distance from Aviemore's center. Tours were put on hold due to COVID-19, but it's hoped they will start up again soon. In the meantime, you can pop into the brewery shop to buy a few bottles for a post-hike drink.

Accommodations
BADAGUISH WIGWAM
AND CAMPSITE
Badaguish Outdoor Centre, Aviemore; tel. 01479 861 285; www.badaguish.org; £75 wigwam for 2

In the outdoor center of Badaguish, long popular with large, organized tours, there's space enough for everyone here. Besides, once you retreat to your wigwam (more like a wooden hut, with beds that switch to seating during the day, and a kitchenette for making a cuppa), you'll soon forget about everyone else. With mountain scenery to enjoy amid the Glenmore Forest Park and lots of space to explore, it's a good alternative to camping. You will need to bring your own sleeping bag and pillow/sheets. (Pre-COVID they were available for hire from £10 per person, so it's worth checking if they are again.)

THE CAIRN HOTEL

Main Road, Carrbridge; tel. 01479 841 212; https:// cairnhotel.co.uk; £100 d

Traditional rooms with white cotton bedspreads topped with tartan throws, widescreen TVs, fluffy towels, and fancy toiletries make this 14-room inn feel like a bargain. Downstairs, the pub is a buzzing meeting place, and its restaurant is always well-stocked with local Highlands produce.

DALRACHNEY LODGE HOTEL

Grantown Road, Carrbridge, Aviemore; tel. 01479 841 252; https://dalrachney.co.uk; £150 d, possible 2-night minimum

Just 15 minutes outside Aviemore on the periphery of the attractive village of Carrbridge, which Queen Victoria described as the "jewel of the north," this former Edwardian hunting lodge is a lovely haven to retire to at the end of the day. Once visited by King George V, the beds are good, there are luxurious Floris toiletries (favored by the Royal Family) in the bathroom, and the lounge is a great setting for a nightcap, with its wing-backed armchairs, tartan curtains, and open fire.

★ KILLIEHUNTLY

Killiehuntly, Kingussie; tel. 01540 661 619; https:// killiehuntly.scot; farmhouse room £395 d including breakfast and dinner, Geordies Cottage £1,750 per week, The Bothy £1,310 per week

For a closer experience of the rewilding projects underway in the Cairngorms, book a stay at this lovely Victorian farmhouse or in one of the nearby self-catering stone cottages that are part of the Wildland portfolio, a conservation organization that is committed to a 200-year project to help nature restore itself.

Rooms are uncluttered and gorgeous, with clean Scandi-inspired palettes of grey and soft pink, bare floorboards covered in thick rugs, and huge comfy beds. Some do share a bathroom, but an honesty bar, wood-burner in the drawing room, plus supper served most evenings (check when booking) more than makes up for this. For more privacy, the two Geordies cottages sleep five, and the Bothy

sleeps four. It's not the cheapest, but a stay here is your holiday, rather than just a place to sleep, with nature walks, calming views, and endless opportunities for wild swimming and wildlife encounters.

Getting There

The main route into the Cairngorms is the well-driven A9—a main road that leads all the way from Inverness in the north through to the south of the park, and vice versa. From Inverness it's 30 miles (48 km; 45 minutes) along the A9 to Aviemore, while to reach Aviemore all the way from Edinburgh is a distance of 128 miles, following the M90 before joining the A9 (206 km; 2 hours 45 minutes) or 84 miles (135 km; 1 hour 50 minutes) from Perth along the A9.

There are alternatives to this direct route, particularly if you'd like to make some detours. The **Snow Roads,** for instance, is much more scenic. And then there's the A939 from Nairn, on the Moray Firth coastline, which brings you to Grantown-on-Spey (23 miles/37 km; 35 minutes)—handy for the Malt Whisky Trail.

Within the Cairngorms, there are train stations at Aviemore, Carrbridge, Kingussie, Newtonmore, and Dalwhinnie, which have regular connections to Edinburgh (2 hours 50 minutes to Aviemore; £45.60 single, £54.60 return), Perth (1 hour 30 minutes to Aviemore; £30.60 single, £40.70 return), Stirling (2 hours 5 minutes to Aviemore; £37.90 single, £52.90 return), and Inverness (40 minutes to Aviemore; £13.80 single, £23.50 return). Trains from Glasgow sometimes change at Perth. In addition, trains from London to Inverness stop at Aviemore and Kingussie.

From Inverness, the M91 bus with Scottish Citylink will get you to Aviemore in just 50 minutes (single £6.60). From Perth, it will be the M90 that you'll need (2 hours 10 minutes; £12.60), and from Aberdeen, you'll need to go to Perth first and catch the M90 from there. There is a good network of buses within the park, particularly from Aviemore, run by Stagecoach (www.stagecoachbus.com/about/

☆ The Snow Roads

www.snowroads.com

Many people have the impression that Aberdeenshire roads are quite tame, and perhaps even a little boring compared with west coast roads. Ascending a huge hill on the A93 from Balmoral as you drive to Perth, feeling your back press against the car seat as you go up and up the road before reaching the top, you'll realize that impression is all wrong.

The Snow Roads is a 90-mile (145-km) route from **Blairgowrie** in the south all the way to **Grantown-on-Spey** in the north, traversing the highest public roads in Scotland, and is so called as even in summer you can still see snow on the mountain tops. The old military roads of the route form part of a network built in the 18th century by General Wade to enable government forces to respond quickly and deploy to key locations if there were any future Jacobite risings. The section from Ballater to Blairgowrie is the most treacherous, once considered so dangerous that it earned the nickname the Devil's Elbow, due to double hairpin bends. But it's also majestic, with beautiful scenery all around. The road has since been straightened out, and the old tracks of the hairpin bends are instead used by walkers and some daring cyclists, though the gradient is still hair-raising, and you can visit the breathtaking **Devil's Elbow Viewpoint** near Blairgowrie.

Considered something of a secret passage to the Highlands, particularly for visitors to Royal Deeside, the Snow Roads route traverses the beautiful **Glenshee,** whose Gaelic name of Gleann Shith translates as "glen of the fairies," before flattening out somewhat as you drive north from Royal Deeside to Grantown-on-Spey. It's a much nicer and quieter route to follow than the busy A9. It can be a bit daunting in winter, and if there has been heavy snowfall the roads may be impassable. If the roads are open, then as long as due care is taken, it can be a beautiful place to drive in winter.

north-scotland). Check the website for time-tables. Traveline (www.traveline.info) is also a good resource for planning your routes to and from towns and villages within the park.

ROYAL DEESIDE

It was in this part of the Cairngorms that Queen Victoria cemented her love affair with Scotland, putting roots down here at Balmoral, which she had renovated from modest country home to grand castle. Today it's still a favored holiday home for the Royal Family—Her Majesty The Queen and her family spend Christmas here every year—and so the area has earned a royal tag.

It's a genteel kind of place, where the road softly skirts fertile farmland, passing under canopies of trees, and alongside rivers, where it feels as though some salmon may leap out at any moment. Views of the Cairngorm hills and thick native pinewood forests are lovely. Strictly speaking, Royal Deeside—or simply Deeside to some—stretches west from Aberdeen, but the main areas of interest in

the park are Ballater, home to Balmoral, and Braemar slightly west, where the famous Highland Games take place each September (and where one of Scotland's best hotels is sited).

The Victorian village of **Ballater,** set along the River Dee, is a pleasant little place that still displays some remnants from its time as a tourist hotspot for Victorian visitors, including its Old Royal Station, once used to transport Queen Victoria and other members of the Royal Family to nearby Balmoral Castle. Eventually the visitors tailed off and the train station closed in 1966, then in 2015 there was a devastating fire in the station building. Later that year, the village was hit by severe flooding. Since then, Prince Charles has spearheaded a campaign to breathe new life into Ballater, restoring old buildings and improving the food and drink offering in a bid to return it to a tourist village worth visiting.

Surrounded by mountain scenery and located deep in the Cairngorms National Park, the pretty little village of **Braemar** is a good

Queen Victoria in Scotland

Victoria made no secret of her love of Scotland. From her very first visit here in 1842, she was hooked, and she referred to Balmoral, which her beloved Albert had built for her, as "my dear paradise in The Highlands." There are many stories about Victoria and Albert leaving the comfort of Balmoral and going on tour into the countryside, often trying to go incognito, staying in inns in the Highlands, undetected by their subjects. Anyone who watched TV's *Victoria* will know that not only did Victoria like to escape to the Highlands with her children and husband to avoid the public eye, but also following Albert's death it gave her a great deal of comfort and became a place of retreat.

Here are some ways to get a more authentic taste of the region as Victoria would have known it.

- Take a ride on the **Royal Deeside Railway** (www.deeside-railway.co.uk) at Milton of Crathes—a heritage steam train that goes along some of the route that once went all the way to Ballater, which is how Victoria would regularly travel to Balmoral. There's a very sweet tearoom there today.

- Following Albert's death, Victoria had cairns erected all over rural Deeside, in some of her favorite beauty spots, and at Loch Muick you can follow a trail round the edge of the water and pass by **Glas-alt-Shiel,** the property that became known as "widow's house," as it was here that Victoria spent much of her time following her husband's death. In recent years it has been open as a bothy, but it is currently closed. To view it from the outside, park up at the Spittal of Glen Muick car park (Ballater).

- There is also a life-size **statue** to Victoria's confidante and personal attendant John Brown in the grounds of Balmoral, and you can visit his grave in the churchyard of Crathie Kirk.

base for those wanting to combine a visit to Balmoral with some serious hillwalking and landscapes worthy of an oil painting. Its L-plan style **castle** (tel. 01339 741 219; www.braemarcastle.co.uk; 10am-5pm Weds.-Sun. Apr.-June and Oct., 10am-5pm daily July-Sept.; adult £10, child £4, family £22; closed first Sat. in Sept. for Braemar Gathering) was originally a hunting lodge built by the Earl of Mar, who hoped to put a stop to the rising power of the Farquharsons, before falling into the hands of that family after the property was confiscated by the Crown from the Earl of Mar for his part in the Jacobite rising of 1715.

Sights

BALMORAL CASTLE

Ballater, AB35 5TB; tel. 01339 742 534; www.balmoralcastle.com; early Apr.-early Aug. 10am-5pm (last admission 4pm); adult £15, child 5-16 £6, guidebook £5.95

By far the biggest attraction in Royal Deeside is the Royal Family's holiday home of Balmoral. Each spring until early August, the

beautiful grounds and a small section of the interior are open to the public.

To visit, you should prebook tickets and then park up in the car park (£3) in Crathie, a tiny little village, where there is a post office and the small church where the Royal Family attend a service every Christmas Day. It's in the graveyard of this church that you can visit the grave of one of Queen Victoria's closest friends John Brown, where the inscription on the headstone reads:

That friend on whose fidelity you count,

That friend given you by circumstances

Over which you have no control

Was God's own gift.

Well done good and faithful Servant.

From the church, it is just a couple of minutes' walk to the little stone bridge that crosses the River Dee to the ticket office. Even if you've booked online, you'll need to queue, and once in through the gates, you still have

1: Balmoral Castle **2:** Braemar Highland Games Centre

to walk 10 minutes toward the stables, where you'll have to queue again to collect your audio guide. You must pay a deposit (or leave car keys) to take an audio guide, which means you have to queue again at the end to give back the audio guide and collect your bail.

Still, irks aside, as long as you are reasonably fit, the walk to the stables (all flat along the side of a tarmac road) is very pretty and there is a good chance of spotting red squirrels—I saw one before I was even through the gate. The audio guide, which is good, if a little long in places, takes you round the exterior of the property and the grounds. The castle's largest room, the Ballroom, where Ghillie's Balls (where servants dance with the upper class) have been held since Queen Victoria's time, can be visited, and there are regularly exhibitions held in the stables. However, the best thing about a trip here is indeed strolling the grounds and peering up at the palatial home with its numerous pepper pot turrets around a soaring seven-storey tower, and wondering about what really goes on inside.

There are a couple of kiosks to grab a coffee and a snack as you walk round, but it's worth it to wait for the new **café.** The light and airy space, with a pitched roof, wooden beams, and shabby chic white tables and chairs, is pleasingly informal and the food is very good, with generous portions.

BRAEMAR HIGHLAND GAMES CENTRE

The Duke of Rothesay Highland Games Pavilion, Princess Royal & Duke of Fife Memorial Park, Broombank Terrace; tel. 01339 749 220; www. highlandgamescentre.org; by appointment only; adult £5, child £1

This center had the unfortunate timing of opening in 2018, not long before the pandemic, and at present it is only open by appointment, though hopefully it will reopen more regularly soon. With free parking and a good café, it's a great space to learn more about the history of the Braemar Gathering, as well as indulge your interest in the Highland games more generally.

Tours
HIDDEN DEESIDE TOURS

Collection from accommodation; tel. 7920 801 546; www.hidden-deeside.com; £200 half-day tour, £400 full-day tour

These small personal tours for up to four people (the cost is split between you) will take you into the heart of Royal Deeside, in search of fairy-tale castles, mysterious stones, and literary links. You can visit the house where Robert Louis Stevenson wrote his classic tale *Treasure Island* and have a go at dowsing rods at a Neolithic stone circle.

YELLOW WELLY TOURS

Balnellan House, Braemar; tel. 07971 287 366; www. yellowwellytours.com; £350 private 4-hour tour for up to 6 people

These bespoke, chauffeur-driven tours are led by guide Simon, something of a local character, who more often than not can be found wearing yellow wellies with his pair of chocolate cocker spaniels in tow. Simon knows the area inside out, particularly Braemar Castle as he is chair of the organization that looks after the castle. Let Simon plan a half- or full-day adventure for you, where he will tell you tales of royal escapades and local folklore, and take you to castles, mountains, and ancient standing stones.

Hiking
MUIR OF DINNET, LITTLE ORD TRAIL

Hiking Distance: 2.7 miles (4.4 km)
Hiking Time: 2 hours
Trailhead: Burn O'Vat car park
Information and Maps: www.deesidewalks. com/2012/12/muir-of-dinnet-little-ord-trail.html

An easy to moderate walk along a mainly flat path, this trail will bring you close to some ancient relics in Royal Deeside, including stone circles, a crannog (a manmade on-the-water dwelling probably built in the Iron Age), and a beautiful carved Celtic cross, known as the Kinord Stone. It's a circular walk that sets off from a car park on a quiet road, a 10-minute (6-mile/10-km) drive east of Ballater on the

Fishing the River Dee

The River Dee, which meanders through Royal Deeside, is considered the top spring salmon river in the world, and in Deeside, catches for Atlantic salmon are generally higher than anywhere else.

If you are an experienced angler and would like to go it alone, then the **Fish Dee** website (www.fishdee.co.uk) has details on the best places to fish for salmon and also has a section on trout fishing. It also outlines fishing regulations, including when the fishing season starts and ends (Feb.-Oct.—check specific dates for year of travel), and good catch and release practice.

If you'd prefer a guided fishing expedition, the **Monteith Guided Salmon Fishing** (tel. 0131 618 7058; www.salmon-fish-scotland.com/River-Dee-Guided-Salmon-Fishing; from £395 per person for full-day expedition, lower prices for larger groups) provides guided salmon fishing experiences with expert fishers. You can also check Fish Dee for local ghillies or ask at your hotel about recommendations (larger hotels sometimes have their own ghillie).

A93 and B9119, and passes through woodland, grassland, and alongside a loch.

BEN MACDUI AND DERRY CAIRNGORM

Hiking Distance: *18 miles (29 km)*
Hiking Time: *9-11 hours*
Trailhead: *Linn of Dee Car Park*
Information and Maps: *Walk Highlands has a very good route description and map at www.walkhighlands.co.uk/cairngorms/ben-macdui.shtml*

Part of the Cairngorm plateau, this is the second highest mountain in Britain and its terrain is much wilder and less hospitable than Ben Nevis. There are numerous ways to approach it, and many travelers come from the northern side near the ski resorts, but in fact, it's probably best approached from the east in Deeside. This trek sets off from the Linn of Dee car park and leads up through an open glen to an exposed plateau. It's a long old walk and one that should only be attempted by seriously experienced hikers who have prepared properly.

Skiing

GLENSHEE SKI CENTRE

Cairnwell, Braemar; tel. 01339 741 320; www.ski-glenshee.co.uk; parking £3

Just a few miles outside Braemar, this ski and snowboard center has the largest lift system in Britain, and the runs extend over three valleys and four mountains, with a mix of nursery slopes, intermediate runs, and a couple of black runs. The ski season varies but usually runs from December through early April. In summer, even when there's not enough snow to ski, you can take the Cairnwell Chairlift up and down for epic views, while The Tea at the Shee is open daily 8am-4:45pm. In winter, when they are accessible, there are two further cafés: Meall 'o' Dhar Café, in the middle valley, and Cairnwell Café.

Entertainment and Events

BALLATER HIGHLAND GAMES

Monaltrie Park, Ballater; info@ballaterhighlandgames.com; www.ballaterhighlandgames.com; August; adult £10, child £3

Held on the second Thursday in August each year, with both the 2020 and 2021 events canceled, these games, which have been held since 1864, will hopefully return in 2022. The games, which in recent years have been attended by Prince Charles, Duke of Rothesay, attract around 6,000 people each year, with piping competitions, Highland dancing, heavyweight competitions, and more, to entertain the friendly crowd.

BRAEMAR GATHERING

The Princess Royal and Duke of Fife Memorial Park, Braemar; tel. 01339 741 527; www.braemargathering.org; first Sat. in Sept.; adult from £12, child £2

Think of all the images you have in your mind

of the Highland games, and chances are they come from here, the most famous Highland games in the world. Starting in 1832 (though gatherings of one type or another took place for centuries before this in Braemar), Queen Victoria attended the games each year and was enthralled by the spectacle of the piped bands and Highland dancers, and the sheer pageantry of it all. Little has changed since. During the day, there are traditional competitions, from piping to dancing to the tug o' war, caber toss, and hammer throwing, as well as the legendary hill running competition—which is how Highland chiefs picked their fastest messengers centuries ago. With limited options, accommodation in Braemar books up well in advance, so get your room sorted before booking travel.

Food
★ FARQUHARSON'S BAR & KITCHEN

2-4 Invercauld Road; tel. 01339 741 955; www. facebook.com/farquharsonsbarandkitchen; 12pm-10:30pm daily; entrées £4.50

Opened in 2019 by the chief of Clan Farquharson—centurion Captain Alwyne Farquharson—this pub in a converted shop is a much-needed addition to the village. So far, the verdict is good: staff are friendly and the food comforting—pies, fish and chips, burgers mainly. This is a good place to fuel up following a day in the hills.

THE BOTHY BRAEMAR

Invercauld Road, Braemar; tel. 1339 741 019; www.facebook.com/The-Bothy-Braemar-1536437353245804; 9am-5:30pm daily; coffee £2, sandwiches £5.50

This great little café is attached to an outdoor center. There's a raised terrace for alfresco dining, with views over the river. The coffee is good, sandwiches come with crisps and salad, and the cakes are yummy. It's the type of place you can just as easily come and read the paper as refuel for your next adventure. There is also a Bothy in Ballater.

★ ROTHESAY ROOMS

Ballater Station, Station Square; tel. 01339 753 816; https://rothesay-rooms.co.uk; 12pm-2pm and 6pm-9pm Thurs.-Fri., 6pm-9pm Weds., 12pm-3pm Sun.; entrées £12

In the heart of the community of Ballater, this exceptional restaurant was borne out of a local crisis. Following a terrible storm in December 2015, in which the River Dee burst its banks, destroying many homes and businesses, a pop-up restaurant opened with support from Prince Charles, funded by relief donations to help rejuvenate the village and kick-start much-needed new business. Now, the restaurant, which has been listed in the Michelin Guide for the past four years, has relocated from its temporary home to the Old Royal Station, where it will once again serve up high-end field-to-fork cooking when it reopens.

CLACHAN GRILL

5 Bridge Square, Ballater; tel. 01339 755 999; http://clachangrill.co.uk; 3pm-11pm Weds.-Sat., 12pm-10pm Sun.; lunch mains from £9.95, 2-course evening meals from £29.95

A great find in the town of Ballater, this casual restaurant in a pretty-as-they-come pink and grey stone building has plenty of tartan and stag heads inside, and the food is reliable hearty Scottish fare, all sustainably sourced—succulent steaks and catch of the day, with some satisfying vegetarian options too. Plus, for families, kids eat free until 6pm (with a full-paying adult).

Accommodations
BRAEMAR CABINS

7-9 Invercauld Road; tel. 01339 741 242; https://braemarcabins.com; £50 d, minimum stays may apply

For affordable accommodation in Braemar, try these log cabins. They are actually higher spec'd than their outward appearance would suggest, with even the smallest having room for a double bed, a kitchenette, a sofa, and a bathroom with shower. There is constant hot water and underfloor heating to keep you snug.

STAY AT BALMORAL

Balmoral Castle, Ballater; tel. 01339 742 534; www. balmoralcastle.com/cottages.htm; from £705 per week

The next best thing to getting a personal invite to stay with the Queen, these cottages in the grounds of Balmoral, hired out for a week at a time, are enchanting. Some 5 miles (8 km) west of the castle in Queen Victoria's cherished Ballochbuie Forest, they're like a Victorian time capsule, with wrought iron bedsteads, tiled fireplaces, a freestanding bath, and a wood-panelled lounge with open fire. The cottages may sometimes be closed when the Royal Family is in residence, which does make you wonder who might be staying there?

★ DOUNESIDE HOUSE

Tarland; tel. 01339 881 230; https://douneside house. co.uk; from £200 d

A little outside Royal Deeside, but worth the journey, this former family home is now part of a trust and operates as a nonprofit hotel. Lady MacRobert, the lady of the house, turned the family home into a hotel providing accommodation for serving military who needed a break, after her eldest son died in an aviation accident in 1938 and her two younger sons were killed in action during the Second World War. Today the house is open to other guests, though military personnel get special disposition.

The grand country house, which looks out over an infinity lawn, underwent a major refurbishment in 2016, marrying the period features of the house with modern luxuries. Rooms are large—the Lady MacRobert suite has a triple aspect—and are furnished with antique bureaus, thick rugs, and beds with Hypnos mattresses. Downstairs, the three AA Rosette Conservatory restaurant is an elegant setting for fine dining, with calming garden views. There's also a piano lounge, a drawing room, and a bar for downtime. Possibly the biggest draw of the house, though, are the beautiful grounds, which include an arts-and-crafts garden and a Japanese-inspired tranquil rock garden.

★ THE FIFE ARMS

Mar Road; tel. 01339 720 200; https://thefifearms. com; from £250 d, minimum stays may apply

A Victorian pile, built in the 19th century to accommodate the many visitors who came to the tiny Highland village of Braemar after Queen Victoria bought Balmoral, the Fife Arms has long been synonymous with Royal Deeside. However, since being taken over by its current owners, Iwan and Manuela Wirth, and reopened in 2018, this hotel's reputation has pulled in people whether they are interested in visiting Balmoral or not.

Part lavish hotel, part art gallery, this property has been carefully curated and extended to tell the village's story, as well as the wider story of Scotland. There is a room dedicated to Robert Louis Stevenson, who spent several months in Braemar, and of course Victoria's influence is clear to see—there is even a bust of the queen among the more than 14,000 art works. The 46 guest rooms and suites are furnished with antiques and rich and plush fabrics—there are freestanding copper baths in the five-star royal suites. Guests can also book treatments in the spa.

Getting There

By car, Ballater is just an hour's drive west of Aberdeen, along the B9077 and then the A93 (42 miles/68 km). Braemar is one hour and 25 minutes west of Aberdeen by car, along the B9077 and then the A93 (58 miles/93 km). Ballater and Braemar are just 16 miles (25 km) apart on the A93; the drive takes around 25 minutes.

Sadly, there is no train station in Braemar, and the Victorian station in Ballater hasn't been working since the 1960s. Royal Deeside is reachable by bus from Aberdeen, getting to Ballater in a little over 2 hours (Stagecoach no. 201 from Union Square Bus Station; single £11, return £19.80).

Moray Speyside

Named after the river that runs through it, Moray Speyside (often just Speyside) is a region just north of the Cairngorms National Park, which runs all the way north to the rugged Moray coastline. It has a high number of distilleries—51 and counting, more than half of Scotland's distilleries are here—due largely to the abundance of water, from its rivers and secluded glens, and the fertile farmlands, which are perfect for growing barley.

If you are coming to Speyside for the distilleries, that might be all you do here, and that's fine. But if you spend a day or two seeing other sights in the area, such as Ballindalloch Castle, you will get a more rounded feel of the region. With good pathways and cycleways running throughout the region and many of the distilleries located close to each other, it's easy to travel Speyside without a car, which is just as well, considering all the whisky on offer.

ORIENTATION

In the southeastern corner of the region, about 1.5 hours from Inverness and 1 hour from Aberdeen, **Dufftown** is the main town for anyone wishing to follow the Malt Whisky Trail, with six distilleries in and around it (including the world-famous Glenfiddich distillery). Just 5.5 miles (8.9 km) northwest of Dufftown, **Aberlour** is a handsome riverside town with some fine Victorian buildings. Meanwhile, **Craigellachie,** which is walkable (under 2 miles/3.2 km) from Aberlour along the Speyside Way, is another small, pretty town that has a lovely boutique hotel and is home to Speyside Cooperage. About 20 minutes (12 miles/19 km) northeast of Craigellachie, **Keith** is home to Strathisla, the oldest continuously operating distillery in the Highlands. The biggest town in Moray is **Elgin,** which is renowned for its cathedral and cashmere and is some 13.5 miles (22 km) north of Craigellachie, while **Forres,** some 12 miles (19 km) west of Elgin, is another large Moray town, close to the seaside village of Findhorn.

As the distances between each place isn't huge, you may prefer to base yourself in just one of these towns for the duration of your visit rather than move from hotel to hotel. Elgin, Forres, and Keith all have train stations, with Scotrail links to Inverness and Aberdeen.

TOP EXPERIENCE

DISTILLERIES

The River Spey, which runs through Speyside and is fed by the soft water that tumbles down off the mountains, is integral to the whisky produced in this fertile valley, which combined with warmer weather than most parts of Scotland helps produce smooth yet complex whiskies. Speyside whiskies are known for being lighter and sweeter than whiskies from other regions, sometimes with a little smokiness, more often with fruity notes. Some of the whiskies here have been around so long they are part of the landscape, and their names—Glenfiddich, Macallan, etc.—are familiar even to those with little knowledge of whisky. Others are newer, smaller operations, which have earned excellent reputations in a relatively short amount of time. Below I've tried to include a variety of distilleries (mainly on the Malt Whisky Trail, but a couple just off it), where you can see a range of techniques and hopefully notice a difference in the tastings.

Tours
SIMPLY SPEYSIDE

Pickup from Speyside available; tel. 07816 185 978; www.simplyspeyside.co.uk; tours daily year-round; half day £90, full day £150

Whether you want to visit a few big brands, get a balanced view of the region with a tour of three classic distilleries, or see how differently things are done between the huge distilleries

Moray Speyside

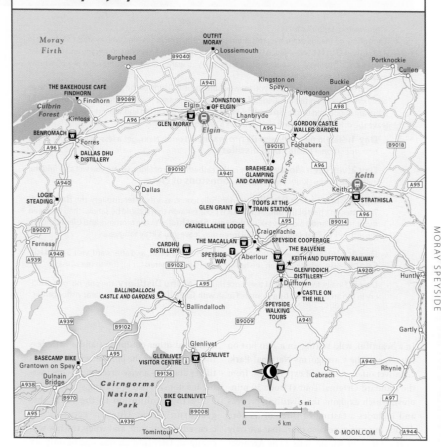

and the small ones, these chauffeur-driven bespoke tours have you covered. Please note, the cost does not cover lunch or entry to the distilleries—you're paying for a driver, transport, and expert guidance.

SPEYSIDE TOURS

Dufftown; tel. 01340 820 892; www.speysidetours.co.uk; full day £145; dine-at-home meals from £30
While whisky is undoubtedly the main reason people visit this region, it's by no means the only reason. What I love about these tours, run by husband-and-wife team Michelle and Andrew, is that they combine visits to both the distilleries that make Speyside famous (they both grew up in Speyside and have worked in the whisky industry) with trips to the countryside, which many visitors forget. They also provide a gourmet picnic made up of lots of local produce, and if you're staying in a self-catering place nearby, you can even order their full dine-at-home experience.

Dufftown and Around
GLENLIVET

Ballindalloch; tel. 01340 821 720; www.theglenlivet.com; 9:30am-5pm Tues.-Sat., 10am-5pm Sun.-Mon.; tours from £15

☆ The Malt Whisky Trail

https://maltwhiskytrail.com

Though by no means definitive, this themed trail, which includes nine whisky sites of interest in and around **Dufftown**—seven working distilleries, plus the Speyside Cooperage and the Dallas Dhu Historic Distillery—is a good place to start if you want a taste (quite literally) of why whisky making is so integral to life here.

If you have five days or more, you may be able to visit all nine of the attractions. You can obviously drive between the distilleries if you're prepared to save your tastings for later, or many of them are connected by the **Speyside Way,** which can be cycled and walked—or take a tour to leave the driving to someone else. Below is a proposed route.

- **Day 1:** Start in the north with **Benromach,** in Forres. Next, get a lesson in history at the non-operational **Dallas Dhu distillery.**

- **Day 2:** Visit **Glen Moray** distillery in the cathedral city of Elgin, where you will also find the mill of the famous knitwear company, **Johnstons of Elgin.**

- **Day 3: Glenfiddich Distillery** is rightfully iconic, as is its sister distillery, the **Balvenie.** The latter isn't part of the official trail but is close enough that it could be sandwiched between a visit to Scotland's oldest working distillery, **Strathisla,** in the morning, and Glenfiddich in the afternoon. That said, a tour of all three may leave you a little fatigued.

- **Day 4: Glen Grant,** in the village of Rothes, is worth a visit, and afterward, visit **Speyside Cooperage,** where you can see how the casks are prepared for maturing the whisky.

- **Day 5:** Finally, farther west of the cooperage is **Cardhu Distillery,** the only historic distillery in the area founded by a woman. Finish with **Glenlivet,** with its excellent visitor center.

In a beautiful, wild setting, in a glen just on the edge of the Cairngorms National Park, Glenlivet offers a range of experiences, from the standard Original Tour (1 hour 30 minutes), which explains the distilling process and includes a tasting of three of its core drams, to some expensive tours that are only worth it for true whisky fans. (The Archives tour, for instance, includes tastings of rare bottlings for £100.)

GLENFIDDICH DISTILLERY

Dufftown, Keith; tel. 01340 820 373; www. glenfiddich.com; 10:30am-4:30pm daily; tours £20

Glenfiddich first began making whisky in 1887, when the first drop of spirit fell from its copper stills on Christmas Day. The distillery was the long-held ambition of William Grant, who together with his nine children and a stone mason, built the distillery from scratch. Before making whisky, Grant had spent around £120 buying the stills and other equipment and a little less than £700 to buy the land on which the distillery stands—a wise investment considering it's not stopped operating since.

During Prohibition in the 1920s, his grandson Grant Gordon actually increased production, and when the law was changed, Glenfiddich was one of only six Scottish distilleries still in operation. The iconic triangular bottle was launched in the 1960s, and shortly afterward, William's great grandson, Sandy Grant Gordon, came up with the idea of a single strand whisky, which kickstarted the single malt boom: Before then it was all about blends. In 1969, Glenfiddich also became the first distillery to open up to visitors, and thus whisky tourism was born.

Today, the distillery's best-selling whisky is 12-Year-Old, the only whisky that isn't bottled on site. Tours of the distillery begin with a history lesson, before talking you through the whisky-making process and then taking you to see both the new and the old still rooms. After the tour, you are taken to the grand Whisky Lounge for a tutored tasting of a flight of whiskies. You might like to extend your visit with lunch on the Robbie Dhu terrace, which overlooks the distillery's single burn.

THE BALVENIE

Dufftown; tel. 01340 822 210; www.thebalvenie.com; check the website for opening times and latest prices

The sister distillery to Glenfiddich, the Balvenie's 12-Year-Old Doublewood is a personal favorite. It's also the only distillery in the Highlands that still maintains the "Five Rare Crafts" it always has: homegrown barley, its own malting floor, copper stills, its own on-site cooperage, and a master of malt who is the longest serving in the industry. Since both Glenfiddich and the Balvenie are within walking distance of Dufftown, you can always combine a visit to the two.

Aberlour and Around
THE MACALLAN

Easter Elchies, Aberlour; tel. 01340 318 000; www. themacallan.com; 2.5-hour Discovery Experience £50, 7-course dining £95, drinks extra

Not included in the Malt Whisky trail, but a distillery that really should be visited, is The Macallan, near Aberlour. Apart from the internationally renowned status of this brand—bottles of The Macallan have been known to go for as much as £1.5 million—it has also hugely invested in its visitor experience in recent years, with an award-winning visitor center.

Remarkably for such a big name, The Macallan actually has some of the smallest stills in Speyside, which The Macallan says helps provide the rich, fruity, full-bodied flavors characteristic of The Macallan, which is aged in sherry-seasoned oak casks. It's an intriguing distillery to visit to see first-hand its green ethics in play: Already, 80 percent of its

energy comes from renewable and non-fossil fuel, and it plans to be fully carbon neutral by 2030. In addition, the distillery only uses barley from the UK that meets the Gold standard with SAIP (Sustainable Agriculture Initiative Platform).

Aside from running tours, the distillery also offers some evening dining experiences in its Elchies Brasserie, with seven-course tasting menus. And of course, a wee dram in the Macallan Bar, taking in panoramas of the Speyside Hills, is highly recommended.

CARDHU DISTILLERY

Knockando; tel. 01479 874 635; www.malts.com/ en-row/distilleries/cardhu; 10am-5pm Tues.-Sat.; tours from £15

The Speyside home of one of the world's best-known whisky brands, Johnny Walker, was founded by two women: Helen and Elizabeth Cumming. Cardhu sometimes can be seen for sale as a single malt, but more usually as part of the Johnny Walker blends. The Cardhu Flavour Journey, with tutored tastings of drams and a cocktail, is a good introduction to the distillery. In the small town of Knockando, it's just a 15-minute (10-mile/16-km) drive southwest of the Macallan distillery.

GLEN GRANT

Rothes; tel. 01340 832 118; www.glengrant.com; 10am-3pm Mon.-Sat.; check website for latest prices

At this distillery, you can enjoy a history lesson, whisky tasting, and a garden walk in one afternoon. The Grant brothers, who set up the distillery in 1840, were smugglers turned good—not just that, but James Grant led the Raid on Elgin in 1820, the last major clan revolt, and the family's Highland heritage is celebrated throughout the distillery. It was a later family member (also James Grant, but known as The Major) who introduced the lovely Victorian garden. It's just 20 minutes (11 miles/18 km) north of the Macallan distillery.

Keith
STRATHISLA

Seafield Avenue, Keith; tel. 01542 783 044; www. chivas.com/en-GB/visit-strathisla; 12pm-4:30pm Weds.-Mon.; Stroll of Strathisla £15, Chivas: The Blend £30

The oldest continuously operating distillery in the Scottish Highlands, this distillery, known for its Chivas Regal whisky, first opened in 1786 when the local flax industry began to wane. Today, it offers some interesting variations on the standard tours offered by distilleries, including the Strathisla Stroll (1 hour), in which you'll get a tour of local landmarks as well as the grounds to get a sense of place and its influence on the whisky, and The Blend (1 hour), in which you can blend your own whisky.

Elgin
GLEN MORAY

Bruceland Road, Elgin; tel. 01343 550 900; www. glenmoray.com; tours 9:30am, 11:30am, 1:30pm, 3:30pm Mon.-Sat. Apr.-Oct., only Sat.-Sun. out of season; £7

They have been making whisky at Glen Moray for 120 years, and it's smooth and fruity, an easy-drinking whisky. You'll get to taste two as part of your tour, which will be led by one of the distillers themselves. You'll also get a chance to look inside the warehouses, where the whisky matures.

Forres
BENROMACH

Invererne Road, Forres; tel. 01309 675 968; www. benromach.com; check website for latest prices

One of the few Speyside whiskies you're likely to taste with a smokey character, at Benromach the whisky is handcrafted and distilled in first-fill casks. Tours were paused in 2020-2021 due to the pandemic, but are due to begin again in spring 2022, and even if not, you can always pop into the shop to pick up a bottle.

1: Glenfiddich Distillery **2:** bottles of Glenlivet whisky **3:** Glen Grant **4:** Ballindalloch Castle

OTHER SIGHTS
Dufftown and Around
★ **BALLINDALLOCH CASTLE AND GARDENS**

Ballindalloch; tel. 01807 500 205; www. ballindallochcastle.co.uk; 10am-4pm Sun.-Thurs. Easter-late Sept.; adult £12, child £6, under 5 free

It's quite remarkable really that Speyside is so synonymous with whisky that a castle of this grandeur should go so largely unnoticed. Just a 10-minute drive southwest of Aberlour, Ballindalloch has been continually lived in by the family who founded it: the Macpherson Grants. It originally began life as a relatively modest tower house in 1546 and was significantly extended in the 1800s in the Scottish Baronial style, "an early Victorian confection," as present owner Guy Macpherson-Grant describes it.

At the time of my visit the house was closed for essential interior works, but I found the grounds to be exquisite, with a beautiful walled garden and a rock garden, and walkways bursting with the bright color of rhododendrons, balanced by the less showy lemon-drop laburnums. Even when admiring the castle from outside you can pick up on other details—the pediments on top of the roof, for instance, include the initials of the generations of the family, and above the tower doorway is the Macpherson family's motto: "Touch not the cat bot a glove," meaning, presumably, think twice before meddling in the Macphersons' business. Meanwhile, above this on the doorway is "Ense et Animo," the more restrained Grant side of the family's motto, "in sword and in spirit."

The house is now open again and you can take a self-guided tour through the dining room, the drawing room, the smoking room, and the library, plus some of the old bedrooms, and try to piece together the family's story by the portraits on the wall. I'm told the tours take about 40 minutes, but you should leave at least an extra hour to explore the gardens.

KEITH AND DUFFTOWN RAILWAY

Dufftown Station; https://keith-dufftown-railway.co.uk; departures 10:30am, 1:30pm, 3:30pm; single: adult £7, child £3.50; return adult £11, child £5

Clattering along an 11-mile (18-km) stretch of railway between Dufftown and Keith, also known as the "Whisky Line," this two-carriage diesel train will take you past fields of barley integral to the area's whisky production, through deep glens and past forests and green undulating hills (40 minutes each way). The pandemic has left the already volunteer-run railway vulnerable to closure, so if you do enjoy your trip, make sure you donate to secure its future.

Aberlour and Around
SPEYSIDE COOPERAGE

Dufftown Road, Craigellachie; tel. 01340 871108; www.speysidecooperage.co.uk; tours on the hour 9am-3pm Mon.-Fri.; £4 per person

An often-overlooked aspect of whisky production is cooperage—the art of making the barrels for maturing, which includes shaping, shaving, and charring the casks—a skill that has been used for over 5,000 years. During these 45-minute tours you'll watch a 4D video before going through to a viewing gallery where you can see coopers at work.

Elgin
ELGIN CATHEDRAL

King Street, Elgin; tel. 1343 547 171; www.historicenvironment.scot/visit-a-place/places/elgin-cathedral; 10am-4pm daily; free

Scotland is full of majestic ruins, it's true, but the remains of this 13th-century cathedral are among the most highly regarded. Like many of the stately ruins of religious builds you see scattered around Scotland, the Elgin Cathedral met its maker, so to speak, after the Protestant Reformation in the 16th century, but became an attraction again in the 19th century, when tourist interest in Scotland was on the increase.

The ruins have numerous points of interest, including its beautiful, intricate west front, with glassless windows now framing only sky;

an almost life-size statue of a bishop in the nave; and, in the graveyard, the tallest gravestone in Scotland, standing at 16 feet (5 m) high. You can climb the towers of the chapter house and west front for wonderful views, and there's a shop and information point where you can learn more about the history of the cathedral.

Forres
DALLAS DHU DISTILLERY

Mannachie Road, Forres; tel. 01309 676 548; www.historicenvironment.scot/visit-a-place/places/dallas-dhu-historic-distillery; 9:30am-5:30pm daily Apr.-Sept., 10am-4pm Sat.-Weds. Oct.-Mar.; adult £6, concessions £4.80, child £3.60, under 5 free

Though it's no longer a working distillery, Dallas Dhu is now open as a heritage site as part of the Malt Whisky Trail. Here, you can see how whisky was made in the 1900s, including a visit to the malt barn and the kiln where the peat was once dried. This is a good alternative to a whisky tour if you're traveling with children.

HIKING AND CYCLING

To hire a bike in Speyside, there's **Outfit Moray** in Lossiemouth, on the Moray coast (Shore Street, Lossiemouth; tel. 01343 549 571; https://outfitmoray.com; 9am-5pm Mon.-Fri.; from £20 a day), while in Grantown-on-Spey, **Basecamp Bike** hires out mountain bikes (5 The Square, Grantown-on-Spey; tel. 01479 870 050; www.basecampmtb.com/bike-hire; 9:30am-5:30pm Tues.-Fri. and 9:30am-1:30pm Sat.; mountain bikes from £25 per day, £15 for children, e-bike £50 per day).

SPEYSIDE WAY

Distance: *85 miles (137 km)*
Time: *5-6 days*
Trailhead: *Newtonmore*
Information and Maps: *www.speysideway.org*

This long-distance route, for walkers, cyclists, even horseriders, largely follows the path of the River Spey, all the way from Newtonmore, on the edge of the Cairngorms, to Buckie on the Moray Firth coast. Of course, en route, it passes through Speyside, where you can stop to tour some of the distilleries, and there's no need to do it all: You could just choose a section.

Though cyclists can follow the route quite happily from Aviemore to Nethy Bridge, you are asked to switch on to the B9102 between Cromdale and Ballindalloch. At Ballindalloch you can rejoin the route to Fochabers. The Speyside Way website seems a little outdated, but Harvey Maps (www.harveymaps.co.uk) shows the whole route on one double-sided folding map.

BIKE GLENLIVET

Glenlivet Bike Trails, Kirkmichael, Ballindalloch; tel. 07963 217 793; www.glenlivetestate.co.uk; bike hire 10am-4pm daily July-Aug., 10am-4pm Thurs.-Sun. May-June and Sept.; half day adult £18, under 16 £10, full day adult £25, under 16 £15, electric bike £40 full day

Single-track dirt trails through dense forest with steep declines make mountain biking on the Glenlivet Estate a lot of fun. There are three main trails: the blue route (good for beginners, but also more experienced cyclists, as there is some climbing and some downhill for amazing views), the slightly more challenging red trail, and most difficult orange trail, which has been labeled "the best freeride trail in Scotland," with lots of jumps and berms. Bikes can be hired from the Glenlivet café May-September.

EVENTS
DUFFTOWN HIGHLAND GAMES

Mortlach School Field, Hill Street, Dufftown; www.dufftownhighlandgames.com; late July; adult £8, concessions £4, under 5 free

There were no Highland games in here in 2021, but organizers are hoping 2022's event will take place. Among the usual collection of piping and dancing competitions, the Dufftown event also includes a hilltop race over 14 miles (23 km), which can be fun to watch.

SPIRIT OF SPEYSIDE WHISKY FESTIVAL

Various locations, Speyside; tel. 07789 671 635; www.spiritofspeyside.com; May; prices vary from free to £70 for behind-the-scenes tours and special tastings

The largest whisky festival in the world has been held virtually since the pandemic outbreak, with the exception of its main spring event, which moved to autumn in 2021. Hopefully the whisky festival will return to its usual spring slot in 2022, when visitors can expect lots of tastings and immersive events in Speyside. There is also now a sister event held each September, **Distilled Food & Drink,** where whisky distillers, gin distillers, and various brewers and food producers all come together under one roof. Keep an eye on the website for more details.

SHOPPING
Elgin
JOHNSTON'S OF ELGIN

New Mill; tel. 01343 554 099; www.johnstonsofelgin.com/retail/visit-us/elgin-mill; 9am-5pm daily

Whisky isn't the only thing they make in Speyside. Johnston's of Elgin also opened its first mill in Elgin in 1797 and very quickly became known for its Estate Tweeds, popularized by Queen Victoria, which it still makes today. You can visit the mill and buy some beautifully crafted wools or cashmeres.

Forres
LOGIE STEADING

Logie Estate; tel. 01309 611 378; www.logie.co.uk; 10am-5pm daily

This collection of art galleries, independent book and antiques shops, craft studios and cafés are set in a 1920s model farm steading in a series of sandstone buildings, in the Findhorn Valley. You could happily spend an afternoon here, browsing the shops and enjoying a nice lunch. There are also good walks along the Findhorn River and a playground for the kids. Keep an eye out for occasional events and pop-ups.

FOOD

Aberlour and Around
★ TOOTS AT THE TRAIN STATION

51 New Street, Rothes; tel. 01340 832 200; www.stationhotelspeyside.com; 12pm-2pm and 5pm-8:30pm daily; entrées £7

This small restaurant with lots of dark wood cabinetry, scores of whisky bottles behind the glass, and even its own ale, is a good dining option in the little town of Rothes, not far from the Glen Grant Distillery. The menu consists largely of steaks, seafood, and salads, with all the produce sustainably sourced—the restaurant manager often brings in vegetables and herbs from his own garden.

Keith and Around
GORDON CASTLE WALLED GARDEN

Fochabers; tel. 01343 612 317; www.gordoncastle. co.uk/cafe; lunch 11am-2:30pm, afternoon tea 2pm-4pm; cakes £2.75

This café in the grounds of Gordon Castle, in north Speyside, specializes in farm-to-table dining, with most of the produce being grown in the kitchen gardens. Think homemade soup, well-filled sandwiches, pies, and very good coffee. After lunch, walk round the walled garden—one of the largest and most impressive in the whole of Britain.

Elgin and Around
THE BAKEHOUSE

91-92 Findhorn; tel. 01309 691-826; www. bakehousecafe.co.uk; 10am-5pm Mon.-Thurs., 10am-7pm Fri.-Sat., 10am-3pm Sun., pizza nights 5pm-7pm Fri.-Sat.; bread loaves from £2, pizza from £8.50

In the picturesque coastal village of Findhorn, you'll find this whole foods café and market, which has quickly established itself at the heart of the local community. The regular market, which sprang up in the middle of lockdown, is here to stay and mainly sells local fruit and veg, complemented by freshly baked bread and other goodies every day. Each Friday and Saturday evening the café also runs pizza nights—call ahead to book.

ACCOMMODATIONS

Dufftown and Around
CASTLE ON THE HILL

Parkhead Steading, by Auchindoun Castle; tel. 01340 821 248; www.castleonthehill.co.uk; Bothy £110 per night, Byre £130 per night

No, you will not be staying in the ruined castle, which is opened to the elements, but in one of two cottages in converted barns with gorgeous views of the castle, just a short drive from Dufftown. There's the cozy Bothy, a two-bed apartment (sleeps 4) with nice touches, such as a window seat and a balcony, and the Byre, which comes with a wood-burning stove, underfloor heating, and a private sunken seating area with firepit outside.

Aberlour and Around
★ CRAIGELLACHIE LODGE

Craighellachie; tel. 01340 881 900 or 07514 179 035; https://craigellachielodge.co.uk; £130 d

On arrival in Craigellachie Lodge, there's a small, cozy bar to the right and the dining room to the left. Rooms are large with Roberts radios, robes and slippers, and huge beds with plump cushions and expensive sheets. It's designed to make you feel relaxed—with seats arranged around the window for garden views, and a huge bathroom with separate shower and standalone bath. There's a tight left turning that's hard to spot as you approach this guest house from the cooperage—the signage is due to be improved—and then a steep gravel track up to the house, which feels very private.

Keith and Around
BRAEHEAD GLAMPING AND CAMPING

Firwood Lodge, Braehead; tel. 01343 880 219 or 07944 579 776; www.braeheadglamping.com; shepherd's hut £80 per night

With a mix of nine wooden glamping pods, one yurt (with more planned), and a shepherd's hut, this is a good base for outdoorsy types. The Bothy Barn provides a communal area for cooking and dining, with log burner and clothes drying (much needed after a wet day outside). Each pod also comes with a firepit, and there are disposable BBQs and extra duvets available. There are also three tent pitches available for the hardcore campers.

INFORMATION AND SERVICES

The main **Malt Whisky Trail** website (https://maltwhiskytrail.com) is a great resource for planning your itinerary before travel, as is **Visit Moray Speyside** (https://moray-speyside.com). Once here, there is a **visitor center** in Glenlivet (www.glenlivetestate.co.uk/visitor-attractions/visitor-centres). Unfortunately, the Speyside Visitor Centre (www.speysidevisitorcentre.scot) has remained closed throughout the pandemic but with luck it will open again soon.

GETTING THERE

Speyside is easily accessed from either Inverness or Aberdeen airports. From Inverness Airport, it's 60 miles (97 km) to Dufftown, a journey time of 1 hour 20 minutes, following the A9 south and then joining the A95 heading east at Carrbridge. From Aberdeen International Airport to Dufftown it's just one hour (47 miles/76 km), taking the A96 northwest from the city and joining the A920 at Huntly.

The nearest stations to Speyside are Aviemore, Keith, and Elgin. From Inverness, there are direct trains to Aviemore (36 minutes; £13.80 single), Elgin (40 minutes; £14.10 single), and Keith (1 hour; £19.30 single). Meanwhile, Aberdeen has direct trains to Elgin (1 hour 28 minutes; £9.40) and Keith (1 hour 8 minutes; £9.40 single). Trains from Aberdeen to Aviemore change at Inverness. All trains run by Scotrail (www.scotrail.co.uk).

Stagecoach (www.stagecoachbus.com) runs several buses through the region, connecting the various whisky towns, including the no. 36 (which stops at Elgin, Rothes, Craigellachie, Aberlour and Dufftown), the no. 34/34X (which connects Aviemore to Grantown-on-Spey), and the no. 10, which connects Aberdeen to Inverness with stops in Fores, Elgin, and Keith.

Glasgow

It's not as visually arresting as Edinburgh, but what Glasgow lacks in old-world charm it makes up for with culture, from its exceptional museums (which are largely free) to its architecture—the handsome red sandstone buildings of the Victorian era, and the Art Nouveau-inspired "Glasgow Style" developed in the early 20th century by Charles Rennie Mackintosh. As Scotland's largest city, Glasgow also has one of the best shopping scenes in Britain and has world-leading live music venues. It is a UNESCO City of Music, after all.

Glasgow is a master of reinvention. The city experienced economic turmoil in the 1930s, followed by the virtual collapse of its shipbuilding industry in the 1960s, and the closure of its steelworks, coal mines, and factories in the 1970s, causing unemployment levels to escalate, but Glasgow wasn't down for too long. By the 1980s the city had recovered

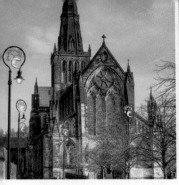

Highlights

Look for ★ to find recommended
sights, activities, dining, and lodging.

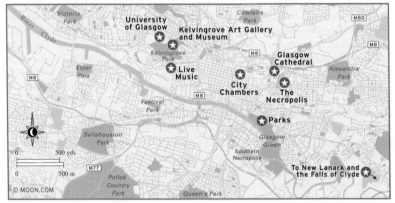

★ **City Chambers:** This elaborate palazzo with its white marble staircase gives the Vatican a run for its money, and its free tours are one of Glasgow's best-kept secrets (page 199).

★ **Glasgow Cathedral:** Visit Glasgow's oldest building—the finest large medieval church to survive the Scottish Reformation with its roof intact (page 204).

★ **The Necropolis:** Along with your visit to the cathedral, don't miss the chance to wander around this elegiac city of the dead (page 206).

★ **University of Glasgow:** Tour this grand neo-Gothic university, said to be J. K. Rowling's inspiration for Hogwarts, and poke through the treasures at the Hunterian Museum (page 207).

★ **Kelvingrove Art Gallery and Museum:** Set in a stunning late-Victorian building that looks more like a palace than a museum, this treasury of Scottish art and natural history is a must for any visit (page 210).

★ **Parks:** Explore the hidden gardens, open spaces, and woodland walks that give Glasgow its nickname "Dear Green Place" and find your own quiet spot (page 214).

★ **Live Music:** From world-class concert halls to underground clubs jammed with up-and-coming bands and low-key pub sessions, you haven't experienced Glasgow until you've heard it sing (page 231).

★ **New Lanark and the Falls of Clyde:** Just 30 miles (48 km) out of the city centre, this World Heritage site is a perfectly preserved mill village with pretty riverside walks through a wildlife reserve to spectacular waterfalls (page 240).

to such an extent that it was named the first European City of Culture in 1990, and UK City of Architecture & Design in 1999.

Today, it is an exciting, innovative metropolis where the old warehouses of the 18th-century Merchant City have been turned into swish restaurants and bars, and the once down-trodden East End is emerging as a hipster haven. In the south of the city you can see hairy coos (Highland cattle), and no trip to Glasgow (or Glesga as locals would have it) is complete without a visit to the city's West End—home to some of its best historic attractions as well as a spirited student population and traditional pubs, where you can discover for yourself why Glasgow is considered the friendliest city in the world. If all that liveliness has taken its toll, then take the train out of the city to the 230-year-old World Heritage site of New Lanark, a conservation mill village surrounded by fertile woodland that is home to the cascading Falls of Clyde.

Glasgow is a lot more down to earth than Edinburgh (many Glaswegians describe Edinburgh as "Aw fur coat an nae knickers," which loosely means that despite appearances Edinburgh is no classier than Glasgow), and some visitors can be put off by Glasgow's grittier, post-industrial look. But it is the city's working-class roots that give it a steely determination that ensures it is never down at heel for too long, and you're unlikely to ever encounter a more authentic city.

ORIENTATION

Built on a grid system, Glasgow's city centre, around Buchanan Street and the rest of the Style Mile that bleeds into the Merchant City, is surprisingly easy to navigate. And while many of the central attractions can be explored on foot or bike, the brilliant Subway system connects you to other parts of the city in mere minutes, too.

City Centre

When most people talk about the city centre, they are referring to the streets north of the River Clyde as far as the M8, which curves around the north and western fringes. The eastern boundary is marked by the Saltmarket and High Street. The city's principal plaza, **George Square,** is Glasgow's civic heart and home to the majestic **City Chambers.** It's a good place to start your exploration of Glasgow, with most of the city centre's main attractions—the **Style Mile, Mackintosh at the Willow,** and the **Gallery of Modern Art (GOMA)**—lying to the west of George Square.

Merchant City

The sophisticated Merchant City cuts through the city centre, with chic restaurants and bars that buzz with after-work drinkers and smartly dressed visitors any night of the week. Amid its cobbled lanes, which roughly speaking stretch west from the High Street all the way to Queen Street, from below George Square and as far south as Trongate, you'll also find some incredible architecture and some real hidden gems, such as the **Britannica Panopticon,** the oldest surviving music hall in the world.

East End

To the east of the city centre, from the High Street on, you'll find the medieval heart of Glasgow, home to some of its oldest surviving buildings, including the indomitable **Glasgow Cathedral** and **Provand's Lordship.** For generations, this was one of Glasgow's more run-down and poorer districts, but flickers of gentrification can be seen, where well-preserved tenement buildings meet some very good restaurants. Southwest of here you can visit the **Barras Market,** where working-class Glasgow can be seen in all its colorful and brash glory, as well as the famous **Barrowland Ballroom.** South

---

Previous: Kelvingrove Art Gallery and Museum; Glasgow Cathedral; People's Palace and Winter Gardens glasshouse.

again, along the banks of the Clyde, you will find **Glasgow Green,** the city's oldest park.

West End

Everything west of Charing Cross is considered the West End, and it would be a shame to visit Glasgow and not venture west at least once. It's here that you will find some of the city's biggest historic charms, such as the magnificent **Kelvingrove Art Gallery and Museum** and the Gothic revival allure and medieval mystery of the **University of Glasgow,** both of which sit around the leafy edges of **Kelvingrove Park.**

In **Finnieston,** a neighborhood that sits between the city centre and Kelvingrove Park, there is an ever-changing food and drink scene, and who knows what bargains you might happen upon in the vintage shops? However, it's **Hillside,** the trendy heart of the West End, just north of Kelvingrove, where you'll find most of the fun bars and lots of independent shops along the main drag of Byres Road. **Clydeside,** on the northern bank of the River Clyde, forms another district of the West End, just southwest of Finnieston. In recent years it has benefited from regeneration, which began with the building of the now iconic **Riverside Museum** in 2011.

Southside

On the south of the River Clyde, this area is gradually becoming more appealing to visitors. Amid the streets of tightly packed tenement buildings, there is plenty of green space, a buoyant café scene, and lots of cultural and heritage attractions, including Charles Rennie Mackintosh's **House for an Art Lover** and **Pollok House.** Several bus routes serve the Southside from the city centre, or you can jump on a bike and be there in no time.

PLANNING YOUR TIME

You need to allow at least two days to see the main attractions in Glasgow—three or four if you want to venture to some of its cooler, less central neighborhoods and sights. If you only have a day, a stroll through the **Merchant City** from **George Square** is a must, as is visiting some of the major Mackintosh buildings, such as the restored **Mackintosh at the Willow** on Sauchiehall Street or **The Lighthouse.** You won't want to miss the **Gallery of Modern Art** either, if only to take a photo of the cone-headed Duke of Wellington statue, an example of Scottish self-determination that won through. The **hop-on hop-off bus** is great for taking in the main attractions if you're short of time, including the **cathedral, Necropolis, Riverside Museum,** and **Kelvingrove Art Gallery and Museum,** though you won't have much time to explore them in a day.

For two days or more, spend one day in the city centre, incorporating the cathedral and Necropolis in the East End, and then give yourself a full day in the West End, so you have plenty of time to look at specific exhibitions and gallery rooms in the Kelvingrove, as well as the **Hunterian,** the **University of Glasgow,** and some of the area's very cool thrift stores. If you're in Glasgow a little longer, chill-out in the Southside or take a nature walk in the north, but not before you've visited the famous **Barras Market** over east.

Glasgow

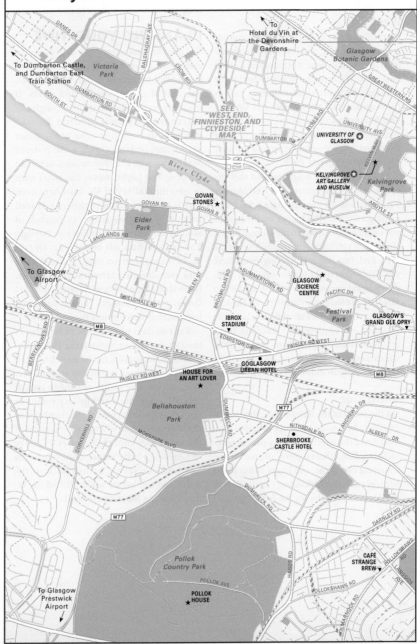

To Dumbarton Castle, and Dumbarton East Train Station

To Hotel du Vin at the Devonshire Gardens

Glasgow Botanic Gardens

DANES DR

Victoria Park

BALSHAGRAY AVE

CROW RD

DUMBARTON RD

SOUTH ST

GREAT WESTERN RD

BYRES RD

UNIVERSITY AVE

SEE "WEST END, FINNIESTON, AND CLYDESIDE" MAP

DUMBARTON RD

UNIVERSITY OF GLASGOW

KELVIN WAY

River Clyde

KELVINGROVE ART GALLERY AND MUSEUM

Kelvingrove Park

ARGYLE ST

GOVAN STONES

GOVAN RD

GOVAN R

Elder Park

LANGLANDS RD

To Glasgow Airport

SHIELDHALL RD

HELEN ST

BROOMLOAN RD

SUMMERTOWN RD

GLASGOW SCIENCE CENTRE

PACIFIC DR

Festival Park

GLASGOW'S GRAND OLE OPRY

M8

IBROX STADIUM

EDMISTON DR

PAISLEY RD WEST

M8

BERRYKNOWES RD

GOGLASGOW URBAN HOTEL

PAISLEY RD WEST

HOUSE FOR AN ART LOVER

DUMBRECK RD

M77

CORKERHILL RD

Bellahouston Park

MOSSPARK BLVD

NITHSDALE RD

ST. ANDREW'S DR

ALBERT DR

SHERBROOKE CASTLE HOTEL

DUMBRECK RD

M77

DARNLEY RD

POLLOKSHAWS RD

HAGGS RD

CAFÉ STRANGE BREW

LANGSIDE AVE

Pollok Country Park

POLLOK AVE

POLLOKSHAWS RD

To Glasgow Prestwick Airport

POLLOK HOUSE

KILMARNOCK RD

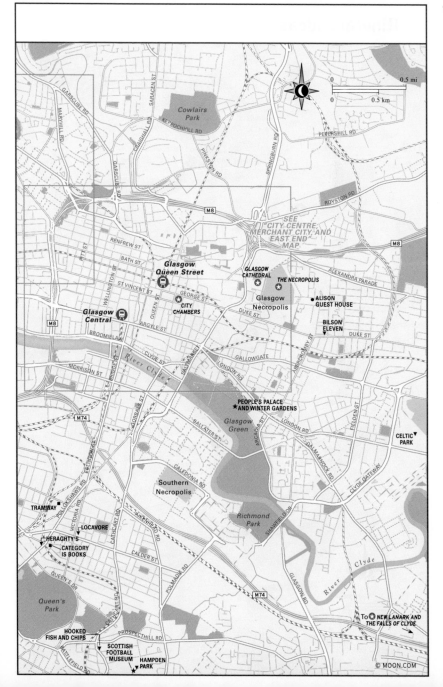

© MOON.COM

Itinerary Ideas

GLASGOW

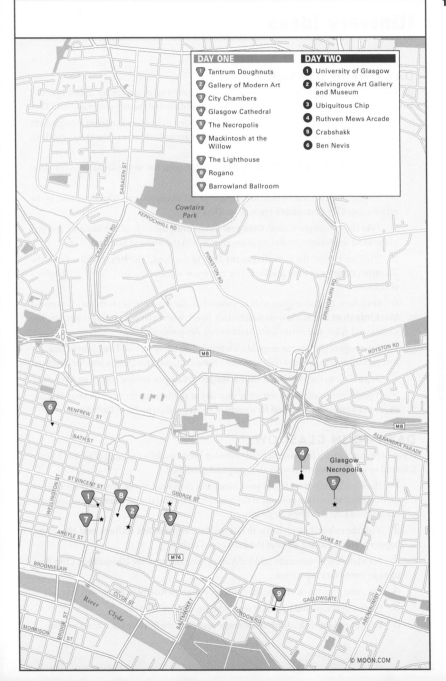

DAY ONE

1. Tantrum Doughnuts
2. Gallery of Modern Art
3. City Chambers
4. Glasgow Cathedral
5. The Necropolis
6. Mackintosh at the Willow
7. The Lighthouse
8. Rogano
9. Barrowland Ballroom

DAY TWO

1. University of Glasgow
2. Kelvingrove Art Gallery and Museum
3. Ubiquitous Chip
4. Ruthven Mews Arcade
5. Crabshakk
6. Ben Nevis

GLASGOW

© MOON.COM

Itinerary Ideas

DAY ONE IN GLASGOW

It's difficult to do Glasgow justice in a day, but you'll have a lot of fun trying. Spend your day visiting some of the major sights, mostly clustered in and around the city centre and East End.

1 Start your day by picking up a high-carb breakfast to go from **Tantrum Doughnuts** in the city centre. Their doughnuts are the perfect accompaniment to the shop's excellent coffee.

2 Pass by the **Gallery of Modern Art** and doff your hat to the Duke of Wellington outside.

3 It's just a block north of here to George Square, where you can take a free tour of the ostentatious **City Chambers** (daily at 10:30am).

4 Take the 15-minute walk to **Glasgow Cathedral,** the city's oldest building and one of the most impressive pre-Reformation churches in the whole of Scotland.

5 Stroll up behind the cathedral to the "city of the dead," the **Necropolis.** From the Victorian cemetery's lofty position, you can enjoy some of the best views of Glasgow's skyline.

6 From here, it's a 30-minute walk or a short bus ride (no. 38 or 57) to the newly restored **Mackintosh at the Willow** on Sauchiehall Street, where you can eat finger sandwiches, scones, and cakes and sip tea from Mackintosh-designed crockery.

7 For more insight into the mark Mackintosh left on Glasgow, visit **The Lighthouse,** his first public commission and now Scotland's National Centre for Design and Architecture.

8 Step back into the 1930s for dinner at **Rogano,** Glasgow's oldest surviving restaurant.

9 If you're not totally worn out from your day of sightseeing, then put on your dancing shoes and head to the East End for a night of revelry at **Barrowland Ballroom.**

DAY TWO IN GLASGOW

If you have a second day in Glasgow, head to the hip West End for a morning of art and history followed by an afternoon of vintage shopping and good food.

1 Have a leisurely breakfast at your hotel, and then head to the West End for the late morning tour around the grounds of the neo-Gothic **University of Glasgow,** which some say inspired J. K. Rowling's Hogwarts.

2 Visit the cultural powerhouse that is the **Kelvingrove Art Gallery and Museum,** hopefully even catching some of the daily organ recital.

3 For a late lunch, venture to cobbled Ashton Lane and see if the **Ubiquitous Chip** lives up to its exemplary reputation.

4 For some post-lunch vintage shopping, pop into the **Ruthven Mews Arcade.**

5 Enjoy a delicious and laid-back seafood dinner at **Crabshakk.**

6 End your night with a traditional music session at the **Ben Nevis** across the road.

Sights

CITY CENTRE
★ City Chambers
George Square; tel. 0141 287 4018; www.glasgow.gov. uk; 9am-5pm Mon.-Fri., tours 10:30am and 2:30pm Mon.-Fri.; free

Step inside this magnificent building on George Square for a taste of the Victorians' penchant for opulence. Built to house the city's council chambers following the closure of its former tollbooth, it is at times excessively ornate to modern eyes, but to 19th-century society it was deemed absolutely necessary to showcase the wealth and power of Glasgow to the rest of the world.

The building, which was opened by Queen Victoria in 1888, is the creation of William Young and came at great expense—at £500k it far exceeded the original £100k budget, but you don't have to look far to see where the money was spent. In the foyer there is a mosaic floor decorated with the Glasgow Coat of Arms, which depicts the miracles of Glasgow's patron saint, St. Mungo (versions of which you will see throughout the city), while the ceiling here is embellished with 1.5 million half-inch (12.7-mm) Oppenheimer ceramic tiles.

The three-story Italian white marble staircase is the building's real draw. The largest of its kind in the western world, it has often stood in for the Vatican on-screen. All of the above can be explored on your own during council opening hours if you're short of time, but much better is to join one of the two daily **free tours** run by knowledgeable guides, who will explain the history of the building, tell tales on some of its famous past guests, and shed a little insight into the workings of the city council. Tours last about 45 minutes.

In the actual chamber itself (which you can only visit on a tour) you can sit in councilors' chairs or have your photo taken in the seat of the Lord Provost—the city's elected figurehead. Look carefully by the seats in the chamber, and you will see a small hole on each shelf in front. For many years the council upheld a tradition of holding a flower in each one when the council was in session. One story behind the flower is that when Queen Victoria came into the chamber as part of the opening ceremony, there were some members of the public here, and she is said to have preferred the smell of the flowers to them.

The **Banqueting Hall** is enormous, with many paintings on the wall, an abundance of leather-embossed gold leaf, and huge chandeliers. It was in this room that Billy Connolly was given the Freedom of the City of Glasgow, as was Nelson Mandela when he visited in 1993. Overall, it is a remarkable place. The tours are delivered with wit and panache, and everywhere you look there is another stunning detail to take in. It really is a work of art.

Centre for Contemporary Arts
350 Sauchiehall Street; tel. 0141 352 4900; www. cca-glasgow.com; 11am-12am Tues.-Sat.

Set in an 1868 building by Glasgow's greatest neoclassical architect, Alexander "Greek" Thomson, it's always worth seeing what's on at this arts center during your stay. Its diverse program includes photography shows, music recitals, short films, and carefully curated art exhibitions, and it is frequented by high-brow residents in the know.

MERCHANT CITY
The Lighthouse
11 Mitchell Lane; tel. 0141 276 5365; www. thelighthouse.co.uz; 10:30am-5pm Mon.-Sat., 12pm-5pm Sun.; free

Designed by Charles Rennie Mackintosh, this building once housed the *Glasgow Herald* newspaper and is today home to Scotland's National Centre for Design and Architecture (though it has remained closed throughout the pandemic). It takes its name from the tall tower that glowers out over the city and is seen as a beacon of Scotland's creative industries.

City Centre, Merchant City, and East End

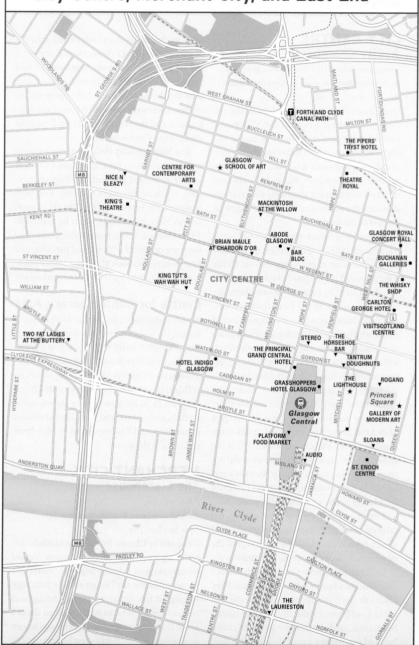

FORTH AND CLYDE CANAL PATH

WEST GRAHAM ST

BUCCLEUCH ST

THE PIPERS' TRYST HOTEL

MILTON ST

PORT DUNDAS RD

MAITLAND ST

SAUCHIEHALL ST

HILL ST

GARNET ST

GLASGOW SCHOOL OF ART

CENTRE FOR CONTEMPORARY ARTS

NICE N SLEAZY

BERKELEY ST

RENFREW ST

THEATRE ROYAL

HOPE ST

KING'S THEATRE

KENT RD

BATH ST

PITT ST

BLYTHSWOOD ST

MACKINTOSH AT THE WILLOW

SAUCHIEHALL ST

GLASGOW ROYAL CONCERT HALL

ABODE GLASGOW

BRIAN MAULE AT CHARDON D'OR

BAR BLOC

BATH ST

BUCHANAN GALLERIES

ST VINCENT ST

HOLLAND ST

W REGENT ST

WEST NILE ST

THE WHISKY SHOP

KING TUT'S WAH WAH HUT

DOUGLAS ST

CITY CENTRE

W GEORGE ST

CARLTON GEORGE HOTEL

WILLIAM ST

ST VINCENT ST

HOPE ST

RENFIELD ST

VISITSCOTLAND ICENTRE

LITTLE ST

ARGYLE ST

BOTHWELL ST

N CAMPBELL ST

WELLINGTON ST

THE HORSESHOE BAR

TWO FAT LADIES AT THE BUTTERY

STEREO

TANTRUM DOUGHNUTS

CLYDESIDE EXPRESSWAY

WATERLOO ST

THE PRINCIPAL GRAND CENTRAL HOTEL

GORDON ST

HOTEL INDIGO GLASGOW

CADOGAN ST

GRASSHOPPERS HOTEL GLASGOW

THE LIGHTHOUSE

ROGANO

HYDEPARK ST

HOLM ST

BROWN ST

JAMES WATT ST

Princes Square

Glasgow Central

GALLERY OF MODERN ART

ARGYLE ST

MITCHELL ST

QUEEN ST

PLATFORM FOOD MARKET

SLOANS

ANDERSTON QUAY

AUDIO

MIDLAND ST

JAMAICA ST

ST. ENOCH CENTRE

HOWARD ST

River Clyde

CLYDE ST

CLYDE PLACE

PAISLEY RD

CARLTON PLACE

KINGSTON ST

COMMERCE ST

BRIDGE ST

OXFORD ST

NELSON ST

WALLACE ST

WEST ST

TRADESTON ST

CENTRE ST

THE LAURIESTON

GORBALS ST

NORFOLK ST

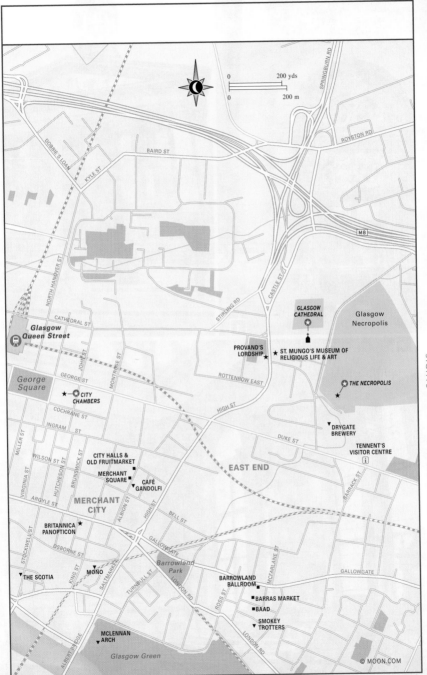

0   200 yds
0   200 m

SPRINGBURN RD

DOBBIE'S LOAN

KYLE ST

BAIRD ST

ROYSTON RD

NORTH HANOVER ST

M8

STIRLING RD

CASTLE ST

CATHEDRAL ST

GLASGOW CATHEDRAL

Glasgow Necropolis

Glasgow Queen Street

PROVAND'S LORDSHIP

ST. MUNGO'S MUSEUM OF RELIGIOUS LIFE & ART

JOHN ST

MONTROSE ST

GEORGE ST

ROTTENROW EAST

George Square

★ CITY CHAMBERS

★ THE NECROPOLIS

COCHRANE ST

HIGH ST

INGRAM   ST

DUKE ST

MILLER ST

WILSON ST

BRUNSWICK ST

CITY HALLS & OLD FRUITMARKET

DRYGATE BREWERY

TENNENT'S VISITOR CENTRE

EAST END

VIRGINIA ST

HUTCHESON ST

ALBION ST

MERCHANT SQUARE

CAFÈ GANDOLFI

ARGYLE ST

MERCHANT CITY

HIGH ST

BELL ST

BARRACK ST

STOCKWELL ST

BRITANNICA PANOPTICON

OSBORNE ST

GALLOWGATE

KING ST

SALTMARKET

Barrowland Park

MCFARLANE ST

GALLOWGATE

THE SCOTIA

MONO

TURNBULL ST

LONDON RD

BARROWLAND BALLROOM

ROSS ST

BARRAS MARKET

BAAD

SMOKEY TROTTERS

MCLENNAN ARCH

ALBERT BRIDGE

Glasgow Green

LONDON RD

© MOON.COM

City Centre Mural Trail

www.citycentremuraltrail.co.uk; open 24/7; free

One great way to see the city is to follow the mural trail, where you can see colorful and often fun street art round many a corner; it may just be the first official trail of its kind in the world. The murals have helped rejuvenate the city and add splashes of color and humor to vacant buildings.

THE ROUTE

The full route covers almost 6 miles (9.6 km), from the cathedral in the East End through to the M8 on the edge of the West End, and from the banks of the River Clyde in the south of the city centre, right up to Cowcaddens at the north of the city. It includes 29 pieces, so it might be a bit much for an afternoon, but there is no reason you can't split it up over a couple of days. Many of the most famous pieces of graffiti can be found in the city centre, and plotting a route to take them in (along with breaks for refreshments or other sightseeing) is a great way to orient yourself, especially if you like street art. Download a map from the website, or simply let your eye guide you as you wander around the city centre.

HIGHLIGHTS

Locals have their favorites, but must-sees include the **Fellow Glasgow Residents** mural (on Ingram Street), which transformed a run-down car park into something quite beautiful, and the famous **Glasgow Panda.** The black and white animal brings smiles to all who search him out in a secret corner on Gordon Lane, just off Buchanan Street, and is born out of the joke that there are more pandas in Scotland than Conservative MPs (which though not strictly true at the moment, may be again soon). And make sure you visit each of the three murals added to celebrate the 75th birthday of one of Glasgow's favorite exports, the Big Yin, Billy Connolly, which depict the comedian at different stages of his career and can be seen at Osborne Street, Dixon Street, and Gallowgate.

Though sections of the building are sometimes closed off for public functions, on the whole The Lighthouse is one big creative space where you are free to wander. The permanent **Mackintosh Interpretation Centre** tells the story of the building, Mackintosh's part in it, and how it was transformed into what you see today. A highlight of the building is undoubtedly the exposed stonework of the **tower,** which can be ascended via a dizzying spiral staircase. At the top is an external viewing platform where you stand beneath the ogee arch of the roof. To access the tower stairs, go past the Mackintosh Interpretation Centre. The indoor viewing platform on floor 6 has floor-to-ceiling windows and is also worth a gander. If you're lucky someone may even be playing the piano as you take in the city views.

Gallery of Modern Art (GOMA)

Royal Exchange Square; tel. 0141 287 3050; www. glasgowlife.org.uk/museums/venues/gallery-of-modern-art-goma; 10am-5pm Mon.-Thurs. and Sat., 11am-5pm Fri. and Sun.; free

Housed in the former mansion of one of Glasgow's richest Tobacco Lords (wealthy merchants and slave traders), William Cunninghame, this contemporary art gallery is sometimes maligned for offering style over substance. Nevertheless, it is popular with locals, and with four galleries, a café, and a shop, it is a good place to while away a couple of hours. In particular, it is a good place to see works by the "New Glasgow Boys"—a generation of figurative painters who studied at the Glasgow School of Art in the 1980s and whose

---

1: the entrance to Glasgow City Chambers
2: Gallery of Modern Art **3:** council chamber, City Chambers

work tends to focus on the working-class side of Glasgow.

Truth be told, though, many people who head to GOMA don't actually come inside at all. Instead, they are drawn to the **statue of the Duke of Wellington** outside, which is distinctive because the Duke is wearing a bright traffic cone on his head. Of course, this wasn't the intention of the sculptor, Carlo Marochetti. The cone appeared as part of a student prank in the 1980s; despite repeated efforts to remove it, it was always returned, so much so that the council gave up (there was even a popular online campaign to keep it). And so, it remains one of the most photographed spots in the whole of the city and a sign of the subversive nature of some residents. You'll even find it on postcards around Glasgow.

Britannica Panopticon

*117 Trongate, 1st Floor; tel. 0141 553 0840; www.
britanniapanopticon.org; tours 12pm-5pm Tues.-Sat.;
free*

This beautiful building on Trongate, with arched windows supported by columns, is home to one of the oldest music halls in the world. It's where Stan Laurel (of Laurel and Hardy fame) made his stage debut. Pop in to have a look or a drink at the bar, or talk to the friendly volunteers who will tell you about how audiences would cram into the hall in the Victorian era, armed with old turnips and other vegetables, ready to throw at performers who didn't have them rolling in the aisles. There are also occasional cabaret and comedy shows that really bring the venue to life, though throwing things these days is strictly forbidden.

EAST END
★ Glasgow Cathedral

*Castle Street; tel. 0141 552 8198; www.
glasgowcathedral.org; 10am-4pm Mon.-Sat.
(closed for lunch 1pm-2pm) and 1pm-4pm Sun.; free
(donations welcome)*

To the east of the city centre, the mighty Glasgow Cathedral, known by many names—the High Kirk of Glasgow, St. Kentigern's, and most affectionately, St Mungo's after the patron saint of Glasgow, who is believed to have built a church on this very site—has been a place of worship for more than 800 years. The first stone of the cathedral was laid in 1136 and dedicated to King David I, with the current building consecrated in 1197.

It is considered the best preserved large medieval church in Scotland, after surviving the turbulent Scottish Reformation remarkably intact. Indeed, it is the only cathedral on the Scottish mainland to have survived the uprising without losing its roof. Glasgow Cathedral remained unscathed during both the Battle of Glasgow in 1544 and the Reformation, not because it was overlooked by would-be attackers but because it was so loved by the people of Glasgow that the tradespeople of the city took up arms to protect it.

Today, it is a splendid example of a medieval cathedral. Its gray stone has darkened with age and is adorned with dozens of arched windows. The central stone spire (added after an earlier wooden spire was destroyed) is the pinnacle of this most precious building.

Inside, the rood screen (a rarity to still be found in Scottish churches) acts as a partition between the long nave and the chancel at the head of the building, where you will find the altar. A flight of stone steps takes you down into the dark crypt, the symbolic burial place of St. Mungo, while throughout the building there is beautiful stained glass, though much if it is more modern than you might think. Revealed in 1999, *The Millennial Window* by John Clark is on the north wall of the nave and includes text from the New Testament etched into pictures of birds taking flight, seen as a symbol of hope.

As in all cathedrals and places of worship, keep noise to a minimum, and please note that only visitors attending the morning service should come on Sunday mornings (11am); for everyone else, the cathedral opens at 1pm on

1: Glasgow Cathedral **2:** The Necropolis

Charles Rennie Mackintosh and the Glasgow School of Art

When you hear the term Glasgow Style in reference to architecture, it is pretty much all down to this one man: Charles Rennie Mackintosh. Challenging the very staid Victorian expectations of how buildings should be, he created some of the city's most exquisite edifices, including his masterpiece, the **Glasgow School of Art** (167 Renfrew Street), of which unfortunately little remains following two terrible fires.

Mackintosh was born in the city's poor East End in 1868 to a working-class family. In 1889 he took on a job as a trainee draftsman at architectural practice Honeyman & Keppie. In 1892, while still working at that firm (he was later made a partner), Mackintosh became a night student at the Glasgow School of Art, where he met his future wife, fellow artist Margaret Macdonald, as well as her sister Frances Macdonald and Herbert MacNair (Frances and Herbert later married, too). They collectively came to be known as The Four—a group of artists who went on to define what is known as the Glasgow Style. In 1897 Mackintosh won a competition to remodel and develop his alma mater; his winning design caused his reputation to rocket.

Once widely considered Charles Rennie Mackintosh's greatest achievement, with the wooden library the pinnacle of his Art Nouveau showpiece, the Glasgow School of Art was sadly devastated by a fire in 2014, and then again by a second major fire in the summer of 2018, less than a year before it was due to reopen following a painstaking restoration process. This most recent fire has blindsided the city and those involved in the project; at present it is really not known what future, if any, there is for the building (or at least Mackintosh's design) as plans are on hold until a report into the cause of the second fire is released. In the meantime, here are some of the best ways to get a glimpse of Mackintosh's Glasgow Style:

- The **Charles Rennie Mackintosh Society** (www.crmsociety.com/tours-events/special-mackintosh-tours) now offers walking tours of the city centre on most Fridays at 2pm, starting at the Mackintosh at the Willow on Sauchiehall Street and visiting other Mackintosh buildings before ending up at the excellent art and design space The Lighthouse on Buchanan Street.

- An afternoon tea at the famously stylish **Mackintosh at the Willow** teahouse is one of the best ways to get a sense of the architect's work (page 225).

- Today home to Scotland's National Center for Design and Architecture, **The Lighthouse** is so named for its tall tower, which Mackintosh originally designed to serve as a water tower for the building (page 199).

- Visit a re-creation of the home Mackintosh lived in with his wife at the **Hunterian Museum** (page 210).

Sundays. Guided tours, which last about an hour, are sometimes available with volunteer guides on-site if you ask nicely. They are free, but donations are welcome.

★ The Necropolis

Castle Street; www.glasgownecropolis.org; always open; free

Overlooking the cathedral on the second highest hill in Glasgow, this sprawling cemetery dates back to 1832, when it was built as a burial place for the rich merchants of the city. At the time, Glasgow's population was near a bursting point, having soared from 83,000 in 1800 to around 200,000 by 1830—a problem that brought both cholera and typhoid epidemics.

The wealthy residents wanted a place that reflected the status of Glasgow at the time, and so they took inspiration from Paris's Père Lachaise cemetery; many of the tombs and monuments were designed by Alexander "Greek" Thomson, known for his extravagant Greco-Egyptian style. It covers 37 acres (15 hectares) with more than 50,000 past residents of Glasgow buried here, although just 5 percent have a memorial erected. Look out for the Celtic headstone of one Andrew McCall (a close friend of Charles Rennie Mackintosh's father), thought to be the designer's first ever creation. The prominent statue of Scottish Reformer John Knox actually predates the cemetery.

The **free tours** each month are often fully booked, so be sure to reserve your place a couple of months in advance during peak months by emailing tours@glasgownecropolis.org. Tours on Friday nights are the most atmospheric and will tell of the past lives of Glasgow's anatomists, inventors, writers, and artists. The Necropolis is a Weegie (slang for people from Glasgow) favorite for views of the city, and you can easily visit here and the nearby cathedral in a few hours.

Provand's Lordship

3 Castle Street; tel. 0141 276 1625; www.glasgowlife. org.uk/museums/venues/provands-lordship; 10am-5pm Mon.-Weds. and Sat., 11am-5pm Fri. and Sun.; free

The oldest house in Glasgow, one of the few remaining examples of medieval architecture in the city, and known affectionately as the "auld hoose," Provand's Lordship is dressed much as it would have been during the 17th century (with furniture gifted by shipping magnate and art collector Sir William Burrell). One of the highlights is the serene and pretty Tudor-style **St. Nicholas Garden,** a lovely place to escape the city and read a book. Look out for the carved faces in the cloistered walkway known as the **Tontine Heads,** which were once scattered across the city but were reunited here in 1995. There are no facilities as such, but you are free to use the toilets and café across the road at St. Mungo's Museum.

St. Mungo's Museum of Religious Life and Art

2 Castle Street; tel. 0141 276 1625; www.glasgowlife. org.uk/museums/venues/st-mungo-museum-of-religious-life-and-art; 10am-5pm Mon.-Weds. and Sat., 11am-5pm Fri. and Sun.; free

Fitting for a city that was founded as a place of worship, this unusual museum explores the significance of religion in people's lives both in Scotland and across the world. It's at times poignant because religion has formed the basis of many of the divisions across the city, from the Scottish Reformation to the bitter rivalry between football fans of the mainly Catholic Celtic and the predominantly Protestant Rangers. The museum is a short walk from Provand's Lordship, the cathedral, and the Necropolis.

Tennent's Visitor Centre

161 Duke Street; tel. 0141 202 7145; www. tennentstours.com; 9am-6pm Mon.-Sat., 10am-4pm Sun.; brewery tour £12.50; heritage centre free

Craft beer may be sneaking its way into more and more Glasgow pubs, but there are some that will never sway from what they know, and what they know is Tennent's. At the Wellpark Brewery in the East End, where brewing in some form or other has taken place for 450 years, you can learn all about how this much-loved Scottish beer—brewed since 1885—is made in the free heritage centre and see how methods have changed and adapted throughout history.

Brewery Tours, which take around 90 minutes, are well worth the fee, and you (of course) get to try some of the beer at the end. It also offers a slice of nostalgia for anyone who spent their youth in Scotland as there is an impressive collection of vintage packaging as well as film footage of some classic old adverts. The Visitor Centre is located just in front of the Necropolis and Glasgow Cathedral, so could be a great way to lift the dour mood. Wear flat shoes as you'll be entering working areas.

WEST END
★ University of Glasgow

University Avenue; www.gla.ac.uk/explore/visit/ attractions; guided tours 2pm Tues.-Sun.; guided tours adult £10, child £5, concessions £8, under 5 free, family ticket £25

Could this be the inspiration behind J. K. Rowling's Hogwarts? The neo-Gothic design

GLASGOW SIGHTS

West End, Finnieston, and Clydeside

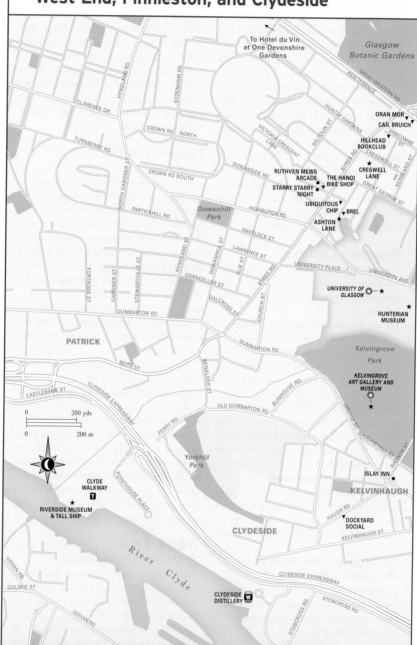

To Hotel du Vin
at One Devonshire
Gardens

Glasgow
Botanic Gardens

HYNDLAND RD

SYDENHAM RD

KEW TERRACE

GREAT WESTERN RD

CLARENCE DR

CROWN RD NORTH

HUNTLY GARDENS

ORAN MOR
CAIL BRUICH

UNICOMBE ST

TURNBERRY RD

VICTORIA CRESCENT
LANE

SALTOUN ST

BYRES RD

HILLHEAD
BOOKCLUB

CRESSWELL ST

KERSLAND ST

CROWN RD SOUTH

DOWANSIDE RD

RUTHVEN MEWS
ARCADE

CRESWELL
LANE

NORTH GARDNER ST

PARTICKHILL RD

Downhill
Park

HIGHBURGH RD

THE HANOI
BIKE SHOP

GREAT GEORGE ST

STARRY STARRY
NIGHT

UBIQUITOUS
CHIP

BREL

HAVELOCK ST

ASHTON
LANE

HYNDLAND ST

LAWRENCE ST

DOWANHILL ST

ELIE ST

UNIVERSITY PLACE

UNIVERSITY AVE

FORTROSE ST

GARDNER ST

STEWARTVILLE ST

CHANCELLOR ST

BYRES RD

CHURCH ST

DALCROSS ST

UNIVERSITY OF
GLASGOW

DUMBARTON RD

DUMBARTON RD

HUNTERIAN
MUSEUM

PATRICK

BEITH ST

Kelvingrove
Park

BENALDER ST

BUNHOUSE RD

KELVINGROVE
ART GALLERY AND
MUSEUM

CASTLEBANK ST

CLYDESIDE EXPRESSWAY

OLD DUMBARTON RD

ARGYLE ST

SAUCHIEHALL ST

RADNOR ST

FERRY RD

0   200 yds

0   200 m

Yorkhill
Park

ISLAY INN

KELVINHAUGH

CLYDE
WALKWAY

POINTHOUSE PLACE

HAUGH RD

DOCKYARD
SOCIAL

RIVERSIDE MUSEUM
& TALL SHIP

CLYDESIDE

KELVINHAUGH ST

GOVAN RD

River Clyde

CLYDESIDE EXPRESSWAY

STOBCROSS RD

GOLSPIE ST

CLYDESIDE
DISTILLERY

STOBCROSS RD

GOVAN RD

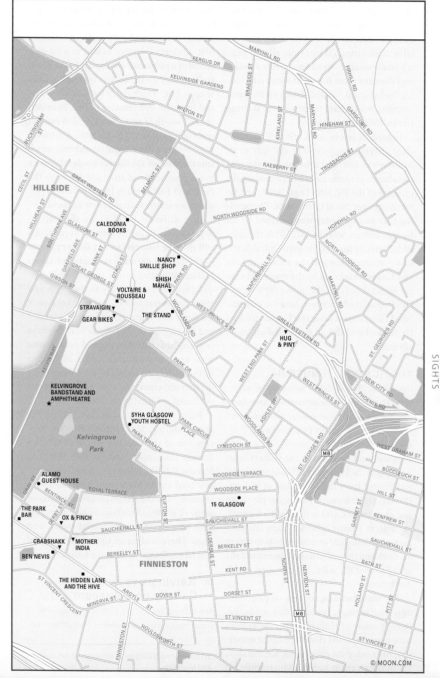

© MOON.COM

of the University of Glasgow, with its crow-stepped gables, pointed turrets, and conspicuous spire that can be seen for miles around, attracts admiring glances from all that pass. It's small wonder—it has more listed buildings than any other British university, including the beautiful, vaulted cloisters with fluted columns, which have taken a recent starring role in TV's *Outlander*.

Indeed, it is one of Scotland's four ancient universities, second in age only to St. Andrew's in Fife, and it has seen many special alumni graduate from here, including the inventor of the TV, John Logie Baird, and famous explorer David Livingstone. The building that you see today was designed by Sir George Gilbert Scott in 1870, with the spire added later by his son, Sir John Oldrid Scott. However, one lodge and the decorative Lion and Unicorn staircase by the memorial chapel were taken from the university's former building on the high street, long since demolished. Tours leave from the University East Undercroft and should be booked online in advance.

THE HUNTERIAN MUSEUM

University of Glasgow, Gilbert Scott Building; tel. 0141 330 4221; www.gla.ac.uk/hunterian; 10am-5pm Tues.-Sat.; museum and art gallery free, Mackintosh House adult £8, concessions £6, prices vary for special exhibitions

This compact museum in the Gilbert Scott Building of the University of Glasgow campus was created from the collections of William Hunter, an 18th-century Glasgow physician and obstetrician, and is filled with fascinating objects. Hunter collected many anatomical and pathological specimens to help him in his work and the collection has been carefully added to over the years. You can even see his death mask.

The main building focuses on paleontology, archaeology, geology, and medicine, though many of Hunter's other collections have been dispersed elsewhere in the university; his zoological collections, for instance, are in the Graham Kerr Building, while his

collection of books and manuscripts are kept in the University of Glasgow Library. Young visitors will love seeing Scotland's first dinosaur footprint as well as a life-size model of a plesiosaur on display. In the **Main Gallery** look for the ancient mummy of Lady Shepen-hor, which dates back 2,500 years, and the fossilized remains of the "Bearsden Shark," which is an astounding 330 million years old. Another highlight is the **Antonine Wall: Rome's Final Frontier exhibit,** which tells the story of the Roman border that once ran across Scotland from the Clyde to the Firth and Forth, much like Hadrian's Wall, which separated Scotland from England.

In a different building on the university campus, across University Avenue, you will find the **Hunterian Art Gallery,** home to the largest permanent display of James McNeil Whistler works in the world, bequeathed to the university in the 1930s and 1950s for several reasons, not least because of the American-born artist's Scottish ancestry and his support of the famous Glasgow Boys (a group of artists who painted rural scenes with unknown figures). Other highlights in the gallery include *The Entombment* by Rembrandt, a moving oil painting that depicts the burial of Christ by torchlight.

For a fee you can also visit, within the same building, **Mackintosh House,** a re-creation of the Glasgow home of Charles Rennie Mackintosh and his wife Margaret Macdonald, which was very near the university. Look out for Mackintosh's personal writing desk—one of his most luxurious creations, made of ebonized mahogany and sycamore with mother-of-pearl, silvered metal, and glass. There is often an impressive series of special exhibitions held at the museum, too.

★ Kelvingrove Art Gallery and Museum

Argyle Street; tel. 0141 276 9599; www.glasgowlife. org.uk/museums/venues/kelvingrove-art-gallery-and-

---

1: University of Glasgow **2:** Kelvingrove Art Gallery and Museum

museum; 10am-5pm Mon.-Thurs. and Sat., 11am-5pm Fri. and Sun.; free (some temporary exhibits may charge)

This handsome museum is one of the city's most popular attractions and is not to be missed. Set within the lovely Kelvingrove Park (designed by the former head gardener of Chatsworth House) and just a short stroll from the University of Glasgow, its grand exterior—with numerous red sandstone towers topped with finials—is one of the city's most recognizable landmarks, built between 1888-1901 in the Spanish Baroque style.

Inside it doesn't disappoint either, with 22 galleries displaying some 8,000 objects. The interior is effectively split into two, with art galleries on one side displaying an impressive collection of Dutch and Flemish Masters (look out for the Van Gogh), as well as the foremost collection of works by the Glasgow Boys, a group of late 19th-century artists who were disillusioned by formal painting techniques and subjects and chose to paint rural scenes with unknown figures instead. Works of note by female artists include Mary Cassatt's 1885 painting *The Young Girls* and *Two Children* by Joan Eardley, a 1963 piece that mixes paint with collage, and bears some similarity to the former artwork. The museum on the other side focuses on natural history and world culture with Sir Roger the Elephant, a stuffed elephant that has been part of the museum for over 120 years. It's a particularly poignant exhibit—you can still see one of the bullet holes from when he was executed on the orders of the owner of Glasgow zoo. The **Kelvingrove organ** in the center hall is also a highlight: In 2016 footage of organist Chris Nickol playing David Bowie's *Life on Mars* on the day of Bowie's death went viral. Attending one of the daily organ recitals (1pm Mon.-Sat., 3pm Sun.) is highly recommended.

Glasgow Botanic Gardens

730 Great Western Road; tel. 0141 276 1614; www. glasgowbotanicgardens.com; 7am-dusk daily, Kibble Palace 12pm-4pm daily; free

These lovely gardens, originally opened to assist the teachings of the university, are free to roam. A delightful mix of formal gardens and more remote paths that venture into wooded areas, the Botanic Gardens are where most Westenders come for a brush with nature.

Amid the grounds you'll find several striking glasshouses, including the huge domed **Kibble Palace,** which extraordinarily once stood on the banks of Loch Long—a sea loch in Argyll and Bute—but was transported here in the late 19th century. Inside Kibble Palace are lots of exotic plants and flowers, including a tree fern collection and orchids, and hidden among the fauna are some elaborate marble sculptures, not least the statue of Eve by Italian sculptor Scipione Tadolini.

Clydeside Distillery

The Old Pump House, Queen's Dock; tel. 0141 212 1401; www.theclydeside.com; 11am-5pm Weds.-Sun., tours on the hour, last tour at 4pm; adult £15

This shiny new whisky distillery (it opened in 2017) is part of the heralded redevelopment of the Clydeside area of the city and uses traditional techniques, such as hand-distilling to create its single malt. The ambition here is personal: owner Tim Morrison, who has a background in whisky-making across Scotland, wants to revive whisky-making in Glasgow, in the very dock built by his great grandfather. Visitors on the main distillery tour (which lasts an hour) will hear all about this personal journey and the history of the whisky industry in Glasgow, take a tour around the distillery, and be able to enjoy views of the Clyde from the gleaming glass Still House. At the end of the tour, you'll also be able to sample three drams from across Scotland. Other pricier tours are available, which include food pairings and more tastings. There is also a good café and shop on-site.

Riverside Museum and Tall Ship

Pointhouse Place; tel. 0141 287 2720; www. glasgowlife.org.uk/museums/venues/ riverside-museum; museum 10am-5pm Mon.-Thurs.

*and Sat., 11am-5pm Fri. and Sun., tall ship
10am-4:30pm Sat.-Weds., 11am-4:30pm Thurs.-Fri.;
free*

Described as "Glasgow's Guggenheim," this award-winning transport museum is every bit as famous for its stunning exterior as it is for what's inside. With a modern nod to the pleated sheds of the Clyde's heyday, the striking design by the revered late architect Zaha Hadid has added an exciting landmark to the city's skyline. Hadid actually designed the building from the inside out and its interactive displays celebrate Glasgow's engineering traditions while offering lots of hands-on exhibits. Jump aboard a vintage Glasgow tram or take a walk through Glasgow streets of old.

Plus, moored outside is the city's tall ship *Glenlee,* which is also free, and with its steel hull and trio of powerful masts, it recalls the Clyde's once thriving shipbuilding industry. On board you can explore life below decks, including the Captain's Cabin, and there is a good play area for under-fives. A short audio guide tells of the history of the ship.

SOUTHSIDE
Pollok House

2060 Pollokshaws Road, Pollok Country Park; tel. 0141 616 6410; www.nts.org.uk/visit/places/pollok-house; 10am-5pm (last entry 3:30pm) Thurs.-Mon. Apr.-Oct., 10am-4pm Thurs.-Mon. Nov.-Feb.; adult £8.50, concessions £6

It was at this elegant 18th-century stately home, set within Pollok Country Park, that discussions first took place to set up a National Trust for Scotland to care for some of the nation's most special heritage places in the 1930s. Like something from the pages of a Jane Austen novel, though the current house was designed by William Adam in 1752, the site and grounds were the ancestral home of the wealthy Maxwell family for 700 years.

Two giant lion sculptures greet you as you ascend the steps into the Georgian gardens. Inside there is a magnificent collection of paintings on view, including an impressive array of Spanish art, plus pieces by Scottish artists Raeburn and Guthrie, as well as

beautiful silverware and furniture to admire. Refuel with a scone or cake and a coffee in **The Edwardian Kitchen** café.

House for an Art Lover

Bellahouston Park, 10 Dumbreck Road; tel. 0141 353 4770; www.houseforanartlover.co.uk; 10am-5pm daily, but subject to change; adult £6.50, child £5

Set within the expansive grounds of Glasgow's **Bellahouston Park** and originally designed as a country-style retreat, today this exciting art space celebrates the best of art, design, and architecture. Built in the late 1980s from designs by Charles Rennie Mackintosh on the site of 18th-century mansion Ibroxhill House, it is a multi-use venue where you can come for a lovely lunch, see art by emerging Glaswegian artists in the galleries and studios, admire the design flourishes of Mackintosh and his wife, Margaret Macdonald, and wander the sculpture garden right outside the house.

All visitors are given an audio guide, and in the former stables of the house you can access the **Heritage Centre,** which showcases the local history of Bellahouston Park and its surrounding area. Make time to stroll the grounds of the park itself, which includes a Victorian walled garden, a good playground, and an Alice in Wonderland-style maze for children. Please note that hours of operation may differ due to private events.

Govan Stones

Govan Old Church; tel. 0141 440 2466; www. thegovanstones.org.uk; 1pm-4pm daily Apr.-Oct.; free but donations welcome

Possibly one of the most humbling experiences you can have in Glasgow is visiting this small church in the south of the city. On display are some of the city's most ancient artifacts, which were discovered here in 1855. Comprising 31 early medieval stones, first carved between the 9th and 11th centuries, the Govan Stones feature intricate etchings of warriors and crosses that tell the story of the Viking rulers of the Kingdom of Strathclyde. The collection's outstanding piece is undoubtedly the **Govan Sarcophagus,** which may have been intended to hold the remains of the founder of the previous church on the site, and the recent discovery of three more stones suggest that even more lie beneath the graveyard.

Glasgow Science Centre

50 Pacific Quay; tel. 0141 420 5000; www. glasgowsciencecentre.org; 10am-5pm daily late Mar.-late Oct., 10am-3pm Wed.-Fri., 10am-5pm Sat.-Sun. late Oct.-late Mar.; adult £12, child £10, Glasgow Tower additional £3.50 (£6.50 on its own), planetarium additional £3 (£5.50 on its own)

A little away from the city centre (it costs about £5 in a taxi) on the south side of the River Clyde, this huge attraction is spread across three floors and has more than 300 interactive exhibits. It's a great place to amuse children (particularly on a rainy day), who will love the **Bodyworks** exhibition where they can burn off some energy on the hamster wheel or even perform a virtual autopsy. In a **Question of Perception,** both adults and kids will enjoy the mind-boggling illusions where you can grow or shrink and see the whole universe tilted. The center is also home to a planetarium, an IMAX cinema,

a good shop, and a café. Many people head out this way to ascend the 417-foot (127-m) **Glasgow Tower,** which is the tallest fully rotating freestanding structure in the world and affords panoramic views across the city.

Scottish Football Museum

Hampden Park; tel. 0871 200 2233; www. scottishfootballmuseum.org.uk; 10am-5pm daily; adult £13, child £5, family £30, under 5 free

Get some sense of what the game of football (or soccer) really means to the people of Scotland at **Hampden Park,** Scotland's national stadium. In the museum you can sit in the old dressing room and listen to a rousing address from Craig Brown, the nation's most celebrated football manager, and see the original Scottish Cup, the first national football trophy in the world. Meanwhile, stadium tours will give you the chance to sit in team locker rooms, walk the down the tunnel, feel the excitement and pride that players walking onto the pitch have with the full support of the "Hampden Roar," and even take a shot on goal. Make time for the **Hall of Fame,** too, where you can learn about some of the true greats of Scottish football.

Sports and Recreation

★ PARKS

Glasgow has more than 90 parks and green spaces, living up to its nickname of "Dear Green Place," so there are lots of opportunities to walk, cycle, and run, or just to sit and get away from the hustle and bustle of the city for a few hours. Many of the parks also have museums, art galleries, and other sights worth visiting.

East End
GLASGOW GREEN

Greendyke Street, Saltmarket; www.glasgow.gov.uk/ glasgowgreen

While by no means the prettiest of Glasgow's parks, Glasgow Green, a 136-acre

(146-hectare) site of open land in the East End that reaches down to the River Clyde, is pretty hard to beat in terms of history. It was here that Bonnie Prince Charlie and his Jacobite army camped between 1745 and 1746, and where the Suffragette Movement regularly met in the 1870s. The Green is dominated by a column celebrating the victories of Admiral Horatio Nelson, and you can still see the cast-iron washing poles, which look like neatly arranged tree saplings from a distance and were used by women

1: People's Palace and Winter Gardens **2:** Riverside Museum and tall ship *Glenlee* **3:** Georgian buildings around Kelvingrove Park **4:** Queen's Park, a popular green space for Southsiders

from the poor East End to hang their washing out to dry until the 1970s.

To the west, the **People's Palace and Winter Gardens** (tel. 0141 276 0788; www.glasgowlife.org.uk/museums/venues/peoplespalace; 10am-5pm Mon.-Weds. and Sat., 11am-5pm Fri. and Sun.; free) is an incongruous French Renaissance-style building with attached glasshouse. It first opened in 1898 to provide a cultural space for residents of one of the city's most cramped and destitute areas. Upstairs, you can take a trip through Glasgow's social history via a thoroughly engaging series of exhibits. Downstairs, you can have coffee and cake in the Winter Gardens, or just have a gentle walk amid the tropical flowers.

On the edge of Glasgow Green, you'll see the **McLennan Arch,** a triumphant arch framed by a pair of Ionic columns. Its presence often baffles visitors. What building was once here? The arch actually once formed part of the old Assembly Rooms, the fashionable place to be seen in Georgian society, a few streets away on the north side of Ingram Street. When the Assembly Rooms were demolished in the late Victorian period, the arch was saved and first moved to Greendyke Street and then moved to this spot in 1922.

West End
KELVINGROVE PARK

6 Professors' Square

Over in the West End and connecting some of the area's biggest sights, including Kelvingrove Art Gallery and Museum and the University of Glasgow, and with the River Kelvin running through it, this possibly wins the prize of Glasgow's prettiest park. It was designed by Sir Joseph Paxton, but at only 85 acres (34 hectares) it is tiny compared with its Southside cousin, Queen's Park (also designed by Paxton). However, what it lacks in size it makes up for in splendor. Part of the appeal of Kelvingrove is that, whether you're walking by the river or catching some shade beneath the Suffragette Oak—a tree planted a century ago to honor the women who made

women's suffrage possible—you're never far from some beautiful architecture, such as the salubrious **Park District** that curls around the northeast corner of the park and is redolent of Edinburgh's New Town, though it was built sometime later. The **Kelvingrove Bandstand and Amphitheatre** (Kelvin Way; tel. 0141 287 4350; www.facebook.com/KelvingroveBandstand; ticket prices vary) in the park is also a great place to watch summer concerts, though spots for this special concert experience are understandably hugely in demand.

South Side
QUEEN'S PARK

520 Langside Road

When Southsiders want a lazy afternoon lying around reading the papers, catching up with friends over a picnic, or going for a walk, this is generally their place of choice. Set along the busy Pollokshaws Road, the 140-acre (57-hectare) park is easily accessible, yet it doesn't take long to escape the sound of traffic. Laid out in the mid-19th century, this mix of neatly manicured lawns and more natural grassy slopes was named after Mary, Queen of Scots (a battle was fought here in her name), and its grand style is typical of the Victorian era, with a boating lake, glasshouses, and aviary. Make time to climb up **Camp Hill** for views over the city; on a clear day you can see Ben Lomond beyond the Campsie Fells if you know what you're looking for. And don't be afraid to sneak a shortcut through some leaf-covered trails—it's all part of the fun.

POLLOK COUNTRY PARK

2060 Pollokshaws Road

The largest park in Glasgow (360 acres/146 hectares) and also the only one that can be described as a country park, this haven of tranquility on Glasgow's Southside is made up of 140 acres (57 hectares) of woodland, along with more formal gardens that include perfectly clipped yew hedges and herbaceous borders, around **Pollok House**—a reminder that it was once a grand estate.

Many people come here to see the herd of Highland cattle in the fields to the south-west of the museum building, and many more come to have a go on one of the three mountain bike tracks. Avid *Outlander* fans may also note that key scenes from the TV show were filmed here.

BELLAHOUSTON PARK

16 Dumbreck Road

Another giant of a park in the Southside, this 169-acre (68-hectare) green site, just north of Pollok Park, offers bowling greens, a Victorian walled garden, a sunken garden, an Alice in Wonderland-style maze, and a pitch and putt; its wide-open spaces also make it a popular choice for large outdoor concerts. However, it's a little tired compared with some of Glasgow's other green spaces, and the highlight is without a doubt the incredibly stylish **House for an Art Lover,** an art gallery and exhibition space inspired by the designs of Charles Rennie Mackintosh but built long after his death.

WALKING

CLYDE WALKWAY

Distance: *4 miles (6.4 km)*
Walking Time: *2 hours*
Trailhead: *Riverside Museum*
Information and Maps: *www. southlanarkshire.gov.uk/downloads/download/258/ clyde_walkway*

At some 40 miles (65 km) long altogether, this riverside route takes you from the center of Glasgow all the way to the tumbling Falls of Clyde in New Lanark. Most people won't attempt it all, but those who do will find the route quite straightforward and will probably stop at Cambuslang, Strathclyde Loch, Maudslie, and New Lanark. The stretch of this route in Glasgow, starting at the Riverside Museum and tall ship and heading east, is a novel way to see much of the city. The route is waymarked and mainly paved, and takes you along the river, opposite Glasgow Science Centre and its tower, through the heart of Glasgow's once busy shipbuilding and cargo

centers, marked by the iconic Finnieston Crane, and all the way to Glasgow Green in the East End.

CYCLING

FORTH AND CLYDE CANAL PATH

Distance: *18 miles (30 km)*
Cycling Time: *1.5 hours*
Trailhead: *Cowacaddens Subway Station*
Information and Maps: *www.sustrans.org.uk/ ncn/map/route/route-754*

This canal path, which runs all the way from Glasgow to Edinburgh, offers lots of opportunity for cycling along a flat, traffic-free route. If you're just after a little afternoon exploration, then the section from Cowcaddens Subway Station in the north of the city centre to the canal-side village of Kirkintilloch, northeast of Glasgow, offers a reasonable 9-mile (15-km) route (18 miles/30 km round-trip) through gentle countryside and allows for a pit stop at the **Stables Pub** in Kirkintilloch, which was built to serve the watermen and horses who worked the canal. The route follows a section of the National Cycle Network (route 754) and is well signposted from Cowcaddens; though the path is narrow (about 3.3 feet/1 m across), it's an easy ride on tarmac and some cobblestones.

GEAR BIKES

19 Gibson Street; tel. 0141 339 1179; https://gearbikes. com; 10am-6pm Mon.-Sat., 12pm-5pm Sun.; £20 a day, £80 a week

At this bike hire place in the city's West End, all bikes—currently Ridgeback hybrids, but they do update the range regularly—come with lights, a tool kit, pump, helmets, and locks all included in the price.

GLASGOW BIKE TOURS

Meet at Drygate Brewing Company, 85 Drygate; tel. 0778 668 3445; https://glasgowbiketours.co.uk; adult £39-55, child £20

If you want to explore Glasgow on two wheels but don't really know where to begin, then these guided tours, which set off from the East End, could be a good option. The standard

The Old Firm Rivalry: Celtic vs. Rangers

It's no secret that the rivalry between Glasgow's two biggest football teams, Celtic and Rangers, runs deep. While many Glaswegians treat it as a bit of fun, many others don't, so you're better off avoiding the topic if it comes up in the pub. Traditionally, Celtic fans come from the Catholic side of the community, largely made up of the descendants of Irish immigrants who began arriving in Glasgow in droves in the 19th century, as they fled the Great Famine, while Rangers fans tend to hail from the Protestant community. Often rivalry among fans has been entwined with politics.

It hasn't always been the case that the two clubs don't get on. When Celtic was first formed in 1888, the two clubs seemed to be friendly enough; however, as Celtic—an outwardly Catholic club with a strong Irish Republican outlook—started to establish itself as a serious contender in the game, the rivalry stepped up, leading to larger crowds in the stands. A satirical cartoon in 1904 first used the label "Old Firm" and hinted that the rivalry was seen as a money-spinner by the two clubs. However, it was the 1912 opening of a shipyard on the Clyde by Belfast shipbuilder Harland & Wolff (who built the *Titanic*) that is largely thought to have brought Irish politics into play. Harland & Wolff was notorious for excluding Catholics from its workforce, so it brought scores of Irish Protestant workers, who gravitated toward Rangers. As sectarian violence spread across Ireland between Republicans (mostly Catholics) and Unionists (mostly Protestants), football supporters in Glasgow allowed their vitriol to spill out onto the stands. Indeed, such was the strength of belief that for many years Rangers had an unspoken rule that it would not knowingly sign a player from the Catholic community.

On Derby days police presence in Glasgow is stepped up, and, though the heady days of sectarian clashes seem to be fading into memory, there is still friction. Celtic fans, for instance, still like to wind Rangers fans up about the fact Rangers' holding company went into liquidation in 2012 and the club had to apply to enter the third division of the Scottish League. Celtic fans joke that the Old Firm Derby is no more, since Rangers is now a new club. And so, the war rumbles on.

three-hour Sightseeing Tour (10:30am or 2:30pm daily; adult £39, child £22) takes you from the city centre, along the Clyde waterfront, and through leafy Kelvingrove Park to the trendy West End, taking in all the major sights. The 4.5-hour Sightseeing & Whisky tasting tour (by request with a 2:30pm start; £75) does all of the above but also incorporates a stop-off at a Glasgow pub for a few wee drams. Private tours are also available.

SPECTATOR SPORTS

Spectator sports are taken seriously here, particularly when it comes to football, so be careful about ribbing anyone about their team. But, if you happen to be in town when there's a match, do go and see the famous Scottish passion firsthand.

CELTIC PARK

Parkhead; tel. 0871 226 1888; www.celticfc.net; tours 11am, 12pm, 1:45pm, 2:30pm Mon.-Sun. (except *home matchdays), matchday tours 9:30am, 10am, 10:30am, 11am Sat.; tours adult £13.50, under 12 £8* This football stadium in the Parkhead area of Glasgow's East End is Celtic's home ground and has been since 1892. It is often referred to simply as "Parkhead" or sometimes "Paradise." You can purchase tickets for home matches online or by calling the ticket line (from around £20). Some tickets are available on the day of the match at the Celtic ticket office, but queues can be enormous. To reach the ground, get the train from Glasgow Central to either Dalmarnock or Bridgeton, both of which are within 15 minutes' walk of the ground.

IBROX STADIUM

150 Edmiston Drive; tel. 0871 702 1972; www.rangers. co.uk; tours 10:30am, 12:30pm, 2:30pm Fri.-Sun. (except home matchdays); tours adult £15, child £5 Rangers' home ground is in the Southside of the city in the Govan area and is served by

Ibrox Subway Station. Tickets for home games can be purchased online or by calling the hotline. There are also tours of the grounds, during which you can visit the locker rooms and climb the marble staircase to the trophy room.

TOURS
GLASGOW CENTRAL STATION TOUR
Gordon St.; tel. 07734 647 381; www. glasgowcentraltours.co.uk; £13

This fascinating walking tour takes you underneath the city proper into the railway vaults of this iconic station and through the basements and boiler rooms. You will learn the story of the city through the context of its main station and will even visit the eerie deserted old Victorian platform. The brilliant

guides know how to tell a story and will have you in both floods of laughter and tears. The tours are popular, so book well in advance. Over 12 years old only.

WALK THE GLASGOW MUSIC MILE
78 Whitecrook St., Clydebank; tel. 0131 558 2715; https://glasgowmusiccitytours.com; adult £17, child £12

Immerse yourself in the sound of the city on one of these insightful tours that take in some of Glasgow's most influential music venues. The two-hour tours take you from the Royal Concert Hall to King Tut's Wah Wah Hut where you can take a selfie on the very stage where Oasis and Blur played as young unknowns.

Performing Arts and Entertainment

CONCERT HALLS AND EVENT VENUES
City Centre
GLASGOW ROYAL CONCERT HALL
2 Sauchiehall Street; tel. 0141 353 8000; www. glasgowconcerthalls.com/glasgow-royal-concert-hall; box office 10am-6pm Mon.-Sat.

Seen as a symbol of the regeneration of Glasgow following its City of Culture status in 1990, this concert hall is now home to the Royal Scottish National Orchestra. It's a high-tech space to hear music from the genres of classical, pop, folk, and rock, and everyone from B. B. King to Johnny Cash and Van Morrison have graced its stage.

Merchant City
CITY HALLS AND OLD FRUITMARKET
Candleriggs; tel. 0141 353 8000; www. glasgowconcerthalls.com; box office 10am-6pm Mon.-Sat.

As its name suggests, these dual venues once formed part of a market complex, and were used to host large public gatherings, with

the likes of Charles Dickens and Benjamin Disraeli holding court. The Old Fruitmarket was a working market until the 1970s, but since 2006 both venues have been operating as performance spaces, with the Grand Hall of the City Halls auditorium home to the Scottish Symphony Orchestra, while the Old Fruitmarket has leaned more toward the experimental side of contemporary music.

East End
★ BARROWLAND BALLROOM
244 Gallowgate; tel. 0141 552 4601; barrowland-ballroom.co.uk; times vary, but often 7pm-11pm

Opened by "Barras Queen" Maggie McIver, Barrowland has been a fixture in Glasgow since 1934. Though the original building burned down in 1958, the rebuilt ballroom opened in 1960 and has been one of the city's favorite music venues ever since. Everyone from David Bowie to The Clash, U2, and the Foo Fighters have performed here, attracted no doubt by the famous sprung dance floor, fantastic acoustics, and faded glamour. Today gigs are played out in the main hall or in the smaller Barrowland 2 bar downstairs, with big names (both contemporary and old school) regularly on the set list.

THEATER
City Centre
THEATRE ROYAL

282 Hope Street; tel. 0141 332 9000, box office 0844 871 7677; www.glasgowtheatreroyal.org.uk

Despite appearances (the building was massively redeveloped in 2014 so looks a lot newer than it is), this is Scotland's longest-running theater and home to Scottish opera and ballet. Opera season runs October-June with the new program announced each April. Ballet season is year-round. While on the outside the building may look ultra-modern, inside its auditorium, where the Victorian horseshoe wall remains, all the grandeur of yesteryear is still apparent. It's a beautiful setting for some world-class performances.

KING'S THEATRE

297 Bath Street; tel. 0844 871 7615; www.atgtickets. com/venues/kings-theatre

Designed by renowned theater architect Frank Matcham, who designed many London theaters, including the London Coliseum, this historic theater presents an unusual façade with both Art Nouveau and baroque features. It is the go-to place for touring productions in Glasgow.

Southside
TRAMWAY

25 Albert Drive; tel. 0141 276 0950; www.tramway. org; art exhibitions 12pm-5pm Tues.-Fri., and 12pm-6pm Sat. and Sun., show times vary but often 7pm-11pm

Housed in a former tram shed and originally opened to host Peter Brook's *Mahabharata,* this venue has lost little of its avant-garde reputation. Considered one of the most exciting theaters in Glasgow, it's a top-notch place for seeing contemporary and risk-taking shows. It also hosts regular daytime contemporary art exhibitions.

COMEDY CLUB
West End
THE STAND

333 Woodlands Road; tel. 0141 212 3389; www. thestand.co.uk; tickets from £3

Like its sister venue in Edinburgh, this venue is popular for established comedians to try out new material. Keep an eye out for Glaswegian comics such as Kevin Bridges coming back to home turf; the atmosphere is electric (even though the air is often blue).

Barrowland Ballroom

Festivals and Events

SPRING

SOUTHSIDE FRINGE

Various locations; www.southsidefringe.org.uk; May; prices vary

This community festival held each May takes place across several Southside venues, and includes around 100 events. There are theater performances, special food and drink tastings, and lots of live music. Many events are free.

SUMMER

WEST END FESTIVAL

Various locations; tel. 0141 341 0844; www. westendfestival.co.uk; June or September; prices vary

The city's largest cultural event used to take place in its coolest quarter each June (though in 2021 September was chosen, so it's worth checking for future dates) with as many as 400 events across 80 venues. Tickets for many events can be purchased individually and are largely free (you can also just turn up), so it's a great chance to dip in and out and see what this bustling area has to offer.

WINTER

CELTIC CONNECTIONS

Various city centre venues; tel. 0141 353 8000; www. celticconnections.com; January; prices vary by performance

Lifting the post-Christmas gloom is this annual celebration of Celtic music across the genres of folk, roots, and world music that takes place over 18 days across numerous venues, from Oran Mor to the City Halls. More than 300 events take place, including collaborative shows, exhibitions, ceilidhs, and spontaneous sessions, all continuing late into the night.

Shopping

CITY CENTRE

Glasgow is the undisputed shopping capital of Scotland, with everything from major brands, independent boutiques, and designer labels along its **Style Mile,** a Z-shaped mile-long route between Argyle Street and Sauchiehall Street that takes in hugely popular malls including the **Buchanan Galleries** (220 Buchanan Street; tel. 0141 333 9898; www.buchanangalleries.co.uk; 9am-6pm Mon.-Sat., 10am-6pm Sun.) and **St. Enoch Centre** (55 St. Enoch Square; tel. 141 204 3900; www. st-enoch.com; 9am-6pm Mon.-Sat., 10am-6pm Sun.), as well as store-lined plazas like **Princes Square.** You'll find leading British stores here, including **House of Fraser** (Buchanan Street), which has the largest beauty hall in Scotland.

Take note that shops in the centre are generally open Monday-Friday until at least 5pm, 10am-6pm on Saturday, and sometimes shorter hours on Sunday (smaller independents may also have reduced hours). Late-night shopping is on Thursday, when most shops will be open until at least 7pm.

THE WHISKY SHOP

220 Buchanan Street; tel. 0141 331 0022; www. whiskyshop.com; 10am-5pm daily

Once you've worked your way around some of Glasgow's many whisky bars and have found a dram you like, come here to pick up one to take home or arrange for international delivery to your home address.

MERCHANT CITY

For more high-end one-off items, head to the Merchant City.

MERCHANT SQUARE CRAFT FAIR

71 Albion Street; www.merchantsquareglasgow.com; market runs 11am-6pm Sat., 12pm-6pm Sun.

Each weekend this covered courtyard hosts a craft and design fair, which is a great chance to browse handcrafted goods, all made right here in Glasgow. It's perfect for picking up authentic souvenirs and though it has been closed during the pandemic, it should be back soon.

EAST END

BARRAS MARKET

244 Gallowgate; tel. 0141 552 4601; www. theglasgowbarras.com; 10am-5pm Sat.-Sun.

This old East End market sprouted up in the early 20th century when an entrepreneurial young lady by the name of Margaret Russell (known as the Barras Queen, later Maggie McIver) and her husband James McIver began renting out horses and carts to traders who would fill them with goods for sale in some of the more affluent parts of the city. Eventually, they moved on to static barrows or *barras,* and so the market was born. Despite developing something of a negative reputation over recent decades, the Barras is still a popular destination for tourists, as well as hip young things who come to peruse the stalls of bric-a-brac, vinyl, and secondhand clothes.

BAAD

54 Calton Entry; tel. 0141 237 9220; www. baadglasgow.com; 12pm-12am Tues.-Sat., 11am-10pm Sun.

For something a bit different and to get a feel of the creative communities in Glasgow, head to Barras Art & Design (BAaD), a cool space amid the old market with huge graffiti murals and home to lots of start-ups, including a record shop and pop-up studios for picking up local artwork. This is certainly a place to watch—you may even catch one of the gigs that take place here sporadically.

WEST END

For quirkier, edgier stuff—particularly clothing and funky jewelry and furniture—you can't beat the West End.

Shopping Streets

THE HIDDEN LANE AND THE HIVE

1081 Argyle Street; www.thehiddenlaneglasgow.com; hours vary, most businesses open Sat. 12pm-5pm, with some weekday hours, Hidden Lane Tearoom 10am-4pm Mon.-Fri., 10am-5pm Sat., 12pm-5pm Sun.

This secret lane in Finnieston features works from over 100 artists' studios and has a real local feel. You can shop for unique pieces at Shona Jewellery or stop off in the Hidden Lane Tearoom before perusing one of the many craft workshops. Meanwhile, The Hive, also hidden behind the main throng of Argyle Street, is a four-story building that is home to lots of independents.

Bookstores

VOLTAIRE & ROUSSEAU BOOKSELLERS

12 Octago Lane; tel. 0141 611 8764; https:// voltaireandrousseaubooks.com; 10am-6pm Mon.-Sat.

You need to possess a certain level of patience to browse the disordered shelves and piles of books at this bookshop in the Hillhead area of the West End, but you will be rewarded with lots of amazing finds and plenty of things that you never knew you needed.

CALEDONIA BOOKS

483 Great Western Road; tel. 01141 334 9663; www. caledoniabooks.co.uk; 10:30am-6pm daily

For rare books, including out-of-print titles, come to this shop, also in the Hillhead area. There are lots of publications on Scottish history and literature. It's a great place to stock up on books to swot up on (or study intensely).

1: Princes Square forms part of the Style Mile
2: Buchanan Street Subway **3:** Barras Market

Gifts and Souvenirs
NANCY SMILLIE SHOP
*425 Great Western Road; tel. 0141 334 0055; www.
nancysmillieshop.com; 10am-5:30pm Mon.-Sat.,
11:30am-5pm Sun.*

This Hillhead boutique sells a range of ceramics, jewelry, and hand-blown glass as well as some lovely tweed throws. It's a good place to pick up Scottish gifts that aren't too tacky.

Antiques and Vintage
RUTHVEN MEWS ARCADE
*57 Ruthven Lane; www.visitwestend.com/discover/
the-lanes; 11am-5:30pm Mon.-Sat., 12pm-5pm Sun.*

A small arcade featuring just 10 outlets, it nevertheless has a good ratio of antiques and vintage goods, from mid-century furniture to subversive art and memorabilia.

STARRY STARRY NIGHT
*19 Downside Lane; tel. 0141 337 1837; www.
starrystarrynightvintage.co.uk; 10am-5:30pm
Mon.-Sat., 11am-5pm Sun.*

This Aladdin's cave has retro and vintage clothing dating all the way from the Victorian era, right up to the 1980s, including bejeweled flapper dresses and dazzling costume jewelry.

SOUTHSIDE
Bookstores
CATEGORY IS BOOKS
*34 Allison Street, G42 8NN; www.categoryisbooks.
com; 11am-6pm Thurs.-Sun.*

An independent LGBTQIA+ bookshop that celebrates queer culture, with books, magazines, comics, films, and art on sale, as well as lots of badges. If you want to learn about the LGBTQIA+ community and events in Glasgow, this is a good starting point.

Food

As Scotland's largest city, Glasgow offers cuisine from all over the world. You may have heard of the deep-fried Mars Bars (which are exactly as you might expect—Mars Bars covered in batter and deep fried), but did you know that Glaswegians are partial to deep-frying all manner of foods? Deep-fried pizzas and deep-fried chips are all fair game, too.

But you would be wrong, so wrong, to think that Glaswegian food is all unhealthy. Known as the vegan capital of Britain, Glasgow restaurants feature tasty healthy super foods, and, as there is a large student population, a lot of it is very well priced. Finnieston in Glasgow's West End is undoubtedly the foodie center of Glasgow and there are always new places opening up here, from cheap eats to inventive fine-dining restaurants. If it's local dishes you are after, then look for some of the modern Scottish menus, while you can also experience many of the outside influences that have made their way onto the food and drink scene, including Indian cuisine.

CITY CENTRE
Traditional Fare
TWO FAT LADIES AT THE BUTTERY
*652-654 Argyle Street; tel. 0141 221 8188;
twofatladiesrestaurant.com/buttery; 12pm-10:30pm
Tues.-Sat., 12pm-10pm Sun.; entrées £9*

Ignore the name for a moment; this old-school Finnieston restaurant offers the archetypal fine dining experience, with mahogany walls and tartan carpet creating a very homey feel. Mains err on the traditional side (grilled lemon sole or Scottish beef fillet), but this is one place where you'll definitely want to leave space for dessert. Opt for the Grand Dessert and you'll be presented with a sharing platter of all the desserts on the menu (bar the cheeses), so you may want to take it easy on the starters.

Fine Dining
BRIAN MAULE AT CHARDON D'OR
*176 West Regent Street; tel. 0141 248 3801; www.
brianmaule.com; 5pm-9:30pm Weds., 12pm-2:30pm*

and 5pm-9:30pm Thurs.-Fri., 12pm-2:30pm and 4:30pm-9:30pm Sat.; entrées £11.75

The menu at this smart city centre restaurant focuses on the abundance of natural produce available in Scotland, from hand-dived scallops to wild game and Scottish beef. Dishes are undeniably fresh with a French classic style, such as spiced pork belly, garlic squid, and cumin jus or roast Scotch sirloin with crushed turnip.

Afternoon Tea
★ MACKINTOSH AT THE WILLOW TEA ROOMS

215-217 Sauchiehall Street; tel. 0141 204 1903; www. mackintoshatthewillow.com; tea rooms 11am-5pm daily (afternoon tea 12pm-4:30pm), Salon de Luxe 2pm sitting Thurs.-Sun., rooftop terrace 12pm-7pm daily, tours 10am and 11am daily, exhibition 10am-4:30pm daily; afternoon tea £23.95, Salon de Luxe afternoon tea £45; cocktails £8.50, tour £7.50, exhibition £5.50

Charles Rennie Mackintosh designed these famous tearooms for his friend Miss Cranston in 1903-1904, and, though the building has changed hands several times, it remains resolutely Mackintosh. In June 2018 it reopened, having been closed for several years while the Willow Tea Rooms Trust undertook major restoration work to return the tea rooms to their heyday after the building began to deteriorate.

Mackintosh and his wife, Margaret Macdonald, designed everything, from the chairs to the menus, and even the waitress uniforms and cutlery. Set across three floors, the 200-seater restaurant is the height of Edwardian elegance. There is a front and back saloon, a billiards room, and a gallery that floods with light, but the most beautiful room and the best place to have afternoon tea is the famously opulent Salon de Luxe, where once you had to pay a penny extra to enter. In this room you will find original Mackintosh stained-glass doors with purple paneling and leaded frieze decorated in the Art Nouveau style. Margaret designed the tearoom with her husband and a gesso panel with the quote

"O ye, all ye that walk in Willowwood" (from the sonnet "Willowood" by Dante Gabriel Rossetti) by her hand takes pride of place opposite the fireplace.

You'll get a choice of a good range of white, black, green, and fruit teas, while the selection of finger sandwiches (egg, cucumber, and ham and mustard), scones, and cakes come on a tiered stand. There's also now a nice roof terrace for cocktails.

Next door to the tearoom, a shop sells Mackintosh souvenirs and hosts a good exhibition. You can also book one of the 45-minute tours of the tearoom, run by volunteers from the Charles Rennie Macintosh Society, who can explain the history behind some of the design flourishes and the restoration process.

Vegan
STEREO

22-28 Renfield Lane; tel. 0141 222 2254; www. stereocafebar.com; 12pm-9pm daily; small plates £5.50

One of the city's best-loved vegan restaurants, Stereo also doubles as a gig venue and occupies the basement and lower floors of the former Daily Record building, designed by Charles Rennie Mackintosh. Choose from light bites such as sticky cauliflower wings, sharing platters, or one of the cakes (all baked in house). If you're really hungry, it's hard to resist one of the seasonal pies (mushroom and spring vegetable, for instance), and you can rest assured everything is completely free of animal produce.

MERCHANT CITY
Traditional Fare
CAFÉ GANDOLFI

64 Albion Street; tel. 0141 552 6813; www. cafegandolfi.com; 8am-5pm Mon., 8am-10:30pm Tues.-Sat., 9am-5pm Sun.; entrées £7

This Glasgow institution serves delicious food using the freshest Scottish ingredients. Revolving doors lead to a beautiful room of heavy oak furniture designed by the late Glasgow School of Art graduate Tim Read, and the food is worthy of such a grand setting.

Classic dishes include Stornoway black pudding followed by house-smoked venison. There is also a good choice of pasta dishes.

Steak and Seafood
★ ROGANO

11 Exchange Place; tel. 0141 248 4055; www. roganoglasgow.com; 12pm-11pm daily; entrées £10.50

Over 80 years old, Rogano is part of the furniture of Glasgow. Located just off Royal Exchange Square, it famously boasts the same Art Deco style as the *Queen Mary* (a ship built on the Clyde at the same time) and is the city's oldest surviving restaurant. The **Oyster and Cocktail Bar** is a must, while dishes like the chilled Scottish *fruits de mer* have been served here since 1935.

Food Market
★ PLATFORM AT ARGYLE STREET ARCHES

The Arches, 253 Argyle Street; tel. 0345 241 6253; https://argylestarches.com/platform.; 12pm-10pm Fri.-Sat., 12pm-6pm Sun.; dishes £7

Once home to a world-renowned club, the Arches has been transformed into an independent street food market, open Friday and Saturday night and Sunday afternoon. Freshly cooked food is served in a hidden underground location (the doorway is under the arches behind Glasgow Central Station and looks more like the entrance to a cool office), where a DJ spins tunes and there's a microbrewery on-site. Many of the stallholders already have establishments in Glasgow, so it's a good chance to try a variety of dishes under one roof before you book a table—it's a darn bit cheaper, too.

Light Bites
TANTRUM DOUGHNUTS

28 Gordon Street; tel. 0141 248 1552; www. tantrumdoughnuts.com; 8:30am-6pm Mon.-Fri., 10am-6pm Sat. and Sun.; doughnuts £2

This donut shop is so popular it has two locations (the other is in the West End), and the premise is simple: delicious, indulgent donuts that are handmade. The donuts are made by actual pastry chefs using brioche dough that is proofed for 16 hours. Try the peanut butter and jam one or the "old fashioned" almond glaze buttermilk donut.

EAST END
Fine Dining
BILSON ELEVEN

10 Annfield Place; tel. 0141 554 6259; https://bilsoneleven.co.uk; 6pm-8pm Thurs.-Sat.; tasting menu £100 per person, £70 extra for the drink pairing

Loosen your belt if you're planning to dine here, as it's tasting menu only and the restaurant advises you allow 3-4 hours to complete your dinner. Housed in an old tenement building in the gradually gentrifying Dennistoun area of the east end, dining here is an intimate event, as dinner is served in the house's drawing room. Dishes use Scottish ingredients and are playful in their presentation.

Light Bites
SMOKEY TROTTERS

Back of Randall's Antiques, entry Stevenson Street, Barras Market; 11am-9pm Weds.-Sat., 11am-6pm Sun.; burgers £8.50

For the best burgers in town, surely no one can outdo this laid-back joint, tucked in behind one of the antique emporiums at Barras Market (I found it by accident but there is a sign pointing to it on Stevenson Street). They do fries with "just salt pal," grilled cheese sandwiches, and rice dishes, but really you'd be doing yourself a disservice if you didn't try one of the burgers, such as the Hot Mother Clucker with crispy fried chicken, buffalo sauce, and blue murder mayo. Delicious. "Nae meat" burgers are available, too.

WEST END

The cobbled backstreet of **Ashton Lane** in the student mecca of the West End is very pretty and is a living example of the city's ability to reinvent itself. It was once a run-down,

---

1: Step back to the 1930s with dinner at Rogano.
2: Ubiquitous Chip is on pretty Ashton Lane.

largely forgotten street, but the arrival of one of Glasgow's most popular restaurants, the Ubiquitous Chip, in the 1970s encouraged other independent businesses to follow. It has since become a bustling passageway of bars and restaurants, firmly on the tourist trail. Follow the lane north and you'll come onto **Creswell Lane,** a similarly attractive cobbled lane that has lots of small boutiques and shops and that, for some reason, fewer tourists seem to find.

Modern Scottish
OX AND FINCH

920 Sauchiehall Street; tel. 0141 339 8627; www. oxandfinch.com; 12pm-1am daily; plates from £7

This 2018 Michelin Bib award-winning restaurant in Finnieston serves up small plates of immaculately presented food for sharing. There is slow-cooked lamb shoulder served with an almond and mint yogurt, or charred leeks with poached egg, as well as a really good choice of vegetarian and vegan dishes.

Traditional Fare
UBIQUITOUS CHIP

12 Ashton Lane; tel. 0141 334 5007; www. ubiquitouschip.co.uk; 12pm-1am daily; entrées £11, brasserie £7.45

Arguably Glasgow's most famous restaurant, this Ashton Lane stalwart, with its cobblestone floors, nooks and crannies, and covered courtyard (with fishpond), is an unforgettable place to eat. The food showcases the best of Scotland, too, from homemade haggis to Orkney smoked salmon and scallops from Islay. There is also a brasserie-style menu, with slightly more affordable prices.

STRAVAIGIN

28 Gibson Street; tel. 0141 334 2665; www.stravaigin. co.uk; 4pm-12am Tues., 12pm-12am Weds.-Fri., 11am-12am Sat.-Sun.; entrées £8.50

This boundary-pushing restaurant, which offers a casual approach to eating well, is renowned for inspiring culinary curiosity, but it also knows when to stick with what works: its homemade haggis has been on the menu since 1994. Its vegetables are grown on its own small holding in Ayrshire and the atmosphere is lively and vibrant, making it a good place to break bread with friends.

French
CAIL BRUICH

725 Great Western Road; tel. 0141 334 6265; www. cailbruich.co.uk; lunch 12pm-4:30pm Thurs.-Sat., dinner 6:30pm-12am Weds.-Sat.; tasting menus from £75 per person

The proud owner of Glasgow's only Michelin star, this West End restaurant offers a French-style menu with resolutely fresh ingredients and flavor combinations that are well thought out. There are seasonal tasting menus (two courses from £22). The service is discrete, and mains include dishes like rabbit with black garlic, violet artichoke, foie gras, and white asparagus. For something more casual, check out their new sister small plates restaurant, **Bar Brett,** one of the most exciting new Glasgow dining spots.

Seafood
★ CRABSHAKK

1114 Argyle Street; tel. 0141 334 6127; www.crabshakk. com; 12pm-12am daily; entrées £9.95

This established restaurant that was in Finnieston long before it was cool to be here sticks to doing what it does well: serving seafood and fish suppers with finesse. Seared scallops with anchovies or salt and pepper squid are good for sharing, and everyone should try the Crabshakk fish club sandwich at least once.

Asian
SHISH MAHAL

60-68 Park Road; tel. 0141 334 7899; www. shishmahal.co.uk; 12pm-2pm and 5pm-11pm Mon.-Thurs., 12pm-11:30pm Fri.-Sat., 5pm-10pm Sun.; entrées £4.95

This restaurant proudly boasts that chicken tikka masala was created here. With this in mind, it's nigh on impossible to resist sampling the restaurant's take on the dish, but, if you can, there is a range of Punjabi and South Indian dishes to choose from as well.

THE HANOI BIKE SHOP

*8 Ruthven Lane; tel. 0141 334 7165; https://
hanoibikeshop.co.uk; 12pm-11pm Mon.-Thurs.,
12pm-12:30am Fri., 11am-12:30am Sat., 11am-11pm
Sun.; entrées £6.65*

Tucked away on the quirky Ruthven Lane in the city's West End, this no-frills eatery serves fresh, vibrant Vietnamese street food with a menu designed for sharing.

MOTHER INDIA

*28 Westminster Terrace; tel. 0141 221 1663; www.
motherindia.co.uk; 12pm-10pm Mon.-Thurs. and Sun.,
12pm-10:30pm Fri.-Sat.; entrées £7.50*

Offering its unique "twist on tapas," this casual dining restaurant in Finnieston is one of Glasgow's most popular. It's recommended you choose three or four dishes between two people, but everything on the menu sounds so good, it's hard to stop yourself from going overboard.

Food Market
DOCKYARD SOCIAL

*95 Haugh Road; dockyardsocial.com; 5pm-11pm Fri.,
12pm-11pm Sat., 12pm-8pm Sun.*

It was only a matter of time before Finnieston got its own street food market, and as you might expect, this one, which opened in December 2017 just a short walk from Kelvingrove Park, comes with a side of conscience. While for many customers, the focus is on different vendors serving global comfort food—there are 12 different stalls, and food allergies and dietary preferences are well catered for—organizers also hope to create a training school to help disadvantaged people in the city get on their feet.

Good karma and all, the market is housed in an old warehouse building with a rolling program of live music and DJs providing a musical backdrop. It's a trendy hangout where you can kick back and choose between an array of Scottish pop-ups while you sip on craft beer or a seasonal cocktail.

SOUTHSIDE
Fish and Chips
HOOKED FISH AND CHIPS

*1027 Cathcart Road; tel. 0141 649 3994; www.
hookedtogo.co.uk; 12pm-10pm Mon.-Sat., 4pm-10pm
Sun.; entrées £3.35*

This fish-and-chip shop near Mount Florida rail station is really handy for Hampden Park and features some interesting spins on normal chippy classics, including breaded haddock with pesto, sweet potato fries, and homemade mushy peas and tartare sauce. Don't miss the melt-in-your-mouth mac and cheese balls.

Cafés
LOCAVORE

*349 Victoria Road; tel. 0141 378 1682; https://
glasgowlocavore.org; 7:30am-8pm daily; salads from
£4.50*

Housed in a sustainable grocery store, this café is perhaps the only fully organic café in the city (though I'm sure others will soon follow). Dishes are dependent on what is available in the café's organic market garden as well as excess produce in the shop, to ensure as little waste as possible. Expect salads, soups, stews, and a good choice of vegan and vegetarian dishes. You can also pick up fresh bread and organic fruit and veg.

CAFÉ STRANGE BREW

*1082 Pollokshaws Road; tel. 0141 440 7290; www.
facebook.com/cafestrangebrew/timeline; 9am-5pm
Mon.-Sat., 9am-4pm Sun.; entrées £5.50*

Set in the Shawlands area of Southside, this café serves up good coffee as well as a range of yummy brunch dishes. Don't be put off by the long queue—it does move fast and is worth it for the tasty cakes (many of which are gluten-free) and the baked eggs.

Nightlife

There are no two ways about it: Glaswegians love a drink. Scottish writer Jack House, known as Mr. Glasgow, famously declared, "The Glasgow invention of square-toed shoes was to enable the Glasgow man to get closer to the bar." It's also a young city; almost a quarter of its population is aged between 16 and 29. Perhaps because of its youthful inhabitants, in terms of sheer variety of nightlife, Glasgow is rarely bettered.

At the **Teuchters' Triangle,** a collection of convivial pubs with Highland roots in the West End, you can experience the famous Glasgow good humor and hospitality. For clubbing, try the high-octane venues on **Sauchiehall Street.** When it comes to live music, those in the know go to King Tut's Wah Wah Hut for an intimate (if rather sweaty) gig or the sprung dance floor of the 1960s Barrowland Ballroom. Merchant City is home to the city's very own **"pink triangle,"** just south of George Square, the center of Glasgow's growing gay scene.

Wherever you end up, make sure you are dressed for the occasion; while there is a cool, understated vibe at many bars and clubs, the term Glasvegas refers to the fact that many Glaswegians like to get dolled up for a night on the tiles (particularly on a Saturday night). The average cost of a pint is £4, while a small glass of wine is anything upward of £4.50.

CITY CENTRE
Bars and Pubs
THE SCOTIA
112-114 Stockwell Street; tel. 0141 552 8681; www. scotiabar-glasgow.co.uk; 12pm-12am daily; pints of beer from £3.30, single malt whiskies from £3
It was here that a wide-eyed young man by the name of Billy Connolly first cut his teeth on the comedy circuit. Reputedly Glasgow's oldest pub—it's been around since 1792—it has all the fixtures: wood beams, barstools,

and brass pumps. Plus, aside from the regularly scheduled music, there are also some impromptu sessions.

NICE N SLEAZY
421 Sauchiehall Street; tel. 0141 333 0900; www. nicensleazy.com; 12pm-3am Mon.-Sat., 1pm-3am Sun.; entry often free, some gigs from £6; pints of beer from £3.30, cocktails from £4.50
Let's get one thing straight: you're not coming here to be wined and dined, so take a clue from the name. This dive bar has an amazing jukebox and booths, and it's a bona fide jumping joint. There is hand-scrawled graffiti on the walls and a disco ball, and, although it wouldn't kill bar staff to break into a smile every now and then, it's still one of the most fun nights out you can have in Glasgow.

Live Music
★ KING TUT'S WAH WAH HUT
274a St Vincent Street; tel. 0141 221 5279; www. kingtuts.co.uk; 4pam-12am daily; gigs from £8; pints of beer from £3.25
As the place where Oasis was discovered, this dark, underground (literally) gig venue has achieved cult status. Every band starting out wants to play here because they know they'll be playing to a captive audience (as well as some record company spies), and you do get the sense that any minute you might just see the next big thing.

Nightclubs
BAR BLOC
117 Bath Street; tel. 0141 574 6066; www.bloc.ru; 11am-3am daily; events free, pints of beer from £2.90, cocktails from £4.95
Refreshingly, all the gigs and events at this city centre bar-club are free and the lineup is varied. There is live music or DJs seven nights a week playing an eclectic range, from rockabilly to indie, to folk and jazz. It looks the part,

☆ Best Places to Hear Live Music

King Tut's Wah Wah Hut

For a long time, Glasgow without music was impossible to imagine. During lockdown, though, the city's bars and clubs were quiet and it didn't suit the place. Now things are creeping back to normal and no matter what night of the week you arrive in the city, you can be assured of an exceptional choice of music taking place in pubs and clubs across Glasgow (much of which is free). There's simply no such thing as a quiet night out in Glasgow, Heaven forbid. Here are some of the top places to hear live music, whatever mood you are in.

- **King Tut's Wah Wah Hut:** It's over 25 years since a little-known band called Oasis was signed by Alan McGee here in 1993, but this 300-capacity venue is still considered at the forefront of new music (page 230).

- **Mono:** With live music most nights of the week (mostly up-and-coming bands, with free entry), this is a slightly cooler, more left-field venue on the eastern fringes of the city centre. There's a good variety of music, from funk and soul to indie rock and dance (page 232).

- **Barrowland Ballroom:** Set in a 1930s music hall, this slightly kitsch and utterly retro venue in Glasgow's East End, with its sprung dance floor, is like a time machine back to the heady days of early rock 'n' roll. You can't miss it—just look for the huge neon sign (page 219).

- **Ben Nevis, Islay Inn, and Park Bar:** While there are lots of pubs around the city where you can hear Scottish folk, nowhere does it better than the trio of pubs that make up what is known as the Teuchter's Triangle on Argyle Street in the West End (pages 233, 234, 233).

too, with neon lights and records stacked behind metal cages, giving it both an anarchic and disco feel.

MERCHANT CITY
Bars and Pubs
THE HORSESHOE BAR

17-18 Drury Street; tel. 0141 248 6368; www. thehorseshoebarglasgow.co.uk; 9am-12am daily; pints of beer from £3.50, wine from £11.99 a bottle

Fancy it is not, but this Victorian bar, which, as you might have guessed, is shaped like a horseshoe, is nothing short of a Glaswegian institution—if the football is on, the place is heaving. Once one of the city's grandest gin bars, it is now one of its busiest pubs and an easy pit stop when shopping on nearby Buchanan Street. Be prepared to hang around the enormous bar, the longest in Europe, until a table becomes available, and, with daily deals such as two meals for £8, there are few places offering better-value food.

SLOANS

108 Argyle Street; tel. 0141 221 8886; www. sloansglasgow.com; 11am-12am Mon.-Thurs. and Sun., 11am-1am Fri.-Sat.; pints of beer from £4, single malt whiskies from £3.50

One of the oldest pubs in the city (it dates from 1797), Sloans is hidden down an alleyway just off the city centre end of Argyle Street. Inside, the oval bar is a good place to meet friends, while in summer drinkers spill out onto the cobbles. The biggest attraction of Sloans, however, is the weekly ceilidh held every Friday in the ballroom across the cobbles. It's a lively party where you'll be swung about to shrieks of laughter and the fun is undeniably infectious.

Live Music
★ MONO

12 Kings Court; tel. 0141 553 2400; www. monocafebar.com; 11am-11pm Sun.-Thurs., 11am-1am Fri.-Sat.; many events free, other gigs from £8; beer from £4, small wine from £4.50

This stripped-back café-bar has an exposed microbrewery and an award-winning vegan restaurant—the macaroni and cheese is especially good. During the day it is a cool place to chill out or browse the record store (run by Stephen McRobbie from indie band The Pastels), while from 7:30pm onward it's a good place to catch new music, often for free.

Nightclubs
AUDIO

14 Midland Street; www.musicglue.com/ audioglasgow; 6:30pm-11:30pm, until 3am on club nights; from £7, some events free, beer and wine from £3

This tiny venue underneath the railway arches is a great place to see loud punk and metal bands. The crowd is dressed down, which is just as well as it's a little grotty, but with acoustics this good no one seems to care. You have to shout to be heard at the bar, though, or else get good at miming and mouthing your order.

EAST END
Bars and Pubs
DRYGATE BREWERY

85 Drygate; tel. 0141 212 8815; www.drygate.com; 5pm-12am Mon.-Thurs., 12pm-12am Fri.-Sun.; tours £10

This brewery, which also offers tours on Sundays, serves beer, pizza, and burgers in its very cool Peaks Bar, which has views over the brewhouse. Ideal for beer connoisseurs, all beers are brewed on-site using a range of techniques and you can try a selection with one of the beer flights. There are also occasional gigs and DJ nights.

WEST END
Bars and Pubs
ORAN MOR

Top of Byres Road; tel. 0141 357 6200; https:// oran-mor.co.uk; 9am-2am Mon.-Weds., 9am-3am Thurs.-Sat., 11am-3am Sun.; pints of beer from £3.80, single malts from £3.50

This old church has been converted into a unique venue, bar, and restaurant. Aside from the Whisky Bar, which offers 280 single malts, there is also the late-night brasserie and two restaurants. Most visitors come here to see the incredible mural ceiling in the auditorium by artist and writer Alastair Day, but, if you can, try to attend one of the *A Play, A Pie, and A Pint* shows, which are popular with local students.

HUG & PINT

171 Great Western Road; tel. 0141 331 1901; www. thehugandpint.com; 12pm-12am daily; pints of beer from £3.50, bottle of wine from £14.95, main courses from £5

A firm favorite with Finnieston locals, this pub does comfort vegan food with aplomb (dishes are typically designed to be shared), and it has an exciting music schedule, with some impressive names such as Billy Nomates. The venue also supports up-and-coming performers, be they spoken word artists, musicians, or comedy acts.

BREL

Ashton Lane; tel. 0141 342 4966; www.brelbar.com; 12pm-12am Mon.-Thurs. and Sun., 12pm-1am Fri.-Sat.; pints of beer from £4.60, bottle of wine £18.95

Among the many cool restaurants and bars in and around Ashton Lane, this little gem stands out, not least because of its fab beer garden. In summer months there are also regular barbecues and a good lineup of live acts, while in winter hide away indoors and indulge in one of their fondue and raclette nights. It's not the cheapest pub around, but it's a cool place to be.

Live Music

★ THE PARK BAR

1202 Argyle Street; tel. 0141 339 1715; www. parkbarglasgow.com; 11:45am-12am daily; pints of beer from £3.50, single malts from £3.50

At the west end of Argyle Street, you will find the city's largest number of proper pubs, including this gem, which forms part of what is known as the Highland (or Teuchter's) Triangle. It's famed for its traditional music; Thursday is the regular music night and is an informal affair, followed by band nights on Friday, Saturday, and Sunday. Music starts around 9pm each night.

★ BEN NEVIS

1147 Argyle Street; tel. 0141 576 5204; www.facebook. com/TheBenNevisBar; 12pm-12am Mon.-Sat., 12:30pm-12am Sun.; pints of beer from £3.50, single malts from £3

This is one of the city's best bars for whisky and traditional music, a winning combination. With wooden floors and bare stone walls, it has a very old-school Scottish charm

Brel, Ashton Lane

and is small enough to make you feel a part of things once the gathered musicians get going on one of the side tables. It's the kind of place you can come into on your own and soon make friends for the evening.

★ ISLAY INN

1256 Argyle Street; tel. 0141 334 7774; www.islayinn. com; 11am-12am daily; pints of beer from £3.50, single malts from £3.50

During the day this traditional inn is a little on the sleepy side, but come evening there's good music and a typically talkative group of locals. If you're peckish, tuck into one of the homemade burgers, but it's the music that really draws the punters. There are jam sessions on Monday and Thursday evenings, an open mic on Sunday, and live bands play on Friday and Saturday nights.

Nightclubs
HILLHEAD BOOKCLUB

17 Vinicombe Street; tel. 0141 576 1700; https:// hillheadbookclub.co.uk; 11am-12am Mon.-Fri., 10am-12am Sat. and Sun.; pints of beer from £3.75, cocktails from £7.50

Hillhead Bookclub is evidence of just how cool the West End has become. This multi-faceted venue hosts some of the city's best DJs Wednesday-Sunday, but it is so much more than just a club. Pop-up vintage fairs are held regularly, and on Sunday mornings, you can often see trendy 20- and 30-somethings trying to undo the damage from the night before, drinking Bloody Marys and attempting to read the newspaper—all to a rockabilly-rock 'n' roll soundtrack. Come for "mate's rates" drink deals Monday-Thursday.

SOUTHSIDE
Pubs
THE LAURIESTON

58 Bridge Street; tel. 0141 429 4528; www.facebook. com/TheLaurieston; 11am-11pm daily; pints of beer from £3.50, single malts from £3.50

Stepping into this weathered but warm pub is like stepping into the set of a 1960s British cop show. Little has changed over the years—the circular bar with Formica tables remains and the pub still has a separate lounge area, with wood paneling, red bench seats, and tartan carpet. Indeed, vintage touches abound, including a machine for heating pies and old Glasgow photos on the wall. It's well-located for pre- or post-drinks at the nearby Citizen's Theatre and a friendlier bunch of punters you never did find.

HERAGHTY'S

708 Pollokshaws Road; tel. 0141 423 0380; www.heraghtysbar.com; 11am-12am Mon.-Sat., 12:30pm-12am Sun; pints of beer from £3.45, single malts from £3.50

In the popular Strathbungo neighborhood, this family-run Irish pub, which first opened its doors in 1890 and has been in the Heraghty family since the 1970s, claims to pour the best pint of Guinness in the whole of Glasgow. It's moved with the times, too, and stocks a good range of craft beer as well as several Scottish gins.

Live Music
GLASGOW'S GRAND OLE OPRY

2-4 Govan Road; tel. 0141 429 5396; www. glasgowsgrandoleopry.co.uk; 7pm-12am Fri.-Sat., sometimes Sun.; cover charge £5; pints of beer from £3.50, wine from £4 a glass

Taking inspiration from the famous Nashville venue, this country and western dive bar first opened its doors in the 1970s, and, though it's become a little more ironic than in its '70s heyday, it's an awful lot of fun, with fantastic live music and typical entertainment including bingo, a shoot-out, and line dancing.

Accommodations

This being a major city, accommodation options are wide. As expected, you pay more the more central you are, but prices are a lot more reasonable than in Edinburgh. Most guesthouses and hotel rooms come en suite, but, if you are staying in a hostel, then you will have to share a bathroom and often leave your room to do so.

If you are just in Glasgow for a couple of days, you will probably want to stay in and around the Merchant City or the city centre for a chance to see the main attractions, plus explore one or two other areas. Many well-known hotel chains have places within easy reach of either Glasgow Central Station or Queen Street, and, if you can stay mid-week, then prices will drop substantially. Likewise, try to avoid school holidays (Easter and late July-early September) as these are peak times. If you're most interested in the city's cultural highlights, such as the Hunterian and the Kelvingrove, then it makes sense to stay in the West End, while the Southside is a good option for a relaxing few days where you can lap up the laid-back café culture.

CITY CENTRE
Under £100
THE PIPERS' TRYST HOTEL

30-34 McPhater Street; tel. 0141 353 5551; www. thepipingcentre.co.uk/stay; £78 d, £90 with breakfast

This small hotel within the National Piping Centre offers superb value for money for a city centre hotel, with clean and welcoming rooms (a wee dram comes as standard) if not the most exciting decor.

£100-200
★ ABODE GLASGOW

129 Bath Street; tel. 0141 221 6289; www. abodeglasgow.co.uk; £114 d, £134 with breakfast

This 59-bed hotel is housed in an attractive converted townhouse. In the center of

the hotel is an amazing cage lift, and rooms are bright and clean with large bathrooms. Breakfasts are tasty—the full Scottish is recommended, and you can even order a smoothie on the side. Plus, it's just a 10-minute walk to Glasgow Central Station and within staggering distance of King Tut's Wah Wah Hut.

CARLTON GEORGE HOTEL

44 West George Street; tel. 0141 353 6373; www. carlton.nl/en/hotel-george-glasgow; £126 d, £158 with breakfast

A highlight of a stay at this vibrant boutique hotel is having afternoon tea (from £14.95 per person) in the Windows Restaurant, which has splendid views of George Square. Another plus, which does make the price a lot more appealing, is complimentary minibars in all the rooms, plus decanters of gin, whisky, and vodka. Oh, and all beds are king size.

MERCHANT CITY
Under £100
GRASSHOPPERS HOTEL GLASGOW

87 Union Street; tel. 0141 222 2666; www. grasshoppersglasgow.com; £98 d

If you're arriving into Glasgow by train, you couldn't find a much more convenient place to stay. Rooms feature period details such as high ceilings and cornicing, and they have bright, cheerful decor. It's a good affordable option if you want to stay central.

£100-200
★ GRAND CENTRAL HOTEL

99 Gordon Street; tel. 0141 413 9115; https:// grandcentral.vocohotels.com; £123 d

Also very close to Glasgow Central but with a bit more gloss is this historic railway hotel, which has hosted many an illustrious guest, including Frank Sinatra and Winston Churchill. The hotel's Champagne Central bar harkens bag to the Golden Age of travel with views over the station. Rooms are tastefully decorated.

HOTEL INDIGO GLASGOW

75 Waterloo Street; tel. 0141 226 7700; www. hinglasgow.co.uk.; £155 d

Housed in one of Glasgow's first-ever power stations, this smart and colorful hotel is inviting. Minibars are stocked with free soft drinks (pay a little more and you'll get free beer and wine, too) and beds come with Egyptian cotton sheets. You'll find Aveda toiletries and rainfall showers in the bathrooms. There's also a mini gym on-site, plus a 12pm check-out time.

EAST END
Under £100
★ ALISON GUEST HOUSE

26 Circus Drive; tel. 0141 556 1431; www. visitscotland.com/info/accommodation/alison-guest-house-p216551; £40 d

If you want to visit the cathedral and other historic sites in the East End, then this budget guesthouse is a steal. With doubles from £40 (with breakfast) and a genuinely personal reception from hosts Ann and Kenny, this Victorian villa offers budget accommodation that is clean, comfy, and welcoming. Plus, breakfast is cooked to order and the couple and their family will be only too happy to guide you to the best places to visit. Be warned, though, they don't respond much to emails, so ring to book.

WEST END
Under £100
GLASGOW YOUTH HOSTEL

7-8 Park Terrace; tel. 0141 332 3004; www. hostellingscotland.org.uk/hostels/glasgow; £59 private twin, £26 shared room, cooked breakfast £7

This hostel overlooking Kelvingrove Park is basic but in a good location. Beds are wooden framed and rooms (including bathrooms) are clean. Wi-Fi is patchy and is not available in the dorms, so you have to use one of the communal areas to get online.

★ ALAMO GUEST HOUSE

46 Gray Street; tel. 0141 339 2395; www. alamoguesthouse.com; £95 d

This impeccably presented family-run guest-house offers astounding value for money. Set in a Victorian building, it is effortlessly refined, with period cabinetry, Victorian carved armchairs, and even four-posters in some rooms. Plus, breakfast, which is included, can be enjoyed while admiring views of Kelvingrove Park and the University of Glasgow.

£100-200
15 GLASGOW

15 Woodside Place; tel. 0141 332 1263; http://15glasgow.com; £130 d

This luxurious B&B comes with super king beds and with many of the 19th-century property's original features, including wooden shutters and fireplaces. Guests have access to a private garden opposite, and considering breakfast is included, it's a pretty good price.

HOTEL DU VIN AT ONE DEVONSHIRE GARDENS

1 Devonshire Gardens; tel. 0141 378 0385; www. hotelduvin.com/locations/glasgow; £144 d

Uber-cool rooms veer on the decadent side with this trusted hotel brand. Beds come with hand-sprung mattresses and Egyptian cotton sheets, and rooms are decorated in warm hues with sumptuous fabrics. Bathrooms include freestanding baths and walk-in monsoon showers. The hotel is located on a pretty tree-lined Victorian terrace, where you can enjoy its sophisticated whisky room.

SOUTHSIDE
£100-200
SHERBROOKE CASTLE HOTEL

11 Sherbrooke Avenue; tel. 0141 427 4227; www. sherbrookecastlehotel.com; £176 d

This beautiful Scottish baronial four-star hotel in acres of its own grounds is not actually as expensive as you might think. Its turrets offer a fairy-tale feel to the place, but rooms aren't overly romantic, with classic colors and no superfluous furnishings. Afternoon tea (£39.90 for two) can be taken each day between 1pm and 4pm in the lounge, library, or Morrisons Room.

GOGLASGOW URBAN HOTEL

517 Paisley Road West; tel. 0141 427 3146; www. goglasgowhotel.com; £183 d

Well-located for the Ibrox Stadium if you are considering going to a match or taking a tour of Rangers' ground, these modern rooms are cool and minimalist (though lacking a little character), but beds are fitted with Egyptian cotton sheets and there are full-length mirrors in each room. This hotel attracts a business crowd and sports fans.

Information and Services

VisitScotland iCentre (tel. 0141 566 4083; www.visitscotland.com/info/services/glasgow-icentre-p332751) is located at the south entrance of Buchanan Street Subway Station. Staff can advise on everything from accommodation providers to travel to entrance tickets for attractions.

People Make Glasgow (https://people-makeglasgow.com) is the official guide to the city and is packed with tips, inspiring articles, events and festivals, and up-to-date news.

Similarly, **Glasgow Life** (www.glasgowlife.org.uk) is a charity that aims to inspire people to get out and explore and is particularly insightful when it comes to museums and cultural spaces.

As you travel around town, be sure to make good use of the many fliers and freebie magazines in the pubs and cafés, particularly in the West End and Southside. The two best magazines for gigs and exhibitions are *The Skinny* and *The List*.

Getting There

BY AIR

With two airports, Glasgow is extremely well served for air travel.

GLASGOW AIRPORT

Paisley, www.glasgowairport.com

Located just 8 miles (12.9 km) west of the city, this is the main airport where most visitors to Glasgow will arrive. It has direct flights from North America with **United Airlines** and from Canada with **Air Transat.**

A flight from London takes just an hour, and there are dozens of flights per day. **Ryanair** (www.ryanair.com) flies direct to Glasgow Airport from London Stansted; **British Airways** (www.britishairways.com) flies from London Gatwick, London Heathrow, and London City; and **easyJet**

(www.easyjet.com) flies from London Gatwick, London Stansted, and London Luton.

The **Glasgow Airport Express 500** is the official airport bus and leaves from just outside the terminal building every 10 minutes (15 minutes; adult £8.50, child £4.50). Buses run from 4:45am-11pm seven days a week, except on Christmas Day, and the best way to get a ticket is through the FirstBus app. From the city centre, you can get the return bus from Buchanan Bus Station or George Street. You can also prebook a taxi with **Glasgow Taxis** (tel. 0141 429 7070; www.glasgowtaxis.co.uk) or pick one up just outside the terminal building (although the former is cheaper, around £27).

GLASGOW PRESTWICK AIRPORT

Aviation House, Prestwick; www.glasgowprestwick. com

Located 32 miles (51 km) southwest of the city centre, this airport has inbound flights from many European hubs but none from London. Trains run three times an hour to Glasgow Central Station (50 minutes; £8.30 one-way).

BY TRAIN

Many people traveling from London choose to travel by train. **Glasgow Central** (Gordon St., www.scotrail.co.uk/plan-your-journey/ stations-and-facilities/glc) and **Glasgow Queen Street** (North Hanover Street, George Square; www.scotrail.co.uk/plan-your-journey/stations-and-facilities/glq) are both centrally located stations.

There are more than 20 direct trains from London Euston with **Avanti West Coast** (www.avantiwestcoast.co.uk) to Glasgow Central daily, that take around 4.5 hours and cost anywhere in the region of £30-80 each way. More romantic (though a little more expensive) is the **Caledonian Sleeper train** (www.scotrail.co.uk/plan-your-journey/ travel-connections/caledonian-sleeper). The train journey takes 7.5 hours, but, as it's overnight, you hardly mind. It costs from £45 oneway (though it can cost a lot more last minute, particularly if you want a cabin). There is just one sleeper train per day.

From Edinburgh, a train runs every few minutes into either Glasgow Queen Street or, less regularly, Glasgow Central. Journey time varies from 50 minutes to 1.25 hours, and tickets cost just £12.90 one-way. From Inverness, roughly one train runs per hour into Glasgow Queen Street (3.5 hours; from £8.30 one-way). Four trains a day run from Fort William to Glasgow Queen Street (3.75 hours; from £23.50 one-way). All tickets can be booked through **ScotRail** (www.scotrail. co.uk).

BY CAR

From **London,** the most direct route to Glasgow by car is to take the M40 to just outside Birmingham where you'll join the M6 all the way to Gretna Green, just across the Scottish border, and then take the A74 up to Glasgow (415 miles/668 km; 7.5 hours).

From **Edinburgh** follow the M8 west for 47 miles (76 km; one hour). From Stirling, Glasgow is a 27-mile (43 km) drive southwest along the M80, which takes just 30 minutes.

From **Mallaig** on the west coast of Scotland (the main jumping off point for Skye), it's 3.5 hours (152 miles/245 km), first east along the A830 to Fort William where you need to pick up the A82, which takes you all the way down through Loch Lomond before joining the M8 into the city. From Fort William, the journey time is just 2.5 hours (109 miles/175 km).

If you're coming all the way from **Inverness,** it's actually quite straightforward as you can take the A9 all the way down to Stirling and pick up the M80, which, despite covering 169 miles (272 km), only takes just over three hours.

Getting Around

Glasgow is built on a series of drumlins (hills), so while walking is a good way to orient yourself, you may find it takes some exertion.

As with most major cities, you should avoid driving in Glasgow where possible—parking is difficult and pricey. There's always traffic, so with an excellent Subway system, good buses, bikes, and sights that are within easy walking distance of each other, there's really no need for a car.

BY SUBWAY

The circular **Subway** (www.spt.co.uk/travel-with-spt/subway) system, actually one of the oldest underground systems in the world, is an easy way to get around the city. Purchase tickets in a machine at the Subway station; these need to be tapped in and out at card reader panels as you enter and leave stations. With just two lines—one clockwise and the other counterclockwise—it's pretty hard to get lost.

Journeys cost from just £1.55 one-way, while an **all-day ticket** costs £4.20 adult (child £2.10, under 5 free). If you are going to be here for a few days, you might want to think about getting a **Subway Smartcard,** which can be refilled. You will need to supply a passport-size photo for this and register on the **SPT website** (www.spt.co.uk/travelcards/subway-smartcard). Once you obtain a card, you can top it up on the **Bramble-powered website** (www.mybramble.co.uk) or in a ticket machine at a Subway station.

In addition to the Subway, there are lots of train stations connecting different parts of the city. An **SPT Roundabout** ticket (adult £7.40, child £3.70) gives you unlimited access to all the Subway and train stations and is valid after 9am on weekdays and all day on weekends or public holidays. You can buy these tickets at the ScotRail train stations or Subway stations.

Subway stations are dotted around the city centre, West End, and East End, with a few in the more northerly parts of Southside. With just 15 stations on the circuit, it takes just 24 minutes to go around them all. To find a Subway station above ground, you should look for the logo, which is an orange S against a white background within a gray circle and then an outer orange circle.

BY BUS

A very good bus system reaches all of the spots that the Subway doesn't serve (particularly handy if you are staying in the Southside). The main bus company is **First Glasgow** (www.firstbus.co.uk/greater-glasgow), which operates more than 100 routes through the city. Buses are a mix of double- and single-deckers, and always have the bus number and final destination displayed on the front. There are timetables on the FirstBus website (www.firstbus.co.uk) or, better, download the **FirstBus app,** which will help you plan your journey with real-time bus updates. You can pay on board using your contactless debit card, or buy in advance through the app.

If you're traveling as a family and using public transport, a **Daytripper ticket** (£23.20 for two adults and up to four children, £13.10 for one adult and up to two children) can be quite useful as it gives unlimited travel on most buses, Subway trips, and trains, and it can be purchased online from the **SPT Store** (www.spt.co.uk/tickets/day-tickets/daytripper), though it can only be used after 9am on weekdays.

Many first-time visitors use the **City Sightseeing** hop-on hop-off bus (https://city-sightseeing.com/en/92/Glasgow; one day £16, two days £17; 9:30am-4:30pm). With 21 stops taking in the biggest attractions and unlimited rides within a set time frame, two tours are offered: the live guide, which allows you to interact and ask questions, and the audio guide. Headphones are provided for the latter, so you can just plug in and chill out, or jump off if somewhere sounds interesting. You can't miss the buses—big red double-deckers with the City Sightseeing logo on the side. Main stops include George Square, Glasgow Cathedral, the Riverside Museum, the Buchanan Galleries, and the Kelvingrove Art Gallery and Museum. Buy tickets on the City Sightseeing website.

BY BIKE

It is possible to cycle around the city though you will have to familiarize yourself with the rules of the road. Roads are busy with cars, so make sure you keep to the left-hand side of the road and clearly indicate when turning or pulling out. The city council has some cycle routes listed on its website (www.glasgow.gov. uk/article/19355/Plan-a-route) and the very good Next Bike scheme has bikes and docking stations throughout the city (www.nextbike. co.uk/en/glasgow).

BY TAXI

You can hail a black taxi from anywhere in the city, and you'll recognize legitimate taxis as they will have a telling "taxi" sign—when this is lit up, you know the taxi is free to hail. Glasgow isn't huge, so you can expect to pay around £10 to travel from the Southside to, say, the West End. There are also taxi ranks outside both Glasgow Central and Queen Street stations.

Greater Glasgow

★ NEW LANARK AND THE FALLS OF CLYDE

This perfectly preserved old mill town is a remnant of the busy cotton industry brought to Glasgow and its surrounds on the River Clyde. New Lanark was founded in 1786 by David Dale, a local businessman, and Richard Arkwright, the famous entrepreneur who had already transformed the cotton industry in England. Though Dale was considered enlightened for his time, the majority of his workforce was made up of children alongside Highlanders who had been removed from their land during the notorious clearances.

You can visit the World Heritage site of New Lanark and the Falls of Clyde for free, but, if you would like to see the museum exhibits and inside the many buildings that make up the visitor center, you will need to pay the entry fee.

New Lanark Village

New Lanark Road; tel. 01555 661 345; www. newlanark.org; visitor center 10am-5pm Apr.-Oct., 10am-4pm Nov.-Mar.; adult £5, child free

Today, you can tour many of the mill buildings, including the schoolroom where Dale's son-in-law Robert Owen created the world's first infant school. You can also see the historic spinning mule in operation, and the village store where you can learn about Owen's revolutionary idea of selling quality goods at affordable prices to workers. Make sure to try some New Lanark ice cream, too.

Falls of Clyde

New Lanark; https://scottishwildlifetrust.org.uk/ reserve/falls-of-clyde; free

The Falls of Clyde are a series of linns, or waterfalls, located in a wildlife reserve that runs from the south of the heritage village of New Lanark and have attracted such famous visitors as William Wordsworth and J. M. W. Turner, who were mesmerized by their beauty. The four waterfalls that make up the Falls of Clyde are the upper falls of Bonnington Linn, Corra Linn, Dundaff Linn, and the lower falls of Stonebyres Linn; they are spaced out amid the serene wildlife reserve that follows the path of the River Clyde, at times rumbling, sometimes rushing. Look out for birdlife, including dippers, ravens, and kingfishers, as

Day Trips from Glasgow

Destination	Travel Time	Why Go?
Stirling (page 110)	30 minutes by train	Stirling's castle and picturesque old town are like a mini taste of Edinburgh that you can get without checking out of your Glasgow hotel.
Dumbarton Castle (page 243)	30 minutes by train	This fortress dramatically situated on the River Clyde has roots to the Middle Ages.
Perth (page 138)	1 hour by train	The "Fair City" of Perth makes for an interesting contrast with the grit and bustle of Glasgow.
Loch Lomond and the Trossachs National Park (page 290)	1 hour by train	If you're pressed for time, the West Highland Line makes it easy to visit this national park on a day trip from Scotland's largest city.
New Lanark and the Falls of Clyde (page 240)	1 hour by train, plus 10-minute bus ride	You'll get a unique view into industrial history in this well-preserved 18th-century mill town.
Dunfermline (page 121)	1.25 hours by bus	Wandering amid the ivy-covered walls of Dunfermline Abbey and Palace makes for a romantic day trip.
Ayrshire (page 263)	1 hour by train, plus 15-minute bus ride	Alloway, just a bus ride away from Ayr (Ayrshire's central hub), is the center of all things Robert Burns, Scotland's most famous poet.
Arran (page 276)	1 hour by train, plus 1-hour ferry ride	It takes some doing to visit the Isle of Arran in a day, but you'll be rewarded by what many call Scotland in miniature.

well as otters along the riverbank and signs of badgers who forage here. In the evenings Daubenton's bats are known to feed along the river.

FALLS OF CLYDE HIKE
Distance: 3.75 miles (6 km)
Time: 2 hours round-trip
Trailhead: Dundaff Linn

Information and Maps: www.walkhighlands. co.uk/glasgow/falls-of-clyde.shtml

The route is clearly signposted from the village of New Lanark. Follow the badger signs south through the village with the river on your right until you reach the first of the waterfalls, Dundaff Linn, at the far end of the village, which is where the woodland walk to Corra Linn, the tallest and most impressive

of the waterfalls, and beyond begins. Though the path is nicely laid out and sturdy for the most part, there can be some steep climbs, and you'll need to be wary of the wooden boardwalks that can be slippery following heavy rainfall (sometimes they are even submerged). It's worth it, though, for the views and the sense of calm. You can choose to walk back the way you came from New Lanark here or continue following the path up and over the river before coming back on the opposite bank past Bonnington Linn to New Lanark. This full route should take around two hours.

Getting There and Getting Around

There are two direct trains from Glasgow Central Station to Lanark Station every hour (50 minutes; £7.30 one-way). From Lanark Station you can get the no. 135 bus right into New Lanark village (tel. 0155 577 3533; www.stuartscoaches.co.uk, £3.50 each way), which takes around 10 minutes and runs every hour at 27 minutes past the hour (subject to change). Make sure you check return times for the bus with **Traveline** (www.traveline.info), so that you can make your returning train.

To drive from Glasgow, it's just 32 miles (51 km) southeast to Lanark. Leave the city on the M8, heading east, before joining the M74 south. Leave the M74 at junction 9 and take the B7086 into New Lanark.

DUMBARTON CASTLE

Castle Road, Dumbarton; tel. 0138 973 2167; www.historicenvironment.scot/visit-a-place/places/dumbarton-castle; 9:30am-5:30pm daily Apr.-Sept., *10am-4pm Sat.-Wed. Oct.-Mar. adult £6, child £3.60, under 5 free*

In the heart of the ancient Kingdom of Strathclyde, just 15 miles (24.1 km) from Glasgow, lies this former stronghold, which sits on a volcanic plug (much like Edinburgh Castle). Once known as "Alt Clut" or "Rock of the Clyde," and later renamed "Dun Breatann" from the Gaelic for "fortress of the Britons," it was a significant fortress in the Middle Ages that initially stood to protect from Norwegian Vikings, whose frontier lay just 10 miles downriver (and who once ruled the Western Isles as well as islands in the River Clyde), and later the English.

Today, not much is left of the 13th-century castle, built by Alexander II of Scotland, but you can still climb the 557 steps to the top of White Tower Crag for views as far as Ben Lomond. Plus, it offers good insight into 18th-century military tactics, and you can see some of the artifacts from the castle in the Georgian Governor's House. Grab a coffee by the main entrance to keep your hands warm as you walk around, as much of the site is exposed.

Getting There

It's just a 30-minute (20.5-mile/33-km) drive west of Glasgow to Dumbarton Castle along the M8 and then the M898 before joining the A82 at Old Kilpatrick. Alternatively, you can get the train with **ScotRail** (www.scotrail.com) from Glasgow Queen Street to Dumbarton East (30 minutes; £4.60 one-way), from where it is a 12-minute walk to the castle. Trains runs every 5-10 minutes.

1: New Lanark **2:** Corra Linn at the Falls of Clyde

Southern Scotland and the Borders

Too easily missed, southern Scotland is often sped through by visitors crossing the English border by train or car, heading to some of the bigger tourist draws of Glasgow, Edinburgh, and the Highlands. But stop awhile en route and you'll find much to enjoy in this region. From the soft green hills of Ayrshire—the homeland of that most Scottish of poets, Robert Burns—to the overlooked (and much better for it) "Scotland in miniature" Isle of Arran, southern Scotland is filled with natural attractions and historic landmarks, with rarely a queue in sight.

Cutting through the region, the Southern Uplands is a mountain chain noticeably more forested and also more rounded than the Highlands. These hills give way to arable valleys, making this

Highlights

Look for ★ to find recommended sights, activities, dining, and lodging.

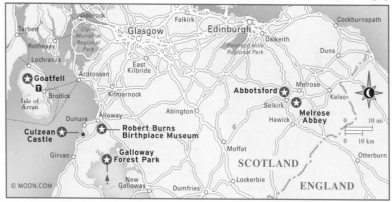

★ **Abbotsford:** This palace of curiosities was the beloved home of Sir Walter Scott, a shrine to all the weird and wonderful things that inspired him (page 253).

★ **Melrose Abbey:** So significant was this 12th-century abbey that it was here that Robert the Bruce insisted his heart be buried (page 254).

★ **Robert Burns Birthplace Museum:** Visit the thatched home of the Scottish bard and pore over original manuscripts in the nearby museum (page 263).

★ **Culzean Castle:** You could spend all day exploring this remarkable cliff-top castle and its sprawling parkland (page 265).

★ **Galloway Forest Park:** Switch off from the outside world in this forested wonderland and watch the night sky's amazing light show (page 269).

★ **Goatfell:** A climb up the Isle of Arran's highest hill, walking distance from the ferry terminal, is easy to do on a day trip from the mainland (page 278).

Southern Scotland and the Borders

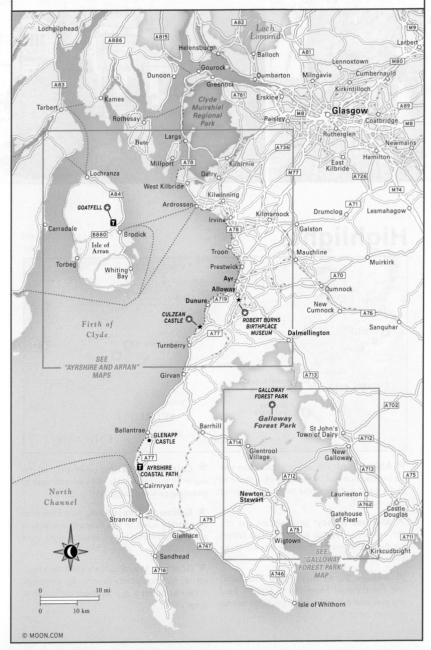

Lochgilphead

Loch Lomond

A82

M9

Larbert

M80

A886

A815

Helensburgh

Balloch

A81

Lennoxtown

Cumbernauld

Dunoon

Gourock

Dumbarton

Milngavie

Kirkintilloch

A89

A83

Kames

Greenock

A761

Erskine

M8

Glasgow

Coatbridge

M8

Tarbert

Rothesay

Clyde Muirshiel Regional Park

Paisley

Rutherglen

Newmains

Bute

Largs

A736

East Kilbride

Hamilton

Millport

A78

Kilbirnie

A726

M74

Lochranza

Dalry

A77

Drumclog

A71

Lesmahagow

GOATFELL

West Kilbride

Kilwinning

Kilmarnock

Drumclog

A841

Ardrossan

Irvine

A78

Galston

Carradale

Brodick

Troon

Mauchline

Muirkirk

B880

Isle of Arran

Prestwick

Ayr

A70

Torbeg

Whiting Bay

Alloway

Dunure

A719

Cumnock

ROBERT BURNS BIRTHPLACE MUSEUM

New Cumnock

A76

Firth of Clyde

CULZEAN CASTLE

A77

Dalmellington

Sanquhar

Turnberry

SEE "AYRSHIRE AND ARRAN" MAPS

Girvan

A713

GALLOWAY FOREST PARK

A702

Ballantrae

Barrhill

Galloway Forest Park

St John's Town of Dalry

A712

GLENAPP CASTLE

A714

Glentrool Village

New Galloway

A77

AYRSHIRE COASTAL PATH

A712

A713

A75

Cairnryan

Laurieston

North Channel

Newton Stewart

Gatehouse of Fleet

A762

Castle Douglas

Stranraer

A75

Wigtown

Kirkcudbright

Glenluce

A747

SEE "GALLOWAY FOREST PARK" MAP

A711

Sandhead

A716

A746

Isle of Whithorn

0   10 mi
0   10 km

© MOON.COM

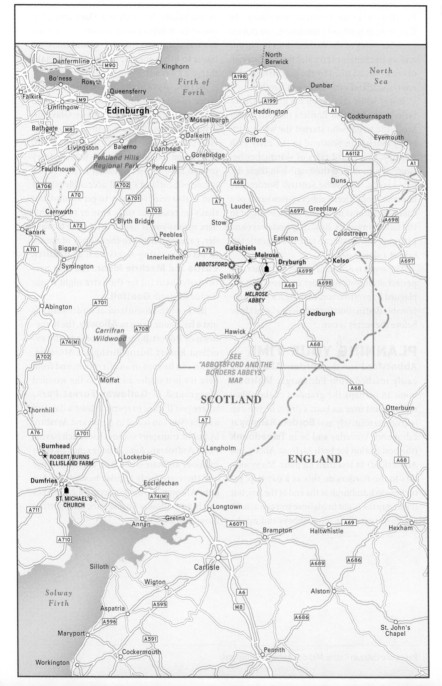

Scotland's chief farming territory. In Galloway, in Scotland's southwest, you can experience some of the darkest skies in Europe and a surprisingly pretty and deserted stretch of coastline, warmed by the gulf stream, that enjoys Scotland's most clement weather.

It was while staying on his grandparents' farm in the Scottish Borders that Sir Walter Scott, the writer who started the wave of literary tourism in Scotland in the early 19th century, first heard tales of skirmishes between the Scots and the English in these debated lands. Today the Scottish Borders are home to magnificent abbeys—remnants of a time when it was necessary to show might in the face of invaders, linked by cycleways and pathways where you can take in the gentle terrain at a slower pace.

The south is Scotland's quietest corner, the perfect antithesis to busier quarters that are plagued by overtourism, making it a more sustainable destination for travelers who get here before the secret is out.

PLANNING YOUR TIME

Abbotsford and the **Borders Abbeys** are easily reached from Edinburgh. **Melrose,** home to perhaps the grandest of the abbey ruins, is just over an hour's drive, or you can hop on the relatively new **Borders Railway** at Edinburgh Waverley and be in **Tweedbank** (the best station for both Melrose Abbey and Abbotsford) in less than an hour. Many visitors to the Borders do this as a day trip, returning to Edinburgh at the end of the day, but if you stay the night in Melrose you can also fit in one or two of the other abbeys and maybe

even a bucolic bike ride too. Once arrived in one of the Borders towns, it's very easy to walk around the towns themselves and there are buses to other abbeys, but a car does make things a lot easier.

Arran, Ayrshire, and **Galloway** are more easily combined into one trip, and your best starting off point is Glasgow. From Glasgow, it's just a 40-minute train ride (50 minutes by car) to **Ardrossan,** where you can catch the 50-minute ferry over to Brodick on the Isle of Arran. Arran is one of Scotland's most accessible islands and is also relatively easy to get around, but that's no reason to rush. One or two nights here means you'll have a little time to wander, gaze, and listen to the sounds of nature in between seeing sights such as **Brodick Castle** and **Machrie Moor.** You'll be particularly thankful for the extra night if you decide to climb **Goatfell.**

Back on the mainland at Ardrossan it's just a half-hour drive to **Alloway,** the hometown of Robert Burns and home to the excellent Robert Burns Birthplace Museum, which can be seen in an afternoon, and from here it's just under an hour to the wooded playground of **Galloway Forest Park,** where you'll want to spend at least a day and a night. You can travel to Arran and Ayrshire by public transport without too much hassle. From Ardrossan, Ayr can be reached by train in about an hour (changing at Kilwinning) and there are fairly regular buses from Ayr onto Alloway. However, having a car makes reaching Galloway Forest Park (and getting around it) a lot easier.

Itinerary Ideas

DAY TRIP TO THE BORDERS

The Borders Railway makes Abbotsford and the Borders Abbeys an easy day trip from Edinburgh, but stay a night and you'll have time to take in southern Scotland's pastoral atmosphere on a longer countryside walk or visit more of the religious ruins that characterize this region.

1 From Edinburgh, it's under an hour's ride on the train to **Tweedbank Station,** a 20-minute walk (or quick cab or taxi ride) from the home of Sir Walter Scott, your first destination of the day.

2 Spend a few hours admiring the curiosities and treasures housed in **Abbotsford,** the neogothic manor Scott spent over a decade constructing. You can grab breakfast or an early lunch at Ochiltree's Café, the on-site cafeteria.

3 From here, it's an hour's walk, 30-minute bus ride, or 6-minute cab journey to the magnificent ruins of **Melrose Abbey,** where you can wander grounds, chapels, and other buildings dating to the 12th century.

4 In central Melrose, enjoy a creative, seasonal dinner at **Provender,** before heading back to the train station for the return trip to Edinburgh.

ARRAN AND AYRSHIRE

It's possible to get a good overview of the Isle of Arran in just a day, but if you want to climb **Goatfell,** it's recommended to spend two days here, as the hike takes the better part of a day. You'll want a rental car for this two-day itinerary to explore Arran and the remote countryside around Galloway Forest Park, home to dark skies and wild woodland.

Day 1

1 Set off early from Glasgow to **Ardrossan Harbour,** an hour-long drive, and catch one of the morning ferries over to Brodick on Arran. You can have a cooked breakfast on the ferry.

2 From Brodick, it's a 50-minute walk or an 8-minute drive to **Brodick Castle, Garden, and Country Park,** a Scottish baronial-style castle with formal grounds and pretty woodland trails where you can sometimes spot red squirrels.

3 Pop in for lunch at the friendly and lively **Wineport,** a short walk from the castle.

4 After lunch, take the 30-minute drive to **Machrie Moor** to see the impressive standing stones dating from around 3500 to 1500 BC.

5 Drive back to Brodick and check into the spick and span **Rosaburn Lodge** guest house, whose idyllic gardens overlook the River Rosa.

6 Try some Scottish-style tapas at the **eighteen69 Restaurant** within the Auchrannie Estate and round off your evening with an Arran malt nightcap.

Day 2

1 Breakfast in the guest house and take the early ferry back to Ardrossan Harbour. From here, head to Alloway, a 40-minute drive south, where you can visit the **Robert Burns**

Itinerary Ideas

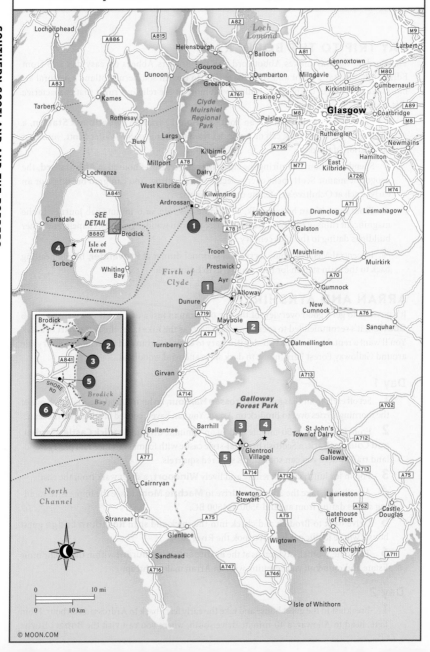

© MOON.COM

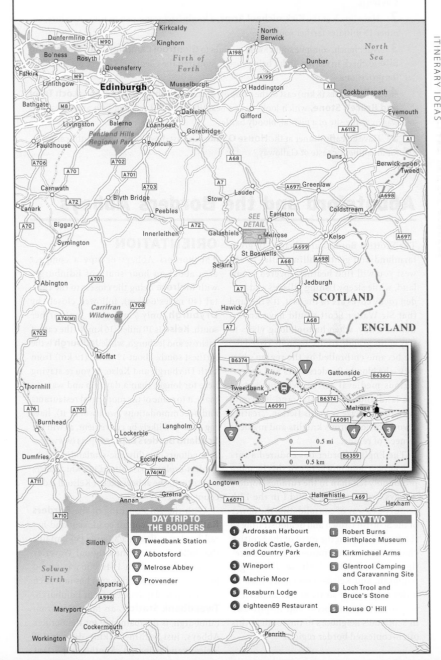

DAY TRIP TO THE BORDERS	DAY ONE	DAY TWO
1 Tweedbank Station	1 Ardrossan Harbourt	1 Robert Burns Birthplace Museum
2 Abbotsford	2 Brodick Castle, Garden, and Country Park	2 Kirkmichael Arms
3 Melrose Abbey	3 Wineport	3 Glentrool Camping and Caravanning Site
4 Provender	4 Machrie Moor	4 Loch Trool and Bruce's Stone
	5 Rosaburn Lodge	5 House O' Hill
	6 eighteen69 Restaurant	

Birthplace Museum, home to the thatched Burns Cottage where the famed Scottish poet was born.

2   Have lunch at the **Kirkmichael Arms,** a lovely backwater pub in rural Ayrshire, another 15 minutes farther south.

3   After lunch, continue south for 45 minutes to **Glentrool Camping and Caravanning Site** to check in for the night, being sure to stop into the Glentrool Gallery & Craft Shop for provisions.

4   Drive 5 miles (8 km) east of the campsite and take an afternoon stroll up to **Loch Trool and Bruce's Stone,** which looks over a beautiful tranquil scene of loch and forest that was once the site of a pivotal, bloody battle.

5   Have an early dinner at the **House O' Hill** pub, just down the road from the campsite, for an authentic taste of Galloway.

Abbotsford and the Borders Abbeys

The Scottish Borders are cloaked in green farmland and gentle rolling hills. To the west you will find heather-covered moorland, while sleepy fishing villages and hidden rocky coves are to the east. It's the land that Sir Walter Scott would have known well as a boy, when he took long visits to stay at his grandparents' farm in Tweedale. He became enthralled by the region's history (the bloody Borders Wars and the notorious medieval reivers who plundered the land and settlements), and he would later romanticize it in his fiction, creating a world of chivalrous knights and maidens in need of rescue.

The English border has endured a turbulent past, and nowhere can this be more profoundly felt than in the ruinous Borders Abbeys, built by King David I in the 12th century as a way of consolidating the power of the Scottish Crown and demonstrating to the English Crown the force of the Scottish church. The concentration of elaborate religious buildings at Melrose, Dryburgh, Jedburgh, and Kelso—none more than 12 miles (19 km) or so from one another—was intended to impress and inspire awe in Scotland's neighbors to the south in this often-contested border region.

ORIENTATION

The Borders Abbeys occupy a compact area about an hour south of Edinburgh, with **Melrose** being the closest to the capital (40 miles/64 km), followed closely by **Dryburgh,** only 7 miles (11 km) farther south. **Kelso** is 10 miles (16 km) to the east of Melrose and Jedburgh, while **Jedburgh** is the farthest south, about 12 miles (19 km) from both Dryburgh and Kelso. If you're staying here for longer than a day trip and want to make it to some of the more rural restaurants and accommodations (well worth it), having a car will likely be convenient, as will the **Scotland Borders Explorer** pass (www.goscotlandtours.com/historic-scotland/scottish-borders-explorer-pass.html; £16), which offers access to all the abbeys except Kelso at a discounted rate.

With the 2015 opening of the **Borders Railway** (www.scotrail.co.uk/scotland-by-rail/borders-railway), a 35-mile (56 km) line that follows part of the original Waverley Route that opened in 1849 but was forced to close in the 1960s, this area has now been opened up to day-trippers from Edinburgh. **Tweedbank Station,** an hour ride from Edinburgh, is the main stop for the Borders Abbeys, just within walking distance of Melrose and Jedburgh. Another important stop on the railway is **Galashiels** (52 minutes from Edinburgh, the stop before Melrose), which has more bus connections to the other abbeys. The **Borders Buses app** (www. bordersbuses.co.uk) is a good resource for cheaper online tickets and ease of travel. Or, consider traveling on two wheels; The distances between the Abbeys are not huge, and the **Borders Abbeys Way** connects most of them on a scenic hiking/cycling route.

MELROSE

The attractive town of Melrose, which sits at the foot of the Eildon Hills, is something of a gateway town for those who want to visit Abbotsford (the home of Sir Walter Scott), Melrose, or any of the other Borders Abbeys. It is also the birthplace of Rugby Sevens, a fact celebrated with the jubilant Melrose Sevens Festival that takes place here in April, attracting rugby fans worldwide.

As the closest abbey to both Edinburgh and the end of the Borders Railway line, at Tweedbank Station, Melrose is one of the most visited. Tweedbank is just about evenly situated between Abbotsford (a 30-minute walk to the west) and Melrose Abbey (35 minutes to the east), or you can take a cab or one of the many buses that stop at the station en route to or from the area's most visited sites. If you'd like to spend more time discovering the Borders region, Melrose is the most obvious overnight base, with convenient access to the other abbeys and a good choice of places to stay and eat, as well as being incredibly pretty in its own right. VisitScotland's iCentre in Melrose is no longer open, so **VisitScotland's website** (www.visitscotland.com/destinations-maps/scottish-borders) should be your first stop when planning a trip here.

Sights
★ ABBOTSFORD

Melrose; tel. 01896 752043; www.scottsabbotsford. com; 10am-4pm March and Nov., 10am-5pm Apr.-Oct.; house, chapel, and gardens adult £11.70, under 17 £5.10, concessions £10.70, gardens only adult £5.90, child £3.10, concessions £5.40

Sir Walter Scott is rightly remembered as having ignited a fashion for literary tourism in Scotland in the 19th century with his historical fiction books, yet writing was only one of his obsessions. He was also an ardent collector, with a particular interest in—though not limited to—the Jacobites, and his home on the banks of the River Tweed is a museum of his vast collection.

Clearly, early years spent visiting family in the Borders had an impact on Sir Walter Scott, for it was here that he chose to build his beloved home. Scott described the house on the banks of the River Tweed as "a Dalilah of my imagination." He spent 14 years transforming an old farmhouse into the whimsical baronial manor house you can see today, complete with castle turrets and gables. Among a long list of designers and craftspeople, Scott enlisted architect William Atkinson, who later remodeled Chequers in Buckinghamshire (the British Prime Minister's second home), to help realize his vision.

Today, it is the embodiment of Gothic romance—look for the **Juliette balcony** by Scott's bedroom, and the **Rapunzel-style tower** that overlooks the River Tweed. Inside, it's a treasure box of curiosities and antiquities, with animal skulls jostling for position with old weaponry and artifacts that may well have belonged to some of the most famous figures in Scottish history that Scott brought so vividly to life. Examples include Rob Roy's gun and Montrose's Sword, Scott's most treasured item. The **library,** made up entirely of books amassed by the man himself, includes almost five thousand chapbooks, alongside unique items such as a 15th-century illuminated manuscript recounting legends relating to English and Welsh saints, books on witchcraft, and large sections on both the Covenanters and the Jacobites.

You can enter the **study** where Scott wrote his later works and even sit at the writing desk at which he wrote his celebrated Waverley novels. The exquisite **Chinese Drawing**

Abbotsford and the Borders Abbeys

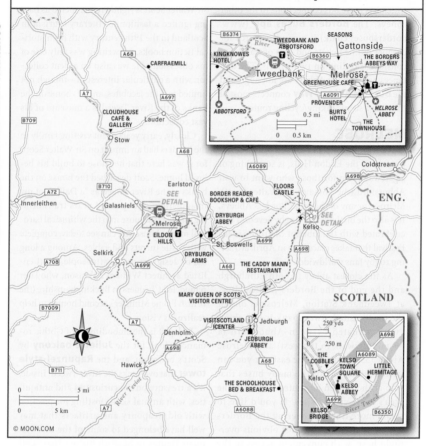

© MOON.COM

Room, with hand-painted wallpaper, was where Scott would entertain evening guests, such as William Wordsworth, J. M. W. Turner and Lord Byron. Scott died at Abbotsford in 1832, and just a few years later his family opened it up to the public. Among its early first guests were King George IV and Queen Victoria. Allow 2-3 hours for your visit.

The onsite cafeteria, **Ochiltree's Café** (Abbotsford, Melrose; tel. 1896 752 043; www.scottsabbotsford.com/eat; 10am-5pm (last orders 4pm) daily; pot of tea £1.80, cakes £4, mains £11.95), has a seasonal menu of Scottish dishes such as haggis bon bons, plus

sandwiches, teas, and coffee; sit on the balcony if the weather allows.

★ MELROSE ABBEY

Abbey Street; tel. 01896 822 562; www. historicenvironment.scot/visit-a-place/places/ melrose-abbey; 10am-5pm daily Apr.-Sept., 10am-4pm Oct.-Mar.; adult £6, child £3.60, under 5 free, concessions £4.80

The most famous of all the Borders Abbeys and arguably the most magnificent ruin in the whole of Scotland, Melrose was founded

1: Abbotsford 2: Melrose Abbey

by King David I in 1136, making it Scotland's first Cistercian monastery. Though its original grandeur was destroyed by the invading English army of King Richard II in 1385, you still get some sense of the scale of the original abbey, and many of the decorative sculptures are incredibly well-preserved.

The rose-stone remains you see today are largely from the early 15th century and are in the Gothic style. Inside, there are remnants of the ornate stone vaulting above the presbytery at the east end, where the high altar once stood. Part of the nave as well as the monks' choir and transepts remain, too, and you can see where carved stone once separated the glass in the windows. The exterior is covered in unusual masonic carvings depicting hobgoblins, angels, and cooks with ladles—there's even a pig playing the bagpipes. It is considered one of the most elegant of all Scotland's surviving abbeys.

Most visitors come here on pilgrimage to pay respect to Scottish king Robert the Bruce, whose heart is said to be buried in the **chapter house,** having been discovered during an archaeological dig in the 1990s and reinterred. Of course, there's no certainty that it is indeed the warrior-king's heart, but only the most hardened visitor would dare challenge the romantic tale. The **Commendator's House,** built a fair bit later (1560), is relatively intact compared with the rest of the abbey, and today functions as a museum displaying artifacts found throughout the grounds. There's also a small shop and **visitor center,** where you can pick up a map that will help you make your way around the abbey and find the most memorable sculptures. Last entry is half an hour before closing.

Hiking

If you're planning to do any walks in the Scottish Borders, be they short ambles or long-distance routes, the **Walk Scottish Borders website** (https://walkscottishborders.com) is invaluable. There's also a sister website (https://cyclescottishborders.com) for cycling in the region.

TWEEDBANK AND ABBOTSFORD

Hiking Distance: 3.5 miles (5.5 km) round-trip
Hiking Time: 2 hours round-trip
Trailhead: Tweedbank station
Information and Maps: https://walkscottishborders.com/route/tweedbank-and-abbotsford

Though the first section of this walk isn't the prettiest, it's relatively easy, and will get you to Abbotsford in good time if you've arrived by train. Turn right out of the station, cross the road, and take the next left onto Craw Wood. Follow the road until the end of the estate and then take the tarmac path that runs between the houses. At the junction, turn right and take the subway under Tweedbank Drive. Keep following the path as it edges round Gunknowe Loch, where you can look for ducks and swans. Follow the loch-side path between the houses to the road where there's a bus stop. Turn right and keep walking to the roundabout, cross over it, and Abbotsford is in front of you through the gate ahead. After exploring the house and grounds, you can return to Tweedbank via the **Borders Abbeys Way** (BAW, turn left out of the visitor center), following an old path toward the River Tweed. Just before you reach the river, bear right up a track and pass under a road bridge. Follow the BAW through woodland and then along the riverbank, all the way back to Tweedbank. Go up the steps just before you reach the railway viaduct and turn right to get back to the station.

EILDON HILLS

Hiking Distance: 6 miles (9.5 km) round-trip
Hiking Time: 3-4 hours round-trip
Trailhead: Nutwood car park
Information and Maps: www.walkhighlands.co.uk/borders/eildon-hills.shtml

This steep hill walk to visit the peaks that gaze over Melrose should take around half a day. To start, take the lane toward Melrose's Market Square and turn left at the mercat cross, following signs for the golf club. Follow the road under the bypass and keep your eyes peeled for a sign on a lamppost that tells you where to turn left onto a path between some houses and gardens.

The path soon climbs a long flight of steps, and once you've reached the top of these the path will continue to go up between fields. You'll pass through two gates and continue climbing up the next field, and then at another gate you need to follow the sign to the right (it should be marked with the logo of the three peaks of the Eildon Hills as well as the white cross for St Cuthbert's Way, which follows the same route at this point) and keep going until you reach the col between two of the three hills.

Keep on the path until you reach the saddle between the hills and then leave the St Cuthbert's Way and take the wider, more obvious path that bears to the right and climbs up Eildon Mid Hill. The final climb to the summit is rockier. You'll know you've reached the summit as there's a trig point and a view indicator.

You can return to Melrose the way you came, or retrace your steps until there's a track to the right that forms part of the **Borders Abbeys Way.** Follow this as it curves to reach the A6091, where if you turn right you can pass under the subway. Continue under the old railway and then turn left on a path that will eventually bring you down to the road in Newstead. Take a sharp left and then turn right onto a footpath known as the Priorswalk (it should be marked by the three hills sign), which will lead back to Melrose, where you should take the right-hand branch of the road and look for the footpath that will take you all the way back to Melrose Abbey.

Festivals and Events
MELROSE SEVENS FESTIVAL
The Greenyards, High Street, Melrose; https:// melrose7s.co.uk; April

This is the oldest Rugby Sevens competition in the world. When it's on, this event attracts teams and spectators from across the world. Having been canceled two years running now, everyone is hoping 2022 will be the year it returns.

Food
GREENHOUSE CAFÉ
6 Buccleuch Street; tel. 01896 800 360; www. facebook.com/greenhousecafemelrose; 8:30am-4pm Weds.-Sun.; coffee £2, main dishes £7.95

Handmade sandwiches, well brewed tea, and a daily specials board make this a smart choice for lunch for anyone visiting nearby Melrose Abbey. It's got a surprisingly bright and modern interior, with color-clashing and loud wallpaper ensuring this is no stagnant dusty café. There's a decent vegetarian menu, and staff won't make you feel silly for having dietary requirements.

PROVENDER
West End House, High Street; tel. 01896 820 319; https://provendermelrose.com; 11:30am-2:30pm and 6pm-9pm Mon.-Sat., 12pm-3pm and 6pm-8pm Sun.; mains £15

Offering a fusion of Scottish, British, and French gastronomy, this centrally located Melrose restaurant appears casual, but the menu is anything but. Every care is put into providing a seasonal and very appealing menu that doesn't overcomplicate things. There is a good choice of seafood dishes (seared squid with garlic, spinach, and olive, or grilled native lobster served with french fries and garlic butter) as well as a lot of fresh vegetables (asparagus and broad beans in spring) and, of course, Borders lamb. It's a little on the pricey side, but it is a place worth splashing out on.

BORDER READER BOOKSHOP & CAFÉ
Old Melrose; tel. 01835 824 597; www.border-reader. co.uk; 10:30am-5pm daily

This cute little secondhand bookshop and café about 2 miles (3.2 km) outside Melrose, just off the A68 on the way to Dryburgh, is set within an old dairy farmhouse and is a suitably quiet venue for a good browse through some of the 5,000 books available on its neat shelves, with a cup of tea in hand. There's also a little farm shop on-site.

The Borders Abbeys Way

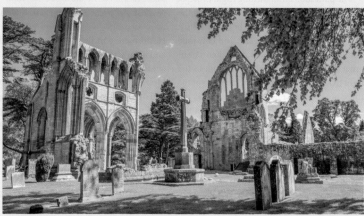

Dryburgh Abbey

Hiking Distance: *68 miles (109.4 km) round-trip*
Hiking Time: *7 days round-trip*
Trailhead: *Melrose Abbey*
Information and Maps: *www.scotborders.gov.uk/bordersabbeysway*

This route links the four abbeys of Melrose, Jedburgh, Dryburgh, and Kelso and travels past idyllic pastoral scenes of farms and meadows. It can be broken down into smaller sections. Most visitors start at Melrose, from where you can either walk one section or stop for a night near each abbey before starting the next stage. The route can be walked, cycled, or explored by car; using local buses will help you cover more ground over a shorter time than on foot.

If you would like to attempt all four of the abbeys, then you will need to leave yourself at least seven days and maybe consider booking a self-guided tour with a company like **Macs Adventure** (www.macsadventure.com; from £525 for seven days, six nights), which will provide detailed maps, organize accommodation en route, and transfer your bags to your next destination for you.

KELSO TO JEDBURGH

For those with less time, a good section is the 13.5-mile (22-km) stretch from Kelso to Jedburgh, on a mix of riverside paths, tracks, and road. En route you'll pass by **Roxburgh Castle** (Kay Brae, Kelso TD5 8LT; www.borderarchaeology.co.uk/home/sites/roxburgh; open 24 hours; free), once one of Scotland's most powerful strongholds (now in ruins) over the Victorian Roxburgh viaduct, and a well-preserved section of Roman Dere Street, which once ran all the way from Perth in Scotland to York in England.

DRIVING THE ROUTE

If driving to this region of the Lowlands, I recommend starting in Kelso (just 44 miles/70.8 km southeast of Edinburgh), the least complete of the abbeys, heading southwest to Jedburgh before traveling northwest to Dryburgh, and finally visiting Melrose, which is widely considered the most magnificent abbey. This route is around 50 miles (80 km) in total; to reach Kelso, head out of Edinburgh on the A1 before joining the A68, A697, and A6089 all the way to the town.

★ SEASONS

*Gattonside; tel. 01896 823 217; https://
seasonsborders.co.uk; dinner from 6pm Weds.-Sun.,
lunch 12pm-2pm Fri.-Sun.; mains £11*

As its name suggests, the focus at this restaurant, 2.5 miles (4 km) outside Melrose, is on seasonal produce, and the menu is well worth the £5-7 taxi ride. Run by husband-and-wife team Roger and Bea, the attention to detail is impressive. Roger even cures his own meats and makes his own preserves, and the couple will make you feel right at home. Prices are pretty fair too.

★ CLOUDHOUSE CAFÉ & GALLERY

*23 Townfoot; tel. 01578 730 718; https://
cloudhousecafe.co.uk; 10am-3pm Mon.-Thurs. and
Sat-Sun., 10am-4pm Fri.; cakes £2.25*

This charming café in the sweet village of Stow, 10 miles (16 km) northwest of Melrose, is run by smiling staff. This is the place to stop for good coffee and delicious cakes that would put your granny to shame. The homely, slightly worn interiors—bare floorboards with upcycled wooden chairs and reclaimed wooden tables—adds to the appeal.

Accommodations

KINGKNOWES HOTEL

*Selkirk Road; tel. 01896 758 375; www.kingsknowes.
co.uk; £110 d*

You can enjoy views of Abbotsford from this romantic baronial mansion on the banks of the River Tweed. The 12 elegant bedrooms are traditionally decorated with the occasional antique furnishing—the Scott Suite has the best view—and the food and drink on offer are of high quality.

★ CARFRAEMILL

*Lauder; tel. 1578 750 750; www.carfraemill.co.uk;
£90-120 d*

This countryside inn on the edge of the Lammermuir Hills is just 30 minutes south of Edinburgh and is exceptionally kid-friendly. Rooms are spotless, dressed in soothing shades with teddy bears on the bed, and there are lots of toys and books to keep the kids

busy in the country-style Jo's Kitchen, so parents can enjoy their meal without fear of the kids running riot. There are also doubles for couples, who may prefer to eat in the more grown-up Bistro restaurant.

BURTS HOTEL

*Market Square, Melrose; tel. 01896 822 285; www.
burtshotel.co.uk; £120-148 d*

This upmarket hotel housed in an 18th-century listing building in the center of Melrose has bundles of character. There are 20 en-suite rooms (7 singles), with modern tartan furnishings in the bedroom and Arran Aromatics toiletries in the bathroom. Downstairs the bar (with its open fire) serves food, plus there is a more formal restaurant.

THE TOWNHOUSE

*Market Square, Melrose TD6 9PQ; tel. 1896 822 645;
www.thetownhousemelrose.co.uk; £115-190 d*

The Townhouse is well-placed for Melrose Abbey as well as the quaint shops and restaurants of the small town. Clean, comfy, with funky yet grown-up rooms and a good on-site restaurant and bar, The Townhouse is a good base for exploring the Borders towns.

Getting There

By car, it takes just over an hour to reach Melrose from Edinburgh (traffic depending). Take the A7 south from the city bypass for 27 miles (43 km) before joining the B6452 in Galashiels for the last 4 miles (6.4 km) into Melrose.

To get to Melrose and Abbotsford, take the train from Edinburgh Waverley Station (under 1 hour; from £11.50 each way or £12.20 day return) to Tweedbank Station (Melrose; tel. 344 811 0141; www.scotrail.co.uk/plan-your-journey/stations-and-facilities/twb), at the end of the Borders Railway line.

Getting Around

Abbotsford is about a 20-minute walk from Tweedbank station, following the Abbotsford Link signs from the station, or you can take a slower more scenic route along the Borders

Abbeys Way. Melrose's pretty town center is about a 30-minute walk from Tweedbank station, or there are a number of local buses that connect the two, the 60, 67, and 68. The main bus provider is **Borders Buses** (www.bordersbuses.co.uk; £4.75 single, £8.40 unlimited day travel) and buses run around every 50 minutes-1 hour, but with a few to choose from you rarely wait longer than 20 minutes. **Ace Taxi Cabs** (tel. 079 2923 2923; www.acetaxicabs.co.uk; open 24/7; £1.75/£2 per mile) connects locations within the region.

To follow some of the lovely cycle routes in and around Melcrose, such as the **Borders Abbeys Way** to Abbotsford along the banks of the River Tweed, pick up a bike from **Diamond Cycle Centre** (Unit 5, Adam Purves Hub; tel. 01896 758 410; www.stevediamondcycles.co.uk; 9:30am-5:30pm Tues.-Fri., 9:30am-4:30pm Sat.; £20 per day, electric bikes £40 per day).

DRYBURGH ABBEY

Dryburgh; tel. 01835 822 381; www.
historicenvironment.scot/visit-a-place/places/
dryburgh-abbey; 10am-4pm daily Oct.-Mar.; adult
£6, child £3.60, concessions £4.80, under 5 free
Dryburgh's eponymous abbey is not only the burial place of Sir Walter Scott, but is also home to some of the finest Gothic architecture in all of Scotland. This abbey has survived three fires and at least four attacks in its history; amazingly, plasterwork and paintings from the 12th century remain, as well as the two transepts and the West Front. The cloister buildings are some of the best preserved in Scotland, and its location nestled in a loop of the River Tweed is exceptionally tranquil. Last entry is half an hour before closing.

Worth a stop if you're visiting the abbey, the nearby **Wallace Monument** was the first statue erected in Scotland to the national hero. It can be reached by following the Dryburgh road from the nearby village of St. Boswells (where most day-trippers to Dryburgh will stop for lunch) in less than 10 minutes by car, or in 50 minutes on foot. Just after the road crosses the River Tweed, take

the road to the left and keep following signposts for the monument. The statue is perched on a steep incline above the river and is about a five-minute walk through woods from the car park.

Food and Accommodations
DRYBURGH ARMS

Melbourne Place, Newtown; tel. 01835 822 704; www.
dryburgharms.co.uk; £80-110
This traditional pub with rooms in the village of Newtown St Boswells is a cozy place to stay and a good stop-off for a light lunch (food has been paused during the pandemic but should be up and running again by next season). There are just three rooms—two doubles and one family room. The decor is crisp and clean with heavy tweeds. Staff can advise on places a short taxi ride away for dinner, and the pub with its open fire and bare floorboards is the perfect place to come back to after a day's walking.

Getting There and Around
By car from Edinburgh, follow the A68 and then B6360 and B6356 (40 miles/64.4 km, 1.25 hours). It's only 16 minutes (8 miles/12.8 km) southeast of Melrose, taking the A6091 to A68 before continuing to the B6360 and B6356. To get here by public transportation, you'll need to first take the train from Edinburgh to Tweedbank (£11.50 single, £12.20 day return), then take the no. 67 bus from outside the train station to the Agricultural College (25 minutes; £4.75 single, £8.40 unlimited daily). From here it is still just over a 20-minute walk to the abbey.

JEDBURGH

Some say Jedburgh is the bonniest of the Borders towns; if that's true, it's no thanks to its unfortunate location. Being situated just 10 miles (16 km) from the border with England meant historically that Jedburgh was pillaged often and subsequently rebuilt. Today it's a pretty town with colorful restored buildings, including one in which Mary, Queen of Scots, once stayed.

Sights
JEDBURGH ABBEY

4/5 Abbey Bridgend; tel. 01835 863 925; www.
historicenvironment.scot/visit-a-place/places/
jedburgh-abbey; 9:30am-5:30pm daily Apr.-Sept.,
10am-4pm daily Oct.-Mar.; adult £6, child £3.60,
concessions £4.80, under 5 free

Originally founded as a priory in 1138 for Augustinian canons and raised to abbey status in 1154, Jedburgh mixes Romanesque and Gothic architectural styles. It is remarkably intact and gives a good sense of the scale of monastic houses in the 12th century. Stroll its open cloisters and view the findings of modern-day excavations, including the discovery of an 8th-century shrine and the 12th-century Jedburgh Comb. Last entry is half an hour before closing.

MARY QUEEN OF SCOTS' VISITOR CENTRE

Queen Street; tel. 01835 863 331; www.liveborders.
org.uk/culture/museums/our-museums/mary-queen-
of-scots-visitor-centre; 10am-4pm Thurs.-Mon.; free
(£1 donation encouraged)

It was in this 16th-century house that Scotland's tragic queen holed up for a whole month in 1566. Using paintings and textiles linked to the queen, the small, free museum attempts to explain the cult that grew up around her, and how her decision to leave here led in part to her downfall, with the queen lamenting "Would that I had died in Jedburgh." With attractive grounds to wander amid historic pear trees, this is worth an hour of your time. Last entry 40 minutes before closing.

Food and Accommodations
THE CADDY MANN RESTAURANT

Mounthooly; tel. 01835 850 787; http://caddymann.
com; lunch 12pm-2pm Weds.-Sun., dinner served at
6pm Fri.-Sat.; £6.95 entrees

This family-friendly restaurant in a quaint cottage is consistently good and has a daily changing menu that features lots of lovely local produce. Try the Border Tart, and you might as well sample the gin of the month while you're at it.

THE SCHOOL HOUSE BED & BREAKFAST

Edgerston, Camptown; tel. 1835 840 627; www.
theschoolhousebedandbreakfast.com; from £95 d,
three-course dinner £24 per person

The oldest B&B in Jedburgh is housed in a listed building that looks like something out of an Agatha Christie adaptation. There are just four rooms, ensuring a really personal experience and, unusually for a B&B, the owners also offer an exceptionally good-valued dinner, which is served in a minstrel gallery no less. The other standout feature, aside from the neat rooms, is the sweet garden with views over ancient woodland.

Information and Services

Just across from the abbey, this **VisitScotland Jedburgh iCentre** (Murray's Green, Jedburgh; tel. 1835 863170; 9:30am-5pm Mon.-Sat., 10am-4pm Sun.) can arm you with maps, Scotland Borders Explorer passes (useful if you're planning to visit all the abbeys), and even bus tickets.

Getting There and Around

If you're driving from Edinburgh, take the A68 and then the B6358; it should take a little over an hour. From Melrose, it's a 25-minute drive (12 miles/19.3 km), also on the A68 and B6356. By public transport, after taking the train from Edinburgh to Tweedbank, then take the no. 68 bus to **Jedburgh Station** (40 minutes; £4.75, £8.40 unlimited daily); unfortunately, Jedburgh is not linked to Edinburgh or Melrose by train.

Once here, there's free parking and you can walk between the sites with ease.

KELSO

The market town of Kelso is itself worth a visit. Sir Walter Scott considered it Scotland's "most beautiful." Highlights include the **Kelso Bridge,** built by John Rennie the Elder (who also built London's Waterloo Bridge), and the William Adam-designed Floors Castle. There's also a good

farmers market on the fourth Saturday of the month (9:30am-1:30pm) in **Kelso town square.**

Sights
KELSO ABBEY

Kelso; www.historicenvironment.scot/visit-a-place/ places/kelso-abbey; 9:30am-5:30pm daily Apr.-Sept., 10am-4pm Sat.-Weds. Oct.-Mar.; free

Kelso was once one of the most powerful religious houses in all of Scotland; during the 12th and 13th centuries, the Abbot of Kelso had precedence over all other abbots in the country. It was here that James III was crowned King of Scots in 1460 following the death of his father at nearby Roxburgh Castle. However, its status didn't stop repeat invasions by English forces, including those during King Henry VIII's infamous Rough Wooing campaign in the mid-16th century. Little remains of the original monastery precinct except for a fragment of the abbey church, but it still gives some indication of how richly decorated the abbey once was.

FLOORS CASTLE

Kelso; tel. 01573 223 333; www.floorscastle. com; 10:30am-4pm Sat.-Sun. of Easter weekend; 10:30am-5pm May-Sept.; adult £15, child free

This stunning castle is the family seat of the Duke of Roxburghe and his family, first built in the 1720s by William Adam to a common layout incorporating two symmetrical wings, and embellished in the 19th century by William Playfair, who added the battlements and turrets. It is a richly decorated stately home, with an impressive collection of fine art, plus newly restored tapestries in some of its grand rooms. Outside, the gardens are beautiful, particularly the impeccable formal Millennium Garden, which includes a French-style parterre with the intertwining initials of the incumbent Duke and Duchess of Roxburghe perfectly etched into the lawn, plus

a pretty walled garden, woodland trails, and an adventure playground. There are cheaper tickets to just visit the grounds.

Food and Accommodations
THE COBBLES

7 Bowmont Street, Kelso; tel. 01573 223 548; https:// cobbleskelso.co.uk; 12pm-11pm (last orders 9pm) Weds.-Sat., 12pm-7pm (last orders 5pm) Sun.; entrées £6.50

Along with straight-up pub food, this restored 19th-century coaching inn just off the main square in Kelso serves a good selection of steaks with Scottish Borders beef matured for 35 days or more, plus burgers, soups, and sandwiches. Upstairs there is also a functional and clean two-bed apartment that sleeps up to four and that costs from £95 per night.

★ LITTLE HERMITAGE

Hermitage Lane, Kelso; tel. 1573 226 711; www.crabtreeandcrabtree.com/properties/ little-hermitage; £705 per week

This self-catering property, hidden away at the end of a lane, is just a five-minute walk from Kelso's cobbled square. Offering contemporary open-plan living, it has a stone- and wood-clad exterior with walls of glass bathing the interiors with natural light. There are two bedrooms, a large kitchen for preparing your own meals using local produce from the village (there's a fishmonger, two butchers and a couple of bakeries), and a large lawned garden that you share with the owner.

Getting There and Around

If you're driving direct from **Edinburgh** (44 miles/70.8 km, one hour), take the A68, A697, and then A6089. From Melrose, it's a 25-minute (14-mile/22.5-km) drive on the A6091, C78, and B6397. By public transport, from Tweedbank, take the no. 67 bus from outside the station to Coledale Car Park (45 minutes; £4.75 single, £8.40 unlimited daily).

Ayrshire

In this farming region of patchwork fields and idling sheep, there's a sense of quiet and calm as you turn off the main A77 artery road to villages such as **Maybole** (home to Culzean Castle) and **Straiton** (a good entry point to Galloway Forest Park), where few tourists venture. The region's most famous export, Robert Burns, was himself of farming stock, and a visit to his birthplace, the family's first smallholding in Alloway, is a highlight of any visit. From here the Ayrshire coast can be explored, from the stirring ruins of Dunure Castle through to the imposing Culzean Castle, a route that can be driven or done on foot along the **Ayrshire Coastal Path.** The views across to Arran (accessed from Adrossan Harbour on the Ayrshire coast, an hour's drive or 45-minute train ride from Glasgow, or an hour north of Ayr) and the distinct boulder of Ailsa Crag, the remains of an extinct volcano, are fantastic.

The **Visit Southwest Scotland** tourism membership organization (www.visitsouthwestscotland.com) pulls together lots of places to visit in Scotland's southwest, including the 300-mile (482 km) **South West Coastal 300,** a driving route that is a quieter, less trampled alternative to the Highland's North Coast 500.

AYR AND VICINITY

Ayr is a reasonably sized yet somewhat tired town, though regeneration plans are afoot. There are still remnants of what was once a grand town in old buildings, particularly those that creep down toward the wide golden sand beach. However, most visitors don't stop here for long, preferring nearby attractions such as **Alloway** (Robert Burns's hometown), just to the south of Ayr, **Culzean,** a typically opulent stately home with expansive grounds located farther south along the coast, or other pretty cobbled villages off the beaten track.

A tourism initiative, the **Coig** (https://thecoig.com), Gaelic for "Five," aims to promote five different routes in and around Ayrshire and Arran and is a good starting point for inspiring places to visit. Route no. 1, **The Shire,** highlights some of the best places to visit in Ayrshire in particular, but be warned, businesses do pay to be mentioned, so don't take everything they say as gospel.

Sights

★ ROBERT BURNS BIRTHPLACE MUSEUM

Murdoch's Lone; tel. 01292 443 700; www.nts.org. uk/visit/places/robert-burns-birthplace-museum; 10am-5pm daily Apr.-Sept., 10am-4:30pm daily Oct.-Mar.; adult £11.50, concessions £8.50, family £27, one-adult family £20

Encompassing both **Burns Cottage,** where the bard was born and spent the first seven years of his life, and a very interesting museum on his life and works, this is a must for Burns fans. The thatched cottage, which dates from 1757, has recently undergone some restoration work, and the gardens around it are being returned to a design similar to what would have existed in Burns's time. From here, it's a 5- to 10-minute walk along **Poet's Walk** to the more modern museum, which has handwritten manuscripts of some of his most loved poems, as well as his father's bible, with the page open on an entry that confirms Robert's birth, saying simply: "Had a son Robert 25th Jan 1759."

One of Burns most famous poems, *Tam O Shanter*, is set in Alloway, and you can visit some of the many sites referenced in the poem, including the spooky **Auld Kirk** (Blackfriars Walk, Ayr; tel. 01292 262 938; www.auldkirk. org), across from the museum, where Tam encounters the witches and warlocks that are to pursue him; and the **Brig o' Doon** (River Doon; open 24 hours; free), south of the museum, where the protagonist finally escapes the clutches of the dark spirit, today

Ayrshire and Arran

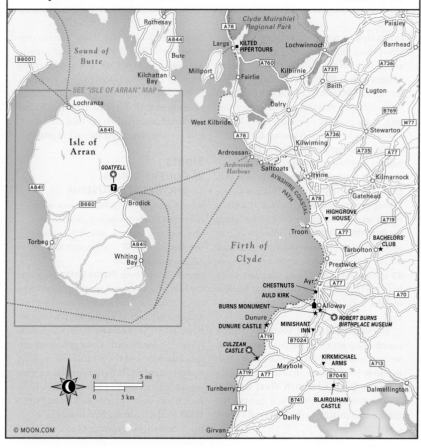

marked by the **Burns Monument.** You'll be given a map of all the locations on entry to the museum.

DUNURE CASTLE

Dunure; open 24/7; free

A ruined castle on Ayrshire's coastal path, Dunure may not have Culzean's grandeur, but it was once the main castle for the Kennedy clan (the Earls of Cassilis), who built Culzean. One can only imagine some of the goings on: Mary, Queen of Scots, is known to have stayed here in 1563, when it would have looked very different from how it does today. Just a few

years later, in 1570, it was the scene of one of the most macabre tales in Scottish history, in which Gilbert Kennedy (the same who had hosted Mary) tortured the abbot of Crossgael Abbey, Allan Stewart, by roasting him over a spit until he signed over lands to him.

Today, its lonesome position overlooking the Firth of Clyde, where it gazes forlornly at Arran, lends it a gloomy atmosphere. The 15th-century beehive-style dovecot, the oldest part of the castle to remain, is a good place to watch the sun go down. *Outlander* fans will know the castle and its harbor as the location for scenes where Claire and Jamie watch as Ian

Robert Burns: Scotland's National Poet

Though he spent much of his life in Edinburgh after the publication of his first book, it was in Ayrshire that Scotland's bard was born, and where he returned many times in his life. Visit some of the spots below to follow in Burns's footsteps.

- **Burns Cottage, Alloway:** This humble thatched cottage, built by his father, was where Robert Burns was born in 1759. Back then it was a simple design—a two-room home where all the family slept and ate, and the children were even schooled. In the late 18th century a byre and barn were added, and later still, in the Victorian era, the building became an alehouse, popular with literary tourists. Today it can be visited on a ticket to the Robert Burns Birthplace Museum, just a short walk away.

- **Auld Kirk, Alloway:** On the main road in Alloway, just across from the Birthplace Museum, is this decaying church and churchyard, where Burns's father and sister are buried—you can just about make out the headstone from the pavement. The 16th-century kirk would already have been in ruin in Burns's time, and it is perhaps local ghost stories and games he played here as a child that fired his imagination when he set the witches dance here in his narrative poem, *Tam O'Shanter*: "Kirk-Alloway seem'd in a bleeze; Thro' ilka bore the beams were glancing; And loud resounded mirth and dancing."

- **Burns Monument, Alloway:** Standing in its own memorial gardens, on the north bank of the River Doon and more importantly overlooking the Brig o' Doon, the bridge where Tam O'Shanter makes good his escape, is this Greek-inspired homage to Burns with nine pillars and a large cupola.

- **Bachelors' Club, Tarbolton** (Sandgate Street; tel. 01292 541 940; www.nts.org.uk/visit/ places/bachelors-club; by appointment only; free): It was in Tarbolton, just 10 miles (16 km) northeast of Alloway (a 20-minute drive on the A77 and A719), that Burns would gather with friends in a men-only debating club in rooms above an old house. Today the 17th-century house with red-shuttered windows has been authentically restored by the National Trust. Downstairs you can see a typical home of Burns's period, with chairs around an open fire and a grandfather clock in the corner, while upstairs you can visit the very rooms where Burns learned to dance and become a freemason.

- **Ellisland Museum & Farm** (Holywood Road, Auldgirth, Dumfries; tel. 01387 740 426; www.ellislandfarm.co.uk; 1pm-4:30 pm Tues., 11am-1:30pm Weds., 11am-3:30pm Sat.-Mon.; £5): Halfway between his birthplace in Ayrshire and his final resting place in Dumfries is the home that Burns built on the banks of the River Nith for his expanding family and where some of his greatest works were written. You can look through memorabilia, walk the grounds that inspired him, or have a cuppa in the pop-up tearoom. From Alloway, it's an 1 hour 20 minute (53-mile/85 km) drive southwest, mostly on the A76.

- **Robert Burns Mausoleum, St Michael's Church, Dumfries:** The large white structure in the graveyard is pretty hard to miss, as almost every other headstone and statue is built out of red stone. Burns died in the town of Dumfries in 1796, seven years after moving here to take up a post as an excise officer. His wife, Jean Armour, is also buried here, as are three of the couple's sons. It's 1.5 hours (60 miles/96.5 km) from Alloway on the A713, A712, and A75.

swims out to Silkies' Island. It's just 15 minutes (6 miles/9.6 km) south of Alloway driving along the Ayrshire coast.

★ CULZEAN CASTLE

Maybole; tel. 01655 884 455; www.nts.org.uk/visit/ places/culzean; 10:30am-4:30pm daily (last entry 4pm) late Mar.-late Oct.; adult £18.50, concessions £13.50, family £46, one-adult family £36

Culzean (pronounced Cullain) is a beautiful castle on the Ayrshire coast built to an L-shaped, Robert Adam design, and set in a precarious-looking cliff-side location with huge gardens and grounds. Built from

1777-1792 for the 10th Earl of Cassillis on the site of an earlier castle, it has been extended many times since, but thankfully many Adam features remain, such as original ceilings with his signature delicate plasterwork and "Adam" green color. Guides can advise on which ones are original and which are revivals.

Of course, Culzean is known for the ghost story of the piper and his dog, who went to check the cave beneath the castle and were never seen again. Guides aren't convinced of the authenticity of the tale, inferring it could have simply been a story constructed to keep locals out of the cave and away from the family's contraband. For a long time the cave has been locked, with a fortification built in front of the entrance, but rangers on the estate now take tours into other caves below the castle where artifacts and human remains have been found, and the odd ghost story or tale of smugglers may be told.

Many visitors also come to stay in the Eisenhower apartment—the top floor of the castle was given to the US President as a thank you gift for his efforts in the war. Eisenhower came four times; his first visit was in 1946, and he came in 1959 as President. He called it his Scottish White House. When he died it reverted to the National Trust, which runs the castle, and it can now be hired out for holiday stays.

Official **tours** of Culzean take place twice a day, or you can go around on your own with one of the tablet-style multi-media guides, which include fun behind-the-scenes videos. And while the interiors offer up all kinds of stories on the family's past (the **Armoury Room** you first enter is particularly impressive), the grounds outside are also magnificent.

It's a huge estate, with wildflower meadows, formal gardens, and a double walled garden, but fear not, you don't have to walk all the way from the car park to the castle and beyond (though it's a nice thing to do if you are up to it): there are golf buggies and trailers to take you around. The deer park is a major feature of the estate, a legacy of the 11th Earl, a wealthy American who inherited the estate and whose money saved Culzean from decay. He was a little bit of a show-off and so brought over all sorts of animals, including buffalo and raccoons (the latter are said to have escaped); this tradition has been continued to some extent with red and fallow deer and llamas. Culzean is just 20 minutes farther down the coast from Dunure Castle, an 8-mile (12.8-km) drive.

Hiking

AYRSHIRE COASTAL PATH

Distance: *92 miles (148 km) one-way*

Time: *6-9 days*

Trailhead: *Glennapp, southern Ayrshire*

Information and Maps: *www.walkhighlands. co.uk/glasgow/ayrshire-coastal-path.shtml*

This coastal route was opened in 2008, with large stretches passing by long beaches and dramatic seaside cliffs, as well as plenty of castles. It took more than four years to develop, in honor of the 100-year anniversary of Ayr's Rotary Club. Linking to several other paths, including the **Mull of Galloway Trail, Clyde Coastal Path,** and **Firth O Clyde Rotary Trail,** there are several sections of this long-distance route that are accessible on a day hike, particularly the **Maidens to Dunure section** (6.2 miles/10 km; 4.5-5 hours), which takes you past Culzean and Dunure Castles.

The southern part of the path is generally considered more scenic and more challenging, while the northern half is more industrial, as it approaches the endpoint in Skelmorlie (34 miles/54.7 km west of Glasgow; 1-hour drive). The starting point, Glennapp, is about an hour south of Alloway (33 miles/53 km). Check the Walk Highlands website for more information on where to stay and stock up on supplies en route.

1: Robert Burns Birthplace Museum 2: Dunure Castle 3: Culzean Castle 4: the view from Glenapp Castle

Tours

KILTED PIPER TOURS

*2 Middleton Drive, Largs; tel. 01475 272 060; www.
kiltedpipertours.com*

This small company can organize 1-2-day
Robert Burns trips or a broader Ayrshire day
trip, which sets off early and takes in views of
Ailsa Craig and passes through **Galloway
Forest Park.** Depending on the number of
people on your tour, you may be able to make
specific requests.

Food

MINISHANT INN

*28 Main Road, Minishant; tel. 1292 442 483; www.
theminishant.co.uk; 4pm-10:30pm Thurs.-Fri.,
12pm-10:30pm Sat., 12:30pm-10pm Sun.; entrées
£5.95*

Portions are generous in this blink-and-you'll-
miss-it place on the main road from Alloway
to Maybole. It might not look like much from
outside, but if you're after a decent fill with
straight-up pub grub, then you won't be
disappointed.

★ KIRKMICHAEL ARMS

*3-5 Straiton Road, Kirkmichael; tel. 1655 750 200;
www.kirkmichaelarms.co.uk; 12pm-9pm daily; entrées
£7.50*

This is a true community pub in the village of Kirkmichael, about 20 minutes (8
miles/12.8 km) inland from Culzean Castle,
with unfussy interiors but jolly staff and
regulars. There's beer from the Ayr Brewing
company on the hand pump and decent pub
grub—burgers and steaks—all freshly prepared and good value too. Try the haggis
scotch eggs to start and a pie if you're really
hungry.

HIGHGROVE HOUSE

*Old Loans Road, Troon; tel. 01292 312 511;
www.highgrovehouse.co.uk; breakfast/brunch
9am-11:30am daily, lunch 12pm-2:30pm Mon.-Sat.,
dinner 5pm-9pm Mon.-Sat., all-day dining 12pm-9pm
Sun.; entrées £7.95*

With a glass terrace affording lovely views of
the Ayrshire coast, this fancy restaurant 20

minutes (10 miles/16 km) north of Ayr always
has a good choice of seafood on the menu,
with locally landed fish coming in every day.
There's also a grill menu, and the early bird
deals are really good value. There are also
eight good-sized rooms, though the decor is
more functional than homely.

Accommodations

CHESTNUTS

*52 Racecourse Road, Ayr; www.chestnutshotel.com;
from £70 per night*

With just 10 rooms, this family-run hotel, a
few minutes' walk from Ayr's seafront, is set
in a smart former mansion. Staff are attentive
and the food in the main restaurant is decent,
though the decor is a little old-fashioned in
places.

BLAIRQUHAN CASTLE

*Straiton, Maybole; www.blairquhan.co.uk; from £350
for a three-night stay*

Accessed via a narrow single-track road,
under a canopy of trees, the eight cottages
on this estate certainly feel hidden away, but
while they are well-equipped and functional,
they have little of the romance of the castle
in whose grounds they sit. Guests are free to
roam the estate and there are some suggested
routes in the guest book, but they need to
steer clear of the lawn in front of the castle
when it is being hired out, and unfortunately
they don't get to take part in any of the estate's activities.

★ GLENAPP CASTLE

*Ballantrae, Girvan; tel. 01465 831 212; www.
glenappcastle.com; £350 d*

Not for the budget-conscious, this five-star
hotel stands head and shoulders above others
around it. Its Scottish Baronial-style turrets
and battlements are very pleasing to the eye,
and its setting amid a forest of giant redwood
trees with views over to the Isle of Arran give it
the kind of country-style seclusion that other
properties lack. Rooms are regal in style, with
floor-length floral curtains, canopied beds,
and antique furnishings, and the restaurant

deserves its fine-dining status. Staff can organize all manner of country pursuits and activities, from falconry to deer stalking, and from helicopter rides to a sea safari. The location is also convenient for trips into Galloway Forest Park, or you can join one of the hotel's winter stargazing excursions.

Getting There and Around

Ayrshire is easily accessible from Glasgow, and whether you're traveling by train or car, you can be here in around an hour. Once you arrive, a car is useful, though you can manage on local buses to some extent or book a local tour guide. From **Glasgow** (38 miles/61 km), you'll need to get on the M8 to leave the city and then join the M77 and the A77, which will get you to Alloway in about 45 minutes.

From **Glasgow Central,** trains take around an hour (£9.30 single) to Ayr. From Ayr, it's just over 15 minutes by bus (or X77 toward Glasgow; £3 single) to Alloway, where you will find most of the Robert Burns attractions.

★ GALLOWAY FOREST PARK

This thick and lush forest about 18 miles (30 km) inland from the Ayrshire coast is known for having some of the darkest skies in Europe, leading it to be designated a Dark Sky Park in 2009, while its more recent Biosphere status recognizes its significance as a place for people and nature to come together in harmony. Covering about 300 square miles (776 square km), very few people live in the park, meaning its skies really are as black as can be, and studded with bright stars and clear constellations (as long as there's no cloud cover), with an uninterrupted view of the Milky Way a real possibility.

The best times to visit are winter, early spring, and autumn, when the days are shorter—though you can still go stargazing very late in the day in summer, it can sometimes feel like the skies never get fully dark at this time of year. However, you'll want to venture here during the daytime, too, when

you can visit tumbling waterfalls and tranquil lochs, admire peaceful and natural scenes, and maybe spot red deer and wild goats on your travels.

Visiting the Park

Galloway is home to three visitor centers in the southern and western parts of the park; these are the best places to find more information about stargazing, and are close to many of the park's best and most accessible sights and hikes. The visitor centers also provide facilities like toilets and cafés. **Glentrool** (http://scotland. forestry.gov.uk/forest-parks/galloway-forest-park/glentrool-visitor-centre), about an hour (35 miles/56 km) south of Ayr, is closest to lovely Loch Trool and sights related to the Scottish Wars of Independence. **Kirroughtree** (https://forestryandland. gov.scot/visit/forest-parks/galloway-forest-park/kirroughtree-visitor-centre), a further 30 minutes (15 miles/24 km) south of Glentrool, is the main gateway to the park and its outdoor activities center. Finally, **Clatteringshaws** (https://forestryand-land.gov.scot/visit/forest-parks/galloway-forest-park/clatteringshaws-visitor-centre) is 25 minutes (14 miles/22.5 km) east of Kirroughtree and is conveniently located to **New Galloway** (71 miles/114 km; 1 hour 40 minutes south of Glasgow, or 1 hour south of Ayr on the A713), east of the park, which has a good concentration of accommodations and restaurants.

Besides the visitor centers mentioned above, visit the official **Galloway Forest Park website** (https://forestryandland. gov.scot/visit/forest-parks/galloway-forest-park) for information on navigating the park and different walking and cycling trails available.

LOCH TROOL AND BRUCE'S STONE

North shore of Loch Trool; https://forestryandland. gov.scot/visit/forest-parks/galloway-forest-park/ bruces-stone-loch-trool

This loch, in the heart of the forest, near the

Galloway Forest Park

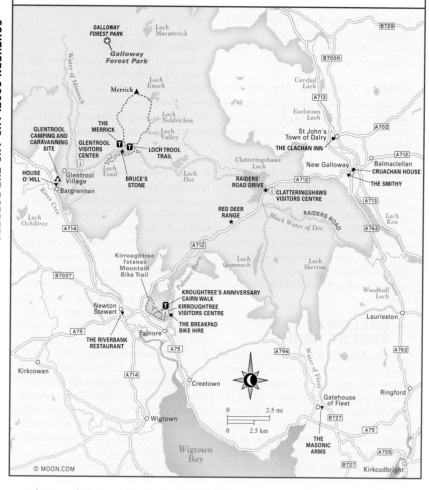

© MOON.COM

settlement of Glentrool, is often described as the "quiet place." Ancient oak woodlands stretch down to the shoreline and the loch is fed by clear water that pours down from the Galloway Hills via rocky beds giving the area a timeless and untampered feel.

Follow the signs for "Bruce's Stone" from Glentrool and park up at the car park on the north side of the loch after around 4 miles (6.4 km). From here's it's a short walk up the hill to Bruce's Stone, a giant granite boulder

that commemorates Robert the Bruce's victory over the English Army here in 1307 during the Scottish Wars of Independence. The stone is also the start point for the walk up The Merrick.

RAIDERS' ROAD DRIVE

Clatteringshaws Visitors Centre; https://forestryandland.gov.scot/visit/forest-parks/galloway-forest-park/raiders-road-forest-drive

This 10-mile (16 km) forest drive, which

Food Foraging

Food foraging is a big thing across Scotland. It was already growing in popularity as food provenance started to have a bigger impact on menus, and gin makers began foraging for local botanicals to make their drinks taste "of" a place. The need to become more resourceful during the pandemic meant more people began growing their own fruits and vegetables, and many began looking to the natural spaces around them for ingredients. Some chefs are now using this trend to their—and our—advantage.

LEARN FROM THE BEST

Though southern Scotland's natural woodlands, seas, and hills are alive with edible possibilities, it can be hard for the novice forager to know where to start. This is why it's a good idea to take a tour. Mark Williams, of **Galloway Wild Foods** (www.gallowaywildfoods.com), leads regular events (check website for schedule; events last around 3 hours, booking ahead recommended; £30-60 per person) and teaches private courses (minimum 3 hours per course; from £100 per hour) in Galloway and beyond, in which he takes visitors on trips in search of wild foods, fungi, and even seaweed that they can eat. Courses range from day trips exploring the tidal salt marsh of Galloway's Solway Firth, as well as woodlands and hedgerows (where you'll cook what you find), to a gourmet foraging weekend.

BECOME A BUSHCRAFT MASTER

With **Arran Bushcraft & Survival** (www.arranbushcraftandsurvival.co.uk) on the Isle of Arran, you'll not only learn to look around you and use your environment to be self-sufficient but also find out how to forage for basic ingredients and how to cook them over a campfire. Courses range from 1-2 days (£75-160 per person).

RESTAURANTS THAT USE FORAGED INGREDIENTS

There are lots of good restaurants in southern Scotland that use seasonal, locally foraged ingredients but perhaps none does it better than **Mr Pook's** (38 King St; tel. 01556 504 000; www.mrpooks.co.uk; 12pm-2pm and 5:30pm-9pm Weds.-Sat.; entrées £10), some 25 minutes (15 miles/24 km) southwest of Galloway Forest Park in Castle Douglas, on the A75. Since opening in 2018, chef Mr "Ed" Pook has been offering the region on a plate, using raw ingredients where possible to give a taste unique to the region. Obviously, the menu is dependent on what he can get his hands on, but foraged samphire, mushrooms, wild raspberries, and bee pollen have been known to feature.

follows the River Dee and much of an old drove road that features in a novel by Scottish author S. R. Crockett (contemporary of both J. M. Barrie and Robert Louis Stevenson) is a great way to see a good amount of the park without having to travel too far. Following a largely single-track gravel road, from Clattinshaws to Loch Ken, it's not a drive that should be rushed, as there's a good chance of seeing red kites in the sky above, or wandering roe deer. **Otters Pool,** about halfway along the route, is a nice place to pull over for a picnic lunch, a toilet break, or just a cooling paddle in the rock pools (sightings of otters are rare). The road is only open from April to October (though it can be cycled year-round), and there is a small fee of £2 to use it.

RED DEER RANGE

The Queen's Way (north side of the A712), near Clatterinshaws; https://forestryandland.gov. scot/visit/forest-parks/galloway-forest-park/ red-deer-range

About 60 deer live on this range, so if you've not managed to see any yet, come here and view them through the hide for free. Though they're not wild as such, it's still a thrilling experience to encounter one this close up.

Stargazing

There are three **visitor centers** positioned throughout the park in some of the darkest locations, so wrap up warm, bring a flask of something hot to drink and a camera, and enjoy.

GLENTROOL

Glentrool, Newton Stewart; tel. 0300 067 6800; http://scotland.forestry.gov.uk/forest-parks/ galloway-forest-park/glentrool-visitor-centre; 10:30am-4pm daily

With a nearby campsite, this is perhaps the best place to enjoy the park's dark skies, and at twilight or first thing in the morning there's a really good chance of spotting roe deer or red squirrels. To get there, take the road that passes north from Glentrool village.

KIRROUGHTREE

Forest Drive, Newton Stewart; tel. 1671 402 994; https://forestryandland.gov.scot/visit/forest-parks/ galloway-forest-park/kirroughtree-visitor-centre; 11am-2:30pm Mon.-Fri., 10am-4pm Sat.-Sun.

Signposted from the A75 at Palnure, this is the gateway center for many arriving in the park, particularly those wanting a little adventure. Though you'll want to venture after dark to see nature's light show, it's a good place to come during the day, too, when you can pick the brains of staff, watch red squirrels and birds from the hide, or take one of the other woodland walks or mountain bike trails.

CLATTERINGSHAWS

Clatteringshaws House, New Galloway, Castle Douglas; tel. 7860 773 502; https://forestryandland. gov.scot/visit/forest-parks/galloway-forest-park/ clatteringshaws-visitor-centre; 11am-3pm daily

This visitor center is in a picturesque location overlooking Clatteringshaws Loch and its water birds.

BIOSPHERE DARK SKY RANGER

www.freelanceranger.com/stargazing.html

Elizabeth Tindal is one of the first Biosphere Dark Sky Rangers to be appointed, and can arrange bespoke stargazing trips. Whether you simply want someone to guide you, to set up a campfire to keep you warm and tell stories around, to plan a special nighttime feast, or to make it a really memorable experience, Elizabeth can make it happen.

Hiking

KIRROUGHTREE'S ANNIVERSARY CAIRN WALK

Hiking Distance: *1.5-mile (2.5-km) loop*
Hiking Time: *1 hour*
Trailhead: *Kirroughtree Visitor Centre, Forest Drive*
Information and Maps: *https:// forestryandland.gov.scot/images/pdf/rec_pdfs/ Galloway-Forest-Park-Map-and-Trail-Guide.pdf*

This circular route offers a moderate walk, setting off from and returning to the Kirroughtree Visitor Centre, which takes you to a magnificent viewpoint. The walk along firm gravel paths takes you in through mature woodland and up moderate gradients to a cairn that was put up to mark the park's 50th anniversary. You return via Bruntis Loch, but keep an eye out for mountain bikes, which share the trail.

LOCH TROOL TRAIL

Hiking Distance: *5.5-mile (8.8-km) loop*
Hiking Time: *2.5-3 hours*
Trailhead: *Caldons car park, 2 miles (3.2 km) east of Glentrool Visitor Center*
Information and Maps: *www.walkhighlands. co.uk/galloway/loch-trool.shtml*

Encircling the famous loch, once the scene of a bloody battle and today a serene body of water where nature is at her best, this is a moderate walk that climbs and descends more than you might think. The trail starts by crossing a bridge over the Water of Trool, after which you turn left at each of the junctions and then cross a second bridge. Follow the track and it forks left, then look for marker posts for the Southern Upland Way, where you'll turn left and go over another

1: Galloway Forest Park **2:** Galloway Forest Park is a Dark Sky Park. **3:** Bruce's Stone **4:** the view from Bruce's Stone

small bridge before forking right onto a path that goes up through trees before revealing the first view of the loch. From here the trail is well-waymarked and you can do a short detour to Bruce's Stone. The path is a mix of hard surface tracks and beaten earth.

THE MERRICK

Hiking Distance: *8.25 miles (13.2 km) round-trip*
Hiking Time: *4-5 hours*
Trailhead: *Car park near Bruce's Stone, Loch Trool; 3 miles (4.8 km) east of Glentrool Visitor Centre*
Information and Maps: *www.walkhighlands. co.uk/galloway/merrick.shtml*

This is the tallest hill in southern Scotland and forms part of the brilliantly named Range of the Awful Hand (so called because of its resemblance to a hand and its knobbly fingers).

The first section follows a good hill path, but in the later stages the ridge path is just bare earth, so proper hiking boots are essential. To begin, park at the end of the public road up Glen Trool and follow the road up to the right, to Bruce's Stone. From here, return to the road and take the path that goes diagonally uphill marked Merrick Trail. The route is beautiful, passing by waterfalls that you can't always see but can definitely hear, above burns, and through dense forest. You'll see isolated bothies and traipse along deserted ridges with views over Galloway Forest Park and as far afield as Northern Ireland and the Isle of Man.

Cycling

THE BREAKPAD BIKE HIRE

Kirroughtree Forest Visitor Centre; tel. 01671 401 303; www.thebreakpad.com, standard bikes from £25 per day, electric bikes from £35 per day

Conveniently located at Kirroughtree Visitor Centre, this bike service can not only repair your bicycle but also has a decent selection of mountain bikes and electric bikes to hire, including kids' models. Staff can advise you on the best routes to take and give some safety tips.

KIRROUGHTREE 7STANES MOUNTAIN BIKE TRAIL

Cycling Distance: *6.3 miles (10 km)*
Cycling Time: *1-2 hours*
Trailhead: *Kirroughtree Visitor Centre*
Information and Maps: *https:// forestryandland.gov.scot/images/pdf/rec_ pdfs/7stanes_Kirroughtree_trail_map__info.pdf*

Offering some of the best mountain bike riding in the whole of Scotland, Kirroughtree offers routes for beginners right through to adrenalin junkies. The **Larg Hill** route is suitable for all (even kids) who are confident on their bikes, but you will need some basic off-road riding skills. It's a winding, exhilarating route, mainly on single track that includes some small rock drops for added excitement.

The trail map above also outlines other routes, including the "severe" Black Craigs, which should only be attempted by very experienced riders.

Food

THE RIVERBANK RESTAURANT

Goods Lane, Newton Stewart; tel. 01671 403 330; www.facebook.com/pages/Riverbank-Restaurant/109046719156927; sandwiches £4.95

Generously filled fresh sandwiches, baked potatoes, and soft spongy cakes served alongside excellent coffee are the specialties of this café near Kirroughtree (4 miles/6.4 km; 10 minutes west of the visitor center). A meal here will set you up for the day before your foray into the forest.

THE SMITHY

High Street, New Galloway; tel. 01644 420269; www. thesmithy-newgalloway.co.uk; 10am-4pm Weds.-Mon. early March-early Nov.; sandwiches £5.40

This tearoom 10 minutes (6 miles/9.6 km) east of Clatteringshaws serves freshly made sandwiches and dishes and has a lovely setting next to Mill Burn at the head of Loch Ken. You can have lunch or a late breakfast while listening to the meditative sound of the waterfall. Fruit scones or savory cheese scones with a cup of tea are a good mid-morning snack, or you can order a hot dish such as scampi or pie and choose three sides from a possible six.

THE HOUSE O' HILL

Bargrennan; tel. 01671 840 243; www.houseohill. co.uk; entrées £5.95

The only pub actually within the park, just a mile (1.6 km) down the road from Glentrool, this pub prides itself on using local ingredients, including fish, meat, and cheeses, and is a good choice for a post-walk or cycle dinner. There's also home-baking and afternoon tea for slightly lighter meals and two simple but comfy rooms for overnight stays.

THE MASONIC ARMS

10 Ann Street; tel. 01557 814 335; www.masonicarms. co.uk; entrées £7

Choose between the bright and contemporary sunroom or the more traditional and cozy bar area at this pub and restaurant in an 18th-century building, with clues to its masonic past in the stonework. There are daily specials and a good variety of local produce, from creamy farmhouse cheeses—best enjoyed with a pint of real ale or whisky by the fire—to steak, game, and seafood, served by professional yet friendly staff. It's a bit of a detour from the park, a 30-minute (17-mile/27-km) drive southeast of Kirroughtree.

> TOP EXPERIENCE

Accommodations and Camping
★ GLENTROOL CAMPING AND CARAVANNING SITE

Bargrennan, Newton Stewart; tel. 01671 840 280; www.glentroolcampingandcaravansite.co.uk; tent pitch £11 plus £4 per person, caravan pitch £11 plus £4 per person, static caravan £85 per night

To really make the most of the 300 miles (483 km) of wilderness on offer at the Galloway Forest Park, there's no better place to stay than in this peaceful campsite, with a stream running alongside, where you can really embrace the glittering night sky. There's a small **shop** on-site, a food prep area, clean communal showers and toilets, and free Wi-Fi. If you don't have camping gear, there are also two two-bedroomed static caravans for hire with their own toilets and shower rooms. Though there is no food on-site, the **House O'Hill** pub is just a few minutes' walk away. Cash is preferred, and there's a three-night minimum stay.

CRUACHAN HOUSE

Kenbridge Road, New Galloway; tel. 0164 442 0865; www.cruachanhouse.com/en-GB; £160-196 d

At this delightful B&B in an Arts and Crafts-style cottage, owners Hazel and Roger invite guests to make themselves very much at home and will provide tea and cake on arrival. Rooms are large and airy with big beds and period features, and bathrooms with deep baths, separate showers, and lots of nice smellies. The pretty three-acre gardens are nice for a morning stroll or evening's stargazing. There's even a summerhouse, where you can enjoy a nightcap, and the lounge has a lovely window seat that is ideal for a lazy afternoon reading. Cooked breakfasts are as good as you will find anywhere. It's conveniently located to Clatteringshaws Visitor Center, a 10-minute (6-mile/9.6-km) drive east.

THE CLACHAN INN

8-10 Main Street, St John's Town of Dalry; tel. 1644 430 241; www.theclachaninn.co.uk; £65 s, £85 d, family room £125

This pub with rooms in the cute village of St John's Town of Dalry, just north of New Galloway, is a great find. The pub is a delight, with wooden floorboards, an open fire, worn but comfy seating, a good range of ales and craft beers on tap, and a decent choice of Scottish gins and whiskies. Far from your standard pub fare, dishes include venison or peat-smoked haddock, as well as typical British pub snacks such as pork crackling and pickled eggs. There are six non-showy rooms, each with an en-suite, at reasonable prices.

Getting There and Around

From **Glasgow**, it's just under two hours to

Galloway Forest Park. Take the M77 and then A77 southwest of the city into Ayrshire and turn left onto the B7045 just past Minshant, which will take you all the way into the park to Loch Trool. From Ayr, it's an hour's drive south to Galloway Forest Park (35 miles/56 km).

You can get the train from Glasgow to Dumfries (1 hour 45 minutes; £18.40 single) or to Girvan (1 hour, changing at Ayr; £11 single). There are some buses that will take you toward the park, but with no public transport within the park, you will need to be prepared to walk or cycle a lot. From Dumfries Train Station, for instance, it's a three-hour cycle to Clatteringshaws Visitor Centre, while from Girvan you could cycle to Glentrool in 2.5 hours.

Arran

It's often said that Arran is Scotland in miniature. If you want to see castles, soaring hills, and ancient sites, then come to 167-square-mile (432-square-km) Arran, which has it all. Just off the mainland in the Firth of Clyde between Ayr and Ardrossan, Arran is one of the most accessible of all Scotland's isles. It's an easy weekend trip from Glasgow—at a push, you could even do it in a day.

Brodick Harbour, in a sheltered inlet right about in the middle of the eastern coast of the island, is where ferries arrive to Arran from Ardrossan. The town of **Brodick** itself is Arran's central hub, with its highest concentration of shops, restaurants, and accommodations, and it sits in the shadow of **Brodick Castle,** which overlooks the little bay and buildings below. The main road through town, the **A841,** also happens to be the Ring Road that runs the length of the island; it would be a 2-hour drive (without stops) if you wanted to drive it all, about 60 miles (96 km) in all. The **B880,** also known as the String, cuts through the middle, and can be a useful shortcut.

Goatfell, Arran's highest point at 2,834 feet (864 m), is the island's other major draw, also easily accessible from Brodick, just under 7 miles (11 km) round-trip from the castle. Attractions on Arran's northern coast include **Lochranza,** home to the popular distillery, as well as the charming fishing cottages known as the **Twelve Apostles.** West of Brodick you'll find **Machrie Moor,** mysterious stone circles from the Neolithic era.

GETTING THERE AND AROUND

Arran is a lot easier to get to than you might suppose. You can reach Arran by ferry from **Ardrossan Harbour** (Harbour Street, Ardrossan; tel. 0344 811 0141), accessible from Glasgow in less than an hour, and from Edinburgh in just 90 minutes. From **Glasgow,** it's 33 miles (53 km) along the M8, A737, and A78; from **Edinburgh,** the drive is 79 miles (127 km), and you just need to join the M8 a little earlier. There are also direct trains to Ardrossan Harbour from Glasgow Central Station that take under 50 minutes (£8.30 single). From Edinburgh, you'll need to add on the price and time of a connection to Glasgow Central from Edinburgh Waverley (£13.50 single).

Though it has a couple of pleasant beaches and great views of Arran, there's not much reason to hang around Ardrossan—it's a fairly standard port town. The ferry from Ardrossan to Arran, run by CalMac (www.calmac.co.uk/ports/brodick), takes 55 minutes and costs £3.90 for a single on foot (plus £15.55 if you're taking a car) and arrives at **Brodick Harbour** on Arran.

Once on Arran, if you don't have a car, walking is an option between a couple of places, but you may have to rely on the

Isle of Arran

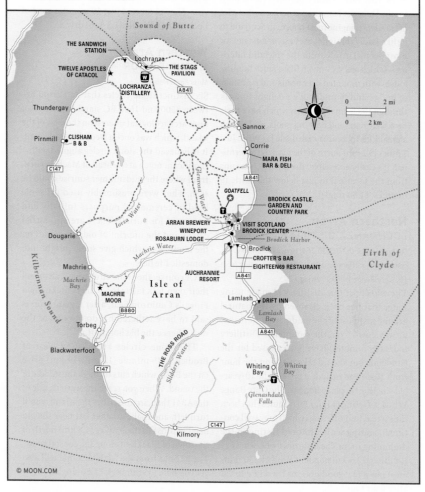

Sound of Butte

THE SANDWICH STATION

TWELVE APOSTLES OF CATACOL

Lochranza

THE STAGS PAVILION

LOCHRANZA DISTILLERY

A841

Thundergay

Pirnmill

CLISHAM B & B

C147

Sannox

Corrie

MARA FISH BAR & DELI

Glenrosa Water

Iorsa Water

GOATFELL

A841

BRODICK CASTLE, GARDEN AND COUNTRY PARK

ARRAN BREWERY

WINEPORT

ROSABURN LODGE

VISIT SCOTLAND BRODICK ICENTER

Brodick Harbor

Dougarie

Machrie Water

Brodick

CROFTER'S BAR

EIGHTEEN69 RESTAURANT

AUCHRANNIE RESORT

A841

Machrie

Machrie Bay

MACHRIE MOOR

Isle of Arran

Kilbrannan Sound

B880

Lamlash

DRIFT INN

Lamlash Bay

Firth of Clyde

Torbeg

THE ROSS ROAD

A841

Blackwaterfoot

C147

Sliddery Water

Whiting Bay

Whiting Bay

Glenashdale Falls

C147

Kilmory

© MOON.COM

0   2 mi
0   2 km

---

sporadic taxis. Alternatively, **SPT** (www.spt. co.uk/travel-with-spt/bus/bus-timetables) has a timetable of all bus services connecting different parts of the island, many of which meet the ferries. The buses are run by Stagecoach (www.stagecoachbus.com; book through the app or buy on board, £1.50 single or unlimited travel with a £4 Day Rider ticket) and some are very handy, including the 322 from the ferry terminal to Machrie (for seeing the standing stones), and the 324

that will take you from the ferry terminal right to the castle gates.

SIGHTS
Brodick
BRODICK CASTLE, GARDEN, AND COUNTRY PARK

Brodick; www.nts.org.uk/visit/places/brodick-castle-garden-country-park; 10am-5pm daily early Apr.-Oct.; adult £14.50, concessions £10.50, family £38.50, one-adult family £27.50

Having recently completed major restoration work, this 19th-century baronial castle built for the Dukes of Hamilton is perhaps what a lot of travelers imagine most houses in Scotland to be like (sadly this is not the case, at least not for most people). Aside from the splendid interiors—which feel very much like a fancy hunting lodge, with mounted deer heads and paintings of horses and hounds—it's a delight to walk through the formal gardens, which have their own waterfalls and bathing pools, and there's a great kids' play area called Isle be Wild. Just 2 miles (3.2 km) north of the main ferry terminal, it's easily accessible; the no. 324 bus runs from the terminal to just below the castle (9 minutes; £1.50 single).

Northern Arran
LOCHRANZA DISTILLERY

Lochranza; tel. 01770 830 264; www.arranwhisky. com; 10am-4:30pm Sun.-Thurs. Mar.-Nov.; tours from £8, Core Range Whisky Tasting £20

The whisky at this distillery is made using water that has been cleansed by the natural granite and peat of the landscape as it makes its way down from the mountains. Distillery tours (45 minutes) have been paused for the pandemic but should take place on the hour from 10am and include a taste of the 10-year-old single malt, plus a liqueur. The Core Range Whisky Tasting (1 hour 30 minutes) has been the virtual tour offering (which may well continue), ending with a tutored tasting in the dramming room.The little town of Lochranza (14 miles/22.5 km north of Brodick; 30 minutes) has a few good options for a bite to eat after your tour.

TWELVE APOSTLES OF CATACOL

Catacol; www.visitarran.com/what-to-see-do/ arran-attractions/the-twelve-apostles-in-catacol

If you find yourself in this tiny village on the north coast of Arran, then chances are you've come to see this terrace of understated fishermen's cottages. Look at the houses closely and you will notice that all of the top windows are slightly different. Apparently, this was so that when the fishermen were at sea their wives could signal to them and they would know whose wife it was. Now that's romance for you. They're located just 10 minutes west of Lochranza, a 3-mile (4.8-km) drive.

Western Arran
MACHRIE MOOR

Moss Farm Road

Six distinct stone circles that date from between 3500 and 1500 BC stand in an area of huge archaeological interest on the west of the island, which was once a Neolithic settlement. It is believed the stone circles aligned with a significant notch at the head of Machrie Glen, from where the midsummer sunrise could be seen. They were presumably used for some kind of ceremonial purposes initially and later used for burials. There are also burial cairns and the imprint of old hut circles on the landscape, which give some insight into domestic life here.

Of course, the stone circles have attracted their own folk tales, too. One is nicknamed Fingal's Cauldron Seat, after a giant who is said to have tethered his dog to one of the rocks, hence the big hole in it.

The stone circles are located west of Brodick, a 45-minute (12-mile/19-km) drive on the B880, which cuts through the middle of the island. When you reach the western side of the A841 that circumscribes the island, you'll turn left, and make another left near the old derelict Moss Farm, 3 miles (4.8 km) north of the town of Blackfoot along the coastal route. The 322 bus from the ferry terminal will also get you here (35 minutes; £1.50 single).

HIKING
Brodick
★ GOATFELL

Hiking Distance: *6.5 miles (10.4 km) round-trip*
Hiking Time: *4.5-6 hours*
Trailhead: *Isle of Arran Brewery*
Information and Maps: *www.walkhighlands. co.uk/arran/goatfell.shtml*

The highest point on the island, this naturally

1: Brodick Castle and Goatfell 2: hiking on Goatfell

rugged mountain, whose jagged and unusual pyramid-like peaks dominate much of the island's landscape, is a destination of choice for hill walkers and climbers, and is currently looked after by the National Trust. Most visitors to Goatfell set off near Brodick Castle. The path is reached by a track that runs past Arran Brewery.

There are good footpaths most of the way (many have been repaired in recent years). Please use them—the area is starting to suffer from overuse, and people veering off the main routes risk upsetting the natural habitats of heath and dwarf juniper trees, whose fragrance wafts through the air as you walk. En route, look for tiger beetles, emperor moths, and of course the buzzards and golden eagles up above. It's a strenuous, almost 3,000-foot (900-m) elevation gain, but you'll see plenty of families on the hike, and it should be doable for people with a relatively good level of fitness.

The last section of the walk is very rough, over and around granite boulders. The view from the top is one of ragged hillscapes and curvaceous coastline—with the Paps of Jura in the distance and even Ben Lomond. On your way back, be sure to head to **Arran Brewery** for a well-earned pint of ale.

Southern Arran
GLENASHDALE FALLS

Hiking Distance: *3 miles (4.8 km) round trip*
Hiking Time: *1.5-2 hours*
Trailhead: *Ashdale Bridge, Whiting Bay*
Information and Maps: *www.walkhighlands. co.uk/arran/glenashdale-falls.shtml*

The relatively simple 3-mile (4.8-km) trek to these lovely waterfalls (also known as Eas a' Chrannaig) also takes you to the twin chambered cairns known as the **Giant's Graves,** from where you can look across to Holy Isle and the Firth of Clyde. The trailhead is about 25 minutes (10 miles/16 km) south of Brodick, and the path is well signposted from the little town of Whiting Bay. It goes through pretty woodland, dipping and rising regularly until you reach a choice of two viewing platforms for the dual falls. At the lower one, follow the signs to reach the Giant's Graves.

FOOD
Brodick
EIGHTEEN69 RESTAURANT

Auchrannie Resort, Auchrannie Road, Brodick; tel. 01770 302 234; www.auchrannie.co.uk/eighteen69. html; Thurs.-Sun. dinner from 5pm; small plates £8

One of the dining options on offer at the Auchrannie Resort, this is Scottish small

Glenashdale Falls

plate dining at its best and is a great way to try lots of different local flavors in one sitting. There's a reasonable choice of veggie dishes (slow roasted portobello mushroom with tomatoes, lentils, and spinach, for instance), plus cold plates, meat, and fish dishes. Don't leave until you've tried the baked Cullen skink pie.

WINEPORT

Cladach, Brodick; tel. 01770 302 101; www.wineport. co.uk; food served from 11am-7pm daily; light bites £8
This bar/bistro with a large outdoor eating area is popular in summer, and with walkers of Goatfell either before or after a hike. Wherever possible, they use local produce, such as cheese from Arran Dairies and meat from Arran Butchers.

Northern Arran
THE SANDWICH STATION

A841 Lochranza; tel. 07393 602 806; https:// thesandwichstation.weebly.com; 8:45am-4pm Mon.-Sat., 8:45am-3.30pm Sun.; sandwiches £4.50
As you might expect, this place does sandwiches very, very well, and nothing else (except for the soup of the day). Artisan breads including sourdough and focaccia come from a local bakery, and the tasty fillings are sourced as locally as possible—the smoked fish comes from Skipness Smokehouse, while cheeses and salad leaves come from right here on the island. This is a well-priced top-notch lunch stop.

THE STAGS PAVILION

Lochranza; tel. 01770 830 600; www.stagspavilion. com; 5:30pm-8:15pm Thurs.-Mon.; entrées £5.95
Deer roam freely outside this restaurant in the popular town of Lochranza, but it's worth a pit stop just for the homemade food that combines Scottish ingredients with Italian chef Rino's homeland influences. With mountains just behind, it has an Alpine feel, and you can order Scottish comfort food such as Arran lamb slow-cooked, or go for more classic Italian dishes.

MARA FISH BAR & DELI

Shore Road, Corrie; tel. 01770 810 555; www. mara-arran.co.uk; 4pm-8pm Tues. and Fri., 9am-4pm Weds.-Thurs. and Sat., 10am-4pm Sun., closed in winter; mains £10
With a name that translates from the Gaelic for The Sea, you know you're in for a treat here. With the aim to encourage more sustainable Scottish fishing, this takeaway-style joint (there are a few outdoor seats) 15 minutes (6 miles/9.6 km) north of Brodick offers meals cooked to order, prepared using the catch of the day. Dishes include hake cooked with ginger, lobster bisque, and fish tacos, and it's a contender for the best fish and chips you've had in your life.

Southern Arran
DRIFT INN

Shore Road, Lamlash; tel. 01770 600 608; https://driftinnarran.com; 12pm-9pm Thurs.-Sat., 12:30pm-9pm Sun.; platters from £9.50
This coastal pub has a garden offering sea views, just 10 minutes (3.5 miles/5.6 km) south of Brodick. Most people come here for the tantalizing platters: the fish ones come with a duo of gravlax, fish cakes, and homemade bread, while the veggie platters, with beetroot and chickpea pate, and a trio of Arran cheeses, are hard to resist.

BARS
CROFTERS ARRAN

Shore Road, Brodick; tel. 01770 302 579; https:// croftersarran.com; 11am-12am daily
Formerly known as Fiddler's, this bar does good pub food with lots of veggie and vegan options, and it's worth booking a table if you want to be sure of having a seat on a music night. Local musicians play everything from folk to Americana and jazz, and you may even catch the odd touring band on your visit.

ARRAN BREWERY

Cladach, Brodick; tel. 1770 302 353; www. arranbrewery.co.uk; 10am-5pm Mon.-Sat., 12:30pm-4:30pm Sun. Apr.-Sept., 10:30am-4:30pm Mon.-Sat. winter, tours daily 11am and 2pm; tours £15

Located between Brodick Castle and Goatfell, this is an almost obligatory stop for everyone who visits Arran. Join a guided tour to see how the beer is made, followed by a tasting, or just pop in and buy some local ales from the shop.

ACCOMMODATIONS
Brodick
ROSABURN LODGE

Brodick; tel. 01770 302 383; www.rosaburnlodge. co.uk; £100 d, Rosa Suite £120 d

This attractive riverside guesthouse is a charming base just outside Brodick. With just three rooms, it's quiet and unhurried, yet within walking distance to good restaurants, shops, and pubs. Rooms are simple and decorated in fresh creams and soft shades, and the breakfast room has glorious garden views. From the Rosa Suite, which has nine windows, you can see the peak of Goatfell. Don't forget to ask the owners, Paul and Leen, for a packed lunch if you're considering climbing Arran's highest hill.

AUCHRANNIE RESORT

Auchrannie Road, Brodick; tel. 01770 302 234; www. auchrannie.co.uk; £159 d in spa resort

Indulge yourself at this four-star spa resort, just 1 mile (1.6 km) from Brodick. The spa has two swimming pools, a sauna, and steam rooms, plus a full list of relaxing treatments. Rooms are contemporary and high end; some suites even have outdoor hot tubs on their own private terraces. The resort also

has more traditional rooms in the country house hotel, and some self-catering lodges. Plus, guests arriving on foot will be picked up or dropped off at Brodick ferry terminal for free.

Northern Arran
CLISHAM BED & BREAKFAST

Pirnmil, Arran; tel. 01770 850 294; www. arran-clisham.co.uk; £74 d

In this utterly charming family home that provides bed and breakfast across just two rooms, the service is faultless, with host Diane going above and beyond to make you feel at home. Not far from Lochranza (7 miles/11 km south; 20 minutes), beds at this four-star B&B in the peaceful village of Pirnmill on the northwest coast of Arran are comfortable and the full cooked breakfasts will set you up for the day. Just make sure you're back in time to watch the sun set over the Kilbranan Sound toward the Kintyre Peninsula from your bedroom window. Payment is by check or cash only and the B&B is closed from end of October until April.

INFORMATION AND SERVICES

In Brodick, right by the harbor, you'll find the **Visit Scotland Brodick iCenter** (The Pier; tel. 01770 303 774; www.visitscotland. com/info/services/brodick-information-centre-p332591; 9am-4:30pm Tues.-Sat.). If it's open, this is a good point of reference for your time on Arran.

Loch Lomond and the Inner Hebrides

It's surprisingly easy to find space for seclusion, nature walks, and wild adventures in Scotland, even if you're starting off in a city.

From Glasgow, Loch Lomond and the Trossachs National Park is the obvious choice. Indeed, it's so close that its southern fringes were once called Glasgow's "green lung." Encompassing some 720 square miles (1,864 square km) of lochs, glens, mountains, and woodland, which are home to 25 percent of Britain's threatened bird, animal, and plant species, Scotland's first national park can be reached from its most populated city in as little as half an hour. With some exciting re-wilding projects underway, as well as numerous places to camp, trek,

Highlights

Look for ★ to find recommended sights, activities, dining, and lodging.

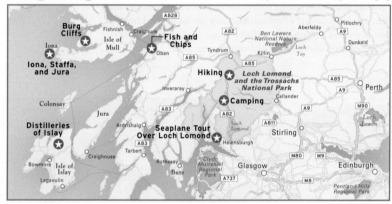

★ **Hiking Loch Lomond and the Trossachs National Park:** Bag one of the park's 21 Munros, or trek along some of its 22 lochs (page 297).

★ **Seaplane Tour Over Loch Lomond:** Get a bird's-eye tour of the national park for a real sense of the sublime (page 299).

★ **Camping:** Whether you want to pitch up your tent in the wild or at a campsite with more creature comforts, there are wonderful places to camp in Loch Lomond and the Trossachs National Park (page 304).

★ **Fish and Chips in Oban:** This well-connected port is known as the Seafood Capital of Scotland for very good reason (page 308).

★ **Burg Cliffs:** Time, water, and wind have done their work on the Ardmeanach Peninsula of Mull's west coast, creating striking rock formations (page 313).

★ **Iona, Staffa, and Jura:** The less visited, less populated islands of Iona, Staffa, and Jura are well worth a visit, or even better a peaceful night or two (page 316).

★ **Distilleries of Islay:** Hop from distillery to distillery on this beautiful isle and enjoy drams of peat-tinged whisky, aged to perfection (page 322).

cycle—even swing through the trees—it's a natural wonderland that you could happily spend a week or more exploring.

It was amid the crumpled hills and glistening lochs of what is today the Loch Lomond and the Trossachs National Park that Sir Walter Scott first began his love affair with Scotland, and were it not for his *Lady of the Lake* ode, inspired by his travels through the region, the Highland Revival of the 19th century may never have begun.

To the west lies the Inner Hebrides, one of the best places in Scotland to spot native wildlife. Local small-scale tours will let you get to the heart of the region and give you the opportunity to support fragile local economies. And make sure you visit some of the west's best isles, including the spiritual isle of Iona and the whisky isle of Islay, which are more accessible than you might think.

ORIENTATION

Loch Lomond and the Trossachs National Park—just 25 miles (40 km) north of Glasgow, 20 miles (32 km) west of Stirling, and 30 miles (48 km) west of Perth—crosses the diagonal Highland Boundary Fault, which many people take as the division between the Highlands and the Lowlands. The park is expansive, covering 720 square miles (1,865 square km) in total. To the west, the port town of **Oban,** from where you can access many of Scotland's islands, including **Mull,** is just 36 miles (58 km) from the north end of the park. **Islay** is best accessed from Kennacraig on the Kintyre Peninsula, some 55 miles (89 km) south of Oban.

PLANNING YOUR TIME

Loch Lomond and the Trossachs National Park is large (720 square miles/1,865 square km), and though many travelers simply pass through it as they journey on up to Fort William and then Mallaig for the ferry over to Skye (either by train or car), it really is worthy of a few days of your time, particularly if you are partial to walking or camping. That said, the area around **Balloch** and **Luss** is very touristy. Though they are useful places to stock up on supplies and they have some good restaurants and cafés, aim to travel to the north or east side of the park if you want a little more peace. If you plan to spend some time in the national park, come prepared with hiking boots, camping supplies, and, depending on the time of year, a swimsuit in case you want to take a dip in the loch.

Both **Islay** and **Mull** should be taken slowly; you will also need to factor in ferry timetables and crossings to each, so allow for a minimum of around three days in each place (a week is even better).

You'll do best with your own rental car in this region, though Loch Lomond and the Trossachs National Park is traversed by the famous **West Highland Line** (www.scotrail.co.uk/scotland-by-rail/great-scenic-rail-journeys/west-highland-line-glasgow-oban-and-fort-williammallaig) and so is easy enough to get to from Glasgow on public transport. Once in the national park, regular ferries across the lochs, bicycle rentals, and your own two feet may just get you where you need to go.

Loch Lomond and the Inner Hebrides

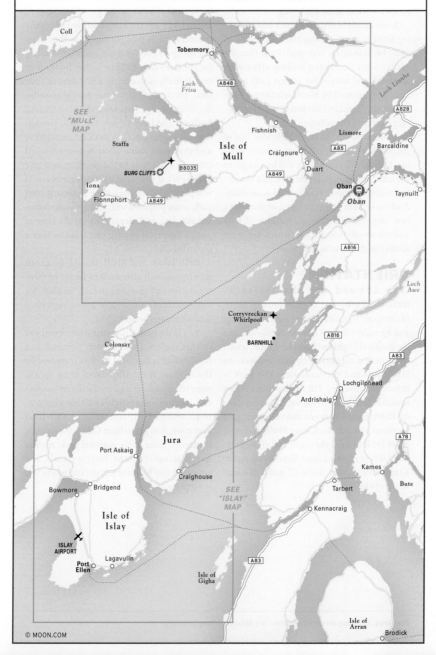

© MOON.COM

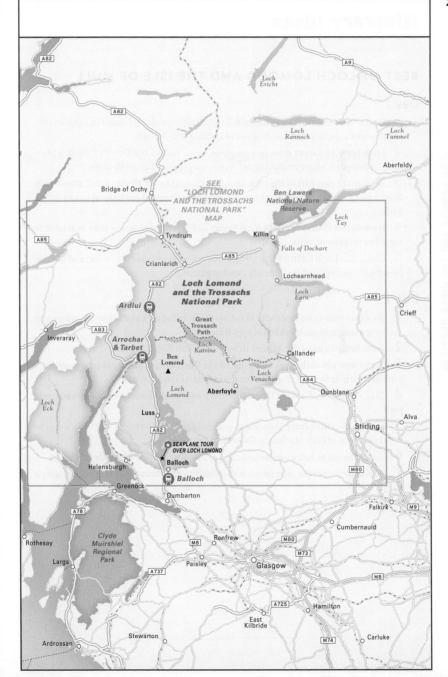

Itinerary Ideas

BEST OF LOCH LOMOND AND THE ISLE OF MULL

Day 1

1 Start with breakfast at **Roast's Café,** a surprisingly good café located in a garden center; this spot is particularly handy if you're arriving into Balloch.

2 From here, it's a short drive or a couple of hours' trek to **the Devil's Pulpit,** a place steeped in legend, where unnerving red waters surge around an eerily shaped rock.

3 Head to the east part of the park for a trip aboard the *Sir Walter Scott* steamship from Trossachs Pier for a taste of how Victorians first viewed the natural beauty of the park.

4 Have dinner at the **Pier Café** (only Friday and Saturday); you may even be treated to some live traditional music.

5 Check into **Loch Katrine Eco Lodges** for camping with added comfort and indulge in some stargazing from your private viewing platform.

Day 2

1 It's a half-hour drive first thing to the northeast of the park and **Mhor 84,** where you can have a scrumptious breakfast of eggs Benedict.

2 From here, it's just a five-minute drive to visit **Rob Roy's grave.**

3 Travel west out of the park along the A85 to Oban where you should treat yourself to probably the best fish and chips of your life at **Oban Fish & Chips.**

4 Take a (prebooked) tour of **Oban Distillery** and sample some of its 14-year-old single malt.

5 Head to the Oban Ferry Terminal to grab a ride over to the Isle of Mull. Pay a visit to the ancient seat of Clan Maclean at **Duart Castle.**

6 Treat yourself to half a lobster and chips at the local haunt of **Hebridean Lodge.**

7 Check into one of the snug rooms at the **Strongarbh House,** just above Tobermory's harbor.

Itinerary Ideas

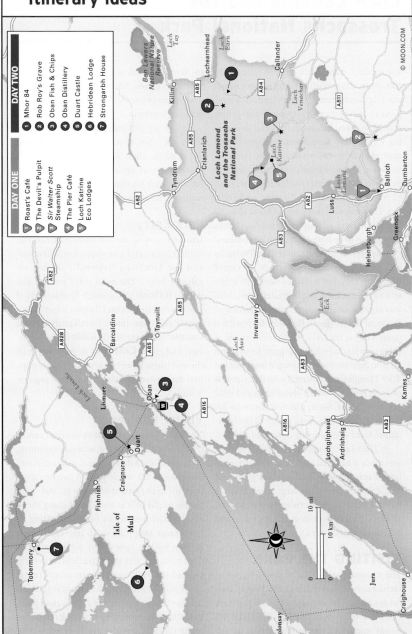

© MOON.COM

DAY ONE

1. Roast's Café
2. The Devil's Pulpit
3. *Sir Walter Scott* Steamship
4. The Pier Café
5. Loch Katrine Eco Lodges

DAY TWO

1. Mhor 84
2. Rob Roy's Grave
3. Oban Fish & Chips
4. Oban Distillery
5. Duart Castle
6. Hebridean Lodge
7. Strongarbh House

Loch Lomond and the Trossachs National Park

For outdoor enthusiasts, there is little not to like about this sprawling national park where the Highlands meets the Lowlands. It's a region of marked contrasts, with the gently rolling lowland landscape of the south giving way to steep mountains in the north and myriad lochs, rivers, woodland, and forests in between. Munro-baggers are spoiled with 21 peaks to choose from (that's a lot more than Skye), including Scotland's most southerly, Ben Lomond, and there are no fewer than 22 lochs for water adventures, plus Scotland's only lake is to be found in the park's confines.

Way back in the 18th century, the Trossachs was a largely unknown enclave in the center of the country, but a chance visit here at the end of the century by Sir Walter Scott, who was regaled en route with tales of heroics of the local Robin Hood, Rob Roy, inspired his poem *Lady of the Lake*, which tells the tale of three men (including an incognito King James V) who fight for the affections of local woman Ellen Douglas, interspersed with descriptions of a war between the Lowland Scots and rival Highland clans. Soon, travelers began to descend on the Trossachs in search of the landscapes Scott so eloquently described.

In 2002 Loch Lomond and the Trossachs was made a national park, and now there are lots of accommodations amid its glens and fertile forests, as well as large areas of space for wild camping, boat cruises across its lochs, and lots of bike-hire places, hiking trails, and adventure sports to try.

VISITING THE PARK

The national park's **official website** (www. lochlomond-trossachs.org) is a hugely useful resource. The site offers tips on places to camp and where to access services, and it has handy maps and recommendations for inspiring scenic routes that can be downloaded for free. The park is well-serviced: there are picnic benches, barbecue stands, toilets, and scenic viewpoints all around (mostly well-waymarked).

If you are planning to **camp** in one of the park's hot spots between March and September, then **book a permit** well in advance as spaces are limited (www. lochlomond-trossachs.org/things-to-do/ camping/get-a-permit).

Park Entry

Unlike many of the national parks in the United States and elsewhere, Loch Lomond and the Trossachs National Park has no gates or fences. The main entry point to the park is **Balloch** in the south (particularly if you're traveling from Glasgow), but many people also come into it from **Tyndrum** and **Crianlarich** in the north, **Killin** in the northeast, and either **Callander** or **Aberfoyle** in the east (these latter two are particularly popular for visitors coming from Edinburgh or Stirling).

Visitor Centres

The **Loch Lomond Shores** tourism center (Ben Lomond Way; www.lochlomondshores. com; 10am-6pm daily) is by far the most visited place in the whole park. It can be rather overrun in the height of summer, and some people might balk at the idea of going shopping in such a naturally beautiful setting (it has a large shopping mall, Jenner's, which is open 9:30am-6pm daily). Nevertheless, it does serve as a very useful nucleus for getting around the park on public transport (most buses stop here, and the Balloch train station is a short walk away), and it's also a good place to stock up on necessities and book one of the many tours or services available across the park—plus there's free parking.

The **VisitScotland iCentre** (The Old Station Building; tel. 01389 753 533; 10am-5pm daily) is located just opposite Balloch train station. Staff will furnish you with a map and give you some ideas of how to spend your time here.

Seasonal Considerations

If you are coming during the summer months, keep one step ahead of the fearsome midges (irritating flies that tend to travel in swarms) by checking out the **midges forecast** (www.smidgeup.com/midge-forecast).

Winter can be a surprisingly rewarding time to visit the park, when the Munros and other hills are capped with snow, frost covers the tips of trees, the lochs take on an icy blue, and there is barely anyone else around. It can also be a good time of year to spot red deer as they come down to lower spots for easier grazing, but I wouldn't recommend climbing or hiking the hills at this time of year—stick to the woodland trails unless you're very experienced—nor would I recommend camping. This is the perfect time of year to hunker down in a warm inn. The roads can get icy in winter, particularly away from the main routes, and even the more northerly section of the A82 can get hazardous.

ORIENTATION

The national park stretches over 720 square miles (1,865 square km), with a boundary length of 220 miles (350 km). It is divided into four distinct areas. **Loch Lomond** itself, the park's centerpiece, is the largest stretch of inland water in Britain, and though this is the most touristy of all four areas, it is still very beautiful.

Breadalbane in the northeast, which runs into Perthshire, is home to small villages with a real local feel, as well as forest walks, and dramatic views. It's a tranquil place, where you can visit the grave of celebrated outlaw Rob Roy (whom Sir Walter Scott immortalized) or trek to the roaring **Falls of Dochart**.

The **Trossachs**, just south of Breadalbane, encompasses both the **Queen Elizabeth Forest Park** and the **Great Trossachs Forest National Nature Reserve,** both of which offer Narnia-like trails beneath huge canopies of trees.

The fourth area is the **Cowal Peninsula** in the west of the national park, on the far side of **Loch Long,** which includes the **Argyll Forest Park,** home to magical forest trails and the oddly shaped peak of Ben Arthur, known as the Cobbler.

If you don't mind crowds, **Luss** and **Tarbet** are the best bases for the western shores of Loch Lomond, while on its eastern shores, **Balmaha** has some good camping. If you want to leave as small a footprint as possible, stay at one of the places east of Loch Lomond. The west side of the park can get saturated with tourists at busy times and residents of the slate village of Luss have even at times asked for people to stay away. For the Trossachs, both **Aberfoyle** and **Callander** are good entry points. To the northeast, **Killin** and **Balquhidder** are good bases. **Arrochar** is a good place to stay if you would like to venture into the Cowal Peninsula.

SIGHTS
Loch Lomond

www.lochlomond-trossachs.org

At 22.6 miles (36.4 km) long, Loch Lomond is Scotland's largest loch by surface area—27.5 square miles (71 sq km). It has a funnel shape, with a broad expanse of water at its southern end, narrowing to a fjord-like finger the farther north you go. Within its waters there are more than 30 islets, and it is flanked by mountains, including the mighty Ben Lomond to the east, which is best seen from the western shore. The views become more majestic as you travel north along the western A82 from Balloch in the south to Ardlui, with the road rounding the shoreline to reveal reflections of the Highland hills.

INCHCONNACHAN

Near Inchtavannach, Loch Lomond

A visit to this little island on the west side of Loch Lomond is a must, if only to see the

Loch Lomond and the Trossachs National Park

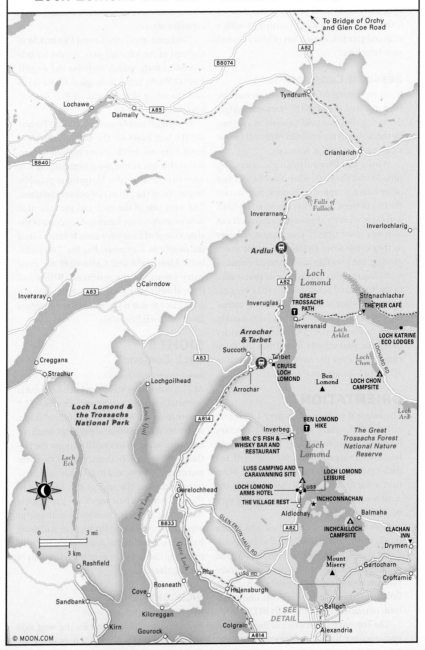

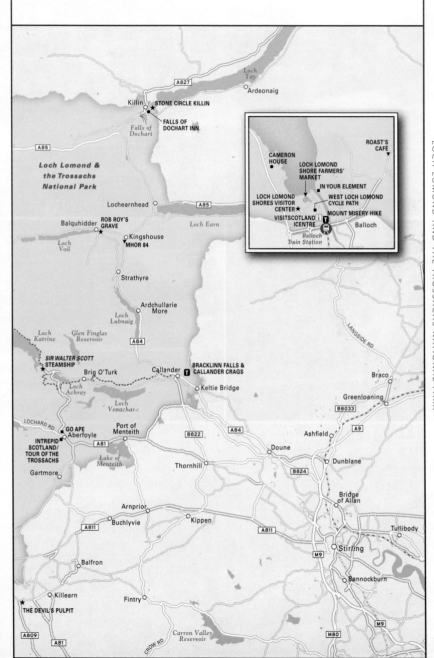

Loch Tay

A827

Ardeonaig

Killin

STONE CIRCLE KILLIN

FALLS OF DOCHART INN

Falls of Dochart

A85

Loch Lomond & the Trossachs National Park

Lochearnhead

A85

Loch Earn

Balquhidder

ROB ROY'S GRAVE

Kingshouse

MHOR 84

Loch Voil

Strathyre

Ardchullarie More

Loch Lubnaig

Loch Katrine

Glen Finglas Reservoir

A84

LANGSIDE RD

SIR WALTER SCOTT STEAMSHIP

Brig O'Turk

Callander

BRACKLINN FALLS & CALLANDER CRAGS

Braco

Loch Achray

Keltie Bridge

Greenloaning

Loch Venachar

B8033

LOCHARD RD

GO APE Aberfoyle

Port of Menteith

B822

A84

Ashfield

A9

INTREPID SCOTLAND/ TOUR OF THE TROSSACHS

A81

Doune

Lake of Menteith

Thornhill

B824

Dunblane

Gartmore

Bridge of Allan

Arnprior

Kippen

Tullibody

A811

Buchlyvie

A811

Stirling

M9

Balfron

Bannockburn

Killearn

Fintry

THE DEVIL'S PULPIT

A809

A81

CROW RD

Carron Valley Reservoir

M80

M9

Inset map:

ROAST'S CAFÉ

CAMERON HOUSE

LOCH LOMOND SHORE FARMERS' MARKET

IN YOUR ELEMENT

LOCH LOMOND SHORES VISITOR CENTER

WEST LOCH LOMOND CYCLE PATH

VISITSCOTLAND i ICENTRE

MOUNT MISERY HIKE

Balloch

Balloch Train Station

colony of wallabies that have lived here since the 1940s—it's one of the very few places outside Australia where the marsupials run wild. Of course, the wallabies are not indigenous, meaning their presence does cause some controversy: some locals want them culled as they say they threaten the native capercaillie population (the island is one of the few places in Scotland where the giant grouse can be seen in the treetops).

Passenger boats don't stop here, but you can reach it by hired motorized boat (with skipper) or kayak from **Loch Lomond Leisure** (Luss), which also runs guided speedboat tours. A boat trip through The Narrows, the strait between Inchconnachan and the neighboring isle of Inchtavannach, is thought to be one of the prettiest places to cruise on the loch. Once on the isle, you are free to wander at leisure or simply paddle around its tranquil shores.

FALLS OF FALLOCH

Inveranan, near Ardlui

In the north of the park, these falls, the bottom of which are reached via a very easy 10-minute amble from the small car park, are often known by the slightly more romantic name of Rob Roy's Bathtub. The falls spill into pools below from a height of 30 feet (9 m) and, even following particularly long dry spells, they're usually still in spate. Whether the bandit himself ever bathed here, we'll never know, but today the deep plunge pool beneath the waterfall is popular with swimmers who can cope with the cold waters.

Please don't attempt to jump or dive in from above the waterfalls, as this can be dangerous. There are plenty of other, safer spots for a plunge; for example, you can carefully climb down the rocks to the right of the falls (as you look at the waterfall).

1: Loch Lomond **2:** Falls of Falloch **3:** Falls of Dochart **4:** Ben Lomond

The Trossachs and Loch Katrine

THE GREAT TROSSACHS FOREST NATIONAL NATURE RESERVE

Enter at Inversnaid or Brig O' Turk; www.lochlomondtrossachs.org/things-to-see/great-trossachs-forestnational-nature-reserve

There is much to enjoy in one of the UK's largest nature reserves, including Loch Katrine, which sits in the center of the reserve and was the inspiration for Sir Walter Scott's *Lady of the Lake* poem, in which he wrote: "The Summer dawn's reflected hue / To purple changed Loch Katrine blue; / Mildly and soft the western breeze, / Just kissed the lake, just stirred the trees."

Camping is possible along the shores of the loch, though in summer there are a few bylaws in place, which means you may have to get a permit. The reserve is best entered from either Inversnaid to the west or Brig O'Turk to the east. It's crossed by the 30-mile (48 km) **Great Trossachs Path**—a walking or cycling route between Callander in the east of the park and Inversnaid at Loch Lomond in the west. From Inversnaid, many other routes snake off into looped trails through woodland and along lochside paths.

LOCH KATRINE AND THE *SIR WALTER SCOTT* STEAMSHIP

Trossachs Pier; tel. 01877 376 315; www.lochkatrine. com/cruises/loch-cruises; two-hour return cruises 10:30 am daily from Trossachs Pier, 11:30am daily from Stronachlachar; round-trip adult £18, child £10, under 5 free, concessions £16.50, family £46, one-way adult £15, child £8.50, under 5 free, concessions £13.50, family £38, bikes £2 extra

This freshwater loch hidden away in the center of the park at the heart of the Great Trossachs Forest National Nature Reserve—an area the size of Glasgow—is where you can board the famous steamship that has operated since 1900. The loch itself is miniscule compared with Loch Lomond, just 8 miles (13 km) long, but it's in many ways much prettier than its bigger sibling. Thick clumps of forest line its banks, and its waters often glisten a vivid blue,

Rewilding the Great Trossachs Forest

Within the confines of Loch Lomond and the Trossachs National Park is the Great Trossachs Forest National Nature Reserve, one of the UK's largest nature reserves. Here a huge woodland regeneration plan is unfolding, returning heavily grazed land and plantation forestry to more natural landscapes through a mix of planting and natural regeneration. Highland cattle have even been brought in to trample the ground and spread the seeds from the trees, including birch, oak, willow, and Caledonian pine.

The 200-year project, begun just a decade ago, aims to restore native woodland; unlike modern forestry, it is not densely packed with trees but has decent amounts of space in between, as well as moorland, grassland, and montane scrub. The project is designed to encourage repopulation of indigenous wildlife, and dragonflies, golden eagles, and pine martens can already be seen. It's also hoped that rare species such as the Scottish wildcat and red squirrels will thrive, too. So far, since the start of the project, black grouse numbers have soared by 700 percent.

reflecting the surrounding hills and mountains in their surface.

The Clyde-built *Sir Walter Scott* steamship, powered by a triple-expansion engine, is the last of its kind still in operation in Scotland. Passengers can view its workings as they glide across the loch just as Victorian day-trippers once did. The cruise from Trossachs Pier, at the southern end of the loch, to Stronachlachar on the northwest bank takes two hours round-trip; one-way trips are also available. On the cruise, watch for **Queen Victoria's Royal Cottage,** a Gothic stone building that was intended to house the monarch when she visited the loch in 1859 but was never used because the 21-gun salute to welcome Her Majesty shattered all the windows. Also en route you can see the peaks of Ben A'an and Ben Venue, and at the northwest tip of the loch you can alight at **Glengyle,** the birthplace of Rob Roy MacGregor.

Bikes can be taken on board (though you should book them in advance), and there is a car park at Trossachs Pier. Many people book a one-way ticket from Trossachs Pier to Stronachlachar and cycle back along the scenic northern shore of the loch, where there is very little traffic. Bike hire is available with **Katrine Wheelz at Trossachs Pier** (www.katrinewheelz.co.uk; £20 per day).

THE DEVIL'S PULPIT
Blair Court, A890 Dumgoyne 5, Glasgow

This gorge, ever so slightly outside the Trossachs border in the south of the park, is popular with day-tripping Glaswegians. Rich in myth and legend, the odd-shaped rock where red-tinged water gushes by is said to be where the devil once stood to deliver his sermon with swirling blood around. It's also thought to have once been a secret meeting place for Druids. Of course, the redness of the water is down to the sandstone beneath, but with a narrow gorge and the right light, it certainly takes on a fearsome atmosphere.

Breadalbane
ROB ROY'S GRAVE
Balquhidder Old Kirk

In the northeast of the park in this otherwise unremarkable graveyard lie the remains of one of Scottish folklore's biggest heroes, Rob Roy MacGregor, alongside the bodies of his wife and two of his sons—or so we are led to believe. Thousands of tourists make the pilgrimage to this quaint stone church on the outskirts of the village of Balquhidder each year, but many locals, particularly those of the rival MacLaren Clan, say the grave is a fake and nothing more than another example of MacGregor propaganda. Clan loyalties run deep in these parts, even after all these years.

The grave is found ever so slightly to the east of the ruins of the old kirk. The new parish church, which can be visited and holds some interesting mementoes as well as a detailed account of William Wordsworth and his sister Dorothy's visit, sits just above. The graves of Rob Roy (real name Raibert Ruadh MacGhriogair) and his family are guarded by a low black rail and the headstone is etched with the words "MacGregor Despite Them" in reference to the clan name that was outlawed.

FALLS OF DOCHART

Killin

These beautiful waterfalls, which tumble along the River Dochart, create white water as they break over the many rocks before crashing down under the bridge in the village of Killin. The best place to view them is from the bridge, where the sound of the rushing water as it makes its way to Loch Tay can be deafening. Look for the island in the middle of the river downstream from the bridge. Known as Innis Bhuidhe, it is home to the burial ground of the chiefs of Clan MacNab.

STONE CIRCLE KILLIN

Killin

If you're visiting the Falls of Dochart, it's worth going the extra half a mile (0.8 km) to the nearby stone circle of Killin. From the village, head east along the river to the stone circle (which is actually more an oval shape composed of six dark gray slabs covering an area of around 33x28 feet (10x8.5 m), that sits in a sheep field on farmer's land to your right). There is little known about the stone circle, though some slabs have cup marks, suggesting it is prehistoric, and there is some evidence of restoration, probably in the 18th or 19th century. The landowner is happy to let visitors come and stand in the field; just make sure you close the gate behind you.

ENTERTAINMENT AND EVENTS

LOCH LOMOND HIGHLAND GAMES

Balloch Country Park; tel. 01389 757 616; www. llhgb.com; July; adult £5, child and concessions £3, family £13

At the southern entry to the park, in the village of Balloch, these traditional Highland games take place in July. In addition to the usual piping, dancing, and caber toss, it also hosts two tugs-of-war (you can enter if you can persuade some teammates) and the 262.5-foot (80 m) Scottish Sprint Championship. Not to be taken too seriously, it's a fun day out even if you are just spectating.

★ HIKING

You can take numerous walks in and out of the park—both the **West Highland Way** and the **Rob Roy Way** pass through it—where meandering streams and lush forests are yours to explore. But, though on the whole the routes are waymarked, it doesn't take you long, once you turn off a minor road or start to ascend a mountain, to feel very isolated. While this may be just the effect you are looking for, make sure you are properly equipped with lots of drinking water, a map, sunblock, a hat, and midge repellent (particularly in summer). Here is a taster of some of the best walking experiences to be had.

Meanwhile, **Walk Highlands** (www. walkhighlands.co.uk) provides detailed route maps of some of the most popular walks in and around the park. This expansive park is best enjoyed on foot, by bike, or on the water, though a car is really useful if you want to cover longer distances. You really should allow yourself a few days here.

If you are planning to attempt one of the Munros or longer mountain hikes, **Mountaineering Scotland** provides an easy-to-follow guide on the essential skills (www.mountaineering.scot/safety-and-skills).

Around Loch Lomond

BEN LOMOND HIKE

Distance: *7.5 miles (12 km) round-trip*

Time: *4.5-5.5 hours*

Trailhead: *Rowardenanan car park*

Information and maps: *www.walkhighlands. co.uk/lochlomond/ben-lomond.shtml*

There are an incredible 21 Munros across The Loch Lomond & The Trossachs National Park —almost 10 percent of Scotland's total— so it's an ideal place to bag your first one. Scotland's most southerly, Ben Lomond (3,196 feet/974 m) looms over Loch Lomond and is a popular hike, as it's relatively straightforward. Though it is popular, if you set off early in the morning, there's a good chance you can take in views of the length of Loch Lomond from its summit on your own.

The path, for the most part, is clear (though it narrows in places) and starts from just behind the information building in the car park. From here you will climb through oak woods first, followed by an area of cleared forest (which is being regenerated) and then open hill. Soon Loch Lomond will come into view on your left, and as you ascend at a steady gradient the views of the loch will become more spectacular. Keep following the path, which starts to zigzag up the mountain (less steeply than before), and then follow the ridge of the mountain before a steep ascent to the top, when the eastern corrie (hollow area between hills) will come into view.

MOUNT MISERY HIKE

Distance: *6.5 miles (10 km)*

Time: *2-2.5 hours*

Trailhead: *Balloch train station*

Information and Maps: *www.hill-bagging. co.uk/mountaindetails.php?rf=5011*

For day-trippers from Glasgow who are looking to squeeze a walk into their visit, the ascent to Mount Misery—named for the women who gathered on its summit in vigil for the men who perished in the Battle of Glen Fruin of 1603—is very doable.

From Balloch train station, turn right along the platform. Go past the Tullie Inn and then turn right again and cross the bridge. Follow the road past the Balloch House, on your left-hand side. Follow the signs for Balloch Country Park. Turn into the park on your left-hand side and walk up the path in the direction of Balloch Castle. Take the path to the right just before the castle, follow for a few yards, and then turn right again. Follow this path all the way to the North Lodge exit of the park and then turn left up the hill, past the children's hospice of Robin House, which will be on your right.

This road continues for around 2 miles (3.2 km) until Lorn Mill Farm, which will be on your right, while ahead is the peak of Mount Misery (also known as the summit of Knockour Hill) for superb views of Loch Lomond and its islands. In total (there and back) this route climbs around 400 feet (122 m). Most of the route is hard paths with no mud, so it can be done in trainers.

GREAT TROSSACHS PATH

Distance: *30 miles (48 km)*

Time: *2-3 days*

Trailhead: *Inversnaid (on Loch Lomond) or Callander*

Information and Maps: *www.lochlomond-trossachs.org/things-to-do/walking/long-distance-routes/great-trossachs-path*

You can choose to do just a small section of the Great Trossachs Path, or walk or cycle its length. The path is waymarked, and although it is rough and stony in places, it's easy to follow with lots of good smooth sections (around Loch Katrine, it's tarmac). The path also connects to the West Highland Way, which links Glasgow to Fort William, and the Rob Roy Way, which goes all the way to Pitlochry in north Perthshire, meaning long-distance walkers and hikers can plot an epic route.

The Trossachs and Loch Katrine

BRACKLINN FALLS AND CALLANDER CRAGS

Distance: *4 miles (6.5 km)*

Time: *2-2.5 hours*

Trailhead: *Bracklinn Falls car park, off Bracklinn Road*

Information and Maps: *http://incallander. co.uk/bracklinn-falls-and-callander-crags*

This walk takes you through pretty woodland, past waterfalls (of course), and atop crags for views over the town of Callander and toward Loch Lomond and the mighty Ben Lomond. Set off from the Bracklinn Falls car park, from where it is well signposted to the falls. You will cross the peat-tinged river by bridge, and then you need to watch for a path to the left that rises into the woods upstream of the river. The track curves around as it ascends the hill. As long as you don't turn right you shouldn't get lost. After half a mile (0.8 km) the track will drop down and pass by a waterfall and the deep Scouts Pool beneath the bridge.

On the other side of the bridge go through the gate and follow the path all the way up to the road, where you'll turn left and walk for around a mile (1.6 km). Keep an eye on the numbers of the telephone poles—shortly after number 34 you'll see the path for Callander Crags marked; this path will take you all the way to a ridge at the top. The cairn here was built to mark Queen Victoria's Jubilee, but you won't care too much about that while you're catching your breath and looking out toward Ben Lomond to the north or Stirling Castle to the southeast. Follow this path back down to the minor road, turn right, and follow it all the way back to the car park.

OTHER SPORTS AND RECREATION
★ Seaplane Tour
LOCH LOMOND SEAPLANES

1 John Street Lane, Helensburgh; tel. 01436 675 030; www.lochlomondseaplanes.com; 9am-5pm daily Jan.-Mar., 8:30am-6:30pm daily Apr.-Sept., 8:30am-5pm daily Oct.-Dec.; Classic Discovery tour £119, Premium Discovery £139, Classic Explorer £149, Premium Explorer £169

Board one of these light aircrafts for a memorable tour from above. Taxiing on Loch Lomond, outside Cameron House Hotel, these tiny seaplanes seem like speedboats at first, picking up momentum as they whizz across the water, but pretty soon the nose of the plane starts to rise and you are airborne. Once in the air, the pilot acts as a tour guide, pointing out some of the sights down below, from old ruined castles, to lochs, glens, and mountain peaks. Afterward, you can reflect on the experience over a glass of prosecco. Discovery tours last 40 minutes (30 minutes in flight) and cover a distance of around 70 miles (113 km), giving aerial views of the park. On an Explorer tour (60 minutes), you will cover a larger distance and may head all the way out to the west coast of Scotland. Trips are dependent on weather, and routes may change. Occasionally, flights do need to be canceled at short notice, so if your schedule isn't flexible, it's worth going for a Premium ticket for an additional cost, which allows a full refund if your flight gets canceled.

Adventure Sports
GO APE

The Lodge-Forest Visitor Centre Queen Elizabeth Forest Park, Aberfoyle; tel. 01603 895500; https:// goape.co.uk; 9:30am-3 hours before dark weekdays Mar.-Oct., 8:30am-3 hours before dark weekends; adult £33, child (10-15 years) £25, minimum age 10

This adventure playground in the Trossachs is utterly exhilarating. To enter the treetop course, you first zipline over a 148-foot (45-m) drop for 1,060 feet (323 m) with gorgeous views on the ride (if you're brave enough to keep your eyes open). There are several treetop adventures that see you scaling heights, walking tightropes, and even jumping off ledges, which will make you feel very Lara Croft/Tarzan. After all that there is an even longer zipline to complete to return to the start point where you can calm down with a cuppa in the lovely café. If you have time (an hour or so extra), take the short forest trail from the visitor center, passing by moss-covered tree trunks to reach a hidden-away waterfall and a wildlife hide—this is actually where I saw my first red squirrel.

INTREPID SCOTLAND

Main Street, Aberfoyle; tel. 07964 909666; www.
intrepidscotland.com; foraging from £30 for a half
day, cycle safari £15 for 2 hours

This small company, run by one of the national park's rangers and a small team of local experts, is a fantastic way to engage more with nature in the park. Tim and friends run foraging sessions to go in search of fungi and edible plants to make jams, jellies—even alcoholic drinks—as well as campfire cooking classes, fishing excursions, and cycle safaris that take in wildlife and great scenery.

Sailing and Watersports
LOCH LOMOND LEISURE

Luss; tel. 0333 577 0715; https://lochlomond-
scotland.com; kayaking from £20 (1 hour), speedboat
£70 (30 minutes), speedboat tour from £160, bike
from £14/2 hours or £30/day, wetsuit £2

If you want to get out on the water on your own, then this hire company based on the shore in Luss is a good option. You can rent out kayaks for a laid-back, gentle experience, or, for a bit more excitement, get a speedboat (which comes with its own skipper). Lifejackets are provided as are paddles for kayaks. The company also offers guided speedboat tours to some of the islands within the loch, and bike hire from a few hours to several days is available, too.

IN YOUR ELEMENT

Loch Lomond Shores, Balloch; tel. 0333 600 6008;
https://iye.scot; canoeing £30 (1.5 hours), gorge
walking £40 (2.5 hours), river sledging £45 (2.5
hours), TreeZone adult £25, under 18 £18

This company, based in Balloch, runs lots of outdoor activities, from canoe tours to thrilling gorge walks. You'll be provided with all necessary equipment; just make sure you have swimwear and suitable shoes.

1: sea plane taking off from Loch Lomond
2: Start a hike or activity from Aberfoyle.
3: treetop adventure with Go Ape 4: a cruise on Loch Lomond

Cycling and Mountain Biking

There are infinite possibilities when it comes to cycling through the park, from well-worn routes to off-road options. There are plenty of places to hire bikes if you don't have yours with you, and most ferries will accommodate them if you want to travel from one side of the loch to the other at no additional fee. The **Loch Lomond and the Trossachs National Park website** (www.lochlomond-trossachs.org) offers lots of suggested routes, all of which come with their own downloadable route card.

On Loch Katrine, visit **Katrine Wheelz** (Trossachs Pier, Loch Katrine; tel. 01877 376 366; www.katrinewheelz.co.uk; 9:30am-5pm daily; bike from £20/day or £90/week), or **Wheels Cycling Centre** (Invertrossachs Road, Callander; tel. 01877 331 100; https://scottish-cycling.com; 10am-4pm Mon.-Tues. and Thurs.-Sat.; full day £20).

WEST LOCH LOMOND CYCLE PATH

Distance: *17 miles (27 km) one-way*
Time: *1 hour 30 minutes*
Trailhead: *Balloch visitor center*
Information and Maps: *www.lochlomond-*
trossachs.org/things-to-do/cycling/cycling-routes/
west-loch-lomond-cycle-path

This is an easy route for beginners or reluctant cyclists who nevertheless want to cover a lot of ground in the park. Starting at the visitor center in Balloch, the route pretty much follows the west shore of Loch Lomond, through the heritage village of Luss and all the way to Tarbet. It's mainly flat along a waymarked path, though one section of it does run alongside the exceedingly busy A82.

TOUR OF THE TROSSACHS

Distance: *31 miles (50 km) round-trip*
Time: *3 hours*
Trailhead: *Aberfoyle*
Information and Maps: *www.lochlomond-*
trossachs.org/things-to-do/cycling/cycling-routes/
tour-of-the-trossachs

For those who want to exert themselves a lot more, this hard, circular route takes you in a counterclockwise direction from Aberfoyle, north through Queen Elizabeth Forest Park, before skirting the north and west coast of Loch Katrine and heading back south, past Loch Arklet, and along the eastern shore of Loch Chon and the northern shore of Loch Ard to Aberfoyle.

Setting off from Aberfoyle, the route sorts the wheat from the chaff early on by launching riders straight into the steepest path of the day—the challenging **Duke's Pass**, a sweat-inducing 2.4-mile (3.8 km) climb that has gradients of 6-11 percent and lots of sharp ramps. Those who do manage it are rewarded with fabulous alpine views, as they ride past numerous rocky crags before winding down a road that twists and turns before joining a single-track road (be alert as traffic may still come from the opposite direction) to Stronachlachar. Adventurous riders can continue on by climbing another road to Loch Ard via Loch Arklet and Loch Chon, which brings you all the way back to the beginning at Aberfoyle. If this feels a bit much, you can take the ferry from Stronachlachar to Trossachs Pier to rejoin the start of the route back to Aberfoyle, effectively cutting out around 6 miles (11 km).

Cruises
CRUISE LOCH LOMOND
The Boatyard, Tarbet; tel. 01301 702 356; www. cruiselochlomond.co.uk; adult from £13
Offering cruises on the loch aboard one of six vessels, this family-run business has a range of itineraries, which set off from one of four locations. The 90-minute Rob Roy Discovery (£15) from Tarbet on the western shores of Loch Lomond, near Arrochar, includes a whisky coffee (for adults, and just instant coffee at that), which you can sip while being regaled with legends of the outlaw who supposedly hid in some of the caves. The large passenger boats have twin decks with an enclosed saloon below as well as an open deck on top, and, though they can get busy in summer, there's plenty of room for everyone.

The company also has bird-watching cruises and runs a **waterbus** (one-way from £10) between the east and west of Loch Lomond; it's quite common for people to use the waterbus simply to get from one side of the loch to the other, rather than doing a cruise. Crossings include Tarbet to Rowardennan (best for Ben Lomond) and Luss to Balmaha, along with lots of other routes. Cruise Loch Lomond also rents out bikes, with helmets and repair kits, at very reasonable rates (£13 for up to three hours, £17 per day).

FOOD
There are lots of good places to eat within the national park, from humble cafés where you can stop mid-walk to cozy inns where you can replenish following a major hike. There's even the odd fine dining option to enjoy when you've had enough of working up a sweat on muddy trails.

Around Loch Lomond
LOCH LOMOND SHORE FARMERS' MARKET
Ben Lomond Way; https://lochlomondshores.com/ events/loch-lomond-shores-august-market-every-sunday; 10am-4pm first and third Sunday of the month
Stalls are piled high with fresh local produce at this market, a great place to pick up supplies for a picnic or dinner round the campfire. Get there early to get the best offerings, which include pies baked that morning and delicious smoked fish.

CLACHAN INN
Drymen; tel. 01360 660 824; www. clachaninndrymen.co.uk; 11am-12am Mon.-Thurs., 11am-1am Fri.-Sat., 12pm-12am Sun.; entrées £5.95
In the pretty village of Drymen (not far from the Devil's Pulpit) is Scotland's oldest licensed pub, which is popular with walkers on the West Highland Way or the Rob Roy Way, which virtually starts outside the door. In fact, the first licensee of the pub in 1734 was one of Rob Roy's sisters. The food is fresh, hearty, and well-priced, with steak, pies, seafood, and tasty pizzas all on the menu. There

are also some simple but clean rooms if you need somewhere to spend the night.

★ THE VILLAGE REST

Pier Road, Luss; tel. 01436 860 220; www.the-village-rest.co.uk; 10am-9pm daily; entrées £6.25

This casual and inviting café is pretty hard to resist when you are visiting the heritage village of Luss. Set in one of the lovely slate-roofed cottages where workers once lived, it's a good coffee or lunch stop, or a welcoming place to indulge in some comfort food later in the day. If you're in need of a pick-me-up, you'd be a fool not to try the gateaux of haggis, neeps, and tatties smothered in Cognac sauce. The location is handy for anyone staying at the nearby Luss Camping and Caravanning Park.

★ MR. C'S FISH & WHISKY BAR/RESTAURANT

The Inn at Loch Lomond, Inverbeg; tel. 01436 860 678; www.innonlochlomond.co.uk/dining; lunch 12pm-5pm daily, dinner 5pm-9pm; entrées £6.95

Set within the **Inn at Loch Lomond,** a Victorian tavern with rooms just 3 miles (5 km) north of Luss near the banks of Loch Lomond, this informal restaurant serves a good choice of burgers, steaks, and seafood. Kids are well-served with mini pizzas or chicken goujons followed by an ice cream sundae, while grown-ups should try the calamari and chips or a battered haggis supper. It has an extensive whisky menu too, and staff can talk you through it in an unpatronizing way. It's just a shame the views of the loch aren't better.

ROAST'S CAFÉ

Loch Lomond Homes and Garden Centre, Balloch; tel. 01389 752 947; www.lochlomondgc.co.uk/roasts-cafe.php; 10am-5pm daily; full Scottish breakfast £6.50/£12 for two, afternoon tea for two £14

Located within a garden center on Loch Lomond Shores, this is an unpretentious and rather decent breakfast or lunch stop. Service is friendly and prompt, and everything is homemade—there's even an on-site baker—and it offers good-value deals for two.

The Trossachs and Loch Katrine

★ THE PIER CAFÉ

Loch Katrine, Stronachlachar; tel. 01877 386 374; www.thepiercafe.com; 9am-5pm daily, 6pm-8:30pm Fri.-Sat.; entrées £6.25

This café, taken over by the current owners in 2007, has become something of a community hub in the quiet setting of Stronachlachar, overlooking the serene Loch Katrine. The menu includes full cooked breakfasts in the morning to set you up for the day (and porridge, naturally), filled sandwiches, and rolls for those who pop in mid-cycle or walk, right through to stews in the evening on Friday and Saturday. There's a regular program of live traditional music too, the perfect accompaniment to the views.

Breadalbane

★ MHOR 84

Balquhidder; tel. 01877 384 646; https://mhor84.net; 8am-9pm daily; entrées £7, £90 d

This café-cum-bar-cum-restaurant in the northeast of the park serves food all day, starting with its house special eggs Benedict in the morning, through to steaks, burgers, and seafood chowders from lunch to dinner time. It's well-priced home-cooked fare that is good enough to warrant a bit of a detour from your normal route. There are also some clean, affordable, retro-styled rooms.

ACCOMMODATIONS

Most of the grander hotels and guest houses are located in and around Luss, on the western shores of Loch Lomond, and are good if you're just here for a day or two. However, for more seclusion, go deeper into the forest on the eastern side of the park, where there are wonderful campsites and some lovely sustainable places to stay for a wilder/eco-friendlier holiday.

Around Loch Lomond
CAMERON HOUSE

*Loch Lomond, Balloch; tel. 01389 310 777; www.
cameronhouse.co.uk; Cameron Club Lodges from
£180 d (3-night minimum)*

For out-and-out luxury on the banks of Loch
Lomond, Cameron House has always been the
place to go. Sadly, a fatal fire in December 2017
caused extensive damage, but the five-star hotel
reopened in summer 2021 following major restoration. There is a choice of luxury bedrooms
dressed in Scottish fabrics—many of which
have loch views—and more sophisticated suites,
which are all loch-facing, in the main house.
There are also self-catering Cameron Club
Lodges, many of which have private terraces
and balconies, located a few miles away, right
by the spa with its sensational infinity pool,
all of which can be accessed via a free shuttle
bus. Central to the reopening of the hotel is
the new fine-dining restaurant Tamburrini
and Wishart, which promises to have seasonal
produce and world-class seafood at its heart.
Cameron House Marina is also where you can
take a flight with Loch Lomond Seaplanes.

★ LOCH LOMOND ARMS HOTEL

*Main Road, Luss; tel. 01436 860 420; www.
lochlomondarmshotel.com; £195 d*

This impeccably presented country house
hotel, in an old 17th-century coaching inn,
is adorned in Scottish fabrics, with pretty
cushions and woolen throws on the bed. The
best rooms in the house are the Colquhoun
Room, whose name is a nod to the clan that
has made Luss its home since the 13th century, and the Lomond room, which comes
with a romantic four-poster and even has a
separate dressing room. Hospitality trays include shortbread, and there are Cinq Mondes
toiletries in the bathroom.

The Trossachs and Loch Katrine
★ LOCH KATRINE ECO LODGES

*Trossachs Pier, Loch Katrine, Callander; tel. 01877
376 315; www.lochkatrine.com/accommodation/pods;
Loch lodges £80 d, Ben lodges £40 d*

Camping pods are popping up all over
Scotland, and these ones, secreted behind a
veil of trees, are simply lovely. There are eight
pods (or lodges) in total. The pricier Loch
lodges have under-floor heating, en suites,
and their own picnic benches and terraces
(great for stargazing). Meanwhile, the more
basic Ben lodges are still cozy, with electric
heating, but you'll have to share toilet and
shower facilities, and linen is extra. Both options offer a 20 percent discount off the *Sir
Walter Scott* steamship.

Breadalbane
FALLS OF DOCHART INN

*Gray Street, Killin; tel. 01567 820 270; www.
fallsofdochartinn.co.uk; £90 d*

This well-priced three-star hotel in a former
blacksmith's house has fantastic views of the
nearby waterfalls. Rooms are small, but they
have a certain vintage charm. Downstairs,
there's a restaurant and an excellent bar with
white stone walls, wooden floorboards, and an
open fire. You may catch an impromptu folk
music session; otherwise, there's usually some
good Scottish music on the stereo.

TOP EXPERIENCE

★ CAMPING

Experience the ultimate freedom of pitch-
ing up under the stars with no obvious
modern intrusions. Thanks to the Scottish
Outdoor Access Code, you can wild camp
in most of the park (maximum 2-3 nights
in one place) throughout the year. From
March to September, the most popular
lochside areas are subject to bylaws—in this
case, measures in place to protect the areas
from environmental damage—which means
that you'll need a permit (£3) to camp here.
For more information on camping in Loch
Lomond and the Trossachs, visit the **Loch
Lomond and Trossachs National Park**

1: Loch Lomond Shore Farmers' Market
2: the heritage village of Luss

website (www.lochlomond-trossachs.org/things-to-do/camping).

For the camper who wants a little more comfort, lots of sites offer full facilities with hot showers and electric hookups. There are also plenty of good campsites that offer a "wilder" experience with few amenities (just fresh water and composting toilets), many of which are lochside. If you've arrived in Scotland without any camping gear and don't want to buy it all, Rent a Tent, in Edinburgh, which launched in 2019, can supply you with all the gear you need before hitting the road (tel. 0757 978 6854; www.rentatent-scotland.com; from £10 a night for a two-man tent). Alternatively, look for campsites with pre-erected tents.

Around Loch Lomond
★ INCHCAILLOCH CAMPSITE

Inchcailloch; www.lochlomond-trossachs.org/things-to-see/inchcailloch; Mar.-Sept.; £5 per night

This pretty island on Loch Lomond is a nature reserve and an idyllic camping spot. Only 12 people can camp here each night, and permits get booked up quickly. Access is by boat from Balmaha on the eastern shore of Loch Lomond, which must be arranged through **Balmaha Boatyard** (tel. 01360 870 214; www.balmahaboatyard.co.uk). The waterbus service from **Loch Lomond Shores** will also get you here. You'll find a beautiful setting for remote camping, with forest trails through fields of wildflowers (the bluebells in May are particularly lovely). There is no drinking water, so stock up before you leave, and there's no refuse collection, so you will need to take any rubbish away with you. Public toilets are composting only.

LUSS CAMPING AND CARAVANNING SITE

Luss; tel. 01436 860 658; www.campingandcaravanningclub.co.uk; late Mar.-late Oct.; £12.75 per adult per night, 2-night minimum

If you are a more reluctant camper, then you may find comfort in numbers, such as at this lochside campsite on the western shore of Loch Lomond. It's well-facilitated too—there are proper toilets, showers, washing machines,

and wireless Internet. It might lack some of the romance of wilder sites, but you'll be grateful of the pub within walking distance, particularly after a long drive. The site is run by the Camping and Caravanning Club, so only members can bring caravans and camper vans. Anyone can book a tent pitch, though currently it has to be done by phone.

The Trossachs and Loch Katrine
LOCH CHON CAMPSITE

Aberfoyle; www.lochlomond-trossachs.org/things-to-do/camping/find-a-campsite/loch-chon-campsite; Mar.-Sept.; £7 per adult per night, under 16 free

This beautiful, tranquil campsite on the east side of the park, just outside the Great Trossachs Forest National Nature Reserve, is another example of a small, picturesque site with basic facilities and away from crowds. Cloaked in woodland, it sits on the edge of Loch Chon, a sheltered water between Kinlochard and Inversnaid that is said to be home to one of the world's largest population of fairies as well as a shape-shifting kelpie. There are 26 pitches (two of which are accessible), and, unlike many of the wilder campsites, this one allows you to bring your car here. Fire bowls are provided for making a campfire, and there are toilets and clean running water.

GETTING THERE
By Car

From Glasgow, if you're coming by car, it's just a 35-minute drive (25 miles/40 km) from the city to the southerly entry point of Balloch along the M8 and the M898 to Erskine Bridge, where you will join the A82, which takes you all the way into the park.

Travelers setting off from Edinburgh can reach Balloch in an hour and a half (71 miles/114 km), also using the M8 to A82 route. Alternatively, it takes just over an hour to reach Callander in the east of the park from Edinburgh (54 miles/87 km). Take the M9 and B824 to Stirling and then the A84 to Callander.

From Oban you can reach Tyndrum in the far north of the park in an hour by following the A85 east for 36 miles (58 km). From Stirling, it's 22 miles (35 km) west along the A811 (30 minutes) to Drymen in the southeast of the park, while from Perth, it's 44 miles (71 km) west to Balquhidder in the northeast of the park, a journey time of 1.5 hours.

By Train

The national park does try to encourage visitors to travel by public transport where possible. From Glasgow Queen Street, **ScotRail** (www.scotrail.co.uk) has trains every half hour to Balloch, with a journey time of 50 minutes (£5.60 each way). From Edinburgh, it takes two hours to reach Balloch by train, with trains every half hour and a change at Glasgow Queen Street (£17.60 one-way).

The **West Highland train line** (www.scotrail.co.uk/scotland-by-rail/great-scenic-rail-journeys/west-highland-line-glasgow-oban-and-fort-williammallaig) also passes through the park about six times a day (twice on Sunday) and stops at a number of stations. Disembark at Arrochar and Tarbet (1.25 hours; £12.40 one way) to explore the western shores of Loch Lomond or the west of the park, or get off at Ardlui (1.30 hours; £16.30 one way) if you want to visit the north end of the loch.

GETTING AROUND

The best ways to explore the park are on foot, by bike, or by cruise. From Balloch station it's just a 12-minute walk through the park to **Loch Lomond Shores** from where you can catch a cruise or join one of the walking trails.

By Car

You do not need a permit to drive in the national park, and parking is generally good and often free. There are petrol stations throughout the park, including **Lomond Service Station** just outside Balloch, **Dreadnought Service Station** on the Stirling Road in Callander, and **MacTavish's** on Main Street in Arrochar.

The main A82 road links the towns along the western shores of Loch Lomond, including Balloch, Luss, Tarbet, and Arlui, all the way north to Crianlarich and Tyndrum. For Arrochar and the west of the park, turn west onto the A83 at Tarbet. From Crianlarich, you can turn east onto the A85 to explore the north and east of the park more fully. The main road east out of Balloch is the A811. Turn off at Drymen onto the B837 for Balmaha, or carry on for the left-hand turn for the A81 if you're heading to Aberfoyle.

By Bus

Bus routes through the park are relatively good (though far less regular than in the cities, and some only run every two hours). A couple of operators run buses that go through the park, including **Scottish Citylink** (www.citylink.co.uk), which runs a service linking Balloch with Arrochar via Luss along the western shore (no. 976; £6 one-way) in just 25 minutes, though buses are infrequent (about three times a day). **Garelochhead Coaches** (www.garelochheadcoaches.co.uk) runs a direct service from Balloch to Luss (no. 305) roughly every two hours (15 minutes; £3.20 one-way).

By Boat

The main waterbuses in Loch Lomond are run by **Cruise Loch Lomond** (tel. 01301 702 356; www.cruiselochlomond.co.uk), which runs ferries out of Luss and Tarbet between mid-March through the end of October (£10 one-way, £13 return, return tickets valid for five days). Both ferry ports run one service per day across to Rowardennan on the eastern shores of Loch Lomond, which is the jumping off point for Ben Lomond. From Tarbet the ferry leaves at 8:45am, arriving at Rowardennan at 9:30am, with the return ferry departing Rowardennan at 4:45pm and arriving into Tarbet at 5:30pm. For Luss, the ferry departs Rowardennan at 9:30am, arriving into Luss at 10am. The ferry taking you back to Rowardennan departs Luss at 4:15pm, arriving into Rowardennan at

4:45pm. There is also a service from Luss to Balmaha farther south on the eastern shore, running twice a day at 10:15am and 12:30pm, as well as waterbuses that connect Luss and Tarbet.

On Loch Katrine (tel. 01877 376 315; www.lochkatrine.com), there is a round-trip service from Trossachs Pier on the southern end of the loch to Stronachlachar on the north-west shore, at 10:30am each day aboard the *Sir Walter Scott* steamship from late March to early January (£14 one-way, £17 round-trip). From late May until early October, there are also two additional trips (1:30pm and 4:15pm) aboard the modern cruiser *Lady of the Lake* (£11.50 one-way, £14 round-trip).

Oban

Oban is very much a gateway town. Most of the main amenities are clustered round the attractive and bustling harbor, and though it is a pleasant place to meander and watch the boats and ferries come and go in Oban Bay, there's little need to spend more than a day or two here while you are plotting routes to Mull and other islands that are nearby. Oban is well facilitated with several banks and shops.

SIGHTS
Oban Distillery
Oban; tel. 01631 572 004; www.malts.com/en-gb/ distilleries/oban; 12pm-4:30pm daily Dec.-Feb., 9:30am-5pm daily Mar.-Apr., 9:30am-7:30pm daily May-Sept., 9:30am-5pm daily Oct.-Nov.; Sensory and Flavour Finding Tour £10, Exclusive Distillery Tour £75

This small distillery in the center of Oban is one of the oldest single malt distilleries in Scotland, and a good place to spend an hour or so, particularly if it's raining or you're waiting for a connection out to one of the islands. The popular distillery tours should be booked in advance. The one-hour Sensory and Flavour Finding Tour is a good introduction into the process of making Oban whisky and includes a tasting straight from the cask. Meanwhile, the Exclusive Distillery Tour (two hours) gives you access to the warehouse and includes an in-depth tasting in the manager's office. If tours are booked, it's still worth popping in for a tasting at the bar.

McCaig's Tower
Duncraggan Road, Oban

This rather odd Colosseum-like landmark looks a little out of place towering over the traditional Scottish town. Often called McCaig's folly, it was built for local banker John Stuart McCaig in 1897 as a lasting monument to his family. McCaig intended for it to house an art gallery, but it was unfinished by the time of his death and his descendants refused to complete it. Only the outer walls were finished, and today, if you can cope with the steep 10-minute walk up here, it's a pleasant place to take in the views to Oban Bay and its many islands through the arched windows.

★ FOOD
Known as a seafood capital, whether it's fish and chips to take away or lobster served in a posh restaurant, you have to try some of the seafood in Oban. But beware: if you opt for the former, you'll need to take cover (literally), as the seagulls here are vicious.

OBAN SEAFOOD HUT
Calmac Pier, Oban; tel. 07881 418 565; 10am-6pm daily; sandwiches from £2.95

If you are getting on or off a ferry in Oban, you can't help but notice the gaggle of people tucking into trays of seafood under a gazebo by this hut known by locals as the Green Shack. On your way to boarding a ferry, grab a

1: Oban **2:** Oban Distillery **3:** Oban Fish & Chips
4: McCaig's Tower

1

2

THE OBAN DISTILLERY
ESTD 1794

OBAN FISH & CHI
TAKE-AWAY / RESTAURA
EST FISH & CHIPS I'VE EVER TASTED"
RICK STEIN
Award Winning Take-Away

3

4

ready-made prawn or fresh salmon sandwich, but if you have time (and are with a friend) get one of the seafood platters, which is just £12.50 for 2, or £25 for two for the Grand Platter, which includes lobster.

OBAN FISH & CHIPS

116 George Street, Oban; tel. 01631 569 828; www. obanfishandchipshop.co.uk; 11am-11pm daily; entrées £6.30

Oban Fish & Chips serves the best battered fish I have ever tasted. It's perfectly seasoned and just the right side of crispy (still soft enough to bite into) without being too oily. The fish tea special (£11), which is recommended, nay commended, comes with a thick cut of either haddock or cod, served with mushy (mashed peas, a common accompaniment to fish and chips across Britain) or house peas (it has to be the former, surely) and chips. You can also order white pudding, black pudding, Scotch pie, and specialties such as battered Isle of Mull scallops. There is a dine-in restaurant, but they stop seating customers about 40 minutes before closing.

THE WATERFRONT FISHHOUSE RESTAURANT

1 Railway Pier; tel. 01631 563 110; https:// waterfrontfishhouse.co.uk; lunch 12pm-2pm, dinner 5:30pm-9:30pm daily summer, lunch 12pm-2pm, dinner 5:30pm-9pm daily winter; entrées £7.99

A little more upmarket than some of Oban's food establishments, this restaurant still manages to be more relaxed than its menu might suggest. Dig into a steaming bowl of local mussels or Isle of Mull scallops (a must) with smoked paprika butter. Oysters are also farmed locally, just north of Oban, and other dishes vary depending on what's been caught that day.

ACCOMMODATIONS

OBAN YOUTH HOSTEL

Corran Esplanade, Oban; tel. 01631 562 025; www. hostellingscotland.org.uk/hostels/oban; shared room £24 per bed (towels extra), private room £60 d (including towels)

Worth the trek out of town along the esplanade, this hostel is set within a Victorian villa and has waterfront views from its lovely lounge area. Staff are friendly and well-informed, and though the rooms are basic, they are clean. I'd skip the optional breakfast (which you need to pay for anyway) and head into town for something a little more appealing.

★ OLD MANSE GUEST HOUSE

Dalriach Road; tel. 01631 564 886; https:// obanguesthouse.co.uk; £70 d

With just a handful of rooms, this charming B&B in a Victorian villa overlooking Oban Bay is well placed for the town center but manages to feel very quiet. The slightly old-fashioned interiors are nevertheless quite sweet, and the complimentary glass of sherry is a nice touch. Breakfasts are good, and on occasion evening suppers may be arranged.

GETTING THERE

The main reason people come to Oban is its **ferry terminal,** accordingly the center of action in the town, surrounded by seafood restaurants and conveniently located right next to the railway station.

By Train

Trains, operated by **ScotRail** (www.scotrail. co.uk) run six times a day from Glasgow to **Oban Railway Station** on the **West Highland Line** (3 hours; from £19.80 each way). The route is spectacular: mountains peek over woodland and every now and then the lush greenery is broken by a loch, which appears for a few heavenly seconds before disappearing behind a bank of trees again. The trains are a little old and basic, but you'll be willing the train to slow down so you can take it all in. The West Highland Line splits at Crainlarich in the north of Loch Lomond and the Trossachs National Park, with trains for Oban heading west and trains for Mallaig heading farther north.

Coming from Edinburgh, Stirling, or

Perth, you'll need to get a train to Glasgow Queen Street and head to Oban from there.

By Bus

The no. 976 bus with **Scottish Citylink** operates three times a day between Glasgow Buchanan Bus Station and Oban (3 hours; £13.70 one-way). The bus stops en route in Balloch, Luss, Tarbet, and Arrochar. There are no direct buses from Edinburgh.

By Car

It's slightly quicker to drive from Glasgow (97 miles/146 km; 2.5 hours) than to take the bus, and you'll still pass through Loch Lomond and the Trossachs National Park on your way. Just follow the M8 and the M898 from the city center to Erskine Bridge to join the A82, which takes you all the way to Loch Lomond and the Trossachs National Park. Follow the A82 north, all the way through the park until Tyndrum, where you will turn west onto the A85, which brings you all the way into Oban.

From Edinburgh (122 miles/196 km; 3 hours), take the A90 west out of the city to join the M9 all the way to Stirling. From Stirling (86 miles/138 km; 2 hours 15 minutes) take the A84 northwest, into the Loch Lomond and the Trossachs National Park via Callander and up to Lochearnhead in the northeast of the park, where you can take the A85 west all the way to Oban. From Perth (94 miles/151 km; 2.5 hours) it's virtually a straight road along the A85 west.

The Inner Hebrides

This archipelago of more than 70 islands (many of which are very small and uninhabited), which lies off the west coast of Scotland, extends from Skye in the north (see page 346) to **Islay** in the south, and is a place of incredible beauty. **Mull** is the second-largest island in the Inner Hebrides, south of its big sister Skye and the Small Isles. West of Mull's southern tip is **Iona,** best known as the home of the Benedictine Iona Abbey. North of Iona, tiny **Staffa** is uninhabited by humans but serves as a landing point for an adorable puffin population; and medium-sized **Jura** stretches between Mull and Islay.

The islands are rich in heritage, with traditional whisky distilling, crofting, and fishing industries, as well as history. Once the stronghold of the Lords of the Isles—ancestors of Clan MacDonald who ruled much of western Scotland until the 15th century—their ancient seat of Finlaggan on Islay is a must-visit for a glimpse into the region's Gaelic past. Meanwhile, islands such as Mull, Iona, and Jura offer fantastic wildlife experiences and plenty of space for isolation and serenity.

MULL

Mull is perhaps the greenest island you will ever see, and the natural beauty of its often-wild landscape is balanced by its main town of Tobermory, where colorful houses line its harbor. The most visited of all the islands accessible from Oban, Mull is 36 miles (58 km) wide; by Scotland's standards, it's big, meaning there's plenty of space for all those tourists to share. It does take a long time to get around as most of the roads are single-track and winding, so if you are driving, patience is a virtue.

It would take a lot to upset the air of calm on Mull. Otters roam its riverbanks, seals flop around in its sea lochs, and sheep often wander into the road, while cascading waterfalls are the only interruption to the thick slopes of pines and ferns. At the Burg Cliffs—dramatic terraces of basalt rock—you can see the fossilized remains of trees or come across wild deer, goats, and eagles.

Mull

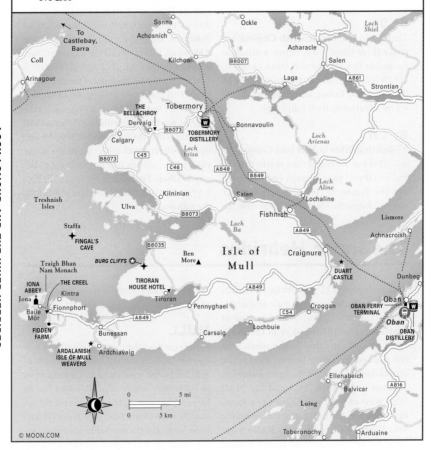

© MOON.COM

Orientation

Irregularly shaped Mull, with several peninsulas extending out west into the Atlantic, has an area of 337 square miles (873 square km) and 300 miles (482 km) of coastline. Ferries arrive in **Craignure,** on the southeastern coast of the island, passing **Duart Castle** on the way to the ferry terminal. The main town is **Tobermory,** home to the distillery of the same name, some 21 miles (34 km) up the island's eastern coast, a 34-minute drive. To the west, one of Mull's most iconic landscapes is the **Burg Cliffs,** 26 miles (42 km; 1 hour 15 minutes) west of Craignure. **Fionnphort** is

right down on the southwest tip of Mull, about 35 miles (56 km) west of Craignure (1-hour drive).

Getting There

Getting to Mull is fairly easy from Oban. **CalMac** (www.calmac.co.uk) runs a route from Oban to Craignure on the south of Mull (45 minutes; £3.60 one-way, plus £13.40 with a car). This is by far the most popular way to reach Mull, and runs several times a day. Arrive at the **Oban Ferry Terminal** (which is a bit like an airport lounge) a minimum of 10 minutes before your scheduled departure (longer if driving). Pick up a copy of the ferry timetables from Oban ferry port. As well as listing all sorts of ferry connections, the timetable also shows how the buses on Mull link with each of the ferries. There is a good café on board serving cooked breakfasts for morning passengers and fuller meals at lunch and in the evening (burgers, macaroni and cheese, baked potatoes, etc.); plus, it has a decent kids' menu.

Getting Around

Many day-trippers to Mull are surprised that they can't walk it all in a day. The best way to get around is to drive, but you'll need to master the single-track roads quickly (learn when to pull aside to the left and when to go). It's pretty hard to pick up any speed here, which should give you time to look out for some of the island's 5,000 wild red deer. From Craignure to Tobermory it's a 40-minute trip north along the A849 and then the A848, while from Craignure to Fionnphort, it's an hour's drive west along the A849.

Buses on Mull are run by **West Coast Motors** (tel. 01586 552 319; www.westcoastmotors.co.uk). The bus takes about 1.25 hours from Craignure to Fionnphort (no. 496, four buses daily Mon.-Fri., three buses on Sat., no service Sun.), the miniscule ferry port for crossing to Iona to the west. From Craignure to Tobermory (no. 95 or no. 49), it takes just under an hour and buses are slightly more regular. Tickets cost £1.40 one-way (£2.30 round-trip). If traveling by bus from Craignure, make sure you check the bus timetable before you book your ferry because only a select few are met by the bus, and this varies very much by the day and time of year.

Taxis are available if you don't have a car and would rather not rely on public transport. **Mull Taxi,** based in Tobermory (call Alan, tel. 07760 426 351; www.mulltaxi.co.uk), will pick you (and your luggage) up from anywhere on the island and gives private tours.

Sights
DUART CASTLE

Isle of Mull; tel. 01680 812 309; https://duartcastle. com; 11am-4pm Apr., 10:30am-5pm May-Oct.; adult £7, child £3.50, family £17.50

The ancient seat of Clan Maclean, this castle is one of the first sights most visitors to Mull see, guarding the island atop a crag that juts out into the Sound of Mull. It's hard to believe it stood in ruin for years before being carefully restored in the early 20th century. Today it looks like a perfectly preserved clan castle, complete with a 14th-century keep with walls 10 feet (3 m) thick. Inside, it's more grand stately home than medieval stronghold. The resplendent interiors, including the magnificent Great Hall, are filled with family heirlooms that give some insight into the lives of the Maclean Clan, while the ghostly dungeons are enough to prickle your imagination. Though the castle is only open to visitors from April to October, you can visit the grounds and walk all the way down to the water's edge, past the lined-up canons, or just inspect the exterior at close quarters year-round.

TOBERMORY DISTILLERY

Tobermory, Mull; tel. 01688 302 647; http:// tobermorydistillery.com; 10am-5pm daily; tasting experiences from £25

Right off the harbor in Tobermory, this small, classically whitewashed distillery surrounded by quaint stone buildings is backed by Mull's green hulls. The distillery, in operation since the 18th century, produces two types of malt, the smoother Tobermory, and the more peated Ledaig, as well as their own Hebridean gin. Tours are fairly informal, with plenty of time to ask the guides questions and sample a wee dram afterward.

★ BURG CLIFFS

Tiroran, Mull; tel. 01681 700 659; www.nts.org.uk/ visit/places/burg

The sight of the Burg Cliffs as you pass along the Ardmeanach Peninsula, on Mull's west coast, is unmistakable. Millions of years of exposure to the Atlantic forces have shaped and sculpted the rock face here into what looks like perfectly lined terraces. You might pass them on a boat from the Isle of Mull to Staffa, but you can't beat walking amid the wild and craggy landscape that makes up much of Mull's west coast, a perfect example of Hebridean wilderness.

A mix of rocky uplands, grassy lowlands, and wind-and sea-battered coast make this a unique place to explore; it is teeming with golden eagles, red deer, wild goats, and even otters along its rocky shoreline. In June, look out for the rare Scotch burnet moth that lives here. Looked after by the National Trust, depending on the season, the cliffs could be a kaleidoscope of color thanks to an abundance of wildflowers, or look barren and foreboding under heavy wintry skies.

Most visitors will want to see the ginormous **MacCulloch's fossil tree,** an imprint left in the cliffs some 50 million years ago, but this does entail a 5-mile walk (10 miles there and back/8 km, 16 km there and back) along a rocky coastal path from the car park at the Tiroran House Hotel. Alternatively, you can see this unique landscape from the scenic B8305 road, which skirts the east side of the dramatic, rocky coast.

ARDALANISH ISLE OF MULL WEAVERS

Ardalanish Farm, Bunessan; tel. 01681 700 265; https://ardalanish.com; 10am-5pm daily summer, 10am-4pm Mon.-Fri. winter

In the southwest of the island, this sheep and cattle farm is where rural life and creativity using age-old techniques combine to produce beautiful and unique tweed and woolen products. The fleece from the Hebridean sheep on the farm and other farms on Mull is woven into beautiful items, from homewares to clothing and accessories, which can be bought in the on-site mill shop. Visitors can also take a tour of the weaving mill or try one of the homemade pasties that include some of the farm's own venison, lamb, and beef (meat can also be bought). From time to time, there are

even short taster sessions if you'd like to have a go at hand-looming.

Food

The **Mull & Iona Food Trail** (http://mullandionafood.co.uk) website connects travelers to businesses that sell both seafood and other locally sourced ingredients, meaning you can have a more authentic eating experience.

★ THE CREEL

Fionnphort Car Park; tel. 01681 700 312; 8am-late daily; entrées £4

This small shack is perfectly positioned for day-trippers to Iona. The building might not look like much, but you really don't want to miss the seafood here, most of which is caught by owner Andrew. With langoustines, dressed crab, kippers, and lobster—much of which is landed just the other side of the pier—it's hard to imagine a fresher catch elsewhere.

THE BELLACHROY

Dervaig, Tobermory; tel. 01688 400 314; www. thebellachroy.co.uk; lunch 12:30pm-2:30pm Fri.-Tues., dinner 6pm-8:30pm Weds.-Thurs.; entrées £5.95

Dating from 1608, this is the oldest inn on Mull and began life as a stopping point for drovers (cattle herders). Set in the pretty village of Dervaig, it's not overly showy. The Bear Pit bar is atypical of a Highlands pub, but the food in the restaurant is good, honest Scottish cuisine: risotto, fish and chips, and steaks, served alongside local real ales, cheeses, and single malts.

HEBRIDEAN LODGE

1 Baliscate, Tobermory; tel. 01688 301 207; www. hebrideanlodge.co.uk; 6:30pm-8:30pm Mon.-Fri.; entrées £7.50

Set on a mezzanine level above a gallery and shop, this restaurant is the go-to place for locals who want some home-cooked fare using

---

1: Duart Castle **2:** Get fresh seafood at The Creel. **3:** local buses meeting the ferry **4:** Burg Cliffs

☆ Island-Hopping in the Inner Hebrides

puffins on Staffa

There are almost 80 islands in the Inner Hebredian archipelago, 35 of which are inhabited, including the Isle of Skye in the north and stretching to Islay in the south. Though taking in all of the Inner Hebrides would be the work of a lifetime, the three islands of Iona, Staffa, and Jura are accessible to the highly visited isles of Mull and Islay and give a taste of what these wild islands have to offer.

IONA

For a retreat from modern life, you can't beat the tiny isle of Iona—just 1 mile (1.6 km) by 3.5 miles (5.6 km)—which has been a place of religious retreat since St. Columba arrived in the 6th century and set up his monastery here, the site of today's Benedictine **Iona Abbey** (Iona; tel. 01681 700512; www.historicenvironment.scot/visit-a-place/places/iona-abbey-and-nunnery; 9:30am-5:30pm Apr.-Sept., 10am-4pm Mon.-Sat. Oct.-Mar., Sunday grounds only; £7.50 adult, £4.50 child). Be sure to check out St. Oran's Chapel and Reilig Odhráin, the graveyard next door, where Scottish kings were buried for centuries, including the infamous Macbeth.

A 15-minute walk north of the abbey is **Traigh Bhan Nam Monach,** otherwise known as the White Strand of the Monks due to its rather dark history. It was here in the 8th century that many monks were slaughtered at the hands of the Vikings. Today an ethereal beauty prevails at this beach, with its white sand, tufts of grasses, and dunes that slope down to blue and turquoise waters.

There's not a huge choice of places to eat on Iona, but everything is fresh and local. Wholesome local produce is served at the **St. Columba Hotel**'s restaurant (Iona; tel. 1681 700 304; www.stcolumba-hotel.co.uk; 11am-9pm Mar.-Nov.; entrées £7). If you can, spend a night here rather than cram it all into a day as most visitors do, and it will feel like you have the island to yourself in the morning.

Getting There

Ferries to Iona depart regularly throughout the day (fewer on Sundays) from the small port of **Fionnphort** on the Ross of Mull, an hour's (33-mile/53-km) drive west of Craignure. The crossing takes just 10 minutes (£1.70 single/£3.40 return). Cars cannot be taken onto Iona, but there is a parking lot at Fionnphort where you can leave your vehicle.

STAFFA

This tiny uninhabited island just 10 miles (16 km) off the coast of Mull is only accessible to day-trippers by boat, which can be boarded in Oban, Mull, or in Iona. It rivals the Giant's Causeway across the Irish Sea in terms of staggering geographical features; most famously, Fingal's Cave is renowned for its striking series of basalt columns. You can see the cave from the sea, but if you want to get closer, you can reach the mouth of the cave via a pathway over rocks, which isn't actually as treacherous as it first looks—the rocks are relatively level and there is a rail to hold on to as you go.

The other highlight of a visit to Staffa is the puffins that live and breed here March-September. To see them, climb the steep steps after you disembark your trip boat to the grassy ridge (again use the handrail) and then turn right (there is a sign to remind you). It's about a 10- to 15-minute walk to their main breeding ground in a bay, helpfully marked with a red/orange buoy. Once here, find a spot a safe distance from the edge of the cliff face and then sit and wait—it can take up to 30 minutes or so for the puffins to start to play ball, but if you visit in May or June, they will eventually do so.

Getting There

There are a couple of companies that offer good day trips to Staffa with well-informed skippers who act as your guides, including Staffa Trips (tel. 1681 700 358; www.staffatrips.co.uk), which offers two sailings a day from Iona and Fionnphort on Mull (9:45am and 1:45pm pick up at Iona, 10am and 2pm pick up at Fionnphort). Cruises last around 3 hours 20 minutes, with at least one hour ashore at Staffa.

JURA

The long narrow isle of Jura is like an arm being held aloft from the torso of Islay. Many people don't actually set foot on Jura but see the Corryvreckan Whirlpool—where water gets squeezed in the Sound of Jura, creating whirling effect and big standing waves—on a boat trip from Oban. Jura Boat Tours takes visitors close to the action from Craighouse on Jura (tel. 07976 280 195; www.juraboattours.co.uk/tours/corryvreckan; tours at 9am Mon.-Tues., Thurs., Sat.-Sun., 2pm Fri. Apr.-Oct.; adult £40, child £25).

After Islay's distilleries, many visitors relish the relative calm of Jura Distillery (Craighouse; tel. 1496 820 385; www.jurawhisky.com; 10am-4:30pm Mon.-Sat. late Mar.-Oct., 10am-4pm Mon.-Fri. Nov.-Mar.; Daily Distillery tour £6, Signature Jura Tour £15), which so far seems to have avoided the tourist map. If you're feeling inspired to write a novel after the tasting, try renting out Barnhill (Northeast Jura; www.escapetojura.com; from £1,000 per week, sleeps eight), the house where George Orwell famously wrote much of *1984*.

Getting There

From Port Askaig on Islay, there's a ferry to Port Feolin on Jura run by SP Ship Management Ltd (£15.40 per vehicle, £3,70 per adult passenger, child £2.10); ring 01496 840 681 for times. It takes just 10 minutes, with views of the Paps of Jura, the island's three distinctive mountains, as you cross. If you haven't come to Jura with your own car, Garelochhead Coaches bus no. 456 (www.garelochheadcoaches.co.uk) runs Mon.-Sat. between Port Feolin and towns on Jura's coast, including Craighouse, which is home to Jura Distillery. They can also be booked for private tours.

local ingredients from the land and sea. The short menu changes regularly, but it almost always includes half lobster with triple-cooked chips. There would be uproar if it was removed from the menu.

TIRORAN HOUSE HOTEL

Mull; tel. 01681 705 232; www.tiroran.com; 12pm-5pm Mon.-Fri.-Sun.; mains £9.95

This is the only country house hotel on the whole of Mull, and the en suite rooms and three self-catering cottages are sweet, with floral curtains and cute details. It's a little out of the way down some country lanes—it's not uncommon to have Highland cattle pass you on the road. Though the hotel's main restaurant hadn't reopened at the time of writing, the **Whitetail Gin Shop** and the café were open, offering artisan foods (bread, jams, etc.) as well as salads, soups, coffees, and other hot mains— in addition to gin, of course. It's a good food and drink stop either before or after a walk on the Burg.

Accommodations
★ FIDDEN FARM

Knockvologan Road, Near Fionnphort; tel. 01681 700 427; www.ukcampsite.co.uk; £10 per adult

Just 2 miles (3 km) from Fionnphort, this campsite on the edge of another of Mull's white sandy beaches, Fidden, is a great place to get away from it all. There's little to do here except sit and watch the ebb and flow of the tide or look out for eagles above or dolphins and whales in the water, but isn't that the point? If you do feel the need to sightsee, catch the ferry to Iona, which has a similarly unhurried vibe. Toilets and showers are on-site.

TOBERMORY YOUTH HOSTEL

Main Street, Tobermory; tel. 01688 302 481; www. hostellingscotland.org.uk/hostels/tobermory; bed in a shared dorm £20, four-person private room £96

Quite possibly the most photographed hostel in Scotland, this budget option is one of the bright properties that forms the colorful parade along Tobermory's harborside. It's well-placed for the attractions of the town—shops, pubs, and restaurants—and many of the rooms have sea views. There's also a little garden out back where you can drink your morning coffee.

★ STRONGARBH HOUSE

Tobermory; tel. 01688 302 319; https://strongarbh. com; £95 d, minimum two-night stay

This lovely period house overlooks Tobermory from up high on its own spacious grounds, with a private path to take you all the way down to the harbor. Inside, a curved staircase leads to the four stylish rooms: dressed in a contemporary take on Victoriana, two even have four-posters. The snug library is a lovely place to unwind after a day exploring, and, though there are tea- and coffee-making facilities in your room, you'll probably want to pop home for the complimentary afternoon tea served each day from 4pm to 6pm.

ISLAY

There is something of a paradox taking place on Islay. Tourism provides a brilliant injection to the economy, but locals fear that, with more distilleries planned over the next few years (there are already nine across its 239 square miles/619 square km) it could turn into something of a whisky Disneyland. Whisky is a big draw, it's true, but, with a wild landscape of bog and peat land as well as fertile farmland, there's much more to the southernmost Inner Hebrides isle, which is not known as the Queen of the Hebrides for nothing.

The people here are among Scotland's friendliest. The Ileach, as they are called, have a strong sense of community and identity, and they're never too busy to stop to say hello or have a blether (idle chat). Other inhabitants include the red stags whose bellows can be heard high on the hillsides in October, abundant birdlife, and the frequently spotted seals.

Getting There
BY FERRY

The ferry to Islay departs from **Kennacraig** on the mainland. From Glasgow (100 miles/161 km; 2.5 hours), take the A82 up

Islay

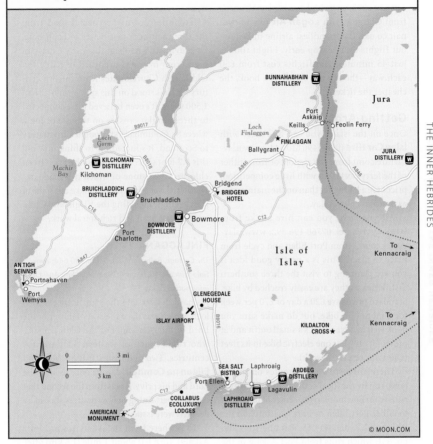

into Loch Lomond and the Trossachs National Park all the way to Tarbet, where you'll turn left onto the A83, which takes you all the way to Kennacraig. From Oban (55 miles/88 km), you can reach Kennacraig in an hour and a half by heading south on the A816 before picking up the A83 at Lochgilphead. From Edinburgh, it's a 3.75-hour drive (150 mi/241 km) along the M9 to Stirling, before turning west onto the A811 to Balloch and then coming up the A82 through Loch Lomond before joining the A83 at Tarbet. Alternatively, there are three buses a day from Glasgow to Kennacraig with **Scottish Citylink** that take 3.25 hours (£18.60 one-way).

From Kennacraig, the ferry crossing takes 2 hours to **Port Askaig** on the east coast of Islay and 2.25 hours to **Port Ellen** on the south coast; there are around four ferries a day with **Calmac** (www.calmac.co.uk). Cars can be taken on both ferry routes. The Port Askaig ferries take just under 2 hours, while the Port Ellen crossings take 2.25 hours. Prices are the same for both ferries: £6.10 one-way and £13.40 round-trip adult passenger, £3.35 one-way and £6.70 round-trip child, plus £33.45 one-way per car.

BY AIR

You can fly to **Islay Airport** (Glenegedale; tel. 149 630 2022; www.hial.co.uk/islay-airport/) from Glasgow with **Logan Air** (www.loganair.co.uk), the friendliest airline in Britain, but flights do book up early. Flight time is just 45 minutes, and flights cost from £50 each way—though the earlier you book, the cheaper the tickets.

Getting Around

Once on the island you can hire a car with **Islay Car Hire** (tel. 01496 810 544; www.islaycarhire.com) from the airport or from either of the ferry ports, but with little competition, prices are a lot higher than on the mainland—as much as £50 per day.

Alternatively, you can hire a bike from **Islay Cycles** (tel. 07760 196 592; www.islaycycles.co.uk) from Port Ellen and cycle from place to place. This is a pretty good idea if you are planning to visit the three southern distilleries, as they are easily reached by bike. Standard prices are £20 a day or £70 per week for a mountain bike, but do make sure you book well in advance; it's a small outfit and at present it only has one electric bike in its fleet (£30 a day or £120 a week).

There are just two **bus** routes on the island, run by the local council: no. 450, which runs from Bowmore in the center of the island to either Port Ellen or Port Charlotte on the Rhinos (£2.75 one-way, £5.50 round-trip), and no. 451, which runs from Port Askaig in the northeast, down to Port Ellen in the south, and then along past each of the three southern distilleries to Ardbeg (£3.85 one-way, £7.70 round-trip). However, buses are not frequent, with two, perhaps three a day, and none on Sunday.

Carol's Cabs (tel. 01496 302 155; www.carols-cabs.co.uk) is the longest-running cab firm on Islay and, in addition to offering a standard taxi service, offers island and whisky tours.

Sights

KILDALTON CROSS

West of Ardmore; free

A few miles down the coastal road from the three southern distilleries of Laphroaig, Lagaluvin, and Ardbeg, this early Christian high cross in the churchyard of Kildalton Old Parish Church dates from the 8th century and has stood on this spot for more than 1,500 years. It's even believed to be connected to three similar crosses on the isle of Iona, where St. Columba first brought Christianity to Scotland. It's incredible to think how old this 8.7-foot (2.65 m) cross is; the gray-green chlorite schist stone of which it is made has weathered well: You can still make out some of the carvings, including the Virgin and Child on the cross head and rich spiral work.

FINLAGGAN

The Cottage, Ballygrant; tel. 01496 840 644; www. finlaggan.org; 10:30am-4:30pm Mon.-Sat. Apr.-Oct.; information center £3

It's hard to overstate the significance of this loch, which was once the seat of power of the Lord of the Isles, chief of the Clan Donald, who ruled much of western Scotland for centuries. Two main isles, **Eilean Mor** and **Eilean na Comhairle,** were once used by the Lord and his privy. It was from the second that charters pertaining to how matters should be decided were issued.

To get here from the A846 (toward Port Askaig), turn left about 1 mile (1.6 km) after Ballygrant. After half a mile (0.8 km) turn left again onto Finlaggan Farm (look out for animals in your pathway) until you come to the information center. You should pay the small fee inside, where knowledgeable staff will also give you useful background on the site. Follow the small path down over a bridge and onto the first island of Eilean Mor, where you can walk amid the ruins of this once ancient seat and settlement, thought to have been destroyed in the 15th century by Clan

---

1: American Monument **2:** Finlaggan **3:** Coillabus Ecoluxury Lodges **4:** Laphroaig Distillery

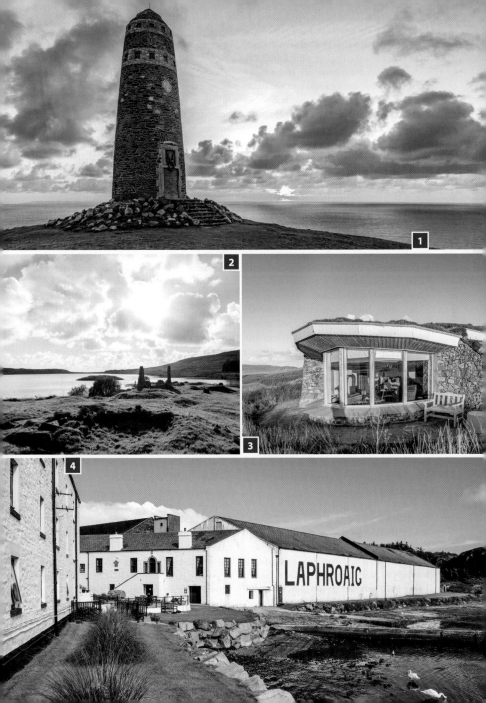

Campbell on the orders of King James V in retribution to an earlier plot between the Lord of the Isles and the English King Edward IV to wrest power from James III. If the visitor center is closed, you can still visit the island of Eilean Mor (Eilean na Comhairle is not accessible), but you should put your fee in the honesty box provided.

AMERICAN MONUMENT
Mull of Oa

This monument commemorates the loss of life of U.S. servicemen in two separate 1918 ship sinkings: the passenger liner *SS Tuscania* on February 5, which was transporting over 2,000 troops to France, and just eight months later *HMS Otranto,* which was ferrying troops to Glasgow. More than 600 people died in the two tragedies, and many are buried at the military cemetery at Kilchoman.

Standing high on a cliff on the Oa Peninsula, the lighthouse-shaped monument includes a plaque with words from then president Woodrow Wilson. It's a half-hour walk to get here from the Royal Society for the Protection of Birds (RSPB) parking spot, through a well-marked but muddy trail that crosses a field of sheep. Once here, it is an exposed but beautiful spot (stay well back from the edge) with views over to Antrim in Northern Ireland, just 25 miles (40 km) across the sea. If you visit for sunset, be sure to leave with enough light to make your way back down to the car park.

Beaches
MACHIR BAY
Kilchoman

With 1.2 miles (2 km) of golden sands, Machir Bay on the island's western coast is one of Islay's most spectacular beaches, especially when it comes to sunsets. It's very accessible too—just a short walk over a bridge and through the dunes from the small car park, making it a great option for kids or the less mobile. It's also a good stop-off before or after visiting Kilchoman Distillery.

★ Distilleries

Islay whiskies are generally renowned for being heavily peated, a holdover from when the island's only abundant source of fuel was peat from the bogland, so it was used to dry out the barley during the malting process. The peat-tinged flavor proved popular, but while the whiskies of the south (Laphroaig, Lagavulin, and Ardbeg) are known for their smokiness, they can be a bit of an acquired taste, and some people find them too medicinal. The whiskies of the north are a lot lighter.

All distilleries are geared up for visitors, and each offers tours, which are competitively priced and include a tasting of at least one of the distillery's expressions. If you are doing a tour of a distillery or two by car, then there are small tasting bottles for the designated driver to take home, so they needn't miss out. It is also possible to cycle between some of the distilleries—hire a bike from **Islay Cycles** (2 Corrsgeir Place; tel. 07760 196 592; www.islaycycles.co.uk; from £20 per day) in Port Ellen in the south—though you still should watch what you are drinking. You can even walk between the three most southerly ones (the farthest, Ardbeg, is only an hour's walk from Port Ellen).

LAGAVULIN DISTILLERY
Lagavulin; tel. 01496 302 749; www.malts.com/en-gb/distilleries/lagavulin; 10am-5pm daily; tours from £15

One of the most photographed distilleries in Scotland, the classic whitewashed distillery complex of Lagavulin, with its iconic red smokestack, sits right on the beautiful Lagavulin Bay. Distillers have been making whiskies known for thier rich, peaty character onsite since at least 1816. Book tours ahead to avoid disappointment.

LAPHROAIG DISTILLERY
Port Ellen; tel. 01496 302 418; www.laphroaig.com; 9:15am-5pm daily Apr.-Sept., 9:30am-5pm daily

Oct.-Mar. (closed weekends Jan.-Feb.); tours from £10

People either love or hate this peaty whisky, made on the south of the island. It is popular, though, and one of the more familiar names, plus you get three drams on the one-hour Laphroaig Experience tour. It's also located just outside the town of Port Ellen, the main entry point to the island, and visitors here often combine a visit to stop-offs at both Ardbeg and Lagavulin, also in the south of Islay.

ARDBEG DISTILLERY

Port Ellen; tel. 01496 302 244; www.ardbeg.com; 9:30am-5pm Mon.-Fri. early Jan.-Mar., 9:30am-5pm daily Apr.-Oct., 9:30am-5pm Mon.-Fri. Oct.-mid Dec., closed Dec. 21-Jan.6; tours from £6

The farthest of the three southern distilleries along the winding road of Port Ellen (though still manageable on foot for many), Ardbeg has been legally distilling whisky for 200 years, and like Laphroaig, its whisky is heavily peated. You can take the Distillery Tour and Wee Taste (1.25 hours; Mon.-Fri. 11am and 3pm, no tours Dec. and Jan.), which start by taking you down to the pier in front of the whitewashed warehouses. Inside, you'll be guided through the whisky-making process step-by-step, before choosing a dram to sample in a charming hidden tasting room. Many visitors stop here for lunch in the very good **Old Kiln Café** (12pm-4pm when distillery is open), which serves well-priced mains, such as fish pie or haggis, neeps and tatties with a creamy pepper sauce.

BOWMORE DISTILLERY

School Street, Bowmore; tel. 01496 810 441; www. bowmore.com; tours 10am, 11am, 1:30pm, and 3:30pm Mon.-Sat., 12:30pm and 2pm Sun. Apr.-Oct., 10:30am and 2pm Mon.-Sat. Nov.-Mar.; tours from £10

The first legal distillery on the island, Bowmore in the center of the town of the same name, malts some of its own barley (about 30 percent) and has the oldest maturation warehouse in the world. On the one-hour tour you'll learn how they've been making their whiskies since 1779 using traditions passed down through generations. There are also more in-depth tastings that incur a higher price, and you can stay on-site in either **The Harbour Inn** (www. bowmore.com/harbour-inn; doubles from £115 d) across the road or one of the **self-catering cottages** (www.bowmore.com/bowmore-cottages; from £105 d) within the distillery complex.

BRUICHLADDICH DISTILLERY

Port Charlotte; tel. 01496 850 190; www. bruichladdich.com; 10am, 1pm, 3pm, and 4pm Mon.-Fri., 10am, 1pm, 2pm, and 3pm Sat., 11am, 1pm, and 2pm Sun.; distillery tours £5, Warehouse Experience £25, Botanist Tour £25 (all one hour)

A huge array of whisky is made at this distillery in the southwest of Islay, from the un-peated Bruichladdich, to the heavily peated Port Charlotte, the eye-watering smokiness of the Octomore, and the distillery's brand of dry gin, The Botanist. The normal (un-peated) whiskies here have a more floral flavor. Tours are famously generous; even on the £5 tour you should be able to try several whiskies. On the Warehouse Experience, taste straight from the cask; the Botanist Tour is a chance to try the distillery's gin.

KILCHOMAN DISTILLERY

Rockside Farm, Bruichladdich; tel. 01496 850 011; www.kilchomandistillery.com; 9:45am-5pm daily late Mar.-early Nov., closed weekends early Nov.-late Mar.; Distillery Tour £7

Islay's renowned farmhouse distillery is a popular place for those wanting to see how whisky is made from start to finish—the distillery harvests its own barley, and even the bottling is done by hand on-site. It's set on a pretty farm, and, with two drams plus a free glass thrown in, it's a value too. The slow distillation process makes an intense and smoky dram. There's also a good **café** on-site.

BUNNAHABHAIN DISTILLERY

Port Askaig; tel. 01496 840 557; https:// bunnahabhain.com; 10am-4pm Mon.-Sat., 12pm-4pm Sun., tour times vary in winter and summer; Quick Look Tour £5, Production Tour £7, Warehouse 9 Experience £25

Near Port Askaig on the north of the island, the whisky distilled at Bunnahabhain is much milder than its southern counterparts, and many find it a better introduction to the distinct malts of Islay. If you're short of time, the Quick Look Tour (30 minutes) will give you an overview of the distilling process and a wee dram, while the Production Tour (50 minutes) goes into a little more detail. One of the most popular tours, though, is the Warehouse 9 Experience (one hour), which includes tastings straight from the cask.

Food

★ BRIDGEND HOTEL

Islay; tel. 01496 810 212; www.bridgend-hotel.com; home-baking from 11am, lunch 12pm-2pm daily, dinner 6pm-9pm; entrées £6.95

This utterly unpretentious restaurant with rooms (£135 d) uses the freshest of local ingredients, including game from the Islay Estates and vegetables from the restaurant's very own garden. Try the medallions of venison or baked hake with shellfish risotto.

SEA SALT BISTRO

57 Frederick Crescent, Port Ellen; tel. 01496 300 300; www.seasalt-bistro.co.uk; morning coffee 10am-12pm daily, lunch 12pm-2:30pm, dinner 5pm-9pm, takeaway 5pm-9pm; entrées £5.50

At this busy bistro-takeaway place, you can stop for a morning coffee if you are on your way to the ferry, sit down for a full-on dinner, or get takeaway fish and chips for an evening stroll.

AN TIGH SEINNSE

11 Queen Street, Portnahaven; tel. 01496 860 224; 12pm-4pm Weds.-Thurs., 12pm-8pm Fri.-Tues.; entrées £5.25

This pub that looks more like a private home than a public place is one of the best places to experience Islay hospitality. It also sells great seafood (a pint of prawns in their shells or fresh crab), and you might even hear the seals outside "singing."

Accommodations

GLENEGEDALE HOUSE

Glenegedale; tel. 01496 300 400; www. glenegedaleguesthouse.co.uk; £160 d

This award-winning guesthouse, halfway between Bowmore and Port Ellen and very close to the airport, has just four rooms in the lavish home of Graeme and Emma, who make you feel every inch as though you are their personal guests. Rooms come with Egyptian cotton sheets and Highland chocolates—you'll even be met with home-baking and tea if you arrive between 3:30pm and 5pm.

★ COILLABUS ECOLUXURY LODGES

The Oa Peninsula, Islay; tel. 07824 567 435; http:// coillabus.com; £1,700 per week

This duo of luxury lodges, hidden away in the wilds of the Oa, offer impeccable accommodation in a remote location. With turf-roofs designed to blend into the landscape, the floor-to-ceiling windows in their living rooms are perfect for wildlife watching, from pheasants to golden eagles and buzzards—it's even possible to hear red deer at night during rutting season. While not cheap, the lodges can comfortably sleep four in two huge en-suite bedrooms, which have a five-star spa feel to them, with your own sauna and an outdoor bathtub (with hot water of course), perfect for an unforgettable stargazing experience.

Western Highlands and the Isle of Skye

The western Highlands region, running from

Glen Coe in the south up to the western edge of Loch Ness and across the sea to Skye, is interwoven with stories, from clan rivalries to Jacobite risings, all under the shadow of some of Scotland's mightiest mountains.

Outdoor adventure hub Fort William is the main jumping-off point for hiking Ben Nevis and exploring the wider area, including Glen Coe, whose mountain scenery is unparalleled. In this vast valley, nature has left its indelible mark in the eight Munros and other big hills that were formed millions of years ago by volcanic eruptions before being carved into shape by gigantic glaciers. Today these mountains watch silently over rushing rivers and the snake of cars passing far below, as

Highlights

Look for ★ to find recommended sights, activities, dining, and lodging.

★ **Driving the Glen Coe Road:** As the A82 twists and curls through Scotland's most scenic glen, you'll want to take a thousand photos (page 332).

★ **Hiking Ben Nevis:** Whether you climb to the top or take a storied walk to view its north face, big Ben is bound to astound you (page 337).

★ **West Highland Line/Jacobite Steam Train:** Board the Harry Potter train for a scenic journey along the West Highland Line to Mallaig before heading to the Isle of Skye (page 342).

★ **Portree:** Skye's picturesque main town has some surprisingly good food and drink offerings (page 353).

★ **Blà Bheinn:** The only one of Skye's Munros not on the Cuillin Ridge, the summit of this mountain is one of Skye's most attainable (page 367).

★ **Hike to the Cleared Village of Boreraig:** This haunting village still shows the stone ruins of a lost community (page 368).

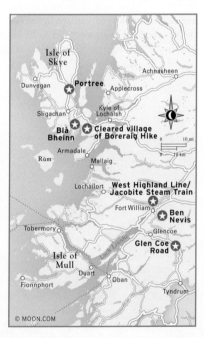

© MOON.COM

though they dare not speak their secrets, and yet memories of the Massacre of Glencoe seem to linger in the air like a sorrowful ballad.

Meanwhile, it was at Glenfinnan that Bonnie Prince Charlie, the romantic figurehead of the '45 Jacobite Rising, raised his father's standard, ready to rouse his followers. This majestic setting, like an oil painting, is best viewed from the window of the Jacobite Steam Train as it curves around the Glenfinnan Viaduct. Forming part of the West Highland Line, one of the most beautiful train routes in the world, it takes you from Fort William to Mallaig, from where it's a short ferry ride across to the Isle of Skye.

Named Skuy (misty isle) by its Norse settlers, Skye is the gateway to the Hebrides—some of the most remote parts of Britain. It's an extraordinary place of epic proportions. Colossal mountains march through the island, splitting it in two, strange, sharp rocks stab at the sky, and no two scenes are ever the same. So surreal is its landscape that it has spawned countless myths and legends—of giants turned to stone, lovelorn fairies, and mysterious kelpies.

ORIENTATION

The **Great Glen**—a diagonal fault line that cuts right through the middle of Scotland—runs from Inverness all the way to **Fort William** at the head of Loch Linnhe. Just 16 miles (26 km) south of Fort William lies **Glen Coe,** a monumental valley where craggy Munros rise to the skies, punctuated with green moorland and icy rivers and lochs. Together with Fort William, Glen Coe forms part of the **Lochaber Geopark,** a region of incredible geological interest that stretches as far west as the Isle of Rum, which lies off the coast of Skye.

Skye is the largest isle in the Inner Hebrides, just off the northwest coast of Scotland. For a long time, it was only accessible by ferry, and the original crossing was from **Kyle of Lochalsh** on the mainland (some 60 miles/97 km west of Drumnadrochit on Loch Ness) to Kyleakin on southeast Skye. Since 1995, however, people can now drive onto the island at Kyleakin via the **Skye Bridge,** just a mile (1.6 km) west of Kyle of Lochalsh. The other year-round way of reaching Skye is to take the ferry from **Mallaig,** farther south on the mainland, which comes into Armadale on the south of Skye. From Easter to October, you can also take a short ferry crossing from **Glenelg,** located between Kyle of Lochalsh and Mallaig on the mainland coast, to Kylerhea, just a few miles south of Kyleakin.

PLANNING YOUR TIME

In the western Highlands, whether you're driving the **Glen Coe Road** or climbing **Ben Nevis,** give yourself at least three days. The route to Skye **from Fort William to Mallaig** deserves at least a full day to ensure you see the main sights (or take the much less traveled route aboard the turntable **Glenelg** ferry). You can reach this western Highlands region from the south, from Edinburgh or Glasgow by car via Loch Lomond and the Trossachs National Park, or via train from Edinburgh or Glasgow to Fort William, where you can board the **Jacobite Steam Train.** It's also easy to get here from Inverness, driving southwest along the shores of Loch Ness.

Whether you arrive by car or ferry, **Skye** is not a place to do in a day or two—it's quite a large island and traveling around it takes time. More time—a week at least—allows you to spread out to secret corners of the isle rather than rush to the same four or five hot spots that every tourist visits. Try basing yourself on the north of the isle for a few days, so you can venture into the **Waternish Peninsula,** and then stay on the south of the island for the remainder of your visit (or vice versa, depending

Western Highlands and the Isle of Skye

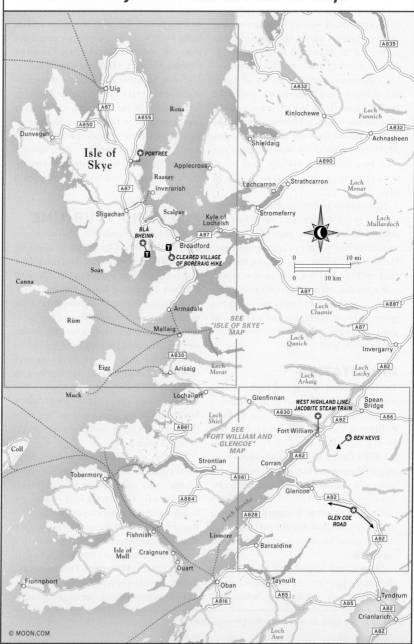

Uig
A87
A850
A855
Rona
Dunvegan
Kinlochewe
Loch Fannich
A832
A835
A832
Achnasheen
Shieldaig
Isle of Skye
PORTREE
Applecross
A890
Loch Monar
Raasay
Inverarish
Lochcarron
Strathcarron
Loch Mullardoch
Sligachan
Scalpay
Stromeferry
BLÀ BHEINN
T
Kyle of Lochalsh
A87
Soay
T
Broadford
CLEARED VILLAGE OF BOREAIG HIKE
0   10 mi
0   10 km
A87
Loch Cluanie
Canna
Armadale
SEE "ISLE OF SKYE" MAP
A87
A887
Rùm
Mallaig
A830
Loch Quoich
A82
Invergarry
Eigg
Arisaig
Loch Morar
Loch Arkaig
Loch Lochy
Muck
Lochailort
Glenfinnan
WEST HIGHLAND LINE/ JACOBITE STEAM TRAIN
Spean Bridge
Loch Shiel
A830
A82
A86
Coll
SEE "FORT WILLIAM AND GLENCOE" MAP
Fort William
BEN NEVIS
A861
A82
Strontian
Corran
Tobermory
A884
Glencoe
A82
A861
GLEN COE ROAD
A82
Loch Linnhe
A828
Fishnish
Lismore
Barcaldine
A82
Isle of Mull
Craignure
Duart
Fionnphort
Oban
Taynuilt
Tyndrum
A816
A85
A85
A82
Crianlarich
© MOON.COM
Loch Awe
A82

Roads to Skye

Most visitors to Skye come from Inverness, or Edinburgh and Glasgow. From Inverness, there are two road options, outlined below. From Edinburgh and Glasgow, you will inevitably drive through the Loch Lomond and the Trossachs National Park and come out near Bridge of Orchy, before continuing the A82 through Glen Coe and then up to Fort William and beyond. Once you get to the waters around Skye, there are a few ways to cross: the ferry from Mallaig or Glenelg (farther up the Sound of Sleat from Mallaig), or the bridge to Skye from Kyle of Lochalsh.

INVERNESS TO KYLE OF LOCHALSH

There are two main driving routes from Inverness to the Kyle of Lochalsh, to cross over the Skye Bridge. The first takes you south down the western shore of Loch Ness, before heading west on the A887 past Loch Cluanie, before dropping down through Glen Shiel, then to Kyle of Lochalsh (80 miles/129 km; 1 hour 50 minutes). The second option (the same distance and time), is to head west from Inverness along the A835, passing inland (along one section of the NC 500) to Achnasheen, down through Strathcarron. On the latter, you also get views of the Torridon Hills from about midway along the route, though the former will take you right past Eilean Donan Castle (admittedly it's not hard to detour there from the other route).

Once you've crossed the bridge (which is approximately 1,600 feet/488 m long, a 5-minute ride), you'll be in Kyleakin on the southeastern corner of Skye, a 45-minute (33-mile/53-km) drive from Portree.

FORT WILLIAM TO MALLAIG

This drive, which takes just an hour (43 miles/69 km), follows a similar route to the last section of the West Highland Line, with some edge-of-your-seat scenery as you go. The official Road to the Isles website (www.road-to-the-isles.org.uk) offers tons of local information and trip inspiration on the route, and the benefit of traveling this section by car rather than rail is that you can stop as many times as you like. The Glenfinnan Viaduct is undoubtedly the highlight, but it's not the only place you'll want to stop—the views over to the Small Isles will certainly tempt you to pull over.

The Mallaig ferry (https://www.calmac.co.uk/article/2121/Skye) crosses to Armadale, almost on Skye's southern tip. It's an hour away (42 miles/68 km) from Portree, and a very beautiful detour off the main road from Armadale, known as the Ord Loop, offers spectacular views of the Cuillin, the mountainous interior of Skye.

THE GLENELG FERRY

https://skyeferry.co.uk

This ferry route is the last manually operated turntable ferry in Scotland and it has offered a car ferry crossing across the narrow channel that separates Skye from Glenelg in Lochalsh on the mainland since 1934. Glenelg is more or less in the middle of Kyle of Lochalsh and Mallaig, a 2-hour (73-mile/117-km) drive from Inverness or a 1 hour 40-minute (70-mile/113-km) drive from Fort William.

This ferry crosses to Kylerhea on Skye, about 22 minutes (10 miles/16 km) by car from Kyleakin and the Skye Bridge.

on your overall route). Most travelers will visit **Portree** at least for an afternoon or dinner, followed probably by the **Trotternish Peninsula**, but by no means does this need to be the focus of your visit. And, if you don't take at least one major walk, you'll only really skim the surface.

The main tourism season runs from April to late October; come a little out of season and you will have many of the beauty spots to yourself and an increased chance of spotting wildlife, though some pubs and restaurants may be closed.

Itinerary Ideas

DAY 1

1 Coming from Inverness and Fort William in your rental car, head toward Glen Coe, stopping at the **Glencoe Visitor Centre** to orient yourself for the spectacular drive ahead.

2 You'll find yourself wanting to pull over at every vista but be sure to stop at the **Three Sisters Viewpoint** to marvel at the three famous peaks.

3 Stop for a pint (non-drivers only), a meal, and maybe even live music at the **Clachaig Inn.**

4 Return to Fort William to check into **Achintee Farm,** your accommodations for the night.

5 For dinner, rub elbows with hikers over hearty pub fare at the **Ben Nevis Inn.**

DAY 2

1 You can drive the route from Fort William to Mallaig in just about an hour, or you can drop off your rental car to ride the Jacobite Steam Train (though you may want to pick up a rental car again for your time on Skye). Either way, be sure to stop off at Glenfinnan to take in the view of the iconic **Glenfinnan Viaduct.**

2 Take the next boat from **Mallaig Ferry Terminal** to Armadale on Skye.

3 Drive straight to Portree for lunch at **Café Arriba.**

4 Head to the tip of the Trotternish Peninsula and park near Staffin to explore the ethereal landscape of the **Quiraing** on foot.

5 Drive on toward the Michelin-starred **Loch Bay** restaurant.

6 End your night in the cozy bar of the **Stein Inn,** your accommodations for the night.

DAY 3

1 In the morning, drive to **Dunvegan Castle and Gardens** for a peek into the historic interior and a stroll around the grounds.

2 Take the hike out to **Claigan Coral Beach,** a lovely 40-minute walk from the car park just down the road from Dunvegan Castle.

3 Reward yourself with lunch at another of Skye's best restaurants, the **Three Chimneys.**

4 Head south for a tour and tasting at the **Talisker distillery,** Skye's oldest.

5 End your last night on Skye with pub grub, traditional music, and a good night's sleep at **The Old Inn.**

Itinerary Ideas

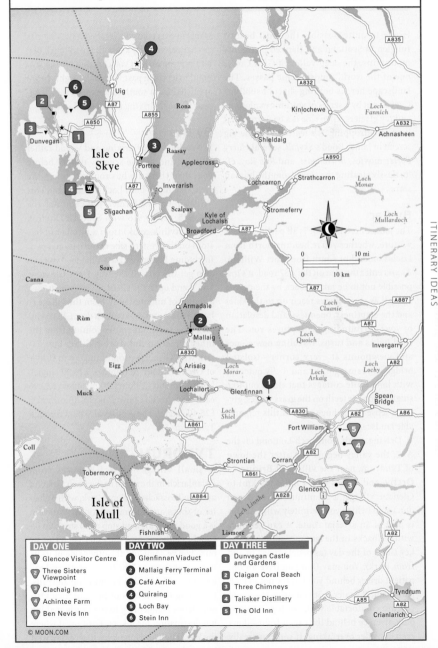

DAY ONE
1. Glencoe Visitor Centre
2. Three Sisters Viewpoint
3. Clachaig Inn
4. Achintee Farm
5. Ben Nevis Inn

DAY TWO
1. Glenfinnan Viaduct
2. Mallaig Ferry Terminal
3. Café Arriba
4. Quiraing
5. Loch Bay
6. Stein Inn

DAY THREE
1. Dunvegan Castle and Gardens
2. Claigan Coral Beach
3. Three Chimneys
4. Talisker Distillery
5. The Old Inn

© MOON.COM

★ Glen Coe Road

Home to quite possibly the most beautiful glen in Scotland and flanked by mighty mountains, the deep valley of Glen Coe is one of the world's most scenic passes. The landscape here is nothing short of sublime. Carved out by a series of volcanic explosions and icy glaciers, Glen Coe is a backdrop that is so jaw-dropping, it's featured on the big screen in James Bond's *Skyfall,* several *Harry Potter* movies, *Braveheart,* and *Rob Roy,* effortlessly stealing the show from the human stars.

By Car

The journey to Glen Coe is all part of the adventure, whether you're heading north from Loch Lomond or south from Fort William. As you enter the glen on the A82 road, it's impossible not to be taken aback by the drama of it all as steep slopes reach up to the skies and the emptiness, openness, and desolation of your surroundings enraptures you. The road twists and turns, revealing new scenes and viewpoints at every corner—isolated bridges, streams, gorges, and rocky outcrops with lone white cottages that stand out like single crocodile teeth on the grass verges, giving a sense of the huge scale of this remarkable landscape.

Driving north from Loch Lomond on the A82, the valley begins just after the town of Tyndrum, near the village of **Bridge of Orchy,** and curves for 24 miles (39 km) to Glencoe village, a 30-minute drive if you don't stop (which you definitely will). As this is part of an arterial route, it can get busy with tailbacks in the summer months or at key times of the day (as people travel to and from work). You may find you have an impatient driver behind you but try not to let it panic you. It's safer that you drive at a speed you are comfortable with, with good stopping distance behind the car in front—don't even consider overtaking. If someone really wants to overtake you, let them take that risk as chances are they know the road much better than you do or if you can, pull into a viewpoint to let them past. The major sights below are listed from south to north, as they'll appear if you're driving from Loch Lomond.

By Bus

If you don't fancy driving and would rather sit back and let the scenery unfold before you, then there are bus routes through the glen, starting in both Loch Lomond and Fort William. For the former, you can catch the 914, 915, or the 916 with Scottish Citylink (www.citylink.co.uk) from a number of bus stops on the western side of the national park (including Balloch or Luss Village)—you can also get the bus all the way from Glasgow. You'll end up at the Glencoe Crossroads, just a couple of minutes' walk from the village (1 hour 40 minutes, 3-4 buses a day; £23.70 single). The same bus routes coming from the other direction link Fort William bus station with Glen Coe, continuing on to Bridge of Orchy (1 hour 10 minutes; £14.90 single), Loch Lomond (2 hours 20 minutes; £25.90 each way), or Glasgow (3 hours 15 minutes; £26.40 single). These buses also pass through Tyndrum.

TYNDRUM

A small village just a few miles from Crianlarich in the north of the Loch Lomond and the Trossachs National Park, with a cluster of shops and accommodations, Tyndrum is a good place for a pit stop or to stock up on supplies either before you enter Glen Coe or once you've come out the other side of it. Its name translates as "the house on the ridge," and it is surrounded by beautiful upland hills, including the Munros of Ben Lui, Ben Oss, and Beinn Dubhchraig to the south, making it a destination for hikers. Positioned where the West Highland Line splits to go either west to Oban or north to Rannoch and Corrour, it's also very well connected, with two train stations.

Shopping
GREEN WELLY SHOP

A82, Tyndrum; tel. 01301 702 089; www. thegreenwellystop.co.uk; 8:30am-5:30pm Apr.-Oct., 8:30am-5pm Nov.-Mar.; petrol station 7am-10pm May-Sept., 8am-9pm Oct.-Apr.

En route to Glencoe from Loch Lomond, shops are few and far between the farther north in the park you go, and then you reach Tyndrum. The Green Welly Shop on the main A82 road just as you enter Tyndrum (on your right-hand side if you're coming from Loch Lomond) has achieved near cult status and is more a Highland mall than a single shop. As well as fuel and snacks, this is the place to stop to buy any outdoor gear or clothing you may be missing. It's hard to miss as it is well signposted and has a giant picture of a green welly on its front.

Getting There

There are two train stations in Tyndrum: Upper Tyndrum Station (Upper Station Road, Tyndrum; 2 hours from Glasgow; £22.80 single) and Tyndrum Lower Station (Lower Station Road, Tyndrum; 2 hours from Glasgow; £22.80 single). The first is on the Fort William branch of the West Highland Line and the second is on the Oban branch. From Upper Tyndrum, it's just over 3 hours to Mallaig for the ferry to Skye (£32.90 single), and from Tyndrum Lower, it's just over 1 hour to Oban (£12.60 single).

LOCH TULLA VIEWPOINT

11.3 mi (18.2 km) from Tyndrum; 18.2 miles (29.3 km) from visitor center

There's a good-sized parking area by this loch near Bridge of Orchy, where you can enjoy views of the water with the Glen Coe mountains behind and a thick bank of pine trees in front. It's pretty much the postcard-perfect image of the Highlands that we've all come to expect.

RANNOCH MOOR VIEWPOINT

15.5 mi (24.9 km) from Tyndrum, 14 mi (22.5 km) from visitor center

This viewpoint near Bridge of Orchy will give you an overview of this vast, flat landscape of blanket bog, sprinkled with infinite lochans and streams and broken up occasionally by bare lumps of rock. You can also appreciate the sense of desolation in what is regularly cited as one of Britain's last wildernesses from the train window on the West Highland Line.

MEETING OF THE THREE WATERS

24.3 mi (39.1 km) from Tyndrum, 5.2 miles (8.4 km) from visitor center

A waterfall at the foot of the Three Sisters, where waters from three sources combine, tumbling (or thundering after heavy rainfall) down over rocks into a pool before joining Loch Achtriochtan. This beauty spot, sometimes called Glencoe Falls, was featured in the James Bond film *Skyfall*.

THREE SISTERS VIEWPOINT

25.2 mi (40.6 km) from Tyndrum, 4.3 miles (6.9 km) from visitor center

Just over a mile (1.6 km) past Loch Achtriochtan is the most popular viewing point of all—so popular there's one on the north side of the road and one on the south side (just as well as it's near a bend in the road). Technically three ridges of the same mountain, Bidean nam Bian, the peaks that form the Three Sisters are individually known as Gearr Aonach (Short Ridge), Aonach Dubh (Black Ridge), and Beinn Fhada (Long Hill). If you can, try to time your visit for early morning, when the mountain peaks will be bathed in sunlight.

LOCH ACHTRIOCHTAN

27.3 mi (43.9 km) from Tyndrum, 2.2 miles (3.5 km) from visitor center

This beautiful loch will be on your right as you drive south through Glen Coe from the village of Glencoe. There is a viewpoint with parking just after it, but if you take the left turn just before it, you'll reach the Clachaig Inn and the filming site of Hagrid's hut from the Harry Potter films.

GLENCOE

Glencoe village itself, on the shores of Loch Leven, is small but surprisingly well facilitated, with views of hills all around. It pretty much consists of a single road, with lots of modern housing at this far end, and older stone buildings the farther into the village you go. The 19th-century Scottish Episcopal **church** was built in the Gothic Revival style. Down a little turnoff from the village, you'll find a moving monument to those who lost their lives in the Massacre of Glencoe.

Sights
GLENCOE VISITOR CENTRE
Glencoe; tel. 01855 811 307; www.nts.org.uk/ visit/places/glencoe; 9:30am-5:30pm Mar.-Oct., 10am-4pm Nov.-Feb.; adult £6.50, concessions £5, family £16.50

While the Glen Coe landscape is obviously free to all, the Glencoe Visitor's Centre does incur a fee, but it offers a very moving introduction to the area and enables you to stand on the sites of the famous massacre as well as find out about the families who once lived here, and the wildlife often found in and around the glen. Plus, for a more immersive experience, you can join one of the **Land Rover Safaris** (from £20 per adult for a 1.5-hour tour) to explore the glen more fully. The Historical Land Rover Safari Tour (set dates each year; adult £25, child £15) takes 2.5 hours and takes you through some of the townships affected by the Massacre of Glencoe as well as a site overlooking the isles where the clan chief is buried.

GLENCOE WAR MEMORIAL
8 Upper Carnoch, Glencoe; free

Set away on a little side street in the little village of Glencoe, this monument to the people killed in the Massacre of Glencoe is very discreet and understated. Erected by a descendant of the MacIain clan in the 1880s when monuments to significant Scottish events and people were very fashionable, the memorial honors those who fell to the sword in this most heinous of crimes. A large stone slab at the bottom explains what it is there for, and includes a slender pillar with a Celtic cross on top.

To reach the monument, it's just a couple

Loch Achtriochtan

of minutes' walk from the village. Go past the Nisa shop with the shop on your left and then turn right after a couple of hundred yards up the lane signposted Upper Carnoch. You can also drive to it, but parking is scarce.

Food and Accommodations
CLACHAIG INN
Glencoe; tel. 01855 811 252; https://clachaig.com; food served 12pm-9pm; entrées £5.95, £100 d

In the heart of Glencoe is this local and tourist favorite, which gets its fair share of weary walkers in need of some sustenance. Food is decent and portions generous. Try the Highland game pie or the haggis, neeps, and tatties. The **Boots Bar** (round the back) is where you go for music, while locals head straight to the small bar next door to it behind an unmarked door. If you don't have kids, don't eat in the lounge—the atmosphere is much better elsewhere. Black Gold (a Scottish alternative to Guinness) is on tap, and there is a huge whisky list to work your way through.

You can book a night or two in one of the 23 bedrooms across the Ossian Wing (the older part of the building), the Bidean Wing (which has mountain views), or The Lodge (good for dog owners), all of which are well-priced. Plus, the Clachaig also manages 12 self-catering properties (from £725 a week for a cottage sleeping four) in and around Glencoe.

Information and Services
Glencoe village's good shop, **Nisa Local**

(Glencoe; tel. 01855 811 156; 8am-7pm Mon.-Thurs. and Sat., 8am-8pm Fri., 8am-6pm Sun.), has an ATM and all the essentials, whether you're staying in a nearby hotel or camping.

Getting There
Glencoe village is just half an hour from Fort William, traveling southwest along the shores of Loch Linnhe, before crossing over the bridge at North Ballachulish and east along the shores of Loch Leven (16 miles/26 km). There are buses between the two with **Shiel Buses** (no. N44; https://shielbuses.co.uk; daily; 40 minutes; £4.50 single).

From Loch Lomond, the drive up through Glen Coe is unforgettable. Head north out of the park along the A82 to Tyndrum, passing Bridge of Orchy, and then Loch Tulla on your left before coming to a huge hairpin bend and climbing up toward the Rannoch Moor, a boggy moorland landscape, and then bearing left into the glen itself. It's just 30 miles (48 km) but it will take around 45 minutes and you'll probably do most of it with your jaw hanging slack.

It is also possible to do the same journey by bus on the no. 914, 915, or 916 with Scottish Citylink (50 minutes from Tyndrum; £14.90 single). There are also regular buses between Fort William and the village of Glencoe with Shiel buses (no. N44; https://shielbuses.co.uk; 40 minutes, six buses per day; £4.50 single).

Fort William and Around

Say Fort William to most people, and there's one place that naturally springs to mind: Ben Nevis—a beast of a mountain that soars over the town and whose head is usually, quite literally, in the clouds.

But the highest peak in the British Isles is just one reason to visit this vast region that falls under the even larger area of Lochaber—an area of huge geographical interest. It is a place of natural contrasts where menacing mountains glower over serene lochs, and the thing it has above all else is space, miles and miles of it, with very few people cluttering it up. It is one great big playground for adventure sports, whether you want to ride a mountain gondola, go kayaking,

Fort William and Glencoe

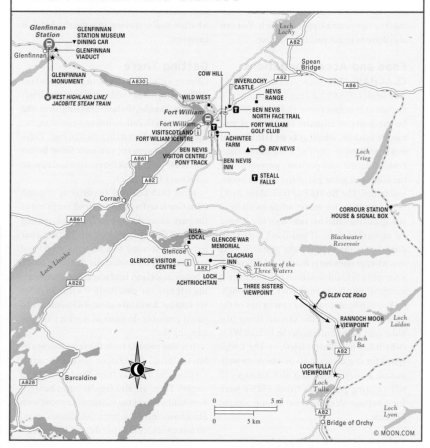

hill-walk to your heart's content, or even ski in winter.

While by no means Scotland's most appealing town, Fort William nevertheless serves as a gateway to those seeking adventure. There are signs it's getting better, with a very good local cinema, more local shops, and improved accommodations. Stock up on necessities here and remember that it's all about the great outdoors, so forgive them their overly tacky gift shops and disappointing modern buildings. It's the jumping off point for the famous Jacobite Steam train, and not far from the legendarily beautiful Glen Coe valley, to the south.

SIGHTS
Ben Nevis

Ben Nevis, Fort William; www.highlifehighland.com/bennevis

Ben Nevis is the highest mountain in the British Isles, and it's rare that you can see its peak—hence its nickname, "the mountain with its head in the clouds." Still, this king of the Grampian Mountains—a mountain range that covers a huge region of the Highlands and spreads southwest to northeast on the eastern side of the Great Glen—also called simply "Ben," is always looming, asking to be photographed. Ben Nevis stands 4,411 feet (1,345 m) above sea level and was once an active volcano that collapsed in on itself millions of years ago. Today the dominant mountain, which lords itself over Fort William and Loch Linnhe below, is a craggy, stern presence, where the hard lines in its rock face seem to dare you to test them.

For those who do make it to the rocky plateau of its summit, look for a cairn (a carefully positioned pile of stones), about 10 feet (3 m) high, which serves as an Ordnance Survey trig point, as well as the ruins of a Victorian observatory—which looks like a rather ramshackle shelter atop a mound of stones—that was once used to chart Scottish weather.

BEN NEVIS VISITOR CENTRE

Glen Nevis Road, Fort William; tel. 01349 781 401
If you're planning to hike or climb Ben Nevis, then you must pay a visit to the Ben Nevis Visitor Centre, which was completely refurbished in 2017. Stop in to check on the daily forecast specific to Ben Nevis, which is updated each morning at 9am. You can also stock up on last-minute snacks here, and it is the best place to park (£4 per car), as most

routes around or up the mountain start here. It can get very busy in summer, so the earlier you get here the better to nab a space, especially during events, such as the Three Peaks Challenge. If you're at all worried, ring the visitor center to see if you can book a car parking space.

SPORTS AND RECREATION

TOP EXPERIENCE

★ Climbing Ben Nevis

Though it is not quite as high as the Alpine mountains, Ben Nevis's high latitude means its summit, so frequently shrouded in mist, is also often capped in snow, thanks to the Arctic-like conditions. Don't be fooled by temperatures on ground level; if you are scaling Ben Nevis, you need to pack warm clothes, whatever the weather. You should also bring lots of water, food for the expedition, good walking boots, a compass, and a map. Make sure you fill out a mountain safety route card and leave it with someone trustworthy before you set off. Unless you are incredibly experienced, don't even consider doing the walk in winter.

hiking on Ben Nevis

WESTERN HIGHLANDS AND THE ISLE OF SKYE
FORT WILLIAM AND AROUND

PONY TRACK

Distance: *10.5 miles (17 km) round-trip*
Hiking time: *7-9 hours*
Trailhead: *Ben Nevis Visitor Centre*
Information and maps: *www.walkhighlands.*
co.uk/fortwilliam/bennevis.shtml

Most visitors who ascend to the summit of Ben Nevis use the Pony Track (erstwhile known as the Mountain Path), which sets off from the Ben Nevis Visitor Centre (also known as the Glen Nevis Visitor Centre) and begins with a steep climb on a track to Lochan Meall an t-Suidhe, which roughly marks the halfway point, before following a zigzag route to the top. This route is straightforward in the sense that there is a relatively clear path to the top. But it is strenuous with steep sections throughout and then stony and rough as you near the top. It is also sometimes possible for the path to disappear under snow, so you will need to be prepared to exercise some navigational skills. The visitor center has useful signs offering advice on how to approach this hike—read them. The route outlined by the Walk Highlands website is detailed and includes maps and GPS waypoints that you can download.

BEN NEVIS NORTH FACE TRAIL

Distance: *11 miles (17.5 km) round-trip*
Hiking Time: *10-11 hours*
Trailhead: *North Face Car Park, near Torlundy*
Information and Maps: *www.walkhighlands.*
co.uk/fortwilliam/carnmordeargarete.shtml

If you don't want to walk in the wake of millions of other tourists and you are a very experienced mountain walker, then this alternative route up the mighty mountain is worth considering. You need to come properly equipped (good boots, maps, compass, walking sticks, and ice-ax or crampons in winter) and be prepared for a lot of scrambling. Those who do come this way will view the graceful arc of the Càrn Mòr Dearg Arête, a curvaceous mountain ridge, which you'll need to traverse by scrambling.

To reach the trailhead, park at the North Face Car Park and walk along the track until you reach a barrier. The track will shortly turn to the left, and you follow the path to the right signposted for the North Face Trail. Continue ahead uphill and keep left at a fork in the trees. Follow the path as it climbs up and swings to the right before leveling out. Keep straight ahead when another path joins, and soon you'll reach the edge of a forest. Carry on left along the path and look out for a sign to the right for "Allt a' Mhuillin and CIC Hut." Take this and keep on the path before joining a track. When you come to the junction, turn right and Ben Nevis will be in front of you.

From now on you will be walking toward the north face of Ben Nevis. Cross a stile and follow the path. Eventually, there will be a boggy path to the left; take this path to begin your ascent to Càrn Mòr Dearg, the first of two Munros you will scale today. The higher you go, the more dramatic the views, and you'll be able to see the many crevices and gullies of Ben Nevis. You'll now climb on to the ridge of Carn Deag Meadhonach and see the pointed peak of Càrn Mòr Dearg. Next, you'll descend slightly to the crest of Càrn Mòr Dearg, which involves some scrambling, not too precipitous, though you will want to concentrate and try not to get too distracted by the awesome view beneath Ben Nevis's cliffs. Once across the ridge, it's a steep climb over boulders and scree to the summit. Your route down should follow the Pony Track.

Tours and Mountain Guides

If you're not confident enough to attempt Ben Nevis yourself—and there's absolutely no shame in that—then there are some very good mountain guides who can take you there.

ADVENTURE NEVIS

3 Bracara, Morar; tel. 01687 460 163; www.
adventurenevis.com; year-round, check website
for organized tour dates; group tours from £70,
Mountain Path from £200 per day for two, North
Face Trail £220 for two

This outfit, run by experienced hill-walker Peter Khambatta—he has walked the Scottish hills for over 20 years and is a Munro completist himself—will take you on guided tours along either the Pony Track or the North Face Trail. You can choose to join a small group, or book Peter or one of his trusted guides to yourself. As well as telling you a little about the history of the area and pointing out geographical features you might otherwise overlook, your guide will also teach you how to read a map and navigate so you might have more confidence to go it alone in future.

WILD ROOTS HIGHLAND GUIDING

Various locations; tel. 07720 398 642; https:// wildrootsguiding.scot; year-round; group journeys from £50 per person, private bookings £160 for 1 person, £220 for 2-3 people

These guided walks run by genuine enthusiast and expert Anna Danby are a breath of fresh air. Rather than lead you up mountains while you exert yourself for the sake of it, Anna prefers to adopt a slower approach to guiding, where you walk a little, stop for a chat, maybe read some poetry, and hear stories about the lifestyles of people that once lived in the area, as well as the area's geology. I did a storytelling wander of some of Ben Nevis's north face with Anna and loved it.

Other Hikes
STEALL FALLS

Hiking Distance: *2.3 miles (3.5 km)*
Hiking Time: *1.5-2 hours*
Trailhead: *Ben Nevis Car Park, Glen Nevis Road*
Information and Maps: *www.walkhighlands. co.uk/fortwilliam/steallfalls.shtml*

This brilliant short walk covers just 2.3 miles (3.5 km) and takes you through Nevis Gorge before arriving at Steall Falls. The path is clear and well-marked throughout, though you should be prepared for some steep drops and rough track underfoot. Park at the Ben Nevis car park at the end of Glen Nevis and look for the path at the far end of the car park, which is signposted to Spean Bridge, Corrour Station, and Kinlochleven. Allow 1.5-2 hours for the round-trip journey (once you reach the falls

return to the car park by the same route). It's a wild walk along a rocky gorge, where you will see glimpses of the river below through gaps in the trees before crossing a grassy meadow to view the waterfalls, above which rises the Munro of An Gearanach.

Golf
FORT WILLIAM GOLF CLUB

North Road, Fort William; tel. 01397 704 464; http:// fortwilliamgolfclub.com; 9am-5pm Mon., 9am-10pm Tues. and Thurs., 9am-6pm Weds., 9am-7pm Fri., 8am-8pm Sat.-Sun.; green fees Mar.-Oct. £30 per player for 18 holes, £15 for nine holes, Oct.-late Feb. £15 per round

There are few more spectacular backdrops to a few rounds than here, in the majestic mountainous region of Fort William. A relatively new course by Scottish standards, this 18-hole course at the base of Ben Nevis only opened in 1976 and has a more relaxed approach than most, but don't be too sloppy—jeans and sports colors won't be tolerated. Visitors are always welcome, though prior booking is essential, and to avoid crowding please don't arrive more than 15 minutes before your allotted time.

Cycling and Mountain Biking
COW HILL

Distance: *7.5 miles (12.1 km)*
Time: *1-2 hours*
Trailhead: *Braveheart Car Park, Glen Nevis*
Information and Maps: *www.ridefortwilliam. co.uk*

This light woodland, where crofters' cows once grazed, is now home to a herd of Highland cattle and is a lovely place for an afternoon's cycle. Setting off from Braveheart Car Park, the route, which suits intermediate and advanced cyclists, includes a little road cycling at first before you reach Cow Hill, where there's a steep climb. But persevere and you'll be afforded amazing views of Fort William. The good news is that the way back is pretty much all downhill.

NEVIS CYCLES

Lochy Crescent, Inverlochy; tel. 01397 705 555; www. neviscycles.com; 9am-5:30pm daily; from £35 per day, £160 per week

This well-facilitated bike-hire company offers full-suspension enduro bikes good for rougher tracks, road and touring bikes, cross-country bikes for adventure cyclists, and a good selection of electric bikes and downhill two-wheelers too. Kids' bikes and child's seats are also available, and there is an option for one-way bike collection if you're planning a long-distance route. Bikes come with helmets, pumps, water bottles, tire levers, and a spare tube. If you're not sure what the best bike is for your trip, ask staff and they'll be able to advise you. The company also runs a hire shop from the Nevis Range mountain gondola station from late March through October.

Winter Sports
NEVIS RANGE

Torlundy, Fort William; tel. 01397 705 825; ski passes £35.50 adult, £23.50 child 5-17; lessons £31 for a two-hour group session, £65 per hour private lesson for two, equipment hire £24.50 per day and £18.50 child

Enjoy skiing and snowboarding on the slopes of Aonach Mòr, Scotland's highest snow sports destination, from December through April (snow depending) with runs ranging from beginner-level to off-piste. Book lessons (either as part of a group or privately for up to two people) to give you the confidence to enjoy the slopes, or simply hire equipment and get ski passes if you have prior experience. The summit of Ben Nevis peering over the top of the neighboring mountains is an incredible backdrop to a day on the slopes.

Wildlife Safaris
WILD WEST

9 MacKay Crescent, Caol, Fort William; tel. 0333 123 2820; www.wildwest.scot; year-round; Big Five Safari adult £69, child £42, Big Five with cruise adult £85, child £50

These eight-hour tours take you into wild landscapes not far from Fort William where you can hopefully see Scotland's "big five" (golden eagles, harbor seals, otters, red deer, and red squirrels). They also furnish you with practical tips on how best to spot wildlife on your own. Guide Ian McLeod also offers half-day excursions and can create custom itineraries.

FOOD
BEN NEVIS INN

Claggan, Achintee, Fort William; tel. 01397 701 227; www.ben-nevis-inn.co.uk; food served 12pm-9pm daily Mar.-Oct. and Thurs.-Sun. winter (closed Nov.); entrées £5.95

Known as the "wee inn at the foot of the Ben," this is where walkers of Ben Nevis come after their trek. It's the kind of place where you won't feel bad tracking in a bit of mud, and the food is suitably hearty, with pub staples such as burgers, fish-and-chips, and more unusual-sounding dishes such as chicken and haggis rumbledethumps. There's a good choice of vegetarian dishes, too.

★ CRANNOG

Town Pier, Fort William; tel. 01397 705 589; www. crannog.net; lunch 12pm-2:30pm daily, evening meals 6pm-9:30pm; entrées £7.95

Set just by the town pier in Fort William, this red-roofed building (once a bait shed) has been providing top-notch Scottish seafood for over 26 years. The menu changes each season, but you can expect the likes of west coast mussels and peppered salmon fillet.

ACCOMMODATIONS
ACHINTEE FARM

Glen Nevis; tel. 01397 702 240; http://achinteefarm. com; £80 self-catering apartment, £110 d

Self-catering rooms on this farm at the foot of Ben Nevis are basic, but they are very cheap too. You'll have to make your own breakfast, but there's a shop a mile (1.6 km) away and the Ben Nevis Inn is very near for dinner. The farm has the charming Shepherds Cottage for hire (sleeps two, £550 per week), plus three B&B rooms in the farmhouse, which are available mid-May-early October.

INVERLOCHY CASTLE

Torlundy, Fort William; tel. 01397 702 177; https:// inverlochycastlehotel.com; £595 d

This beautiful country house hotel in a 19th-century castle surrounded by acres of greenery is a must for royal fans. Queen Victoria stopped here in 1873 en route to Balmoral and was enamored by her surroundings. Each of the 17 rooms and suites, including the one Victoria stayed in, has views of the grounds or loch and is luxuriously appointed. The **Michel Roux Jr. restaurant** is a great place to celebrate a special occasion (three-course set menus £67, men should pack a dinner jacket).

INFORMATION AND SERVICES

Fort William's **VisitScotland iCentre** is in the center of town (15 High Street; tel. 01397 701 801) and can advise on places to stay, bus tickets, cruises, and local activities. For tips on walking in the area, the **Ben Nevis Visitor Centre** (Glen Nevis; tel. 01349 781 401) offers useful maps and the local weather forecast—essential if you're planning to climb Ben Nevis.

GETTING THERE
By Car

From Inverness, Fort William is a 66-mile (106-km) drive south along the A82, with a journey time of around 1.75 hours. From Glasgow it's a 108-mile (174-km) drive north to Fort William pretty much all the way along the A82, which should take about 2.5 hours. From Edinburgh, the drive takes just over three hours (132 miles/212 km). Take the M9 to Stirling to join the A84 into Loch Lomond and the Trossachs National Park as far as Lochearnhead, before turning left onto the A85 and following this west to Crianlarich, where you can take the A82 to Fort William (from Loch Lomond, the trip takes just 1.25 hours).

By Bus

From Inverness you can take the no. 919 bus, with **Stagecoach** (www.stagecoachbus.com; two hours, two per day Mon.-Sat. one per day Sun.; £10.40 one-way). **Shiel Buses** runs the no. 513 (N19) from Inverness to Fort William (https://shielbuses.co.uk; two hours, two per day Mon.-Fri., one per day Sat.; £10.40 one-way). From Glasgow, the no. 914, 915, and 916 with **Scottish Citylink** (www.citylink.co.uk; four per day; £18.70 one-way) takes 3.25 hours to reach Fort William from Buchanan Street Bus Station.

By Train

Many visitors arrive at **Fort William Station** (Tom-na-Faire, Station Square) on the overnight **Caledonian Sleeper train.** One train sets off each night from London (except Saturday) and gets into Fort William in the morning (12.75 hours; £50 one-way, £185 with cabin). There are around four direct trains with **ScotRail** (www.scotrail.co.uk) from Glasgow Queen Street each day (3.5 hours; £13.90 each way). Trains from Edinburgh and Inverness change in Glasgow. From Fort William, it's possible to board the last leg of the famed West Highland Line for Mallaig and the Isle of Skye beyond.

GETTING AROUND

Once here, the best way to get around is by car, on foot, or by bike. There are some **local bus and coach services** (www.lochabertransport.org.uk) but they are infrequent and are generally used to connect Fort William with other towns and villages, such as Glencoe.

Of course, if you've arrived by public transport and want to hire a car, that's possible too. **Practical Car & Van Rental** (www.practical.co.uk/locations/england/scotland/fortwilliam) will meet you at the train or bus station with your chosen vehicle.

Fort William to Mallaig

This route, from the outdoor activity mecca of Fort William to one of the main entry points to the Isle of Skye, is best enjoyed on the West Highland railway line, particularly in summer when the journey can be made aboard a steam train—the one that stars as the *Hogwarts Express* in the Harry Potter series no less. You can also drive this section in around an hour along a route that takes you through what were once among the most isolated townships of Scotland, fringed with omnipresent hills and thick woodland inland, and with unbroken views across to the Small Isles along the coastal stretch.

★ WEST HIGHLAND LINE/JACOBITE STEAM TRAIN

Fort William train station, Tom-na-Faire, Station Square, Fort William; tel. 0344 811 0141; www. scotrail.co.uk; four trains per day Mon.-Sat., one on Sun.; from £15.30 return; Jacobite Steam Train tel. 01524 732 100; www.westcoastrailways.co.uk/ jacobite/jacobite-steam-train-details.cfm; morning service 10:15am and afternoon service 2:30pm late Apr.-late Oct.; adult £31.75 one-way, child £18.75 one-way

Often described as one of the greatest railway journeys in the world, where cinematic backdrops reveal themselves one after another, the West Highland Line is a journey you'll want a window seat for. Look out for red deer, often camouflaged on the mountainsides. In the summer, you can opt to continue traveling the final section, from Fort William to Mallaig, on the diesel train that departs from Glasgow, or disembark at Fort William and do the remainder of the journey on the Jacobite Steam Train. The former is much cheaper (5 hours 20 minutes for the whole journey; £38.60 single); as for the latter, you'll need to first pay to get the train from Glasgow to Fort William (£33.20 single) and then pay to get the Jacobite Steam Train connection (at least another £49

on top), and it will take longer, as you will have to wait for the connection and allow for the slower steam train. However, having done the journey both ways, I must admit, the steam train is special.

From Fort William

The most obvious and most traveled route from Fort William to Mallaig, departure point for the Isle of Skye, is along the West Highland Line; passengers on the Caledonian Sleeper train from London can join this section of the line at Fort William. Trains run four times a day (once on Sundays) and take 1.5 hours (from £7.20 one-way).

Position yourself on the left-hand side of the train as it departs Fort William (ideally by one of the doors) for the best views of the famous **Glenfinnan Viaduct** crossing, and the **Glenfinnan Monument**, which overlooks **Loch Shiel**, whose shores are guarded by imposing mountains. The train will stop here for a while, giving you time to visit the station museum. When the journey resumes, you'll pass **Loch Eilt**, yet another setting for the *Harry Potter* movies. Look out to sea as you approach **Arisaig;** on a clear day the Small Isles should come into view. There are stunning sea views as the line rounds the coast toward Mallaig and **Loch Morar**—the deepest loch in the whole of Scotland, which appears to the right shortly before you reach your destination.

From Glasgow

To fully appreciate the scenery along the West Highland Line, though, you should catch the train from the start of the route in Glasgow (5 hours 20 minutes; £38.60 one-way), and gawp as the train skirts the glimmering

1: view from the West Highland Line near Fort William **2:** Glenfinnan Monument **3:** West Highland Line

Harry Potter Film Locations

While any bona fide Harry Potter fan will no doubt hot-foot it to platform 9 ¾ at London's King's Cross, there is no shortage of Harry Potter filming locations right here in Scotland too.

THE BRIDGE TO HOGWARTS

Perhaps the most famous Harry Potter-related sight is the **Glenfinnan Viaduct,** known as the Bridge to Hogwarts, which the *Hogwarts Express* crosses in *Harry Potter and the Chamber of Secrets* (when Harry and Ron narrowly miss a collision with it in their flying car). The best way to see it is aboard the **Jacobite Steam Train.**

NATURAL SETTINGS

If **Loch Shiel** looks familiar, it may be because it (as well as **Loch Morar,** close to Mallaig) is often used to represent Hogwarts Lake in the films.

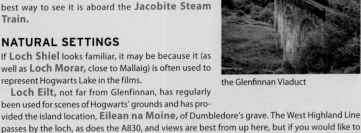

the Glenfinnan Viaduct

Loch Eilt, not far from Glenfinnan, has regularly been used for scenes of Hogwarts' grounds and has provided the island location, **Eilean na Moine,** of Dumbledore's grave. The West Highland Line passes by the loch, as does the A830, and views are best from up here, but if you would like to stand on the shoreline, it's just a 10-minute walk from the roadside, or 30 minutes from Lochailort train station.

The dramatic mountains and valleys of **Glen Coe** have frequently provided backdrops in the films; most memorably, it was opposite the **Clachaig Inn** that Hagrid's Hut was placed in the spring of 2003 for filming of *Harry Potter and the Prisoner of Azkaban.*

---

lochs of **Loch Lomond and the Trossachs National Park** (page 290) and travels past the eye-catching lumpy mountain peak of Ben Arthur, known as the Cobbler (stops near Loch Lomond include Arrochar and Ardlui), before chugging all the way up to Rannoch Moor and on to Fort William.

Before you reach Fort William, **Corrour Station House & Signal Box** (Corrour Station, near Loch Ossian; tel. 01397 732 236; www.corrour.co.uk/station-house; closed Nov.-Mar.; £110 d) is a brilliant stop-off for those who are traveling the West Highland Line and want to pause awhile to take it all in. The Station House restaurant proudly calls itself the most remote restaurant in Scotland, as it is only accessible by those disembarking the train at Corrour Station or anyone willing to walk a very long way to get here (entrees

£7). It's worth it, though: a roaring fire awaits as does homemade food, and the three double rooms in the old signal box (right on the tracks) are cozy; plus, guests can enjoy panoramic views from the sitting room in the old lookout tower.

Tickets

Standard diesel trains have toilets but few other amenities. First-class tickets on the Jacobite Steam Train (adult £59.95 round-trip, child £32.90 round-trip) come with tea and coffee, and there are options for afternoon tea and a cheese board. The best seats are either the private tables for two on the left-hand side in Carriage A or in the "Harry Potter" seats in Carriage D, in vintage compartments that seat six (you'll need a first-class ticket for both these options). However, there is no each-way option for first-class (you need to book a return ticket), so if you want the luxury of first-class and the choice of seats but plan to travel on to Skye, you will need to forfeit your return ticket.

If you are not headed to the Isle of Skye, you can complete the 84-mile (135-km) round-trip from Fort William to Mallaig and back in a day.

GLENFINNAN AND LOCH SHIEL

By raising his father's standard at Glenfinnan, which fired the '45 Jacobite Rising, Bonnie Prince Charlie assured this small settlement on the shores of Loch Shiel's legendary status. It's just as well that he chose such a beautiful backdrop, with the blue loch flanked by lush mountains, an undeniable artist's muse. In 1815, the Glenfinnan Monument, in remembrance of all those clanspeople who lost their lives in the rising, was erected, and then in 1898 the Glenfinnan Viaduct, a mighty curved structure with 21 arches, added another focal point. More recently, of course, it was a choice of location in the Harry Potter films, attracting a never-ending stream of visitors.

Once you alight at Glenfinnan, be sure to pop into the Dining Car at the **Glenfinnan Station Museum** (Station Road; tel. 397 722 295; www.glenfinnanstationmuseum.co.uk; 9am-5pm Mon.-Sat., 10am-5pm Sun.; free), which has a good selection of tea and cakes with an old-school, golden age of train travel feel.

Sights
GLENFINNAN MONUMENT
Glenfinnan; tel. 01397 722 250; www.nts.org.uk/ visit/places/glenfinnan-monument; 10am-4pm daily Nov.-Feb., 9am-6pm daily Mar.-June, 9am-7pm daily July-Aug., 9:30am-6pm daily Sept.-Oct.; adult £3.50, concessions £2.50, family £9

Standing on the banks of Loch Shiel, the Glenfinnan Monument is a poignant tribute to the moment Bonnie Prince Charlie arrived in Scotland in 1745, raising his standard to launch a rebellion that came close to overthrowing the monarchy. The monument stands 15 feet (18 m) high and features a lone kilted clansman on top—a reminder of all those who lost their lives in the ensuing rebellion, fighting for the Jacobite cause.

A good exhibition in the **Glenfinnan Visitor Centre** tells the story of the '45 rebellion, or you can join one of the guided tours to the top of the monument (included in the visitor center price and available when there is staff); in winter you will need to ring ahead to book. It's 62 steps to the top (with no disabled access unfortunately), and there is a narrow hatch to pass through, but if you can manage it, the views of Loch Shiel and its surrounds, including the **Glenfinnan Viaduct,** are amazing. Be warned, the monument and car park can be saturated with Harry Potter fanatics in summer due to the viaduct's starring role in the movies, so if you are coming here to absorb the history, it's best visited out of season.

GLENFINNAN VIADUCT
Glenfinnan; open 24 hours; free

This 21-arched viaduct with a span of 1,000 feet (300 m), which carries trains on the West Highland Line (including the Jacobite Steam Train), is a feat of engineering but is better known as the location for filming scenes of the "train to Hogwarts" in the Harry Potter movies. Today, many people come to visit the **Glenfinnan Viaduct viewpoint,** a half-mile (0.8-km; 15-minute) walk from the Glenfinnan Station Museum, to catch a picture of the Jacobite Steam Train as it passes by.

Food
GLENFINNAN STATION MUSEUM DINING CAR
Station Cottage; tel. 01397 733 300; https:// glenfinnanstationmuseum.co.uk; 9am-4:30pm Mon.-Sat., 10am-4:30pm Sun. May-Oct., evening meals sometimes available; sandwiches £6.60, cakes £2.80

This sweet little restaurant in an old railway carriage harks back to the Golden Age of travel of the late 19th and early 20th centuries. The menu includes toasted sandwiches served with salad or coleslaw, homemade soup, or traditional cakes and treats, such as all-butter shortbread and fruit cake.

Getting There

Glenfinnan is just a 25-minute drive from Fort William along the A830 (17 miles/27 km). You can also travel between the two by diesel train in just over half an hour with Scotrail (www.scotrail.co.uk; £7.20).

MALLAIG

Mallaig is a busy fishing and ferry port that's a great place to catch your breath before you venture out to Skye.

Food
CORNERSTONE RESTAURANT

Main Street; tel. 01687 462 306; https:// seafoodrestaurantmallaig.com; 12pm-2:45pm and 4:45pm-9pm daily mid-Mar.-Sept., opening times may shorten out of season; entrées £6.95

At this seafood restaurant you can tuck into freshly landed prawns, langoustines, mussels, and salmon while enjoying harbor views.

Entrées are well-priced, with good-sized portions—if you're starving, go for the excellent fish and chips. The restaurant fills up quickly when the Jacobite Steam train comes in, so you'd be wise to book ahead.

Information and Services

Pop into the **Mallaig Heritage Centre** (Station Road, Mallaig; 11am-4pm late Mar.-June and mid-Sept.-Oct., 11am-6pm July-mid-Sept.; adults £2.50, kids free) for a local history lesson.

Getting There

Mallaig is just an hour from Fort William (43 miles/69 km), a beautiful drive west along the A830, through Glenfinnan, curving north along the coastline of the Morar peninsula. The train from Fort William to Mallaig takes around an hour and 25 minutes and costs from £14 each way. It's just a 2-minute walk from the **train station** to the **ferry port** in Mallaig. If you arrive in Mallaig by train but would like a rental car to navigate Skye, **Morar Motors** (tel. 01599 534 329; www.morarmotors.co.uk) will deliver it to the ferry port for you.

Isle of Skye

On everyone's favorite island, the drama of the landscape—all jagged peaks and pinnacles, where shimmering lochs and pools are hidden high up in mountain ranges amid secret gullies—seems otherworldly, impossible even. Skye has fired imaginations for generation after generation, with tales of fairies, sprites, and kelpies passed down through folklore to help explain the unexplainable. It's home to Britain's most magnificent mountain range, which covers much of the center of the island, including the taller, sharper, formidable main Cuillin Ridge to the west known as the Black Cuillin, and the slightly more rounded slopes of the Red Cuillin to the east of Glen

Sligachan. It is now also home to some of the best stargazing spots in the British Isles.

Headlines regularly purport overtourism on the island, but you'd be silly to fall for the lie that Skye is busy. Yes, if you want to visit the same five or six sights (the Quiraing, the Old Man of Storr, Fairy Pools, etc.) as everyone else, then you will find yourself admiring beauty spots surrounded by strangers, but it really doesn't take much to find peace and serenity here. Especially given the devastating impact the COVID-19 crisis has had on tourism, it's a good idea to try to map out your own unique journey, taking in other parts of the isle that are equally special.

Isle of Skye

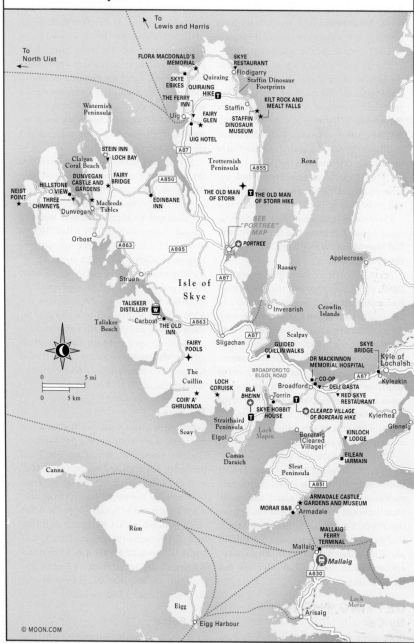

To Lewis and Harris

To North Uist

FLORA MACDONALD'S MEMORIAL

SKYE RESTAURANT
Flodigarry

SKYE EBIKES

Quiraing

QUIRAING HIKE

Staffin Dinosaur Footprints

THE FERRY INN

Uig

FAIRY GLEN

Staffin

KILT ROCK AND MEALT FALLS

STAFFIN DINOSAUR MUSEUM

UIG HOTEL

A87

Waternish Peninsula

Trotternish Peninsula

Rona

A855

STEIN INN
LOCH BAY

Claigan Coral Beach

FAIRY BRIDGE

DUNVEGAN CASTLE AND GARDENS

A850

EDINBANE INN

THE OLD MAN OF STORR

THE OLD MAN OF STORR HIKE

NEIST POINT

HILLSTONE VIEW

THREE CHIMNEYS

Macleods Tables

Dunvegan

Orbost

A863

A885

SEE "PORTREE" MAP

PORTREE

Applecross

Struan

Isle of Skye

A87

Raasay

TALISKER DISTILLERY

Carbost

THE OLD INN

Talisker Beach

A863

Inverarish

Crowlin Islands

FAIRY POOLS

Sligachan

A87

Scalpay

GUIDED CUILLIN WALKS

SKYE BRIDGE

DR MACKINNON MEMORIAL HOSPITAL

Kyle of Lochalsh

The Cuillin

LOCH CORUISK

BROADFORD TO ELGOL ROAD

CO-OP

A87

Kyleakin

0   5 mi
0   5 km

COIR' A' GHRUNNDA

BLÀ BHEINN

SKYE HOBBIT HOUSE

Torrin

DELI GASTA

Broadford

RED SKYE RESTAURANT

Kylerhea

Straithaird Peninsula

CLEARED VILLAGE OF BORERAIG HIKE

Glenelg

Soay

Elgol

Loch Slapin

Boreraig (Cleared Village)

KINLOCH LODGE

EILEAN IARMAIN

Camas Daraich

Sleat Peninsula

A851

Canna

ARMADALE CASTLE, GARDENS AND MUSEUM

MORAR B&B

Armadale

MALLAIG FERRY TERMINAL

Rùm

Mallaig

Mallaig

A830

Eigg

Arisaig

Loch Morar

Eigg Harbour

© MOON.COM

ORIENTATION

Most visitors to Skye arrive at either **Armadale** in the southwest of the island on the **Sleat Peninsula,** via the ferry from Mallaig, or **Kyleakin** in the southeast, via Kyle of Lochalsh and the Skye Bridge.

The island's main town is **Portree,** at the bottom of the protruding **Trotternish Peninsula** on the north of the isle. This pretty harbor town, where colorful houses line the quayside, is the main base for tour providers and getting provisions. To reach Portree you'll join the A87, the busiest of a handful of main roads that connects the corners of the isle. The A87 passes through **Broadford,** another relatively large town with a supermarket and petrol station. The Trotternish Peninsula is where you will find some of Skye's most famous sights, including **the Quiraing, the Old Man of Storr, Fairy Glen,** and **Staffin's dinosaur beach.**

West of Portree, the A850 meets the B886, which turns toward the **Waternish peninsula** on northwest Skye, or you can continue to **Dunvegan Castle.** Farther west, taking the B884 via the A863 will bring you to **Neist Point,** the island's most westerly spot. On the west coast of the Trotternish peninsula, in northern Skye, lies the settlement of **Uig** from where you can catch the ferry to Lewis and Harris and North Uist, both in the Outer Hebrides, from the Uig Ferry Terminal. Uig is a 25-minute (16-mile/26-km) drive north of Portree on the A87.

While north Skye may get the most visitors, the terrain of the south is much gentler and more fertile than the melodramatic bare rock of other parts of the island, and on the Sleat Peninsula you can find space away from the crowds. It's in the center of Skye that you'll find its best assets—the monumental **Cuillin** peaks. Glen Sligachan acts as a natural boundary between the Black Cuillin in the west and the Red Cuillin in the east.

GETTING THERE
By Car

Once only accessible by a ferry crossing from Kyle of Lochalsh, today Skye is one of the easiest islands to get to by car due to the Kyle of Lochalsh bridge, which opened in 1995 and links the mainland to Kyleakin in the south of the Isle of Skye. Just 10 miles (16 km) west of Dornie on the A87, the bridge, which takes just five minutes to cross and has no toll, has made it much easier for islanders to head to the mainland for work; it's also encouraged a whole wave of day-trippers who try to tick off as many of the most famous sights and destinations as possible in 12 hours or so, which I really don't recommend.

Skye is around two hours from Inverness (81 miles/130 km) along the A82 and then A87, or via the route of the Kyle railway line along the A835, the A832, and the A890 (similar time and distance). From Fort William, it's just under two hours (74 miles/119 km) to Kyle of Lochalsh; follow the A82 north to Invergarry where you can pick up the A87 all the way west to Kyle of Lochalsh and simply drive over the bridge. Most people driving from Fort William simply follow the A830 west to Mallaig (43 miles/69 km) for about an hour and get the ferry from there to Armadale. From Edinburgh it's a four-hour drive to Mallaig (185 miles/298 km), and from Glasgow it's a three-and-a-half-hour drive to Mallaig (150 miles/241 km).

By Bus

Citylink (www.citylink.co.uk) runs a few bus services per day to Portree on Skye from Glasgow (buses no. 915 or no. 916 from Buchanan Bus Station; 7 hours; £44.30 one-way) and Inverness (direct bus no. 917 from Inverness Bus Station; 3.5 hours; £26.40 one-way). Tickets can be bought from the ticket office at the bus station, but spaces do fill up, so book a seat online in advance. From Kyle of Lochalsh, bus numbers 917 (twice a day) and 915 (once a day) set off from the harbor slipway (near the Seaprobe Atlantis office) over the bridge (1 hour; £7.50 one-way).

By Ferry

By far the most utilized ferry crossing to Skye

is from **Mallaig,** where the West Highland railway line ends. Ferries with **CalMac** (www.calmac.co.uk) depart several times a day (roughly every hour). The crossing to Armadale in south Skye takes 45 minutes (£3 each way for a foot passenger, plus £9.95 one-way for a car).

The **Glenelg Ferry crossing** (Easter-Oct.), a small independent operation, is considered more scenic, and is much shorter than the one from Mallaig. If you do opt for this route, you're in for a treat as you'll get to ride on Scotland's last manually operated turntable ferry. This ferry route operates every 20 minutes or so (as much as it's needed) 10am-6pm daily April-May and September-October, and 10am-7pm June-August. It costs £15 one-way for a car with up to four people. The crossing takes mere minutes and lands in Kylerhea, just a few miles south of Kyleakin on Skye. To reach Glenelg, turn off the main road from Invermoriston to Kyle of Lochalsh (the A87) at Shiel Bridge and follow the Old Military Road for 9 miles (14 km). From Fort William, it's just an hour's drive to Mallaig, for the ferry to Skye (43 miles/69 km). From Inverness, you're most likely to want to cross the Skye Bridge, but if the romance of a ferry really grabs you, then you could get to Glenelg in 1 hour 45 minutes (73 miles/117 km).

GETTING AROUND

At 639 square miles (1,656 square km), Skye may not sound huge, but, with much of the rocky landscape not navigable to road vehicles and just a clutch of main roads, it can take a long time to get from A to B. Because you'll be astounded at the landscape as you drive (particularly when you get off the main thoroughfares, which will keep you occupied), it's not a place to rush.

By Car

To see as much of the island as possible, get off the beaten track, and travel at your own pace, you need a car. It's a joy to turn off the main roads onto a narrow, single-track road, where there will be far fewer cars, but plenty of sheep to keep you company. There are only a few main roads on Skye, the **A87,** which travels from near Kyleakin (across the Skye Bridge) to Portree being the busiest. At times it can get clogged up and drivers sometimes will go faster than you are comfortable with. In cases like these, stick to a safe speed and be prepared to pull into a viewpoint or other layby if you need to, to let people past. In autumn and

Armadale ferry terminal

winter, the roads can also be icy, so you will need to consider this, especially when navigating twisting sections of road.

You'll need a map—the *Scotland Visitors' Atlas & Guide A-Z* is good—and get into the habit of filling up the tank when you see a petrol station, because you never know when you might see one again. If you didn't travel to the Isle of Skye with a car, you can rent one from **Morrison Car Hire** (Dunvegan Road, Portree; www.morrisoncarrental.com). If you're arriving as a foot passenger on the ferry from Mallaig, you can hire a car from DriveSkye (Armadale; www.driveskye.com), which is within walking distance of the ferry port.

By Bus

Sporadic bus service is operated by **Stagecoach** (www.stagecoachbus.com), and in theory it's possible to travel the island this way, as bus connections do link all the main towns and villages. The no. 52 bus links the two main towns of Broadford and Portree with the ferry terminal at Armadale (£4.20 from Armadale to Broadford; £7.70 from Armadale to Portree). If you are planning to get more than one bus in a day, a Day Rider ticket at £9.20 will save you money and can be bought on board or through the Stagecoach app.

By Taxi

If you want to pop out for dinner or even arrange a bit of a whistle-stop tour of some of the main attractions, then **Gus's Taxis** (tel. 01478 613 000; https://skye-taxis.co.uk) based in Portree can arrange either lifts or more bespoke tours. The fleet of five minicabs can also collect you from the ferry port in Armadale or at the Kyle of Lochalsh train station and bring you over to the island.

Tours

SKYE JEEP TOURS

Pickup in Broadford or Portree; tel. 01599 522 270 or 07976 238 862; https://skyejeeptours.com;

seven-hour tour £225, £75 per person if booking for three

On these road trips aboard a vintage jeep, your driver (usually one half of husband-and-wife team Lynne and Sam) will take you pretty much wherever you want—from the famous sights to a more in-depth exploration of lesser-known places, all while entertaining you with stories, legends, and memories. Tours are limited to three passengers in the vintage jeep and Wrangler, and four in the Cherokee. Tours last a minimum of seven hours, and they will pick you up from either Broadford or Portree. Occasionally, you'll be joined on board by the couple's friendly (and well-behaved) half lab half border collie, Brymer. For the truly adventurous, you can stay in the couple's military pod, Boris, for £66 per night with a minimum stay of two nights.

SKYE ADVENTURE

Pickup in Portree or Sligachan; tel. 07785 962 391 or 07818 884 609; www.skyeadventure.co.uk; from £57

Tours range from Munro-bagging, traversing the Cuillin Ridge, or gorge walking—think scrambling, climbing, and swimming in crystal-clear pools, and jumping and sliding down amazing waterfalls. Guides pick you up from Portree or Sligachan and provide all equipment (including wetsuits). Tours are adapted to match your ability.

SKYE HIGH WILDLIFE

Pickup from hotel on Skye; tel. 01471 855 643 or 07809 580 253; http://skyehighwildlife.com; half day £60 per person, full day £120 per person

Professional photographer Stewart Dawber takes guests off road on his wildlife photography courses, to some of the most remote parts of the island. With Stewart's expertise in tracking wildlife, as well as a lot of patience, you'll be able to get up close to pine martens, otters, red deer, and Highland cows, and take photos worthy of a magazine cover (bring your own camera). Each course is tailor-made, and Stewart will pick you up from your accommodation. Tours are offered year-round; in winter Stewart will even take you to an out-of-the-way bothy for lunch cooked on a wood burner and some local whiskies.

SKYEFARI

Pickup from hotel; tel. 07871 463 755; www.skyefari. com; £90-3,150 per person

If you want to see Skye's "big five" when it comes to wildlife (otters, red deer, golden eagles, sea eagles, and seals), then your best chance is to go to the places where no one else goes. David Lambie, owner and wildlife guide at Skyefari, knows these places better than most and he has permission to use private tracks to reach places normally out of bounds—I also saw an elusive pine marten on my trip. Tours can take place at night, during the day, or he'll plan a bespoke trip for you. He's also good fun and very easy to follow, plus he has top-notch gear from the likes of Swarovski Optic to help aid your search. David has also partnered with the Sonas Collection, so anyone staying at any of its hotels (Duisdale, Skeabost, etc.) gets special deals.

ARMADALE AND SOUTH SKYE

Fools are they who discount the south of Skye—in particular, the **Sleat Peninsula**—and roar through it when they get off the ferry at Armadale from Mallaig, determined to reach Portree and the Trotternish. Known as the "garden of Skye," it's much greener than most of the isle, with its rocky shoreline punctuated with pretty meadows of wildflowers, forests, lonely beaches, and heather-clad hills. There's a slower air about the place, mainly because it gets far fewer visitors, and there's not a lot to do here other than sit and listen to the birds, take bracing walks, learn some Gaelic, or watch out for otters or seals, but that's half the appeal.

Armadale Castle is worth an afternoon of your time, and there are some pretty and deserted **beaches.** Plus, with a hotel that encourages Gaelic language, storytelling, and music, it's a great place to learn about this integral part of local culture.

Sights
ARMADALE CASTLE, GARDENS, AND MUSEUM

Armadale, Sleat; tel. 01471 844 305; www. armadalecastle.com; gardens 9:30am-5:30pm daily, museum 10am-5:30pm, café 9:30am-3:30pm, plus Thurs.-Sat. evenings late Mar.-late Oct., 10am-3pm Weds.-Sun. Mar. and Nov.; adult £8.50, concessions and child £6.95, under 5 free, family £25

Once the family seat of the Macdonalds of Sleat, part of the formidable Clan Donald, this castle, which now stands in ruin, is set amid 40 acres (16 hectares) of well-kept woodland gardens. The castle ruins date from the 19th century, though Macdonalds lived here in an older mansion house from the 1650s onward. Scottish heroine Flora Macdonald was married here in 1750 and just over 20 years later Samuel Johnson and James Boswell visited it. It's an easy stop-off for anyone arriving or departing by ferry at Armadale, particularly those with kids—there's a playground and special trails to follow.

You can't step inside the castle itself because the crumbling walls are fenced off for safety, but you can walk around the splendid gardens, where 100-year-old trees stand watch over beautiful displays of bluebells and orchids, plus herbaceous borders and pretty little ponds. Take a seat on one of the well-placed benches for wonderful views. The museum tells the story of Clan Donald across six galleries, from their position as powerful Lords of the Isles to the subsequent diaspora in the wake of Culloden. On display are broadswords (one of the weapons of choice of clansmen), bagpipes, and a 17th-century firearm reputedly fired at Culloden.

Beaches
CAMAS DARAICH AND LIGHTHOUSE

Road end of the Aird of Sleat

While tourists head to Claigan Beach in northern Skye, locals know that this is Skye's other best beach. It takes a little while to get here, but with golden sands and sparkling turquoise waters, it's worth the effort. The trail starts at the road end of the Aird of Sleat, reached via Newton Bank (left when you come off the Armadale Ferry), where parking is available. Follow the path straight ahead as it crosses boggy moorland. You'll reach a bridge where there is a sign pointing to the left to "sandy beach." From the beach it's not far to the automatic lighthouse on the Point of Sleat. Follow this direction as the path leads steeply uphill; it's a little rough in places, but follow close to the fence and you should be okay. In total the walk should take 3-4 hours there and back (5.25 miles/8 km).

Food and Accommodations
KINLOCH LODGE

Sleat; tel. 01471 833 333; https://kinloch-lodge.co.uk; breakfast 8:15am-9:45am, lunch 12pm-2pm, dinner 6:30pm-9pm daily; 5-course menu £80, afternoon tea £24, 3-course Sunday lunch £40; cookery courses from £25, £340 d

This is grand-style dining in a resplendent room where you slide into period chairs and eat beneath the approving stares of the expensively framed portraits on the wall. Tables are dressed in white linen with candles in the center, and the food by chef Marcello Tully is superb, with shellfish, game, and seasonal vegetables and herbs prepared imaginatively and matched with good wine. Afternoon tea is also available, and from late October to the end of February the elegant Edwardian hotel (you can stay too, if you can afford it) hosts Sunday roasts, followed by a whisky tasting in the bar. Sporadic cookery courses with Marcello are also offered.

MORAR B&B

2 Calgary, Ardvasar, Sleat; tel. 01471 844 378; www.accommodation-on-skye.co.uk; £95 d

This is not your average bed-and-breakfast; just a mile outside Armadale, Morar B&B comes with its own indoor heated swimming pool. Set on a croft within a family home, it also offers views from the terrace, or guests can wander down amid the meadows where there are rare orchids. The nearby bay is a prime place to spot otters, and the family's chickens will keep you company. Rooms are bright and tastefully decorated with statement wallpaper and big prints, giving them a thoroughly modern feel. A stay here is a steal at this price.

★ EILEAN IARMAIN

Isleornsay, Sleat; tel. 01471 833 332; http://eileaniarmain.co.uk; Am Birlinn 5:30pm-8pm daily, Am Praban 5:30pm-9pm daily, ring ahead to check in winter; entrées £6, £191 d

This hotel, with 12 bedrooms and suites, a pub, and a restaurant, is in a fabulous waterside location and you'll be so glad you found it. Resolutely Gaelic in its approach—speaking the language was once a prerequisite to working here and is still encouraged—dishes are satisfyingly Scottish (rack of Scottish lamb and the hotel's own fish pie). You can have a more relaxed walk-in dinner (from the same menu) in the **Am Praban Bar,** where traveling Scottish musicians, students of the Gaelic college, and locals can often be found setting up a Cèilidh session. Opened by the late Sir Iain Noble, a Gaelic language activist, who also opened the nearby Sabhal Mòr Ostaig Gaelic college, it's not so much a restaurant and hotel as it is the heart and soul of the community.

Information and Services
Visit Sleat (www.visitsleat.org) is a useful portal of tourist information.

Getting There
From Portree, it's an hour's drive to Armadale south along the A87 for 25 miles (40 km) before turning right onto the A851 just past Harropool for a further 15 miles (24 km). From Broadford it's just 25 minutes south on the A87 before taking the same turning onto the A851 (16 miles/10 km).

Also from Portree, the no. 52 **Stagecoach** bus runs to Armadale in 1.25 hours (£7.70, three times a day in summer and timed to meet the ferries, fewer trips out of season). From Broadford, it's just a 30-minute bus ride on the no. 52 to Armadale (£4.10 one-way).

Getting Around

Take a left out of the ferry terminal and head 4 miles (6 km) along the east coast of the peninsula to the Aird of Sleat, the end of the road, via Newton Bank, from where you'll need to get your walking boots on to reach the tip of the peninsula. Take a right out of the ferry terminal onto the A851, also along the east coast, to explore Sleat.

Relatively few people venture to the west coast of Sleat, but if you would like to, you'll need to take one of the two roads that cross through the Sleat: the first is on your left by Kilbeg as you travel north, the second a short while after. To travel around the region or a little farther afield, both **James's Taxi and Tours** (tel. 01471 844 717) and **Nicolson Hire Taxi Service** (tel. 01471 844 338) are reliable cab firms and can take you on bespoke tours too.

★ PORTREE

The pretty-as-a-picture town of Portree is Skye's main hub. It's from here that most tours set off, and it is also a good launch pad for many of the main sights on the island, those north along the **Trotternish Peninsula**. A bunch of colorful buildings lines the **harbor,** where you can pick up fish and chips and sit and watch the boats or walk up the hill (known locally as the Lump) for the best views. In town are some useful shops, from gift stores to places to pick up gear, plus lots of places to stay and eat.

Shopping
INSIDE OUT

Varragill House, The Green; tel. 01478 611 663; www. inside-out-skye.com; 9am-6pm Mon.-Sat. year-round, Sun. in summer

If you're planning to hike while you are here or even if you're just ill-prepared for Scotland's unpredictable weather, this place will come in handy. You'll find big-names (Haglofs, Marmot, and Keela) alongside lesser-known U.K. brands, and you can pick up everything from wet-weather gear to walking boots, those all-important walking poles, and the vital Ordnance Survey walking maps.

SKYE BATIKS

The Green; tel. 01478 613 331; https://skyebatiks.com; 9am-6pm Mon.-Sat., 10am-5pm Sun.

This quirky new-age shop has been brightening up the lives of Portree residents and visitors since the 1980s. You can browse and buy batik-style clothing or homewares and bright bags (handmade in Sri Lanka using

Portree

Portree

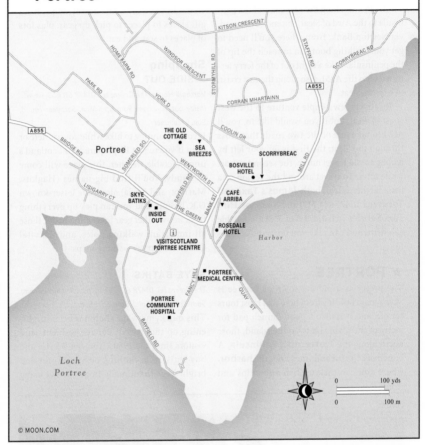

© MOON.COM

traditional methods to wax and dye the cloth). It's a good place to indulge your hippie side, and staff are extremely friendly. They may even offer you a coffee if you smile nicely.

Food
CAFÉ ARRIBA

Gladstone Buildings, Quay Brae; tel. 01478 611 830; www.cafearriba.co.uk; 8am-5pm Tues.-Sat.; flatbreads £4.25

Arguably the best coffee on Skye (made of 100 percent Arabica beans) is at this vibrant and laid-back café—you can't miss the loud blue and orange sign—where you could just as happily pore over your guidebook while nursing a hot drink as you could tuck into a hearty breakfast or good home-cooked lunch. The flatbreads are nice and affordable, and comfort food such as creamy macaroni and cheese or sausage and mash will cheer up the rainiest of days. There are good views of the harbor, and vegetarian and vegan options.

SEA BREEZES

2 Marine Buildings, Quay Street; tel. 01478 612 016; lunch 12pm-2pm, dinner 5pm-9:30pm daily Apr.-late Oct.; entrées £6.50

In a Victorian stone building that forms part

Skye's Food Scene

For many years now, the Isle of Skye has been known for its creative food scene. As to be expected for an island, a lot of Skye's cuisine relies on their local bounty of seafood. Much of the island's seafood used to be exported to other places, leaving little for locals to enjoy, but a change in law means that now chefs can really mine the local area for the best ingredients for their table.

SKYE'S BEST RESTAURANTS

At one point a few years ago, Skye had no fewer than three Michelin-starred restaurants—not bad for an area of this size—and though at present only **Loch Bay** (page 362), in the village of Stein, can lay that claim, there's always a good chance restaurants will reclaim their stars, or new places will land their first. Loch Bay is renowned for its expert cooking of quite simple dishes, using French techniques to bring out the natural flavors of Scottish ingredients.

tarts at Loch Bay

Other restaurants worthy of mention include the **Three Chimneys** (page 364), awarded a Michelin star in 2014. This is one of Scotland's most-loved restaurants, because of its stunning loch-side location and its dishes using the freshest ingredients, where a love of cooking (and eating) shines through. And there's **Scorrybreac** (page 355), a small restaurant in Portree known for using meat from the island and seafood from the harbor below to tantalizing effect.

THE IMPACT OF CORONAVIRUS

In the wake of the coronavirus pandemic, restaurateurs are having to get even more imaginative. It's no secret that social distancing has placed enormous pressure on the hospitality industry in terms of being able to operate at a profit, and the next few years will be very telling as to who will survive long-term. You can help by supporting local restaurants as much as possible when you are here as well as reserving ahead and never ever being a no-show.

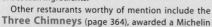

of a conservation area, this small friendly restaurant serves delicious straight-up seafood. Here the freshness of the dishes speaks for itself—there's a squeeze of lemon here and splash of white wine there but no heavy sauces—and the local seafood platters are good for sharing. Some tables have harbor views, too. They currently don't have a website, so bookings are by phone only.

★ **SCORRYBREAC**

7 Bosville Terrace; tel. 01478 612 069; www. scorrybreac.com; 5pm-9:30pm Weds.-Sun.; three courses £42, six courses £60

This restaurant above the harbor is intimate and inventive. Chef Calum Munro first opened in his parents' front room, and it soon became so popular that he found himself here, in prime position in Portree. Fine-dining preparations of cod, polenta, samphire, and lemon use the best local and seasonal ingredients. Settle in for the evening and savor each mouthful. Minimum three courses.

Accommodations
ROSEDALE HOTEL

Beaumont Crescent, Portree; tel. 01478 613 131; www. rosedalehotelskye.co.uk; £125 d

The layout of this hotel seems a little odd until you realize its maze of stairways and corridors and low beams come from combining three separate fishermen's cottages. Rooms are good, if a little plain, some with nice harbor views. There's a decent Scottish Tapas restaurant on-site, and a wee dram is presented to you on arrival, along with some homemade shortbread.

BOSVILLE HOTEL

9-11 Bosville Terrace, Portree; tel. 01478 612 846; www.bosvillehotel.co.uk; £210 d

The recently renovated Bosville is all minimalist seaside chic with a slight Scandinavian-cool edge, right in the center of town. Book a premium double room for harbor views. Downstairs, the Dulse & Rose restaurant serves a good modern Scottish menu, and the Merchant Bar with its wood burner has a good selection of Scottish gins to tempt you.

THE OLD COTTAGE

Suladale, near Portree; www.sykescottages.co.uk; £553 pw

This former crofter's cottage, about 10 miles (16 km) west of Portree, is brimming with character. There's a four-poster bed in the bedroom, and the rest of the accommodation, which includes a cozy living room with wood burner and pitched roof, is spread neatly across one floor. The kitchen is small but functional, and the owner will start you off with enough firewood for at least your first evening.

Information and Services

Portree's **VisitScotland iCentre** (Bayfield House, Bayfield Road, Portree; tel. 01478 612 992; 9am-5pm Mon.-Sat. and 10am-4pm Sun. Apr.-late Oct., 9:30am-4:30pm Mon.-Sat. late Oct.-Mar.) has free wifi and is in the town center. You'll find **Portree Filling Station** (7:30am-9pm Mon.-Sat., 9:30am-6pm on Sun.) on the A87, shortly before you enter the town from the south.

Visit **Portree Medical Centre** (tel. 01478 612 013; 8:30am-5:30pm Mon.-Fri.), near the harbor, for minor complaints. **Portree Community Hospital** (tel. 01478 613 200), also based here, has a Minor Injury Unit, which operates 8am-11pm. For more serious conditions you will likely be transferred to **Dr. Mackinnon Memorial Hospital** in Broadford (26 miles/42 km away).

Getting There

Portree is a 35-mile (56 km) drive from Kyle of Lochalsh over the Skye Bridge and along the A87 (just under an hour). From Armadale Ferry Terminal (where ferries from Mallaig arrive), it's 42 miles (68 km), first north along the A851 before joining the A87 (also just over an hour). From Broadford it's 26 miles (42 km) north along the A87 to Portree (40 minutes).

From the Armadale Ferry Terminal, you can catch the no. 52 bus with **Stagecoach** (www.stagecoachbus.com) to Portree (1.25 hours; £7.70; three times a day in summer, less out of season), which stops at Broadford a short time. From Broadford, it's just under 40 minutes to Portree (£6.10 each way). **Citylink** (www.citylink.co.uk) connects Portree to and from Kyle of Lochalsh on the no. 915, no. 916, and no. 917 (just over an hour; £7.10 each way). The first bus sets off at 11am, with around five in total each day.

Getting Around

Portree itself is perfectly manageable on foot. All the main amenities, restaurants, and bars are centered around the harbor in the heart of town, or a few streets back from it. If you want to venture farther afield and you don't have a car, there are plenty of trip boats operating from here and most tour guides will pick up from Portree, too.

Skye EBikes (16 Borneskitaig; tel. 07460 633 507; Mar.-Oct.; £50 per day, over age 14 only, £100 deposit), based in the far north of the Trotternish Peninsula, hires out electric bikes. They have also handily outlined a Trotternish Explorer route that you can follow to see some incredible sights on the peninsula.

TROTTERNISH AND NORTHEAST SKYE

The craggy landscape of the Trotternish Peninsula extends 20 miles (32 km) north from the town of Portree and is like nothing you have ever seen before, a haven for hikers and explorers. Amid a dream-like landscape that seems to defy all logic are two of Skye's most famous and visited hikes: The Old Man of Storr, a pinnacle that can be seen for miles around, and the Quiraing, a supernatural place, often shrouded in mist, where unbeliev-able rock formations look like they have been placed here by the gods themselves.

From Portree, there are two roads to the peninsula: the old faithful A87, which you can follow for 16 miles (26 km) to the town of **Uig** on the west coast; and the A855, which travels along the more dramatic east coast of the peninsula all the way to **Flodigarry** (21 miles/34 km) before looping round and com-ing back south along the west coast to meet the A87 at Uig.

Driving along the east coast, the first major sight you will come to is **the Old Man of Storr,** 6 miles (10 km) north of Portree. A further 10 miles (16 km) will bring you to **Staffin,** famous for its **dinosaur footprints** and one of the main access points to the be-fuddling rocky wilderness of **the Quiraing.** A further 11 miles (18 km) along the same road will bring you to the turning for **Kilmuir Graveyard** (just behind the Skye Museum of Island Life), where you will find a huge monu-ment to the woman who helped Bonnie Prince Charlie escape, Flora Macdonald. Four miles (6 km) south from Kilmuir is **Uig,** the best entry point for the famous **Fairy Glen.**

Sights
KILT ROCK AND MEALT FALLS
Staffin Road, 1.24 miles (2 km) south of Staffin
On the Staffin Road on the east coast of the Trotternish (about 9 miles/15 km north from Portree) is this dual viewpoint where you can see both the vertical basalt columns of Kilt Rock (as you might expect, they look like the pleats of a kilt; in the right light the colors look

a little like tartan too), and Mealt Falls, which crash down from the rocks to the sea below. Parking is free; though there's not much of it, it's worth a 10-minute stop, if you can find space, if only to hear the soft hum as wind travels through the rocks.

STAFFIN DINOSAUR FOOTPRINTS
An Corran, Staffin, the dinosaur beach
It was on this beach, just outside the old crofting community of Staffin, that fossil-ized dinosaur footprints, believed to belong to a family of Ornithipods, were discovered in 2002. Today, many people make the visit to this otherwise fairly nondescript beach to see the prints. Visit at low tide and look to the right of the big boulders on the flat mud stone (at the bottom of the slipway)—there is a map in the car park that shows you where to look.

To learn more, stop by the esoteric **Staffin Dinosaur Museum** (6 Ellishadder, Staffin; www.staffindinosaurmuseum.com; 9:30am-5pm daily; adult £2, child £1, family £5). Run since 1976, the miniscule museum has a staggering collection of dinosaur fossils, all collected and catalogued by Dugald Ross. Through his research, Ross was able to ascer-tain which dinosaurs once walked here, in-cluding the mighty Stegosaurus. He also offers tours to see the footprints in situ at the beach and can shed light on the most recent dino-saur footprints discovered at nearby Brothers Point, but these are by request and should be booked in advance.

FLORA MACDONALD'S GRAVE
Kilmuir Graveyard
Flora Macdonald is a heroine across the whole of Scotland for the part she played in help-ing Bonnie Prince Charlie flee government forces in the wake of Culloden. Disguising Charlie as an Irish maid by the name of Betty Burk, she transported him to Skye from the Isle of South Uist in the Outer Hebrides, from where he made good his escape. In this small graveyard, a large memorial stands for Flora Macdonald, with the words: "Her name will

be mentioned in history, and if courage and fidelity be virtues, mentioned with honor."

Hiking

THE OLD MAN OF STORR HIKE

Distance: 6 miles (4 km)
Time: 1.5 hours round-trip
Trailhead: Old Man of Storr car park, A855
Information and Maps: www.isleofskye.com/skye-guide/top-ten-skye-walks/old-man-of-storr

Seen from miles away as you drive around the Trotternish Peninsula, particularly on the east side, the Old Man of Storr is a true symbol of Skye. Its unusual formation, which stands out slightly separate from the spires around it, has spawned many a folktale. One story says that it is a giant's thumb, the only bit still seen of him after he was buried in the earth.

Many visitors simply view it from the road, but there's a straightforward walk to the foot of the pinnacle via a graveled footpath. Walk through the gate at the end of the car park and follow the trail up the hillside. Don't worry when the path splits; you can take either side, but the path on the right-hand side is probably best. After a while the gravel becomes muddy and a bit rougher underfoot. When the path splits again, take the left-hand trail and watch out for uneven rocks. Soon the Old Man will appear on your right. The foot of the Old Man of Storr is a wondrous place to drink in the rest of the spectacular scenery of the Trotternish. Only experienced hikers should attempt to climb to its summit, which is very steep and requires some scrambling.

THE QUIRAING HIKE

Distance: 4 miles (6.5 km)
Time: 2 hours round-trip
Trailhead: Summit of the minor road between Staffin and Uig
Information and Maps: www.isleofskye.com/skye-guide/top-ten-skye-walks/the-quiraing

The result of a giant landslide, this natural arena, which soars above the Trotternish Peninsula, is best experienced on foot so you can really get a sense of the scale of the large pinnacles and spires of bare rock that protrude from its surface. Over time, erosions and glaciers sculpted the rock into the bizarre pillars and formations you see today, which have names that give some indication of their appearance, such as **the Needle**—a sinister spiky rock that could be a needle but looks more like a pointed witch's finger beckoning you over, and **the Table**—a smooth, plateau that seems out of place amid the craggy scenery.

A relatively direct walking route to the escarpment can be accessed quite easily from a single-track road at Brogaig, just after Staffin. If coming from the south, take the road to your left just after the Staffin post office. Stay on this road, taking care round the hairpin bends, for 2.5 miles (4 km), until you reach the car park. The same unmarked road can be accessed from Uig by taking the first right after the ferry terminal. Coming from this direction, the drive to the car park is around 4 miles (6 km).

Opposite the car park is the **Flodigarry Path,** which takes you all the way through the 1.25-mile (2-km) wild rocky fortress of the Quiraing. The path is narrow and mainly level, though it will start to drop away steeply to your right, revealing views of Raasay and Applecross. You will cross a burn and then about half a mile (0.8 km) later the path will become steeper as you enter the Quiraing. On your right, you'll see the foreboding prison, which looks like a medieval keep standing guard. It's then up to you how much you explore the individual features of the Quiraing before following the same path back down; you'll need to leave the main path to ascend the slopes to the Needle and, if you keep the Needle to your left, you'll soon reach a gully where there is another path that will take you to the Table.

FAIRY GLEN

Distance: 1.25 miles (2 km)
Time: 1 hour
Trailhead: Fairy glen car park

1: Old Man of Storr 2: The Quiraing

Information and Maps: *www.walkhighlands. co.uk/skye/fairyglen.shtml*

It was in this ethereal landscape near Uig that movie director Steven Spielberg chose to film the 2016 fantasy adaptation of Roald Dahl's classic children's novel *The BFG*. It's not hard to see why: its cone-shaped hills easily convince one that they could be home to magical beings, hence the name. It's an easy hike but leave yourself plenty of time to immerse yourself in the strange scenery of the glen.

This site has become so popular that there is now a dedicated car park. From the south, turn right before the Uig Hotel, signposted for Sheader and Balnaknock, and follow the narrow lane until you see the car park. Park up and then follow the path up the bracken hill ahead. When you've arrived in the magical landscape, there's no specific trail to take, but once you've ascended some of the small hills, you'll want to head to the odd-looking peak in the distance on the left-hand side of the road. Called Castle Ewen, it may look like a ruined castle, but it is in fact just a bizarre-shaped lump of basalt.

With it being a grassy region, it can get very muddy. Ignore guides who claim that moving some of the smaller rocks in the glen to create spirals is an offering to the fairies; all this does is serve to undermine the natural state of the glen.

Food and Accommodations
SKYE RESTAURANT

Flodigarry Hotel, Flodigarry; tel. 01470 552 203; https://restaurant-isleofskye.co.uk; 12:30pm-3pm and 6:30pm-9pm daily; entrées £8.50

Within the Flodigarry Hotel, this fine-dining restaurant presents classic dishes in a relaxed environment, with stunning views of the Quiraing and the Torridon mountains on the mainland. The menu is less fancy at lunchtime—try the Highland beef stew served in a big bun, which should set you up for a big walk—while for dinner you can eat salmon caviar of venison cured in heather honey.

THE FERRY INN

A87, Uig; tel. 01470 542 300; https://theferryinnskye. com; 5pm-10pm Mon.-Sat.; £27 for two courses, £35 for three courses; £170 d

This 19th-century inn has been given a warm and contemporary refurb that feels utterly inviting. Seafood comes fresh—it's landed at nearby Uig Pier—and meat and vegetables are also as local as possible. Dishes are on the fine-dining side, yet with hearty portions. Alongside dishes of roast salmon with mussels, there's also a hearty côte de boeuf to share. Rooms are also exquisite.

UIG HOTEL

A87, Uig; tel. 01470 542 205; www.uig-hotel-skye. com; £75 s, £165 d

Just a five-minute drive from Uig Bay on the western side of the Trotternish, this old coaching inn is now a warm hotel with 11 rooms that are comfortable, if a little plain. Isle of Skye red deer plus scallops from the Hebridean Uist isles are served in the on-site restaurant, which overlooks the bay. This hotel is the obvious choice if you want to visit the nearby Fairy Glen.

Information and Services

If you want to walk on the unearthly landscape of the Trotternish, get a copy of the indispensable **Ordnance Survey map** (Explorer 408, Skye—Trotternish & The Storr), which can be picked up in the **Inside Out** shop in Portree. **Uig Filling Station** (8am-8pm Mon.-Sat., 10:30am-5pm Sun.), right by the ferry terminal, is the only place to refuel on the Trotternish. There is no visitor center on the Trotternish itself, but the **VisitScotland iCentre** in Portree (tel. 01478 612 992) will be able to advise you on travel in the area.

Getting There and Around

From Portree you can do a circular drive either clockwise or counterclockwise, round the peninsula, starting on the west coast or on the east coast; my preference is for the latter. From Portree, take the A855 up the east coast, through Staffin, round the top via Flodigarry, and back through Uig, joining the A87 (49 miles/79 km; 1.5 hours without stopping).

From the ferry terminal at Armadale, it's 59 miles (95 km) to Staffin, and a similar distance to Uig; both journeys take around 1.5 hours. To reach the Trotternish, take the A851 north from Armadale for about 15 miles (24 km) before turning left onto the A87 that will take you all the way into Portree. From Portree you can choose to take either the A855 to Staffin or continue on the A87 to Uig. From Broadford, it's around 42 miles (68 km) to either Uig or Staffin, following the A87 to Portree before making the same decision between the A855 to Staffin or the A87 to Uig. The journey time to either is just over an hour from Broadford.

There are also a couple of daily **Stagecoach** (www.stagecoachbus.com) buses from Portree. The 57A stops at Staffin (30 minutes; £4), Flodigarry (35 minutes; £4.60), and Uig (1.25 hours; £5.35) and runs around four times a day (twice on Saturday and no Sunday service), while the 57C (which travels from west to east) stops in Uig (30 minutes; £5.35) and Kilmuir (35 minutes; £5.35) and runs four times a day, with two buses on Saturday and none on Sunday. If you are traveling from Broadford or Armadale, get the no. 52 bus to Portree and change here for the Trotternish.

NORTHWEST SKYE

Most of the main draws to the northwest of Skye lie in and around the **Waternish peninsula,** just northeast of the region's famous **Dunvegan Castle,** where there are also some excellent restaurants, and some eclectic art studios and craft workshops. A narrow strip of land, it's a quite untouched place where green hills gently sweep down to the blue sea below and corncrakes can be heard (but not seen) making their distinct "crex-crex" mating call under cover of tall grasses.

The entry point to Waternish is marked by a little blink-and-you'll-miss-it bridge known as **Fairy Bridge** shortly after you turn off the main road from Portree to Dunvegan onto the B886. Many people stop here to take photos because of the dubious story that says it was here that the fairy lover of the chief of Clan MacLeod bid him farewell to return to her own people. Instead, venture farther into the peninsula where you can find some real hidden treasures, including the sleepy village of **Stein** on the northeastern shore of Loch Bay, where you can witness some spectacular sunsets.

Farther west of Waternish, the steep cliffs of **Glendale** are alive with seabirds, while its wild meadows are filled with vibrant flowers, from orchids to primroses and bluebells. Look out for the duo of flat-topped hills known as **MacLeods Tables.** According to folklore, the tips of these hills were cut off by St. Columba, the 6th-century Irish missionary who brought Christianity to Scotland.

Sights
NEIST POINT
Duirnish, Glendale; www.glendaleskye.com/neistpoint.php

Skye's most westerly point, at the tip of the remote peninsula of Duirnish, is one of the best places on Skye to see whales, dolphins, and even the occasional basking shark. It's the only real reason to venture this far over (unless you're seeking seclusion) and offers splendid views of the jagged Waterstein Head, and from its stunning cliff-top location you can look over the Minch (Atlantic Sea channel) toward the Western Isles.

It's possible to walk down to the **lighthouse** that stands at Neist Point; just follow the signs to Neist Point and park up at the car park at the end of the road. The path starts just past the weather-beaten shed in the car park. The path itself is well laid out with concrete steps, and handrails, though it is steep. You may be tempted by some of the well-worn trails leading up grassy banks to your right; be wary of exposed cliff-top sections that are unfenced and steep in places. Once you reach the lighthouse, take a moment to examine the bizarre rocks upon which it sits, akin to those at the Giant's Causeway across the sea. Some believe the Causeway continues under the sea, all the way from Northern Ireland to Skye.

DUNVEGAN CASTLE AND GARDENS

MacLeod Estate, Dunvegan; tel. 01470 521 206; www.dunvegancastle.com; 10am-5:30pm daily Easter-mid-Oct.; adult £14, child £9, concessions £11, family £34

The oldest continuously inhabited castle in Scotland, Dunvegan Castle is the ancestral home of the chiefs of Clan MacLeod, and it looks romantic in its loch-side setting, elevated on a basalt outcrop, particularly when covered in a misty haze. You can admire the Victorian revamp of its exterior, with battlements and towers that run the full length of the roof line, as you drive down to Claigan Beach.

However, to see the older parts of the castle, including the 14th-century keep, you need to pay the entry fee. Inside, it's palatial, both in terms of size and design, decorated in opulent 19th-century style. Artifacts on display stir up a sense of Scottish patriotism—there's a lock of Bonnie Prince Charlie's hair here—as well as clan loyalty. The most famous item is the fabled Fairy Flag, an ancient banner that, according to one legend, was gifted to a chief of Clan MacLeod by his fairy wife, and when unfurled in battle helped the MacLeods defeat their enemy. Take time, too, to walk the castle's grounds; laid out in the 18th century, they include 5 acres (2 hectares) that are a riot of color, in stark contrast to the largely barren landscape of Skye. Boat rides out on the loch to see seals and other wildlife are also available for an additional fee (25 minutes; adult £7.50, child £5.50, under 3 free).

Beaches
CLAIGAN CORAL BEACH

Dunvegan

This beach—one of Skye's finest—is just a short drive past Dunvegan Castle down a single-track road that passes by windswept hills strewn with heather until you reach a car park. From the car park it's a good mile-long (1.6-km) trek along a cliff-side path to reach the beach, and you'll inevitably meet sheep and the odd cow blocking the path en route. Walking boots are advised as you will have to cross a couple of streams, but it's utterly worth it. The water looks clear enough to drink, and the "coral," which looks like sand at first, is sun-bleached algae. At low tide you can also walk over to the tidal island of **Lampay.**

Food
STEIN INN

Macleods Terrace, Stein, Waternish; tel. 01470 592 362; https://thesteininn.co.uk; 12pm-3pm and 6pm-9:30pm Mon.-Sat., 12:30pm-3pm and 6:30pm-9pm Sun. Easter-Oct., 12pm-2:30pm Tues.-Sat., 12:30pm-3pm Sun., 5:30pm-8pm Tues.-Thurs. and Sun., 5:30pm-8:30pm Fri.-Sat. winter; entrées £6.95, £125 d

In the little township of Stein on the eastern shore of Loch Bay is Skye's oldest inn. Inside, the whitewashed building is all low ceilings, with a pub area with an inglenook fireplace and a separate, slightly fancier restaurant. Tempting dishes such as Highland venison pie or Isle of Skye scallops are accompanied by good ales on tap. Think ahead and book into one of the inn's five rooms.

★ LOCH BAY

1 Macleods Terrace, Stein; tel. 01470 592 235; www.lochbay-restaurant.co.uk; 12:15pm-1:30pm Weds.-Fri. and Sun., 5:30pm-8:45pm Tues. and Sat., 6:15pm-8:45pm Weds.-Fri. Easter-Oct., 6:15pm-8:45pm Weds.-Sat. Nov.-Dec. 22; 3-course lunch £34, 3-course dinner £43, 5-course fruits de mer £70

Next door to the Stein Inn, this restaurant, which gives a contemporary Scottish twist to classic French cooking, is one of Skye's best, proven by its Michelin Star. It's well worth the drive here down winding roads (all the

1: Dunvegan Castle 2: The Stein Inn 3: shellfish broth at Loch Bay 4: Neist Point

better if you're staying in the Stein Inn). You can expect the freshest seafood—try the fruits de mer—in a traditional crofter's cottage (the seats are even covered in Harris Tweed). Staff are down to earth and friendly, making for an altogether fantastic culinary experience.

THREE CHIMNEYS

Colbost; tel. 01470 511 258; www.threechimneys. co.uk; 12pm-1:45pm and 6pm-9:15pm daily (hours may be reduced in winter), closed mid-Dec.-mid-Jan.; tasting menu £68, £360 d

Another of Skye's finest restaurants, the Three Chimneys (signposted on the B884) makes delicious Scottish dishes using carefully sourced ingredients. It has held three AA red rosettes for 18 years, was named U.K. restaurant of the year in the Good Food Guide 2018 and has previously held a Michelin star. The menu depends on what's in season and what's been caught, from slow-cooked Wester Ross salmon or lemon sole with lobster ravioli.

Accommodations
EDINBANE INN

Off the A850, Edinbane; tel. 01470 582 414; www. edinbaneinn.co.uk; £140 d

Halfway between Portree and Edinbane, this is a great place for traditional music. Sessions take place on Sunday afternoons year-round and on Tuesday and Friday evenings (9pm-11pm) in high season. The pub can be a little noisy, but rooms are freshly decorated and comfortable. There's also a good bar menu. Wifi is available, but phone service is virtually nonexistent. No children under 14.

★ HILLSTONE LODGE

12 Colbost, Dunvegan; tel. 1470 511434; www. hillstonelodge.com; £185 d

The architect of this small B&B knows the power of a view. Floor-to-ceiling windows abound, meaning you can soak up scenes of Dunvegan loch from the moment you fling open the curtains in the morning until you're sipping a whisky in the relaxing lounge as the sun goes down. Rooms are modern and minimal, with Scottish fabrics featured throughout

and Noble Isle toiletries in the en suites. Close to the famous castle and less than a mile's walk to the famous Three Chimneys restaurant, its location is top-notch.

Getting There

From Portree, it's a 30-minute drive to Dunvegan along the A850 (21 miles/34 km). From Armadale, it's an hour and 20-minute drive, taking the A851 for 15 miles (24 km) before turning left onto the A87 for 18 miles (29 km) and then turning left onto the A863 at Sligachan, which you follow for 23 miles (37 km) all the way to Dunvegan. From Broadford the journey time is 55 minutes, again following the A87 to Sligachan and then joining the A863, a total distance of 39 miles (63 km).

From Portree, you can take the no. 56 bus (45 minutes; £5.35), run by **Stagecoach** (www.stagecoachbus.com), to Dunvegan. The bus runs four times a day (no service Sunday).

CENTRAL SKYE AND THE CUILLIN

Cutting through the center of Skye, the Cuillin is considered Britain's most magnificent mountain range and a mecca for walking enthusiasts, with 11 Munros within its fold—12 if you count Blà Bheinn, on the cusp of the Cuillin Ridge. Even if you don't think you can manage scaling one of its peaks, the views of the craggy gray mountains towering over you are still awe-inspiring. And they hide no end of waterfalls, streams, gorges, and lochs. You may come across the odd hiker going in the opposite direction, but if the idea of total isolation leaves you a little nervous, consider booking a tour to guide you through the region. Only experienced walkers and climbers with safety measures in place should attempt trekking or climbing in the Cuillin alone.

A largely uninhabited region of the isle, the center is where Skye is at its most awesome. You'll lose track of the number of eagles you spot swooping down to snatch up prey (you'll see even more "tourist eagles," or buzzards as they are more commonly known), and you'll need a little patience as the resident sheep wander into your path and refuse to budge, seemingly as mesmerized by the sublime beauty of it all as you are.

Orientation

The center of civilization in these parts is in **Broadford,** a reasonably big town by Skye's standards on the east coast. From Broadford, the single-track B8083 passes southwest through the village of **Torrin** before rounding **Loch Slapin** and then winding up and down on the edge of the Cuillin all the way to the fishing village of **Elgol** at the bottom of the **Strathaird peninsula.** From Elgol, you can take a boat trip to the **Small Isles** and **Loch Coruisk** in the heart of the Cuillin.

You can also reach the Cuillin from farther north. **Sligachan** is pretty much where you would hit if you were to put a pin in the center of a map of Skye. It's 16 miles (26 km) northwest of Broadford along the A87 and is probably the most popular entry point into the mountain range. From Sligachan, it's 8 miles (13 km) west to **Carbost** (home to **Talisker Distillery**). It's from around here that you can access the famous Fairy Pools.

Sights
FAIRY POOLS

Carbost, Glenbrittle; www.isleofskye.com/skye-guide/ top-ten-skye-walks/fairy-pools

Probably the most visited sight on Skye, this collection of pools fed by a series of waterfalls is an Instagram favorite: at times the color of the water is emerald green.

Unfortunately, the pools have become a victim of their own success, with thousands upon thousands of people visiting them each year. The ecosystem has really struggled to cope, with the Highland Council initially widening the path to accommodate the tremendous footfall and more recently adding a big visitor car park and toilets. There are other, less visited and equally special pools to see, such as **Coir' a' Ghrundha.** If you must visit the pools, follow a couple of simple rules to prevent even further degradation of the area:

stick to the path (don't be tempted to take off-road shortcuts), and where possible take one of the local tours (too many cars is another problem, and this will cause less impact) with someone like **Tour Skye** (tel. 01478 613 514; www.tourskye.com).

If you want to appreciate the atmosphere of the area, it's also advisable to visit outside high season, or come early in the morning or late at night. The Fairy Pools can be a special place to be under Skye's famously dark skies.

COIR' A' GHRUNNDA

Glen Brittle campsite

The route to this hidden-away pool is not too hard to follow, and it gets easier if you grab yourself a copy of **Ordnance Survey Explorer Map 411: Skye—Cuillin Hills,** which you can buy online from **Inside Out** in Portree.

Setting off from Glen Brittle campsite, follow the main path that goes up behind the toilet block and then take the path that branches right across the burn. From here the path is relatively easy to follow as it takes you up, rising steeply to the left (cairns are there to help mark the way) into the lower corrie (steep-sided hollow). In the lower corrie the ground becomes trickier, with scree and large boulders to navigate. Stick left and high as much as possible; once you reach the waterfall you should be able to scramble up it and into the upper corrie. And there you have it, your own private pool, with no other tourists spoiling your view. The return trip should take 2 hours in total, covering 4 miles (6 km) round-trip. Inexperienced walkers should have no problem finding a local guide to take them here. This trek should only be attempted on a fine day.

BROADFORD TO ELGOL ROAD

B8083 from Broadford

To fully appreciate the majesty of the Cuillin, take the main road from Broadford to Elgol. As the road winds through a natural landscape of hills and unkempt fields where sheep mill about by boggy lochs, there are plenty of

Ethical Tourism on the Isle of Skye

Let's get one thing clear: tourism is key to Skye; if it goes, the impact would have a devastating effect on the local economy. However, overtourism threatens the island's most popular sights. By simply widening your net, you will not only have a more unique experience, but you can also sleep easy at night, safe in the knowledge that you are contributing to safeguarding and protecting this most special island for future generations. Here are some other tips for touring Skye ethically.

- **Look for alternatives:** For example, the Fairy Pools are beautiful, but why not venture to some of the other stunning, less crowded pools on Skye instead, such as Coir' a' Ghrunnda?

- **Take a tour with an ecologist:** Tours with people such as David from Skyefari or a land manager, who understand the environment and nature, are imperative for passing down good information for how to explore the outdoors. They also often have the knowledge and access to much quieter parts of the island.

- **Travel less, experience more:** SkyeConnect, a collective voice for businesses (particularly tourism businesses) on Skye are keen to encourage slow tourism. The new SkyeTime initiative (www.skye-time.com) is still in its infancy, but at its core is the idea that by staying a little longer in one place, taking time to watch wildlife and admire the changing landscape as the light alters, you will enrich your experience of the isle. I couldn't agree more.

passing places to pull over and take in the astounding views of (at first) the rounded tops of the Red Cuillin, and then the spikier summits of Blà Bheinn and the Black Cuillin, making you feel wholly insignificant in comparison.

In total the drive through Torrin, round **Loch Slapin** and up round the far end of the Cuillin and down into Elgol, takes 35 minutes (14.5 miles/23 km). It being a single-track road, though, you'll want to take your time; there's no need to rush scenery like this.

The no. 55 bus comes down here, too, four times a day from Broadford Monday-Friday (50 minutes; £5.25).

LOCH CORUISK

This loch, hidden in the Cuillin, is said to have its own kelpie (water spirit), which isn't very surprising because there is something ethereal about the place. Walking round the edge of the loch (the south side is easiest and offers the best views) will take you 3-4 hours to do a full circuit (4.25 miles/7 km), and it's hard not to spend the entire time looking up at the enormous mountains that encircle it—though you'll have to get here first, which for most people means taking a boat trip. Once a volcanic bowl (its Gaelic name translates as

"cauldron of waters"), over time it was shaped by glaciers. Though at times it's a sinister, bewitching place with ink-black waters, and it must be terrifying in a storm, when the sun is out, the loch glimmers a bright blue, and it's tempting to go for a dip, until you touch its surface and its coldness scolds you.

If you've ever heard The Skye Boat Song, you might be interested to hear that it was while being rowed across the waters of this loch in the 18th century that Miss Annie MacLeod first had its melody sung to her by boatmen. She quickly wrote it down (lyrics were added later by Sir Harold Boulton), and it is now a song that invokes a strong sense of patriotism and longing.

Bella Jane (Elgol; tel. 01471 866 244; www.bellajane.co.uk; adult £28, child £16, under 4 free) runs trips here from its base in Elgol every day from April until late October (when weather allows) at 9am, 10:45am, 12:15pm, and 2pm. The standard round-trip lasts three hours and gives you the chance to see seals (and possibly other marine wildlife) before spending an hour and a half ashore. Experienced hikers can opt for a one-way trip and walk back to Elgol, though you'll need to traverse at least one river and the aptly named Bad Step—a huge boulder precariously perched on an ocean cliffside. Elgol is just over half an hour by car from Broadford (14 miles/23 km). To reach it, you need to turn off the main A87 road onto the B8083 by the Broadford Hotel. This road will then take you down along a largely single-track road to Torrin, skirt Loch Slapin, and then take you up around the back of the Black Cuillin before descending to Elgol.

TALISKER

Carbost; tel. 01478 614 308; www.malts.com/ en-gb/distilleries/talisker; 10am-4:30pm Mon.-Fri. Jan.-Mar., 9:30am-5pm Mon.-Sat. and 10am-5pm Sun. Apr.-June and Sept.-Oct., 9:30am-5:30pm Mon.-Sat. and 10am-5pm Sun. July-Aug., 10am-4:30pm Mon.-Sat. and 11am-4:30pm Sun. Nov.-Dec.; Classic Distillery Tour £10, Talisker Flight Tour £25

The granddaddy of Hebridean distilleries, Talisker single malt whisky is renowned for its full-bodied flavor, inspired by its coastal windswept location. There are tours throughout the day, but to ensure you get on one (especially in summer), book at least 3-4 days in advance. The Classic Distillery Tour (45 minutes) will talk you through the process of making Talisker whisky and give you the chance to have a wee dram, while the Talisker Flight Tour (1.5 hours) gives you a tasting of several different Talisker whiskies. If tours are booked up, you can stop by and have a dram at the bar or buy a bottle to take home with you if you're the designated driver.

Hiking

If you are considering a hike, ensure you have a good map—mobile phones and even compasses often fail to work here. Also, tell someone where you are going and be prepared to turn back if conditions change. Climbing the Cuillin is not for beginners: you will often be scrambling over scree, debris, and bare rock at perilous heights, so you need to know what you are doing, and bring snacks and all supplies you'll need for a challenging hike.

Guided Cuillin Walks (Skye Guides, 3

Luib; tel. 01471 822 116; https://skyeguides. co.uk; three-day 1:1 traverse £800, four-day 1:1 traverse £1,060, five-day 1:1 traverse £1,350, prices reduced slightly as more people take part) offers introductory walks that will take you into the heart of Skye on wildlife-spotting adventures (even camping overnight for the chance to see the Northern Lights), but their specialty is to traverse the Cuillin Ridge, a challenging trek that takes three to five days to complete.

★ BLÀ BHEINN

Distance: *5 miles (8 km)*
Time: *5-6 hours*
Trailhead: *Car park off B8083 road near Loch Slapin*
Information and Maps: *www.walkhighlands. co.uk/munros/bla-bheinn*

As you approach Loch Slapin from Broadford, the hulk of Blà Bheinn, one of Britain's mightiest mountains, glares down at you. It marks the entry to the Black Cuillin proper and is separated from the rest of the range by Glen Sligachan, making it the only one of Skye's Munros not to be part of the Cuillin Ridge. Nevertheless, it displays all the characteristics of the nearby mountain range and is relatively easy to ascend if you are prepared for a bit of scrambling—though inexperienced walkers are advised to go with a guide.

Start your walk at the car park on the far side of the loch if you're coming from Broadford; you'll need to watch for it because it's easy to miss. From the car park, cross the stream and turn left. The mostly gravel path is well-marked initially and follows the river before turning into quite a deep gorge punctuated with several waterfalls. It then gradually starts to wind up and become less clear, zigzagging to the top as you round big boulders. Don't forget to stop to look behind you once the boulder section is complete for stunning views of Loch Slapin and to see how far you've come. En route you'll pass mountain streams and secret corries. The higher you go, the more entrancing the scenery is: With some mild scrambling, go past the vertical rock wall of the Great Prow as you near the top to see the Cuillin range to the northwest and the Red Cuillin to the northeast.

★ HIKE TO THE CLEARED VILLAGE OF BORERAIG

Distance: *6 miles (10 km) round-trip*
Time: *3-4 hours*
Trailhead: *Start at Kilchrist Church on the Broadford to Elgol road*
Information and Maps: *www.isleofskye.com/ skye-guide/top-ten-skye-walks/boreraig*

Among the saddest marks on Scotland's past are the notorious Highland Clearances, in which communities were forced from their land to make way for more profitable sheep farming. On this walk, you can visit one of the cutoff communities that suffered this fate.

The trailhead is near a church located on the Broadford to Elgol road, just a six-minute drive from Broadford, and parking is available in a lay-by (turnout) opposite. To start, walk back in the direction of Broadford and take the first right after the cattle grid. You'll cross a muddy field, after which the path turns to gravel, which leads up a grassy slope, where you will turn right onto the main path. As it rounds the corner, it becomes quite steep for a while, and after 20 minutes or so you will reach the remains of the old turn table of the now defunct marble quarry. Take the path slightly to the left, which climbs uphill and becomes increasingly muddy. After a while, you will come to a gate with a stile to cross, and once through here the path evens out for a while. Gradually, the left-hand side will drop away to reveal a loch and valley below, and the path will become much narrower and at times sodden underfoot. It then rises down again, and there are some narrow sections along the edge of the valley, so tread with care. Eventually, there will be another gate to pass over, and once you're on the other side the path starts to go down steadily. Soon you'll reach a grass-covered wall, and shortly after this you will see the remains of the first house marking the entry into Boreraig.

From here, it's a direct route down into the township. Houses are then spread out to the far west of the bay and a little over to the right, so explore the ruins and stone outlines of former homes and imagine what once was. One point of warning: Before you go too far, get your bearings because it is a little too easy on the way back up to get disoriented and lose the path.

Beaches

TALISKER BEACH

Near Talisker Distillery; www.isleofskye.com/ skye-guide/top-ten-skye-walks/talisker-beach

There is a certain rawness to this black-and-white sand beach in Talisker Bay. Park on the tarmac road into the settlement of Talisker and follow the sign that reads "to the bay." The track runs behind Talisker House, where Samuel Johnson and James Boswell stopped on their epic Hebridean journey in the 1770s, then emerges at the southern end of the bay. Though the beach is largely sandy, there are stones here too and a waterfall on the north side of the bay pours down the rock face. The beach's most impressive facet, though, is its irregular sea stack to the south. The walk takes just 20-30 minutes, and swimming is possible here.

Food

DELI GASTA

The Old Mill, Harrapool, Broadford; tel. 01471 822 646; www.deligasta.co.uk; 8:30am-5pm daily; sandwiches £6.45

Opened in 2016 in an old mill on the outskirts of Broadford, this café has been embraced by locals. The coffee is delicious, and the sandwiches, filled with fresh crabmeat, smoked salmon, and venison, are a step above your normal over-the-counter light bites.

RED SKYE RESTAURANT

The Old Schoolhouse, Breakish; tel. 01471 822 666; www.redskyerestaurant.co.uk; café 12pm-3pm daily, restaurant 5:30pm-late; entrées £7.50

1: approaching the Cuillin from the road past the Fairy Pools **2:** walking to Boreraig **3:** Skye Hobbit House **4:** Blà Bheinn

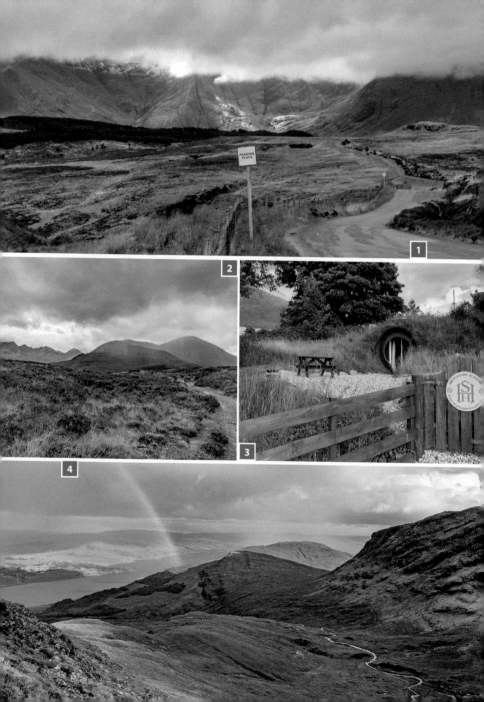

This family-run restaurant, in an idyllic location with views of both the Cuillin and the Applecross hills, has a tempting menu of local dishes as well as a good drinks menu, with plenty of Scottish whisky and gin alongside the wine. Alcohol seems to be a strong theme as even the mussels are whisky infused, but Scottish staples such as cullen skink and Stornoway black pudding will soon soak it up.

Accommodations
★ SKYE HOBBIT HOUSE
9 Torrin, Broadford; tel. 01471 822 078; www. skyehobbithouse.co.uk; Barrel House £15 per person, Round House £20

Tucked away on a little road just before you come into Torrin is this little gem of a place, which offers two options: the cute-as-anything Barrel House, which has twin beds, a table, a bench, and not much else; and the Round House, which sleeps up to four. Prices include pillows and pillowcases (you'll need to bring sleeping bags), drinking water, solar electricity, and use of a compost toilet and communal cooking area. There's wifi in a little shed and even a games room with a pool table; plus, you have amazing views of Blà Bheinn and a fire pit and BBQ to make the most of those long summer evenings.

THE OLD INN
Carbost; tel. 01478 640 205; www.theoldinnskye. co.uk; B&B £100, Bunkhouse £23 per person

At this inn, right by Talisker Distillery, you can stay in the lodge (which offers reasonable B&B rooms) or in the more basic bunkhouse. The inn itself is a music pub, with a jam session every Friday and a more traditional session every Wednesday. Please note the inn is closed from late October until mid-May.

Information and Services
There are a few main towns in central Skye to pick up supplies, get online, and get that all-important phone signal. **Broadford** is probably the best facilitated and is just 7

miles (11 km) from the Skye Bridge. It has a large **Co-op** directly on the A87 (Main Street, Broadford; 7am-10pm daily), with the finest view of any supermarket I've ever come across and an essential 24-hour petrol station. This is also where you will find Skye's main hospital, **Dr. MacKinnon Memorial Hospital** (High Road; tel. 01471 822 491).

Getting There
Broadford is located on the A87; it's pretty much impossible to visit the center or north of Skye without traveling through it. From Portree it's a 26-mile (42-km) journey south along the A87 to Broadford (35 minutes). From Armadale the distance to Broadford is 16 miles (26 km)—take the A851 north up the Sleat Peninsula and then turn left onto the A87 to Broadford (25 minutes).

The no. 52 bus from **Stagecoach** (www. stagecoach.com) passes through Broadford from both Portree and Armadale. From Portree the journey time is 45 minutes (£6.10), and there are three buses a day in summer (two in winter) Monday-Saturday. From Armadale it's a 25-minute journey (£4.10) three times a day (twice in winter with no Sunday service).

Getting Around
From Broadford, you can take the main A87 road for 16 miles (26 km) to reach Sligachan, which should take around 25 minutes. To reach Carbost, turn off the A87 at Sligachan onto the A863, from where it's another 8-mile (13-km) drive, for a total journey time of 35 minutes from Broadford.

A skeleton bus service run by **Stagecoach** (www.stagecoachbus.com) operates between the towns. From Broadford, you can jump on the no. 917 or no. 52 buses, which will get to Sligachan in just over 20 minutes (£4.10). There are no direct buses to Carbost from Broadford, and connections from Sligachan and Portree are sporadic at best. Check **Traveline** (www.traveline.info) for the best route.

Inverness, Loch Ness, and the North Coast 500

The northern Highlands is a place of extreme, empty beauty. Vast landscapes where rock as old as the Earth rises to craggy peaks, which give way to deep glens and wide straths covered in velveteen purple heather in spring and summer, turning golden in autumn before becoming bleak and blanketed by snow in winter. Here, isolated white sand beaches could be in the tropics were it not for the whirring winds, and often the only clue to human habitation is the occasional lonesome bothy or cottage.

It's a place to escape to, to feel the essence of nature, where the sea will at times roar with anger at you and at others lull you with its gentleness. You can see wildlife often evasive in other more populated parts of Scotland—red deer, leaping salmon, rare bumblebees, dolphins and, of

Highlights

Look for ★ to find recommended sights, activities, dining, and lodging.

★ **Culloden Battlefield:** Stand on the site of one of Scotland's bloodiest and most decisive battles—the last stand of the Jacobites (page 390).

★ **Cawdor Castle:** Visit the medieval fortress that Shakespeare bound to King of Scots Macbeth forever more (page 393).

★ **Kayaking on Loch Ness:** Avoid the tour buses by paddling yourself around on Scotland's enormous loch (page 397).

★ **Badbea:** This windswept abandoned settlement is a stark reminder of some of the impact of the Highland Clearances (page 411).

★ **The Flow Country:** One of the largest areas of blanket bog in the world, this patchwork of peat fields and pools is home to amazing birdlife and fauna (page 413).

★ **The Drumbeg Road:** This thrilling 22-mile (35-km) diversion from the North Coast 500 Route takes in breathtaking vistas from Scotland's western coast (page 424).

course, hairy heilan coos (Highland cows)—and walk for days without seeing anything resembling civilization.

To reach this utopia, Inverness, a pretty city set on the Moray Firth with the River Ness running through it, is very much the gateway. For a long time, visitors would come here—the last major town for a hundred miles or more if you're traveling north—settle for a few days, visit nearby major sites, such as the Culloden Battlefield where Jacobite dreams came crashing down in 1746, and then perhaps book a one- or two-day tour into the Highlands. Most visitors to Inverness come on the way to the most famous loch of them all, Loch Ness, to attempt to solve Scotland's "unsolved mystery" of the Loch Ness Monster.

For the last six years or more, however, a huge campaign promoting a 500-mile (800-km) driving route through the upper reaches of the Highlands, has resulted in one of the most exhilarating car journeys imaginable. The North Coast 500 has been an outstanding success, attracting tens of thousands of visitors each year who otherwise wouldn't have come to this part of the Highlands. My advice is to choose a section of the route and do it at leisure, really giving yourself time to slow down and take it all in. If the past year or two has taught us anything, it's that rushing around is not relaxing, and traveling is a privilege.

ORIENTATION

As the main entry point to the Highlands, **Inverness Airport** receives regular flights from London and other international destinations, and its train station is a stop on the **Caledonian Sleeper,** too—you could bypass Glasgow and Edinburgh entirely and come right here. **Inverness** is located on the **Moray Firth** coast at the north end of the Great Glen, a diagonal fault line that runs southwest all the way to Fort William at the head of Loch

Linnhe, connected by a series of lochs and canals including the legendary **Loch Ness.**

There are a few major towns along the shores of Loch Ness; the **A82** runs from the outskirts of Inverness through the hubs of **Drumnadrochit** and **Fort Augustus,** both of which get extremely crowded with tourists, particularly in the height of summer. On the quieter eastern shore of the loch along the **B862** and then the **B852,** villages like **Dores** and **Foyers** are subtler and more genuine.

Once you've done the obligatory search for Nessie and perhaps kayaked on Loch Ness's mysterious waters, you can head out onto the less traveled **North Coast 500** route. Actually covering 516 miles (830 km) in total, departing from Inverness, it can be driven clockwise or counterclockwise, though I recommend the latter, first heading 120 miles (190 km) north to what's almost the Scottish mainland's most northerly point, **John o' Groats.** From there, continue to Scotland's jagged west coast, where the route loops around lochs that dig into the landscape, turning south toward Applecross, where you'll turn back east toward Inverness.

Alternatively, from Applecross, you're not far at all (about 40 miles/64 km) from Kyle of Lochalsh and the **Skye Bridge.** Many people also use Inverness as a starting point for the road to Skye without traveling up to the North Coast 500, driving along the northern coast of Loch Ness before heading west to Kyle of Lochalsh—an 80-mile (128-km) journey in all.

PLANNING YOUR TIME

There is a temptation for many visitors to the area to book a short excursion or whistle-stop tour from Inverness into the Highlands and leave, but this would be doing the region a real disservice. **Inverness** itself, with a few museums, shops, and restaurants, is worthy of a day or two. If you want to visit **Culloden, Cawdor,** or Loch Ness, you'll need to factor

---

Previous: Eilean Donan Castle; memorial cairn at Culloden; Cawdor Castle.

Inverness, Loch Ness, and the North Coast 500

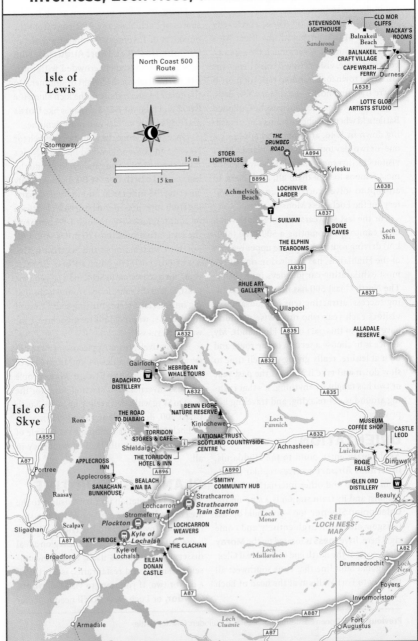

North Coast 500 Route

Isle of Lewis

Stornoway

STEVENSON LIGHTHOUSE — ★ CLO MOR CLIFFS
Sandwood Bay Balnakeil Beach MACKAY'S ROOMS
BALNAKEIL CRAFT VILLAGE
CAPE WRATH FERRY Durness
A838
LOTTE GLOB ARTISTS STUDIO

THE DRUMBEG ROAD
STOER LIGHTHOUSE ★ A894
B896 Kylesku A838
Achmelvich Beach LOCHINVER LARDER A837
SUILVAN BONE CAVES Loch Shin
THE ELPHIN TEAROOMS
A835 A837
RHUE ART GALLERY
Ullapool
ALLADALE RESERVE
A835
A832
Isle of Lewis

0   15 mi
0   15 km

Gairloch HEBRIDEAN WHALE TOURS
BADACHRO DISTILLERY A832
A832 A835
THE ROAD TO DIABAIG BEINN EIGHE NATURE RESERVE
Isle of Skye Rona Kinlochewe Loch Fannich
A855 MUSEUM COFFEE SHOP CASTLE LEOD
A87 TORRIDON STORES & CAFÉ
Portree Shieldaig NATIONAL TRUST SCOTLAND COUNTRYSIDE CENTRE A832
THE TORRIDON HOTEL & INN Achnasheen Loch Luichart Dingwall
APPLECROSS INN A896 ROGIE FALLS
Raasay Applecross BEALACH NA BA A890 GLEN ORD DISTILLERY
SANACHAN BUNKHOUSE SMITHY COMMUNITY HUB Beauly
Sligachan Scalpay Lochcarron Strathcarron
Plockton Strathcarron Train Station
LOCHCARRON WEAVERS Loch Monar
Stromeferry Kyle of Lochalsh SEE "LOCH NESS" MAP
SKYE BRIDGE Kyle of Lochalsh
Broadford THE CLACHAN Drumnadrochit Loch Ness
EILEAN DONAN CASTLE Loch Mullardoch A82
A87 Loch Cluanie Invermoriston Foyers
Armadale A887 Fort Augustus

INVERNESS, LOCH NESS, AND THE NORTH COAST 500

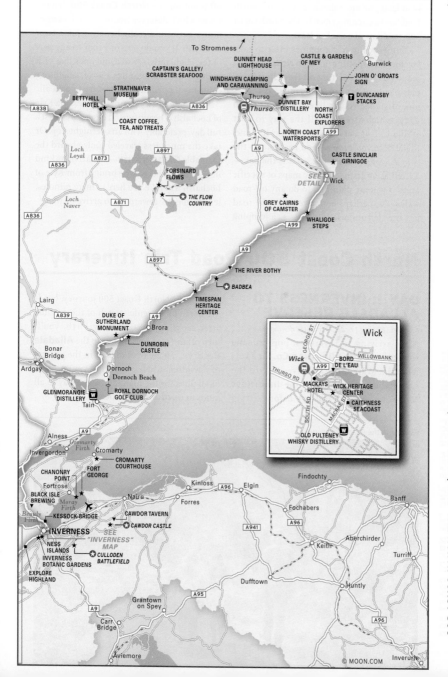

in at least one more day, and to see the north Highlands, circumscribed by the North Coast 500, you'll need a week at least.

Numerous tour companies offer to take you monster-spotting on **Loch Ness,** but with many bus routes setting off from Inverness, plus plenty of car hire companies, as well as long-distance routes like the **Great Glen Way,** which stretches all the way to Fort William, it is very possible to do it alone. Make sure you have a good road map—the *A to Z Scotland North & South* is the best— as well as Ordnance Survey maps of specific areas if you are planning to do any off-road walks. Or, perhaps better yet, take the road less traveled and use Inverness as a jumping

off point for the **North Coast 500** driving route, which deserves five to seven days minimum but would really benefit from a two-week trip. If you do opt for a tour to any part of the Highlands, try to avoid ones that visit multiple destinations; use a local, small tour company if possible and don't try to do it all.

The route to **Skye** from Inverness via Kyle of Lochalsh is beautiful and deserves at least a full day, preferably with an overnight stop. Or take the much less traveled route aboard the turntable **Glenelg ferry**—the last of its kind in Scotland. Though the bridge from Kyle of Lochalsh will take you here in mere minutes, it's much more rewarding to arrive by water.

North Coast 500 Road Trip Itinerary

DAY 1: INVERNESS TO ALLADALE RESERVE

43 miles (69 km); 1 hour 30 minutes driving time

After arriving in Inverness, pop into the **Inverness Coffee Roasting Co.** for a caffeine fix. Walk along the river toward the castle and have a look in the **Inverness Museum and Art Gallery** before setting

off on your North Coast 500 journey, heading north on a scenic stretch of the A9. Just after crossing the Cromarty Firth, you'll turn off the road on a detour to the **Alladale Reserve,** a huge tract of land in the process of rewilding, where you'll find your accommodations for the night and a gateway to all kinds of **outdoor activities.**

walking in the Alladale Reserve

DAY 2: ALLADALE RESERVE TO WICK

93 miles (150 km); 3 hours driving time

Back in your rental car, head back to the North Coast 500 route. Shortly after returning to the A9, you'll pass a very conspicuous and rather controversial statue—the **Duke of Sutherland Monument,** which commemorates George Granville Leveson-Gower, who was responsible for some of the worst of the Highland Clearances that so characterize this region. You'll get a real lesson in the meaning of the dark period in Scotland at **Badbea,** an abandoned village another hour up the road.

After the sobering walk around the former Highland settlement, warm your spirits with a lunch at the **River Bothy,** before sampling some Maritime Malt at the **Old Pulteney Whisky Distillery** in Wick. Tonight you'll stay at **Mackays Hotel,** with comfortable rooms and a delicious in-house restaurant in a 19th-century building.

DAY 3: WICK TO THURSO

45 miles (72 km); 1 hour 30 minutes driving time

It's time to head north. Grab something for breakfast at **Stacks Coffee House & Bistro** before taking the obligatory photo at the **John o' Groats Sign,** followed by a trip to the *actual* northernmost spot in the UK—**Dunnet Head.** After a brisk stroll down to the lighthouse and back, you can try some gin at **Dunnet Bay Distillery** and then head to Manor House in Thurso, where a cozy bed and delicious meal await you.

DAY 4: THURSO TO DURNESS

75 miles (121 km); 2 hours 30 minutes driving time

Today's itinerary begins and ends at beaches that will make you feel like you're at the end of the world. First is **Farr Beach,** a sandy strand that's protected by dunes and treasured by locals. **Coast Coffee, Tea and Treats** is a great place to get your caffeine fix after walking on the sand. Keep heading west to the town of Durness, where you can check into your

lodging at **Mackay's Rooms,** followed by a trip to **Balnakeil Craft Village,** where you can meet local artisans, watch them at work, and possibly buy some of their creations. Watch the sunset from **Balnakeil Beach,** regularly ranked among the best beaches in Scotland.

DAY 5: DURNESS TO ULLAPOOL

95 miles (153 km); 3 hours driving time

As if the drive so far hasn't been exciting enough, today you'll take the thrilling **Drumbeg Road,** which rewards experienced (and careful) drivers with incredible views. Be sure to stop at the **Lochinver Larder** as a reward for your intrepid driving, followed by a hike to the **Bone Caves,** where a treasure trove of animal remains from the glacial period were found. You'll be ready for a pint and some traditional music at the **Ceilidh Place** in Ullapool, where you'll also be sleeping for the night.

DAY 6: ULLAPOOL TO TORRIDON

94-116 miles (151-187 km); 2.5-3.5 hours driving time

Truly daring motorists can attempt the famously hair-raising routes of **Bealach na Bà** or the **Road to Diabaig**—or, skip the steep climbs and hairpin turns and visit the **Badachro Distillery** and go for a hike in the **Beinn Eighe Nature Reserve** instead. Either way, you'll end up at the **Torridon Hotel and Inn** at the end of the day for room and board.

DAY 7: TORRIDON TO LOCH NESS

103 miles (166 km); 3 hours driving time

The last day of driving on the North Coast 500 is somewhat uneventful compared to the dramatic, single-track roads thus far, but it ends with a pretty spectacular reward. Stop off at the **Museum Coffee Shop** in Strathpeffer, housed in a grand, Victorian former train station, before heading straight for **Drumnadrochit** on the shores of Loch

North Coast 500 Road Trip Itinerary

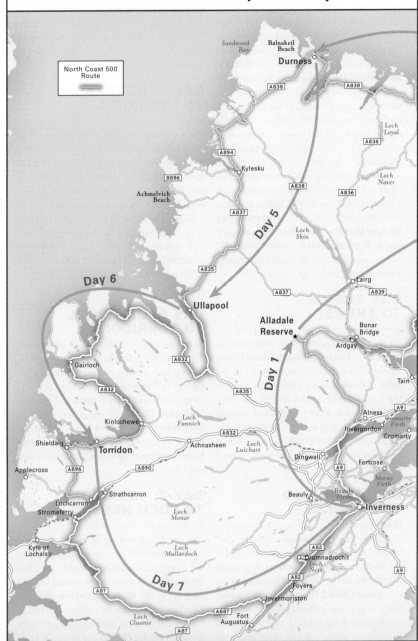

North Coast 500 Route

Sandwood Bay

Balnakeil Beach

Durness

A838

A838

A838

Loch Loyal

A836

A894

Kylesku

A838

A836

Loch Naver

Achmelvich Beach

B896

A837

Loch Shin

Day 5

A835

A837

Lairg

A839

Ullapool

Day 6

Alladale Reserve ★

Bonar Bridge

Gairloch

A832

A832

Ardgay

Tain

Day 1

A835

Kinlochewe

Loch Fannich

A832

Loch Luichart

Achnasheen

Alness

A9

Cromarty Firth

Invergordon

Cromarty

Shieldaig

Loch Monar

Dingwall

Fortrose

Applecross

A896

Torridon

A890

Beauly

Beauly Firth

Moray Firth

Strathcarron

Lochcarron

Stromeferry

Loch Mullardoch

Inverness

Kyle of Lochalsh

Day 7

A82

Drumnadrochit

Loch Ness

A9

Foyers

A82

Loch Cluanie

A87

Fort Augustus

A887

Invermoriston

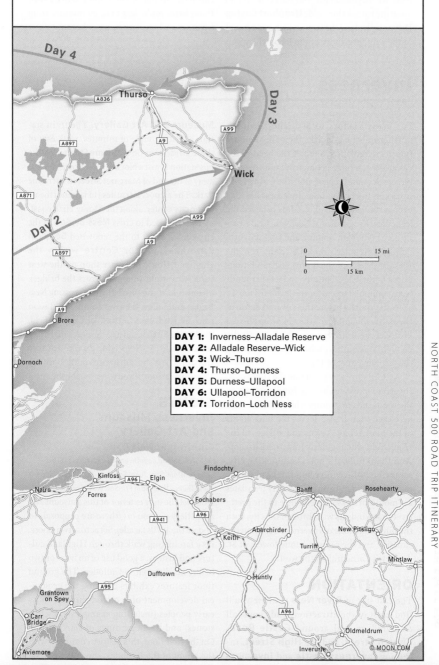

DAY 1: Inverness–Alladale Reserve
DAY 2: Alladale Reserve–Wick
DAY 3: Wick–Thurso
DAY 4: Thurso–Durness
DAY 5: Durness–Ullapool
DAY 6: Ullapool–Torridon
DAY 7: Torridon–Loch Ness

© MOON.COM

Ness, where you can get your bucket list photo amid the ruins of loch-side **Urquhart Castle.** Drive north along the famous loch and around to the southern shore of the loch, where you can have dinner at the homey **Dores Inn.** From here, you're less than 20 minutes from Inverness, where your journey began.

Inverness

For many visitors to Scotland, Britain's northernmost city marks their first venture into the Highlands. Sited at the head of the Great Glen, a huge geological fault line that bisects Scotland diagonally all the way from Inverness to Fort William, Inverness has long been a strategic stronghold. It is believed the legendary King of Scots, Macbeth, held a castle here in the 11th century, and later the royal burgh was regularly raided by clans from the Western Isles and the notoriously ambitious Lords of the Isles. The city and its surrounds were common targets for the Jacobites too. In 1746 and shortly before their overall defeat at the Battle of Culloden, they blew up the old Fort George in Inverness, which, ironically enough, was built to subdue them following the Jacobite rising of 1715.

As the main entry point into the Highlands, Inverness provides all the fundamentals to the thousands of visitors who travel through here each year. It also serves the inhabitants of the more remote towns and villages of the Highlands, who regularly travel here to shop. And thankfully, it's not a bad-looking city; some fine 19th-century buildings can still be found here today. Inverness loosely translates as "mouth of Ness," in reference to the pretty river that winds its way through the city, with the pink sandstone of Inverness Castle on the east side and the red sandstone towers of St. Andrew's Cathedral on the west.

ORIENTATION

The east side of **River Ness** is where you'll find most of the attractions and shops, all clustered on and around **Castle Road, Church Street,** and the **High Street,** including **Inverness Castle** and **Inverness Museum and Art Gallery.** The train station is just a couple of minutes' walk east of these attractions on Academy Street, and the bus station is just a block farther north, tucked away at the end of Margaret Street in Farraline Park. The airport is 9 miles (14 km) northeast of the city center, along the Moray Firth coast.

You will need to cross **Ness Bridge** in the city center to get to the renowned **Scottish Kiltmaker Visitor Centre** within the Highland House of Fraser shop on the west bank (turn right when you cross the bridge). Meanwhile, if you turn left when crossing Ness Bridge and follow the river south, you'll soon reach **St. Andrew's Cathedral.** Farther afield, the **Moray Firth** lies just to the north of the city center, while the **Ness Islands** and **Botanic Gardens** lie a short distance south. Both are accessible on foot, if you're reasonably fit.

SIGHTS
Inverness Museum and Art Gallery
Castle Wynd; tel. 01463 237 114; www. highlifehighland.com/inverness-museum-and-art-gallery; 10am-5pm Tues.-Sat. Apr.-Oct., 12pm-4pm Tues.-Thurs., 11am-4pm Fri.-Sat. Nov.-Easter; free

Don't let the ugly exterior of this museum and art gallery put you off (there are proposals to update the 1970s façade). Set across two floors, it's a fascinating walk through Highland culture and history, a good use of an hour or two before heading out to Culloden. The ground floor features exhibits charting the geological development of Scotland through to its early peoples (including examples of Pictish stones) and the beginnings of clan culture. On the first floor, this history continues with the plight of the Jacobites, showcasing some

Inverness

River

Ness

A82

A82

A82

A82

A82

CHAPEL ST

ROSE ST

RAILWAY TERRACE

STROTHER'S LANE

DOUGLAS ROW

FRIARS' ST

FRIAR'S LANE

CELL ST

HUNTLY ST

QUEEN ST

BALNAIN ST

GREIG ST

GREIG ST BRIDGE

KING ST

HUNTLY ST

DUNCRAIG ST

KENNETH ST

GLENURQUHART RD

KENNETH ST

TOMNAHURICH ST

ALEXANDER PLACE

NESS WALK

BISHOPS RD

NESS BANK

HAUGH RD

CASTLE RD

NESS WALK

INFIRMARY BRIDGE

GORDONVILLE RD

BANK ST

CHURCH ST

POST OFFICE AVE

QUEENSGATE

UNION ST

BARON TAYLOR'S ST

MEALMARKET CLOSE

LOMBARD ST

BRIDGE ST

NESS BRIDGE

ACADEMY ST

EASTGATE

CHARLES ST

ARDCONNEL ST

HILL ST

REAY ST

DENNY S

CROWN ST

ARGYLE ST

ARGYLE TERRACE

MICHELL'S LANE

PORTERFIELD BANK

OLD EDINBURGH RD

CULDUTHEL RD

MAYFIELD RD

SOUTHSIDE RD

CULDUTHEL RD

ARDROSS PLACE

ARDROSS ST

BISHOPS RD

INVERNESS COFFEE ROASTING CO ▼

LEAKEY'S SECONDHAND BOOKSHOP

INVERNESS BUS STATION ■

HOOTENANNY

MUSTARD SEED ▼

VICTORIAN MARKET

🚆 **Inverness**

GIRVANS ▼

ℹ **VISITSCOTLAND INVERNESS ICENTRE**

THE SCOTTISH KILTMAKER VISITOR CENTRE ■

★ **INVERNESS MUSEUM AND ART GALLERY**

CASTLE GALLERY ■

★ **INVERNESS CASTLE**

PITFARANNE GUEST HOUSE ●

To Aberfeldy Lodge →

BAZPACKERS ●

✝ **ST. ANDREW'S CATHEDRAL**

EDEN COURT THEATRE ■

GLENMORISTON HOUSE HOTEL ●

ROCPOOL RESERVE ●

0   150 yds
0   150 m

© MOON.COM

of their traditional weapons (such as dirks) alongside bagpipes and other memorabilia. The first floor is also home to two art galleries that host temporary exhibitions, often from local artists, covering fine art, ceramics, and modern art. There's also a café, a shop, and a useful exhibit (on the ground floor) on Gaelic phrases, so you can show off to your friends back home.

Inverness Castle

Castle Street; tel. 1349 781 730; www. highlifehighland.com/invernesscastleviewpoint; 11am-6pm daily Apr.-May, 10am-7pm daily June-Aug., 11am-6pm daily Sept.-Oct.; £5 adult, £3 under 12

Inverness Castle is a palace of pink sandstone overlooking the city, its current incarnation built in 1847 (after the Jacobites destroyed the medieval castle just before the Battle of Culloden in 1746). It has a series of towers and turrets typical of Scottish Baroque style. The **Inverness Castle Viewpoint,** which ascends 94 steps up the north tower, is the only part of Inverness Castle that is open to the public. Once you make it to the top, the rounded viewpoint is narrow, but it's rarely crowded so there's plenty of space to see everything. It's only really worth it on a clear day; come later in the afternoon for the best chance of having this spot to yourself.

St. Andrew's Cathedral

Ardross Street; tel. 1463 225 553; https:// invernesscathedral.org; 9:30-5pm Mon.-Sat., 10am-3pm Sun.; free

Lovely, red-stone St. Andrew's Cathedral was built in the late 19th century, with plenty of stone ornamentation on the entryways and towers, and an intricately carved wooden chancel piece and supporting arches. The church holds regular concerts and community events, and is actually the northernmost cathedral in the mainland UK.

Inverness Botanic Gardens and Nursery

Bught Lane; tel. 01463 713 553; www. highlifehighland.com/inverness-botanic-gardens; 10am-5pm daily summer, 10am-4pm daily winter; free but donations welcome

This delightful garden, free to visit (though donations are welcome), is small but quaint. In the Tropical House you'll see colorful displays and a waterfall that creates a soothing atmosphere above a pond filled with koi; next door see hundreds of cacti. In the outdoor garden, you'll find a wildflower meadow and carved animals hidden among the shrubs of the raised and ground-level beds.

Ness Islands

Great Glen Way; www.visitinvernesslochness.com/ listings/ness-islands; open 24/7; free

You'll feel a long way from the city center when you reach these pretty islands planted with mature Scots pine and fir, sycamore, and beech trees, but, in actual fact, you can get here on a lovely 20-minute walk along the River Ness (where you can often spot seals playing in the water). Connected by a series of Victorian footbridges, the islands, which also mark the beginning of the Great Glen Way, are free to wander. They're not huge—around half a mile from top to bottom—and you can easily cross them in 10 minutes, but come for a picnic, spend a little longer walking around looking for the tree sculptures (including one of Nessie), or find a spot to sit and watch the fishermen.

SPORTS AND RECREATION

Hiking

THE GREAT GLEN WAY

Distance: *79 miles (127 km)*
Time: *4-7 days*
Trailhead: *Ness Islands*
Information and Maps: *www.highland.gov.uk/ greatglenway*

Setting out from Inverness, this long hiking trail follows the route of the Great Glen, a geographical fault line that dissects the Lowlands and the Highlands of Scotland in a diagonal line all the way to Fort William. Along the way, you'll trek close to the shoreline of Loch

---

1: enjoying Inverness **2:** St. Andrew's Cathedral

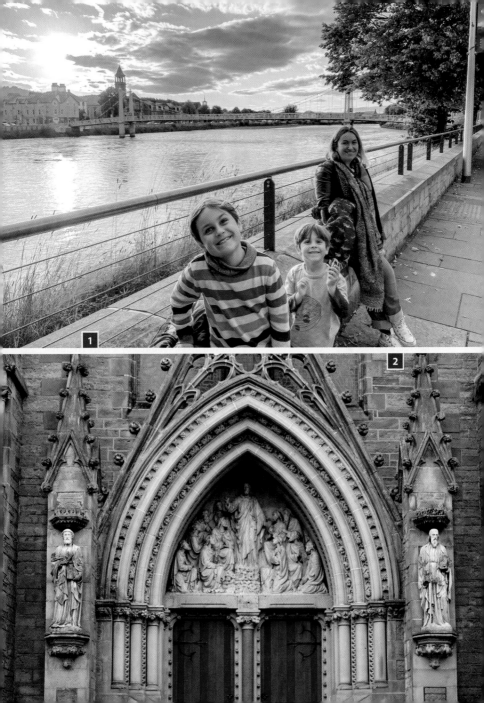

Ness, and then past a series of other lochs and canals that make up the Caledonian Canal. The route is low-level (with some options to head to higher ground) and quite flat (so it can also be cycled and it's also possible to travel the Great Glen Way by boat), passing through forests and some farmland. You'll need to stop overnight along the way if you want to complete it all, and you may wish to do some slight detours—to climb one of the Munros or Corbetts that beckon in the distance, for instance, or to kayak some of the waterways. You can also do the route from the other way, setting off from Fort William, or just do a short section, such as from Drumnadrochit to Invermoriston (14.3 miles/23 km; 4-5 hours), which includes trekking to the highest point of the Great Glen Way for far-reaching views of Loch Ness and Glen Moriston.

Dolphin-Spotting
DOLPHIN SPIRIT TRIPS
Inverness Marina, Stadium Road; tel. 07544 800 620; https://dolphinspirit.co.uk; RIB rides 10:30am-12:30pm and 2:30pm-4:30pm Apr.-June and Sept.-Oct., 9:30am-11:30am, 12:30pm-2:30pm, and 3:30pm-5:30pm July-Aug.; cruiser rides 10am-11:15am, 12pm-1:15pm, 2pm-3:15pm, 4pm-5:15pm Apr.-Oct.; RIB rides adult £34, child £24, family £105, cruiser rides adult £18.50, child £12, family £55, under 4 free

For an exhilarating ride out to the Moray Firth, book one of these two-hour Rigid Hull Inflatable Boat rides where, hopefully, you'll spot some of the resident dolphins or see some passing pods, even some whales. There's also a gentler, more kid-friendly cruise option. Importantly, Dolphin Spirit is accredited by the Dolphin Space Programme, a code of conduct to ensure the dolphins don't endure any undue stress from the boats. Arrive 30 minutes before departure time for the RIB rides and 15 minutes before cruiser trips.

Fishing
YOU FISH SCOTLAND
Inverness; tel. 01463 772 121; https://youfishscotland. com; year-round; salmon fly-fishing from £372 per day

The River Ness is renowned for its great salmon and trout fishing. Whether you're a complete beginner or more advanced, this small company run by the affable Wes and Roz will organize the best trip for you. Your guide—sometimes Wes, sometimes one of his very experienced hands—will collect you from your hotel, and you'll be given a homemade lunch, plus all needed equipment.

FESTIVALS AND EVENTS
INVERNESS HIGHLAND GAMES
Bught Park, Inverness; tel. 01463 785 006; http:// invernesshighlandgames.com; July; adult £8, child and concessions £2, under s free

The program each year at this stalwart Highland event is usually packed. Since 1822, it's usually been held in July in a park on the west side of the river. There are track and field events for participants of all ages, but the highlight is the opening ceremony at midday on the Friday, which features clan chieftains in full dress, followed by a mass Highland fling, which is fast, chaotic, and a lot of fun.

RED HOT HIGHLAND FLING HOGMANAY PARTY
Northern Meeting Park, Inverness; www.highland. gov.uk; free

Everyone is hoping that this free concert, held since 2008 (with the exception of COVID cancellations), will be back soon. Held on New Year's Eve from about 8pm, it attracts as many as 15,000, making it one of the largest Hogmanay concerts in Scotland. As well as live music, there's also an amazing fireworks display. Keep an eye on the Highland Council website for news on the event.

ARTS AND CULTURE
EDEN COURT THEATRE
Bishops Road, Inverness; tel. 01463 234 234; https:// eden-court.co.uk; cinema from £6.50, theater tickets from £13

Easily the Highlands' premier culture hub, this is a real meeting place for locals, who come to catch up over coffee, watch a film, see a play, or view one of the regular free exhibitions. Ticket prices are good compared with theaters in other major cities, and, while there are few West End names, a lot of the shows offer humor and insight into local culture.

SHOPPING

LEAKEY'S SECONDHAND BOOKSHOP

Greyfriars Hall, Church Street, Inverness; tel. 01463 239 947; www.facebook.com/LeakeysBookshop; 10am-5:30pm Mon.-Sat.

There are bookshops and then there is Leakey's. On entering the former church, you can smell the old pages of the thousands of tomes all stacked together, a little higgledy-piggledy, but in sections at least. Release yourself for an hour or two from the pressures of the real world by trawling for bargains or collectors' editions, or reclining into a sofa on the gallery above to try before you buy.

THE SCOTTISH KILTMAKER VISITOR CENTRE

4-9 Huntly Street, Highland House of Fraser, Inverness; tel. 01463 222 781; www. highlandhouseoffraser.com; 9am-10pm daily summer, 9am-6pm daily winter, closed Sun. Jan.-Mar.; kilt-making exhibition adult £2.50, concessions £1.50, under 5 free

As well as a gorgeous array of bright knits and woolen garments from the likes of Harley of Scotland and Glen Appin, and Trinity caps and capes made from Harris Tweed—all sold to you by staff dressed in kilts—you can learn about the art of kilt-making here. Head upstairs to the kilt-making exhibition where you can see some of the shop's kilts being handmade and learn about the precision art, from how much cloth to cut to how to fold and pleat it correctly. Last entry is 45 minutes prior to closing.

VICTORIAN MARKET

Academy Street, Inverness; tel. 01463 710 524; www.thevictorianmarket.com; 8am-6pm Mon.-Sat., 11am-4pm Sun.

This covered market, entered through a doorway on Academy Street near the train station, has seen better days, but still has some pleasant cafés, retailers selling traditional garb, and a few jewelers. It's a slice of 19th-century nostalgia, although it's not quite the original building—that one burned down in 1889, the sole fatality being a dog who refused to leave the shop it guarded.

CASTLE GALLERY

43 Castle Street, Inverness; tel. 01463 729 512; www. castlegallery.co.uk; 9am-5pm Mon.-Sat.

Just a short walk from the city's main museum and gallery is this bright gallery with art works spread across two floors featuring a mix of contemporary pieces from British artists. View paintings of Scottish landscapes alongside studio glass and pieces of jewelry.

FOOD

Traditional

★ HOOTANANNY

67 Church Street, Inverness; tel. 01463 233 651; www. hootanannyinverness.co.uk; 12pm-3pm and 5pm-8pm Mon.-Sat., 12pm-9pm Sun.; entrées £5.45

Most people come to Hootananny in the center of town for the Scottish traditional music sessions that take place every night Sunday-Wednesday 9:30pm-midnight. However, the menu is decent too, with stews, tasty burgers, and homemade haggis meatballs. Book a table for dinner and settle in for the night. On Friday and Saturday live Scottish bands play on the main stage too.

Modern Scottish

MUSTARD SEED

16 Fraser Street, Inverness; tel. 01463 220 220; www.mustardseedrestaurant.co.uk; 12pm-3pm and 5:30pm-10pm daily, early evening menu 5:30pm-7pm daily; entrées £6.95, 2-course early evening menu £14.95

Ask anyone in Inverness for their top three restaurants, and the chances are this will be one of them. The building itself is reason enough to visit: its former guise as a church affords it a double-height ceiling, and period features entwine with modern minimalist

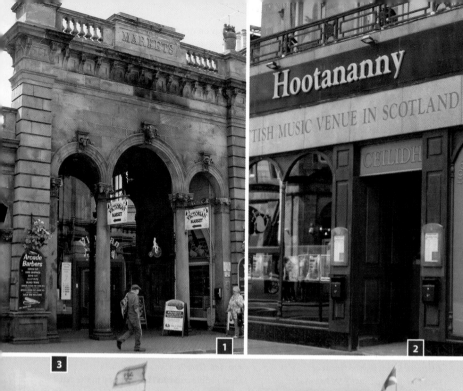

touches to give a fresh feel. That's not to undersell the food, though, which is consistently good, and dishes such as pan-seared Scottish salmon or shellfish gnocchi are fairly priced. In summer book a table on the terrace for lovely river views.

Pub Grub
★ CLACHNAHARRY INN

17-19 High Street, Clachnaharry; tel. 01463 239 806; www.clachnaharryinn.co.uk; 12:30pm-9pm Mon.-Sat., carvery 12:30pm-8pm Sun.; entrées £4.95

Known to locals as "the Clach," this inn is worth a little trip out of town for. In the former fishing village of Clachnaharry, now a quiet backwater of Inverness, you can catch the no. 307 bus here from the Inverness bus station. Its pub fare and portions are large, so come hungry. There's a nice beer garden and great staff, and the bar is almost always humming with locals. The menu is sometimes reduced on Mondays and Tuesdays, and don't arrive too late—they occasionally decide to close the kitchen a little early if it's quiet.

Light Bites
INVERNESS COFFEE ROASTING CO

15 Chapel Street, Inverness; tel. 01463 242 555; https://invernesscoffeeroasting.co.uk; 10am-2pm Mon.-Fri.; coffee £2

A cool espresso bar/bean shop, it's snug in here so not a place to stop for long, though there are a few tables and even a couple of stools by the counter if you'd like to have a little natter with the always-friendly staff as you drink. As the name suggests, they roast their own beans here, and the beans are all sourced ethically from people who work very closely with the farmers and cooperatives. If you're a bit overwhelmed by the choices on offer, ask for a taste before you buy, and staff will be happy to oblige.

1: the Victorian Market **2:** Hootananny
3: traditional Highland Games near Inverness

GIRVANS

2-4 Stephens Brae, Inverness; tel. 01463 711 900; https://girvansrestaurant.co.uk; 9am-6pm Mon.-Weds., 9am-7pm Thurs.-Sat., 10am-5pm Sun.; cooked breakfast £9.50

This is a popular brunch spot on weekends. You'll often find leisurely locals tucking into cooked breakfasts (served all day Sunday), which come with tea or coffee and toast. It's a good lunch spot during the week too, with lovely fresh filled sandwiches and baked potatoes or pastries (though rather cheekily, there is a minimum spend of £4 per person noon-2:30pm).

ACCOMMODATIONS
BAZPACKERS

4 Culduthel Road; tel. 01463 717 663; www. bazpackershostel.co.uk; £22 for a dorm bed, £65 d

You can't get much more centrally located than this hostel, which lies in the lee of Inverness Castle. Rooms are standard for a hostel (dorms and some private doubles and singles are available), but there are nice touches, including the real fire awaiting you on arrival and the full range cooker in the communal kitchen. For £5, staff will even wash and dry your clothes for you.

★ ABERFELDY LODGE

11 Southside Road; tel. 01463 231 120; www. aberfeldylodge.com; £110 d

This homely B&B set in a grand Victorian villa feels a lot less budget than its price. Inside, rooms are clean and bright; two of them have doors that lead onto the nice garden. That said, the building is old, so the hot water has a little knack to it and wifi is only really good in the lounge. If you can see past these things, you'll have a lovely wallet-friendly stay, just 10 minutes from the train station.

PITFARANNE GUEST HOUSE

57 Crown Street, Inverness; tel. 01463 239 338; www. pitfaranne.com; £130 d

Centrally located—the castle is just a five-minute walk away—this B&B on a quiet residential street is a real home from home.

Owners Malcom and Maggie will go out of their way to help you make the most of your time here.

GLENMORISTON HOUSE HOTEL

20 Ness Bank, Inverness; tel. 01463 223 777; www. glenmoristontownhouse.com; £229 d, £269 river view room

Set back from the road along the riverbank, this townhouse hotel has 30 bedrooms, plus three posh self-catering apartments. The Deluxe River View rooms with a huge trio of windows are the nicest, and it's hard to resist the wood-paneled Whisky and Piano Bar, with the city's largest whisky collection. On Saturday you'll be entertained by the resident pianist.

ROCPOOL RESERVE

Culduthel Road, Inverness; tel. 01463 240 089; https://rocpool.com; £250 d

Housed within an attractive but understated Georgian mansion, each of this hotel's 11 rooms comes with a giant bed and in a range of styles, from the decadent to classic or hip. As well as Tassimo coffee machines and Bose Bluetooth sound systems, lots of extra perks can be added, including in-room massages. It even has its own Chez Roux restaurant.

INFORMATION AND SERVICES

The main **tourist office** for Inverness is located near the castle (36 High Street; www. visitscotland.com/info/services/inverness-icentre-p333031) and is a good place to ask about the best tours. A few websites can help plan your visit, including the **official city website** (www.inverness-scotland.com) and **Visit Inverness & Loch Ness** (www. visitinvernesslochness.com). Last, but certainly not least, **Highlife Highland** (www. highlifehighland.com) is a local charity that runs many of the local tours and helps support the heritage of the city.

GETTING THERE
By Air

Inverness Airport (www.hial.co.uk/inverness-airport) lies 9 miles (14 km) east of the city, with several arrivals each day from all London airports, as well as from Manchester, and around one flight a day from Stornoway on the Isle of Lewis with Logan Air (www.loganair.co.uk).

From the airport, you can take the no. 11 or no. 11A bus with **Stagecoach** (£4.40 each way) from Inverness Airport into the city center. Buses are fairly regular (every 40 minutes Mon.-Sat., slightly less regular Sun.), with a journey time of 20-25 minutes. Taxis are also available with **Inverness Taxis** (www. inverness-taxis.com), which take around 20 minutes to reach the city (£12). Car hire is available at the airport with a number of operators, including Arnold Clark (www. arnoldclarkrental.com/airport-car-hire/inverness-airport) and Avis (www.avis.co.uk) from around £140 per week.

By Train

Inverness Train Station is located on Academy Street in the city center. Many people choose to get to Inverness from London aboard the **Caledonian Sleeper** train (www.sleeper.scot), which sets off the night before from London Euston and arrives into Inverness at around 8:40am. There is one train a day, except Saturdays (11.5 hours; £50 one-way, £185 with a single cabin). **ScotRail** (www.scotrail.co.uk) also has trains into Inverness from all major Scottish cities (Perth, Edinburgh, Stirling, and Glasgow). From Edinburgh around seven direct trains run a day (3.5 hours; from £15.50 one-way). From Glasgow six direct trains run a day (3.25 hours; from £11.80 one-way single).

Inverness Train Station is also the starting point for the Kyle Line (www.scotrail.co.uk/scotland-by-rail/great-scenic-rail-journeys/kyle-line-lochalsh-inverness), which splits into two main branches, one heading north along Scotland's eastern coast, ending in

Wick, and the other ending all the way to Kyle of Lochalsh and the Bridge of Skye.

By Car

Inverness is 3.25 hours (157 miles/253 km) north of Edinburgh. Take the M90 north to Perth where you will join the A9, which will take you all the way into Inverness. The journey time from Glasgow is about the same, but you take the M80 out of the city, all the way to Stirling, where you can also pick up the A9 (169 miles/272 km). From Aberdeen, Inverness is a 2.5-hour (104-mile/167-km) drive along the North East coast on the A96. From Fort Augustus, at the foot of Loch Ness, Inverness is an hour (35 miles/56 km) away; from Fort William, it's 2 hours (66 miles/106 km). Finally, from the Skye Bridge and Kyle of Lochalsh, Inverness is 2 hours (80 miles/129 km) away.

Parking in Inverness is fairly easy, with street parking and a good selection of car parks available in the city center.

By Bus

Just a block away from the train station, Inverness Bus Station (Margaret Street) is also accessed from Academy Street and offers all manner of connections.

The no. N19 from Shiel Buses (https://shielbuses.co.uk; two buses per day Mon.-Fri., one per day Sat.; £10.40 one-way) and the no. 919 from Stagecoach (www.stagecoachbus.com; two buses per day Mon.-Sat.; £10.40 one way) travels from Fort William to Inverness Bus Station (2 hours), stopping at Fort Augustus, Drumnadrochit, and Urquhart Castle on Loch Ness. Stagecoach has also recently overtaken a service from Foyers on the eastern shores of Loch Ness to Inverness a few times a day Mon.-Sat. (no. 302; 50 minutes; £3.40 one-way). The no. 917 from Scottish Citylink links Skye with Inverness (journey time 4.25 hours, four times per day; £26.40 each way single) and passes along the western shores of Loch Ness.

GETTING AROUND

Once in the city, you can reach most of the main sights on foot. However, if you're short of time, the CitySightseeing hop-on, hop-off bus (www.citysightseeinginverness.com) encircles the city (adult £10, concessions £8, child £3, under 5 free). Tickets last 24 hours, though buses only run 9:30am-4:15pm. For a quick lift, call or hail Inverness Taxis (tel. 01463 222 222; https://inverness-taxis.com).

Moray Firth

The majority of visitors to Inverness come to visit Loch Ness, which lies just 13 miles (21 km) south of the city and can be reached easily by bus, car, or even boat tour. However, before you head off in search of Nessie, make time to explore some of the major attractions to the east of the city. Here you'll find the scene of one of the most historic battles in British history, Culloden, which has an excellent visitor center; and jutting out onto the Moray Firth is imposing Fort George, which some consider one of the finest military fortifications in the whole of Europe.

Fans of TV's *Outlander* are well served in

the area too. The area's nearby ancient burial site of Clava Cairns was supposedly the inspiration for Craigh na Dun on the show, ensuring its place on bucket lists across the world for at least as long as the show runs. Speaking of fictional connections, when Shakespeare wrote down his account of one of the most notorious of Scottish kings, Macbeth, he used more than a little poetic license by changing the setting to Cawdor Castle, just 15 miles (24 km) northeast of Inverness. From here, you're only kilometers away from the distillery-rich region of Moray Speyside (page 180).

★ CULLODEN BATTLEFIELD

Culloden Moor, Inverness; tel. 01463 796 090; www.nts.org.uk/visit/places/culloden; 10am-4pm Jan.-Feb., 9am-6pm Mar.-May, 9am-7pm June-Aug., 9am-6pm Sept.-Oct., 10am-4pm Nov.-Dec. 23 and Dec. 27-30, 10am-2pm Dec. 31; visitor center adult £11, concessions £9.50, family £27, entry to the battlefield free

There are few experiences more emotive, particularly for members of the Scottish diaspora, than standing on the very battlefield where 1,600 men and boys (1,500 of whom were Jacobites) were brutally slaughtered in an hour, bringing the Jacobite dream crashing down and sending its leader, Bonnie Prince Charlie, running for the hills.

Anyone can step onto the moor itself for no charge. The battlefield, an area of generally flat (though lumpy), open boggy moorland, has been left much as it was prior to that fateful day; it's easy to see how the Jacobites, who favored charging downhill, were left vulnerable. On a cold and wet day when there are few visitors and an eerie sense of calm, it's not hard to imagine the battle cries of the clansmen as they charged forward, claymores in hand, bellowing their clan names as they ran to certain death.

Old Leanach Cottage, which was here back then (government forces burned down the barns that once stood near it when Jacobites hid there), still stands, and reopened in 2019 following major restoration work, which included a new heather-thatched roof. Some sensitive additions have also been made to the landscape, including red and blue flags that indicate where each side stood, a 6-foot (1.8-m) memorial cairn, and headstones to mark the graves of hundreds of clansmen.

If you are at all unfamiliar with the lead-up to the battle or the significance of the Jacobite cause, then paying to enter the visitor center is a must. There is an easy-to-follow path through the exhibits, which are spread out through one interconnected gallery. A mix of sound, stories, and artifacts bring the Jacobite cause to life. About halfway around, you can enter a separate room in which you can take part in an immersive experience. Hemmed in by screens with reenacted footage on all sides, and with surround sound, you really get a sense of the relentless combat in which the Jacobites armed with claymores and dirks were torn down by the better-equipped redcoats. This can make for uncomfortable viewing and is quite graphic in places, so it's not suitable for children.

There's a lot to take in, so give yourself at least a couple of hours here; the audio guide is good, even if it doesn't always seem to tally with the exhibits, so feel free to pause at times to take in the information. It's also worth paying the extra £2 for a tour of the battlefield, where your guide will reveal the personal stories of some of the men and boys who fought that day.

Getting There

To reach Culloden Battlefield it's just a 6-mile (10-km) drive east from Inverness along the B9006, which takes about 15 minutes. There is a car park just outside.

From Inverness, it's very easy to get to Culloden Battlefield by bus. Take the no. 5 bus from Queensgate to Croy and tell the driver you're going to Culloden Moor, not Culloden—the site is a further 10-minute bus ride from its namesake town (30 minutes, hourly, Mon.-Sat.; £3.15 one-way, £4.20 day rider). Or, located between Inverness and the airport, **Sneckie Taxis** (www.sneckietaxis.com) can organize tours to Culloden or work with you to create a bespoke itinerary such as a drive into the Highlands.

CLAVA CAIRNS

Near Inverness, IV2 5EU; tel. 0131 668 8600; visitscotland.com/info/see-do/clava-cairns-p245611; open year-round; free

With the earliest parts dating from around 2,000 BC, this collection of burial chambers in a woodland setting above the River Nairn is utterly beguiling. There are two main sections open to the public that once formed a larger complex. The first is **Balnuaran of Clava,**

The Battle of Culloden

The Battle of Culloden, which ultimately changed the course of Scottish history, took place just 6 miles (10 km) east of Inverness, on April 16, 1746, the culmination of a rising kickstarted by Bonnie Prince Charlie's arrival in Scotland less than a year earlier.

THE JACOBITE UPRISING

Raising the Stuart standard at Glenfinnan on August 19, 1745, Bonnie Prince Charlie staked his family's claim to the British crown and began a hearty uprising to rid Scotland and England of the Hanoverian rule of King George II once and for all. The cause united Highland clans (both Catholic and Protestant), many of whom believed the Stuarts would give Scotland more control over its affairs, and the Jacobites looked on course to win their fight.

RETREAT FROM DERBYSHIRE

After declaring Charles's father, James Francis Edward Stuart, King of Scotland in Edinburgh, and celebrating victories at both the Battle of Prestonpans and Battle of Falkirk Muir, the Jacobites marched south in the hope of launching an invasion on London. They were making steady progress and made it as far as Derbyshire in England—just three days from the capital—but there an about-turn took place. When English and French reinforcements they had been promised failed to materialize, the Jacobite army got jittery and, against the wishes of Bonnie Prince Charlie, decided to retreat. Sadly, this was to be their downfall. Unbeknownst to the Jacobites, King George II's son, the Duke of Cumberland, a fearsome and expert commander (his brutality earned him the nickname "Butcher"), was hot on their heels with a huge army. It was at Culloden that he caught up with them.

THE AFTERMATH

The open moorland of Culloden did not suit the fighting style of the Jacobites, made up predominantly of Highlanders whose best weapon was the element of surprise, leaping down mountains to catch their enemies off guard. Faced with a much larger and much better organized army of redcoats, who were drilled and in line, the Highlanders did the only thing they could—they charged at the enemy, but as they did the redcoats released canon after canon. Since then, the battle site has become a place of pilgrimage for millions of Scots, many of whom became scattered around the globe in the wake of Culloden as a result of the subsequent emigrations.

with an impressive central ring cairn surrounded by standing stones and two passage graves, as well as a kerb ring cairn (a small circle of large kerbstones, with the center filled in) added some thousand years later. The way the graves are aligned—with the three prominent cairns forming a line from northeast to southwest—has led to theories that the midwinter solstice would have been a significant time of the year for the people here.

The second area you can see is **Milton of Clava,** where you can view the remains of a medieval chapel—little more than a collection of large stones today—as well as a prominent standing stone, which may have formed part of another cairn. Today visitors are also drawn to Clava Cairns due to its role in inspiring TV's *Outlander*.

Getting There

Though a little tricky to reach by public transport, these prehistoric burial chambers are an easy detour from Culloden by car (just a 5-minute drive). Simply turn right onto the B9006 when you leave the Culloden Visitors Centre (rather than left to go back to Inverness), then turn right at Culloden Road, follow the road for a couple of minutes, and take the first road on your right (just past Clava Lodge Holiday Homes). The site will be on your right-hand side. The same route can be walked in around 30 minutes.

CLANS
MACGILLIVRA
MACLEAN
MACLACHLAN
ATHOL HIGHLANDERS

FORT GEORGE

Fort George; tel. 0131 310 8702; www. historicenvironment.scot/visit-a-place/places/fort-george; 9:30am-5:30pm daily late Mar.-Sept., 10am-3:15pm daily Oct.-late Mar., closed Sat.-Sun. Dec.-Jan.; museum free, Fort George adult £9, child £5.40, under 5 free

Following the defeat of the Jacobites at the Battle of Culloden, this fortification was built as a base for King George II's army with the intention of preventing any future uprisings. Its most striking feature is the mile of wall that surrounds the fort—though by the time they built it, the rising was over and not so much as a single shot has ever been fired at it. The ramparts provide a great viewing platform for views out to the Black Isle, and you can sometimes spot dolphins, whales, and seals in the waters of the Moray Firth. Elsewhere in the complex, the grand Georgian military buildings are worth a gander, including the grand magazine, originally created to hold 2,672 gunpowder barrels and today filled with a huge weapon collection.

Today Black Watch, the 3rd Battalion the Royal Regiment of Scotland, are based here, so much is off limits. The Highlanders' Museum, free with tickets to the fort, is worth a look for those who like military history. Set across three floors of the former Lieutenant Governors' House, more than 20,000 artifacts and 10,000 documents and photographs in 16 rooms chart the story of some of these Highlanders. In the neatly organized displays you can see campaign medals, including 16 of the regiment's 22 Victoria Crosses, the regimental uniform of King Edward VIII, and, rather unexpectedly, a box once used by Adolf Hitler to file personal papers.

An audio guide is available for the fort. Please note the museum is closed on weekends in December and January, though the fort is open. The ramparts and most of the fort are accessible to wheelchair users, but the museum is largely inaccessible.

1: clan graves at the battlefield site on Culloden Moor **2:** Cawdor Castle

Getting There

Fort George is just 13 miles (21 km) northeast of Inverness. If you're driving, you need to take the A96 toward Nairn before turning left at Newton of Petty onto the B9039, past the airport, and then bearing left onto the B9006 at Ardersier. The journey time is around 25 minutes. The fort is hard to reach by public transport, but local taxi firms will bring you here and collect you at a designated time.

★ CAWDOR CASTLE

Nairn; tel. 01667 404 401; www.cawdorcastle.com; 10am-5:30pm daily late Apr.-early Oct.; adult £11.50, child £7.20, family £33

Before I bring you the bad news, here's some good: Cawdor Castle is a well-preserved 14th-century castle in the style of a rectangular tower house that was constructed around a legendary thorn tree. The story goes that the Thane of Cawdor decided he needed a more powerful castle. He was visited by an oracle who told him to strap all of his gold to the back of a donkey, and wherever that donkey rested he should build his castle. The donkey came to rest by a hawthorn tree, and that is where the castle was built.

Now for some not-so-welcome news: Macbeth never lived here—he couldn't have. He died some 200 years before the current castle was built. There was an earlier castle here, founded in the 12th century, but that was still way after his time. The link to Macbeth seems to have come from poetic license. This news shouldn't put you off, though; the castle, which is still lived in by the Cawdor family, is a fine stately home with all the exquisite paintings and priceless furniture that one might expect of the landed gentry.

It's a sprawling palace, with 11 rooms to visit, and incredibly preserved, with much of the splendor added in the 17th century. The Thorn Tree room, where the fabled tree still stands, is relatively plain with bare brick walls, but the Tapestry Bedroom is richly decorated, with a crimson velvet four-poster bed and huge tapestries on the walls. Outside, the expansive grounds include a walled garden, flower garden, and wild garden. A walk through the Big Wood, a remnant of the ancient Caledonian forest, is also a must, and on bright days, you should also stroll to the summer house of the Dowager Countess Cawdor, Auchindoune House.

Macbeth aside, Cawdor Castle has been home to one or two more dubious characters in its time. To hear scandals and stories of past residents, a tour of the castle with an expert guide (1 hour; £110 for groups of up to 15) is recommended, but they only run on request, so book ahead. Express guided tours (just half an hour; from £30 per person) also run out of season if you ring ahead.

Food and Accommodations
CAWDOR TAVERN

Cawdor, Nairn; tel. 01667 404 777; 12pm-11pm Mon.-Sat., 12pm-10:30pm Sun.; entrees £6.95

In the little village of Cawdor, not far from the castle, is this local tavern where you can eat hearty Scottish dishes such as roast rump steak and the famous chicken Culloden, in which chicken breast is stuffed with haggis, swede puree, and mashed potatoes as well as a delicious whisky cream sauce. It's a fair bit pricier than most pubs but the quality is worthy of it. The pub, once the workshop for the Cawdor Estate, is exactly what you want inside, particularly in the lounge bar where there is a log fire and oak paneling that originally came from the castle's dining room. Highland Country buses no. 7 or no. 12 stop here from Inverness.

Getting There

For Cawdor Castle, take the A96 east out of the city before turning right onto the B9090 to Cawdor (14 miles/23 km; 30 minutes). On weekdays, the no. 252 with **D&E Coaches** (www.decoaches.co.uk) from Strothes Lane (just off Academy Street) in Inverness will get you to Cawdor in 45 minutes twice a day (£3.40 each way, £5.20 return). Get off at Cawdor Primary School, a 10-minute walk away.

Loch Ness

Loch Ness is the tourist hub of the central Highlands. Most visitors come in search of the famous Loch Ness Monster, but, legends aside, this loch is one of nature's great enigmas. Twenty-three miles long (36 km) and around 1 mile (1.6 km) at its widest, it's neither Scotland's largest loch (that is Loch Lomond) nor quite its deepest (Loch Morar claims that title), but it is certainly its biggest body of water—with a depth of 755 feet (230 m) in places, it holds more water than all the lochs in England and Wales put together.

The loch is served by the town of Fort Augustus in the south where a ladder of locks is the nucleus for visitors who like to sit and watch boats come up and down, but they are also useful places to restock and book tours and experiences.

SIGHTS
Drumnadochit
LOCH NESS CENTRE AND EXHIBITION

Drumnadrochit; tel. 01456 450 573; www.lochness. com; 9:30am-5pm daily Easter-June, 9:30am-6pm July-Aug., 9:30am-5pm Sept.-Oct., 10am-3:30pm winter; adult £7.95, child £4.95, under 6 free

If you want to learn more about the myth of Nessie, then a stop here is worth an hour of your time. While it doesn't shy away from revealing some of the more daring hoaxes, it also puts forward a compelling argument that there is something lurking beneath the loch's surface. All visitors take part in a 35-minute audio-visual tour, using a mix of archive materials. To younger tech-savvy minds, it may look a little amateurish, so kids could get a little bored. For the more cynical traveler, the

Loch Ness

Struy

A831

A82

EXPLORE HIGHLAND

FISH
LOCH NESS

B862

ALDOURIE
CASTLE

DORES INN

Dores

ACH-NA-SIDHE

A82

B852

LOCH NESS CENTRE
& EXHIBITION

DRUMBUIE
FARM

A887

Drumnadrochit

LOCH NESS GIFTS

CAFÉ
EIGHTY2

URQUHART
CASTLE

Divach
Falls

A82

B852

N e s s

Inverfarigaig

B862

LOCH NESS
SHORES

THE CRAIGDARROCH
INN

Foyers

WATERFALL
CAFE

Falls
of Foyers

Loch
Mhor

Invermoriston

Loch

A82

B862

SEE
DETAIL

Fort
Augustus

A82

0   2 mi

0   2 km

© MOON.COM

BUNOICH BRAE

A82

MORAG'S
LODGE

Fort
Augustus

CALEDONIAN
CANAL CENTRE

CANAL SIDE

CANAL SIDE

IN YOUR
ELEMENT

CRUISE
LOCH NESS

THE BOTHY

STATION RD

THE CLANSMAN
CENTRE

GLENDOE RD

THE LOVAT

A82

B862

exhibition also includes a lot of background on the geology of the loch, though granted, many of the displays are a little dated. It's not particularly ground-breaking stuff, but on a wet day it can fill in an afternoon and may even trigger a theory or two.

URQUHART CASTLE

A82, Drumnadrochit; tel. 01456 450 551; www. urquhart-castle.co.uk; 9:30am-6pm Apr.-Sept., 9:30am-5pm Oct., 9:30am-4:30pm Nov.-Mar.; adult £9, child £5.40

This ruined castle on the bonnie banks of Loch Ness has endured much warfare and unrest, and today it retains a haunting beauty. With 1,500 years of history, it has drawn romantic poets and writers in search of some of the relics of its past that saw it host lavish royal banquets and withstand countless sieges. St. Columba is said to have visited in the 6th century, and it has spent 500 years as a medieval fortress—changing hands many times during the Wars of Independence between the English and the Scottish. It was finally abandoned in 1692 when the last soldiers marched out, burning it on their way so it could not be requisitioned by Jacobite forces.

Today, some of the magic is lost among the throngs of people who come simply to take well-cropped photos. There is a good visitor center, though; the short film particularly gives a good overview of the history of the place. You can wander the grounds freely, nip in and out of the ruined segments, including the miserable-looking prison cell, and head down to a little pebble beach in front of the castle that looks out over Loch Ness. For the best views, climb the five-story Grant Tower and see if you can spot unusual ripples—large unidentified objects have shown up on sonar here. There's also a decent café and a large shop in the visitor center.

DIVACH FALLS

Drumnadrochit; https://scotland.forestry.gov.uk/ visit/divach-falls

These waterfalls, which drop 100 feet (30.5 m), are just 2 miles (3 km) south of the village and only a short walk from the small parking area (albeit at the end of a single-track road). To get to the car park, follow the A82 south out of Drumnadrochit and turn left onto the Balmaccan Road (it should be signposted to Balmaccan and Divach). Then follow this road for around a quarter of a mile (0.4 km) before staying right to join a single-track unmarked road. The small parking area will be on your right after another mile (1.6 km). The walk to the viewing platform, though just 984.3 feet (300 m), is steep and muddy at times over rough ground. The falls, surrounded by ancient oakwoods, drop from a good height and appear pure and wild.

Eastern Loch Ness
FALLS OF FOYERS

Foyers

This thunderous waterfall was a popular beauty spot among 18th- and 19th-century travelers. Robert Burns wrote of how the "roaring Foyers pours his mossy floods," and later in the same poem, "Still, through the gap the struggling river toils, and still, below, the horrid cauldron boils." There's little to fear today, though. The path is safe and well laid out with steps over steep parts and two viewpoints (upper and lower) as well as proper safety guards. It's pot luck too (depending on how much rainfall there has been recently) whether the falls are gushing or merely trickling, but the woodland around them is a very pretty place to be anyway.

Most visitors enter from the top of the woodland park by the village of Foyers (where there's a good café and shop) and walk down toward the falls, see them, and simply return the way they came—10 minutes there, 10 minutes back. However, for more peace and a better chance of seeing some red squirrels, continue down the path once you've visited the falls, all the way along the walkway, and enjoy the increasing quiet as you go. The bottom part of the woodland park is where squirrels are most frequently sighted, so find a spot, lay down a blanket, sit in silence, and wait. The walk down and back up again should take no more than an hour.

SHOPPING
Drumnadochit
LOCH NESS GIFTS

The Green, Drumnadrochit; tel. 01456 450 695; www. lochnessgifts.com; 9am-9pm summer, 9:15am-5:15pm fall, winter, and spring

Sometimes all you want is an unashamedly tacky gift shop, and that's exactly what you'll find here. Keyrings and soft Highland cattle and Loch Ness Monsters are all here to tempt you, as are scarves in a wide choice of tartans.

Fort Augustus
THE CLANSMAN CENTRE

Canalside, Fort Augustus; tel. 01320 366 444; www. clansmancentre.uk; 10:30am-6pm daily Mar.-Oct., restricted openings in winter

In this old 19th-century schoolhouse at the bottom of Fort Augustus's staircase of locks, this better-than-most souvenir shop sells good-quality tartan scarves alongside the ubiquitous Nessie hats and fridge magnets. More interesting is the Highlanders museum hidden behind a door in the corner of the shop: a replica of a clansman's turf house where intermittent shows describe the traditional way of 18th-century Scottish life. Sadly, at present these shows are only available by prior arrangement for groups of eight or more.

THE CALEDONIAN CANAL CENTRE

Ardchatten House, Fort Augustus; tel. 01320 366 493; 9am-5pm daily

This café-cum-shop-cum-museum has a higher-caliber selection of books, toys, and souvenirs than you'll find elsewhere, plus a small but well-presented museum on the canal. The café offers a choice of light bites and hot drinks for sit-down or takeaway.

SPORTS AND RECREATION
★ Canoeing and Kayaking

There's surely no better way to grasp the scale of Loch Ness than on a boat powered by pure elbow grease. The southern end of the loch is safest, and even with the murmur of cars on the A82 in the distance, it can still feel very peaceful with miles of blue water in front of you and green banks of trees on either side.

Book a guided canoe or kayak tour with an activity provider, or you can rent a kayak from Loch Ness Shores campsite for a solo paddle from £10 per hour. You'll be provided with lifejackets and any other necessary equipment, and you'll also be advised of currents to steer clear of and safe spots to go in for a swim. Loch Ness is vast and very deep, meaning it is extraordinarily cold, so don't take any unnecessary risks. It's also classed as open water, so make sure you keep close to the shoreline, unless you are with a guide.

EXPLORE HIGHLAND

Dochgarroch Lock, Inverness; www.explorehighland. com; 1 4-hour trip per week Easter-Oct.; adult £45, under 18 £30

These four-hour paddling trips are taken aboard tandem kayaks under the guidance of local expert Donald Macpherson. While at times the waters of the loch are eerily still, they can be precarious when the wind picks up; having Donald nearby is very reassuring. Trips are taken weekly from Dochgarroch Lock on the Caledonian Canal, where they continue toward Loch Ness. They are typically offered in the afternoon (1pm-5pm), though sometimes in summer Donald also offers trips 6pm-10pm as well as private trips.

IN YOUR ELEMENT

Fort Augustus; tel. 0333 600 6008; https://iye.scot; adult £22, child £15 per hour

You can take a canoeing tour with your own guide with In your Element, setting off from Fort Augustus on the southern end of the loch, or hire canoes and kayaks from them, which can be delivered to where you are staying, if you'd rather go it alone.

Boat Trips and Fishing
CRUISE LOCH NESS

Canal Swing Bridge, Fort Augustus; tel. 01320 366 277; www.cruiselochness.com; 10am, 11am, 12pm, 1pm, 2pm, 3pm, and 4pm late Mar.-Oct., 1pm and 2pm Nov.-late Mar.; adult £14.50, child £8.50, family £44

These child-friendly cruises are pretty hard to miss—you'll spot their kiosk when you cross the bridge in Fort Augustus. They are a lot of fun; your guide for the 50-minute Daily Cruise will intrigue you with tales of unexplained objects on the sonar, with plenty of jokes thrown in too. Morning cruises are less crowded, but from 1pm onward (especially in July and August), it's wise to book ahead.

FISH LOCH NESS

Dochgarroch Lock, Inverness; tel. 07793 066 455; https://fishlochness.com; Easter-Sept.; from £90 per person

Local ghillie Stuart Macdonald can take groups of up to seven out on four-hour trips that give you enough time to fish and take in the Highland scenery. Wet-weather gear is recommended; Stuart will provide licenses, rods, lifejackets, and tackle.

Hiking

A new walking or cycling route around the loch, the **Loch Ness 360** (https://lochness360.com), incorporates sections of previously existing long-distance trails, including the South Loch Ness Trail and the **Great Glen Way,** and is also a great way of taking it all in while avoiding the tourist crowds. Companies such as **Absolute Escapes** (www.absoluteescapes.com) can arrange baggage transfers for you.

SOUTH LOCH NESS TRAIL

Hiking Distance: *13.5 miles (22 km)*
Hiking Time: *Full day (7-8 hours)*
Trailhead: *Dores, Inverness*
Information and Maps: *https://lochness360.com/section-five*

In recent years there has been a concerted effort to draw tourists to the less-visited eastern shores of Loch Ness. This trail (Section 5) leads from Dores, just outside Inverness, to Foyers, about halfway along the southern shore, and takes in a quieter, slower pace of travel, away from the busy A82. The landscape is a little more unkempt, and, with fewer travelers, you're more likely to see deer wandering the woods. The villages of Dores and Foyers feel much more geared toward ramblers and cyclists than day-trippers. This section is one of six walking routes that encircle the loch to make up the full 80-mile (129-km) Loch Ness 360 route, which can be completed over 6-7 days. An easy add-on would be to overnight in Foyers and then continue the next morning onto Section 4 to Fort Augustus.

FOOD
Drumnadochit
CAFÉ EIGHTY2

Lewiston, Drumnadrochit; tel. 01456 450 400; www.facebook.com/cafeighty2; 9am-5pm Mon.-Sat., 11am-5pm Sun.; coffee from £2, cakes from £2.75

Don't underestimate this wee café in the center of Drumnadrochit, though it's all pastel colors, mismatched chairs and tables, and bunting; it serves the best coffee around. Plus, it has exemplary vegan and vegetarian food. Oh, and cakes. You must try the cakes.

Fort Augustus
THE BOTHY

Canalside, Fort Augustus; tel. 01320 366 710; 12pm-2:15pm and 5pm-9pm (5pm-8pm winter); entrées £5.50

This canal-side pub-restaurant in Fort Augustus is probably its most welcoming. There are a couple of good beers on tap, including Skye Red and Skye Gold, and the menu is reassuringly traditional, with haddock and chips and steak pie on offer. With its stone walls and fireplace, the pub area is cozier than the conservatory, but the whole place feels very rustic and unpretentious.

1: Urquhart Castle **2:** Falls of Foyers **3:** kayaking on Loch Ness **4:** campsite at Loch Ness Shores

THE LOVAT

Fort Augustus; tel. 01456 649 0000; www.thelovat. com; 7:30am-9:30am Mon.-Sat., 12pm-2pm and 6pm-9pm Sun.-Thurs., 12pm-2pm and 6pm-9:30pm Fri.-Sat.; entrées £8.25

This upmarket restaurant in a former railway hotel (now an elegant four-star hotel) is probably Loch Ness's finest. Dishes are of the haute cuisine level and have been awarded three Rosettes, and it shows. Ox cheek, roast grouse, and scallops all appear on the menu regularly and are given the light touch that lets their natural flavors come through. It puts other restaurants in the area to shame.

Eastern Loch Ness
★ THE CRAIGDARROCH INN

Foyers; tel. 01456 486 400; www.thecraigdarrochinn. co.uk; 12pm-2pm and 6pm-8:30pm daily; entrées £4.35

It's worth the 15-minute uphill trek from the Loch Ness Shores campsite to this pub, if only for the views of the campsite and loch, where the more you indulge in the local ale, the more you may believe you've seen Nessie. The food is pretty standard pub grub but good all the same, and there is a kids' menu. You may be tempted to cut through the overgrown trails on your way up to shorten the journey, but, if you want to avoid getting bitten by midges, take the main road up to the left and then take a sharp right once you see the sign after 1,500 feet (457.2 m) or so. Or you can even drive the car all the way up. There are also rooms available (£120 d).

★ DORES INN

Dores; tel. 01463 751 203; www.thedoresinn.co.uk; lunch menu noon-5pm, evening menu 5pm-8:45pm; entrées £4.95

With roses climbing its walls, this white stone building with slate-tiled roof is about as inviting as they come, and inside it gets better. Sit by the fire as you fill up on home-cooked food or take in the views of Loch Ness from one of the window seats. There's a sun terrace and a large beer garden, where you may find yourself rubbing shoulders with locals. Staff

are very friendly—so much so there is a complimentary shuttle service to pick you up and drop you off if you are staying within a 10-mile (16.1 km) radius.

WATERFALL CAFÉ

Foyers; tel. 01456 486 233; http:// foyersstoresandwaterfallcafe.co.uk; 9am-5pm Mon.-Thurs., 9am-7pm Fri.-Sat., 10am-3pm Sun. Apr.-Oct., 9:30am-4pm Mon.-Thurs., 9:30am-7pm Fri.-Sat., 10am-2pm Sun. Nov.-Mar.; sandwiches £7.50

In the village of Foyers, just across the road from the path that leads down to the famous falls, is this cute little café where you can buy delicious homemade cakes, sandwiches, and fresh tea and coffee, or even read one of the books available. In summer, treat yourself to an ice cream from the hut outside where you can help yourself to free sprinkles and sauce. In the telephone box outside, there's even a resident gnome to whom you are encouraged to send postcards; all the postcards he receives are displayed here.

ACCOMMODATIONS
Drumnadochit
DRUMBUIE FARM

Drumnadrochit; tel. 01456 450 634; www. loch-ness-farm.co.uk; £90 d

There are three en suite rooms in this intimate B&B on a working farm; the family breeds Highland cattle, and you can often see cows and their calves grazing outside. In the morning, as you feast on smoked salmon, scrambled eggs, or a full Scottish breakfast, you can gaze out to Loch Ness from the dining room. In the evenings snuggle up by the log fire in the lounge.

Fort Augustus
MORAG'S LODGE

Bunoich Brae, Fort Augustus; tel. 01320 366 289; www.moragslodge.com; £24.50 for a dorm bed, £62 private double

Just outside Fort Augustus, this hostel offers the normal dorm setup alongside doubles, twins, and family rooms and is something of a local legend in its own right. There's a self-catering kitchen (of course), but you can also order a well-priced home-cooked meal before you sample some of the single malt whiskies in the bothy-style bar and dance the night away to some of the live music. It's not your average hostel at all.

Eastern Loch Ness
★ LOCH NESS SHORES

Monument Park, Lower Foyers; tel. 01456 486 333; https://lochnessshores.com; £20 for a tent pitch, wigwams from £65

This is the only campsite with direct shore access, so if you want a campsite on Loch Ness, it has to be here. Owners Donald and Lyn have created a warm, lovely environment where it seems everybody is just delighted to work here, and everyone, whether you have brought your own tent or are staying in one of the onsite wigwams (more a wooden pod) or in a motorhome, is made to feel at home. The toilets and showers are pristine, and you can hire one of the kayaks for just £10 per person to head out on the loch, or try your luck making it up the nearby River Foyers as far as the old Telford Bridge (if conditions are suitable). There is a nice pebble beach from where you can skim stones after a home-cooked dinner that can be purchased from the Airstream van. There are lots of books to read and a fab shop. Fires are allowed, and there are even den-building workshops for kids. Need I go on?

ACH-NA-SIDHE

Wester Drumashie, Dores; tel. 01456 486 639; http://achnasidhebandb.co.uk; £90 d

Just a five-minute drive from the village of Dores, this quiet B&B has both loch and mountain views, a relaxing lounge and TV area, and lovely grounds with horses in a paddock. Family-run, there's little husband-and-wife team Marsaili and Ian and their kids won't do to make you feel at home—including washing and drying your clothes if you've been caught out by the weather.

ALDOURIE CASTLE

Loch Ness; tel. 01463 751 309; www.aldouriecastle. co.uk; cottages (sleeping 2 or more) from £1,000 per week, exclusive 2-night use of the castle £20,000

If you've spotted this Disney-style castle from the water, then you no doubt have fantasies of staying here. The good news is that, if you are loaded and/or have lots of friends to share it with, you can—it is available for exclusive hire. For the rest of us, there are some lovely cottages in the grounds to hire, such as the romantic white-stone Ivy Cottage with pitched roof or the one-story Pier Cottage right on the shoreline. Each of the four cottages is brimming with charm, and you'll get to gaze up at the stepped gables and Rapunzel-style turrets every day during your stay.

INFORMATION AND SERVICES

Sadly, the VisitScotland iCentres in both Drumnadrochit and Fort Augustus are permanently closed. The best physical place to visit to pick up maps, leaflets, and other information is the **Inverness iCentre** (36 High Street, Inverness, tel. 01463 252 401). The website www.visitinvernesslochness.com has lots of inspiration for things to do in the area and useful walking trails.

GETTING THERE AND AROUND

Most visitors to Loch Ness will arrive from **Inverness;** as well as having a well-served airport, it's where the closest train station is. Once here, it's time to get your walking boots on if you don't have a car, as local buses can be unreliable. Alternatively, you could book a private tour with the likes of **Loch Ness Travel** (tel. 01456 450 550; www.lochnesstravel.com), which also offers a taxi service. Expect to pay around £34 for a transfer from Inverness to Drumnadrochit, or, for a full day's excursion (eight hours) from Inverness to Loch Ness, it would cost £500, though you could bring seven friends with you.

By Car

It's just 16 miles (26 km) from Inverness along the A82 to Drumnadrochit (a journey time of half an hour) and 20 miles (32 km) along the B862 and B852 to Foyers (about 45 minutes). Fort Augustus can be reached by following either of these routes on for another 15-20 minutes. From Drumnadrochit, it's a further 19 miles (31 km) to Fort Augustus, while from Foyers it's a further 14 miles (23 km). From Fort William, it's a 50-mile (80-km) drive northeast up the A82 to Drumnadrochit (1.25 hours).

From Glasgow, it's 3.5 hours (139 miles/224 km) to Fort Augustus. Take the M8 north out of the city before picking up the A82, which will take you all the way up through Loch Lomond National Park, through Glen Coe where it becomes the **Glen Coe Road** (page 332), and past Fort William.

The journey time from Edinburgh is 3.75 hours (159 miles/99 km). You'll take the M90 north to Perth and join the A9, which you'll follow all the way through Perthshire to Dalwhinnie, where you fork off onto the A889. Follow the A889 until it turns into the A86, before turning right onto the A82 at Spean Bridge, bringing you to Fort William.

By Bus

A number of buses set off from Inverness Bus Station to Loch Ness, including the no. 513 (or N19) from **Shiel Buses** (https://shiel-buses.co.uk; 30 minutes, every two hours summer, twice a day winter, Mon.-Sat.; from £3.70 one-way to Drumnadrochit) and the no. 919 from **Stagecoach** (www.stagecoach-bus.com; 30 minutes, twice a day Mon.-Sat.; from £3.70 one-way to Drumnadrochit). Both of these buses stop at Drumnadrochit, Urquhart Castle, and Fort Augustus. These buses also link with Fort William in the opposite direction (1.75 hours to Drumnadrochit). Stagecoach has also recently overtaken a service from Foyers on the eastern shores of Loch Ness to Inverness a few times a day, Monday-Saturday (no. 302; 50 minutes; £3.40 one-way). To reach Loch Ness from Glen Coe, you'll need to get the no. 915 or no. 916 bus with Scottish Citylink from Glen Coe to Fort William (about four buses a day) and connect with one of the Loch Ness buses there (30 minutes to Fort William; £8.50 one-way).

The most direct route from Glasgow is to take the train from Glasgow Queen Street station to Spean Bridge (3 hours 30 minutes; from £33.20 single) and then take the Scottish Citylink no. 919 bus to Fort Augustus (40 minutes; £8.30 single). From Edinburgh, you'll have to get the train from Inverness (3 hours 30 minutes; from £28 single) and then travel onward from there.

Inverness to Kyle of Lochalsh

Many visitors tack on the Isle of Skye to their Inverness and Loch Ness travels, crossing over to the island via the bridge between Kyle of Lochalsh on the mainland and Kyleakin on Skye. By car, there are two main routes from Inverness. The most popular and probably most scenic is via the A82, along the shores of Loch Ness, before joining the A887 at Invermoriston and then the A87. It takes around two hours (80 miles/129 km).

Alternatively, the less traveled more northerly route takes you up through the Black Isle to join the A835, past Achnasheen and Strathcarron. For this route you will have to do a little detour along the A87 when you get to Auchtertyre if you'd like to visit Eilean Donan Castle. The distance covered and time traveled are similar.

Once you've reached Kyle of Lochalsh, the Skye Bridge takes just 5 minutes to cross. It's also possible to travel from Inverness to Kyle of Lochalsh by train, on the scenic Kyle Line.

SIGHTS
Eilean Donan Castle

Dornie, by Kyle of Lochalsh; tel. 01599 555 202; www. eileandonancastle.com; 10am-4pm daily Feb.-late Mar., 10am-6pm late Mar.-late Oct., 10am-4pm late Oct.-late Dec., opens at 9am July-Aug. and 9:30am Sept.; adult £7.50, child £4, family £20, under 5 free

Undoubtedly one of Scotland's most photographed and most romantic castles, this is a must-see on your way to Skye. It's located on its own little island at the point where three great sea lochs converge, just a few miles from the bridge to Skye.

Though this 13th-century castle was all but destroyed by the Jacobites, it was carefully restored in the early 20th century, complete with a fearsome portcullis and noble keep, reached via an arched stone bridge. Its atmospheric location has given it starring roles in over 30 films. Many simply stop here for the photo opportunity, but it's also worth paying the entrance fee, crossing over the stone bridge, and exploring the castle, all of which is open to the public. Inside, bare stone walls are adorned with all manner of memorabilia, including cannonballs that the Jacobites fired on the castle in 1719, alongside dirks and dueling pistols and family portraits.

Outside, you can walk around much of the castle exterior via a pathway that branches off to meet narrow staircases and courtyards, and fully appreciate the romantic setting.

FOOD
THE CLACHAN

13 Francis Street, Dornie; tel. 01599 555 366; www. theclachan.com; meals served 6pm-9pm Easter-Oct.; entrées £5.75

Straightforward traditional dishes (steak and Guinness pie or poached salmon served with seasonal vegetables) are served at this pub, just a 10-minute walk from Eilean Donan Castle. The food is well-cooked, well-presented, and well-priced. First come, first served.

WATERSIDE RESTAURANT

The Dornie, 8-10 Francis Street, Kyle of Lochalsh; tel. 01599 555 205; https://dornie-hotel.co.uk/seafood-restaurant-skye; 6pm-9pm Mon.-Sat. and 12pm-2:30pm Weds.; entrées £6.95

If you love seafood, then this place, once by the train station but now relocated to the dining room of the Dornie Hotel, is for you. Owners Jann and Neil MacRae handpick their local suppliers, with Isle of Skye mussels and peat-smoked salmon featuring on the menu. Neil also runs seafood cruises aboard his own fishing boat, Green Isle, cooking the daily

Eilean Donan Castle

catches on board. Seafood doesn't get much fresher than this.

INFORMATION AND SERVICES

Pick up maps and mine for as much info as possible at the **VisitScotland iCentres** in Inverness and Fort Augustus before heading along the A87 because, once you're on the road, services are sparse. For online inspiration and tips ahead of travel, check out the **Lochalsh & the Isle of Skye guide** (www.lochalsh.co.uk). There's also a **visitor center** at Eilean Donan Castle (tel. 01599 555 202; www.eileandonancastle.com/visit/visitor-centre).

GETTING THERE

Kyle of Lochalsh is truly the end of the line, a collection of restaurants, shops, and accommodations that have popped up to catch people on their way to Skye, with a train station right on the Kyle Akin and all roads seeming to lead to the Bridge to Skye, about a mile (1.6 km) to the west.

By Car

Kyle of Lochalsh is just under two hours (80 miles/129 km) from Inverness. There are two main ways to get here, both of which are about the same distance and time: the southern route, which travels along the northern shores of Loch Ness on the A82, turning northwest at the A887 all the way to Kyle of Lochalsh; and the northern route, on the A835, A832, and A890, passing through Strathcarron on the North Coast 500, which is just 30 minutes (20 miles/32 km) north of Kyle of Lochalsh.

By Train

Arcing all the way from Inverness to the shores of Loch Alsh for a distance of 80 miles (129 km), the Kyle Line is a spectacular route to travel between the two (2.75 hours; £13.90 one-way) and is known as the Great Highland Railway journey. As you approach the west coast you can see the dramatic Torridon Peaks to the north, while Skye comes into view to the south. There are some fabulous places to alight en route, including **Plockton.**

The North Coast 500

TOP EXPERIENCE

The marketing campaign behind the North Coast 500 has done its job well. A swell in visitors coming over the past few years has meant that the little visited parts of Scotland on this route have been opened up to tourism—a long time coming, as in the north Highlands you have it all. There are dazzling sandy beaches where you can have the sea to yourself, mountains ripe for adventure, unique ecosystems and wildlife sanctuaries, and lasting reminders of lives once lived, from Pictish carvings to cleared villages.

However, during the coronavirus pandemic, the burgeoning tourism industry here was shown to be vulnerable. When they were riding high, many businesses borrowed to extend and improve their offerings, but closures in 2020 meant that lots of hotels, restaurants, and activity providers really struggled, and some chose not to open at all when they could.

The upshot is that, while tourism is integral to these small communities, the pandemic allowed time for a rethink for both businesses and visitors. The Highlands is not a place to be rushed. The things that make this region so special really lend themselves to slow tourism and ecotourism. Come and visit but stay longer; don't whizz round the 500-mile (800-km) route as so many visitors do. And don't take it too literally either. It's okay to detour—in fact, it's crucial if you really want to have a unique and memorable visit.

ORIENTATION

Though this popular route (technically 516 miles/830 km, rather than exactly 500) can be traveled in either direction, my preference is to travel counterclockwise from Inverness, leaving the rugged and raw landscapes of Wester Ross for the end. Heading northeast from Inverness, you'll start out on the **A9** and eventually the **A99,** relatively well-traveled, two-lane roads. That is, until you get to Wick, where the roads start to get more rural. The A99 becomes the **A836** after John o' Groats, where the road turns to the west, until Kyle of Tongue and Tongue Bridge, after which the road becomes the **A838.** It's also possible to work Loch Ness into the last part of the North Coast 500 route, detouring south from Applecross to Inverness road.

PLANNING YOUR TRIP

To complete the entire route, you'll need at least a week, though that would mean you'd be speeding through; to allow more time for detours and lingering in the charming villages and remote landscapes, two weeks would be ideal. If you have less time, you don't have to follow the route at all, but can instead choose a section and really focus on it. My personal favorite is to cross inland to **Lochcarron** and then work your way north along the west coast to **Ullapool** through **Wester Ross**—a place of large landscapes, rugged coastline, and small settlements, with incredible views over to Skye. From Ullapool you can return to Inverness via the A835 in less than an hour and a half (240 miles/386 km). However, you'll still need a good few days to enjoy this route fully.

Visitor Information

The **official North Coast 500 website** (https://northcoast500.com) is an invaluable tool, with an interactive map to help you get a grasp of the main points of interest, suggested itineraries, and some important notes on road safety. Businesses do sign up to be partners of the route, so remember that ultimately the listings are advertisements. There are also membership options, starting from £15, that promise benefits, including discounts on distillery tours and a NC500 "passport" you can get stamped at 25 major sites.

Road Rules and Safety

Many caravans and motorhomes travel the North Coast 500, and oftentimes the roads are too small for them. Some of the roads, particularly those off the beaten track, can be treacherous at times. Pay attention to the road signs—some roads try to discourage caravans. Use the passing places where safe to do so, not only to let cars coming from the opposite direction pass, but also to let cars overtake you if you're going slower. Winter brings snow and ice, so you'll need to take extra care. I'd advise sticking to the main roads and giving yourself extra time. Some sections of road may become impassable in winter.

Public Transport

Though the North Coast 500 is first and foremost a road trip, parts of it are surprisingly accessible by public transportation, with the **Kyle Line** (www.scotrail.co.uk/scotland-by-rail/great-scenic-rail-journeys/kyle-line-lochalsh-inverness) branching out like a wishbone north and west of Inverness, including several stops along the North Coast 500, such as Wick, Strathcarron, and Plockton. After the Kyle Line ends (in Wick in the north and at Kyle of Lochalsh in the west), buses are pretty much your only option, but they will get you there, as long as you're not set on arriving by a specific time. Buses are mostly run by **Stagecoach** (www.stagecoachbus.com) or Citylink (www.citylink.co.uk).

INVERNESS TO DORNOCH

Miles 0-54; 1.5 hours without stops

Heading out north counterclockwise on the North Coast 500, you soon join a pretty section of the A9, with the road skirting the water and a patchwork of fields, farmland, and gentle hills under canopies of trees. Many travelers stop into **Glenmorangie Distillery,** home to the tallest stills in Scotland, before powering on to **Dornoch,** a compact, well-heeled town with more of a village feel. Once the sleepy capital of Sutherland, Dornoch became world-famous when Madonna chose to christen her son in the town's **cathedral** (www.dornoch-cathedral.com), at a time that she found it twee to do everything as traditionally Scottish as possible. She and Guy Ritchie got married at nearby **Skibo Castle.** Since then it's gained a fantastic five-star hotel and some good restaurants, and its sheltered position means it often enjoys a sunnier climate that other east coast towns and villages, making it an appealing place to stay for a night or two.

Sights
GLENMORANGIE DISTILLERY

Ross-shire, IV19 1PZ; www.glenmorangie.com; tel. 01862 892 477; 10am-4pm Mon.-Fri.; Classic tour £15 (30 minutes), Innovator tour £40 (45 minutes)

This distillery, just past Tain, has been making single malt whiskies on the banks of the Dornich Firth since 1843. It is known for its "giraffe"-style distilleries, the tallest in Scotland, which help produce a smooth and pure whisky. Glenmorangie is a big name in Scottish whisky (which perhaps explains why the price of their tours are comparatively high). The Classic tour includes tasting three of the distillery's most popular expressions, while the Innovator tour lets you try four of its most prized whiskies. If you don't want to fork out for a full tour, you could just pop into the distillery shop and buy some tasters for another time.

Beaches
DORNOCH BEACH

Dornoch

A huge sweep of golden sand just a 10-minute walk from the village of Dornoch through the golf course, this Blue Flag safe beach with low sand dunes is popular with local families and dog walkers. There is a car park, plus toilets and a small children's playground.

Golf
ROYAL DORNOCH GOLF CLUB

Golf Road, Dornoch; tel. 01862 810 219; https:// royaldornoch.com; £210 for a round on the championship course, £50 for the Struie course

A very well-regarded golf club, this natural links course is often cited as one of Scotland's must-play courses. There's a wild, natural beauty to the place, and the welcome is more Highlands warmth than stand-off snobbery. Though golf may have been played here as early as the 17th century, the current club was formed in 1877 and the royal title secured under King Edward VII in 1906. In addition to the main championship course, there's also another 18-hole course known as the Struie, ideal for less serious golfers.

Food and Accommodations
LUIGI'S

1 Castle Street; tel. 01862 810 893; http:// luigidornoch.com; 10am-2:30pm daily, also 6:30pm-9:30pm daily in summer; sandwiches £6.50

This popular café/restaurant serves up fresh mussels daily, alongside homemade burgers, sandwiches, soups, or just coffee/tea and cake. In the summer months, they also do a more formal/slightly more stretching Mediterranean-style menu, with the onus on seafood.

THE COURTROOM DORNOCH

The Carnegie Courthouse, Castle Street; tel. 01862 811 632; www.linkshousedornoch.com/the-courtroom; 12pm-9pm Weds.-Sat., 12pm-4pm Sun.; entrées £7

Madonna's brief flirtation with the town is remembered in the large mural behind the bar at this bistro-style restaurant owned by the same people behind Links House. Service is swift and friendly, and the dishes are more inspiring than the quirky café-esque interior (in the town's old courtroom, no less). There's always at least one local seafood dish on the nicely succinct menu, with local meats and cheeses as well as craft ales from the bar, a

1: Dornoch Beach **2:** Links House

Detour: Black Isle

Not strictly part of the North Coast 500, and not strictly an island either, the Black Isle is just one example of why you shouldn't stick to the driving route of the NC500 rigidly. Just a short drive north of Inverness along the A9, crossing over the Kessock Bridge, this peninsula, surrounded by the Beauly Firth, the Cromarty Firth and the Moray Firth, is easily missed by many who simply drive straight up the main NC500 route, unaware of what lies to the east.

CROMARTY

For many visitors, the charming town of Cromarty, near the tip of the Black Isle peninsula, is a highlight. With traditional whitewashed stone cottages leading down to the harbor, Cromarty is a like a film set of a typical 18th-century port. Tourists gaze adoringly at the more than 200 listed buildings and meander along its narrow lanes of fisherman's cottages, often with colorful floral displays in the front gardens. It was from here in the late 18th and early 19th centuries that many Highlanders left to seek new lives in Canada, America, and Australia following the Clearances. The museum housed in the **Cromarty Courthouse** (Church Street; tel. 01381 600 418; www. cromarty-courthouse.org.uk; 9am-4pm Mon.-Sat.; free) strives to tell their stories.

DOLPHIN-WATCHING

Black Isle is also one of the best places in the whole of Scotland to see dolphins. From Cromarty, **Dolphin Tours with Ecoventures** (Harbour Workshop, Victoria Place, Cromarty; tel. 01381 600 323; Apr.-Oct.; two-hour tour adult £32, child £25, family tickets available) is an accredited operator with the Dolphin Space Programme, meaning the business adheres to a code of conduct that protects the resident bottlenose dolphin population.

If you'd rather not pay for a dolphin-watching boat trip, grab a blanket and a picnic and set up on the narrow neck of **Chanonry Point** (Fortrose, IV10 8SD) for a few hours, and you'll usually be rewarded with some sightings. Visit on a rising tide (about an hour after low tide) and the odds are good that you'll spot dolphins chasing fish in. Although there is a car park, it can get busy, so locals prefer it if you walk here, either along the seafront from the village of Rosemarkie to the northeast or from Fortrose to the west. In July and August, D and E Coaches

pretty garden for rare balmy evenings, and regular music nights, too.

LINKS HOUSE

Golf Road, Dornoch; tel. 01862 811 632; www. linkshousedornoch.com; £225 d, £395 suites
This tasteful five-star positioned next to the golf course is so traditional that it feels as though it's always been here, but it only opened in 2013. Before then, the period mansion had been a private home. The 15 bedrooms, suites, and apartments are spread out over three buildings: the Manse (where you will also find the restaurant, drawing room, and library), the Glenshiel, and the Mews.

Naturally, many of the hotel's guests are golfers, but with its old-world charm and comfort, this makes a very nice stop-off for anyone traveling the NC500 or simply looking for a few days' break. Staff can help arrange activities, such as deer stalking, the McNab challenge (where you try to bag yourself a grouse, salmon, and deer in one day), or wellness treatments in your room.

Information and Services

Visit Dornoch (www.visitdornoch.com) offers tips on things to do in the area and gives relatively up-to-date advice on openings in the area. **Evelix Petrol Station** (Dornoch) is on the A9 and is open 7am-9pm Mon.-Sat.

Getting There

Dorness is an hour north of Inverness, a 45-mile (72-km) drive on the A9. By bus, the X99 Stagecoach will take you from the Inverness

(www.decoaches.co.uk) runs a free shuttle bus that connects Chanronry Point, Rosemarkie, and Fortrose (11:30am-4pm).

LOCAL FOOD AND DRINK

Black Isle is largely a farming region, where there's a growing focus on local food and drink. In Cromarty, **Sutor Creek** (21 Bank Street; tel. 01381 600 855; www.sutorcreek.co.uk; 12pm-9pm daily; entrées £6) is a cute little yellow stone restaurant that's regularly listed in the Michelin guide, with a menu of classic pub dishes—homemade burgers, fish and chips, risotto—done well. **Black Isle Brewing** (Black Isle; www.blackislebrewery.com; tel. 01463 811 871; tours free) have been making beer using barley and hops grown on organic farms since 1998, with daily free tours on request. Finally, **Glen Ord Distillery** (A832, Muir of Ord; tel. 01463 872 004; 10am-5pm May-Oct., 10am-4pm Mon.-Sat and 11am-4pm Sun. Nov.-Feb., 10am-5pm daily Mar., 9:15am-5pm Mon.-Fri. and 10am-5pm Sat.-Sun. Apr.; tasting experience £5, signature experience £10) is the only surviving single malt distillery of the Black Isle, renowned for its Singleton whisky, which is made using Black Isle barley and water from the White Burn to make an amber-colored malt.

INFORMATION AND SERVICES

The **Black Isle website** (https://black-isle.info) has some useful content, and there's a petrol station in Tore open until at least 8pm daily (Muir of Ord).

GETTING THERE

The Black Isle is connected to Inverness by the **Kessock Bridge** and can be reached in minutes by following the A9 north of the city. Fortrose, the village just shy of Chanonry Point, is just over 14 miles (22.5 km) from Inverness (25 minutes by car). For Cromarty, stay on the A832 for a further 9.5 miles (15 km) for a total journey time of 40 minutes. The Black Isle is accessible by bus with the 26A with Stagecoach from Inverness's Farraline Park Bus Station, getting you to Fortrose in around 23 minutes (£3.25 single), and the same bus reaching Cromarty in a little under 50 minutes (£4.70 single).

bus station to Dornoch in just under an hour (£14.40 Dayrider).

DORNOCH TO WICK

Miles 54-116; 1.5 hours without stops

This section of the A9 is really rather pretty, but many visitors pass it by on the race north to reach John o' Groats (which many wrongly attribute to be the most northerly spot on mainland Britain). If you're not in a rush, there are lots of interesting places to stop off at—from Pictish stones to Neolithic burial sites and a couple of very famous castles—while the landscape is as pretty as a picture, with verdant farmland to your left and the sea and the tip of Scandinavia to your right.

This region has a deep-rooted history of distilling—both legally and illegally—and

herring fishing, with the former Viking settlement of Wick very much the heart of both. It is also a place that felt the harsh practices of the Highland Clearance more brutally than most, when unsympathetic landowners forced local people off of the lands where they and their ancestors had toiled for centuries. Stop off at Dunrobin Castle; a heritage center in Helmsdale, Wick, or Dunbeath; or one of the cleared villages to find out about this history.

Sights
DUKE OF SUTHERLAND MONUMENT
Golspie

Not long after leaving Dornoch, you'll encounter "the Manny," one of Scotland's most controversial statues. Like the street names

Detour: Alladale Reserve

Alladale Reserve

Ardgay; alladale.com; tel. 01863 755 338; alladale.com; from £2,750 per week (sleeping up to 12)
A little off the beaten track, this place is worth a detour to see what the early days of a huge long-term rewilding project looks like. Set across 23,000 acres of wilderness, there are four houses available for hire (only one of which is self-catered) within a nature reserve that will one day resemble Scotland as it should be, covered in native trees that will hopefully encourage the return of native wildlife. Until then, it's still an awesome place to take in the long-term vision and see conservation work in action.

Planned on-site activities include guided mountain hikes, trout fishing, clay pigeon shooting, and archery—staff can even arrange off-site tours of distilleries and castles, but frankly, why would you leave before you had to? The three catered cottages come with delicious meals prepared by chef Natasha Buttigieg, delivered to your doorstep. The main **Alladale Lodge** can either be booked exclusively for large groups or as individual rooms. The self-catered property, **Deanich Lodge,** is possibly one of the most remote places you could find to stay in Scotland, the perfect place to disconnect from real life and discover a world of nature and adventure.

GETTING THERE

Alladale Reserve is just over an hour (43 miles/665 km) from Inverness, turning off the A9 onto the B9176 after about 30 minutes. From Dornoch, it's a 50-minute (26-mile/42-km) drive west on the A949.

and statues in Glasgow and elsewhere that stand for people who profited from the slave trade, this statue stands for someone who is viewed as villainous through our modern-day monocles. George Granville Leveson-Gower, the first Duke of Sutherland, was one of the callous landowners who oversaw some of the most brutal of all the Highland Clearances. Looming over the village of Golspie, from its position on top of Ben Bhraggie hill, atop a huge plinth, it's a reminder that in these parts it was often the powerful few who benefited from the land. Though he is much maligned, many people choose to hike it up here (park in the Highlands Wildcat Trail car park, pay the donation, then follow signs for Ben Bhraggie), a roundtrip of around 2 hours with good paths underfoot (2.9 miles /4.7 km). To learn more about the much-detested figure, visit his former home of Dunrobin Castle.

DUNROBIN CASTLE

Golspie, Sutherland; tel. 01408 633 177; www.
dunrobincastle.co.uk; 10am-4pm daily in summer,
10:30am-4pm spring and autumn; adult £11, child £6,
concessions £9

It may look like a fairy-tale castle, but Dunrobin, Scotland's most northerly great house, hides a dark secret. The official seat of Clan Sutherlan, this castle was once home to George Granville Leveson-Gower, the first Duke of Sutherland, who, together with his wife, Elizabeth, the Duchess of Sunderland, cleared his lands of his tenants in the early part of the 19th century to make way for more profitable sheep, sparking a deep sense of displacement that has been passed down through generations.

It is believed that Dunrobin has been here since way before that. The original keep dates back to the 14th century and has been incorporated into the fabric of the house, but the elaborate Scottish baronial style came in the 19th century from Sir Charles Barry, the same man tasked with rebuilding the Houses of Parliament after a major fire. However, a fire here in 1915 led Robert Lorimer to rework the interiors and alter the top of the main tower and clock tower in a more Scottish Renaissance style.

In addition to the house itself, which has 118 rooms (some are out of bounds, as the family still lives here), there is an excellent museum that contains a mind-blowing collection of items, including the heads of lots of animals shot by members of the family, and artifacts brought back from various expeditions. Tickets include entry to the falconry display.

TIMESPAN HERITAGE CENTRE

Dunrobin Street, Helmsdale; tel. 01431 821 327; https://
timespan.org.uk; 10am-4pm daily; adult £4, concessions
£3, under-16 £2, family £10, concessions £3

This heritage center is more forward-thinking than most, hosting regular events and exhibits, including ones on the boom and bust of the local herring fishing industry, the Highland Clearances, a brief gold rush in 1869, and more, giving a varied but real backstory to the region. The museum is also fully accessible, with lifts, ramps, and an Induction Loop system for anyone with hearing difficulties. There is also a good shop, café, bakery, and contemporary art shows.

★ BADBEA

A9, near Ousdale

Driving north on the A9 from Helmsdale, you'll see brown signs for the cleared village of Badbea. Pull into the signposted car park and you can follow a footpath to the former settlement, on the steep cliffs above Berriedale (one-hour return journey (1.25 miles/2 km). Today, most of the houses are little more than a drystone wall. What's particularly poignant about this place is that it wasn't somewhere that people were forced from their homes, but instead it's a place where evicted tenants settled in, in a bid to scratch out a life in the harsh conditions.

Families began to arrive in Badbea in the late 18th century; many of them had been evicted from their homes nearby in Ousdale when the landowner, Sir John Sinclair of Ulbster, decided he would rather use his fertile straths for sheep-farming. Sinclair's method of removal seems to have been anything but sympathetic. A plaque en route to the abandoned township reads that it was first settled by "twelve families whose homes in Sutherland had been destroyed during the Highland Clearances."

By 1814, 80 families lived here but numbers began to dwindle in the late 19th century. In 1911, shortly after the last resident left, a monument was erected to remember the people of Badbea. It's a moving experience standing by it, looking out at the grey angry north sea and imaging what life would have been like here.

GREY CAIRNS OF CAMSTER

A99, Lybster; www.historicenvironment.scot; open 24/7; free

This pair of Neolithic chambered cairns are two of the best-preserved ancient sites in the whole of the British Isles, and yet so few people seem to have heard of them. These sites are set in a bleak and rather lonely peat landscape. You'll need to turn off the A9 about a mile past Lybtser and then follow the A99 for about 4 miles (6 km) deep into the Flow Country. You'll know you're there as grey slabs of stone stand out against the brown moorland. Thought to date from 4,000-2,500 BC, these cairns are incredibly intact (though it's worth noting they have been reconstructed to make them more accessible—there are even roof lights, so you don't need torches).

WHALIGOE STEPS

Cairn of Get Car Park, near Lybster

This famous flight of 365 steps descends steeply down from the cliff-top to one of the most inaccessible harbors in Scotland, perched between two cliffs. Despite being dismissed by Thomas Telford in 1786 as a "dreadful" place for a harbor, the steps, which zigzag down the cliffs, were built shortly afterward and used to haul up basketfuls of fish during the herring boom of the 1800s. Take care walking down them, as they are uneven in places and can be slippery when wet, and it is hard going on the way back up. You can warm up with a cuppa at the **Whaligoe Steps Café & Restaurant** (The Square, Ulbster; tel. 955 651 702; www.whaligoesteps.co.uk) when you're back up top.

WICK HERITAGE CENTRE

20 Bank Row, Wick; tel. 01955 605 393; www.wickheritage.org; 10am-5pm (last entry 3:45pm) Mon.-Sat. Apr.-Oct.

This small museum has been in operation since 1971, run entirely by a team of volunteers. You won't get interactive or high-tech displays, but all the funding in the world couldn't buy you the depth of local knowledge they share. And the collection is seriously impressive. The Wick Society holds the Johnstone Collection: the work of three photographers who documented life in the region between 1863 and 1975, as well as oral histories and rooms made up as they would have been in times gone by.

Badbea

☆ Detour: The Flow Country

This fertile but wet land might just be one of Scotland's last truly wild places. As you drive through the Flow country, having turned onto the single-track A897 at Helmsdale, the sense of desolation is overpowering. This region became a battleground in the 1970s and 1980s between developers and forestry companies and conservationists. The former two groups wanted to exploit tax incentives by planting lots of invasive fast-growing trees, which meant draining the land of its natural resources. Thankfully, conservationists finally won, and today the Flow Country is on the cusp of becoming a UNESCO World Heritage Site as it is home to the largest area of blanket bog in the world; it not only provides essential carbon but also habitats for rare wildlife.

Most visitors will probably gravitate toward **Forsinard Flows** (Flows Field Centre, Forsinard; www.theflowcountry.org.uk; tel. 01641 571 225; visitor center 9am-5pm daily Easter to Oct., reserve always open; free, donations welcome), about halfway along the road. This nature reserve has a good visitor center and the best time to come to see breeding birds is April to June, while insects and peatland plants are at their best June-August.

If you do take the Flow Country turning at Helmsdale, you'll eventually spill out on the north coast at Melvich, which means you will have missed out on a large section of the route, including Wick, John o' Groats, and Dunnet Head, so you may want to travel this section separately.

OLD PULTENEY WHISKY DISTILLERY

Huddart Street, Wick; tel. 01955 602 371; www. oldpulteney.com; 10am-4pm Mon.-Fri.; tours £10, master classes £20

Known as the Maritime Malt, since opening its doors in 1826, Old Pulteney's story has been interwoven with the area's seafaring past. When Wick had a booming trade in herring fishing in the Victorian era, fishermen were known to take stone flagons of the whisky out to sea and then drink more whisky in the pub when they were back on land. This heavy drinking eventually took its toll and the town was placed under prohibition from 1922 to 1947, when many fishermen found themselves out of work. For a while the distillery managed to stay afloat thanks to a good export business and the fact that wayfarers to the town could still enjoy it with a meal. However, the Depression finally forced Pulteney to close up shop from 1930 until 1951.

With its fortunes so linked to the life at sea, it's fitting that Pulteney casks are left open to the sea air. Most visitors to the distillery today are intrigued by the lack of "swan" neck on the wash still, ubiquitous elsewhere. Local legend has it that when it was delivered it was too tall for the distillery and so the manager had the

top cut off—tour guides can offer other, less fun, reasons for this.

CASTLE SINCLAIR GIRNIGOE

Noss Head, near Wick

Once owned by the Sinclair family, the Earls of Caithness, who also owned Rosslyn Chapel, this was once a powerful and opulent castle, with a strategic location on cliffs overlooking the North Sea. Today you can walk to the castle in just 10 minutes from the car park; wear sturdy footwear as there is some uneven ground. The craggy remains of the castle are most spectacular at dusk.

Sports and Recreation

CAITHNESS SEACOAST

Harbour Road, Wick; tel. 01955 609 200 or 07747 404 128; www.caithness-seacoast.co.uk; spring and summer; 1.5-hour trip adult £33, child £24, 3-hour trip adult £55, child £43

These small RIB tours (maximum 12 people) with locals William and Adelaine Munro will help you get closer to the craggy coastline, taking you into sea caves and to the bottom of Whaligoe Steps, and allowing you to see the ruins of Castle Sinclair Girnigoe from the sea. Wheelchair accessible, trips run daily in spring and summer (autumn and winter trips can occasionally be arranged).

Food and Accommodations

★ THE RIVER BOTHY

Ivy Cottage, Berriedale; tel 01593 751 569; 10am-2pm daily mid-Mar.-Dec.; toasted sandwiches £8.50, coffee from £2.20

A delightful café-cum-shop with mismatched furniture, bunting hanging from the counter, wooden floors, and a wood-burner, this place is worth making a very short detour off the A9. Located about halfway between Dornoch and John o' Groats it's also a pretty perfect place for a pit stop. They do huge slices of cake, yummy toasted sandwiches, tea and coffee, plus some bigger meals such as heavily laden burgers too. It's not the cheapest but portions are big, so I'll forgive them that and it's ever so sweet.

BORD DE L'EAU

2 Market Street, Wick; tel. 01955 604 400; www.facebook.com/Bord-de-leau-restaurant-723690517711992; 12pm-2pm and 6pm-11:45pm Tues.-Sat., 6pm-11:45pm Sun.; £5.95 entrées

It might seem a little out of place in the north of Scotland, but this French restaurant, run by French chef Daniel Chretien and his wife, Janice, is the best place to eat in Wick. The interiors are little reminiscent of a 1980s cafeteria, but this is homecooked French food with heart at good prices, plus a great wine list. Dishes include confit of duck, melt-in-the-mouth pâtes, and rabbit stew. Daniel quite often pops out at the end of your meal to see how you found everything, which is always nice.

MACKAYS HOTEL

Union Street, Wick; tel. 01955 602 323; www.mackayshotel.co.uk; £125 d

In the center of the old fishing town of Wick, this independent family three-star hotel is old-school in the best sense of the word. Rooms are clean, with wardrobes (modern hotels take note), bedside tables, mirrors over the dressing table, hospitality trays, and good bathrooms. There are some modern add-ons like digital TVs and good wifi, and the drink that awaits you in your room is very welcome. There is a AA Rosette on-site restaurant and the breakfast is decent. Having been run by three generations of the Lamont family, this hotel is a cornerstone of the community. Also, trivia fans, it's located on the shortest street in the world.

Information and Services

There are lots of shops and petrol stations in Wick, including a Tesco Superstore (North Road, Wick).

Getting There

From Dornoch, Wick is just under 1.5 hours to the north, a 62-mile (100-km) drive on the A9 and A99.

There are several trains per day Monday to Saturday throughout the year from Inverness to Wick on the Kyle Line (4 hours 20 minutes; £22.40 single, £35 return). You'll find the Wick train station right in the center of town, just south of the Wick River, and half a mile (0.8 km) west of the Wick Heritage Centre and the harbor.

WICK TO JOHN O' GROATS AND THURSO

Miles 116-152; 1 hour without stops

The town of John o' Groats, the northernmost settlement in mainland Scotland, has incredible views over to the Orkney Islands to where the town's namesake, Jan de Groot, used to run the ferry over for the princely fare of 2p. Those pennies soon mounted up; local legend has it that he is buried with his diamonds in the town's Canisbay Church. John O Groat's is the end of the epic cycling route from Land's End in the south of Britain all the way to the island's northern point, which means it's always busy with snap-happy tourists and exhausted adventurers. However, there are far more attractive and interesting places to stop off along Scotland's north coast.

To the west, Thurso is a relatively busy

town with some decent seafood restaurants, and is the place to stop for supplies and petrol.

Sights
JOHN O' GROATS SIGN
Wick; open 24/7

It may be a bit naff and you'll probably have to queue for your photo opportunity, but not having your photo taken at this famous white sign, which shows how far you are from New York, Land's End, Edinburgh, Orkney and Shetland, is a bit like visiting London and not taking a picture in front of Big Ben. There will be plenty of other tourists here willing to take your photo, no matter when you visit.

CASTLE & GARDENS OF MEY
Thurso; tel. 01847 851 473; www.castleofmey.org.uk; 10:30am-4pm Weds.-Sun. Apr. to Oct.; adult £12.50, child £6.50, concessions £10, family £35

One of a number of Scottish attractions that remained closed for the whole of 2020, the most northerly castle on mainland Britain, Castle of Mey, was first built in the 16th century by the 4th Earl of Caithness for his second son, William, and became the family seat of the Sinclairs of Mey and later the Earls. However, the Z-plan castle, with its striking corbelled turrets, is best known for being the former home of the Queen Mother, who lived here from 1952 to 1996, gifting it a generous endowment (hence it being impeccably maintained). The gardens, of which the Queen mother was so fond, are protected from the worst of the weather by a 12-foot-high (4-m-high) wall.

DUNNET HEAD
Brough, Thurso

On the tip of this thumb-shaped peninsula, which rises into the Pentland Firth like a hitchhiker hailing a ride, you will find mainland Britain's true northerly point—**Dunnet Head Lighthouse.** Exposed to the elements, it's a breeding spot for seabirds. Look for razorbills, puffins, kittiwakes, fulmars, and guillemots, and on a clear day you can also make out several of the offshore islands.

It takes about 10 minutes to drive here from Dunnet, with the gradually rising road taking you past heathery fields with several lochlans, or small lochs. Dunnet Head can get busy in the height of summer, but come early morning or sunset and it will be quieter. Dunnet Bay, a gorgeous crescent beach with big dunes, right by the village of Dunnet, is also a lovely spot.

DUNNET BAY DISTILLERY
Dunnet; tel. 01847 851 287; www.dunnetbaydistillers. co.uk; £20 per boat shed (seats 2)

This small batch distillery, opened in 2014 by couple Claire and Martin, has steadily been making a name for itself in the busy gin market. What began as a way for the couple to return to work and live in their home county of Caithness has become an award-winning business and a major local employer. Using local botanicals, the Rock Rose Gin cleverly taps into all the local seasons; it's so fresh and zesty that you don't even feel the need to add ice. Tours have been on hold for a while now. Until they are back on, you can book a personal boat shed to hear stories and try tastings of three different gins.

Hikes
DUNCANSBY STACKS
Distance: *5.25 miles (8.5 km)*
Time: *2.5-3 hours round trip*
Trailhead: *John o' Groats*
Information and Maps: *www.walkhighlands. co.uk/sutherland/duncansby-head.shtml*

Lying just to the south of the northeast point of mainland Britain, Duncansby Head, these near-identical pointed sea stacks are a dramatic sight to behold. There is a car park by the lighthouse, or you can walk here from John o' Groats by simply following the coastal path from the famous town. Walk down toward the John o' Groats signpost and turn right to follow the path, which is stony at first and then mainly grassy. As you approach Duncansby Lighthouse, there is a sign pointing to the right for the path to reach the stacks. You can either view the stacks from up high by the lighthouse, or continue on for another

15-20 minutes to get a closer, more exposed view of them.

Beaches
NESS OF DUNCANSBY
John O Wicks

Also known as Shell Beach, this is one of the best places on the whole northern coast to find Groatie Buckies, tiny little cowrie shells that the strong tide leaves behind. Pale pink in color, with a narrow slit on one side and a ribbed back, these shells are easy to identify—"shore-sellers" once came here to find them to sell them to tourists in the Victorian and Edwardian era. Even if you don't find any, time spent here will reward you with other shell treasures. Beachcombing is a great, mindful activity, focusing your search with nothing to disturb you but the sound of the sea. It's not the prettiest beach by any measure, and it has some of the strongest tides in the Pentland Firth, so I wouldn't recommend swimming here, but it has a wild allure, and seals can often be found feeding in its waters.

Surfing
NORTH COAST WATERSPORTS
Dunnet Bay; tel. 07982 649 635; www.northcoastwatersports.com; £30 for a 2-hour lesson, surf retreats from £330 pp or £500 for two

Caithness is renowned for its surfing, so if you would like to have a go on some of the best waves in the UK, then book a lesson with these champion and ISA-trained surf coaches. Lessons usually take place in Dunnet Bay, where you can pick up North Sea swells. Wetsuits and surfboards are provided. More experienced surfers, or adventurous beginners, may want to join one of the three-day retreats, including meals, where you'll stay in the Melvich Hotel and combine surfing with beach yoga.

Tours
NORTH COAST EXPLORERS
Mey House, East Mey, by Thurso; tel. 01847 851 852; www.northcoast.scot; 9am-5:30pm daily Mar.-Oct.; day tours from £200 for two people

These private tours, run by husband-and-wife team Sally-Ann and Robert, are a great introduction to the area and can really take you off the beaten track. Starting with half-day tours and going up to a week, the couple will tailor the itinerary for you, recommending places to stay and where to eat and drink. Robert is very knowledgeable about local history, from the Highland Clearances to ancient burial sites. Tours are run in the couple's Land Rover, with a screen between them and the passengers for safety, and Robert will even give a running commentary as you travel.

Food and Accommodations

Aside from Stacks, the food offering in John o' Groats is not great. For hostels or hotels, you'll need to head a little out of town.

STACKS COFFEE HOUSE & BISTRO
3 Craft Centre, John o' Groats; tel. 01955 611 582; www.stacksbistro.co.uk; 10am-4pm Weds.-Sun.; flatbreads £4.95

Locals love this place, which is run by mother and daughter Teresa and Rebecca, who look after their staff as much as their customers. Everything you see is made fresh, which does sometimes mean you have to wait, but you'll be glad you did. Expect sandwiches and flatbreads made with care and love—the signature Classic Mac is filled with mac and cheese and streaky bacon—spongy cakes topped with huge dollops of icing cream, chili bowls, and soups. This far north, this is exactly the kind of filling comfort food you need.

★ WINDHAVEN CAMPING AND CARAVANNING
Brough, Thurso; tel. 01847 851 927 or 0789 294 803; http://windhaven.co.uk; café open 11am-6pm daily Mar.-Oct.; bed-and-breakfast £77 d, camping £17 per night for a small pitch

This is a surprisingly good little B&B on the road to Dunnet Head Lighthouse. There are just two en suite B&B rooms with a shared

---

1: Dunnet Head **2:** John O' Groats sign **3:** Dunnet Bay Distillery **4:** Duncansby Stacks

Ferries to Orkney

From the northern coast of Scotland (in addition to ferries from Aberdeen), there are three jumping off points to Orkney in the Northern Isles (page 470). Though the ferry is certainly not the fastest way to get there, it is by far the most romantic, and when the conditions are right, you can be on Orkney in as little as 40 minutes.

- **John o' Groats to Burwick, South Ronaldsay:** www.jogferry.co.uk; Jun.-Sept. only, 40 minutes, once a day; £16 each way, foot passengers and bicycles only

- **Gills Bay (west of John o' Groats) to St. Margaret's Hope, South Ronaldsay:** www.pentlandferries.co.uk; 1 hour, three ferries a day; £40 each way car, £17 each way per person

- **Scrabster (near Thurso) to Stromness, Mainland Orkney:** www.northlinkferries. co.uk; 90 minutes, up to three ferries a day; car from £60 each way, passengers £20 each way

living room; the cooked breakfast in the baby-pink and sky-blue adjoining café is excellent, and there are wonderful views of the bay below from the small campsite round the back. Run by Claire, Phil, and Aunty Babs, it's all very friendly, and their dogs Skye and Billy will probably try to guilt you into playing with them. Even if you're not staying, it's a bright and welcome café to stop off at for a coffee or snack, and there are a few local-made gifts to buy, including knitted puffins.

THE GRANARY LODGE B&B

Castle of Mey, Thurso; tel. 01847 851 861; www. castleofmey.org.uk; £130 d

In the grounds of Castle Mey, with sea views of the Pentland Firth toward Orkney, this old brick building—once the granary for the castle—offers 10 B&B rooms (including two suites) of a very high standard. Decor is traditional, with lots of florals, cushions. and period features. There's a beautiful drawing room with real fire and an honesty bar for drinks (always a nice touch), and breakfast is served in the resplendent dining room, where there are several grandfather clocks and triple aspects.

MANOR HOUSE

6 Janet Street, Thurso; tel. 07379 881 307; www. manorhousethurso.co.uk; £114 d

In a renovated, grand 19th-century home, the family-run Manor House has en suite single and double rooms, all with cozy-yet-modern decor. Pristine white walls and bedding contrasts with exposed stone walls. The newly opened bar/restaurant (open breakfast-dinner) will serve updated spins on traditional Scottish food.

Information and Services

Thurso is positively cosmopolitan compared to most Highland towns and villages, so this is the place to stock up on camera batteries, cash, toiletries, and any other essentials. Make sure you refuel; you won't want to go low on the next section. There are several petrol stations in the town (one that's open 24 hours), plus a Tesco and a few other supermarkets, as well as a bike hire.

Getting There and Around

BY CAR

From Wick, you'll follow the A99 16 miles (26 km) north to John o' Groats, keeping to the right when you reach Latheron and the A9 swerves left to head to Thurso. To reach John o' Groats by public transport, you can take the train from along the Far North Line to Thurso (www.scotrail.co.uk; 4 hours; from £13.50 single) and then take the bus along the coast to John o' Groats (no. 80D or no. 280; www.stagecoachbus.com; 35 minutes; £3.80 single). It's just a half an hour drive from John o' Groats to Thurso (20 miles/32 km), traveling west along the A836. The no. 80 bus with Stagecoach North Scotland will get you between the two in just under an hour (£4.75 single, £7.10 return).

BY TRAIN

There are a few trains a day from Inverness to Thurso (www.scotrail.co.uk; 3 hours 45 minutes; single £22.40, return £35). The train station is located just about a mile (1.6 km) south of the waterfront in Thurso.

BY FERRY

The ferry terminal in John o' Groats, where ferries depart for Burwick, South Ronaldsay, Orkney in the summer (June-Sept.) is another spot that feels like it's at the end of the world: literally where the road ends and the sea begins just north of the tiny town center. On the other hand, the Gills Bay Ferry Port, which is really nothing more than a road leading to a dock and the sea, operates ferries to St. Margaret's Hope, South Ronaldsay, year-round. It's between John o' Groats (4 miles/6 km; 10 minutes) and Thurso (16 miles/26 km; 25 minutes), both on the A836. Finally, ferries depart for Stromness, Mainland Orkney from Scrabster Ferry Terminal (Queen Elizabeth Pier; Scrabster, Caithness; tel. 800 111 4422; www.northlinkferries.co.uk), a 6-minute, 2-mile (3-km) drive north of Thurso.

THURSO TO DURNESS

Miles 152-223; 2 hours without stops

Leaving Thurso, you'll follow an at-first gentle rural road for a while, passing the nuclear power station of Dounreay. Before long the coastal road weaves inland, revealing a desolate yet dramatic landscape, moorland broken up by lochans with hills in the distance. The roads are windy here, and if you get stuck behind a slow vehicle then you'll just have to put up with it for a while as overtaking is not advisable.

This gives you more time to acknowledge the Highland cattle and sheep by the side

of the road and take in the scenery, which gradually gets more crumpled as you approach Bettyhill, a resettlement village built by Elizabeth, the Countess of Sutherland, to house those that were cleared from the nearby valley of Strathnaver. After Bettyhill, the road goes inland again before spilling out at the Kyle of Tongue for wonderful views. A few miles farther brings you to the bleak and inhospitable terrain of The Moine, which is being considered as a launch center for satellites by the UK Space Agency. The road returns to the coast as you edge toward Durness, an attractive and busy little part of the Highlands, with beautiful sandy beaches lapped by turquoise waters and grassy cliff-tops offering fantastic views.

Sights

STRATHNAVER MUSEUM

Clachan, Bettyhill; tel. 01641 521 418; www. strathnavermuseum.org.uk

This community museum, run entirely by volunteers, is a great local resource for anyone wanting to learn more about the Highland Clearances in the far north and about the emergence in the area of Clan Mackay (a walk around the graveyard outside the museum will reveal that this is very much Clan Mackay country). The museum is currently undergoing major refurbishment and will remain closed until early 2023.

LOTTE GLOB ARTIST STUDIO

Sculpture Croft, 105 Laid, Loch Eriboll; tel. 07761 220 953; https://lotteglob792300328.wordpress.com; by appointment only, call ahead

Loch Eriboll is not where you'd expect to find an artist's studio, but once you come upon this house on stilts it becomes quite clear why accomplished Danish ceramics artist Lotte Glob chose this spot. Since 1999, the artist has been gradually rewilding her 16 acres (6 hectares) and adding to it with her sculptures. Before your visit, contact Lotte Glob by email through her website or by phone to make an appointment.

Beaches

FARR BEACH

Clachan, Bettyhill

Park by the Strathnaver Museum to reach this beach, which is about a 10-minute walk away. Start with a stroll through **Farr Church,** where you can see the Farr Stone—a Pictish slab that stands just to the west, serving as an impressive gravestone. From the back of the churchyard turn right, past a couple of houses and the Farr Bay Inn on the right and then follow the sign to the left through two kissing gates, which lead to the sand dunes behind the beach. A clear path will bring you to one sand dune, which is like a huge slide down to the beach. With acres of golden sand, this is a really lovely beach that feels like a local treasure.

Food

COAST COFFEE, TEA AND TREATS

Swordly Mill, Swordly, Bettyhill; tel. 07843 682 343; facebook.com/COAST-coffeetea-and-treats_nc500-463716250870926; 10am-4pm daily; coffee £2.20, treats £2.50

Doing exactly what it says on the tin, this trailer van located in a layby as you approach Farr Beach is a great pit stop for tea, coffee, peppermint brownies, and delicious flapjacks. It does get busy, so you'll probably have to drive down the narrow layby to find a parking space or to turn around to come back out. There are a few wooden tables and seats if you want to get out of the car for some fresh air, and the owner is always happy for a chat—when she's not serving, of course.

SCRABSTER SEAFOOD

The Harbour, Scrabster; tel. 07470 004 625; www. scrabsterseafoodbar.co.uk; 2:30pm-6pm Tues.-Sat.; fish and chips £8.95

This seafood bar, which does a roaring trade in takeaway, has visitors coming from far and wide to sample its fresh fish. Specials are dependent on what the local landings are but can include monkfish and prawn scampi or grilled lobster with herb garlic butter. The fruit de mer is a step up on offerings at most fish-and-chip places, though the battered haddock and chips is very well thought of too.

CAPTAIN'S GALLEY

The Harbour, Scrabster; tel. 01847 894 999; www. captainsgalley.co.uk; 2:30pm-7pm Weds.-Thurs., 2:30pm-7:30pm Fri.-Sat.; fish-and-chips £12

For more of a sit-down affair, head next door to the Scrabster's sister restaurant, the Galley, an intimate setting in an old building with bare stone walls that has the same ethos of the fish bar, making simple, sustainable, seasonal food. Owners Jim and Mary Cowrie will often come and chat with you. The menu uses only the freshest seafood, also drawing on Nordic influences in the region.

Accommodations

BETTYHILL HOTEL

Bettyhill, Thurso, Caithness; tel. 01641 521 202; www. bettyhillhotel.com; £130 d

This two-star hotel offers modern, comfortable accommodation, with 20 rooms overlooking stunning Torrisdale Bay. A popular spot for walkers, cyclists, and other adventurers, this property has a bar and restaurant on-site, and usually a steady flow of people to converse with.

MACKAY'S ROOMS

Durness; tel. 01971 511 202; www.visitdurness.com; £149 d; bunkhouse beds £22 per night

A sort of catch-all accommodation company, Mackay's has several places in and around Durness, suiting most budgets. First up there's the boutique B&B with just seven rooms set in a 150-year-old building. The gorgeous rooms are a modern take on traditional Highland interiors, with tweed sofas and chairs, oak floors, and large handmade beds topped with either feathers or super-soft merino blankets. Though there's no dinner available, the locally sourced breakfast menu changes daily and the owners will happily provide a picnic lunch if you're heading out for a big expedition. Meanwhile, the wooden chalet-style Lazy Crofter Bunkhouse offers a mix of shared dorms and two-bed bunk rooms, as well as decent facilities, including a nice living room and a kitchen.

Information and Services

Just before Bettyhill, there is a small **tourist information center** (tel. 01641 521 342; Mon.-Sat. Easter-Sept.) by the Strathnaver Museum. In Bettyhill itself, the general store has fuel, groceries, a post office, and off license.

Getting There

From Thurso it's 70 miles (113 km) to Durness, along the A838 (unless you take any detours), though it will feel longer as the roads are windy. Expect the journey to take around two hours.

DURNESS TO SCOURIE

Miles 223-248; 45 minutes without stops

There are few attractions on this stretch, aside from some lovely beaches, a quirky craft village, and **Smoo Cave**—a sea cave that is a bit of a tourist trap. It's a place to catch your breath before the main road turns south and enters a vast, bleak landscape of huge lumps of quartzite rock and boulders, broken up with icy bogs. If it weren't for the electricity lines, you might be fooled into thinking humans had never made it this far. This is the Highlands at her barest, yet you end up in Scourie—a destination that was once so fashionable that J. M. Barrie and the Queen Mother holidayed here as guests of the Duke of Sutherland at Scourie Lodge.

Sights
CAPE WRATH

tel. 07742 670 196; www.visitcapewrath.com; ferry from 9am on demand daily June-Sept., 11am and 1:30pm May; £7.50 return ferry, van £13 return

Cape Wrath is the most north-westerly point on the British mainland, where the north and west coasts of Scotland collide. It takes its name from the Norse word "hvarf," meaning turning point. Northwest from here, the next place you'd reach would be Iceland.

There is no road to access Cape Wrath on your own. To get here you'll need to take the **Cape Wrath Ferry** from East Keoldale Pier across the Kyle of Durness (10 minutes), where a minibus will be waiting. (The "ferry," by the way, is probably not quite as you imagine it, but rather a small open boat that can only take a few passengers at a time.) The minibus trips take you along an 11-mile (18-km) bumpy track to reach Cape Wrath (50 minutes each way). Once here, you'll have about an hour to look at the **Stevenson Lighthouse** (sadly you can't go inside), marvel at the sheer **Clo Mor Cliffs,** and feel the full force of the Atlantic in your bones before warming up with a cuppa and sandwich at the **Ozone Café.**

Beaches
BALNAKEIL BEACH

Near Durness

Often touted as the most beautiful beach in Scotland, it's no wonder that, unlike many Scottish beaches, you're rarely alone here. Walk to the far end of the beach, around the large grassy rock, for some tranquility. The swimming is safe, and sunsets spectacular.

SANDWOOD BAY

Kinlochbervie; www.walkhighlands.co.uk/sutherland/sandwood-bay.shtml; 8 miles (13 km); 4-5 hours

Another contender for Scotland's best beach, this one is so hard to get to that only the determined make it here. Looking out into the North Atlantic, the waves can get wild, but the pink-tinged sands and the knowledge that you made it after a 4-mile (6-km) trek from the nearest car park in Blairmore will make you feel very smug indeed.

Obviously, with a long journey here, you'll want to wait for a good weather window. To join the path, which is relatively flat and easy to follow, cross the road from the car park, head through the gate, and follow the wide, stony path. This path will take you past Loch Aisir and through peatland in an area protected by the John Muir Trust. With a few streams to cross, you should wear waterproof shoes. It's around a two-hour walk each way.

Shopping
BALNAKEIL CRAFT VILLAGE

1 mile (1.6 km) west of Durness; 10am-6pm daily Apr.-Oct.

This little arts hub is a great place to spend an afternoon. Built in the 1950s as an early-warning center for the MOD (in case of nuclear attack), it was never actually used, so in the 1960s the buildings were requisitioned, initially with the intention of creating small industrial units. When that didn't work out, a newspaper advert called for people with craft skills and business plans to move in for a nominal fee. Today, there are several art studios and craft shops to visit, and you can see skills such as wood turning and stained glass making in action. The **Plastic Lab** can offer tips on becoming plastic-free, and **Durness Deep Time** is an exhibition where you can learn about the archaeology and geology of the area and book guided walks with a geologist.

Food
THE OZONE CAFÉ

Cape Wrath; tel. 01971 511 314; coffee £2.50, sandwiches £3.90

This is the most northerly café in the whole of Britain. John Ure made the news in 2009 when heavy snow meant he and his late wife, Kay, were separated for four weeks over Christmas when she went to buy a turkey and got snowed out. Running this café in the Stevenson Lighthouse, in about as remote a location as imaginable, is no mean feat, but thank goodness John still does. Standing on the edge of the Atlantic as the waves crash against the rocks and the wind howls around you, you'll never want a cup of tea or coffee more.

COCOA MOUNTAIN

Craft Village, Balnakeil; tel. 01971 511 233; www. cocoamountain.co.uk; hot chocolate chaser £6.95

With the most chocolatey hot chocolate I've ever come across, this café in Balnakeil Craft Village specializes in chocolate and not much else. For the full effect, order a hot chocolate chaser, which comes with four chocolates.

Information and Services

In Kinlochbervie, near Sandwood Bay, there is also a petrol station, but it's not open 24 hours (Bervie Stores, The Harbour Kinlochbervie; tel. 01971 521 221). Scourie has a 24-hour fuel station (Scourie; tel. 01971 502 422), as well as a decent local website (scourie.co.uk) for planning your trip.

Getting There

From Durness to Scourie, it's just a 25-mile (40-km) drive south. For the most part you'll still follow the A838, but at Laxford Bridge you'll bear right to join the A894 for the last 6 miles (10 km). Though it's quite a short distance, it will still take 45 minutes.

The **Far North Bus** is a family-run business that offers some useful routes through the northwest Highlands. Route 805, for instance, runs several times a week from Durness to Inverness, passing through Scourie (tel. 01971 511 223 or 07782 110 007; www.thedurnessbus.com; Mon, Tues., Thurs., and Sat. May-Oct., Tues., Thurs., and Sat. Nov.-Apr.). Setting off from Smoo Cave Hotel at 8am, it arrives in Scourie at 9:30am (as long as you request the stop; £5.65 single for this distance) before eventually arriving in Inverness at 11:40am (£20 single for the full route). Buses coming from the other direction set off in the afternoon, arriving into Scourie and Durness in the late afternoon/early evening.

SCOURIE TO ULLAPOLL

Miles 248-317; 2.25 hours without stops

Travel south from Scourie and you'll enter **Assynt,** home to some of the oldest rocks on Earth. It's one of the least populated places in northern Europe—it's largest settlement, Lochinver, is home to just 400 people. As you travel, look out for what appear like ledges in the rock face; geologists call this effect the

1: Balnakeil Beach **2:** Balnakeil Craft Village **3:** seafood at the Kylesku Hotel **4:** view from Drumbeg Road

1

2

WEE
GALLERY

open

3

4

"Glencoul thrust," showing how old rocks can "thrust" up over time. You might find a layer of 500-million-year-old Cambrian quartzite sandwiched between two layers of Lewisian gneiss, which incomprehensibly dates back billions of years. If you like road trips, you won't want to miss the nail-biting Drumbeg Road diversion, which takes you deeper into Assynt country.

Back on the A837, about halfway from Scourie to Ullapool, you'll come to the Bone Caves of Inchnadamph, where in 1928 the bones of Eurasian lynx, brown bear, Arctic foxes, even polar bear, were found—the greatest discovery of the last glacial period in Scotland. In 2004 the **North West Highlands Geopark** (www.nwhgeopark. com) was set up to protect 770 square miles (2,000 square km) of this unique landscape for future generations, as well as enable us to learn more about the geological wonders that can be found here. It's not unusual to see a team of scientists or geologists examining a heap of rock by the side of the road.

Ullapool is a lively fishing and port town— ferries from Stornoway on the Isle of Lewis arrive here—there is no shortage of pubs around the harbor, where you'll often hear impassioned folk music, even the occasional sea shanty.

Sights
★ THE DRUMBEG ROAD
B869, from Kylesku to Lochinver
Not long after you've crossed the Kylesku Bridge, about 15 minutes (10 miles/16 km) south of Scourie, you'll see a right turn signposted toward **Drumbeg.** You don't have to go this way—you can continue along the A894 toward Inchnadamph—but for confident and experienced drivers, this 22-mile (35-km) route is a must and will take around 1 hour 10 minutes in total, but allow more time to stop at some of the beaches en route. The road is narrow and climbs and descends seemingly at will, often leaving little space between you and the cliff edge, but the views are immense, and the excitement is high. Though there are

lots of passing places, as it is largely single-track, you'll have to keep your wits about you as there are plenty of blind corners.

Highlights of the route include **Stoer Lighthouse** (Lairg; www.stoerlighthouse. co.uk); the pretty village of Drumbeg, which has a local store and a great viewpoint; and **Achmelvich Beach** (which itself requires another short detour). Once you come to the end of the B869, turn left and this road will bring you back to the main North Coast 500 route. Those who want more time in this dramatic landscape can make use of the **Clachtoll Beach Campsite** (134 Clachtoll, Lochinver, Sutherland; tel. 01571 855 377; www.clachtoll-beachcampsite.com; open year-round; pitches for 1 adult £17, extra adults £5, children 5-15 £2), an excellent campsite by a beautiful beach with crystal clear waters.

RHUE ART GALLERY
Rhue, Ullapool; tel. 01854 612 460; http://rhueart. co.uk; 10am-5pm Mon.-Sat., call ahead in winter
This well-established gallery on the road into Ullapool hosts regular exhibitions from accomplished artists, particularly those who live in the Highlands and Islands.

Hiking
BONE CAVES
Distance: *2.75 miles (4.5 km)*
Time: *1.5-2 hours*
Trailhead: *Allt nan Uamh Car Park (the Bone Caves), A837*
Information and Maps: *www.walkhighlands. co.uk/ullapool/bonecaves.shtml*
This circular trail is a beautiful and very achievable walk that will take you into the mouth of the limestone "Bone Caves," where Scotland's most famous animal remains were found. From the car park, go through the gate and follow the path past the building. The rough but clear path will take you above a waterfall before gradually ascending upstream. You'll soon see the caves on a steep cliff and when you reach a junction by a large boulder, take the path to the right. The final section is up a steep and narrow path that will take

you to several cave openings. Explore with care and consideration—inside they may be slippery. When you're ready to leave, take the downhill path that continues across the steep slope, bearing left as you go, until you return to the car park.

SUILVAN

Distance: *12.5 miles (20 km)*
Time: *7-9 hours*
Trailhead: *End of public road from Lochinver to Glencanisp Lodge, Lairg*
Information and Maps: *www.walkhighlands. co.uk/ullapool/suilven.shtml*

There are lots of hills and mountains to consider climbing in the north Highlands, but this one, with its unmistakable outline, is possibly the most alluring. Compared to other well-known Scottish hills, it's very "wee," but that's not to say it's easy—in fact if you saw the bulk of its helmet-shaped profile from the sea first, you'd probably rule out attempting to climb it at all. But that's where mountains can be very misleading. Though it's remote and takes the best part of a day to climb and come back down again, it's relatively straightforward. You'd be wise to read Walk Highlands' description of the route in minute detail, and to check out their general advice on climbing in the Highlands. Only attempt this walk in spring and summer, when there is enough light to see you down again. If you're not confident enough to go it alone, book a tour with a guide like **Steve Fallon** (https://stevenfallon.co.uk).

Sports and Recreation
KYLESKU BOAT TOURS

Kylesku, Sutherland; tel. 01971 502 231; http:// kyleskuboattours.com; Apr.-Sept.; 1 hour 45 minutes; adult £30, child £20, under 3 free

Setting off from the little pier just in front of the Kylesku Hotel every day in summer, these small boat tours (4-12 passengers) will take you out on both Glendhu and Glencoul lochs. With a bit of luck, you'll see seals, birdlife, and perhaps even dolphins, as well as the UK's largest waterfall, **Eas a' Chual Aluinn',**

from the water. Your guide will also talk about the history of the area and local fishing techniques. Due to changing weather, you're advised to confirm booking on the morning of your trip.

Food and Accommodations
THE ELPHIN TEAROOMS

Elphin, Lairg; elphintearooms.co.uk; cakes/scones £2.30, tea/coffee £2.20

Just 14 miles (23 km) north of Ullapool, this tearoom with a large car park is a lovely stop-off for anyone driving in Assynt. In summer there are tables outside, perfect for taking in the mountain views as you sip your tea and eat your scones, and sheep and horses from the family's croft may even wander up to say hello. In winter, take a seat inside by the toasty fire and fill up on soup and sandwiches.

LOCHINVER LARDER

Main Street, Lochinver; tel. 01571 844 356; www. lochinverlarder.com; pies £5.95

If ever there was a food best suited from coming in from the cold in the Highlands, it must surely be the pie. Lochinver Larder is known for miles around for their tasty pies and lovely loch views. They have classics like chicken and ham, and steak and ale, plus house favorite venison and cranberry. They even run a "Pies by Post" service for you to enjoy their pies when you are far away from Scotland. I've literally just ordered one while writing this.

THE SEAFOOD SHACK

9 West Argyle Street, Ullapool; tel. 07876 142 623; www.seafoodshack.co.uk; 12pm-6pm daily spring and summer; fish and salad £8

This sustainable seafood van, just set a road back from the harbor in Ullapool, has won a loyal following since opening in 2016 with the sole aim of providing fresh seafood cooked simply. It's run by two young women, Kirsty and Fenella, who were both in their twenties when they started out. They spotted a gap in the market, namely all the fresh seafood being brought into Ullapool before being shipped somewhere else. The small but tempting menu is dependent on what's landed, but often includes fresh lobster, oysters, creel-caught langoustines, and hand-dived scallops from a handful of local suppliers. Each dish comes with lots of salad on the side, making it feel a lot healthier than similar takeaways. There are tables under a canopy, and occasional pop-ups join them, such as local gin makers and the like.

KYLESKU HOTEL

Kylesku, Sutherland; tel. 01971 502 231; https:// kyleskuhotel.co.uk; lunch 12pm-2:30pm Mon.-Sat. and 12pm-5pm Sun., dinner 5:30pm-8:30pm daily; entrées £8.35, £155 d

This place served one of my all-time favorite Scottish meals, though admittedly it's not the cheapest. Situated loch-side once you've crossed over the Kylesku Bridge, this restaurant with rooms has been an inn in some form since 1883. Companionable Tanja and Sonia took over the inn in 2009, turning it into one of the best restaurants in the Highlands. The duo is now off to pastures new, but I've been assured it's in safe hands. The location adds to the enjoyment—large windows overlook the loch and surrounding hills—as does the warm and affable staff, but the food speaks for itself. The focus here is on fresh, local seafood, but the sustainable ethos goes right through the menu, with croft-reared meat. There's also a very good kids' menu and a raised terrace out front if the weather is behaving.

THE CEILIDH PLACE

14 West Argyle Street, Ullapool; tel. 01854 612 245; www.theceilidhplace.com; £100 d

This whitewashed building in the center of Ullapool is a sophisticated small hotel that is sort of a destination in its own right. Aside from smart hotel rooms, there's a bunkhouse, café, restaurant and bar, and a bookshop. There are also regular gig nights. The rooms themselves are comfy, with Roberts radios and a little library, and some come with antique beds and wardrobes. Not all have en suites, but there's a shared lounge and an honesty bar for drinks.

Information and Services

The **Rock Stop Visitor Centre** (A894 Unapool, by Kylesku, Lairg; tel. 1971 488 765; www.nwhgeopark.com) in the North West Highlands Geopark is a good port of call for maps and local info, but sadly, it remained closed for 2020. It should be open again soon but if not, there is a virtual visitor center on the website.

VisitScotland has an **iCentre** (Argyle Street; tel. 1854 612 486; www.visitscotland. com/info/services/ullapool-information-centre-p333161; 9am-12:45pm and 1:45pm-5pm Mon.-Weds. and Fri.-Sat.) in Ullapool, where you can load up on maps and leaflets. There are also volunteer websites run by communities such as Ullapool.com.

Getting There

Ullapool is just 42 miles (68 km) south of Scourie along the A835 (1 hour). It's also only 58 miles (93 km) from Inverness along the A835 (1 hour 15 minutes). It's about an hour and a half from Inverness to Ullapool aboard Scottish Citylink's 961 bus (£14.90 single).

ULLAPOOL TO APPLECROSS

miles 317-424; 3.25 hours without stops

Ullapool is the kind of port town you are in no rush to leave, but leave you must if you want to venture into **Wester Ross,** where a wild beauty prevails. Though it was one of the first parts of Britain to be settled, you wouldn't know it. Aside from mountainous landscapes, corries, lochans and lochs, and the occasional cottage or crofting community, there is little here, and it's all the better for it. **Gairloch** is one of the best places in Scotland to go whale watching, and the drive from Dundonell to Gairloch will leave your jaw gaping. Beyond, the Torridon Hills—which include six Munros in their number—call from afar. These auburn mountains have stood there for millennia and look almost velvet to the touch. Farther south again, you reach Applecross, a region of twisting, snaking roads, including the Bealach na Bà—one of the world's most exhilarating drives.

Sights
BADACHRO DISTILLERY
Aird Hill, Badachro; tel. 01445 741 282; www. badachrodistillery.com; 1-hour tour 2pm Mon., Weds.-Fri.; £20 per person

A short drive from Gairloch along a single-track road will bring you to the small hamlet of Badachro, home to an excellent pub, and also this fledgling distillery that makes craft gins and also whisky—its first single malt was released in 2020. Tours run weekdays (except Tuesday) but even if there are no tours available you can pop in for a chat, a taste, and a look in the small shop. If you like a little love story, you might also be interested to learn that owners Gordon and Vanessa had a whirlwind wedding less than 12 weeks after meeting in the nearby Badachro Inn.

BEALACH NA BÀ
A896, Strathcarron, IV54 8XE

Before you attempt to drive this road, known as the most dangerous in Britain, consider a few things: if it's icy, forget about it. In fact, in winter it's sometimes closed. If it's dark, again, please don't do it. If you're nervous on blind bends or cliff edges, it's probably best to leave it, too. I've traveled the Bealach na Bà a few times, but always as a passenger, and even then my stomach has flipped.

This old pass was cut into the mountain in 1822 to allow cattle to be led over. The route starts on the A896, between Lochcarron and Shieldaig. If you are coming from Lochcarron, you need to take the left-hand road by the Bealach Café, just under 2 miles (3 km) past the Kishorn Seafood Bar. You'll know you're in the right place as the sign says "Road to Applecross" and offers a bit of a warning for anyone having second thoughts. The road goes up over the mountain and is single track all the way. The views en route are very much dictated by the weather—when cloud cover is low and the pass is covered in mist, you can see very little, but the land looks mystical. On days when the sky is clear, the view from the highest point (2,053 feet/626 m) of the valley below, with the serpentine-like river, will make you feel like you've discovered a hidden ancient land. You may even be able to see Skye and the islands of the Outer Hebrides ahead of you. From here, it starts its zigzag descent down again, all the way to Applecross. It's 11 miles (18 km) each way (yes, you do have to drive back again), taking about an hour in total.

If you want to get to Applecross without breaking a sweat, you can take the much gentler coast road (turning up off the A896 toward Ardheslaig, just before Shieldaig), but it will take you a lot longer (50 miles/80 km round-trip, around an hour each way).

THE ROAD TO DIABAIG
From Torridon village

If you tell a local you're taking the drive from Torridon village to the small settlement of Lower Diabaig, you may receive a response along the lines of "Oh you'll be fine. Just fine," said with hardly hidden glee.

From Torridon village, the narrow road to Diabaig climbs inland. At first it skirts Upper Loch Torridon, before snaking farther away from the coast on a series of hairpin bends that often reveal unexpectedly steep hills. But what a scene: a mass of sapphire water framed by grassy moorland and not another soul to be seen. This is what Scottish travel is all about. From here the descent into the tiny harbor hamlet of Lower Diabaig is relatively stress-free.

When you reach it, calm, pretty Lower Diabaig is little more than a few cottages, a red telephone box, a pier, and a café/restaurant (Gille Brighde, The Old Schoolhouse; www.gille-brighde.com; tel. 01445 790 245, 5pm-8pm Weds.-Sat. 12pm-3:30pm Sun., check for winter opening times; entrées £7). The journey is just under 9 miles (14 km) each way, with a total journey time of 50 minutes.

Sports and Recreation
BEINN EIGHE NATURE RESERVE

Kinlochewe, IV22 2PA; www.nature.scot; open 24/7, visitor center 10am-5pm Mar.-Oct.; free

There's more to this region than great drives, and for many it's the perfect playground for adventure. This nature reserve, which covers 19 square miles (48 square km), is Britain's oldest and its nucleus is the Beinn Eighe ridge—an assembly of crooked, craggy peaks and slopes that lie between Loch Macree and Glen Torridon. Here, Caledonian pines as old as 350 years are clumped together, offering a rare glimpse of how Scotland once was, when trees like these would have cloaked huge swaths of the country. Today, the natural setting attracts eagles, pine marten, crossbills, divers, and red deer, and there are lots of walking and cycling trails to follow.

HEBRIDEAN WHALE TOURS

Pier Road, Gairloch; tel. 01445 712 458; www. hebridean-whale-cruises.co.uk; mid-Apr.-mid-Oct.; Whales and Wildlife cruise (2.5 hours) adult £53, child £35; Ultimate Orca 1 (4 hours) adult £84, child £65

There are a few companies offering trips out of Gairloch's pier into the North Minch, but this is the best. As well as potential whale and dolphin spotting you also have a good chance of seeing white-tailed eagles, razorbills, guillemots, and puffins. For the best chance of seeing whales, opt for the four-hour cruise, as it gives you more time to get farther out into open sea.

TORRIDON OUTDOORS

Torridon Hotel & Inn, by Achnasheen, Wester Ross; www.thetorridon.com/torridon-outdoors/our-activities; daylight hours Feb.-Dec.; half-day activities £150 for 2, full-day £250 for 2

This multi-activity tourism provider based out of the Torridon Hotel can assist with everything from guided walking tours—including Munro-bagging among the three mountain ranges of Beinn Alligin, Liathach, and Beinn Eighe—to mountain biking, gorge scrambling, and sea kayaking.

Food and Accommodations
TORRIDON STORES & CAFÉ

Torridon, IV22 2EZ; tel. 01445 791 400; http:// torridonstoresandcafe.co.uk; 10am-5pm Mon.-Sat. May-Oct., 10am-5pm Weds.-Sat Nov.-Apr.; pot of tea £1.20, coffee £2.30, cakes from £1.50

This general store in the blink-and-you'll-miss-it village of Torridon has both a café and a shop. Refreshments include tea, hot chocolate, scones, soup, sandwiches, even a glass of wine or beer. It's a meeting place for locals, and also a fair few passersby, and everyone seems very pleased to be here. The shop has all the essentials—store food, alcohol, toiletries, as well as postcards and stamps—and there is even a handy postbox outside.

APPLECROSS INN

Shore Street, Applecross; tel. 01520 744 262; www. applecrossinn.co.uk; 11:30am-10pm Thurs.-Mon., 3pm-10pm Weds.; entrées £8

This pub is a fantastic reward for anyone driving the Bealach na Bà. It does good seafood and pub grub in a traditional, atmospheric Highland bar. It's usually pretty busy, whatever time of year, but particularly in summer, so book ahead; there are seven nice B&B rooms, too. In summer, grab a pint and some in-the-shell langoustines and take a table outside to soak up the view.

KISHORN SEAFOOD RESTAURANT

Kishorn, IV54 8XA; tel. 01520 733 240; http:// kishornseafoodbar.co.uk; Mar.-Oct.; scallops £8.50, seafood platter for 2 £60

This cute little wooden seafood bar in sky blue with a shaded porch looks like it could be the location for a Caribbean fish fry. But no, it's definitely Scotland: the fish comes straight from the boat, and the setting—with views to Skye and the Applecross hills—is just lovely. People come from all over to try the fish pie, sushi, and overflowing fish platter, best enjoyed with a glass of crisp white wine.

SANACHAN BUNKHOUSE

Kishorn; tel. 01520 733 484 or 07595 851 444; https://ourscottishadventure.com; check in 6pm-9pm;

£20pp in shared room, towel hire £1, sleeping bag hire £5

If you hear people talk about Kishorn Bunkhouse, this is where they mean: a friendly, sociable place with a wood-burner in the lounge and a selection of shared rooms—since January 2021, a new cabin has replaced the bunk house and has space for 12 guests across three rooms. It's basic, but that's reflected in the price, and hot showers are promised. If you like hill-climbing, the great outdoors is literally in your back garden. Owners Sean and Sophie also rent out paddleboards and wetsuits for £15 an hour.

THE TORRIDON HOTEL & INN
By Achnasheen, Wester Ross; tel. 01445 791 242; www.thetorridon.com; £320 d

The Torridon hotel overlooks Upper Loch Torridon, which goes all the way out to sea, and faces several mountains. The 3 AA Rosette 1887 fine-dining restaurant is suitably refined, and the dishes are delicious, with chef Ross Stovold serving up a daily changing four- or seven-course menu. The Whisky Bar is cozy and well-stocked, and the bar staff can guide you through some of the over 350 whiskies. The lounge and bar area are lovely places to unwind, read your book, or play a boardgame (check out the astronomy ceiling in honor of Queen Victoria), and there is even a carefully positioned telescope for guests to use by one of the windows. Guests can also borrow wellies and brollies (boots and umbrellas) by the doors to the hotel to make it easier to walk around the estate.

Information and Services
Visit Applecross.info for pre-planning, as well as the Gairloch & Loch Ewe website (www.galeactionforum.co.uk). The **National Trust Scotland** (www.nts.org.uk/visit/places/torridon) looks after much of the Torridon landscape, so it is also a useful resource. At its **Countryside Centre** on the edge of Torridon village (Torridon, Achnasheen IV22 2EW; tel. 844 493 2229; 10am-5pm Sun.-Fri.) you can speak to local experts.

Getting There
BY CAR
From Ullapool, follow the A832 to Corrieshalloch Gorge, where you take a sharp right onto the A832, which weaves itself to Gairloch (56 miles/90 km; 1 hour 20 minutes). It's by no means a straight route, as the road largely hugs the coast, but it sure is pretty.

For Torridon, stay on the A832 for 30 miles

the lounge at the Torridon Hotel & Inn

Detour: Plockton and Isle of Skye

Plockton

Spending a few nights in the charming village of **Plockton** is a worthwhile detour. Known as the Jewel of the Highlands, the town of Plockton is the kind of place where you may find wandering Highland cattle lazily drinking from a stream on the outskirts on the village.

The **Plockton Inn** (Innes Street; tel. 1599 544 222; www.plocktoninn.co.uk; £140 d) is a traditional-style pub with rooms, a good restaurant, and regular traditional music nights, while the **Plockton Hotel** (41 Harbour St; tel. 1599 544 274; https://plocktonhotel.co.uk; £130 d) is another nice pub with some nice rooms and outdoor seating on a terrace looking out across the bay.

Visit Plockton (https://visitplockton.com) is a really useful website for planning your visit. There is no cash point, so if you need money, you'll have to visit the tiny post office (right at the village hall then right again) on weekday mornings (except Wednesday).

From Applecross, you're actually not far from the Kyle of Lochalsh and the bridge over to Skye, only about 50 miles (80 km) away from Applecross.

If you're headed to Skye from the North Coast 500, Plockton is located on the route from Applecross to Kyle of Lochalsh. From Applecross, it's 36 miles (58 km) southeast to Plockton. You'll need to head over the Bealach na Bà to Tornapress to join the A896 and then take the A890 south at the turning from Strathcarron, following the shores of Loch Carron, before dipping inland toward Achmore and then following signs for Plockton. To reach Plockton from Kyle of Lochalsh, it's just a 15-minute drive north onto Main Street, turning left onto an unmarked road after around 4 miles(6 km) and continuing on for a couple of miles (total distance of 6 miles/10 km). There is a **train station** at the top of the village in Plockton that is part of the Kyle Line and connects to Inverness (2 hours 30 minutes; £24.90 single). To continue on to Skye, you can either take the train to Kyle of Lochalsh, or drive 15 minutes (6 miles/10 km).

(48 km; 50 minutes). From Torridon, turn right onto the A896, passing by the Torridon Hotel & Inn on your right-hand side. Stay on this road for Tornapress and turn right to join the Bealach na Bà for the most exciting route (27 miles/43 km; 1 hour). For a slightly easier route, turn right much earlier, just past Shieldaig onto an unmarked road for the lower coastal road (32 miles/51 km; 1 hour 15 minutes).

BY PUBLIC TRANSPORT

Wester Ross is not the easiest place to get to by public transport. You can reach Strathcarron, 21 miles (34 km) east of Applecross, on the Kyle Line from Inverness (2 hours; £21.40 single, £27.50 return). The 702 bus from Strathcarron will get you to Torridon in about an hour, but it doesn't time well with the trains, so you should make the most of the wait and maybe plan a walk around Strathcarron.

APPLECROSS TO INVERNESS

Miles 434-516; 2.5 hours without stops

This is perhaps the most underwhelming section of the route, but drivers may get a sense of relief at finally driving roads with the occasional two lanes of traffic and no sheer drops over to the side. That said, it's mostly single-track between Strathcarron and Balnacra, so they're not out of the woods yet. Speaking of woods, the road toward Contin takes you past woodland where red squirrels have been reintroduced in the last few years in the hope that they can encourage the growth of native trees (they are known to bury seeds that then grow to become part of the forest).

Before heading back to Inverness, stop off in the Victorian spa town of Strathpeffer, a genteel sort of place surrounded by wooded hills and overlooked by Ben Wyvis. It still bears the hallmarks of its once wealthy past in its architecture, though the railway line no longer runs; the station has cleverly pivoted into a museum and café.

Sights
ROGIE FALLS

Rogie Falls car park, A835 2 miles (3 km) north of Contin; open 24/7; free

Just a mile or so before you reach Contin, coming from the west, this 30-foot waterfall is an easy walk from the car park (five minutes)—just follow the path to the left. For the best views, walk onto the suspension bridge, and then, rather than just getting back in the car, follow the Riverside Trail back through the woods for a slightly longer (0.8 mile/1.3 km) reinvigorating forest walk.

CASTLE LEOD

Strathpeffer IV14 9AA; www.castleleod.org.uk; £5 donation to walk the grounds

Once you pass through Contin, *Outlander* fans should take the next left (A834) to reach this castle, the seat of Clan Mackenzie. Writer Diana Gabaldon says this 16th-century five-story tower house with Victorian and Edwardian additions, surrounded by woodland close to the attractive spa village of Strathpeffer, is where she pointed location scouts to as a possibility for Castle Leoch in the series when filming began. Though Doune Castle was eventually chosen, it's widely believed that this is the place Gabaldon imagined when she wrote her stories. You can only step inside the castle on special open days, listed on the website, or by prebooked private tour (sometimes with the Chief of Clan Mackenzie), though the grounds can be walked throughout the year.

Shopping
LOCHCARRON WEAVERS

Mid Strome, Lochcarron, IV54 8YH; tel. 01520 722 212; 9am-5pm Mon.-Sat. Apr.-Oct., 10am-4pm Mon.-Fri., Sat. by appointment Nov.-Mar.

On the banks of Loch Carron, just as you start to make your way out of Wester Ross, this colorful, reputable shop sells good-quality tartan, knitwear, cashmere, tweed, and kilts.

Food and Accommodations
CARRON RESTAURANT
Cam-allt, Strathcarron; tel. 01520 722 488; www.
carronrestaurant.com; 10am-8:30pm Mon.-Sat. and
10am-3pm Sun. in summer, 10am-5pm Mon.-Sat. and
10am-3pm Sun. in winter; light meals £8.50
Overlooking Loch Carron, this family-run restaurant is a popular stop-off for people traveling from Wester Ross to Inverness and vice versa. You can just pop in for a cuppa or one of the "Five Bakes": shortbread, scones, gingerbread, lemon drizzle, and Florentines are made daily, or for something more substantial try the Scottish smoked salmon platter or the venison burger.

MUSEUM COFFEE SHOP
Strathpeffer IV14 9HA; tel. 07557 505 264;
10am-5pm Tues.-Sun. in spring and summer,
10am-4pm Thurs.-Sun. in winter; cakes £2.95, coffee
£2
The former train station is a reminder of Strathpeffer's affluent past, when Victorians would arrive in droves to soak in its healing waters. Sadly, the trainline no longer comes through here, but it's a relief that the original building remains as the Highland Museum of Childhood and this café is a delight, serving teas, coffees, sandwiches, and standard cafeteria staples alongside irresistible cakes.

Information and Services
The **Smithy Community Hub,** when it is open (Strathcarron, IV54 8YS; tel. 01520 722 952; https://lochcarroncommunity. wordpress.com/category/smithy-hub), is a great place to find out about local events or attend local market days. They do bike hire (from £10 for two hours), but they are still finding their way out of the pandemic, so call ahead to see if and when they will be open. For petrol and shops, you'll be well-served when you reach Inverness, but if you need anything before that, there's a good café in Achnasheen and a petrol station in Contin.

Getting There
It's just 80 miles (129 km) from Applecross to Inverness, starting by crossing over the Bealach na Bà back to Tornapress, where you need to take a right onto the A896, which then takes you through Lochcarron, turning into the A90 as you head toward Coulags, all the way to Achnasheen. At Achnasheen, turn right onto the A832, which becomes the A835 at Garve, past Contin, all the way to Newton of Ferintosh, where shortly afterward you'll take a right turn onto the A9 to Inverness (around 2 hours total journey time).

If you'd like to visit Kyle of Lochalsh from Applecross, you'll need to follow the Bealach na Bà back to the main road at Tornapress, where you turn right onto the A896 and follow this all the way past Lochcarron, turning right onto the A90 to Strathcarron. The A90 will take you all the way to Auchetyre where you turn right onto the A87 and follow this road into Kyle of Lochalsh (1.5 hours; 50 miles/80 km).

The Outer Hebrides

Picture a place where otters are given the right of way, where corncrakes bark from the cover of orchid-freckled green and yellow machair (a low-lying grassy field habitat, unique to Scotland and Ireland, which is set ablaze with flowers in summer), and white sandy beaches look like they've drifted in from the tropics, and you will have a good impression of the Outer Hebrides. For peaceful nature holidays in Scotland, there is no place like it. Often discussed as if they are in the back of beyond, the Outer Hebrides are more accessible than you might think, but just hard enough to get to that they keep all but the most determined away.

The Western Isles are home to some of the most unique communities in Scotland, where crofting—the act of living and working on

Highlights

Look for ★ to find recommended sights, activities, dining, and lodging.

★ **Standing Stones of Calanais:**
Predating Stonehenge, this remarkable ancient site has far fewer visitors (page 443).

★ **Isle of Harris Distillery:** This distillery with a community focus evokes the warm hospitality you'll find throughout the Outer Hebrides (page 453).

★ **Beaches of Harris:** Drive the West Harris coastline north for beach views that will stop you in your tracks (page 454).

★ **Traditional Harris Tweed:** Forget the mills; for an authentic Tweed experience, watch it being handspun at home (page 457).

★ **Barra Runway:** This is the world's only beach runway—you'll never forget the first time you land in Barra (page 464).

★ **St. Kilda:** Birds have replaced people on this remote uninhabited island, a bucket list location for many (page 466).

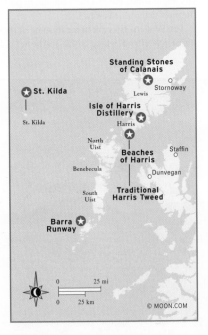

© MOON.COM

small units of land—is still sustainable, and Scottish Gaelic is widely spoken. One of the first places to be settled in the British Isles, the Outer Hebrides may have been hit hard by the Clearances and later depopulation, but residents here consistently report being happier than in most parts of the UK, and tourism is increasingly one of its biggest employers.

With few so-called "attractions," the biggest pull of the Outer Hebrides is the sense of space, quiet, and lack of hurry. Most visitors make a beeline for Lewis and Harris, where the ancient Lewis Chessmen were found near Uig in the 1800s and you can visit the workshop of a weaver to see traditional Harris Tweed being made, but it's worth traveling to some of the even quieter and less visited isles farther south too.

Throughout the isles, a unique Scandinavian/Gaelic culture pervades that can be enjoyed through music, song, and dance in some of the islands' old pubs or at its lively festivals.

ORIENTATION

The Outer Hebrides are sometimes called the **Western Isles,** though confusingly they don't include many of Scotland's western isles (Skye, Mull, or Arran). In my view, it makes more sense if you think of them as Scotland's "far western isles." Shaped a bit like a plume of smoke, this interconnected archipelago of more than 100 islands (about 15 of which are inhabited) rises to the northeast for about 130 miles (210 km) from **Barra Head** in the south to the **Butt of Lewis** in the North. The islands are located about 40 miles (70 km) from the Scottish mainland, across the body of water known as **the Minch.**

The stubby, rocket-shaped dual isle of **Lewis and Harris** is by far the largest of the islands, and the one with the most obvious attractions—ancient standing stones, a diverse landscape, tweed makers, the famous Golden Road, plus Stornoway, a metropolis compared

with the other towns and villages of the isles, and home to one of the Outer Hebrides' three airports. Long separated by the Harris Hills mountain range, despite technically being on the same island, Lewis and Harris developed distinct culture, with Lewis taking up the northern two-thirds of the island and Harris the southern third.

You're not fully south if you arrive at **Barra,** with its airport and hourlong flights to Glasgow, but from here, you can travel farther down to **Vatersay,** the most southerly of the inhabited Outer Hebrides, via a causeway. If you'd like to visit any of the four uninhabited isles farther south—Sandray, Pabbay, Mingulay, and Berneray—you'll need to take a boat from Barra.

North of Barra, via a short ferry crossing, is the isle of **Eriskay**—the real-life setting for the story that inspired Compton Mackenzie's book *Whisky Galore*. North of here is **South Uist**—the second largest isle in the Outer Hebrides—then Benbecula, North Uist, and Berneray; each of these isles is connected by a causeway. Finally, to reach Lewis and Harris, you must catch the CalMac ferry from Berneray to **Leverburgh** in south Harris. From here, it's about 85 miles north (137 km) to the Butt of Lewis, the tip of the northernmost isle.

GETTING THERE
By Ferry
There are several access points to the Outer Hebrides from the Scottish mainland, including, from south to north:

- **Oban** (Inner Hebrides) to Barra and South Uist
- **Mallaig** (Inner Hebrides) to South Uist
- **Ullapool** (The North Coast 500) to Lewis
- **Uig** (northern Isle of Skye) to Harris

All ferries are run by **CalMac** (Caledonian MacBrayne; www.calmac.co.uk) and in

---

Previous: Luskentyre Sands; creating traditional Harris Tweed; Standing Stones of Calanais.

The Outer Hebrides: North and South Uist

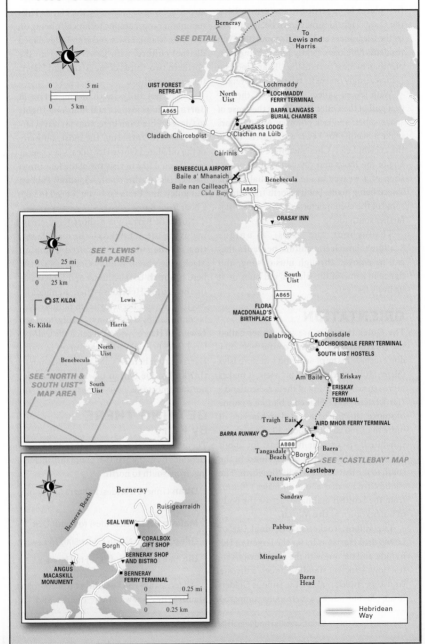

Berneray

SEE DETAIL

To Lewis and Harris

0   5 mi
0   5 km

UIST FOREST RETREAT

North Uist

Lochmaddy
LOCHMADDY FERRY TERMINAL

A865

BARPA LANGASS BURIAL CHAMBER

LANGASS LODGE

Cladach Chirceboist   Clachan na Lùib

Càirinis

BENEBECULA AIRPORT
Baile a' Mhanaich

Benebecula

Baile nan Cailleach
Cula Bay   A865

ORASAY INN

South Uist

A865

FLORA MACDONALD'S BIRTHPLACE

Dalabrog   Lochboisdale
LOCHBOISDALE FERRY TERMINAL
SOUTH UIST HOSTELS

Am Baile   Eriskay
ERISKAY FERRY TERMINAL

Traigh Eais   AIRD MHOR FERRY TERMINAL

BARRA RUNWAY

A888

Tangasdale Beach   Borgh   Barra
SEE "CASTLEBAY" MAP

Vatersay   Castlebay

Sandray

Pabbay

Mingulay   Barra Head

---

0   25 mi
0   25 km

SEE "LEWIS" MAP AREA

ST. KILDA

St. Kilda

Lewis

Harris

North Uist

Benebecula

SEE "NORTH & SOUTH UIST" MAP AREA

South Uist

Berneray

Berneray Beach

Ruisigearraidh

SEAL VIEW

CORALBOX GIFT SHOP

Borgh

BERNERAY SHOP AND BISTRO

ANGUS MACASKILL MONUMENT

BERNERAY FERRY TERMINAL

0   0.25 mi
0   0.25 km

Hebridean Way

The Outer Hebrides: Lewis

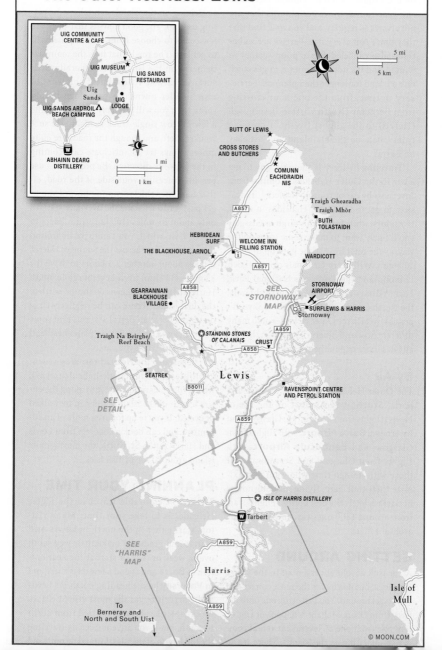

UIG COMMUNITY
CENTRE & CAFÉ
UIG MUSEUM
UIG SANDS
RESTAURANT
Uig
Sands
UIG LODGE
UIG SANDS ARDROIL
BEACH CAMPING
ABHAINN DEARG
DISTILLERY

0   1 mi
0   1 km

BUTT OF LEWIS

CROSS STORES
AND BUTCHERS

COMUNN
EACHDRAIDH
NIS

A857

Traigh Ghearadha
Traigh Mhòr
BUTH
TOLASTAIDH

HEBRIDEAN
SURF
THE BLACKHOUSE, ARNOL

WELCOME INN
FILLING STATION

WARDICOTT

A857

A858

GEARRANNAN
BLACKHOUSE
VILLAGE

SEE
"STORNOWAY"
MAP

STORNOWAY
AIRPORT

SURFLEWIS & HARRIS
Stornoway

STANDING STONES
OF CALANAIS

CRUST

A859

A858

Traigh Na Beirghe/
Reef Beach

SEATREK

Lewis

B8011

SEE
DETAIL

RAVENSPOINT CENTRE
AND PETROL STATION

A859

ISLE OF HARRIS DISTILLERY

Tarbert

SEE
"HARRIS"
MAP

A859

Harris

Isle of
Mull

To
Berneray and
North and South Uist

0   5 mi
0   5 km

© MOON.COM

summer there are usually at least a couple on each route each day. Though ferries do run year-round, in winter months they are not always as regular, and you may find that they don't run every day. Ferries are sometimes also canceled due to poor weather in winter, and it's not uncommon to get stuck on an island for longer than planned. Ferries vary in time, from the one-hour crossing from Berneray (North Uist) to Leverburgh (Harris) to the almost five-hour crossing from Oban, on the mainland, to Castlebay on Barra.

Traveling by ferry is the only way to get a car to the Outer Hebrides. Coming from Inverness by car or train to the ferry, it's feasible to get to the Outer Hebrides in under five hours, while from Edinburgh or Glasgow you'll likely want to make some stops on the way, as the total travel time goes up to about 10 hours. With ferry terminals close to Loch Lomond and the Trossachs National Park, Fort William and the Western Highlands, the North Coast 500, and the Isle of Skye, it's possible to tack the Outer Hebrides onto many different Scotland itineraries, though they really deserve a trip in themselves.

By Air

The Outer Hebrides are home to three airports: **Stornoway Airport** on the Isle of Lewis (flights from Edinburgh, Glasgow, and Inverness); **Barra Airport,** with flights from Glasgow; and **Benbecula Airport,** with flights from Glasgow and Stornoway. For those with limited time who want to maximize their time here, flying into Stornoway or Barra is likely the best option. Flights start from around £100 one-way, and are usually around 1 hour.

GETTING AROUND

A car isn't absolutely essential in the Outer Hebrides, but it is by far the most convenient way to get around. You can bring one onto the ferry from Oban, Mallaig, Ullapool, or Uig, or rent one from one of several car rental companies operating on the islands. There are no trains, buses don't operate every day, and taxis are scarce.

Driving on the islands can take some getting used to. The good news is that there are few roads to choose from, so it's quite hard to get lost. The roads that link the main settlements on the islands are generally well-surfaced tarmac roads, but if you want to visit smaller townships or hidden beauty spots, then you will probably encounter quite a few narrow single-track roads. Make sure you keep left, and though the roads are quite quiet, always try to anticipate cars coming in the opposite direction. Be prepared to use passing places on your side of the road, either to allow vehicles coming toward you to get past, or to let someone overtake you. It's only about 65 miles (105 km) from Barra to North Uist, which you can drive in around three hours. Once across the Sound of Harris, it takes about another 2.5 hours to drive the 83 miles (134 km) from Leverburgh in South Harris to the Butt of Lewis on the far north of the dual island. There can be relatively large distances between petrol stations and some do stay closed on Sunday, so plan ahead and always fill up when you can.

There's also the **Hebridean Way** (www.visitouterhebrides.co.uk/hebrideanway), which runs 185 miles (297 km) along the entire length of the islands and can be walked or cycled. If you're up for even more of an adventure, you can book a boat trip from Lewis and Harris out to **St. Kilda,** the most remote island group of the British Isles.

PLANNING YOUR TIME

The art of enjoyable travel in the Outer Hebrides is to take your time. Many visitors start either in the north in **Lewis and Harris** and gradually make their way south over a week or two, or start at the near bottom at **Barra** and spend a few days there and in **Vatersay** before heading north. As Lewis and Harris is by far the most visited island, this chapter has been organized from north to south, but if you are considering traveling the full length of the isles, I would recommend starting in the south, and flying into Barra from Glasgow (there are also ferry crossings to Barra from **Oban** on the mainland).

If you don't want to constantly be on the move, you may prefer just to stick to a couple of islands, or even just one, rather than attempt them all. Note that given the time it takes to get from place to place, day trips to places like Lewis and Harris are pointless—you'll only see a very small bit of the island and kick yourself that you can't stop for longer. **Visit Outer Hebrides** (www.visitouterhebrides.co.uk) is the main online resource for planning your trip.

One thing worth noting is that religion, which was introduced to the isles by the Celts in the 9th century and embraced by its Viking settlers, is still a cornerstone of island life. Lewis and Harris and North Uist are predominantly Protestant, dominated by Calvinist free churches, and on the southern islands, Catholicism survived the Scottish Reformation. **Sunday closing** is strictly observed (apart from some cases in Stornoway), so you will need to come armed with food and supplies if arriving then. The Eat Drink Hebrides Trail (www.eatdrinkhebrides.co.uk) is a good resource on local food and drinks on the islands.

Whatever you do, don't leave it until you get here to book your **accommodation.** With so few to choose from, rooms book up fast. The same goes for your **car rental,** which should be reserved as far in advance of your trip as possible.

Pretty much everything closes from late autumn to early spring in the Outer Hebrides, including accommodations and restaurants. If you can find a place to stay, though, it can be a beautiful place to cozy down and look out for the Northern Lights. Spring is a beautiful time to visit, when many animals wake from hibernation, migrating birds begin to arrive, and the days start to stretch out—you may even have some nice, hot days. Early spring is particularly good for seeing golden eagles, who can be seen pair-bonding in March. Summer is best for sea swimming, endless days (though beware the midges), and vibrant wildflowers in the machair. For stargazing, quiet, and a good excuse to wrap up by the fire, autumn is appealing (and a good bit cheaper).

Itinerary Ideas

DAY 1

1 Take the morning flight from Glasgow to **Barra Airport** with Loganair, landing on the incomparable beach runway. You can have a cup of tea and brunch at the friendly airport café while you plan your day.

2 Catch the morning ferry over to Eriskay Ferry Terminal on the Isle of Eriskay, where you can have lunch in **The Politician** pub. Ask staff to show you some of the whisky bottles that have survived from the famous *SS Politician* ship, which ran aground here in 1941.

3 Head north to South Uist and pay your respects at **Flora Macdonald's Birthplace.**

4 Stretch your legs and look out for wildlife at **Cula Bay.**

5 Have dinner at the nearby **Westford Inn** and settle in for a traditional music session.

6 Continue north to your treehouse escape and accommodations for the evening, the **Uist Forest Retreat.**

Itinerary Ideas

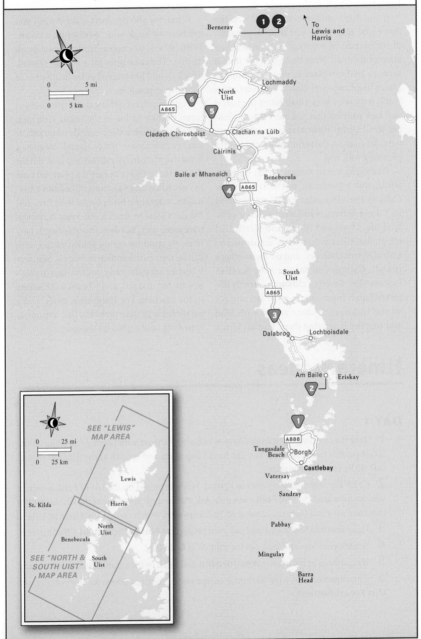

Berneray

To
Lewis and
Harris

0   5 mi
0   5 km

Lochmaddy

North
Uist

A865

Cladach Chirceboist   Clachan na Lùib

Càirinis

Baile a' Mhanaich   Benebecula

A865

South
Uist

A865

Dalabrog   Lochboisdale

Am Baile   Eriskay

A888

Tangasdale
Beach   Borgh

Castlebay

Vatersay

Sandray

Pabbay

Mingulay

Barra
Head

0   25 mi
0   25 km

SEE "LEWIS"
MAP AREA

Lewis

St. Kilda

Harris

North
Uist

Benebecula

SEE "NORTH &
SOUTH UIST"
MAP AREA

South
Uist

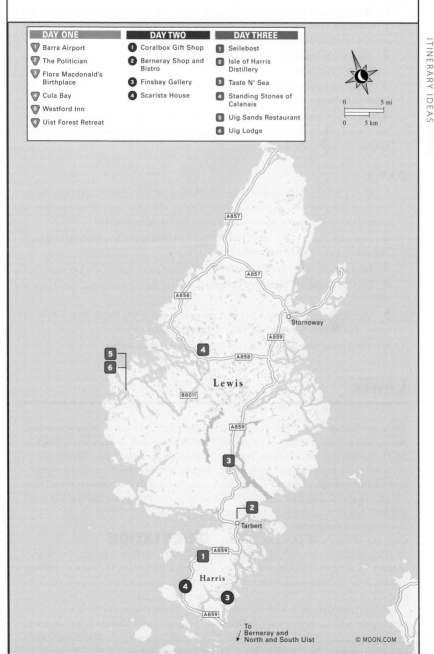

DAY ONE
1. Barra Airport
2. The Politician
3. Flora Macdonald's Birthplace
4. Cula Bay
5. Westford Inn
6. Uist Forest Retreat

DAY TWO
1. Coralbox Gift Shop
2. Berneray Shop and Bistro
3. Finsbay Gallery
4. Scarista House

DAY THREE
1. Seilebost
2. Isle of Harris Distillery
3. Taste N' Sea
4. Standing Stones of Calanais
5. Uig Sands Restaurant
6. Uig Lodge

0   5 mi
0   5 km

A857

A857

A858

A859

Stornoway

A859

5
6

Lewis

A858

B8011

A859

3

2
Tarbert

1   A859

4   Harris

3

A859

To
Berneray and
North and South Uist

© MOON.COM

DAY 2

1 Wake up and eat breakfast in your cabin as you listen to the birdsong. Check out and drive over the causeway to Berneray, where you can pop into the **Coralbox** to browse for some unique gifts and have a blether with the friendly owner.

2 Have a light lunch at the **Berneray Shop and Bistro** before taking the ferry across the Sound of Harris to Leverburgh.

3 Drive the Golden Road, also known as the Bays Road, popping into galleries like **Finsbay Gallery** on the way.

4 Check into **Scarista House** and take a stroll on the glorious beach opposite. Have predinner drinks in the lounge at Scarista House and swap stories with other guests before heading through to the dining room.

DAY 3

1 Have a full Scottish breakfast at Scarista House to set you up for the day before heading north along the west Harris coast, leaving plenty of time to stop and take pictures of some of the most beautiful beaches in the world, including **Seilebost**.

2 Stop off in Tarbert for a tour of **Isle of Harris Distillery** and hear about its long-term ambition to halt depopulation on the island.

3 Have a scenic casual lunch at **Taste N' Sea,** before crossing over into Lewis.

4 Visit the **Standing Stones of Calanais,** possibly the most awesome stone circle in the UK.

5 Continue your journey west to Uig. Time your dinner at **Uig Sands Restaurant** for sunset, and make sure you've reserved a table at the window.

6 You'll spend your last night in the Outer Hebrides at **Uig Lodge**.

Lewis

The largest part of the dual isle of Lewis and Harris, taking up the northern two-thirds of the Outer Hebrides' largest island, at times Lewis feels busy and developed, particularly around **Stornoway,** where the ferry from Ullapool on the mainland comes in, and you will find restaurants, pubs, some high street shops, and a supermarket. At other times, there can be a sense of Armageddon about the place, and driving across the huge expanse of peat bogs and moorland that cover Lewis's interior, it can feel like yours is the only car on the road.

Crossing from Stornoway in the east to the west coast, you'll discover one of Scotland's true treasures, a coastline adorned with historic relics, from ancient standing stones to traditional blackhouse villages and an Iron Age broch, as well as clean, empty beaches. Were it not for a disparate collection of ecohouses, campsites, hotels, and low-key restaurants, you might think you were the only one to set foot on the rippled shores of Uig Sands for centuries.

ORIENTATION

Stornoway, the Outer Hebrides' largest town at around 7,000 people and home to the **ferry terminal** for boats from Ullapool, sits at the top of the natural Stornoway Harbour. The town's **airport** sits just to the east.

Many of Lewis's main attractions are on the east coast, including the **Standing Stones of Calanais** and some of its most spectacular beaches. The Outer Hebrides' northernmost point, the **Butt of Lewis**, is a 45-minute (30-mile/48-km) drive north of Stornoway on the A857. Harris, meanwhile, is about an hour's drive south on the A859.

GETTING THERE

The ferry leaves from Ullapool at **Stornoway Ferry Terminal** in Stornoway, the island's capital and by far the largest city in the Outer Hebrides. The town spreads out around a deep natural harbor, where the ferry terminal is situated. Tickets can be booked through **CalMac** (www.calmac.co.uk; 2.5 hours; £54.05 each way per car, £10 each way adult, £5 each way child).

Flights with Loganair to **Stornoway Airport** (tel. 01851 702 256; www.hial.co.uk/homepage/9/stornoway-airport), located just a 10-minute drive east of the city, set off from Glasgow (www.loganair.co.uk; 1 hour, £125 each way), Edinburgh (1 hour 5 minutes; £100 one-way), Inverness (45 minutes; £75 one-way), as well as from Barra, Islay, Kirkwall on Orkney, and Sumburgh on Shetland.

GETTING AROUND

There is a limited bus service (better in summer), through the local council (www.cne-siar.gov.uk/roads-travel-and-parking/public-transport/bus-services), but if you have a choice, you really will have a better experience with a car. Once on the island, you can hire a car in Stornoway from **Car Hire Hebrides** (www.carhire-hebrides.co.uk), with locations at the airport and in Stornoway proper. Prices are reasonable: you can hire a small car in high season for around £300. The earlier you book, the better deal you'll get.

There are also taxis available through **Stornoway Taxi & Courier Services** (www.stornowaytaxis.co.uk).

SIGHTS
Stornoway
LEWS CASTLE

Lewes Castle Grounds; tel. 01851 822 746; www.lews-castle.co.uk; 10am-5pm Tues.-Sat. Apr.-Sept., *1pm-4pm Tues.-Sat. Oct.-Mar.; free (donations appreciated)*

This castle dating to the mid-19th century looms to the west of Stornoway Harbour, impressive in its meticulously restored state, and now housing self-catering accommodations as well as the **Museum & Tasglann nan Eilean,** which opened in 2016 and is dedicated to the unique culture of the Outer Hebrides, with a number of important objects from the islands' long history.

STORY OF HARRIS TWEED

First Floor, Town Hall, 2 Cromwell Street; tel. 01851 702 269; www.harristweed.org; 10am-3pm Mon.-Fri.

A relatively new tourism venture, this little museum in the Harris Tweed Authority building in Stornoway explains the process of tweed making, the remit of the Harris Tweed Authority. The exhibition, told through video, photos, audio guides, and live demos in summer months demonstrates how interwoven the fabric is with island life. It was closed on my last visit in April 2021, but the signs are good that it will reopen soon.

Western Lewis

TOP EXPERIENCE

★ STANDING STONES OF CALANAIS

Calanais, off the A859; tel. 01851 621 422; www.calanais.org; stones open 24/7, visitor center and café 9:30am-8pm Mon.-Sat. June-Aug., 10am-6pm Mon.-Sat. Apr.-May and Sept.-Oct., 10am-4pm Tues.-Sat. Nov.-Mar.

This impressive stone circle gives Stone Henge a run for its money. Calanais is a collection of 53 grey vertical stones—13 arranged as a stone circle, with a monolith near the middle, and the rest leading out from the circle, creating the shape of a cross—that has intrigued visitors for centuries.

Its location high up on a hill adds to its enchanting atmosphere. In the 17th century, residents of Lewis named the stones "false men," which may have been linked to a legend that

Lewis and Harris: The Island with a Split Personality

Though its official name is "Lewis and Harris," you won't hear locals refer to it as one island, ever. There's a bit of a rivalry between the two sides of the island—mostly in jest, but not always.

AN UNOFFICIAL BORDER

There's no border or signs as such to alert you that you are crossing from Harris to Lewis or vice versa. You'll most likely notice the change in landscape, from hilly Harris in the south to the flat calm of Lewis's peatland in the south, interspersed with countless lochs and lochans, which are blanketed in water lilies in summer. As official as these things get, the boundary between Lewis and Harris is somewhere between Loch Seaforth in the east to Loch Resort in the west. Although modern roads have mitigated this somewhat, difficult-to-cross mountains in North Harris also would have once made it difficult for the two sides of the islands to get to know one another.

CLAN RIVALRY

Historically, Lewis was part of Ross-shire (MacKenzie land), and Harris was part of Invernesshire (MacLeod land), which is perhaps where the sense of separation began. "Lewis looked across the Minch to Wester Ross and Sutherland, while Harris looked to Skye and Uist, and... they developed quite different cultures," says genealogist Bill Lawson, who has lived on the isles since the early 1980s. "Even in the early days of the clans, Harris and Lewis belonged to different families. This continued with the division of the islands between the council areas of Ross and Cromarty (Lewis) and Inverness-shire (Harris and the Southern Isles); until Comhairle nan Eilean (the Western Isles Council) was set up in 1975."

CULTURAL DIFFERENCES

Lawson says that the townships tend to be much larger and more concentrated on Lewis than in Harris, with the Nordic influence in terms of place names and personal names more noticeable. Though many visitors won't notice, the Gaelic between the two islands is very different, with markedly distinct dialects in Harris and Lewis. Lawson says: "Even within Lewis, the Gaelic of Uig bears more similarities to that of Harris than it does to the Gaelic of Point... showing the influence of travel by sea rather than land, as the people of Uig would have had sea links with North Harris."

Generally, Lewis is viewed as the sensible big brother, and Harris is the rebellious little brother. Obviously, however, it depends on whom you ask.

---

they are petrified giants who refused to convert to Christianity. A chambered tomb discovered at the site contained pottery 4,000 years old, dating the stones to at least 2,500 BC.

The Story of the Stones Exhibition in the **visitor center** is interesting and helps place these monoliths in some sort of context. Why they are here remains a mystery, but there are at least 11 smaller stone circles in the vicinity, and Patrick Ashmore, the man who excavated them in the 1980s, believes their placement may have been to capture the moon as it skims the southern hills every 18.6 years, creating a heavenly event "like a great god visiting the earth." You can walk right up to the stones

(about 10 minutes up a walkway from the visitor center) and stand among them for a humbling experience. My advice is to spend 20-30 minutes in the exhibition and then come and spend up to an hour at the stones themselves, taking in the atmosphere and location.

The Callanais stones are located a 30-minute (18-mile/29-km) drive west of Stornoway on the A859 and A858.

ABHAINN DEARG DISTILLERY

Carnish; HS2 9EX; tel. 01851 672 429; https:// abhainndeargdistillery.co.uk; 11am-1pm and 2pm-4pm Mon.-Sat.; tours £10

This craft distillery, near Uig Sands, was the

Stornoway

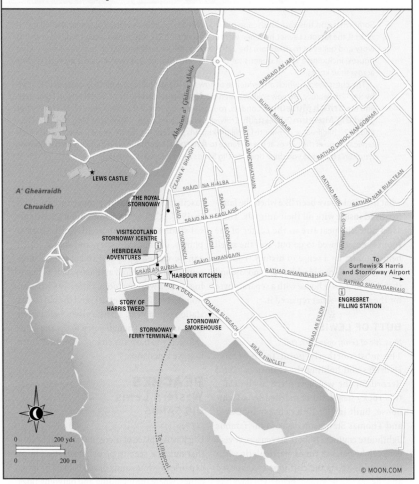

LEWS CASTLE

A' Gheàrraidh

Chruaidh

THE ROYAL STORNOWAY

VISITSCOTLAND STORNOWAY iCENTRE

HEBRIDEAN ADVENTURES

SRÀID AN RUBHA

HARBOUR KITCHEN

MOL A DEAS

STORY OF HARRIS TWEED

STORNOWAY FERRY TERMINAL

STORNOWAY SMOKEHOUSE

To Ullapool

To Surflewis & Harris and Stornoway Airport

ENGREBRET FILLING STATION

Abhainn a' Ghlinn Mhòir

BARRAID AN IAR

SLIGHE MHIORAIR

RATHAD MHICMHATHAIN

CEANN A' BHAIGH

SRÀID NA H-ALBA

SRÀID CHIONNICH

SRÀID CHADH

SRÀID LEODHAIS

SRÀID NA H-EAGLAISE

SRÀID EHRANGAIN

RATHAD CHNOC NAN GOBHAR

RATHAD MINIC

RATHAD NAM BUAILTEAN

A' GHOBHAINN

RATHAD SHANNDABHAIG

RATHAD SHANNDABHAIG

RATHAD AN EILEIN

IOMAIR SLIGEACH

SRÀID EINICLEIT

0   200 yds
0   200 m

© MOON.COM

only distillery in the Outer Hebrides until Harris Distillery opened in 2015, and when it launched its first single malt whisky in 2011 (a baby at just three years old), it was the first legal distillery to do so on the island ever (though whisky was made here illicitly for a long time). Tours, which must be prebooked, take you around the distillery to see how the whisky is handmade, followed by a tasting of the distillery's 10-year-old single malt at the end.

Northern Lewis
THE BLACKHOUSE, ARNOL

42 Arnol; tel. 01851 710 395; www.
historicenvironment.scot; 9:30am-5:30pm Mon.-Sat.
Apr.-Sept., 10am-4pm Mon.-Tues. and Thurs.-Sat.
Oct.-Mar., last entry half hour before closing.; adult
£6, child £3.60, concessions £4.80, under 5 free
This fully furnished thatched blackhouse (traditional Hebridean stone house) was once a family home that has been restored and preserved so that you can step inside for a sense of

The Lewis Chessmen

Somewhere on this vast sandscape of **Uig Sands,** on Lewis's west coast, near the village of Ardroil, the famous Lewis Chessmen were discovered in 1831. The chess pieces, made from walrus ivory and believed to date from the 12th century, are incredibly detailed mini medieval Viking figures, including a trio of queens sat on elaborate thrones and two kings sitting with swords across their knees.

The chess pieces, which are evidence of how this Islamic game was already popular in Europe by the 12th century, are now split between the **National Museum of Scotland** in Edinburgh and the **British Museum** in London. You can view replicas of the chess pieces in the quirky but good **Uig Museum** (5 Eireastadh, Crowlista; www.ceuig.co.uk; 12pm-5pm Mon.-Sat. Apr.-Oct.; adult £2, child free), a 10-minute (3-mile/4-km) drive east of Uig Sands. There is also a giant wood replica of one of the pieces at the entrance to **Ardroil Beach,** the main entry point to Uig Sands (you can't miss it as you drive down to Uig Sands Ardroil Beach Camping).

what life would have been like when the families lived inside with all their animals. Then, as in now, the peat fire in the center of the room is not allowed to go out, and the smell helps conjure up a sense of history. You can also view the ruined blackhouse at no. 39, and the white house—a house with a separate byre for the animals—that replaced it.

BUTT OF LEWIS

Ness, Isle of Lewis; open 24/7; free

The most northerly point in the Outer Hebrides and holding the Guinness World Record for the windiest place in the U.K., this rocky headland is marked by a lighthouse, built in the 19th century by David and Thomas Stevenson, sons of the famous lighthouse engineer Robert Stevenson. A visit here can be hairy at times, particularly when the wind is up, as the cliff tops are exposed and the sea can be violent below. On days like these, tread carefully to the lighthouse and feel the force of the weather before getting back in the car. Longer walks are best left for calm days. It's a 45-minute (30-mile/48-km) drive north of Stornoway on the A857.

COMUNN EACHDRAIDH NIS

North Dell; tel. 01851 810 377; http://cenonline.org; 10am-4:30pm Mon.-Fri., 11am-4pm Sun.; free

In the north of the isle, just a few miles southwest of the Butt of Lewis on the A857, is this fascinating local history museum, founded in 1977. It's a great resource for genealogical studies and has an archive of historical photos, old books, poetry, and songs, which can be viewed by appointment. In the museum you can see old artifacts, such as farming tools, a weaving loom, the early Christian Rona Cross, Barvas pottery, and the old Decca station equipment. There's also a well-priced **café** and shop. Though entry to the museum is free, if you have any change, it's always nice to leave a donation.

BEACHES
Western Lewis
UIG SANDS

Uig Bay

Uig Bay is a place of incredible natural beauty that must be seen to be believed. It's a huge expanse of white sandy beach backed by large dunes, where the incoming and outgoing tides creating a sublime swirling effect on the sand. At low tide, you can walk for miles along the coast, and on sunny days, the turquoise waters glisten seductively. Climb one of the shifting sand dunes for a better view of the beach and seascape for proof that, yes, Lewis can give Harris a run for its money when it comes to beaches.

TRAIGH NA BEIRGHE/REEF BEACH

Cnip

Also on west Lewis, but this time a little north of Aird Uig, this long, sweeping sandy beach is backed by machair. The beach has views over to the isle of **Pabbay** (not to be confused with Barra's isle of the same name), and it's also an excellent beach to look for seashells (particularly at the eastern end). Swimming is safe here, so you may sometimes see families from Stornoway on a beach holiday. A **campsite** (Cnip Grazing, bookable through coolcamping.com), owned by community trust, sits just above the beach. This is one of the beaches where the surfing community of Lewis likes to catch some waves.

Northern Lewis
TRAIGH MHÒR AND TRAIGH GHEARADHA
B895, past the turning for Traigh Mor, northwest Lewis

Not all of Lewis's beautiful beaches lie to the west. The lovely Traigh Mhòr and Traigh Gheardha (sometimes called Garry) beaches, are separated by a rocky promontory on the northeast of the island, looking out onto the Minch. A gorgeous bay of golden sand, with spectacular sea stacks at its southern end, from the car park you can see the **Bridge to Nowhere,** evidence of a failed plan by Lord Leverhulme, a former owner of the island, to connect the east coast of Lewis from Tolsta to the Port of Ness, abandoned in 1921. Today the bridge just leads to a rough path from where there is a tough trek across moorland to Ness. For the best photos of the beach, position yourself on the cliffs near the sea stacks at sunrise or sunset.

SPORTS AND RECREATION
Boat Tours and Cruises
HEBRIDEAN ADVENTURES
22 North Beach, Stornoway; tel. 07871 463 755; www.hebrideanadventures.co.uk; half-day tour from £85 adult, £65 child, 2-6 night cruises from £535 per person

These wildlife boat tours, run out of Stornoway, aboard a converted fishing boat, offer a very real chance of spotting some of Scotland's larger marine life, as well as countless seabirds, as its crew are experts in marine and land-based ecology. Though daytrips are possible (4-7 hours), for the best chance of seeing whales and dolphins, you should book a small cruise (2-6 nights), when you can really tap up the crew for information. On a cruise, you'll have more time to track where wildlife may be, and visit other islands, such as the volcanic Shiant Isles, off Harris's southeast coast, which are famed for their birdlife including puffins and razorbills; Skye; or even St. Kilda. The company is popular, so you'll need to book your trip way in advance.

SEATREK
Miavaig Harbour; tel. 01851 672 469; Apr.-Sept.; www.seatrek.co.uk; 2-hour trip £42 adult, £32 child, 3-hour trip £52 adult, £42 child;

At the moment, cruiser trips from this west coast-based company are paused, but will hopefully be up and running for the 2022 season, when they will include seafood lunches on board. Until then, the two- or three-hour RIB rides are available and include wildlife watching trips to deserted beaches, or a trip to explore the sea caves and lagoon of **Pabbay,** where you can check lobster pots for the day's catch. Fishing trips for novices as well as experienced anglers are also available.

Surfing
Known for its pristine beaches, clear water, consistent waves, reefs, points, and headlands that offer a good variety of waves for a range of surfing abilities, the coastline of Lewis has some excellent surfing. From **September to April,** this region provides challenging surf for competent boarders. **Stornoway** is the main place to find out about the best surfing spots (just pop into **Surflewis** on the outskirts of Stornoway for tips), while **Magic Seaweed** (http://magicseaweed.com) is an excellent website for checking forecasts and surfing reports.

In Uig, **Reef Beach** is one of many spots of Lewis's west coast that attracts surfers.

SURFLEWIS & HARRIS

*10 East Street, Sandwick; 07920 427 194; https://
surflewis.com; surf lessons £45 adult, £35 child,
wetsuit hire £10 per day, surfboards from £15 per day*

If you've ever wanted to learn to surf or just want to brush up on old skills, then these relaxed two-and-a-half-hour sessions (all equipment provided) will give you the confidence to start riding the waves. SurfLewis & Harris also runs SUP lessons and guided snorkeling tours, and it hires out surfboards and wetsuits to both beginner and experienced surfers. The company also has a location in Harris.

HEBRIDEAN SURF

*The Welcome In Filling Station; tel. 01851 840 343 or
07881 435 915; http://hebrideansurf.co.uk; £35 for
2-hour lesson*

These lessons under the guidance of an instructor who knows the surf territory and where to get the best conditions, come highly recommended. Derek MacLeod will take you to empty beaches along the North Atlantic that will suit your level: beginners can practice in a secluded place with waves that aren't too scary, while those with a bit more experience can try to catch some of the area's renowned reef breaks. Price includes board and all safety gear.

FOOD
Stornoway
★ HARBOUR KITCHEN

*5 Cromwell Street, Stornoway; tel. 01851 706 586;
www.facebook.com/HarbourKitchenSTY; 5pm-9pm
Weds., 12pm-2pm and 5pm-9pm Thurs.-Sat.,
12:30pm-3:30pm Sun.; entrées £7.50*

Opened in 2017 by local-born chef Lach Maclean, this excellent Stornoway bistro-style restaurant always has local fresh seafood on its menu—hand-dived scallops and langoustine, for instance—plus local salmon (of course), a couple of meat options, and always a tasty vegetarian option. The kitchen is open, so there is a buzz about the place, and the care given to each dish is evident. Maclean also has plans to open a second restaurant on Bank Street—expect good things.

CRUST

*Achmore; tel. 07762 128 108; www.crustlikethat.
co.uk; 12pm-7:30pm Tues.-Sat.; pizzas from £9*

This blue pizza hut about 10 miles (16 km) outside Stornoway, as you head toward Harris, serves up Neapolitan-style pizzas with toppings provided by other Highlands and islands producers, such as Great Glen Charcuterie. The views of lochs and the Harris hills are amazing, but you do need to order your pizza ahead (the earlier in the day the better, as they do sell out). However, you can just drop in and grab coffee and a brownie.

STORNOWAY SMOKEHOUSE

*Shell Street, Stornoway; tel. 01851 702 723; www.
stornowaysmokehouse.co.uk; 9am-5pm Tues.-Fri.;
pack of double smoked salmon £28*

The last traditional smokehouse in the Outer Hebrides, this is where the legendary Stornoway kippers that you'll spot on many a breakfast menu are smoked—though the Stornoway double smoked salmon is the company's most popular export. Fish is smoked in a traditional brick kiln, in much the same way that it was 150 years ago when this region was the center of Europe's herring industry. Pop into the shop to buy some fish, and if they're not too busy they'll show you the kiln too.

Western Lewis
UIG COMMUNITY CENTRE & CAFÉ

*Crowlista, Aird Uig; tel. 01851 672 444; www.
uigcommunityshop.co.uk; shop 9am-5pm Mon.-Sat.,
café 12pm-4pm Thurs.-Sat; coffee £1.50, sandwiches
£3*

If you've made it as far as Lewis's west coast, then you will be relieved to find this grocery store/café open, as there is little else around. The well-stocked shop has food, wine, and toiletries. The café serves good coffee (to go and sit-in), yummy cakes, homemade soup, and a salmon pâté you'll talk about long after. There is a fuel station—on Sunday when the center is closed, you can still get petrol and pay for it

1: Calanais Standing Stones 2: Harris Tweed weaver Rebecca Hutton 3: Uig Sands Ardroil Beach Camping 4: Uig Sands

Support Community Stores

Though you'll find some larger chain stores in Lewis, it's so important to support local stores on your travels. As well as selling essential items, which are not easily found in more remote parts of the islands, these shops provide real hubs for the community in which they are based. For residents, it's a chance to chat to a familiar face when neighbors are few and far between, and to keep abreast of local news. For visitors, meanwhile, it's an opportunity to get tips from locals, to find out about other services, and to hear Gaelic spoken matter-of-factly.

The Visit Outer Hebrides tourism board is trying to encourage visitors to spend more at these community stores and you will find many of them on the Eat Drink Hebrides Trail (www.eat-drinkhebrides.co.uk). By no means limited to Lewis, they can be found across the islands. Besides the **Uig Community Centre & Café**, which does very well, these are some of the key ones to visit on Lewis.

CROSS STORES AND BUTCHERS

Cross Skigersta Road, Ness; 9am-6pm Mon.-Fri. and 9am-7pm Sat.
On the north of the isle, on the road to the Butt of Lewis, is this fully licensed mini-market, with butcher and deli counter, that sells lots of Scottish-made produce, including its own "Ness" black pudding and Harris gin.

BUTH TOLASTAIDH

North Tolsta; 10am-5pm Mon.-Sat., post office 10am-2pm Mon.-Tues., 10am-1pm Weds.-Fri.
This is a true community store, run by a committee of villagers. At this shop on Lewis's east coast, you'll find all the usual groceries, plus books, newspapers, coal, bottled gas, and a post office.

RAVENSPOINT CENTRE AND PETROL STATION

Kershader; 11am-4pm Mon.-Fri.
In the south of Lewis overlooking Loch Erisort in the under-visited South Lochs region—home to a crofting community where local Gaelic is spoken—is this newly refurbished hostel, shop, café, petrol station, and museum.

via a card machine in the porch—and there is a launderette, a post office, and friendly staff who will happily answer your questions. It's a bit of a lifeline in these parts.

UIG SANDS RESTAURANT

Timsgearraidh; tel. 01851 672 396; 4pm-11pm Weds.-Sat.; three courses £45, children's menu £15
If you are looking for a table with a view, this is it. With a wall of picture windows looking out over the rippling sands of Uig, you may be so distracted you'll forget to order, but order you should. The menu here focuses on local and seasonal ingredients, with an emphasis on seafood; the daily menu is often only decided shortly before service. One day you could have seafood chowder, the next Carloway lobster. Opened shortly before the pandemic, as well

as providing a dining destination for visitors, the restaurant has provided a good number of local jobs.

ACCOMMODATIONS

Though it's a useful place to stock up, Stornoway it's not the best base for a visit to Lewis—there are far more special places. But it can be handy to incorporate an overnight stay here if you are arriving late by ferry, or have an early ferry or boat trip the next day.

Stornoway
THE ROYAL HOTEL

81 Cromwell Street, Stornoway; tel. 01851 706 600; www.royalstornoway.co.uk; £155 d
This whitewashed hotel with views over to Lewes Castle is probably the best place to stay

in Stornoway. It's traditional and well-run, and though a little old-fashioned in places, it's been kept to a reasonable standard and its three-star status is more than fair. Its bright **Boatshed Restaurant** (12pm-4pm and 5pm-9pm daily, takeaway available 12pm-9pm daily; entrées £7.50), with tweed and leather upholstered seating and neatly laid tables overlooks the harbor and is one of the very few places in Lewis where you can dine on a Sunday. Though the menu is a little disjointed, there is a good selection of seafood plates, plus burgers and veggie dishes.

Northern Lewis
WARDICOTT

Light Hill, Back; tel. 07941 765 406 or 01851 820 715; www.wardicott.co.uk; £120 d

With just three bedrooms—two doubles and a twin—this guesthouse on Lewis's east coast offers a real personal experience. All rooms have en suite baths, Egyptian cotton sheets, and wardrobes. There's a huge guest lounge with white sofas positioned around the fireplace, and the home-cooked breakfasts include Charles MacLeod Stornoway black pudding. There is also the option of booking an evening meal (£27 for three courses).

Western Lewis
GEARRANNAN BLACKHOUSE VILLAGE

Gearrannan, Carloway; tel. 01851 643 416; www. gearrannan.com; cottages from £115 per night (minimum 2-night stay), dorm beds from £20

Just a 15-minute drive from the Calanais Standing Stones, these self-catering cottages within an old blackhouse village that was once home to crofting families is like a slice of living history. Though a little pokey, the low cottages are big on charm—with double drystone walls, thatched roofs, window seats (some with sea views), and fuel stoves to cook on—but also modern luxuries like underfloor heating. There's also a hostel for more affordable accommodation. While here, make sure you stop by the village **café** for home-baked goods and the shop for some unique gifts—you may even be able to see a demo of traditional weaving.

UIG LODGE

Uig; tel. 01851 672 396; www.uiglodge.co.uk; £160 d

A relative newcomer to Lewis's accommodation scene, the Victorian-era Uig Lodge offers a little country estate grandeur to the isle. Views of the rippling white sands and blue sea of Uig Sands against the green hills in between are mesmerizing and the **Uig Sands Restaurant** (owned by the same people) is a short walk away. The lodge is intended primarily as an exclusive-use house, perfect for traveling families or outdoorsy groups, but the pandemic led it to open rooms on a B&B basis when not fully booked. The rooms have a modern Scottish feel to them while staying true to their Victorian roots.

★ UIG SANDS ARDROIL BEACH CAMPING

Ardroil Sands, Uig; tel. 07377 525 193; www. ukcampsite.co.uk; tents £5 per pitch, motorhomes/ campers £15

This campsite overlooking an impossibly beautiful tidal beach along Uig Sands will take your breath away. Pop £5 in the porch at the house with a red roof at the top of the road if the owner is not at home (no need to book), and you can camp atop the dunes and make use of the clean toilets and drinking water. Showers are available for £1 and in the morning, after you've fired up the camping stove for your first cuppa of the day, head down to the beach for an invigorating stroll. Stop off at the **Uig Community Centre** en route for supplies. There are also pitches for motorhomes and campers.

INFORMATION AND SERVICES

Explore Isle of Lewis (www.isle-of-lewis. com) has some useful hyper-local info, and there is a **VisitScotland iCentre** by the harbor in Stornoway (26 Cromwell Street; tel. 01851 703 088; 9am-5pm Mon.-Sat., closed for half-an-hour at 12:30pm, Apr.-Oct., contact the iCentre for out-of-season hours). Stornoway is where you will find most of the isle's best facilities: There is a big Tesco supermarket right by the ferry port and a couple of Co-ops on Cromwell Street and MacAulay Road. If you need a bank, the Royal Bank of Scotland on North Beach is open Mon.-Fri.

It's wise to fill up your tank whenever you see a petrol station, and keep in mind that finding one open on Sunday may be a challenge. Useful stations around Lewis include **Engrebret Filling Station,** on the outskirts of Stornoway (Sandwick Road; tel. 01851 702 303; 6am-11pm Mon.-Sat., 10am-4pm Sun.), which also has a cash machine, bakery, grocery, and outdoor equipment shop; to the north, **Welcome Inn Filling Station** and convenience store (Barvas; tel. 01851 840 343; 7am-10pm Mon.-Sat.); and Uig Community Centre on the west coast.

Harris

Often grouped together with its reluctant sibling Lewis, Harris is a place that really earns its place in your heart. It's quieter and even more rural than Lewis, with a far smaller population.

North Harris is sparsely populated, with small townships gathered along the coastline and the interior largely treeless and barren, with erratics (giant boulders deposited by the process of glaciation) and the mountainous Harris Hills peering down over peat bogs as you follow the mainly single-track roads. In the south, its west coast beaches are famous for their pure white sands and iridescent waters, which shift from turquoise to teal, cobalt to lime, dependent on the sun. On the rugged east coast, there's a growing creative scene developing on what's becoming known as the Golden Road, with painters and sculptors, jewelry makers, and more setting up shop among its rocky bays and inlets.

ORIENTATION

Though it's nowhere near as built up as Stornoway, Tarbert, positioned on a narrow ithsmus between West Loch Tarbert and East Loch Tarbert, is Harris's hub, receiving ferries from Uig on the Isle of Skye. About 20 miles (32 km) to the south along Harris's western coast is Leverburgh, where ferries for Berneray depart.

GETTING THERE

The main route into Harris is by ferry. From Uig on the Isle of Skye, the CalMac ferry (www.calmac.co.uk; 1 hour 40 minutes; car £32.80 each way, adult £6.70 each way, child £3.35 each way) arrives at **Tarbert Ferry Terminal.** Or, you can arrive by ferry from Ullapool to Stornoway, from where it's a 50-minute drive south (36 miles/58 km) to Harris along the A859. Independent coach operator Lochs Motor Transport runs several buses a day between Stornoway and Tarbert, Monday to Saturday, which take an hour (bus no. W10; tel. 01851 860288; www.lochsmotor-transport.co.uk; £4.80 single, pay on bus with contactless or cash).

To the south, the port town of Leverburgh and its **Leverburgh Ferry Terminal** receive ferries from Berneray (80 minutes; adult £3.80 each way, child £1.90 each way, car £14.40 each way).

GETTING AROUND

Once here, a car is the obvious way to travel but not altogether essential. **Carhire Hebrides** has a pickup location outside the Essence of Harris shop near the ferry terminal (tel. 01851 706 500; www.carhire-hebrides.co.uk; from £30 per day, plus a surcharge of £60 as this is not the hire firm's main base). The bus services here are slightly more reliable than in other parts of the isles. Bus routes and timetables can be viewed

Harris

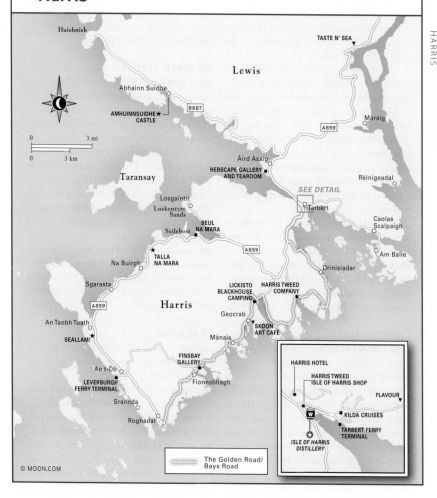

The Golden Road/
Bays Road

© MOON.COM

through the council website Comhairle nan Eilean Siar (www.cne-siar.gov.uk/roads-travel-and-parking/public-transport/bus-services/). The **W10 Harris Spine route,** for instance, travels from Leverburgh through Scarista, Luskentyre, past Meavaig at the Golden Road junction to Tarbert for £3.20 each way (£1.60 child) and runs several times a day Monday-Saturday.

SIGHTS
Tarbert
★ ISLE OF HARRIS DISTILLERY

Tarbert; tel. 01859 502 212; www.harrisdistillery.com; tours 10am, 12pm, 2pm, and 4pm Mon.-Thurs. and 10am Fri.; adult £12, child £6 (over 5 only)

As soon as you come off the ferry from Skye, you'll see this modern distillery, opened in 2015. It now forms part of the **Hebridean Whisky Trail** (https://hebrideanwhisky.com)

but it also does a fine gin. From the instant you walk in, you'll smell the peat fire burning—a symbol of the warm Hebridean welcome you'll receive. Join the 1-hour 15-minute tour and tasting, or visit the canteen or the shop to pick up a bottle.

This distillery has done a lot for the local community. Owner Anderson Bakewell opened it with the aim of stemming the issue of depopulation on Harris by creating a sustainable business that gave young people a place to flourish. With clear soft water and great weather for soil, Harris was a great location for a distillery, despite the fact none of the locals employed to distill had ever done it before, so they were sent all over Scotland to train.

While the distillery waited for its whisky to mature, it started selling gin, and they employed a botanist to go through the isle to see what was growing and what could be used for botanicals. As the lady in question was a wild swimmer, sugar kelp became one of the ingredients.

Eastern Harris
THE GOLDEN ROAD/BAYS ROAD

C79 from Tarbert

Starting just south of Tarbert and running to Leverburgh on the southern tip of Harris, the C79 shows off the east coast of South Harris, which varies hugely from the west coast. Here, it's less about Caribbean-esque beaches and more about rugged rocky coastline, where sheep lazily graze and the weather comes in and goes as if on a whim. The twists and turns of this mainly single-track road require patience and attention from drivers. Along the 25-mile (40-km) route, you'll find a reasonable number of galleries and craft shops, including **Skoon Art Café** and **Finsbay Gallery.** Though it takes just 45 minutes to drive without stops, you could easily spend the better part of the day gallery hopping and taking in the views.

Popular folklore says that the Golden Road got its nickname because this side of Harris was once so rocky and impenetrable that it

cost a lot of money (and manpower) to build the road. That said, this name may trigger an eyeroll from a local. You may endear yourself more to locals if you call this route simply the Bays Road, or even just the Bays.

Western Harris
TALLA NA MARA

Opposite Niseaboist beach, A859; tel. 01859 550 258; www.tallanamara.co.uk; 9am-5pm Mon.-Fri.

The name of this creative space on the west coast of south Harris means "center by the sea." This architecturally interesting timber building, founded in 2017, was intended as a real hub for the West Harris community, though COVID threw a little wrench in the mix. When things are up and running again, there will be live gigs, art exhibitions, plus a good restaurant and a collection of artist studios and craft shops. There are also several camping pitches for caravans, motorhomes, and camper vans, but no tents. Tent pitches are available at nearby Horgabost campsite (tel. 01859 550 386).

SEALLAM!

Northton; tel. 01859 520 258; 10am-5pm Mon.-Fri. in summer, 10am-5pm Weds.-Fri. in winter; adult £3, concessions £2.50

This local history museum is an invaluable resource in the geology, social history, and genealogy of the Outer Hebrides. There is a permanent display, plus changing exhibits to hold the interest of repeat visitors. The research work of Consultant Genealogist Bill Lawson is ongoing (he's written dozens of books), and one of the latest projects he's working on is looking into the emigration areas of Canada and Australia. There is also a small craft shop and café.

★ BEACHES
Western Harris
LUSKENTYRE SANDS

Harris

Chances are that you've seen this beach before. It's an Instagram favorite, but for once there really is no filter needed; the sand is that white and the sea does shimmer in more shades of blue than you can count. Of course, the water here is a little cooler and a little bit iffy in terms of swimming. Still, the views of the North Harris hills and the wrinkled sands that seem to reach out for days when the tide is out, are hypnotic. It's a 20-minute (10-mile/16-km) drive from Tarbert on the A859.

SEILEBOST
Seilebost
While many people claim neighboring Luskentyre Sands is the most spectacular beach on Harris, I beg to differ. Seilebost next door—whose dunes turn at a right angle into Luskentyre, creating one huge mass of beach at low tide—is to me even more show-stopping. As you approach from the south, its myriad shades of blue and green water against the white sand appear luminous and make pulling into the viewpoint on your left irresistible. Take care pulling into and out of the car park, as the road bends around just afterward and you'll have to tuck yourself in well. To reach the beach itself, you can walk the path signposted to Seilebost school shortly afterward on your left. You

should also take care walking on the sand at low tide as there can sometimes be quicksand. Seilebost is located just across the water from Luskentyre Beach, a 15-minute (5-mile/8-km) drive, or 16 minutes (10 miles/16 km) from Tarbert on the A859.

Northern Harris
HUISHNISH
Harris
Though South Harris beaches are legendary, there are some beautiful beaches elsewhere, such as this one (or rather two) on the west coast of North Harris, where a little clutch of houses and a block with toilets, showers, and shelter, at the end of a 12-mile (19-km) single-track road is the only civilization for miles around. The road can be off-putting for those who like their roads straight with few surprises, but take it easy and you will be rewarded with a real sense of end-of-the-road adventure, passing by the Scottish baronial **Amhuinnsuidhe Castle** (tel. 0859 560 200; www.amhuinnsuidhe.com) on the way. When you get here, not only will you most likely have the sand and sea of two quiet beaches backed by machair to yourself, but the views are spectacular.

Seilebost Beach

SPORTS AND RECREATION
ROAM OUTER HEBRIDES

Scalpay, Pontoons; tel. 07845 136 867; http://roamouterhebrides.co.uk; half-day adult £65, child (12-16) £55, full-day adult £85, child £75

One of the best ways to explore Harris is from the water, and on these sea-kayaking adventures you'll be able to take it slow amid the indented coastline, stopping for tea or snacks at a sheltered beach or cove, and seeing seabirds, seals, and maybe even an otter or porpoise or two. Available for everyone, from beginners to experienced sea kayakers, each trip is tailored to you. Just wear swimwear and a warm top, and bring a towel and change of clothes.

SHOPPING
Eastern Harris
FINSBAY GALLERY

1 Ardvey, Finsbay; tel. 01859 530 244; www.finsbaygallery.co.uk; 10am-5pm Tues.-Fri.

This small gallery, one of several on the Bays, is packed with contemporary artworks that are invariably inspired by the local landscape and nature, but often are created by artists who are based elsewhere. The owner curates her collection, which usually includes a mix of paintings, linoprints, and photography, and she is always available for a bit of a natter, too.

Western Harris
HEBSCAPE GALLERY AND TEAROOM

2A Ardhasaig; tel. 01859 502 363; www.hebscapegallery.co.uk; 10:30am-4:30pm Mon.-Fri.

This photography gallery, which you pass on the A859 shortly after crossing over to North Harris, sells prints and souvenirs featuring the landscape photos of fine art photographer Darren Cole LPRS, as well as a selection of other local gifts. Its position high above West Loch Tarbert affords gorgeous views, so you may want to savor it all as you enjoy a barista coffee or home-baked cake.

FOOD
Tarbert
FLAVOUR

Unit 1, Iomairt An Obain, Urgha; tel. 07388 366 361; dinner served at 7pm; £65 pp

At this special restaurant, chef Chris Loye will take you on a culinary journey inspired by his international adventures but using locally sourced ingredients where possible, through an eight-course guided menu that may just be the meal of your holiday. The sea-view setting is spectacular but it's the unique flavor combinations, personal service, and interaction with chef and exceptional presentation that really seal the deal.

Eastern Harris
SKOON ART CAFÉ

4 Geocrab; tel. 01859 530 268; www.skoon.com; 10am-4:30pm Tues.-Sat.; cake/scones £3.50

In the heart of the Bays, this café, in a renovated croft house, is part lunchtime spot, part art gallery, and part community hub, with occasional music nights. It sells original oil paintings by local artist Andrew John Craig and is a welcome option for those gasping for a cuppa and a slice of cake before viewing other galleries along the route. On a good day, you may spot Skye across The Minch, and there is seating outside to fully appreciate this.

Western Harris
CROFT 36

36 Northton; tel. 01859 520 779; https://croft36northton.wixsite.com/home; 11am-7:30pm; seafood from £5 a box

For fresh produce on Harris, swing by this deli with sustainability at its core, housed in a wooden shack and run by a lovely, smiley couple, Julie and Steve. Think butteries handmade by Jane fresh from the oven, strawberry tarts using fruit from the couple's croft, or even boxes of squat lobster or langoustine.

☆ Harris Tweed

You can't come to Harris without buying some Harris Tweed. The cloth is unique to this island, and it's the only fabric in the world protected by an act of parliament and governed by an "orb of authenticity."

The fabric, consisting of wool dyed before being spun on a traditional loom and blended to create yarn that is both hard-wearing and beautiful, has been made on the island for centuries. It was originally created to provide warmth for farmers and others battling the harsh coastal weather, and it was not unheard of for Harris Tweed to be used as a kind of currency, with rents sometimes paid in lengths of cloth. Over time, it became fashionable among the upper classes, and it was woven into luxury clothing for shooting parties and the like.

Today, it is revered as a durable, complex, sustainable, and yet luxurious fabric. Though you can buy a roll of Harris Tweed to make your own items at home, it's much more common to buy clothing or bags that have been made from the cloth here on the isle. Prices range from £5 for a purse, to hundreds for a suit. For those in a hurry, there is a **Harris Tweed** shop in Tarbert (Caberfeidh; tel. 0859 502 040; www.harristweedisleofharris.co.uk; 9am-5:30pm Sat.-Sun.) right by the ferry port, but it is very much geared toward passing tourist trade. It's much better to visit a Harris Tweed maker, or stop off in one of the smaller shops below.

making Harris Tweed at Taobh Tuath Tweeds

TAOBH TUATH TWEEDS

Northtown, South Harris; www.taobhtuathtweeds.com; free
Rebecca Hutton is a traditional Harris Tweed maker who weaves her carefully chosen dyed and spun wool in a shed in her garden. Her house is the first on the left as you enter the little village of Northton in South Harris. If her van is outside, you can be pretty sure she's home, and happy to show you around. Rebecca sells her wares direct from her shed, through her website, or through a local shop in Leverburgh and though she uses a traditional loom and applies the same techniques as used for centuries on the isles, she is relatively new to weaving, starting out in 2012 when the Harris Development Ltd. offered training to attract new people to the industry.

HARRIS TWEED COMPANY

Grosebay; tel. 01859 511 108; www.harristweedco.co.uk; 9:30am-5:30pm Mon.-Sat., closed in winter
Stop off in this small shop in a white building on the Bays Road, where much of the tweed is woven by Donald John Mackay MBE and made into stylish clothing and accessories.

BORRISDALE TWEED

Obbe Road, Leverburgh; tel. 01859 520 208; www.borrisdale.co.uk; 12pm-6pm Tues.-Thurs., 12pm-7pm Fri.-Sat.
Somewhat incongruous on the edge of the small town of Leverburgh as it drifts into the nearby settlement of Borrisdale, this smart shop gives a design twist to the island's traditional tweed and uses Harris Tweed sourced from independents. The prices are quite high, but the minimalist design of the bags, scarves, and homewares shout quality.

Leverburgh
THE ANCHORAGE

The Pier, Leverage; tel. 01859 520 225; www.anchoragerestaurant.co.uk; 12pm-8:30pm Tues.-Sat.; entrées £8.50

Known for miles around for its fish and chips, this restaurant by Leverburgh Pier (near the ferry terminal), is served well by the fishing boats that land their catch nearby, and so generally all the seafood is pretty good. There are also meat and vegetarian options, and a kid's menu.

Northern Harris
TASTE N' SEA

Bowglass; tel. 07444 729 113; www.facebook.com/tastensealochseaforth; 12pm-7pm Weds.-Sat.; shellfish from £7, soups £5

The food truck trend has not passed Lewis by, and at this one it's not your standard takeaway fare. No, here you can buy dishes such as Cullen skink and scallop linguine, with the menu dictated by what seafood comes in. Handily located on the main A859 road in North Harris, with views over Loch Seaforth, it's a worthy pitstop.

ACCOMMODATIONS
Tarbert
HARRIS HOTEL

Tarbert; tel. 01859 502 154; www.harrishotel.com; £129 d

Incredibly handy for those arriving by ferry from Skye, this old-fashioned family-run hotel has huge rooms and a reasonable restaurant with white linen tablecloths and a small bar, which is well-stocked with whisky. In the bar, guests can see a pane of glass etched with the signature of *Peter Pan* author J. M. Barrie, who stayed here in 1912. There are also two sunrooms and a pretty garden.

Western Harris
SCARISTA HOUSE

Scarista; tel. 01859 560 200; https://scaristahouse.com; £200 d

This traditional guest house is delightfully welcoming, with staff who are warm and relaxed. There is a lounge with fire where you meet for canapes and drinks before the set dinner (7pm each evening; £45 for three courses) and there is also a drawing room upstairs for nightcaps, where guests are encouraged to chat and mingle. With views of the coast, the dining room (which is two connected rooms), with its bare white floorboards, varnished wooden tables, fireplace, and candlelight is homely and not overly fancy. The set menu at Scarista includes four courses (though you can opt for dessert or cheese instead of two courses). With three courses for £49 and four for £58, it's neither too expensive nor a snip but just right.

BEUL NA MARA

12 Seilebost; tel. 01859 550 205; guest house £55 per person per night; cottages from £900 per week

Probably the best view of any B&B you've ever stayed at, this sweet guest house overlooking Luskentyre and Taransay Bay is run by Catherine Morrison, who has taken over where her mother left off—running what was one of the first B&Bs. Incredibly well-priced (particularly if you are traveling alone), the rooms in the house are bright and clean and all have en suite, while both the conservatory and TV lounge have clear, beautiful views of one of the isle's most amazing beaches. There are also two self-catering houses, which sleep five and six people.

Eastern Harris
LICKISTO BLACKHOUSE CAMPING

1 Lickisto; Bedouin tent £65 per night, yurt £80, blackhouse bothy £100, pitches from £14

At this campsite in the Bays on a rocky croft around two 150-year-old blackhouses, there is a choice of yurts or a Bedouin tent, which feature log fires, all spaced out for privacy and to allow guests to embrace nature. There is also the Blackhouse Bothy for a cozy, old-worldly stay, with bare brick walls, a double bed and a wood-burner, plus a kitchenette, and pitches for both motorhomes and tents. Owner Grieg is knowledgeable and friendly, but showers and toilets are communal, and watch out for those midges in summer.

INFORMATION AND SERVICES

Sadly, there is no longer a VisitScotland iCentre in Harris—the closest one is in Stornoway on Lewis. For more local advice, you can also use the **Explore Isle of Harris** website (www.explore-harris.com).

In Tarbert, where the ferry from Skye arrives, there are some useful facilities, including a general store, a mini-market, a car-charging station, and cash points. To reach the center of the small village, drive straight off the ferry and then take a sharp right, which will take you up above the ferry terminal. For petrol or diesel, ignore this right, continue straight, take a right onto the main road, and then take the first right (by the Harris Hotel) to Harris Garage (tel. 01859 502 441; 8:30am-6pm Mon.-Fri.).

In Leverburgh, **Harris Community Shop** (www.harriscommunityshop.co.uk; 9am-6pm Mon.-Thurs., 9am-7pm Fri.-Sat.) has fuel, a good grocery store with toilets, and a gift shop, close to where the ferry arrives from Berneray.

Uist

These isles just south of Lewis and Harris—Berneray, North Uist, Benbecula, and South Uist, sometimes collectively known as Uist—are some of the most peaceful isles you will come across on your travels. Personified by the rich machair that grows along their west coast, colored by wildflowers in spring and summer and the empty moorland of its largely inhospitable east coast, and with a sparse population, you can often just sit and watch as wagtails hop across the grass, or listen for the distinctive call of the corncrakes or cuckoos.

Berneray (not to be confused with the uninhabited isle south of Barra) is connected to Harris by ferry, and from here, causeways over the tidal strands take you to North Uist, Benbecula, and South Uist. The highlight of this island is its western beach that takes up much of that side of the coastline, where you can often see seals basking on the rocks. It's a low-lying island, well-suited for walking, with beautiful views.

North Uist, the next isle, has the highest density of Neolithic tombs on the isles. Benbecula, the birthplace of the celebrated heroine Flora Macdonald, sits between North Uist and South Uist, the second largest isle in the Outer Hebrides, which in turn connects to Eriskay, by another causeway.

SIGHTS

Berneray

ANGUS MACASKILL MONUMENT

Berneray

In the south of Berneray is this cairn monument to "Giant" Angus Macaskill, who at 7 feet 9 inches (2.4 m) was the world's tallest man. Born in Berneray in 1825 in a house that once stood where the monument is today, Macaskill was so famous that Queen Victoria requested an audience with him in Windsor Castle, in which she declared him "the tallest, stoutest and strongest man to ever enter the palace." Though he later emigrated to Canada, where he became known as the Nova Scotia Giant, he is still remembered in these parts.

North Uist

BARPA LANGASS BURIAL CHAMBER

Langass, North Uist; open 24/7; free

This Neolithic stone burial chamber dates from around 5,000 years ago, and is thought to be the burial place of a former chieftain. Indeed, it may have been a communal tribal resting place, though it's never been investigated by modern archaeologists. Though it's too dangerous to step inside the chambered cairn, which looks like a huge pile of stones from afar, you can shine a torch in for bit of a look. There is also a stone circle nearby called **Pobull Fhinn,** about a mile walk (1.6 km) to the south, which is worth a look.

South Uist
FLORA MACDONALD'S BIRTHPLACE
Kildonan, South Uist; open 24/7; free

Another local who is remembered fondly is Flora Macdonald, the young lady who helped Bonnie Prince Charlie escape the Western Isles dressed as her milk maid, following the Jacobite defeat at the Battle of Culloden. Today her birthplace is marked by a cairn, set within the drystone outline of her home.

BEACHES
Berneray
BERNERAY BEACH
Berneray

This huge sweep of white sand on Berneray's western coast, a 50-minute walk (2.5 miles/4 km) from the Berneray Ferry Terminal, is backed by machair-topped dunes and with views over to the Harris Hills, and was once embarrassingly mistaken for a Thai beach by the Thai Tourist Board—they used it to represent Kai Bae Beach on brochures.

With 3 miles (5 km) of shell sand to walk along, hemmed in by machair for most of the way, it's a great place to listen for corncrakes and to spot other wildlife.

Benbecula
CULA BAY
7 Nunton, Benbecula

With parking and an area that is accessible for wheelchair users, this beach on the west coast of Benbecula is about 2 miles (3 km) south of the airport and main town of Balvanich. Fringed by machair, it's a good, quiet spot to watch for ground nest wading birds such as oyster catchers, lapwings, and redshank. Also a lovely location to watch the sunset.

SHOPPING
Berneray
CORALBOX GIFT SHOP
3 Backhill, Berneray; tel. 07826 097 599; www.ecwid. com/store/coralbox; 10:30am-5pm Weds.-Sat.

Thank goodness this gift shop on the shore of Bays Loch has not been a victim of the pandemic. Run by Eilidh, a young local photographer who set up shop in 2015 to sell gifts using some of her photos, alongside other handmade Hebridean products, the wooden shop has become a local landmark and Eilidh

Barpa Langass burial chamber

cleverly kept up interest during the pandemic thanks to her live web cams, which showed local wildlife and sea scenes to those itching to get back.

FOOD
Berneray
BERNERAY SHOP AND BISTRO

*5a Borve, Berneray; tel. 01876 540 288; www.
bernerayshopandbistro.co.uk; café 10am-4pm and
6pm-8:30pm Mon.-Sat., shop 9am-5pm Mon.-Sat.;
breakfast rolls £3.25, pizzas £8.50*

Open seasonally, this local café, formerly called the Lobster Pot, is a fabulous spot for breakfast, lunch, or dinner. There are breakfast rolls, pizzas, and a good selection of seafood. There is also a good grocery shop, open all year round with local produce on the shelves, including North Uist's Downpour Gin.

North Uist
HAMERSAY HOUSE

*Lochmaddy, North Uist; tel. 01876 500 700; www.
hamersayhouse.co.uk; brunch 10:30am-1:30pm Sat.,
dinner 5pm-9pm Weds.-Sun.; entrées £6*

A smart bistro from the people who run Langass Lodge, with lots of pastas on the menu that use local ingredients as much as possible. Service is excellent and quality consistent. There are also some nine nice rooms (including a family one) if you'd like to stay (£110 d).

WESTFORD INN

*Claddach Kirkibost, North Uist; tel. 01876 580 653;
https://westfordinn.com; 4:30pm-8:30pm Tues.-Sun.,
12pm-2pm Sat., 12:30pm-2:30pm Sun.; entrées £6.95*

Regularly winning awards for its food and generally amiable atmosphere, this pub with its wooden tables and wood-burner serves good sharing platters—both the crofter's board, with its mix of local meats and smoked fish, and the Taste of Uist seafood platter are recommended. There are also sometimes traditional music sessions in the bar, and it's a rare place where you can eat out on a Sunday.

South Uist
ORASAY INN

*Lochcarnon, South Uist; tel. 01870 610 298; https://
orasayinn.com; 12pm-8pm; entrées £8*

Today also a hotel, the Orasay Inn began primarily as a restaurant in the 1980s and the kitchen is still headed up by owner Isobel. The dining room may feel a little like a time warp, with napkins still placed in glasses and dated decor, but don't worry about that. The food is good and fresh, seafood comes in off the boats, beef comes from the hotel's own fold of Highland cattle, and other produce is sourced carefully from local suppliers. Portions are generous and you can enjoy views over to Skye and Rum as you dine.

Eriskay
THE POLITICIAN

*3 Balla, Eriskay; www.facebook.com/ampolitician1;
food served 12pm-8pm; entrées £5*

This pub is best known as the *Whisky Galore* pub, as it takes its name from the real ship that ran aground in 1941, the *SS Politician*, spilling 22,000 cases of malt whisky, which inspired the tale. It was built long after the incident, but does contain some of the artifacts salvaged from the ship, including some original bottles of whisky. With new ownership as of 2018, plans are afoot to turn this pub into a real community hub, and it is now open year-round. Food is all homecooked, with an emphasis on seafood.

ACCOMMODATIONS
Berneray
SEAL VIEW

*Berneray; tel. 01876 540 209; www.sealview.com;
£80 d, family room £90*

A stone-built house overlooking the Bays Loch seal colony in the Sound of Harris, this property offers the possibility of spotting seals in the loch or even otters hunting along the shoreline as you tuck into breakfast. There are just two rooms—a family room and a double—both well-priced, though only the family room has a sea view.

North Uist

LANGASS LODGE

Locheport, North Uist; tel. 01876 580 285; www. langasslodge.co.uk; £130 d/£165 king-size

A former shooting lodge near Barpa Langas burial chamber and Pobull Fhinn, this small hotel has been under the same ownership for two decades and has a well-deserved excellent reputation. Choose between more traditional rooms in the main lodge or the larger, slightly more modern rooms (with a view) in the Hillside annex. The restaurant is good, especially in terms of seafood. Owner Niall hand-dives the scallops that sit before you himself, while his wife Amanda gathers many of the mussels and cockles.

UIST FOREST RETREAT, NORTH UIST

Taigh na Coille, Claddach Valley, North Uist; tel. 01876 560 894; www.uistforestretreat.co.uk; £1,250 per week

This is one of the newest accommodation options on the northwestern coast of Uist, and days can be spent here walking some of the many trails on the grounds. You may also be able to spot any or all the Outer Hebrides' birds of prey. Each self-catering treehouse has views over the treetops and sandy beaches in the distance. Some treehouses come with private terraces or freestanding baths where you can take in the view as you bathe, but it will cost you for this level of comfort and beautiful setting, and you'll need to book well ahead.

South Uist

SOUTH UIST HOSTELS

North Glendale; tel. 07964 681 901; www. southuisthostel.co.uk; cabin £75 per night, bunkhouse £55, chalet £65

This affordable hostel, with the choice of a self-catering cabin, a bunkhouse, or chalet, will help your budget stretch further without scrimping on views. Set on a working croft on the shore of Loch Boisdale, on the east coast of South Uist, it is a place where the mountain meets the sea. In 2021 the owners introduced a self-contained cabin with a small double, a single bed, and a fold-down bunk, which would suit a family. The bunkhouse, which sleeps up to six, is ideal for a group of backpackers, while the chalet provides the most space.

INFORMATION AND SERVICES

The main town for Uist is **Balivanich** in Benbecula, but it's all relative, so don't expect too much. Located near the airport, the town offers a number of shops, plus a cash point, a petrol station, hospital, and post office.

The website **Explore North Uist** (www. isle-of-north-uist.co.uk) offers some inspiration for visits.

If you want to embrace the Gaelic culture of the islands, then it's worth checking out **Ceolas** in South Uist (Taigh Gleus, Daliburgh; tel. 01878 700 154; www.ceolas. co.uk; 9:30am-5:30pm Mon.-Sat.), not far from the Lochboisdale Ferry Terminal, which offers Gaelic courses and serves as a hub for the community. Staff should be able to point you in the direction of some good traditional music (some gigs are held here).

GETTING THERE AND AROUND

CalMac Ferries from Leverburgh on Harris arrive at **Berneray Ferry Terminal** several times a day (80 minutes; adult £3.80 each way, child £1.90 each way, car £14.40 each way). From Uig on Skye, the CalMac ferry arrives a couple of times a day into **Lochmaddy Ferry Terminal** on North Uist (1 hour 45 minutes; adult £6.70 each way, child £3.35 each way, car £32.80 each way). There is also a daily ferry from Mallaig on the mainland to **Lochboisdale Ferry Terminal** on South Uist (3 hours 30 minutes; adult £11.05 each way, child £5.55 each way, car £61.15 each way). **Eriskay Ferry Terminal** then connects to **Aird Mhor Ferry Terminal** on Barra (www.calmac.co.uk; 40 minutes; adult £3.25 each way, child £1.65 each way, car £11.25 each way).

Loganair also has flights from Glasgow

(www.loganair.co.uk; 1 hour; £119 each way) to **Benbecula Airport** (Balivanich; tel. 0870 602 051; www.hial.co.uk/benbecula-airport), on the western coast of Benbecula, a few times a day.

Tiny Bernerary and Benbecula are small enough to get around on foot, but to travel the 50-mile (80-km) length between Berneray Ferry Terminal in the north to Lochboisdale Ferry Terminal in the south, you'll need a rental car. There are some buses through the council website (www.cne-siar.gov.uk/roads-travel-and-parking/public-transport/bus-services/uists-benbecula-berneray-and-eriskay-timetables/), but a car will give you more freedom. Rental providers include Western Isles Classic Car Hire on North Uist (tel. 01876 525 007; https://westernislesclassiccarhire.com), Ask Car Hire just outside the Benbecula Airport (tel. 0870 602 818; www.askcarhire.com), and Laing Motors Car Hire, conveniently located right by the Lochboisdale Ferry Terminal.

Barra

At the southern end of the Outer Hebrides, in some ways Barra feels like the most accessible of all the isles thanks to daily flights from Glasgow, which take around an hour. Barra's 14,500 acres (5,875 hectares) are a mixture of mountains and sandy beaches, with an eye-catching ruined castle, which has earned it the cringe-worthy nickname "Barradise." You'll often find nonchalant cows idling on a beach, while turquoise seas lap the shore. From here, it's easy to reach **Vatersay,** the most southerly inhabited isle in the archipelago, via a narrow road connecting the two islands.

GETTING THERE

Barra is connected to the Isle of Vatersay to the south by a causeway, about 3 miles (5 km) south of **Castlebay,** Barra's main town. It's where you'll find the **Castlebay Ferry Terminal,** with boats bound for Oban (www.calmac.co.uk; 4 hours 45 minutes; adult £15.55 single, child £7.80 single, car £72.05 single). Even farther south there is a chain of islands—Sandray, Pabbay, Mingulay, and Barra Head (sometimes called Berneray), all now uninhabited—which can only be reached on a boat trip from Castlebay.

Barra Airport (tel. 01871 890 212; www.hial.co.uk/barra-airport) is in Eoligarry in the north of the island, with daily flights from Glasgow with Loganair (www.loganair.co.uk; 1 hour 15 minutes; from £80 each way). The airport is just a five-minute drive from **Aird Mhor Ferry Terminal** for Eriskay, in case you are planning onward

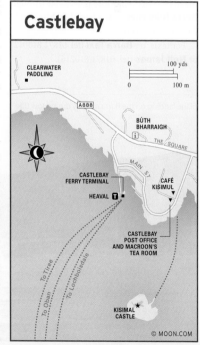

Castlebay

travel (www.calmac.co.uk; 40 minutes; adult £3.25 each way, child £1.65 each way, car £11.25 each way).

GETTING AROUND

The **A888** is a ring-road that runs right round Barra. It can get very narrow in parts, so please be prepared to use the passing bays. The road takes about half-an-hour to drive around (12.9 miles/20.8 km). Car hire is available from **Barra Car Hire** (tel. 01871 890 313), about 2.5 miles (4 km) south of the airport. Leave a message if they don't answer, and they'll ring you back. Don't even think about waiting to hire a car until you get here—they are in very short supply.

To really enjoy this island, though, you should lace up your walking boots and head for the sands and pastures that make Barra one of the loveliest isles to wander—you could walk it all in a little over four hours, and this is the start of the Hebridean Way, which runs all the way up to the very tip of Lewis and can be hiked or cycled. Bike hire is available through **Barra Bike Hire** (www.barrabikehire.co.uk; from £18 per day).

For taxis, try **Barra Taxi** (tel. 01871 810012) or **Neil James** (tel. 01871 810216).

SIGHTS
★ Watching the Planes Land at Barra Airport

Traigh Mhor beach, Eoligarry, Barra

Even if you don't land here yourself, it's worth watching as the planes land on Traigh Mhor beach on the north of the island of Barra between the tides (check the airport website for arrival times: www.hial.co.uk/barra-airport). It's the only airport in the world where the beach itself is the runway, and the faces of the happy (and relieved) passengers as they disembark are priceless. For obvious reasons, you are not allowed to wait on the runway for scheduled flights (you'll know when one is due because the airport windsock will be flying or there will be a strobe light on the air traffic control tower). Grab a cuppa or a bite to eat in the airport **café** and watch the show.

Kisimal Castle

Castlebay, Barra; tel. 01871 810 313 for sailing times; 9:30am-5:30pm daily Apr.-Sept.; adult £4.80, concessions £3.60, under 16 free

Known as the "castle in the sea," the medieval ruins of Kisimul sit on a small island off Castlebay, Barra's main town. The seat of Clan Macneil, it's the only significant castle of the period to survive in the Outer Hebrides. If you

plane landing on the Barra runway during low tide

The Hebridean Way

www.visitouterhebrides.co.uk/hebrideanway

This long-distance route runs the length of the Outer Hebrides, from the southern tip of Vatersay in the island's main town, also called Vatersay, to the Butt of Lewis, and if you follow the full journey, you'll pass through 10 islands, take two ferries, and cross over six causeways. It can be walked or cycled, with slightly different routes for each. Whether you're hiking or biking, due to a prevailing wind from the southwest, it's advisable to travel the route south to north.

THE CYCLING ROUTE

The cycling route covers 185 miles (297 km) on roads that are quiet and relatively flat, though they get busier and hillier as you cycle through Harris and Lewis. It takes a minimum of six days to cycle, though a week to 10 days allows more time to dally. The *Official Hebridean Way Cycling Route Map* is your oracle for completing this journey (find it at www.sustrans.org.uk/find-other-routes/the-hebridean-way).

THE WALKING ROUTE

It is also possible to hike the Hebridean Way, from Vatersay to Stornoway on Lewis. Covering 156 miles (252 km), it does vary from the cycle route, taking you away from the roads across sandy beaches, up through rugged terrain, and past ancient ritualistic sites and deserted townships. The toughest section is from Leverburgh up to Seilebost, as you will cross lots of wet boggy ground and there is a steep climb at the end, but the views of Harris's west beaches are out of this world. You will need to allow a full two weeks to complete it, though you could just do a section. Make sure you get yourself a copy of *The Official Guide Walking the Hebridean Way* (https://hebridean-way-shop.myshopify.com), which breaks the route down into sections.

would like to enter the castle, you will need to take the five-minute crossing over by boat. Once there, make sure you climb up to the battlements for panoramic views. Ferries take off from the jetty in Castle Bay (look for the small open boat) and are timed to run during the castle's opening hours, with the last one setting off an hour before closing. At the time of writing, the castle still hadn't reopened post pandemic, and the Great Hall was undergoing maintenance, so check the status before making plans.

BEACHES

TANGASDALE BEACH

A888

Also called Halaman Bay, this curved beach is among the finest on Barra, and its silvery sands are overlooked by the Isle of Barra Hotel, the scene of incredible sunsets. There is a car park and a small shop; it's safe for swimming, and there are rockpools to explore.

TRAIGH EAIS

Eoligarry; tel. www.visitouterhebrides.co.uk/see-and-do/traigh-eais-p523261

This beach, not far from the airport, is exposed to the full force of the Atlantic and as such has some of the highest sand dunes in Britain. Overlooking the beach is the house built by *Whisky Galore* author Compton Mackenzie in the 1930s, and the author's grave can be visited in Cille Bharra (St. Barr's) graveyard. *Whisky Galore* is a comedy novel (later adapted for film under the title *Whisky Galore!*) that tells the story of a fictional island that has run dry of whisky in 1943, and what happens when a ship carrying thousands of bottles of whisky runs aground off its shore. The story was inspired by the real wreckage of *SS Politician*, which ran aground off Eriskay in 1941 with 260,000 bottles of whisky on board.

☆ St. Kilda: The Remotest of the British Isles

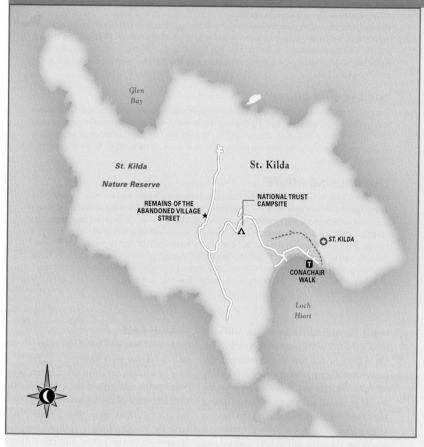

Glen
Bay

St. Kilda

St. Kilda

Nature Reserve

NATIONAL TRUST
CAMPSITE

REMAINS OF THE
ABANDONED VILLAGE
STREET

☆ ST. KILDA

CONACHAIR
WALK

*Loch
Hiort*

The most remote island group in the British Isles, St. Kilda, a collection of five islands, is known as much for its huge seabird colony (numbering around a million in spring and summer) as it is for the evacuation of the last of its human inhabitants in 1930—a startling lesson in social history.

It's a challenge getting there, waiting for weather windows, and crossing unpredictable seas, so consider what a challenge it would have been to live here. However, its people managed the feat for generation after generation, living on the isle for 2,000 years continuously, and as such it is one of the most documented islands in the world.

For many travelers, reaching St. Kilda is the realization of a long-held ambition. Its spectacular seascape, which includes the highest sea cliffs in Britain and the highest sea stack, is certainly a strong pull, and wandering its empty old main street and trying to hear yourself over the noisy birds is also unforgettable.

REMAINS OF THE ABANDONED VILLAGE STREET

For a long time, St. Kilda's islanders were self-sufficient, surviving largely off seabird meat and other natural resources. The inhabitants took a communal, practical approach to life, with daily jobs decided by parliamentary meetings. In the 17th century, crofting came to St. Kilda, as did religion, and in the 19th century the first wave of tourists arrived. There are many theories as to the reasons behind the request for evacuation in 1930; perhaps the residents, who'd begun to learn about a life outside the isles, just wanted to spread their wings, or maybe it was more that the war years had stolen so many of their able-bodied men that life on the isles was no longer sustainable. With the last of the former residents having died in 2016, we may only be able to speculate.

A visit to Village Street, which overlooks Village Bay, a huge crescent of beach backed by those giant sea cliffs on the main island of Hirta, is like walking through a ghost town, with the roofless houses all that is left of the once busy community.

ruins on Village Street

CONACHAIR WALK

Distance: *3.5 miles (5.5 km)*
Time: *3.5 hours*
Trailhead: *Pier, Village Bay*
Information and Maps: *www.walkhighlands.co.uk/outer-hebrides/village-bay-conachair.shtml*
Depending on how you travel to St. Kilda, your itinerary will hopefully leave time for this 3.5-hour walk, which skims close to the cliff edges and is very steep in places. Conachair is the highest point on the isles and will give you a bird's eye view, of, well, thousands of birds.

NATIONAL TRUST CAMPSITE

Hirta; tel. 01463 732 645; www.nts.org.uk/visit/places/st-kilda/planning-your-visit; £20 per pitch
The only accommodation available is a small campsite run by the National Trust for Scotland, where each person can stay for a maximum of five nights. There are shared toilets and showers, and drinking water, but little else, so you will need to bring a camping stove and enough food to sustain you as well as hardy clothing and a good tent; make sure you bring extra supplies in case your return boat ride is delayed due to the weather.

GETTING THERE AND AROUND

The only way to reach St. Kilda is by boat. You can book a tour (or single way passages if you want to stay) with one of the following providers. The **National Trust for Scotland** (www.nts.org. uk/visit/places/st-kilda) has everything you need to know about visiting the isles.

- **Kilda Cruises** (Pier Road; tel. 01859 50 2060; www.kildacruises.co.uk; 8am departure, 2 hour 45 minute crossing, 11.5-hour trip in total; £235), which departs from Leverburgh on Harris.

- **Sea Harris** (tel. 01859 502 007; www.seaharris.com; trips depart 8am and return 7pm. Apr.-Oct.; adult £220, child £180), which runs trips from Leverburgh Ferry Terminal on Harris.

- Or, you could bypass the other Outer Hebrides isles altogether and set off from Skye with **Go to St. Kilda** (Stein, Waternish; tel. 07789 914 144; www.gotostkilda.co.uk; 6:30am briefing, 4-hour crossing, 14-hour trip in total; £260).

SPORTS AND RECREATION

Hiking

HEAVAL

Distance: *3.25 miles (5.25 km)*
Time: *2-3 hours*
Trailhead: *Castlebay, Barra*
Information and Maps: *www.walkhighlands. co.uk/outer-hebrides/heaval.shtml*

The highest hill on Barra, the walk to Heaval is relatively straightforward, though it is steep. Setting off from Castlebay and facing the sea, turn left and walk along the road past the bus stop, post office, and jetty. At the junction, turn right onto the A888 and then follow the main road for just shy of 1.5 miles (2 km; you'll see the conical Heaval up ahead) to a new build house where there is a car park behind (if you don't want to walk the first bit you can just park up here). Leave the road just after the car park and head up into the moorland to the left and you will pretty much just climb up toward the summit from here across boggy ground to start with, though it gets drier the higher up you go. You'll need to bear right as you head up toward the statue of Virgin Mary and child (you can get good views of Castlebay here). From here the path gets steep and rocky. Avoid the path to the right to the summit and keep to the left and it's slightly easier going. To get back to Castlebay, simply retrace your steps.

Kayaking

CLEARWATER PADDLING

Castlebay; tel. 01871 810 443; www. clearwaterpaddling.com; June-Aug.; one-week kayaking trip from £450

Clearwater Paddling, based out of Castlebay, offers a range of week-long guided sea kayaking tours, if you'd like to see the island from the sea. They also offer some wild camping expeditions and multi-activity tours that include coasteering, stand-up paddleboarding, and surfing. Its sister company, **Isle of Barra Surf and Coastal Adventures,** offers shorter kayaking trips and water sports (Castlebay; tel. 01871 810443; www.barrasurfadventures.co.uk; from £45 for a half-day kayaking trip).

FOOD AND ACCOMMODATIONS

CASTLEBAY POST OFFICE AND MACROON'S TEA ROOM

Post Office; tel. 01871 810 312; www.facebook.com/ CastlebayPostOffice; 9am-4:30pm Mon.-Fri.; cakes and scones £2

Within the local post office is this small tearoom, where you can grab a cuppa and some home baking (the scones are a must) and watch the comings and goings of local life in Castlebay. The tearoom has had very restricted opening due to the pandemic, but hopefully things are getting better. Be aware, though, that this is a small business so it may close at short notice due to illness/unexpected things.

CAFÉ KISIMUL

Main Street, Castlebay; tel. 01871 810 645; www. cafekisimul.co.uk; lunch 12pm-4pm, dinner seatings at 6pm or 8pm Mon.-Sat., dinner seatings 5:30pm and 7:30pm Sun. Apr.-Oct.; entrées £6

This popular restaurant serves up Indian and Italian-inspired dishes using Hebridean ingredients. The hand-dived pakora scallops are particularly good—so good that residents on Tiree and Coll are known to have ordered takeaway to be delivered by the CalMac ferry. The restaurant runs regular music nights, too.

HEATHBANK HOTEL

A888, North Bay, Barra; tel. 01871 890 266; www. barrahotel.co.uk; £130 d

On the north of Barra and close to the airport, this family hotel has six neat and functional en-suite rooms, including the new garden Log Pod, as well as a bar and on-site restaurant. In summer there are often traditional music nights, and a good number of locals drink in the bar, so there is usually someone around to tap up for ideas about local sights and activities.

ISLE OF BARRA BEACH HOTEL

Tangasdale Beach, Barra; tel. 01871 810 383; www. isleofbarrahotel.co.uk; £185 d

Probably the best located of all of Barra's hotels, this family-run establishment by Tangasdale Beach is a real treat. There are frequent reports of dolphin spotting from guest rooms, though you're probably just as likely to see them from the restaurant or lounge. Bedrooms aren't overly fancy but comfy, and there is a bit of a nautical theme throughout, with blue and white striped pillows and anchor accessories—even the building was designed to look like an upturned ship.

INFORMATION AND SERVICES

There are some lovely ideas for things to do on the locally run **Isle of Barra website** (https://isleofbarra.com). The town of Castlebay is where you will find most facilities, including the post office, petrol station, bank, doctor's surgery, and hospital.

Bùth Bharraigh in Castlebay is a good first port of call (tel. 01871 817 948; www. buthbharraigh.co.uk; 10am-6:30pm Mon.-Fri., 10am-4:30pm and 6pm-7pm Sat., 12pm-4pm and 5:30pm-6:30pm Sun.), and is becoming the nucleus of life on Barra and Vatersay. Crucially, if the ferry is delayed for some reason, they will reopen out of hours to serve those customers. In fact, this social enterprise not only acts as a store for essentials, but also as a visitor center, helping to find beds for people who arrive and signposting them to local activities. It's also a place where members of the community can meet, supporting local businesses by showcasing their wares, and they offer training, work experience, and employment to locals.

Orkney

Scotland's Northern Isles are composed of two

low-lying island groups, Orkney and Shetland. These are often lonely places, bordering on the bleak, where at times you're more likely to come across an ancient broch (stone tower) or mysterious standing stone dating back millennia than you are a living, breathing person.

Orkney, closer to the Scottish mainland and much more visited, is a quiet, calm place, where birds congregate, ancient stones stand by the side of the road, and craftspeople busy themselves in their studios, preparing themselves for the next intake of tourists. But it's also a green, cultivated place, with much of the land given over to farming and fields stretching out on either side as you travel its country roads.

These isolated islands can sometimes feel as if they've been

Highlights

Look for ★ to find recommended sights, activities, dining, and lodging.

★ **Island-Hopping the Northern Isles:** Connected by ferry (and the world's shortest commercial flight), travel to Orkney's northern islands and you'll be truly off the beaten path (page 482).

★ **Ring of Brodgar:** Visit this stone circle in the gloaming to experience the mysterious atmosphere of this landscape (page 487).

★ **Skara Brae:** This 5,000-year-old village is the most intact Neolithic settlement in western Europe (page 487).

★ **Old Man of Hoy:** This distinctive sea stack off the island of Hoy is a terrific destination for an invigorating hike (page 488).

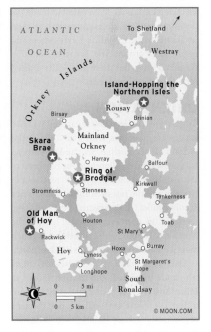

borrowed from somewhere else, and in a sense, they have. From the 8th century onward, the Vikings settled here, making this their base for carrying out expeditions across other parts of Scotland. Originally exiled pirates, successive Norse kings and earls made these remote isles their home and evidence of this time can be seen across the islands, in place names and old settlements.

But, of course, the history and habitation of these isles stretches much further back than the Vikings, to archaeologists' delight. There is no end of prehistoric sights to discover and explore, from world-famous ones such as Skara Brae on Orkney's Mainland, to lesser-known ones where the crowds will be much thinner, if not non-existent.

Today, the friendly people of the Northern Isles make their money through farming, tourism, and offshore oil (though not necessarily in that order), and many of those you meet don't originate from here but made the decision to pull up stakes and move here. And what's not to like? Wildlife is everywhere and nature is all around you. It can be cold this far north, sure, but there are locally crafted textiles to take the edge off.

ORIENTATION

Covering just under 1,000 square miles (2,600 square km) together, with over 2,000 miles (3,200 km) of coastline, Scotland's Northern Isles are scattered obliquely to the northeast of the mainland, as though trying to reach out to Norway and the rest of Scandinavia. Orkney is only 6 miles (10 km) north of the Caithness region of the northern mainland (part of the North Coast 500), while **Shetland** is much more remote, a further 116 miles (187 km) north.

Orkney is made up of 70 islands, 20 of which are inhabited, and the one known as **Mainland** is by far the largest, at 202 square miles (520 square km)—almost half the area of the entire Orkney Island group. Still, distances are not huge here—it's only a 25-minute

drive or so between **Kirkwall** on the east coast, Orkney's central town and home to the main ferry terminal as well as the airport, to the arty harbor town of **Stromness** on the west coast, where the Northlink Ferry between Orkney Mainland and Scrabster on the Scottish mainland lands and departs.

Farther south, there are a few islands connected to Orkney Mainland by a series of causeways known as the **Churchill Barriers** (opened by the then British Prime Minister Winston Churchill in 1945, primarily to provide protection to the anchorage of Scapa Flow, an important naval base in both the First and Second World Wars). Today the Barriers make traveling to the south isles of **Lamb Holm, Glimps Holm, Burray,** and **South Ronaldsay** relatively easy. To the north, interisland flights help make some of the off-lying islands more accessible, including what is often celebrated as the shortest flight in the world (with a flight time of 90 seconds—sometimes less) between the Islands of **Westray** and **Papa Westray.**

GETTING THERE

Traveling to Orkney is a lot easier than you might think, and once you reach it, it's also relatively easy to travel between the islands of the island group.

By Ferry

Orkney is connected to the mainland by ferry from a few locations. It's always advisable to book ferries online before travel.

- **NorthLink Ferries** (www.northlinkferries.co.uk) operates a ferry to Kirkwall from **Aberdeen** (6 hours, 1 ferry per night Tues., Thurs., Sat., Sun. Apr.-Oct., nightly ferry Thurs., Sat., Sun. Nov.-Mar.; from £140 with car), and to Stromness from **Scrabster** (near Thurso on the northern mainland off the North Coast 500; 90 minutes, 3 ferries per day Mon.-Sat., 2 per day Sun. mid-May-Aug., 2 ferries per day daily for the rest of

---

Previous: the neolithic village of Skara Brae; Old Man of Hoy; the Ring of Brodgar.

the year; car from £60 each way, passengers £20 each way).

- **Pentland Ferries** (www.pentlandferries. co.uk) runs boats from Gills Bay (west of John o' Groats) to St. Margaret's Hope, on South Ronaldsay (1 hour, 3 ferries per day; £40 each way car, £17 each way per person).

- **John o' Groats Ferries** (www.jogferry. co.uk) runs ferries for foot passengers and bicycles only between **John o' Groats** and Burwick, on the southern tip of South Ronaldsay, in summer (40 minutes, twice a day June-Sept.; £16 each way).

By Air

More efficient than taking the ferry to Orkney are flights run by **Loganair** (www.loganair.co.uk) to **Kirkwall Airport** (tel. 01856 872 421; www.hial.co.uk/kirkwall-airport) from Glasgow, Edinburgh, Aberdeen, and Inverness—all with flight times under an hour.

GETTING AROUND

Cars are not essential in the Orkney Islands, though they are probably the best way to get around. Compared with some parts of rural Scotland, driving in the Northern Isles is uneventful. The terrain is generally flat, though you will still encounter the occasional single-track or narrow road. If you didn't bring your own car via ferry, be sure to book a rental car well in advance, as supplies are limited.

It is possible, though not easy, to travel the isles by Orkney's very limited bus service; you can view all the bus routes through the local council's website (www.orkney.gov. uk/Service-Directory/B/Bus-Services.htm). That said, as the archipelago is largely flat and nothing is ever too far away, cycling is a good option.

PLANNING YOUR TIME

While it's tempting to design a busy itinerary to ensure you see as much as possible in the Northern Isles, it's not ideal. Much of the beauty of these islands is found when taking things slow, and Orkney really deserves a week or so in itself, allowing you enough time to see the sights, take some walks, and see some wildlife.

The obvious place to base yourself is **Mainland,** specifically in charming **Stromness,** close to the biggest attractions and the **Heart of Neolithic Orkney.** To the east, the main city of Kirkwall offers a good choice of accommodations and is somewhat livelier. For those who want to stay farther south, there are some nice places in and around the cute port town of **St. Margaret's Hope,** on South Ronaldsay, where ferries to and from Gills Bay arrive and depart.

Spring to summer is undoubtedly the best time to visit the Orkney Islands, for the long days that seem to drift into one another with only a few hours of real darkness in the height of summer, and for the large numbers of migrating **seabirds,** including puffins, who come here to breed between April and early August. In **winter,** in between the long, dark nights, you may be surprised by an unexpected crisp day with a bright blue sky, and of course this is the best time to see the **Northern Lights.**

It's worth remembering that tourism is still very much in its infancy in the Northern Isles. Unless you've booked onto a tour for several days, don't come and expect your hand to be held. Outside the main towns of Kirkwall and Lerwick, the isles are largely wild, with just coast and sea, birds, and wind for company. Signposts are few and far between. Make sure you book somewhere to stay before you come and plan a little where you might eat and on what days—you don't really have the luxury of spontaneity here, with a limited number of stores and restaurants.

Before 2020, Orkney Mainland was a regular stop-off for many cruise liners, and when cruise ships docked there could be as many as an extra 7,500 people on the island. When I visited in 2020, I met few people who missed the cruise ships—apparently only a handful of businesses financially benefited—and many more who thought this was an opportunity for Orkney to reset and rethink how it wanted tourism here to work in the future.

Orkney

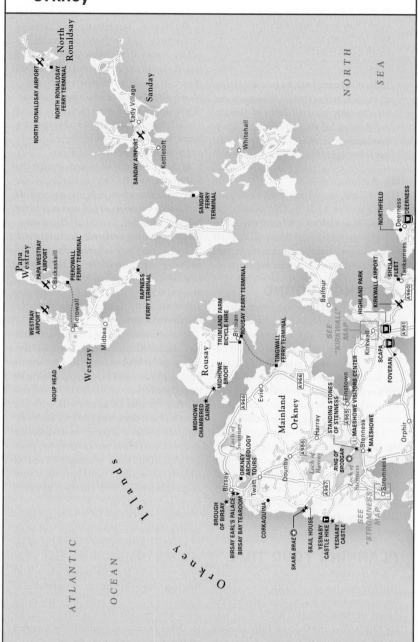

North Ronaldsay

NORTH RONALDSAY AIRPORT
NORTH RONALDSAY FERRY TERMINAL

Sanday

Lady Village
SANDAY AIRPORT
Kettletoft
Whitehall

SANDAY FERRY TERMINAL

NORTH SEA

NORTHFIELD
DEERNESS
Deerness

Papa Westray
PAPA WESTRAY AIRPORT
Backaskaill
PIEROWALL FERRY TERMINAL
Pierowall

RAPNESS FERRY TERMINAL

TANKERNESS
KIRKWALL AIRPORT
SHEILA FLEET
A960

WESTRAY AIRPORT
Pierowall
Midbea
Westray

TRUMLAND FARM BICYCLE HIRE
Brinian
ROUSAY FERRY TERMINAL

Balfour

HIGHLAND PARK
"SEE KIRKWALL" MAP
Kirkwall
A961

NOUP HEAD

Rousay
MIDHOWE BROCH

TINGWALL FERRY TERMINAL

SCAPA
FOVERAN

MIDHOWE CHAMBERED CAIRN

Evie
A966

Mainland Orkney

A965
Finstown
STANDING STONES OF STENNESS
MAESHOWE VISITORS CENTER
Stenness
MAESHOWE

Orphir

ATLANTIC OCEAN

Orkney Islands

Loch of Swannay
ORKNEY ARCHAEOLOGY TOURS
Twatt
Dounby
Harray
Loch of Harray

Birsay
BROUGH OF BIRSAY
BIRSAY EARL'S PALACE
BIRSAY BAY TEAROOM
CORKAQUINA

A986

A967
Loch of Stenness
RING OF BRODGAR

"SEE STROMNESS" MAP
Stromness

SKARA BRAE
SKAIL HOUSE
YESNABY CASTLE HIKE
YESNABY CASTLE

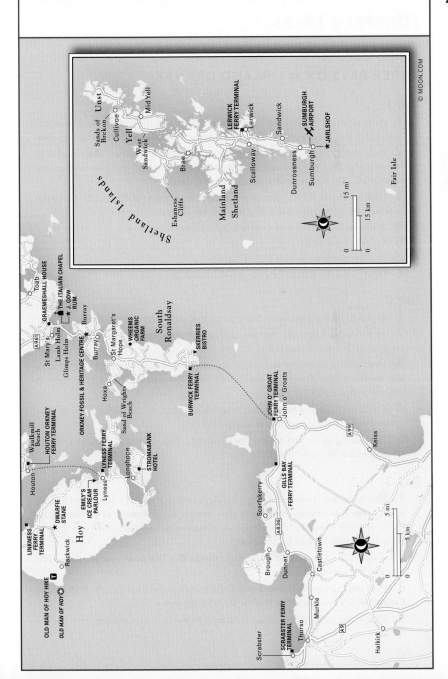

ORKNEY

© MOON.COM

Shetland Islands

Unst
Sands of Brekon
Cullivoe
Mid Yell
Yell
West Sandwick
Brae
Eshaness Cliffs
Mainland Shetland
Scalloway
Sandwick
LERWICK FERRY TERMINAL
Lerwick
Dunrossness
Sumburgh
SUMBURGH AIRPORT
JARLSHOF
Fair Isle

0   15 mi
0   15 km

Toab
GRAEMESHALL HOUSE
THE ITALIAN CHAPEL
J. GOW RUM
Burray
St Mary's
A96
Lamb Holm
Glimps Holm
Burray
St Margaret's Hope
WHEEMS ORGANIC FARM
South Ronaldsay
SKERRIES BISTRO
ORKNEY FOSSIL & HERITAGE CENTRE
Hoxa
Sand of Wrights Beach
BURWICK FERRY TERMINAL
JOHN O' GROAT FERRY TERMINAL
John o' Groats
A99
Keiss

Waulkmill Beach
Houton
HOUTON ORKNEY FERRY TERMINAL
LINKNESS FERRY TERMINAL
Rackwick
DWARFIE STANE
Hoy
EMILY'S ICE CREAM PARLOUR
LYNESS FERRY TERMINAL
Lyness
Longhope
STROMABANK HOTEL
OLD MAN OF HOY HIKE
OLD MAN OF HOY

Scarfskerry
GILLS BAY FERRY TERMINAL
Brough
Dunnet
Castletown
A836
SCRABSTER FERRY TERMINAL
Scrabster
Thurso
Murkle
A9
Halkirk

0   5 mi
0   5 km

Itinerary Ideas

THREE DAYS ON MAINLAND ORKNEY

Day 1

1 After arrival in St. Margaret's Hope from Gill's Bay on the north coast of mainland Scotland by ferry, grab a coffee and a bite to eat from **Robertsons Coffee Hoose & Bar.**

2 Head north to one of the island's quirkiest attractions: the **Italian Chapel,** built by Italian prisoners of war who were brought here to build the Churchill Barriers that connect the islands you've been driving on to Mainland Orkney.

3 Head west to check into your accommodations and have a pub lunch at the **Ferry Inn** in Stromness, afterward watching the boats come and go in the harbor.

4 Walk over to the **Pier Arts Centre** to see some excellent fine art.

5 Visit the **Ring of Brodgar** at gloaming (dusk) when the setting sun paints the sky shades of pink and purple behind the pillars

6 Head back to Stromness for a dinner of local produce at the family-run **Hamnavoe.**

Day 2

1 Don your hiking boots today, before heading to **Julia's Shed** for a takeaway picnic.

2 First, drive up Mainland's western coast to **Yesnaby Castle** sea stack, found along a craggy coastline of cliffs and calling seabirds.

3 Next, visit the incredible Neolithic settlement of **Skara Brae,** contemplating the same sea view that the people who lived here would have 5,000 years ago. Find a place nearby to enjoy your picnic.

4 Check the tide times for arrival at **Waulkmill Beach,** reached down a narrow road at low tide, for sandy footprints and safe swimming.

5 Grab dinner in the **Stromness Hotel,** paying tribute to local poet and favored son George Mackay Brown with a pint or two.

Day 3

1 Have breakfast at your hotel before heading north to Birsay. If you've timed it right, it will be low tide, so you can take your time crossing to the **Brough of Birsay,** watching for all kinds of weird and wonderful sea creatures that have found their way into the rockpools on either side of the causeway.

2 Back on Orkney Mainland, a visit to the **Birsay Bay Tearoom** is a must, as is a slice of one of its cream-filled sponges.

3 Head east to Kirkwall, Orkney's main town, where a stop at the impressive **St. Magnus Cathedral** will give you a view into the area's Viking past.

4 Have a fresh-as-they-come seafood dinner at **Foveran** before catching a ferry back to the mainland.

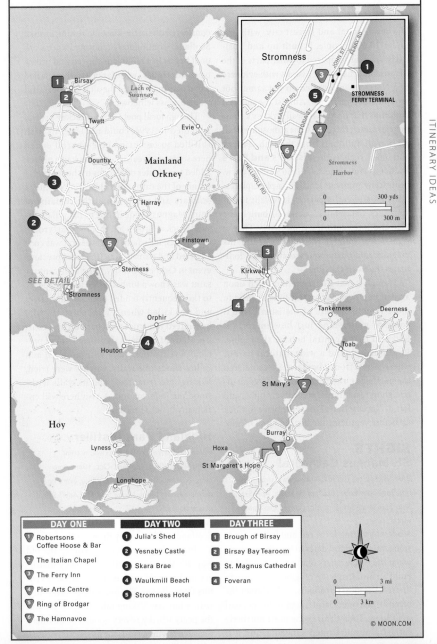

Itinerary Ideas

Stromness

STROMNESS
FERRY TERMINAL

Stromness Harbor

0   300 yds

0   300 m

SEE DETAIL

DAY ONE	DAY TWO	DAY THREE
1 Robertsons Coffee Hoose & Bar	**1** Julia's Shed	**1** Brough of Birsay
2 The Italian Chapel	**2** Yesnaby Castle	**2** Birsay Bay Tearoom
3 The Ferry Inn	**3** Skara Brae	**3** St. Magnus Cathedral
4 Pier Arts Centre	**4** Waulkmill Beach	**4** Foveran
5 Ring of Brodgar	**5** Stromness Hotel	
6 The Hamnavoe		

0   3 mi

0   3 km

© MOON.COM

Kirkwall

Orkney's capital and largest city, with just under 10,000 people, is built up and positively buzzing compared to other parts of the islands. But it has a long history, with evidence of a Norse town founded on the same spot around 1,000 years ago. Amidst the modern buildings that make Kirkwall Orkney's commercial center, there are some atmospheric old lanes with buildings from the 17th century and older, such as the **Bishop's and Earl's Palaces** (Watergate; tel. 01856 971918; www. historicenvironment.scot/visit-a-place/places/ bishop-s-and-earl-s-palaces-kirkwall; 10am-4pm Tues.-Sat.; adult £5, child £3), built in the 12th and 16th centuries, respectively. They're right across from St. Magnus Cathedral, the magnificent Romanesque structure that dominates the town's skyline.

Though it may not seem like much upon arrival in Orkney, after traveling around to more remote corners of the island, you'll come to understand just how important Kirkwall is as a central hub for the region. Positioned around a wide, natural harbor where ferries from Aberdeen, Shetland, and the northern Orkney isles are received, it offers good restaurants, some lively pubs, and lots of places to stay. This is the place to stock up before venturing farther out into Orkney.

SIGHTS
St. Magnus Cathedral
Broad Street; tel. 01856 874 894; www.stmagnus. org; 9am-6pm Mon.-Sat., 1pm-6pm Sun. Apr.-Sept., 9am-5pm Mon.-Sat. Oct.-Mar., closed 1pm-2pm in winter; free

Made of striking local red and yellow sandstone, this cathedral dates to the 12th century, when the Norse rulers of the time decided to build an awe-inspiring religious structure to impress the local Orcadians, and to honor the recently martyred Saint Magnus, former earl of Orkney. Today, this is the most northerly cathedral in the United Kingdom, and it is considered one of the most interesting in all of Scotland. Continuously renovated since work on it began in 1137, inside the red and yellow brick continues, with fantastically detailed wood carvings behind the altar and beautiful stained-glass windows.

Though local poet George Mackay Brown, who died in 1996, could not have his wish fulfilled to be buried here—burial ended here some years earlier—he has had a plaque added to a cluster of plaques in the southeast corner of the cathedral celebrating Orkney's scholars and writers, and the remains of Saint Magnus reside in one of the pillars inside. Mackay Brown felt that the martyrdom of Magnus, for whom the cathedral was constructed and named, was "the most precious event in Orkney's history." The 12th-century saint was known for his desire to bring peace to the frequently feuded over Northern Isles and was killed when a rival chieftain who had agreed to a truce went back on his promise. Many of Orkney's significant, if not precious, events took place within its red and yellow sandstone walls: witches were tried, Vikings hid from foes, and its walls withstood the Reformation. A visit here will enrich any visit to Orkney.

Highland Park Distillery
Holm Road; www.highlandparkwhisky.com/ en/distillery; 10am-4pm Apr.-Oct., 10am-4pm Mon.-Fri. Nov.-Mar., tours on the hour, every hour during opening times; Viking Soul Tour Adult £15, concessions £10

At this traditional distillery—one of Scotland's oldest—they draw on the islands' Viking heritage to produce whisky the old way. It's the most northerly whisky distillery in the world, and as such it attracts visitors from all over. The tours are entertaining, with a fair few Viking tales thrown in, and the peaty whisky is very good. The distillery repeatedly wins awards for its special releases,

Kirkwall

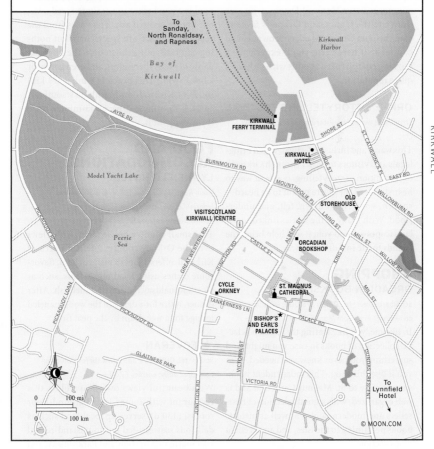

and the bottles have become sought after by whisky collectors.

Scapa Distillery

St. Ola; tel. 01856 873 269; www.scapawhisky.com; tasting 1pm daily; tasting £25

Another distillery, less famous than Highland Park but worth a visit, if only for the comparison, Scapa is a small artisanal distiller, just 2 miles (3.2 km) outside Kirkwall on the shore of Scapa Flow. Tours were paused during the pandemic, but daily tastings have been running (and the shop is open), and the small, helpful team can answer any questions you may have about production.

ENTERTAINMENT AND EVENTS
ST. MAGNUS INTERNATIONAL FESTIVAL

Various locations across the islands; www.stmagnusfestival.com; late June

Run since the 1970s, this festival takes place in the final weeks of June, when the days seem never-ending. There's a mix of music, theater, dance, storytelling, and literature that celebrates the rich heritage of

ORKNEY
KIRKWALL

the isles. It has become part of the fabric of the isles since it was started by classical composer Peter Maxwell Davies, who was drawn to the region, and Orkney's favorite son, the poet George Mackay Brown. If you can make it here then, you'll experience a buzzing energy that's at odds with Orkney's quiet reputation.

ORKNEY STORYTELLING FESTIVAL

Stromness; www.orkneystorytellingfestival.co.uk; Oct.

This warm and inclusive festival, which brings locals and visitors together through Orkney's oral tradition of storytelling, is a great way to hear stories as they were meant to be heard—spoken, not written down, felt, and understood. With many of the stories linked to the landscapes around you, it will help bring the islands to life in a different way.

SHOPPING
ORCADIAN BOOKSHOP

50 Albert Street; tel. 01856 878 000; www.orcadian. co.uk/shop; 9am-5pm Mon.-Sat.

If, like me, you like leafing through an eclectic collection of books in case you might find something you never knew you needed, then you'll like this shop. This independent bookshop is close to St. Magnus Cathedral and is well organized, with a good selection of bestsellers and modern books, as well as historic books pertaining to the isles, and an excellent maps section.

BEACHES
WAULKMILL BEACH

Unmarked road off the A964, Orphir

The single-track tarmac road down to Waulkmill Beach has wildflower meadows on either side and feels like you are reaching a secret place. There are a few houses down near the steps to the beach, however, so parking can be a little tricky (please be mindful of people needing to get out) but is usually manageable. The steps down to the beach are narrow and steep (you'll see them on the right-hand side, if you reach the manicured gardens by the

houses, you've come too far) but they are quite safe as there is a small barrier. I'm told this road is a good place to see short-eared owls, but I never spotted any. The views from the road of the beach are spectacular, but nothing can beat going down onto the huge expanse of sands themselves, and even going for a brief swim. This beach is 8 miles (13 km) south of Kirkwall on Mainland's southern coast, a 15-minute drive or 35-minute cycle if you're up for it.

FOOD AND ACCOMMODATIONS
LYNNFIELD HOTEL

Holm Road, St Ola; tel. 01856 872 505; www. lynnfield.co.uk; lunch 12pm-1:30pm, dinner 6pm-8:30pm; entrées £7

This small country house hotel, with views over the Orkney countryside just north of Kirkwall, offers a superb menu of light, flavorsome dishes using local ingredients, such as North Ronaldsay mutton and shellfish. After dinner, retire for a drink in the wood-paneled lounge for a wee dram by the peat fire.

★ FOVERAN

St Ola; tel. 01856 872 389; www.thefoveran.com; 6pm-8pm daily; entrées £7.50

With beautiful views over Scapa Flow, this restaurant with rooms (eight ground-floor rooms; £130 d), serves up local food such as delicious seaweed-fed mutton, island-reared beef marinated in Highland Park whisky, and smoked fish from Jollys of Orkney, in its modern dining room. Without a doubt this is one of the best places to eat in Orkney.

OLD STOREHOUSE

Bridge Street Wynd, Kirkwall; tel. 01856 252 250; www.thestorehouserestaurantwithrooms.co.uk; 5:30pm-10pm daily; entrées £7.50

In the center of Kirkwall in an old brick storehouse, this relaxed restaurant is known for its scallops and seafood twists on classics, such as haddock Scotch eggs. There's also a separate

For a bit more adventure and even more quiet and birdlife, the northern Orkney Isles reward intrepid travelers. **Orkney Ferries** (www.orkneyferries.co.uk) runs ferries from Kirkwall on Mainland to the islands, and there are frequent, quick, and relatively affordable flights to some of the islands with Logan Air (www.loganair.co.uk), but you will need to do a fair bit of planning ahead, as there is not a lot of infrastructure in these islands. Arrive hungry and you may find the island's only café has closed for the week; the same goes for guesthouses and hotels.

Here are some of the main isles worth visiting:

ROUSAY

www.visitrousay.co.uk
Just 2 miles (3 km) north of Mainland, this island has been described as the Egypt of the north due to its density of archaeological sites—numbering more than 150. Highlights include **Midhowe Broch** (tel. 01856 841 815; www.historicenvironment.scot/visit-a-place/places/midhowe-broch; open 24/7; free), the remains of a settlement from the Iron Age, including a water tank, fireplace, and visible rooms; and the 5,000-year-old **Midhowe Chambered Cairn** (www.historicenvironment.scot/visit-a-place/places/midhowe-chambered-cairn; open 24/7; free), whose separate burial stalls are protected by a modern stone building.

A ferry connects **Tingwall Ferry Terminal** on Mainland with **Rousay Ferry Terminal** (30 minutes, up to 6 per day; passenger £4.25, cars £13.60). Tingwall is a 20-minute drive north of Kirkwall, and Rousay Ferry Terminal is on the eastern coast of the island, where it's possible to rent a bike (try **Trumland Farm Bicycle Hire,** just to the west of the ferry terminal) to cycle to Midhowe Broch (5 miles/8 km) if you didn't come with a car.

WESTRAY AND PAPA WESTRAY

westraypapawestray.co.uk
Wildlife abounds along the coast of Westray, with seals seen so regularly you almost get used to it, and a very good bird reserve at **Noup Head** (Noup; tel. 01856 850 176; www.rspb.org.uk/noupcliffs; open 24/7; free). However, one of the biggest lures to this isle is to catch the small

vegan and vegetarian menu, but you may have to ask. There are also eight luxury rooms to stay in, but they're on the pricey side during summer (£240 d).

KIRKWALL HOTEL

Harbour Street, Kirkwall; tel. 01856 872232; www.kirkwallhotel.com; £165 d
In a commanding Victorian building overlooking the harbor, this stalwart of Kirkwall's hotel scene has recently undergone huge renovation (the restaurant was overhauled in 2019), with plush new interiors in a modern Scottish style. There are 37 bedrooms, plus fresh catches in the Harbour View restaurant, and a huge choice of whisky in the Highland Park bar.

INFORMATION AND SERVICES

VisitScotland Kirkwall iCentre (The Travel Centre, West Castle Street, Kirkwall; tel. 01856 872 856; www.visitscotland.com/info/services/kirkwall-icentre-p333251; 9am-5pm Apr.-late Sept.; check for winter hours) by the bus station, has leaflets and information on everything from ferry and bus timetables to local attractions). For inspiration before you travel, go to www.orkney.com.

GETTING THERE

Nightly Northlink ferries (www.northlinkferries.co.uk) sail to **Kirkwall Ferry Terminal** from Aberdeen, departing in the early evening and arriving in Kirkwall late at night (6 hours; from £140 each way with car). If

flight to nearby Papa Westray, known as the shortest flight in the world, since the aircraft is only airborne for 90 seconds. Once here, aside from the amazing birdlife, there are several fascinating ancient sites, including the Knap of Howar and the remains of a Neolithic farmstead, which is older than the pyramids.

In addition to ferries to Rapness on Westray from Kirkwall (1.5 hours, once daily; passengers £8.35, cars £19.70), there are daily flights from Kirkwall to **Westray Airport** (1 Sand O Gill; tel. 01857 677 271; 20 minutes; from £37 one way). To get to Papa Westray from Westray, the famous 90-second flights depart once or twice a day (£17); you can also fly from Kirkwall (20 minutes; £18) or Northern Ronaldsay (10 minutes; £17). In the summer (May-Sept.), ferries also run between Pierowall on Westray to Papa Westray (25 minutes; 3-6 per day; £4.15).

SANDAY

www.sanday.co.uk

A peaceful island with lots and lots of white sandy beaches and sweeping bays, Sanday is one of the largest of the Orkney Islands and is home to a bustling (and happy) community of crofters and crafters, who may try to persuade you to move here.

Ferries run from Kirkwall to Sanday (1.5 hours; passengers £8.35, cars £19.70), or you can fly to **Sanday Airport** from Kirkwall once or twice per day (20 minutes; from £37 one-way).

NORTH RONALDSAY

northronaldsaytrust.com

Orkney's most isolated island is famous for its seaweed-eating sheep, who feast on as many as seven different types of seaweed. It's worth trying to come during the annual **North Ronaldsay Sheep Festival** (www.nrsheepfestival.com), when workshops are held demonstrating crafts and skills long forgotten elsewhere.

Once a week (on Friday), ferries run to North Ronaldsay from Kirkwall (2.5 hours; passengers £8.35, cars £19.70), or you can fly to **North Ronaldsay Airport** (www.orkney.gov.uk/Service-Directory/T/airfields.htm; 20 minutes; from £18 one-way).

you've taken one of the ferries from Scotland's north coast, you can then drive to Kirkwall from St. Margaret's Hope on South Ronaldsay (15 miles/24 km; 25 minutes); Stromness to the west (15 miles/ 24 km; 20 minutes); or Burwick, also on South Ronaldsay (21 miles/34 km; 30 minutes). Bus service on Orkney is reasonably good; you can travel from St. Margaret's Hope to Kirkwall in just 30 minutes on the Stagecoach bus X1 (www. stagecoachbus.com; buses roughly once an hour; £3.40 single,). From Stromness, you can take the X1 coming from the other direction, which will also get you to Kirkwall in around 30 minutes (£3.60 single).

Kirkwall Ferry Terminal is also the departure point for ferries to Shetland and the Northern Orkney Isles. An excellent ferry network is provided by **Orkney Ferries** (www.orkneyferries.co.uk).

Kirkwall Airport (tel. 01856 872 421; www.hial.co.uk/kirkwall-airport) is just a 10-minute (4-mile/6-km) drive east of central Kirkwall. Either the no. 3 or the no. 4 bus from Stagecoach will get you from the airport to Kirkwall town in just 10 minutes (buses every half an hour; £1.70 single).

GETTING AROUND

Compact Kirkwall is small enough to get around on foot, but to venture to some of the distilleries, restaurants, and accommodations outside the city center, you'll likely want a car. Orkney Car Hire in Kirkwall (Junction Road, Kirkwall; tel. 01856 872 866; www.orkney-carhire.co.uk; from £62 per day) has a fleet of hire cars, but it's limited, so if you're not coming to Orkney with your car, be sure to book well ahead.

Alternatively, you could use a bike to explore the area around Kirkwall (and really much of Mainland). As well as stocking lots of the bigger bike brands (Giant, Raleigh, Orbea), **Cycle Orkney** (Tankerness Lane, Kirkwall; tel. 01856 875 777; www.cycleorkney.com; 9am-5:30pm Mon.-Sat.; adult from £20 per day, child from £10 per day) also rents out a small number of bespoke bikes. Prices are low and include helmets and locks, and the company can also do repairs if you've brought your own bike and need something fixed.

Stromness, West Mainland, and Hoy

While much of Orkney is flat and green, the wildest, most dramatic landscape can be found in the west of the archipelago. Near Marwick Head and reaching south through Yesnaby on Mainland, the land is more rugged, with coastal scenery comprising old red sandstone cliffs where there are blow holes and sea stacks, and often angry, boiling seas. Along much of this coastline, you can also see one of Orkney's most iconic landmarks in the distance, the Old Man of Hoy—a dramatically skinny sea stack off the island of Hoy, to the south. It's also visible from the characterful harbor town of Stromness, home to an excellent art gallery and some decent places to eat.

Perhaps Stromness's most famous native son, there has probably never been more of an advocate of the charms of Orkney than poet George Mackay Brown, who drew on his homeland in much of his work; he often said that he learned more as a child in the freedom of his landscape of sea, sky, and neverending shoreline than he did in the classroom. Mackay Brown wrote with precision of the ordinary people of Orkney—fishermen, drinkers, local characters—and today Stromness still retains its traditions and slowness. Mackay Brown would still very much recognize it.

Heading inland from the western coast, you'll find yourself in what's known as the Heart of Neolithic Orkney, a UNESCO World Heritage Center with an incredible density of ancient sights, including Skara Brae, known as the best-preserved Neolithic settlement in Western Europe, and the Ring of Brodgar, a mysterious circle of ancient standing stones.

Reached by ferry from Stromness (on foot and bike only), Hoy is often the one island travelers choose to visit, outside of Mainland and the ones connected to it by causeway. It's just about doable on a day trip and compared with the rest of the island group, it's rugged and dramatic—the word "Hoy" means "high."

SIGHTS
Stromness
PIER ARTS CENTRE
Victoria Street, Stromness; tel. 01856 850 209; www.pierartscentre.com; 10:30am-5pm daily; free

Opened in 1979 as a place to house the impressive fine art collection of author and philanthropist Margaret Gardiner, this gallery has since attracted world-wide acclaim. Pieces in the permanent collection include those by Barbara Hepworth and Alfred Wallis, as well as contemporary artists such as Sylvia Wishart, the local-born landscape artist who also illustrated much of poet George Mackay Brown's work. There are also regular rolling exhibits and it's a must-visit for anyone passing through Stromness.

STROMNESS MUSEUM
52 Alfred Street; tel. 01856 850 025; www.stromnessmuseum.co.uk; 10am-5pm daily Apr.-Sept., 10am-5pm Mon.-Sat. Oct., 11am-3:30pm Mon.-Sat. Nov.-Mar.; adult £5, child £1

A great example of a small museum, the exhibitions here cover all things Orkney, from

Stromness

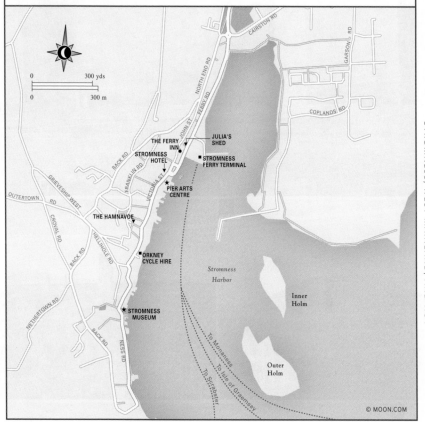

Stromness Harbor

Inner Holm

Outer Holm

JULIA'S SHED

THE FERRY INN

STROMNESS HOTEL

STROMNESS FERRY TERMINAL

PIER ARTS CENTRE

THE HAMNAVOE

ORKNEY CYCLE HIRE

STROMNESS MUSEUM

CAIRSTON RD

GARSON RD

COPLANDS RD

NORTH END RD

JOHN ST/FERRY RD

BACK RD

FRANKLIN RD

VICTORIA ST

GRIEVESHIP WEST

OUTERTOWN RD

CROVAL RD

BACK RD

HELLIHOLE RD

NETHERTOWN RD

BACK RD

NESS RD

To Stromness
To Moaness
To Isle of Graemsay
To Scrabster

0   300 yds
0   300 m

© MOON.COM

geology to history, including artifacts from the former whaling industry and World War I. Employees are uniformly passionate about the subject matter and happy to answer any questions you may have about Stromness, North Isle culture, or anything else.

Heart of Neolithic Orkney

On a thin strip of land between **Loch of Stenness** and **Loch of Harray,** running some 8 miles (13 km) west to Mainland's west coast, the Heart of Neolithic Orkney is composed of a chamber tomb (Maeshowe), two majestic stone circles (the Standing Stones of Stenness and the Ring of Brodgar), and the

Neolithic settlement of Skara Brae, so well preserved it's almost one of a kind. This area is UNESCO World Heritage listed for its concentration of sites that are all around 5,000 years old, giving a spine-tingling view into what life was like so long ago—and none of it more than a 15-minute drive from Stromness.

MAESHOWE

Ireland Road, Stenness; tel. 01856 851266; historicenvironment.scot; 10am-4pm daily; tours £5.50 adults, £3.30 children

Rising from a green field like an unnaturally rounded hill, the mound that covers this Neolithic chambered cairn, or burial

1
2
3
4

monument, is some 24 feet (7 m) high. Surrounded by a circular ditch, the approach to the monument is dramatic and humbling, as you imagine the countless hours of labor that must have gone into designing and constructing the tomb so many years ago.

Inside, after stooping or crawling through its 36-foot-long (11-m-long) entryway, which is only 3 feet high (1 m high), Maeshowe only grows more impressive, with its spacious central chamber and three side chambers composed of slabs of sandstone estimated to weigh up to 30 tons (27 metric tons). Maeshowe's most show-stopping feature only reveals itself once a year, at the winter solstice, when the entrance passage perfectly aligns with the sun, and illuminates the entire cairn. On the more human side, there's also some 12th-century graffiti inside Maeshowe, left by a group of Vikings who came inside to weather a blizzard.

Note that the inside of Maeshowe is only accessible on 45-minute guided tours, and that tours ceased during the pandemic and were still not running at the time of writing. Check online for the current situation and try to book tours ahead when they are running. Tours leave from the nearby **visitor center** (Maeshowe, Stonyhill Road) a mile (1.6 km) up the road, which is free to visit and stayed open throughout the pandemic, with toilets, a café, and a gift shop. It's good place to learn about the clever architecture of the cairn and theories as to why it was built.

STANDING STONES OF STENNESS

B9055, Stenness; www.historicenvironment.scot; open 24/7; free

Though only four upright stones remain of what was once a circle with 12 5,000-year-old stones, this is possibly the oldest henge monument in the British Isles. The remaining four upright grey slabs are up to 20 feet (6 m) in height and would once have formed a ceremonial site.

1: the Stones of Stenness **2:** Maeshowe **3:** Ring of Brodgar **4:** Skara Brae

★ RING OF BRODGAR

B9055, Stenness; tel. 01856 841815; www. historicenvironment.scot; open 24/7; free

More visually pleasing and atmospheric than Stenness today due to its completeness, is this stone circle, just a mile west (1.6 km) and dramatically situated on a thin isthmus between Loch of Stenness and Loch of Harray. This site dates to around 2500 BC (around 500 years after the Stones of Stenness and the other nearby sites), but 36 of the original 60 stone pillars survive, as well as at least 13 burial mounds, making you feel on approach as though you are encroaching on some ancient meeting. Though the stones that make up this ring are smaller than those at Stenness, at up to 10 feet (3 m) tall, they are arranged in an almost perfect circle, a rarity for this kind of Neolithic site, rivaling the much more famous Stonehenge.

As is usual for Neolithic sites, we don't know for sure what the circle was used for—one theory is it could have used for celebrations of past and present communities, and another that it was used to observe the moon—but it feels like a deeply spiritual place regardless, particularly if you visit either at sunrise or just before sunset.

TOP EXPERIENCE

★ SKARA BRAE

Sandwick, Orkney; tel. 01856 841815; www. historicenvironment.scot; 9:30am-5:30pm Apr.-Sept., 10am-4pm Oct.-Mar.; adult £9, child £5.40 (free late June-late Aug.), concessions £7.20

It is hard to comprehend that this village, which was home to a thriving community overlooking the lovely Bay of Skaill long before the pyramids were built, lay hidden for so long. Thankfully, a storm in 1850 uncovered it, revealing the most intact Neolithic settlement in Western Europe.

You'll start at the excellent **visitor centre,** where interactive exhibits and a reconstructed dwelling give context for the excavation ahead (there's also toilets as well as a café and gift shop). Artifacts found on-site and displayed at the visitor center, including tools and pottery, have led experts to believe the people who lived here were farmers, hunters, and fishermen, while other objects like gaming dice and jewelry help to bridge the yawning gulf of time.

Walking above the dugout houses on modern paths built to protect this precious site, you can still see the outlines of where beds and fires would have been—and even furnishings, like stone dressers—when these were people's homes over 5,000 years ago. The view from the sea-facing side of the village is still the same one that residents would have looked out on too, which is hard to fathom. The site is estimated to have been inhabited for around 600 years, probably by no more than 50 people at a time but was abandoned for unknown reasons around 2500 BC.

From April to October, your ticket also gives access to nearby **Skaill House** (tel. 01856 841 501; www.skaillhouse.co.uk), the finest mansion on Orkney, whose 19th-century owner was the first person to discover Skara Brae, and in the walled garden you can watch falcony displays.

The West Coast
BROUGH OF BIRSAY

*Birsay Orkney; tel. 01856 841 815; www.
historicenvironment.scot; 9:30am-5:30pm
mid-June-late Sept.; adult £6, child £3.60,
concessions £4.80; under 5 free*

For around two hours at low tide (check the Historic Environment website for times), you can walk on a concrete causeway across to the tidal island of Brough of Birsay, which lies off the northwest coast of Mainland, surveying the rockpools as you cross. On our visit, we saw a seal swimming, huge jellyfish, and lots of anemones and other sealife. Once across the 500-foot (150-m) divide, you'll find the remains of a Viking house and monastery on the island, and it's a steep walk up to the top and the lighthouse, where you'll want to hold onto your hat. Park at the Brough of Birsay car park, a 20-minute (14-mile/23-km) drive

north of Stromness, in view of the 16th-century ruins of the **Birsay Earl's Palace.**

SPORTS AND RECREATION
Hiking
YESNABY CASTLE

Distance: *1 mile (1.6 km)*
Time: *40 minutes*
Trailhead: *Yesnaby Road*
Information and Maps: *www.orkney.com/plan/itineraries/west-coast-walk-itinerary*

Yesnaby is not actually a castle, but rather an exposed sea stack with natural arch dramatically rising from the sea. You can pull up at the small car park to walk to this landmark on the craggy coastline; just follow the path south (left as you look at the sea). Take care as you walk the cliff path south, where jagged cliffs teem with seabirds, passing several rocky inlets. The path to Yesnaby Castle only takes about 20 minutes each way, but add on extra time to stop for photos or find somewhere safe to perch to breathe in the sea air. The walk description on the website also expands on other walks along this stretch of coastline, which you could combine for one much longer walk from Yesnaby to Stromness (11 miles/18 km, 4-5 hours one way).

★ OLD MAN OF HOY

Distance: *5.75 miles (9.25 km)*
Time: *3 hours*
Trailhead: *Rathwick Car Park, Hoy*
Information and Maps: *www.walkhighlands.co.uk/orkney/old-man-of-hoy.shtml*

The main attraction on the island of Hoy is its eponymous Old Man, a sandstone column in the sea, which is one of the most recognizable of all of Orkney's landmarks (or should that be seamarks?). At 450 feet (137 m) it is the tallest sea stack in Europe, and because of this, it attracts daredevils who attempt to climb it. I wouldn't recommend this myself, but it's certainly worth the walk to get up close to it.

1: Old Man of Hoy **2:** Corkaquina cottage **3:** cake at the Birsay Bay Tearoom **4:** Yesnaby Castle

To get here, you'll need to either take the foot/cycle ferry from Stromness to **Linksness** on Hoy's northern coast, or the car ferry from Houton on Mainland's southern coast (15 minutes; 8 miles/13 km east of Stromness) to **Lyness,** on the eastern tip of Hoy. From Lyness, it's a 30-minute (13-mile/21-km) drive to Rathwick Car Park; from Linksness, it's possible to walk all the way to Rathwick Car Park, though for this hike (16 miles/26 km in total), you will need to allow seven hours round-trip. A good alternative might be to hire a bike in Stromness from **Orkney Cycle Hire** and cycle from Linksness, a 30-minute cycle from Rathwick Car Park. Either way, on route, you'll pass the **Dwarfie Stane,** a huge slab of stone with a hollowed-out entry that lies in a valley between Rathwick and Quoys, which according to Orcadian oral tradition, was once the home of a giant and his wife. The story goes that they were blocked in by a rival giant and the giant inside gnawed his way out, but it's what's known as a rock-cut tomb.

Tours
ORKNEY ARCHAEOLOGY TOURS

Bayview, Birsay; www.orkneyarchaeologytours.co.uk; May-Sept.; 2-day/3-night tour from £1,095, 1-week holiday from £1,795 per person

While not cheap, these all-inclusive tours and holidays (except for travel to the isles) with one of two qualified archaeologists, with extensive excavation experience, are good for those who really want to delve deeper into Orkney's past. Starting with two-day tours and going up to week-long excavation holidays, they will take you to Neolithic sites that other visitors won't see.

Scuba Diving
KRAKEN DIVING

Birsay, Orkney; tel. 07933 492 349; www. krakendiving.co.uk; 4-day PADI course from £700, snorkel safari from £60 per person, guided dive from £170

Scapa Flow, the body of water that surrounds Orkney Mainland and the South Isles, creating a sheltered anchorage, has been used as a

harbor since at least the time of the Vikings when it was given the name Skalpafloi (bay of the long isthmus) and has been an important naval base since the Napoleonic wars of the 18th century. In the First and Second World Wars, blockships, battleships, and U-boats were scuttled and sank here, and so the array of shipwrecks that it is possible to dive is astonishing. Kraken is the only dive school in Orkney, so it's worth considering. As well as offering guided dives and the chance to gain your PADI, the company is now offering snorkel safaris around some of the blockships you can see protruding from the water as you cross the Churchill Barriers. For both guided dives and snorkel safaris, a photographer can be hired for around £50.

FOOD
Stromness
JULIA'S SHED

Ferry Road, Stromness; tel. 01856 850 904; juliascafe.co.uk; 9:30am-4:30pm Mon.-Sat., 10am-4:30pm Sun.; £6.50 crab rolls, salads £6.95

Very much a grab-and-go or grab-and-sit-outdoors as the harbor buzzes around you kind of place, Julia's Shed has friendly staff, and the freshly made rolls and salads—with crab or hot cured salmon—are mouth-watering. There's good coffee and cake, too.

THE HAMNAVOE

35 Graham Place, Stromness; tel. 01856 850606; service from 7pm; entrées £8.50

This local favorite has remained closed for much of the pandemic, but I have everything crossed they will soon be able to reopen. It's an intimate restaurant, specializing in seafood, with personal service courtesy of owners Neil and Sarah Taylor.

STROMNESS HOTEL

15 Victoria Street, Stromness; tel. 01856 850 298; www.stromnesshotel.com

Though it has become a little tired over recent years, Mackay Brown's favored watering hole has recently been bought by the Payman Club—a consortium of luxury hotels—so I suspect a makeover is on the cards, and its Scapa Flow restaurant (which had been reliably good, if not overly fancy) may get an overhaul. One to watch.

The West Coast
★ BIRSAY BAY TEAROOM

Palace, Birsay; tel. 01856 721 399; www. birsaybaytearoom.co.uk; 10:30am-4pm Thurs.-Sun.

Delicious cakes—chocolate, rose and vanilla flavored, Victorian sponge, and the like—teas, coffees, and deep-filled sandwiches and toasties are what you'll find at this lovely tearoom. You can look out over toward the Brough of Birsay as you dine, across a field of cows that leads down to a beach. It's the perfect spot for a drizzly day as you can birdwatch in the warmth, but do book, as it's extremely popular.

Hoy
EMILY'S TEAM ROOM & ICE CREAM PARLOUR

Lyness; tel. 01856 721 399; www.emilystearoomhoy. co.uk, 10am-5pm Tues.-Sat.

It's almost obligatory for visitors to stop off ether on arrival or prior to departure at Emily's Ice Cream Parlour for a scoop from this pretty painted green and grey house near where the ferry departs and arrives in Lyness.

ACCOMMODATIONS
Stromness
★ THE FERRY INN

10 John Street, Stromness; www.ferryinn.com; £130 d

Though you may want to pop into the pub at the nearby Stromness Hotel for a pint in honor of George Mackay Brown and other locals from the past, this inn is the better place to stay. There are 20 well-serviced en-suite rooms, with few frills but comfy nevertheless, and the pub downstairs has a warmth about it, plus a good menu.

The West Coast
CORKAQUINA

Marwick Bay; www.orkney-cottages.co.uk; £800 per week

There isn't exactly an over-abundance of accommodation in the Orkney Islands—even on Mainland—and what you do find is generally a little old-fashioned though hospitable and authentic. For the best value, I recommend self-catering, and we loved this cottage, with views over Marwick Head, which looked abandoned as we approached but was perfectly comfy inside (with underfloor heating a bonus).

Hoy
STROMABANK HOTEL

Longhope; www.stromabank.co.uk; £120 d

If you'd like to extend your stay on the lovely island of Hoy, the Stromabank Hotel is the only accommodation on Hoy that is open year-round, and is a lovely place to base yourself, with good deals out of season.

INFORMATION AND SERVICES

There is a large supermarket on the outskirts of Stromness, as well as a petrol station and other facilities, including a post office and local shops. For general visitor information, however, your best bet is the Kirkwall VisitScotland iCentre. For more on Hoy, check out the local website hoyorkney.com

GETTING THERE AND AROUND

The ferry from Scrabster, just 2 miles (3.2 km) north of Thurso on Scotland's north coast, arrives at Stromness Ferry Terminal, in Stromness's pretty harbor lined by stone buildings (www.northlinkferries.co.uk; 1 hour 30 minutes, 3 ferries per day Mon.-Sat., 2 on Sun. mid-May-Aug., 2 ferries per day daily for the rest of the year; car from £60 each way, passengers £20 each way). By car, Stromness is just 20 minutes (15 miles/24 km) from the main town of Kirkwall. From Kirkwall, you can take the X1 bus with Stagecoach to Stromness, which will get you here in around 30 minutes (www.stagecoachbus.com; £3.60 single).

The main way to reach Hoy is on the car

ferry from Houton in Orphir, a 15-minute (8-mile/13-km) drive east of Stromness, to Lyness on Hoy (www.orkneyferries.co.uk; 40 minutes; car £8.93, adult £2.82, concessions £2.12, infant £1.41), but there is also a foot passenger-only ferry from Stromness to Linksness on north Hoy. This ferry is run by Orkney ferries, takes a similar time, and costs the same.

GETTING AROUND

Though a car makes traveling through this part of Mainland (and really all of Orkney) easier, with relatively flat terrain and short distances between sights, cycling is another great option. Visit **Orkney Cycle Hire** (54 Dundas Street; tel. 01856 850 255; www.orkneycyclehire.co.uk; 8am-5pm daily; bikes from £10 per day) for all your bike rental needs. It's just a 30-minute cycle to Maeshowe, making cycling from Stromness through all the Heart of Neolithic Orkney sights and back in a day quite feasible (21 miles/34 km; about 2 hours with no stops).

If you don't fancy cycling, then the 8S bus with Stagecoach will get you from Kirkwall to the Ring of Brodgar in 55 minutes (£3.40 single). Coming from Stromness, the same bus takes 45 minutes (£3.80 single). From here, you can walk to the Stones of Stenness (1 mile/1.6 km; 17 minutes) and then on to Maeshowe (a further 1 mile/1.6 km; 17 minutes). Skara Brae is a little bit more out on its own, but you can get off the 8S bus after just 10 minutes from Stromness (£2.70 single) while from Kirkwall it's a 36-minute journey on the no. 8S bus (£3.80 single).

East Mainland and the South Isles

The small islands of (running north to south) Lamb Holm, Glimps Holm, Burray, and South Ronaldsay make up the South Isles, and they are accessed from East Mainland by the four iconic causeways known as the **Churchill Barriers.** The causeways were built in the 1940s to protect Navy battleships anchored in Scapa Flow from German U-Boats, but ironically, they weren't officially completed until May 12, 1945—four days after V-E Day.

This area is still home to some World War II sites that will satisfy any history buff, and **St. Margaret's Hope,** on South Ronaldsay, is a charming and quirky little place that's worth stopping off at (either when you arrive from Gills Bay by ferry or on a return visit), with lots of groatie buckies—elsewhere known as cowrie shells, little pink oval shells washed up on the beach—and lobster pots lining the slipway.

SIGHTS
East Mainland
DEERNESS DISTILLERY

Newhall, Deerness; tel. 01856 741 264; www.deernessdistillery.com; 10am-4pm Mon.-Fri. May-Sept.; free

If whisky is not your thing, then steer a course for this distillery, way over east, that produces hand-crafted vodkas, gins, and liqueurs. You can come and see the stills or pop into the well-stocked shop. It also offers takeaway tea, coffee, and snacks.

Lamb Holm
THE ITALIAN CHAPEL

Lamb Holm, Orkney; tel. 01856 781580; www.orkney.com/listings/the-italian-chapel; 9am-5:30pm daily; £3, under 12 free

This pretty white chapel looks out of place against the flat green pastures and vivid blue waters of the Scapa Flow, and it's the story of its construction, rather than necessarily the building itself, that ensures its place as one of Orkney's most visited places. The chapel is two Nissen huts, which were transformed into a place of worship by artist Domenico Chiochetti. He and his fellow Italian prisoners of war were brought here after their capture in North Africa during World War II, to construct the Churchill Barriers to close off four entrances to Scapa Flow that made Royal Navy ships anchored here vulnerable. The painting above the altar in the chapel was based on an image of Madonna and child by Nicolo Barabino that Chiochetti had on a prayer card given to him by his mother before he left Italy.

J. GOW RUM

*Lamb Holm, Orkney; tel. 01856 781580; http://
jgowrum.com; 10am-4pm Mon.-Sat; free*

After a visit to the chapel, stop into the nearby J. Gow Rum distiller, where you can taste rum made right here in Orkney. There are no tours at present, but I suspect this will soon change.

Burray
ORKNEY FOSSIL AND HERITAGE CENTRE

*Burray; tel. 01856 781 714; www.orkneyfossilcentre.
co.uk; 10am-5pm Tues.-Sun. Apr.-early Oct.; adult
£5.10, child £3.40*

You will see this fascinating local museum on the roadside to the right as you travel toward St. Margaret's Hope from Kirkwall. It's of particular interest for anyone who wants to know more about the significance of Scapa Flow, or to hear about life for the Italian prisoners who were based in Burray during World War II and built the famous Italian Chapel. It also goes much further back in time, with lots of intriguing fossils.

SHOPPING
SHEILA FLEET

*The Kirk Gallery & Café, Tankeress; tel. 01856 861
203; https://sheilafleet.com/pages/the-kirk-gallery-
cafe-orkney; 10am-5pm Mon.-Sat., 11am-5pm Sun.*

Orkney jewelry-maker Fleet designs and makes all her gold, silver, and platinum pieces right here on Orkney Mainland in her workshop by the sea. Inspired by the natural world of the isles, you can browse and buy her pieces in this renovated former parish church, where there is a beautiful light-filled gallery attached to a very good café.

BEACHES
SAND OF WRIGHTS BEACH

B9043, South Ronaldsay

There are lots of nice beaches on Orkney mainland, and this crescent-shaped sandy one near St. Margaret's Hope, overlooked by Hoxa Head, where you can just make out wartime buildings, is one of the loveliest. Backed by wildflowers, this beach has a small car park, but there is rarely anyone else here, unless you happen to visit during the third Saturday in August when the annual **Boy's Ploughing Match** takes place, which sees locals test their handmade miniature ploughs out on the sand. Participants attempt to draw a perfectly tilled furrow, while children dress in brightly colored costumes to represent harnessed horses. It's a bizarre but fun tradition on this otherwise quiet beach.

FOOD

All the food listings below are on South Ronaldsay.

★ THE MURRAY ARMS

*Back Road, St. Margaret's Hope; tel. 01856 831 205;
12pm-10pm daily; entrées £6*

This great local pub in the village of St. Margaret's Hope on South Ronaldsay serves seafood sourced from its own boats. The catch is landed daily at the end of the road, giving the restaurant food miles of almost zero. The hot seafood platter is a great pick-me-up after a day's exploring, and you can choose to eat in the small bar area in front, or the slightly more discreet restaurant out back. Make sure you book a table.

SKERRIES BISTRO

*South Ronaldsay; www.skerriesbistro.co.uk;
12pm-4pm Sun.-Fri. and 6:30pm-8pm Mon.-Weds.
and Fri.; entrées £6*

Crabs and lobster are brought in daily to this restaurant just a 10-minute drive from St. Margaret's Hope, from nearby Burwick Harbour. Aside from the fresh and healthy menu, the main reason to visit here is to experience the incredible glass modular building that houses the restaurant, which was transported to South Ronaldsay in 2013 and sits just 260 feet (80 m) from the cliff edge, with a brilliant outdoor terrace when weather allows.

ROBERTSONS COFFEE HOOSE & BAR

Church Road, St. Margaret's Hope; tel. 01856 831889; 12pm-10pm Fri.-Sun.; afternoon tea £13.95

For a quick pit stop on weekends, this family-run café/bar offers a warm Orcadian welcome in St. Margaret's Hope. You can sit in for a sandwich and coffee or afternoon tea or grab something to go. It's also open for drinks into the evening.

ACCOMMODATIONS
East Mainland
★ NORTHFIELD

Deerness; tel. 01856 741 353 or 07720 650 189; www.orkneybedandbreakfastnorthfield.com; £70 d

A beautifully decorated guesthouse with just three rooms (one double and two twins), each with a sea view, this is exceptionally good value. There's a guest lounge with a dual aspect and huge windows looking out over acres of countryside, and the breakfast menu is made up of produce from local suppliers, helping to support the wider community.

★ GRAEMESHALL HOUSE

Holm, off B9052, Kirkwall; tel. 01856 781 220; www.graemeshall-house.co.uk; £100 d (2-night minimum stay)

Six miles (10 km) outside Kirkwall, this smart 17th-century house, recently a private museum, now offers an air of grandeur to Orkney's accommodation offerings. There is a beautiful library and a private chapel, and

breakfast is served in a dining room with wood paneling dating from 1630. The rooms come with antique beds and high-quality sheets, with robes, slippers, and coffee machines, and really at this price, it's a steal.

South Ronaldsay
WHEEMS ORGANIC FARM

Eastside, South Ronaldsay; www.wheemsorganic. co.uk; bell tents £30 per night; camping pods £40 per night, cottage £420 per week, camping pitches from £9, camper van pitches from £12

An organic farm and small holding with eco holidays at its heart, Wheems offers a mix of camping and caravan pitches, bell tents, camping pods (all with access to a shower and toilet block and a kitchen area), and even a cottage on-site. Facing south and east on a cliff-side location in South Ronaldsay, with sandy beaches just minutes away, it is a lovely spot for a peaceful break under huge Orkney skies. Guests can also buy eggs and vegetables from the farm. Bell tents and pods don't come with bedding. There is also campervan hire available.

GETTING THERE AND AROUND

The Pentland Ferries service (https://pentlandferries.co.uk) from Gills Bay on the north coast of Scotland's Mainland arrives into St. Margaret's Hope in South Ronaldsay (1 hour, 3 ferries per day; £40 each way car, £17 each way per person), while John o' Groats Ferries (www.jogferry.co.uk) runs ferries for foot passengers and bicycles only between **John o' Groats** and Burwick, on the southern end of South Ronaldsay, in summer (twice a day June-Sept., 40 minutes; £16 each way).

From Kirkwall, St. Margaret's Hope is a 25-minute (15-mile/24-km) drive, while Burwick is just a bit farther, at 35 minutes (24 miles/37 km). Stagecoach bus X1 (www.stagecoachbus.com; £3.40 single) will take you to Kirkwall from St. Margaret's Hope in just 30 minutes. There are currently no buses running from Burwick to Kirkwall.

1: seafood platter at The Murray Arms **2:** The Murray Arms **3:** the Italian Chapel

Highlights of Shetland

Just 50 miles (80 km) to the northeast of Orkney is the archipelago of the Shetland Islands, which feels even more like a world unto its own. With about 100 islands (16 of which are inhabited), and 1,679 miles (2,700 km) of coastline, life on Shetland is inextricably linked to the sea. It's a place where whales can often be seen off the coast—the minke whale particularly. Nature, wildlife, silence, and solitude can all be enjoyed in the Shetland Islands, but so too can banter and music and culture—you just need to know where to look.

There is a strong sense of solidarity among the famously friendly Shetlanders: Visitors are regularly welcomed into people's homes for "tea and fancies." A good starting point, if you don't happen to bump into someone who invites you in, is to look out for posters/leaflets about any forthcoming Sunday Teas being held in village halls (local shopkeepers will usually know if any are coming up). **Visit Shetland** (www.shetland.org/visit) is another excellent resource for finding out about island life, places to visit, and volunteering opportunities.

Orientation

Like Orkney, Shetland's largest island is called **Mainland** (374 square miles/970 square km). Its largest town and ferry terminal, **Lerwick,** is about halfway up the island's craggy eastern coast, while the **airport** lies about 30 minutes to the south. One of the other most-visited islands is **Yell** (82 square miles/212 square km), the second largest of all the Shetland Islands, known for its beautiful beaches.

Lerwick is where you will find the most civilization, and it is within driving distance of pretty much everywhere on Mainland, making it a smart choice to base yourself. If you would rather hole up somewhere for a week or two and are not too bothered about logging in some driving time, I might advise

Northmavine, an area to the north (34 miles/55 km north of Lerwick, a 45-minute drive) that is home to some small settlements and is within easy reach of the spectacular Eshaness Cliffs.

WILDLIFE WATCHING

The best way to see wildlife on the isles—which includes **otters, whales, puffins,** and more—is with a local guide, who can take you to the spots where they are most often seen. Local experts such as Brydon Thomason of **Shetland Nature** (tel. 01595 760 212; www.shetlandnature.net; 6-7-hour tours from £120 per person) often combine wildlife spotting trips with photography lessons, and general lessons on the natural environment of the islands.

SHETLAND ARTS & CRAFTS TRAIL

shetlandartsandcrafts.co.uk/craft-trail

The Shetland Islands have a long history of textiles and here they do it all, from sheep shearing to wool dyeing, knitting, and weaving. The Shetland Arts & Crafts Trail is a great way to meet people and hear about the local craft traditions.

JARLSHOF

Samburgh, Mainland; tel. 01950 460 112; www. historicenvironment.scot/visit-a-place/places/ jarlshof-prehistoric-and-norse-settlement; 9:30am-5:30pm daily Apr.-Sept., 9:30am-4:30pm daily Oct.-Mar.; adult £6, children £3.60

Orkney doesn't have the monopoly on ancient sites in the Northern Isles, as the incredible Neolithic settlement of Jarlshof, on the southern tip of Mainland (a 24-mile, 30-minute drive south of Lerwick and only a mile south of Sumburgh airport), proves. Here, you'll find evidence of human habitation from the Iron Age right up to Viking occupation and beyond.

ESHANESS CLIFFS

Shetland ZE2 9RS; www.shetland.org/visit/do/
outdoors/walk/eshaness-circular

This peninsula in the west of Mainland (a 39-mile/63-km, hourlong drive northwest from Lerwick) is a rocky place, with a volcanic coastline shaped by the relentless North Atlantic that includes blowholes, craggy sea stacks, and narrow inlets known as geos, making it among Britain's most dramatic coastal landscapes. There are incredible views in all directions as you walk north from the **lighthouse** (www.shetlandlighthouse.com/eshaness-lighthouse; open 24 hours; free), with vertical rockfaces providing popular nesting places for birds. Do stay well back from the edge, as the wind and the sea take no prisoners here.

BEACHES OF YELL

The north island of Yell (the second largest of all the Shetland Islands) is known for its high number of ancient brochs (12 in total) and its gorgeous beaches, lauded for their beauty and cleanliness. **Sands of Brekon** (Cullivoe, northeast Yell) has the largest area of sand dune and dune grassland in Shetland, and its white sands, turquoise waters, wind shelter, and sunset views, make it an obvious choice.

West Sandwick (West Sandwick Beach Car Park, Shetland, ZE2 9BH) is tucked away behind dunes, so many visitors don't realize it's there. It has soft white sand, speckled with occasional shiny fragments of mica, and wonderful views across to Mainland.

Getting There

Yell is located just north of Mainland, connected by ferry (run by the local council; www.shetland.gov.uk/ferries; 25 minutes; £6 return, hourly) from Toft, 30 miles (48 km) north of Lerwick, 40-minute drive. The ferry arrives in Ulsta on Yell, from where it is a 21-mile (34-mi), 30-minute drive to Sands of Brekon, and a 7-mile (11-km), 12-minute drive to West Sandwick.

GETTING THERE
By Ferry

The ferry is probably the most romantic way to travel to Shetland, as it gives you the idea of the scale of the distance between the islands and the Scottish mainland. **Northlink Ferries** (www.northlinkferries.co.uk; one ferry per evening year-round; from £150 for one person and a car) runs a service from Aberdeen on the Scottish mainland, traveling overnight to **Lerwick.** The ferry crossing

Jarlshof

takes 12-14 hours (depending on weather). Ferries are also available from Kirkwall on Orkney Mainland to Lerwick through Northlink Ferries (5 hours 30 minutes, nightly ferry Mon., Weds., Fri. Apr.-Oct., nightly ferry Thurs., Sat., Sun. Nov.-Mar.; from £110 for one person and a car).

By Air

The quickest way to get to Shetland, however, is to fly into **Sumburgh Airport** (Virkie; tel. 01950 461 000; www.hial.co.uk/sumburgh-airport), also on Shetland's Mainland, where there are up to five flights a day from Aberdeen (1 hour), three flights a day from Edinburgh (1 hour 30 minutes), and two flights a day from Glasgow (1 hour 30 minutes). There are also a couple of flights daily from Kirkwall (40 minutes) and a couple from Inverness, which briefly stop in Orkney (1 hour 45 minutes). All flights are run by Logan Air (www.loganair.co.uk), and tickets range from £65 to £120 one way, depending on point of origin and time of booking.

GETTING AROUND

Once arrived in Shetland, if you didn't bring your car, you can rent one from companies such as Avis (Bolts Car Hire Ltd., Sumburgh Airport; tel. 01950 460 777), which is a 30-minute (23-mile/37-km) drive south of Lerwick, the main town. A car is preferable, but there is a surprisingly good number of **taxis** (www.shetland.org/visit/plan/getting-around/taxis), while the overall bus network is managed by **ZetTrans** (tel. 01595 744 868; www.zettrans.org.uk), with individual routes run by different providers, often self-starters. Download the ZetTrans app and it will tell you all you need to know about the comprehensive bus network and can be used even in areas of no phone service. Fares start from £1.80 for a single and tickets can be bought on board in cash or on card. A top-up card can also be bought, which gives a 20 percent discount off fares.

Background

The Landscape

GEOGRAPHY

Located at the top of the British Isles and connected to England by land, Scotland covers an area of 30,421 square miles (78,789 square km), about a third of the United Kingdom's landmass. According to Marine Scotland (https://marine.gov.scot), it has somewhere in the region of 900 islands (most of which are uninhabited and many of which are very small), creating thousands of miles of coastline. Some of the larger island groups include the Orkney Islands and the Shetland Islands, which scatter far into the North Sea from the northeastern tip

of the Scottish mainland, and the Hebrides, commonly divided into two subgroups—the Inner Hebrides and the Outer Hebrides—which lie off Scotland's west coast. Scotland is also home to some of the wildest and least inhabited parts of Europe.

Scotland's mainland is divided into three main topographic areas: the Highlands, the Central Lowlands, and the Southern Uplands. The latter two are generally grouped together in an area known as the Lowlands, and this is where the vast majority of the population lives. This area, as you might guess, comprises much lower land in comparison to the Highlands, though it is certainly not flat—here you will find fertile rolling hills and narrow, gentle valleys. Meanwhile, the east coast of Scotland has a much smoother outline, distinct from the more rugged and craggy west coast.

The area known as the Highlands, which covers much of north and west Scotland, is bisected by the Great Glen Fault. Northwest of the Great Glen is an ancient plateau where peaks have eroded over time and dramatic glens have been sculpted by glaciers. The far northwest of Scotland is particularly barren, and some of the oldest rocks in all of Scotland have been worn down to create imposing sea cliffs sweeping down to vast sea lochs and numerous inlets. Southeast of the Great Glen is Scotland's highest mountain, Ben Nevis.

Lochs

Think of Scotland and one undoubtedly thinks of its lochs: freshwater inland lakes that are landlocked, or strong arms of the sea that ebb and flow with the tide and provide a continuation of the region's rich marine life. The country has over 30,000 freshwater lochs, ranging from those with huge surface areas, like Loch Lomond, to legions of small lochans, which often punctuate wide open plains or can be found on higher land or in peaty areas. They were formed by glaciation following the last Ice Age, between 10,000 and 13,500 years ago, when ginormous sheets of ice that had covered much of the country began to melt, filling valleys that had been carved by the ice. There is a particularly high density of lochs in the north and west of the country, as it was here that much of Scotland's most dramatic geological and tectonic events took place.

As there are so many lochs in Scotland, it makes sense that they are so inextricably linked with Scottish folklore, myths, and legends. Nature and mythology often go hand in hand in Scotland, with stories being retold as a way of explaining the seasons and the unpredictable weather; teaching respect for wildlife and the elements, and awe and appreciation of the landscape; and serving as warnings to stay away from dangerous places. There are, of course, the highly questionable myths of monsters at Loch Ness and Loch Morar, and chilling tales of kelpies (water spirits) that lure unsuspecting victims to their watery graves, but there are also countless other stories and superstitions, passed down through families, that are sometimes otherworldly, often melancholy, and occasionally romantic.

CLIMATE

The saying goes that in Scotland you can see four seasons in a day, but some might argue that you could see four seasons in an hour. Though it is sometimes hard to tell the difference between the seasons—it is perfectly possible to have bright, warm days in autumn, it often rains in spring and summer, and in certain high terrains you can see snow on the mountains throughout the year—they roughly occur at these times: spring (March-May; max. temps. 45-55°F/7-13°C), summer (June-August; max. temps. 59-63°F/15-17°C), autumn (September-November; max. temps. 46-57°F/8-14°C) and winter (December-February; max. temps. 41°F/5°C).

Scotland has a high latitude, which means you can enjoy long summer days; indeed, in

Munro 101

Many visitors to Skye come to bag one or more of its 12 Munros—mountains (or hills as they often call them in Scotland) whose summits are **3,000 feet (914 m) or higher.** With 282 Munros across the whole of Scotland, **Munro-bagging** (climbing to the top of a Munro) is a popular pastime in Scotland and a real achievement when you can scale these huge mountains, for spectacular views and unblemished scenery en route.

Munros get their name from Sir Hugh Munro, a mountaineer who set about surveying and scaling them in the late 19th century and who inspired generations of others who followed in his hard-worn footsteps. Those who complete all 282 are known as **Munroists** or **Compleatists.** If you do manage to complete them all (or even one), you might want to move on to some of the other hills in Scotland, which are classified as follows: **Corbetts** (hills between 2,500 feet/762 m and 3,000 feet/914.4 m, with a drop of at least 500 feet/152 m on all sides), **Grahams** (hills of 2,000 feet/610 m-2,500 feet/762 m with a drop of 150 feet/46 m on all sides), and **Donalds** (hills in the Lowlands of over 2,000 feet/610 m).

the far north of Scotland there's sometimes no complete darkness at all in summer. Winters can get very cold indeed, causing ice and snow to fall and making getting to and from some of the more remote parts very tricky. It's not uncommon for Highland passes to become impassable or for people to become stranded in one place as single-track roads get blocked up. It's worth noting that, though across Scotland snow fall averages 15 to 20 days a year, in the Highlands this rockets to as much as 100 days of snow. Winter is a good time of year to try snow sports in Scotland with ski resorts in both Glencoe and Fort William. It's also the best time of year to enjoy Scotland's dark skies and possibly even see the Northern Lights.

The other thing to remember is that, although Scotland is a reasonably small country, its terrain is varied, and so weather can be very changeable between the regions. It also rains a lot, but people are philosophical about it; as they say here, "today's rain is tomorrow's whisky."

ENVIRONMENTAL ISSUES

Scotland's allure is also its curse. Its wild, open spaces and beautiful beaches that go on for miles have certainly turned the heads of visitors over recent years, and before the pandemic tourism was on the rise, often to the detriment of the landscape. There were reports of littering, people trampling away from footpaths, abandoning tents, rubbish, and other camping gear, and the great outdoors being used as a great big toilet.

Though Scotland both welcomes and relies on tourism, its ecosystems are not necessarily cut out for a lot of foot traffic. This is one reason it's good to get off the beaten track where possible and find your own adventure. You should also listen to the guidelines when it comes to hiking and wild camping to ensure you leave as small a footprint as possible, including following the National Trust for Scotland's mantra: "I love this place, I leave no trace." When you leave a place, it should be as though you were never there.

Much of Scotland's once raw landscape has been affected by farming, sheep grazing, and deforestation, with trees often cut down to provide first agricultural land, and later charcoal for the country's busy ironworks. There is concerted effort being made across parts of Scotland to return the landscape to its natural state, such as the major rewilding project underway at the Great Trossachs Forest National Nature Reserve and ongoing work at the Cairngorms National Park. It's hoped that, by restoring and regenerating natural areas, wildlife that was once driven nearly to extinction can return.

Plants and Animals

TREES

Scotland's long history of deforestation is complex, to say the least. Native trees such as ancient oakwoods, Scots pine, and birch do still exist, but they are found in pockets on more remote peninsulas or protected areas. And, while the vision of Highland mountains thick with pines may look beautiful, these woods are often too densely packed and don't allow enough room for wildlife to grow and thrive.

Projects are underway to restore Scotland's once sprawling Caledonian Forest, which has suffered immensely from over-grazing by sheep and deer. Conservation charity **Trees for Life** (https://treesforlife.org.uk) is committed to expanding and relinking the remnants of these ancient woodlands through a program of natural regeneration (restricting access to grazing animals to allow seedlings to grow and mature properly), replanting native trees, and removing non-native trees. It relies on a steady stream of volunteers to help it in its task to encourage young native trees such as Scots pine, oak, birch, rowan, hazel, and juniper, to grow in Scotland again and to revive this all-important eco-system.

FLOWERS

In spring, Scotland's meadows are carpeted with bluebells and other wildflowers; in summer a rich purple haze of heather contrasts against the lush greenery of the hillsides. In the machair of western Scotland, wildflowers set the coastline ablaze with color.

Other flowers to look for include the thistle, the national flower of Scotland. This purple prickly weed can be found on many heraldic symbols; though, with several varieties, it's difficult to decide which one is the actual symbol of Scotland. One legend of the thistle tells of how a sleeping party of Scots warriors were alerted to an ambush by Norse invaders when one of the Vikings stepped on the spiky plant, and, though there is scant evidence to back it up, you shouldn't let that get in the way of a good story.

MAMMALS

Scotland's unique mammals include large red deer, which are most commonly seen in the Highlands, as well as smaller roe deer, red squirrels, pine martens, badgers, and foxes. Though many people think of Scotland and envisage a mighty stag silhouetted against a misty mountain, there is some debate as to how much deer stalking is good to keep numbers down and give other wildlife a chance without damaging the deer numbers themselves.

Red deer stag stalking season runs from July to mid-October, with the hind stalking season taking place mid-October to mid-February, though most commercial operations take place August to October. If you are planning to do any hill-walking during stalking season, it is worth checking if there is any shooting taking place on the estate at the same time, so you don't risk disturbing any stalking activities. The best way to do this is to check with the Heading for the Scottish Hills access service (www.outdooraccess-scotland.scot/Practical-guide/public/heading-for-the-scottish-hills).

SEALIFE

With thousands of miles of coastline, Scotland's seas are teeming with marine wildlife. Along the west coast, many boat trips will take you out to see grey seals and common seals, often spotted lazily basking on rocks, as well as harbor porpoises, otters, dolphins (both common and bottlenose), and minke whales, which you are most likely to see from May to September. The Moray Firth, just north of Inverness, is home to Scotland's

1: thistle 2: red squirrel 3: hedgehog

largest resident population of bottlenose dolphins. Migrating orcas can sometimes be seen off Scotland's north and east coasts, particularly around the Orkney Islands (May to September is your best chance of seeing them), while a resident pod of eight orcas can be seen off the coasts of Skye and the Small Isles year-round.

BIRDS

Scotland's skies are busy with birdlife. On Skye, Mull, and Islay, eagles are regularly sighted (Mull is particularly good for sea eagles, or white-tailed eagles as they're also called). Other sea birds, such as puffins, are also abundant (particularly on Staffa and around the Treshnish Isles) from April to mid-August. Buzzards are the most commonly sighted bird of prey in Scotland and can be seen all year, though they tend to soar and display more in spring. Meanwhile, the elusive capercaillie can still be found in the Loch Lomond and the Trossachs National Park, and here too the numbers of black grouse are currently on the rise.

For the best of Scottish birdlife, visit Orkney, where you can see all manner of migrating birds, from Arctic terns to guillemots, razor bills, and great skuas, which mob the islands' sea cliffs for breeding. There are 13 bird reserves in total across the island group.

INSECTS

Midges are by far the most complained about group of insects found in Scotland, and they are copious in the Highlands and the west. Traveling in swarms, they range from mildly irritating to a downright nuisance, especially May-September (although it's the biting females from June onward that you want to be particularly wary of). Midges like warm, slightly damp air (often after it's rained), and dusk is their favorite biting time. If you're planning to do any camping at all, particularly in summer, you will want to protect yourself against the midges—Avon Skin So Soft spray is the protection of choice for me (odd, but true), while others swear by Smidge repellant. Make sure you wear long trousers and long sleeves, and if you're sitting outside your tent in the evening, burning a citronella candle can help, too.

In rural Scotland lots of other insects can be found, including mosquitos, horseflies, ants, beetles, ladybirds, birch flies, and black flies (these last two can also be annoying), as well as bees, wasps, spiders, butterflies, dragonflies, and grasshoppers. While you may get the odd bite, there's not much to be worried about when it comes to Scottish insects, although a bite from a tick—a nasty little insect often found in wooded and bushy areas and which carries Lyme disease—can make you very sick if not treated. If you do get bitten by a tick, try to remove it using either a tick removal device or finely tipped tweezers. It's also worth familiarizing yourself with the symptoms of Lyme disease (www.nhs.uk/conditions/lyme-disease) if you have been bitten (similar to the flu, symptoms often show up a couple of weeks later), so you can get treated as soon as possible.

History

Scotland's history is emotive, long, at times brutal and savage, but often told with a sense of pride and patriotism. It has been invaded and settled more times than you can count, and its people have been dispersed to all corners of the globe—as many as 29 million people in the United States claim some Scottish ancestry, with many more in Canada, Australasia, and South Africa. It is this sense of belonging and connection to the land that binds its people and has led to the romanticization of its famous heroes, from fearless warriors to enlightened thinkers. While in other parts of the UK patriotism is a thorny issue, it's rare to meet a Scotsman or Scotswoman who is not proud of where they are from.

ANCIENT HISTORY

The first people to settle in Scotland were the hunters and gatherers of the Stone Age, around 10,000 BC, shortly after the last Ice Age. They were nomads who wandered the land, surviving on what they could—wild animals, seasonal berries, and fruits. It's also likely that these wanderers were able seamen, and so the numerous isles off Scotland's west coast were undoubtedly attractive to them, with plenty of inlets to travel between. It's interesting to note that, despite the many different people who arrived in Scotland thereafter, DNA evidence shows that the bloodstock has changed little since these early hunter-gatherers arrived; thus, Scottish people are mostly descended from them. Eventually, early farmers arrived, but not until around 4,000 BC. They then began clearing forests for arable land, and so began Scotland's long story of deforestation.

It's thought that it's through these early Neolithic people—who began to rely on specific patches of land for survival—that the first signs of clan life sprung, as people "belonged" to a certain home turf for the first time. These Neolithic people also built stone burial chambers (cairns) for their dead, the remains of which can be seen around Scotland, such as Clava Cairns near Inverness and Orkney's Maeshowe. Later, people also began creating tools and weapons of bronze, an idea that probably came to Scotland via Europe.

ROMAN INVASION

The Romans first attacked Scotland in AD 79, and the country's recorded history began shortly thereafter. Though the Romans tried to subjugate Scotland, or Caledonia as the Romans called it, ultimately, they failed. On arrival, they named the indigenous people, whom they considered savages, Picts (meaning painted people). In reality, the pre-Christian Picts were probably made up of lots of different tribes. In AD 83 or 84 the Romans, led by Julius Agricola, fought the Caledonians, led by a fearsome chief known as Calgacus, at the Battle of Mons Graupius (the Grampian Mountains). Though according to the Roman historian Tacitus the Romans won this battle and colonized much of southern Scotland, their style of attack was not suited to the terrain of the Highlands, and further attempts to bring the north of the country under control failed.

As a result, the Romans built the huge stone barrier between England and Scotland known as Hadrian's Wall, largely to keep the northern savages out of their empire. They later built the 37-mile (60 km) Antonine Wall, another great hulk of a barrier, from the Clyde to the Forth, to try to exert control. Eventually, in AD 410, the Romans retreated from Scotland and Britain, having never really conquered the north and leading many to hail it the first episode of Scotland's unwavering might.

POST-ROMAN SCOTLAND

In AD 563 St. Columba arrived in Scotland, setting up a monastery on the tiny Isle of Iona, off the west coast of Mull, and also visiting Skye, where he preached Christianity. Celtic people from Ireland, known as Gaels, had already settled in the west of Scotland. By the 5th century these early Celts (also known as Scoti) ruled a huge area of Scotland known as Dál Riata (or Dalriada) from the center of their kingdom in Kilmartin Glen, Argyll. By AD 800 Vikings, accomplished seamen from Scandinavia (mainly Norway and Denmark), began crossing the North Sea and settling in parts of Scotland, particularly in the west, around Skye. Later, the Picts and the Gaels began to forge a new kingdom known as the Kingdom of Alba. In 843 Kenneth MacAlpin became the first King of Scots, ultimately uniting the nation of Scotland into the country we see today.

Following MacAlpin, the role of king was passed down through a Gaelic system of tanistry (in which eligible men were elected to the role, though blood was often spilled too). Macbeth, King of Scotland from 1040-1057, whom Shakespeare painted as some kind of bloodthirsty social climber, was probably no worse than his peers. By the 12th century, Scotland, increasingly influenced by England, became a feudal society, and under this new system the role of king became a hereditary right in Scotland.

WARS OF INDEPENDENCE

Scotland has long had a fragile relationship with its southern neighbor, England. The larger and more powerful country of England saw itself as superior, and its monarchs considered themselves overlords of Scotland, an idea that riled many a Scottish king or warrior. In 1286, there was a succession crisis in Scotland following the death of King Alexander III, which enabled power-hungry King Edward I of England to take some control. A tussle for the Scottish crown between John Balliol and Robert the Bruce led the guardians of Scotland (a group of noblemen given temporary control of the country) to ask the English king to decide who should be king.

Edward I dutifully chose Balliol, but not before he had convinced the guardians to recognize him as overlord of Scotland.

John Balliol's reign was thwarted by Edward's constant demands, which undermined the Scottish king, and it soon became clear that Edward saw Scotland as nothing more than a vassal state. In 1294, seeing trouble on the horizon, Balliol formed a treaty with England's other enemy, France, essentially agreeing that the two nations would support one other against the English. This partnership became known as the Auld Alliance and continued in some form or other until the 16th century.

On hearing of the Franco-Scottish negotiations, Edward was furious, and in March of 1296 he mounted an attack on Berwick, a town which then stood just across the Scottish border. The following month the English defeated the Scottish at the Battle of Dunbar. By July, Balliol was forced to abdicate.

Edward I's bold move to take Scotland for himself infuriated many Scots people, not least a warrior known as William Wallace, who managed to garner support for a fight for independence, with the aim of returning Balliol to the throne. Together with military leader Andrew Moray, Wallace led Scots troops, largely made up of clansmen from the Highlands, to a huge victory against English troops at the Battle of Stirling Bridge in 1297. Unfortunately, despite the Scottish victory, a determined Edward I continued a vicious assault on Scotland, eventually forcing William Wallace into hiding. By the time Wallace arrived back in Scotland a few years later, momentum had been lost and in 1305 Wallace was betrayed to English forces; he was captured just north of Glasgow, tried for treason in London's Westminster Hall, and hung, drawn, and quartered. His head was placed on a spike in London Bridge and parts of his body distributed among Scottish cities as a warning to future would-be revolters.

But the fight wasn't over. Robert the Bruce, himself a clever political maneuverer, was crowned King of Scotland in 1306, and in

1314 he and his army defeated Edward II at the Battle of Bannockburn, just outside Stirling. Six years later, in 1320, the Declaration of Arbroath, a letter on which the U.S. Declaration of Independence is thought to have been based, was signed by Scottish nobles and barons and delivered to Pope John XXII, requesting that he acknowledge Scotland as an independent sovereign state from England. Though largely symbolic, its intent was clear, and for a while, Scotland was left largely alone.

THE LORD OF THE ISLES

Though much of Scotland now formed part of one country, for a long time much of the western isles and a large part of the western mainland were ruled by a separate entity known as the Lord of the Isles, whose ancient seat was at Finlaggan on the Isle of Islay. The title dates back to the Viking occupation of Scotland, when Somerled, the son of a Gael and a Norse settler, fought off the Norse ruler of the region, Olaf, securing the kingdom for himself and his descendants, the Macdonalds.

The power of the Lord of the Isles, which reached its peak in the 15th century, began to dwindle after one ruler, John Macdonald II, made a treaty with King Edward IV of England in 1462 in a bid to overthrow the Scottish king, James III. When King James IV came to the throne a couple of decades later, he began the process of dismantling the power of the Lord of the Isles for good.

THE STUARTS

In 1542, Scotland was thrown into turmoil when King James V of Scotland died, leaving his six-day-old daughter, Mary, Queen of Scots, the heir apparent. At the time, religious reform was sweeping across Europe; in England King Henry VIII had set up the Church of England following his divorce from Catherine of Aragon, making it a Protestant country. Nervous Catholics acted quickly, and Mary was crowned Queen of Scotland in the Chapel Royal at Stirling Castle in 1543, aged just nine months.

King Henry VIII of England saw a chance to unite the crowns of Scotland and England through the marriage of Mary and his son Prince Edward (later King Edward VI of England), who himself was aged just six. The Scots rejected the proposal and a period of unrest ensued; Henry sent troops to attack Edinburgh in December of that year, and later attacked other parts of Scotland, in a bid to change their mind. This struggle became known as the Rough Wooing.

In 1558 Mary's mother, Mary of Guise, arranged for her to marry the Dauphin of France, in order to strengthen the Catholic line. Mary left for France and didn't return to Scotland until 1561, following the death of her husband. By this time Scotland was in a state of religious unrest. Mary quickly remarried, this time to Henry Stuart, Lord Darnley, a jealous man; in 1566 he entered into a Protestant conspiracy to have Mary's favorite and secretary David Rizzio murdered at the Palace of Holyroodhouse in Edinburgh. The following year Darnley himself was killed in an explosion in Edinburgh, and when Mary then married the Earl of Bothwell, whom many suspected of murdering Darnley, her fate was sealed.

Scotland turned against Mary, thanks in no small part to the vitriolic words of John Knox, leader of the Scottish Reformation and Mary's sworn enemy. Mary was arrested and forced to abdicate in favor of her son, King James VI, who was just 13 months old. She escaped to England, where for a while she lived under the protection of her cousin Queen Elizabeth I of England, though she never saw her son again. Eventually Elizabeth (who never actually met her cousin) grew scared that Mary could claim the throne of England for herself and had her executed at Fotheringhay Castle in Northamptonshire in 1587.

When Elizabeth died in 1603 with no children, King James VI of Scotland succeeded to the throne of England as King James I, thus uniting the two countries in what is known as the Union of the Crowns. In 1707, the Act of Union brought the two countries even closer by creating a single Parliament to rule

Scotland and Britain from Westminster, effectively creating Great Britain.

THE JACOBITES

It was some years prior to the Act of Union that the wheels of the Jacobite cause began turning. During the Glorious Revolution of 1688, in which King James VII of Scotland (King James II of England) was deposed and replaced with William of Orange and his wife Mary II (James's own daughter), many Scottish patriots felt outraged. James, a Catholic, had hoped to return Catholicism to Scotland, but after William of Orange launched an attack on him, he had gone into hiding. It was now left to his supporters to retaliate, which they duly did in 1689. Led by Viscount Dundee, James's supporters (the name Jacobite means "supporter of James") mounted a successful Highland charge against William's forces at the Battle of Killiecrankie in 1689. However, Dundee was killed in the battle, and without a leader the cause simmered.

William of Orange's government was characterized by a series of economic disasters and proved unsympathetic to the needs of its Scottish subjects (in fact, many Scots felt humiliated by the way they were treated by the English Parliament), and so Jacobites who believed in James's hereditary right to the throne were soon joined by anyone who had a grudge against the king. The signing of the Act of Union with England in 1707 (this time under the reign of Queen Anne) brought yet more supporters.

During the Jacobite Rising of 1715, one of Scotland's most influential politicians, the Earl of Mar, raised the standard for the Stuarts when George I of Hanover succeeded to the throne, in the hope of reclaiming it for James Francis Edward Stuart, the son of King James II who was known as the "Old Pretender." During the Jacobite Rising of 1745 (known as the '45), the "Young Pretender," Bonnie Prince Charlie, arrived from exile in Italy to raise the Stuart standard in Glenfinnan. Sadly, this final major uprising led to the overall defeat of the Jacobite cause at the Battle of Culloden, which took place just outside Inverness on April 16, 1746.

COLLAPSE OF THE CLAN SYSTEM

Following Culloden, the British government, by now under the reign of King George II, wanted to ensure no rebellions on such a scale could be mounted again, and so, many measures were put in place to undermine and eradicate traditional Highlands clan culture. The Tartan and the Dress Act of 1746 outlawed the wearing of kilts, just one of many measures meant to control the clans. In addition, British forts were placed along the Great Glen to ensure British troops could leap into action as soon as possible, aided by the notorious "Wade's Roads" introduced throughout the Highlands by General Wade. Highland clans were brought into the military fold, with Highland regiments in the British Army, such as the Black Watch, being created some years earlier.

The most effective and also heartbreaking measure was the Highland Clearances that took place over the course of a century. Through a mix of often brutal forced clearances, the Hanoverian government undid centuries of clan culture, in which a connection with the land as a sense of belonging was ingrained, in a spectacularly short space of time.

ENLIGHTENMENT

An intellectual movement known as the Enlightenment took hold in Scotland in the wake of Culloden. From the 1750s onward, Scottish philosophers, scientists, engineers, doctors, and writers (such as David Hume, Adam Smith, and Robert Burns) were sharing and debating ideas in and around Edinburgh, many of which had a huge impact on the way the world works today. So influential were the leading figures of the movement that French author-philosopher Voltaire was quoted as saying, "We look to Scotland for all our ideas of civilization."

HIGHLAND REVIVAL

One name that sprang up out of the Scottish Enlightenment was Sir Walter Scott—a well-connected Scottish writer and historian whose historic fiction spawned a culture of literary tourism to places such as Loch Lomond and the Trossachs, which in turn was instrumental in the Highland Revival of the 19th century.

Keen to build on the union between Scotland and England and improve relations between the two nations, King George IV embarked on an ambitious state visit to Scotland in 1822, all stage-managed by Sir Walter Scott. As it was the first time a reigning monarch had visited Scotland since Charles I in 1633, George went all out, wearing a kilt for the occasion and improving his reputation in Scotland hugely, creating a certain brand of Scotland in the process. Later, Queen Victoria, who famously fell in love with Scotland and had the huge palace of Balmoral Castle built in Aberdeenshire, cemented the role of Scotland as a fashionable place to be, and people traveled from all over to partake in Scottish customs that were once maligned and outlawed but had come to be considered quaint and twee.

Interestingly, though Highland games and clan tartans are now symbolic of Scotland, it's unclear how popular these were with traditional Highland clans—indeed, the idea of a certain tartan being associated with a particular clan was probably a Scott invention.

BEGINNINGS OF INDUSTRIALIZATION

The union with England brought more trading opportunities to Scotland, and there was a real effort to improve agricultural practices from the mid-18th century on. Around this time Glasgow became the center of the world's tobacco trade, and rich merchants built lavish buildings in the city center. One inconvenient truth is that much of the wealth that Glasgow—and indeed Scotland—built up over this period came off the back of the slave trade, and many well-connected Scots people even emigrated to the Americas to run plantations and profit further from exploitation.

Robert Burns himself even considered a move to Jamaica to be bookkeeper at a plantation in a bid to pay off his debts.

Despite the racism and exploitation that in some ways fueled Scotland's economy, many Scottish people did fight for the abolition of slavery, and Scotland was progressing in other ways at pace. People became much more concentrated in cities, and industries such as mining and shipbuilding provided much-needed work for the urban populations until the 1960s.

MODERN-DAY SCOTLAND

Much of the view of present-day Scotland has been romanticized by films such as *Braveheart,* and people are still drawn to its trove of historic sites, from ruined castles burned to the ground by the Jacobites to prehistoric relics. However, Scotland is also a hugely exciting and innovative country—without Scotland, we would have no flushing toilets (thanks to Alexander Cumming), telephones (thanks to Alexander Graham Bell), or TVs (thanks to John Logie Baird).

It's also a cultural powerhouse, with world-class museums and art galleries, some of the best festivals in the world, and an increasing presence on the world stage. It's a progressive nation as happy to look to its past as it is to imagine a new future. All in all, it's a place that, once it has you in its hold, is very hard to forget.

In 2014, Nicola Sturgeon, the leader of the Scottish Parliament, led a hearty referendum campaign for Scotland to vote for independence from the rest of the UK. It was a close-fought battle, with the outcome 55 percent to 45 percent, but ultimately, the people of Scotland chose to stay as part of the UK. Since then, the referendum on leaving the EU, referred to as Brexit, took place in 2016. Despite the majority of people in Scotland voting to remain in the EU, the majority of the UK did not (albeit by a small margin of 52 percent to 48 percent), so Scotland, along with the rest of the UK, officially left the EU on January 1, 2021.

Government and Economy

GOVERNMENT

Since 1999 Scotland has been devolved from the rest of the UK in some areas. This basically means it has its own government, elected by the people, which sits at the Scottish Parliament in Edinburgh and makes decisions over certain aspects of Scottish life, including how its budget is spent. The current leader is Nicola Sturgeon of the Scottish National Party (SNP), a center-left party with social democracy at its heart. The SNP is the largest political party in Scotland (it currently has 64 seats in the Scottish Parliament and 45 in the House of Commons) and had quite a monopoly on politics north of the border for a few years, though its stronghold is starting to weaken and in 2019 it lost many seats in the general election. Despite the outcome of the 2016 referendum on whether Scotland should remain part of the UK, Sturgeon still believes in independence for Scotland, and support for it has grown since Brexit, so never rule out another referendum.

The second largest party in Scottish politics is the Scottish Conservative & Unionist Party—a right-leaning political party. It was once said there were more pandas in Scotland (the two in Edinburgh Zoo) than Conservative MPs (just the one). Now the same joke could be made about the center-left Labour Party.

ECONOMY

Scotland has a GDP of £166.8 billion and one of the lowest unemployment rates in Europe, at 4.2 percent.

Tourism contributes £6 billion, 5 percent of Scotland's GDP, each year. Other key industries in Scotland are technology and engineering (which currently is more likely to mean software than ships), the financial services industry (which employs many people in Edinburgh and Glasgow, and which contributes around 7 percent of Scotland's overall GDP), and the oil and gas industries, which employ more than 100,000 people. In 2019, oil and gas extraction alone were worth around £8.8 billion to Scotland's economy. Scotland has large oil reserves and is the biggest producer of petroleum in the EU, though the industry has been in decline for several years. With a shift away from fossil fuels, the energy industry is now looking toward more sustainable alternatives, with a focus on offshore wind, storing energy, carbon capture, and ways of decarbonizing heat and transport.

Britain has now left the EU, and the full impact on the economy is hard to know at this early stage, particularly when coupled with the issue of coronavirus restrictions and the impact they have had on the economy. Early signs since Britain left the EU show that the economy has been hit, with the introduction of new tariffs causing delays to supply chains and border delays of goods (including, ironically enough, petrol) making headlines.

On top of Brexit, obviously the full extent of the coronavirus pandemic is yet to be fully seen, though the standstill of international tourism has been a huge blow. Though visits by U.K. residents have increased (between lockdowns), it's not enough to make up the shortfall suffered in 2020 and 2021.

One good news story is that the export tax that had been added to Scottish goods going to the US has now been lifted. The export of food and drink (Scotch whisky, Scottish salmon etc.), is considered four times as important to the Scottish economy as it is to the rest of the U.K.

People and Culture

DEMOGRAPHY AND DIVERSITY

Scotland is not a particularly diverse country, with 96 percent of the population identifying as white, and 83.9 percent specifically as "White: Scottish," according to the last available census results from 2011. Other substantial ethnic groups are Asian (2.7 percent), African, Caribbean, or Black (1 percent), and mixed or other ethnic groups (under 1 percent). However, the percentage of people in Scotland from minority ethnic groups is growing; it had doubled to 4 percent from 2 percent in 2001. Results from the 2021 census will be published in 2022.

Scotland does also have a bit of an issue with an aging population, with the number of people over 65 (16.8 percent) outnumbering people under 15 (16.1 percent) for the first time at the time of the last census.

In more rural communities, the issue is more pronounced, according to 2020 data from the National Records of Scotland. A large part of this is caused by the depopulation of these communities, with young people and families often moving away to seek new opportunities. In March 2021, the Scottish Government released a report in which it set out plans to address the depopulation issue, by creating packages to encourage families to settle in Scotland, as well as the falling birthrate, including easier access to fertility treatments for those with a child already.

CLAN CULTURES

While Highland culture was largely detangled and picked apart from the late 18th century onward, with restrictions placed on clans, and displacement and mass emigrations resulting in people leaving their ancestral lands, the sense of belonging to a place still rings true to many Scots people, wherever they live in the world. Today, people travel the world over to visit places associated with their clan, from the battlefield of Culloden, where they can pay respect to lost lives, to castles associated with their people. Thanks to the Highland Revival of the 19th century, there is now a tartan associated with each clan, which is worn like a badge of honor.

RELIGION

The largest faith in Scotland is Christianity, which accounts for 53.8 percent of all faiths according to the 2011 census. Scotland is a Presbyterian country, with the Church of Scotland recognized as the national church. The other main Christian denomination is the Roman Catholic Church (the dominant religion until the Scottish Reformation), which is still very popular in traditionally Gaelic areas, such as the Hebrides and western Scotland. The third most popular branch of Christianity is the Scottish Episcopal Church. There are also lots of smaller Presbyterian churches.

Other religions are gradually establishing here due to a gingerly increasingly diverse population, but they are still small in comparison (Islam: 1.4 percent, Hinduism: 0.3 percent, Sikhism: 0.2 percent, and Buddhism: 0.2 percent). In reality, though you will see cathedrals and churches in cities, and most towns and villages will have a parish church, Scotland is not an overtly religious country.

LANGUAGE

Though the main language spoken in Scotland is English, some like to call it Scottish English: It's much the same as standard English, with the same spellings, but has a lot of variation in slang and pronunciation. For example, words like *wee* (small) and *muckle* (large or much) are part of common parlance in Scottish English but not in standard English.

As many as 30 percent of the population speaks Scots, sometimes referred to as Lowland Scots, as it is largely spoken in the east and south of the country. It encompasses four main dialects, which are then divided into 10 subdialects, such as "Doric," "Buchan," and "Glesca." Scots is a variation of northern Anglo-Saxon, which was once the widest spoken language in Scotland, in the leadup to the union with England in 1707. But when Scotland and England formed a union, Scots and Gaelic were both suppressed, leading English to become the accepted norm to be spoken in courts and towns, where more commerce took place. Despite the language disappearing, some educated Scots sought to retain it, including, of course, Rabbie Burns, who wrote almost solely in the Scots language.

Today most Scottish schools include Scots as part of their literacy and English curriculum as a way of encouraging youngsters to engage with their lessons and to learn about Scottish culture, identity, history, and expression. Similarly, Gaelic is still spoken in pockets of Scotland, particularly in the Outer Hebrides and parts of Skye. Once a dominant language in Scotland, it has been spoken here for over 1,500 years, but having been intrinsically tied in with clan culture, the language began to fade with the dismantling of the clan system in the late 18th century. It is now considered "definitely endangered" by UNESCO. That said, bit by bit over recent decades, people have begun to understand the importance of preserving Gaelic as a language and the culture around it. In 2018 the Scottish Government invested millions of pounds in promoting it through educational and cultural projects and broadcasting, and tourism providers are starting to recognize the appeal of this unique ancient language to visitors. In southern Skye, on the Sleat Peninsula, the Sabhal Mòr Ostaig Gaelic college has been a huge success since it was founded in 1973 by the late Sir Iain Noble, a keen Gaelic activist. Since then, the Gaelic community has not only survived but thrived in the village of Eilean Iarmain—the pub of the same name is a great place to find out about the Gaelic origins of local place names, which will enrich your travels around the isle.

THE ARTS
Literature

Sir Walter Scott is celebrated for having introduced literary tourism to Scotland with his depictions and romanticism of Highland clans and the landscape they called home, but he is also largely responsible for the romantic view we have of Highland culture, particularly through his novel *Rob Roy,* which tells of the plight of the Jacobites.

Scotland has long been associated with great works of literature, from the stirring poems of Robert Burns to the adventurous imaginings of Robert Louis Stevenson. Contemporary fiction is not to be overlooked either. Irvine Welsh may paint a slightly bleaker view of Scotland than Scott, but the dialect in which he writes, and the honest depictions of inner-city life, are no less captivating. Ian Rankin and Val McDermid rank among Scotland's best thriller writers, while Iain Banks, who writes under two guises (Iain Banks for mainstream fiction and Iain M. Banks for science fiction), is nothing short of a literary hero.

Writers from more marginalized communities are still a little like hen's teeth in Scotland, unfortunately. The Scottish BAME Writers Network is doing great work to get voices of people of color heard, and the recent Scots Makar (poet laureate), Jackie Kay, (who ended her tenure in 2021) has been magnificent in helping widen the appeal of poetry in Scotland. In addition, her 1998 novel *Trumpet,* in which she tells the story of transexual trumpet player Joss Moody, is sensitively handled. There is still much work to be done, and the process for appointing Kay's successor is being changed to encourage more diversity.

Contemporary fiction in Scotland has a good history of finding and celebrating working-class voices, from Ali Smith to James Kelman and, most recently, Douglas Stuart, whose debut novel *Shuggie Bain* won the 2020 Booker Prize. And in terms of literature and writing from an LGBT+ perspective, more and more works are joining the cannon all the time. Jo Clifford's *The Gospel According* to Jesus, Queen of Heaven, a reimagining of familiar stories with a trans woman Jesus, is still popular 12 years on, while *Wain* by Rachel Plummer (2019) is a beautifully inclusive book in which well-known Scottish folktales are retold from an LGBT+ perspective.

Visual Arts

Henry Raeburn, portrait painter to King George IV, was an excellent portraitist, who captured the likenesses of key players of the day, including Sir Walter Scott, whom he painted in 1822, and the Reverend Robert Walker, the star of arguably his most famous work, *The Skating Minister,* on display in the Scottish National Gallery in Edinburgh.

Of course, Charles Rennie Mackintosh's contribution to the Glasgow landscape and to the applied arts is huge. It's important to remember that Mackintosh was also keenly influenced by his wife Margaret Macdonald, her sister Frances Macdonald, and Frances's husband James Herbert MacNair. Together, they made up The Four, a group of accomplished and daring artists who met at the Glasgow School of Art in the 1890s and went on to create what was referred to as the Glasgow Style.

Around this time a group of artists known as the Glasgow Boys, featuring the likes of James Guthrie, who interpreted and expanded on impressionist and post-impressionist paintings of the day, also emerged from the school. Much later, the New Glasgow Boys of the 1980s also from the Glasgow School of Art, became known for their honest, often gritty portrayals of daily life.

Though you may see the occasional piece representing people of color, often there are no artworks by people of color at all in a gallery, such as at the Scottish National Gallery. I spoke to someone there who told me that as part of the gallery's commitment to equality, diversity, and inclusion, the gallery is "reviewing the previous ownership of artworks, artists, their subject matter, sitters depicted, and existing interpretation." I was also told they will be looking at issues of colonialism, slavery, and their legacies.

Music and Dance

While contemporary Scotland, particularly in Glasgow and Edinburgh, is a melting pot of difficult musical styles and dance trends, from techno to thrashing guitar music, pop, and classical, folk music has long been at Scotland's heart. The bagpipes are a traditional instrument, long associated with the Highland clans; indeed, they were played when clans went into battle. There are two main styles of music played, the *Ceòl Mór* and *Ceòl Beag,* Gaelic for "big music" and "light music," respectively. The former is slower, featuring a simple melody, while Ceòl Beag features jigs and reels and is what you are more than likely to hear at ceilidhs—lively dance and music events that take place on occasion in the Highlands and more regularly in the cities.

Many inns in Highland villages, as well as pubs in Glasgow and Edinburgh, feature regular traditional music nights whereby gathering musicians sit and play round a table. Often it is improvised, and there are fiddles, accordions, and guitars as well as occasional singing—from laments to more rousing sing-a-longs—and the odd bagpipe. If you can sing or play and know a folk song or two, you are more than welcome to join in.

Essentials

Transportation

GETTING THERE

Scotland has five international airports: Glasgow, Edinburgh, Aberdeen, Inverness, and Glasgow Prestwick, which between them serve 150 destinations across the world, so the obvious way of getting here is by air. Depending on your departure airport, you may find there are more options flying into London, where there are lots of domestic flights departing to each of the airports above (apart from Glasgow Prestwick). There is also the option of getting the train from London to Scotland, either during daytime hours,

with several trains to each of the main cities each day, or overnight on the Caledonian Sleeper train.

From the United States and Canada

Several airlines fly direct to Scotland from North America. From New York (JFK) you can fly direct to Edinburgh with Virgin Atlantic (www.virginatlantic.com) and Delta (www.delta.com). Delta also has flights from JFK to Glasgow via Amsterdam. United Airlines (www.unitedairlines.co.uk) runs flights from New York/Newark to Edinburgh and Glasgow, from Chicago to Edinburgh, and from Washington DC to Edinburgh.

Virgin Atlantic (www.virginatlantic.com) has flights from Orlando to Glasgow in summer, and you can fly with American Airlines (www.americanairlines.co.uk) from Philadelphia to Glasgow, changing at London Heathrow.

From Canada, Air Canada (www.aircanada.com) flies from Toronto to Glasgow and Edinburgh (stopping in London Heathrow or France). Air Transat (www.airtransat.com) also flies from Toronto to Glasgow in summer and runs summer routes from Calgary, Montreal, and Vancouver to Glasgow. WestJet (www.westjet.com) has flights from Halifax to Glasgow at often absurdly low prices.

Flight time from the east coast of the United States is around eight hours. From Toronto, flight time is around nine hours, more with stopovers.

Some direct flight routes are just seasonal, and you will certainly find more options between May and October, although prices out of season (late October, November, and January-April) can be a lot cheaper if you book in advance.

From London, the United Kingdom, and Ireland

BY AIR

There's no shortage of flights between London and Edinburgh, with several flights every day from each of the main London airports (Gatwick, Heathrow, and Stansted). There are also regular flights to Inverness from Heathrow, Gatwick, and Luton.

Though the main budget airlines of easyJet (www.easyjet.com) and Ryanair (www.ryanair.com) don't offer much in the way of comfort, with an average flight time of just under 1.5 hours, it's probably not necessary to go much fancier, and if you book in advance and are happy to travel midweek, you can usually get return flights for around £50-100. For a tad more comfort, British Airways (www.britishairways.com) is a bit better. Flights from London to Scotland can usually be purchased for around £100-150.

Traveling between Ireland and Scotland is very easy. From Northern Ireland, there are regular flights from Belfast to Glasgow with easyJet, and there are direct flights to the city from both the City of Derry (50 minutes) and Donegal (1 hour) with Loganair (www.loganair.co.uk).

Edinburgh can also be reached direct from Belfast International with easyJet. Dublin has direct flights to Edinburgh with Irish airline Aer Lingus (www.aerlingus.com; 1 hour 5 minutes), a much better option than Ryanair. From Cork, in the south of Ireland, Aer Lingus flights take just over an hour and a half.

BY CAR

From London and other parts of the United Kingdom, it is perfectly possible to drive to Scotland as long as you are prepared for a fair bit of motorway driving. From London, it's an 8-hour journey up to Glasgow without stops, so you should allow 9-10 hours with one decent stop halfway.

Previous: Life in the slow lane on Harris.

Coronavirus in Scotland

At the time of writing in autumn 2021, most of the COVID restrictions in Scotland had been lifted, the result of a successful vaccination program. However, the country, particularly the tourism and hospitality industries, were still feeling the effects of the pandemic, with the loss of a large part of peak season devastating to some.

In terms of the rules, social distancing is no longer required (except in health care settings), but as of October 1, 2021, anyone over the age of 18 needs to show evidence of having had two vaccinations if they wish to go to large events or nightclubs. Plans for a proposed "vaccine passport" were thrown out in September.

If you are traveling from a non-red list country (check your country's status here: www.gov. scot/publications/coronavirus-covid-19-international-travel-quarantine/pages/red-amber-and-green-list-countries) and are fully vaccinated, then you will need to fill in a passenger locator form (PLF) and take a COVID-19 PCR test within two days of arrival. If you are not vaccinated, you will need to quarantine for 10 days. In addition to taking a COVID-19 PCR test before your second day in Scotland, you'll also need to take one on day eight.

While the country adapts to post-pandemic living, face masks are still mandatory in many public indoor places for anyone over the age of 12 (unless they are exempt for some reason). In restaurants and bars, the expectation is that you still wear them while walking around, though obviously they can be removed while eating and drinking. It's likely that this restriction will gradually be lifted, too. Customers are expected to comply with test and trace schemes by supplying contact details for restaurants and bars.

Now more than ever, Moon encourages its readers to be courteous and ethical in their travel. We ask travelers to be respectful to residents, and mindful of the evolving situation in their chosen destination when planning their trip.

BEFORE YOU GO

- Check that your country of departure is on Scotland's **non-red list;** If it's on the red list, you cannot travel.

- Make sure to bring **proof of vaccination** and a booking reference for your **negative PCR test.**

- Check local websites (listed below) for **local restrictions** and the **overall health status** of the destination and your point of origin. If you're traveling to or from an area that is currently a COVID-19 hot spot, you may want to reconsider your trip.

The best route leaves London on the M40, which you stay on for just under 18 miles before joining the M6, which will take you all the way over the Scottish border (you won't even notice you're crossing it), where you pick up the A74 all the way into Glasgow.

BY TRAIN

Probably the most enjoyable way to travel between London and Scotland is by train; ticket prices can be compared through Trainline (www.thetrainline.com), which includes services by all operators.

The main operator for Glasgow is Avanti West Coast (www.avantiwestcoast. co.uk), which leaves from London Euston to Glasgow Central and takes 4.5 hours. There are several trains a day, and seats (always reserve one when you book a ticket) are fairly comfortable. There is a buffet cart on board for refreshments (not included in the price) and wifi (though this can be sketchy). Tickets can be booked up to three months in advance and can cost as little as £30 each way, but be warned: last-minute ticket prices rocket to as much £125 each way. It's also worth checking out first-class tickets because often these are not much more than

- If you plan to fly, check with your airline and the destination's health authority for updated **travel requirements.** Some airlines may be taking more steps than others to help you travel safely. Also be aware that available flights may be less frequent, with increased cancellations.

- **Check the websites** of any museums and other venues you wish to patronize to confirm that they're open, whether their hours have been adjusted, and to learn about any specific visitation requirements, such as mandatory reservations or limited occupancy. Even outdoor locations sometimes have restrictions.

- Pack **hand sanitizer,** a **thermometer,** and plenty of **face masks.** When traveling within the country, consider packing snacks, bottled water, and anything else you might need, to limit the number of stops along your route, and to be prepared for possible closures and reduced services.

- **Assess the risk** of entering crowded spaces, joining tours, and taking public transit.

- **Expect general disruptions.** Events may be postponed or canceled, and some tours and venues may require reservations, enforce limits on the number of guests, be operating during different hours from the ones listed, or be closed entirely.

RESOURCES

In addition to the local resources listed below, be sure to check the websites of local tourism groups for up-to-date information on openings and closures, as well as travel advice.

- **NHS COVID-19 App:** covid19.nhs.uk

- **NHS Inform – COVID-19:** www.nhsinform.scot/illnesses-and-conditions/infections-and-poisoning/coronavirus-covid-19

- **Scottish Government COVID data:** www.gov.scot/publications/coronavirus-covid-19-daily-data-for-scotland

- **VisitScotland** has useful advice for travelers on the current situation: www.visitscotland.com/travel/

standard class but come with a free meal and drinks.

Trains to Edinburgh set off from London King's Cross with London North Eastern Railway (www.lner.co.uk), and prices, times, and amenities are similar.

For a little more adventure (and to save on a night's accommodation), book a cabin on the Caledonian Sleeper (www.sleeper.scot) train that sets off from London Euston at night, arriving into Scotland in the morning. You can choose to disembark in Edinburgh, Glasgow, Aberdeen, Inverness, or Fort William. Prices may seem high at first (from around £130 each

way), but when you consider you'll be saving on a hotel, it often works out.

From Europe
BY AIR

There are excellent year-round flights from most major European cities, including Paris, Brussels, Berlin, and Rome, into both Glasgow and Edinburgh. In addition, you can fly to Inverness from Amsterdam, Bergen, or Zurich, among others. The main European hubs for flight connections to Scotland are London Heathrow, Paris Charles de Gaulle, Amsterdam Schiphol, Frankfurt am Main,

Iceland's Reykjavik-Keflavik Airport, and Madrid Barajas.

BY CAR

While it is possible to drive to Scotland from Europe, it is a bit of a slog. From Brussels, for instance, it is just over a two-hour drive to reach the Euro Tunnel, which in itself is easy and takes just an hour to cross the English Channel. Once in England, it's a short drive through Kent before skirting London to the east and heading up to Scotland via the M20 and then A1. Though this drive is straightforward enough, it's an 11-hour journey without stops, so you should definitely consider overnighting somewhere en route, such as York.

BY TRAIN

Much of Europe is well facilitated by trains, making rail travel a real possibility. From Brussels, it's just a two-hour rail journey on the Eurostar (www.eurostar.com) into London, where you could pick up a connection to Glasgow, Edinburgh, or Inverness. Tickets can be excellent value too, starting at around £50 for a single ticket from Brussels to London. Eurostar trains from Paris to London take 2.5 hours, and there is now a direct route from Amsterdam to London as well that takes just 3.75 hours.

From Australia, New Zealand, and South Africa

Generally, the best way to get to Scotland from Australasia is to fly via the Middle Eastern hubs. Flight time is around 22 hours, perhaps more depending on transfers. It's likely you'll also have to change in either London or at another European airport. However, Emirates (www.emirates.com) offers lots of routes, including a daily flight from Auckland to Edinburgh via Dubai, meaning there's no need for another changeover in London or Europe.

From Africa, the best way to reach Scotland is via one of the European or Middle Eastern hubs. British Airways has long-haul flights from Johannesburg to London Heathrow, where you can connect to Scotland.

GETTING AROUND
By Car

For maximum freedom and some of the best road journeys ever, you can't beat having your own car.

CAR HIRE

There are car hire companies at all major airports; it's best to go with a recognized name because, although other companies may offer what appear to be cheaper deals, by the time you add on insurance, it's likely you'll be out of pocket. While it used to be possible to leave car hire until you arrive—it was unlikely all the cars would ever be out on hire—I wouldn't risk it anymore. There have been reports of a shortage of hire cars as some rental firms didn't update their fleets, either because they weren't expecting such demand, or because they couldn't access finance. Booking early also ensures you get the better deals. If you want to get a good idea of prices, Travel Supermarket (www.travelsupermarket.com) is pretty trustworthy, and companies such as Avis (www.avis.co.uk) and Europcar (www.europcar.co.uk) are fairly reliable. Arnold Clark (www.arnoldclark.com), a Scottish car hire firm with bases at all the main airports/cities, offers very personable service.

A lot of cars are manual transmission, but you can request an automatic, which tends to be more expensive. While car hire itself costs £10-30, you may need to pay extra for insurance if your credit card doesn't include this (from around £10 a day). You'll need to pay extra for GPS and child safety seats if you need them. You will need to have your driver's license with you, as well as a credit card in the main driver's name with a decent credit limit, which will be taken as a deposit. You should also be prepared to show your passport.

RULES OF THE ROAD

In Scotland (and the rest of the United Kingdom) you need to drive on the left-hand side of the road. Make sure you adhere to speed limits because speed cameras lurk in unsuspected places. Usually, there will be a sign stating the speed limit in miles per hour. In the absence of a sign, assume a speed limit of 30 mph in built-up areas and 70 mph on motorways. Thankfully there are no toll fees on Scottish roads and bridges.

Google Maps and the like are all well and good when they work, but it's not unusual to lose signal when driving Scotland's rural roads, so having a good old-fashioned paper map you can actually hold is essential. It never hurts to top up the tank when you see a filling station, even when you're not running too low. Outside the big towns and cities, it's not often certain where the next fuel station will be, and even if you find one, who's to say it will be open?

Once you enter rural Scotland or more remote areas, there's a good chance you will have to drive down single-track roads, meaning you'll have to pull over into passing places to allow other traffic to pass (sometimes this means even pulling over to let eager cars behind you overtake). If a car coming in the other direction on a single-track road flashes its lights, this means the driver is offering to pull in to let you pass. Always remember to say thank you.

By Air

Sometimes, if your time is limited, a quick domestic flight may be your best option, particularly to some of the more far flung areas, such as the Outer Hebrides or Northern Isles. Loganair (www.loganair.co.uk), Scotland's only airline, offers a good selection of domestic flights on small passenger jets, with staff who offer the most genuine of welcomes.

By Train

A relatively good train system in Scotland links the main towns and cities. Glasgow is by far the best-connected city in Scotland, with several trains a day to pretty much all main towns and cities—Perth, Stirling, Inverness, Dundee, Fort William, etc. Edinburgh is reasonably well-connected and is also less than an hour from Glasgow (about three trains an hour) if you do need to pick up a connection.

Train fares in Scotland are priced quite reasonably—it will cost in the region of £30 to travel from Edinburgh to Inverness (a journey time of 3 hours 30 minutes), while to travel between Edinburgh and Glasgow (50 minutes) costs around £13.50.

If you don't want to drive, or at least not drive long distances, then traveling by train is a good option, and you can enjoy the views as you go. ScotRail (www.scotrail.co.uk) has tickets and details on timetables and connections. You should always buy a ticket before you board a train, where possible.

By Ferry

Of course, if you want to visit the islands (except Skye where there is an option of a bridge), then you will need to use the ferries. Though there are a couple of smaller operators (mentioned in this book where necessary), the main ferry operator is Caledonian MacBrayne, or CalMac (www.calmac.co.uk), which transports cars and passengers between the mainland and isles.

Locals often use ferries like buses, to travel back and forth to the mainland for shopping and work from their island home, and the ferries are very well-run and punctual. On occasion ferries may have to be canceled due to rough weather, but this is more of an issue in winter, so if you fancy island hopping, you are probably safe if you stick to the spring and summer months.

By Bus

The main bus service for traveling between cities is Scottish Citylink (www.citylink.co.uk). Local bus services are usually served by Stagecoach (www.stagecoachbus.com). If in doubt about a journey, check Traveline (www.traveline.info), an excellent resource for planning your route from point A to point B via public transport.

Though bus service can be a bargain, traveling by train is often preferable when possible—you're less at the mercy of traffic, so they tend to be quicker. That said, buses are useful for reaching smaller towns and villages, and can be a lifeline if you don't have a car.

Visas and Officialdom

You should always check the U.K. and Foreign and Commonwealth Office's website (www.gov.uk/government/organisations/uk-visas-and-immigration) before you book travel for the latest advice about entry and visa requirements into the United Kingdom.

UNITED STATES AND CANADA

At present, travelers from the United States and Canada do not need a visa to visit Scotland (or indeed any part of the United Kingdom) if they are visiting for six months or less. If you are planning to stay for more than six months, then you will need an entry clearance certificate, obtained from the British embassy in your home nation before you travel.

The American consulate is located in Edinburgh (3 Regent Terrace; tel. 01315 568 315; edinburgh-info@state.gov). There is no Canadian consulate in Scotland, so all enquiries should go through the High Commission of Canada in London (Canada House, Trafalgar Square; tel. 02070 046 000, ldn@international.gc.ca).

EUROPEAN UNION/ SCHENGEN

Now that the UK has effectively divorced from the European Union (EU), freedom of movement in terms of people coming here to work or live is no longer as easy as it once was, and it remains to be seen how much things will change over the coming years in terms of holidays, too. At present, residents of EU countries, non-EU member states of the European Economic Area (EEA; Norway, Liechtenstein, and Iceland), and Switzerland are all free to enter the United Kingdom with no visa for short trips and holidays. Members of the Overseas Countries and Territories (OCT) are also exempt from needing a visa to enter the United Kingdom.

Consulates for several European countries can be found in Edinburgh, including the French Consulate (11 Randolph Crescent; tel. 0131 225 7954; contact.edimbourg-fslt@diplomatie.gouv.fr), the Consulate General of the Federal Republic of Germany and Honorary Consulates of Germany (16 Eglinton Crescent; tel. 01313 372 323; info@edin.auswaertiges-amt.de), the Netherlands Consulate (Baird House, 4 Lower Gilmore Bank; tel. 07731 553 120; hon.consul@netherlands-consulate.co.uk), and the Spanish Consulate (63 North Castle Street, Edinburgh; tel. 01312 201 843; cog.edimburgo@maec.es).

AUSTRALIA AND NEW ZEALAND

Visitors from Australia and New Zealand also do not need a visa to visit Scotland for six months or less. For stays longer than six months, you will need an entry clearance certificate, obtained from the British embassy before you travel.

The Consulate of New Zealand is located in Edinburgh (c/o Blackadders, 5 Rutland Square; tel. 01312 228 109; nzconsulscotland@gmail.com), but as of 2014 there is no longer an Australian Consulate in Scotland. All enquiries must go through the Australia High Commission in London (Strand, London; tel. 02073 794 334).

SOUTH AFRICA

Travelers from South Africa will need a Standard Visitor visa (www.gov.uk/standard-visitor-visa) to enter the United Kingdom, whether you are coming for a holiday, to visit friends and family, or for business. The standard cost for this visa is £95 and will normally allow you to stay for up to six months. You can apply up to three months before you travel and will normally get a decision within three weeks of applying. There is no South African consulate in Scotland. All enquiries should go through the High Commission of the Republic of South Africa in London (South Africa House, Trafalgar Square; tel. 02074 517 299).

CUSTOMS

Most goods in Britain (except for food and books) are subject to Value Added Tax (VAT), which is not always obvious but included in the advertised price. Visitors from non-EU countries can claim a lot of this money back (though not on hotel bills unfortunately) before they leave the United Kingdom. To benefit from this, you should get a VAT 407 form from the vendor at the point of sale (a lot of bigger retailers geared toward overseas travelers will have these) and then show this and your receipt to Customs before you leave. For more information, see www.gov.uk/tax-on-shopping/taxfree-shopping.

Festivals and Events

Exciting cultural events take place across Scotland throughout the year, though some months tend to have more than others. Here are some of the best.

AUGUST IN EDINBURGH

August is the busy time for festivals in Edinburgh (www.edinburghfestivalcity.com), when five artistic and cultural festivals converge to create one almost nonstop extravaganza of music, comedy, dance, art, and literature. The biggest of the five are the Edinburgh International Festival and the Edinburgh Fringe Festival, and the others running at the same time are the Edinburgh Military Tattoo, the Edinburgh Art Festival, and the Edinburgh International Book Festival.

NEW YEAR'S FESTIVALS AND EVENTS

Hogmanay (www.edinburghshogmanay.com) is a big deal in Scotland, but it doesn't have the monopoly on New Year's celebrations. Lots of exciting events ring in the New Year, including the Red Hot Highland Fling in Inverness (www.invernessfestivals.com).

Even if you are not staying in a city on New Year's Eve, there is a good chance you will be brought into the Scottish fold with the tradition of First Footing. This tradition dictates that the "first-footing" (i.e., first person to take a step) across the threshold of a house in the new year should come bearing presents in the shape of a wee dram, a lump of coal, and a coin.

OTHER FESTIVALS
CELTIC CONNECTIONS

Glasgow; www.celticconnections.com; Jan.-Feb.
An annual music festival of Gaelic and Celtic music held across various venues in Glasgow.

SPIRIT OF SPEYSIDE WHISKY FESTIVAL

Speyside; www.spiritofspeyside.com; May
At the largest whisky festival in the world, visitors can expect lots of tastings and immersive events.

ST. MAGNUS INTERNATIONAL FESTIVAL

Orkney; www.stmagnusfestival.com; June
In the long days of summer on the Northern

Isles, this festival brings together a mix of music, theater, dance, storytelling, and literature to celebrate the rich heritage of the region.

Braemar; www.braemargathering.org; September

Possibly the first organized Highland Games, this annual event has had the royal seal of approval since Queen Victoria visited in the 19th century.

Recreation

HIKING AND TREKKING

There are infinite possibilities for hiking in Scotland, whether you want a gentle amble through bucolic landscape, or to bag your first Munro. If you are going it alone, then Walk Highlands (www.walkhighlands.co.uk) is an essential resource of routes and advice, with trails reviewed by people who have actually completed them.

However, hiking in Scotland—especially in the Highlands—is not to be taken lightly, and each year many people get into trouble because they are not experienced navigators. Even if you have printed off a trail description and are armed with an Ordnance Survey (www.ordnancesurvey.co.uk) or a Harveys map (www.harveymaps.co.uk), it is your responsibility to ensure you plan ahead, are realistic about your (and your group's) abilities, come equipped with a compass, are dressed in the appropriate clothing (hiking boots, wet-weather gear, etc.), and have taken safety measures. Together with Mountaineering Scotland (www.mountaineering.scot), Walk Highlands (www.walkhighlands.co.uk/safety) has issued some essential safety advice, which I recommend familiarizing yourself with before embarking on any hillwalking or climbing in Scotland.

If all this sounds a bit serious, then book a guide to escort you on your expedition.

CYCLING

The real challenge for cyclists in Scotland, of course, is the epic Lands' End to John o' Groats 874-mile mission—from the southernmost to northernmost points in the mainland U.K. Others like to cycle the North Coast 500. For the rest of us, there are infinite cycle trails in the national parks (Loch Lomond and the Trossachs National Park, and The Cairngorms) and, in many places, some really good cycle tours as a way to both get around and appreciate your surroundings. Edinburgh and Glasgow are both surprisingly good places to cycle, and so are the relatively flat islands of the Inner and Outer Hebrides, County Fife, and Moray Speyside.

GOLF

Though St. Andrews in Fife is undoubtedly the home of golf in Scotland, there are prestigious courses all over, many of them ancient in origin; in fact, Scotland has over 400 golf courses.

The Scots are widely celebrated for having introduced the world to the game of golf—it has been played here since at least the start of the 15th century. Early courses were often just simple tracks overgrown with bushes and heather, but today they are generally a lot smarter. Golf only really became popular outside Scotland from the 19th century onward, when a boom for tourism to Scotland began. Suddenly, it became fashionable to partake in traditional Scottish pastimes.

Today, lots of tour companies offer trips to see some of the more famous and celebrated of Scotland's golf courses. For example, Golf Scotland (www.golfscotland.com) organizes transfers and trips to the famous Old Links course in St. Andrews.

CAMPING

Wild camping is possible pretty much all over Scotland, thanks to the Outdoor Access Code, which in essence allows you to camp on most parts of unenclosed land, but you should adhere to the "leave-no-trace" motto, which means taking your rubbish with you and removing all signs of campfires. There are a few exceptions—parts of Loch Lomond and the Trossachs National Park are subject to bylaws in the summer months to avoid overcrowding—and common sense should prevail (so don't camp right by someone's house or block someone else's view unless you want a hostile reception).

If going wild is a bit too much for you, Scotland has some excellent campsites—some with luxury bell tents and on-site activities, and others that are more stripped back but still have toilets and showers. Almost all of them are set in beautiful locations. Cool Camping (coolcamping.com/campsites/uk/scotland) is a useful resource for finding the perfect campsite.

Food and Drink

Scotland is quite rightly famed for its national dishes, such as haggis (a dish of spiced sheep's heart, liver, and lungs, which tastes a lot nicer than it sounds) served with neeps (swede, or rutabaga) and tatties (potatoes). However, over the last decade Scottish cuisine has become somewhat more refined. Restaurants in Scotland have long been responding to an increased interest in food provenance, and Local fare now takes pride of place on menus, from Aberdeen Angus beef to shellfish still salty from the sea, to Stornoway black pudding and Arbroath smokies (a type of smoked haddock). Vegans and vegetarians are excellently catered for in major cities, particularly in Glasgow, which is shedding its reputation for serving up deep-fried Mars bars and actually has a thriving and hugely exciting vegan food scene.

Other dishes you should look for on menus are Cullen skink, a deliciously creamy fish stew, and Cranachan, a dessert made of oats, cream, whisky, and raspberries.

SEAFOOD

With miles and miles of coastline, it is fitting that seafood now features heavily on menus in Scotland, particularly along the coast and on the islands. For a long time, although the seas around Scotland were rich with fish and shellfish, locals could barely get a look before the day's catch was ferried off elsewhere, a part of Scotland's huge export business. Now, finally, locals (and visitors) are able to taste it too, and it's not uncommon to see a fairly modest seafood shed (such as the Seaside Shack in Ullapool or Oban's Seafood Hut) by a port, where you can buy really tasty seafood for far less than you'd pay in the restaurants.

WHISKY AND GIN

Whisky is to Scotland what tea is to England. Whisky production takes place across five main regions: Campbeltown, the Highlands, Islay, the Lowlands, and Speyside. Each region brings its own flavors to the whisky. On the Isle of Islay, for instance, where whisky making goes back centuries, distilleries draw on heavily peated malt.

However, whisky isn't the only drink produced here—70 percent of the gin produced in the United Kingdom is made in Scotland, including James Bond's favorite tipple, Gordon's. And as gin is the fastest growing spirit in Scotland, new distilleries are popping up all the time. It's also been a badly kept secret for a few years now that rum will be the next big thing in Scotland, with a few distilleries quietly opening throughout the country.

DINING OUT

There are restaurants and cafés in all big towns and cities, and as expected the larger the place the more variety there tends to be. In Glasgow and Edinburgh, you can find a wide range of international cuisines alongside modern Scottish restaurants, which at the higher end of the scale often borrow from French cooking techniques. At the cheaper end, there are more casual coffee shops, cafés, and bistros, as well as a fair few street food-style places popping up, and lots of good gastro pubs.

Generally speaking, eating out in Scotland is an informal, inclusive affair. You'll be just as welcome in most places in jeans and a t-shirt as you would a shirt and tie. If you're planning to eat in a posh hotel restaurant, or a fine dining or Michelin-starred restaurant though, then you probably will feel more comfortable looking a bit smarter. Many pubs serve food all day, and cafés during daytime opening hours, though some pubs will have select food serving times (the kitchen usually closes an hour or two before closing). In restaurants, there are often two seatings—a lunchtime one, which does vary, but is usually for 1-2 hours between 12pm and 3pm, and dinner service, which usually starts after 6pm; 7pm-9pm is the busy period, and few restaurants accept bookings after 9pm.

Many restaurants add a service charge onto the bill (about 12.5 percent is standard) but this is worth checking. If service is not included, it's customary to add around 12.5-15 percent in tips, and it's helpful if this is in cash as then it's more likely to go directly into the pockets of waitstaff at the end of their shift. Unless you've experienced exceptionally bad service or under-par food, you shouldn't withhold a tip. Unlike in the US, there's no need to tip if you're just having drinks, though if you're having table service for a whole evening then you might like to leave something before you go.

PICNIC SUPPLIES AND GROCERIES

Food provenance—homegrown fruit and veg, locally reared meat, and fresh seafood—is big news in Scotland at the moment, with lots of very good artisan food producers, from cheesemakers to bakers to smokeries. Because of the pandemic, a lot of food and drink producers have pivoted their businesses since 2020, so it's not uncommon to hear of deliveries along the more organic, independent line, and if you are staying in a rural location, there will usually be a good farm shop or farmer's market nearby. When booking into a campsite or self-catering property, ask the owner where to buy good local food and they'll usually have some excellent suggestions.

Accommodations

A wide range of accommodations is available throughout Scotland, from high-end hotels to quaint B&Bs and cozy self-catering properties. This being a land of big open spaces, there are also plenty of places making the most of the incredible scenery and offering more rustic and basic places to stay, from bothies for the brave (simple shelters located in remote locations that offer a "camping with walls" experience) to cozier camping pods for those who still need a few home comforts, such as a kettle and heating.

History lovers will revel at the chance to stay in a bona fide castle or Victorian shooting lodge, while those who long for comforts of a more traditional kind will be happy in an old crofter's house, as long as there is a real fire to warm up by.

Most hotels and B&Bs are happy for you to stay for just one night (although this may vary on weekends, particularly in cities), while a lot of self-catering cottages have a minimum weeklong stay in spring and summer and shorter stays of three nights or more out of season.

Breakfast is normally included unless stated otherwise (except in camping pods and self-catering places), and for the most part you can book your stay with a credit card with no funds taken until you leave (again not generally the case with self-catering).

Conduct and Customs

For the most part, Scottish people are very friendly and welcoming and keen to show off their homeland; however, there are some things you should be aware of. First, though it is officially part of the United Kingdom, a large percentage of Scottish people consider themselves a part of an independent nation, and will take umbrage at being called British. Always err on the side of caution and be careful to make a distinction between the English and Scottish—the recent Scottish referendum over whether it should officially separate from the rest of the United Kingdom was a close-run thing and is still very raw for many. In general, politics can be quite a divisive subject, particularly if the conversation heads into the murky waters of Brexit, so best steer clear.

Similarly, sport can bring out the passionate side of even the meekest character.

Manners are important. Saying please and thank you and looking someone in the eye when you talk to them will take you a long way, whether it's someone you've stopped for directions or the taxi driver taking you back to your hotel.

Many Scottish superstitions center on traditional professions. Fishermen, for instance, observe many omens to keep them safe at sea. The words *rabbit, pig,* and *salmon* are deemed bad luck (perhaps because they were powerful symbols of Celtic gods), and many a sailor has turned around and headed back home after seeing a minister or even a woman on the way to their boat.

Health and Safety

As with all major cities, Glasgow and Edinburgh aren't without their problems. While Edinburgh particularly is relatively safe, you would do well to steer clear of the Meadows, Grassmarket, Cowgate, Tollcross, and Lothian Road after dark. Similarly, you'll need to keep your wits about you in Glasgow late at night, particularly around Sauchiehall Street when all the pubs and clubs kick out. The city does also have a bit of a drug problem, and neds (Scottish slang for gangs of men often looking for trouble) should be avoided. Social problems are less common in more rural areas where you will feel pretty safe; you'll be taken aback by how warmly local communities welcome you.

VACCINATIONS

Prior to the pandemic, you did not need any vaccinations to visit the United Kingdom. Now, it's not mandatory to be vaccinated against COVID-19, but if you're not, you will need to quarantine for at least 10 days on arrival (more if you test positive) and you may not be able to attend large indoor events.

HEALTH CARE

At present all EU citizens are also entitled to free health care at National Health Service (NHS) hospitals and clinics on production of a European Health Insurance Card (EHIC). In addition, there are reciprocal arrangements with residents of Australia and New Zealand.

However, visitors from the United States, Canada, and South Africa, as well as lots of other non-EEA countries, do need to ensure they have travel insurance and/or health care to cover them for their visit. If you are coming into Scotland from overseas and have a medical emergency or accident and need to be treated by an accident and emergency department, you will not be liable for the initial urgent treatment, but it's possible that any further care, such as the admittance to hospital, would incur a charge; therefore it's important to take out insurance before you travel.

Healthcare in the UK is provided by the National Health Service (NHS), which enables residents to access healthcare for free. Certain NHS care is free to overseas holidaymakers, including emergency care in either a hospital or GP (General Practitioner's) surgery, plus emergency transport to get there, sexual health services, and treatments for some infectious diseases, which are in the best interests of public health.

Residents from the European Economic Area (EEA) are also eligible for additional free treatments, provided they are traveling with an up-to-date European Health Insurance Card (EHIC).

If you have a healthcare concern while in Scotland, your first step should be to visit a pharmacy (providing you don't suspect it is infectious or contagious). If you can't get to a pharmacy, you can call NHS24 on 111, and someone will assess your symptoms and advise whether you need to escalate it to an emergency and ring 999 or try to get an appointment at a GP (general practitioner) at a local surgery.

In addition, if you run out of any medicines you regularly take while you are here, you should be able to make an emergency appointment with a GP. You can phone the NHS inform Helpline on 0800 22 44 88 or go to www.nhs24.scot to find the nearest GP surgery.

Practical Details

WHAT TO PACK

There's a hackneyed phrase in Scotland: there's no such thing as bad weather, just the wrong clothes. With weather unpredictable to say the least, you need to be ready, whatever the weather. Unfortunately, this means packing lots. If you're visiting from April to September, you'll need **jumpers (sweaters)** and **coats** to keep you warm but also **shorts** and **t-shirts** (the sun does come out occasionally here, and you'll want to be prepared when it does). If coming in winter, a good range of **thermals, jeans, trousers,** and **layers** should serve you well. If you are planning to do any reasonably rough walking, you will need a good pair of **hiking boots,** some kind of **insect repellent** for the dreaded midges—locals swear by Avon Skin So Soft for keeping them at bay—and long sleeves to minimize the biting when they are at their hungriest (summer evenings).

You'll also want a good **camera** to capture the incredible sights, possibly some **binoculars** if you want to be able to identify some of the wildlife you do spot, and of course some **swimwear** for all that wild swimming.

MONEY

As in the rest of the United Kingdom, the currency is the British pound sterling. You may notice a slight difference in some of the notes north of the border to those found in England; the Bank of Scotland prints its own notes, which feature prominent Scotsmen and the occasional Scotswoman. Although they look different from English notes, they are still legal tender in the whole of the United Kingdom, though you may have a problem trying to convince a bus driver or local shopkeeper in England of that.

As of late 2021, £1 was worth USD$1.36, €1.18, CAD$1.71, AUD$1.86, NZD$1.96, or R 20.28, but with constant fluctuations these rates change all the time. For the most up-to-date **exchange rates,** go to www.xe.com.

The best exchange rates can be found in banks, and most reasonably sized towns will have one (though not many villages—indeed some more remote places just have a mobile bank that visits once a week that aren't really geared up for currency exchange). You'll need to visit during business hours (usually 9am-4pm Mon.-Fri., with occasional Sat. morning openings in the cities). Post offices, which operate similar business hours to banks, are another option, and Marks & Spencer also does decent rates of exchange inside its stores. If you need to get cash outside normal business hours, you can visit a bureau de change, but these do give the worst rates (even if they make a big fuss about the fact you won't be charged to change your money).

Alternatively, you can take money out of an ATM (cash machine) connected to one of the main high-street banks (Royal Bank of Scotland, Lloyds, etc.) using a debit card that doesn't charge an overseas transaction fee (check with your home bank). ATMs can be found all over Glasgow and Edinburgh.

Credit Cards and ATMs

Though you can pretty much pay for anything with a credit or debit card in Glasgow and Edinburgh, in more remote parts of Scotland (along the west coast and parts of Skye) where Internet access is sketchy to say the least, cash is king, so it is always a good idea to carry just enough on you for a day or two. ATMs are everywhere in the cities, and there's one in most towns, but in some little villages locals rely on the little post office for money, which is only possible if you have a U.K. bank card.

VISA and Mastercard are the most readily accepted credit cards in Scotland. Some smaller enterprises don't accept American Express, although this is improving, and you

may be charged a small fee (around 50p) if you use your card to make small purchases (under £10), particularly in smaller establishments.

Budgeting

Scotland is not a particularly cheap place to visit and realistically you will have to budget at least £100 per day, unless you are planning to stay in hostels throughout your stay and cook some of your own meals. A budget of £100-£150 per day would leave some room for booking tours and paying fees into attractions, live gigs, etc.

- Small coffee: £2.40
- Bottle of water: £1.50
- Sandwich: £5.50
- Local bus/train ticket: £1.80
- Museums: free
- Pint of beer: £4
- Dinner: £25
- Hotel room: £80-100

COMMUNICATIONS
Phones and Cell Phones

Before you leave home, make sure your mobile phone is compatible with the United Kingdom's GSM technology, as otherwise you may not be able to use a lot of your phone's functions. In Glasgow, Edinburgh, Inverness, and most big towns you are likely to have good phone reception. However, in large parts of the Highlands it is virtually nonexistent, so if you are traveling around, you need to get out of the habit of relying on your phone for navigation or as a point of contact. If someone might need to get hold of you, forward them the number of your accommodation.

Internet Access

Wireless Internet, 3G, and 4G are all good in the cities, less so in smaller towns, and pretty terrible on the islands. Get into the habit of checking email when you are somewhere built up (even if this means planning ahead a little), and when you're out of range, simply enjoy the fact that you are no longer ruled by that tiny machine in your pocket.

Shipping and Postal Service

You may be surprised to learn that even the tiniest of villages tends to have a post office, albeit one that's just an adjunct to a local shop. You can normally find somewhere to get stamps to send postcards home, but for anything a bit more involved (wiring money, for example) you might have to do a little bit of research or head to a larger town.

While you are allowed to bring a liter of alcohol home with you in your checked luggage, you may prefer to take advantage of some of the shipping packages offered by whisky vendors, such as Royal Mile Whiskies (www.royalmilewhiskies.com), which can arrange for up to six standard 70 cl (23.7 oz) bottles of whisky to be sent to your home in one shipment (this is a legal limitation and more shipments can be arranged). At £49 for the shipment of one bottle, or £164 for seven, it's not cheap, but it can save you a lot of hassle when on holiday. Alternatively, you could wait until you get home—the United States has a good market of single malts and blended Scotch at the moment. In addition, many high-end kilt and tartan retailers also ship around the world.

OPENING HOURS

Normal shop opening hours are 9am-5pm Monday to Saturday, with a little variation either end. In cities, such as Glasgow and Edinburgh, you can expect most shops to be open around 10am-4pm at least, on Sundays too, but in more remote areas Sunday closing is common. Indeed, in the Western Isles where the Free Church of Scotland has quite a strong hold, it was virtually forbidden for shops to open (or for people to do any work at all) on Sunday until recently.

Thursday is often late-night shopping in cities, particularly when it comes to shopping malls and big department stores, and shops will often stay open until 8pm. Large supermarkets, such as Sainsbury's and Tesco, often stay open as late as 10pm, which is useful if you are arriving late and need to stock up for a cottage or house.

Traditionally, pubs open from 11am to 11pm Monday to Saturday, and from 12pm to 10:30pm on Sunday; however, a relaxing of licensing laws back in 2005 means that pubs can apply for an extension to these hours, and most pubs will stay open until at least 12am (or 1am on Friday and Saturday) as long as there are enough customers.

Public Holidays

Each year in Scotland a set number of days is put aside for public holidays, when lots of businesses will close (although in tourism hot spots many will still stay open), and hotels and restaurants may become busier and require a bit more forward planning. So raucous are Hogmanay celebrations across Scotland that both New Year's Day and January 2 are deemed public holidays each year. If a public holiday (such as St. Andrew's Day, which is officially November 30) falls on a weekend, it is normally substituted for a weekday, usually the following Monday. The Scottish public holidays for 2022 are below. (If you're traveling in a different year, you will want to verify dates for that year.)

- **April 15:** Good Friday
- **April 17:** Easter Sunday
- **May 2:** Early May Bank Holiday
- **June 2:** Spring Bank Holiday
- **August 29:** Summer Bank Holiday
- **November 30:** St. Andrew's Day
- **December 25:** Christmas Day
- **December 26:** Boxing Day
- **January 1:** New Year's Day
- **January 2:** Day after New Year's

WEIGHTS AND MEASURES

The United Kingdom uses metric measurements (grams, kilograms, milliliters, or liters) on all goods sold here, with a few exceptions.

Beer and cider from the pump are still sold in pints or half-pint measures, milk in glass bottles normally comes in pints, and precious metals are measured by troy ounce.

Time Zone

Scotland is on Greenwich Mean Time, which makes it Eastern Time + 5 and Pacific Standard Time +8. It does also have Daylight Savings (British Summer Time) from March to October, when it springs forward one hour ahead of GMT.

Electricity

Plug sockets in Scotland and the rest of the U.K. come with three pins, so you will need to bring a plug adapter G to plug in your electronic devices over here. Standard voltage is 230V, frequency 50 Hz. You should be able to pick up a plug adapter at the airport or an electrics shop/supermarket when you get here if you forget to bring one.

TOURIST INFORMATION
Tourist Offices

Throughout Scotland, **VisitScotland** (www. visitscotland.org) operates satellite tourist offices known as **iCentres** that are open year-round. You won't find an iCentre in every town or village, but there is usually one not far from major attractions and it's a good place to book tours, find local restaurant and hotel recommendations, and even buy public transport tickets if you are not confident booking them online.

The overriding tourist board for the whole of the United Kingdom is **VisitBritain** (www. visitbritain.com), but for more specific information on Scotland, **VisitScotland** is the place to go.

Maps

Ordnance Survey (OS) maps (www.ordnancesurvey.co.uk) are the most exhaustive and useful for hikes and long walks and are absolutely essential if you plan to attempt any of the Munros. **Harveys Maps** (www.harveymaps.co.uk) are also very useful, and some find them a lot clearer than the OS ones. Both sets of maps can be picked up from a good bookshop or a well-stocked outdoors shop, as well as purchased online before you travel.

Traveler Advice

ACCESS FOR TRAVELERS WITH DISABILITIES

While big attractions such as Edinburgh Castle and the Palace of Holyroodhouse are well adapted for disabled visitors, because of the nature of some of the sites in Scotland, not all of them are suitable for people with mobility issues, and Scotland does so far seem a bit slow on the uptake in terms of making places more accessible.

Tours are a good option for people with limited mobility, and obviously some are better than others. Equal Adventure Developments (www.equaladventure.org), based in Aviemore, is one organization committed to ensuring disabled travelers don't miss out on the sense of adventure in Scotland and can arrange outdoor activities and adventure sports. In Edinburgh, local guide Margot McMurdo offers tours that cater to disabled travelers (www.aboutscotland.com/tour/guide/access.html).

Wheelchair users and blind or partially sighted travelers, you are eligible for a big discount on trains with the Disabled Persons Railcard (www.disabledpersons-railcard.co.uk), for you and a friend. In theory, all trains should have wheelchair assistance, but in practice this isn't always the case, especially in quieter stations that are not always manned (particularly out of high season).

Uneven ground around many ruins and cleared or abandoned villages have often been left as they were, and many of the walks and hikes are unsuitable for wheelchairs.

Most hotels and places to stay will try to have accessible rooms, and, where this is not possible, proprietors normally make it clear on their website. However, it is advisable to ring and check if you are at all unsure.

TRAVELING WITH CHILDREN

Children love the wide-open spaces and freedom that being in Scotland affords. Wildlife is abundant, in the skies, seas, grasses, and moors, much to their delight. Simply going for a woodland walk can be a huge adventure, searching for trails or faeries and obviously looking out for a certain mysterious monster along the shores of Loch Ness.

Most restaurants and pubs have tapped into family tourism and usually offer a kid's menu, though it can be a bit heavy on the nuggets and burgers. If you're not eating in a pub, it's common practice to make sure any kids are taken home by 7pm, but if you're dining in, it's not normally an issue. Children under three often go free into attractions, travel on buses and trains is free for children under five, and you are rarely if ever asked to prove it. If your children are over five, ScotRail offers a Kids Go Free Ticket that allows an adult to travel with two kids aged 5-15 for just the price of an adult fare.

WOMEN TRAVELERS

Scotland is a relatively safe place to travel as a woman, with low crime rates in much of rural Scotland, but there are still some things you should do to stay safe.

Obviously, in larger cities such as Glasgow and Edinburgh where social issues are more prevalent (petty crime, drug abuse, heavy drinking), it pays to be a bit cautious. Don't leave your drink unattended and don't walk alone at night if you can avoid it, particularly in an area you are unfamiliar with or if you are intoxicated. Don't accept a minicab off the street. If you need to get a cab, book one from a trusted number (better still, ask the

pub or restaurant to ring one for you) or hail an official taxi, which is easy to identify by the "TAXI" light on top. In a just world, all women should be safe to go out at any time of day or night without fear of being attacked. If you are a victim of an assault, remember: it is never your fault and you should report it to the police as soon as you can.

SENIOR TRAVELERS

Travelers over the age of 60 can expect concessions at most paid-for attractions and leisure activities, such as the cinema. If a discount is not offered to you, it's always worth asking.

Be aware that many of Scotland's more historic sites can have uneven ground around them, and a lot of attractions, particularly ruined castles and historic properties, do involve a fair bit of walking, which requires a good level of fitness.

LGBTQ TRAVELERS

Scotland is a relatively open-minded country, accepting people as they come, so LGBTQ+ tourists can look forward to a warm welcome like everyone else. Some hotels and B&Bs are very vocal about being gay-friendly, but don't take that to mean that the less vocal establishments aren't—it's a rarity that you will come across any hostility.

February in Scotland is LGBTQ month, and there are lots of events taking place in major cities to celebrate. In June, Edinburgh's vibrant and embracing Pride Scotia takes place, while Glasgow's Pride takes place in July in Kelvingrove Park. Both cities have bubbling gay scenes, with cool bars and clubs attracting diverse crowds.

If you want to find out more about the lesbian, gay, bisexual, and transgender scene in Scotland, go to www.lgbt.scot.

TRAVELERS OF COLOR

With major universities and a booming tourism industry, Scotland is gradually becoming more multicultural. That said, it still falls way behind England in terms of geographical spread of different ethnicities. Most people of color live in busier, more built-up places such as Glasgow and Edinburgh, and the islands and more remote communities are still predominantly white. Scotland is generally very tolerant, and you should not expect to come across any overt racist behavior, though sadly, everyday racism and unconscious bias can still be encountered.

Jackie Kay, formerly Scotland's Makar (national poet), spoke out in 2020 in an interview with STV Player series *In Conversation with Bernard Ponsonby* on racism in Scotland and how it has changed since she was a child. "Even just the other day, this taxi driver said, 'Where are you from?' and I said Glasgow and he went, 'Oh, how do you explain that tan?'…

The image of a Scottish person isn't me, and I think that we need to try and change what we think of when we think of a Scottish person."

Similarly, Courtney Stoddart, a spoken word performer, who has had a meteoric rise to fame since first performing at a Black Lives Matter rally in 2019, said in an interview with online magazine *Bella Caledonia* that much of her early inspiration came from the trauma of growing up as a mixed-race woman in Scotland, where she was often subjected to both overt and covert racism.

If you do experience racism in Scotland, you can report it to the police, as it is a hate crime.

Resources

Glossary

Below is a list of terms, followed by their definitions, that are used frequently within Scotland and the pages of this guide.

ben or beinn: a mountain, as in Ben Nevis

blackhouse: a traditional thatched cottage found in the Highlands or islands, usually with thick drystone walls; there was normally a fire in the middle of the room with no chimney, so the smoke went through the roof and caused the soot to blacken the interior, hence the name.

bog: a freshwater wetland of soft ground, made up of decaying plant matter known as peat—a common fuel

bothy: a Scottish hut or basic dwelling, usually located in the mountains or more remote areas, where rural workers once sought refuge but which are now often used by hikers or campers looking for shelter

brae: a steep hillside or slope

broch: a circular stone tower, unique to Scotland, that dates from the Iron Age

burn: a watercourse, smaller than a river, that is often the main source of water for a village or settlement

cairn: found throughout Scotland, these mounds of stones are often used as a landmark (such as on the summit of a mountain); there are also lots of prehistoric chambered cairns, believed to have once been used for burials

caol: from the Gaelic for "narrow." Pronounced "kweil," it is sometimes used to refer to a strait or a firth

ceilidh: pronounced "keili," this is a lively social event with Gaelic music, singing, and dancing

clan: a close-knit group of families, usually originating from the Scottish Highlands, who share a kinship and a connection to the same ancestral ground

coire or corrie: a round hollow, often found on mountainsides or valleys

coorie: a Scottish word meaning to snuggle, or get cozy, which is sometimes now used to describe a wellness trend that encourages embracing small Scottish pleasures

coos: slang for cow, when referring to Highland cows (Heilan' coo)

corbett: the name given to mountains in Scotland 2,500-3,000 feet high (762-914 m)

crag or creag: rock or rockface

crannog: an ancient home, often built on stilts, found in Scottish lochs

crofter: a person who farms a croft (plot of land)

dram: a small drink of an alcoholic spirit—in Scotland, usually whisky

faerie: an alternative spelling of *fairy*, a mythical being that appears in many a folktale

first-foot: the first person to cross the threshold of a house on New Year's/Hogmanay

firth: narrow inlet of the sea

gillie: someone who accompanies you on a fishing or hunting trip

glen: a narrow valley

gloaming: dusk or twilight

Highlands: This refers to a region that encompasses much of the northern two-thirds of Scotland and includes many mountain ranges. The Highlands was traditionally home to clans, many of whom descended from the Gaels. Since the mid-19th century, it has been sparsely populated.

Hogmanay: the name for New Year's Eve in Scotland; the term originated in the 17th century, perhaps of Norman French origin

howe: a depression in the landscape, usually a basin or valley

howff: a welcoming meeting place, normally a pub

kelpie: a sinister water spirit that often pops up in Scottish folklore, normally taking the form of a horse and often taking pleasure in the drowning of sailors. There is said to be one in Loch Coruisk on the Isle of Skye.

kilt: a knee-length pleated skirt of tartan, traditionally worn by Highlanders

kirk: a church; sometimes used to differentiate between the Church of Scotland and the Church of England

kyle: a narrow strait or channel of water

laird: estate owner

loch: in Scotland it can be used to describe a lake (often landlocked) or an inlet of the sea

Lowlands: a relatively low-lying region that lies south and east of the Highlands

machair: a fertile grassy plain enriched by sand and shells blown in from the coast, where wildlife and wildflowers are in abundance

manse: the home or, more often, former home of a minister of the clergy

munro: a mountain in Scotland that is at least 3,000 feet (914 m) high

mushy peas: a side dish of mashed peas, which usually accompanies fish and chips

Scotch: related to Scotch whisky, this is malt or grain whisky made in Scotland that must be aged for a minimum of three years. Most Scottish people do not respond well to being labeled "Scotch" themselves (stick to Scottish or Scots); they prefer to reserve the term for whisky or Scotch eggs (a hard-boiled egg wrapped in sausage meat, covered in breadcrumbs, and deep-fried; it isn't actually uniquely Scottish but eaten all over the UK)

shiel: a basic, rough shelter, typically used by shepherds on high ground

single malt: whisky containing water and malted barley from a single distillery

sporran: part of Highland dress, this small pouch hangs from round the waist at the front of a kilt

strath: a valley, wider and usually more shallow than a glen

tartan: woolen cloth woven in a pattern of checks or crossed lines that is usually associated with a particular Scottish clan or region

thane: a historical title often held by a clan chief, who was awarded land by the Scottish king

tweed: a rough woolen cloth, renowned for its hardiness; originating from Scotland, it is typically woven of spun wool of different colors, giving it a speckled finish

weegie: a slang term for someone from Glasgow. It can sometimes be seen as derogatory, so use it sparingly

wynd: a narrow passageway

Scottish Phrases

The main language spoken in Scotland is English, but of course, even if all the people you encounter speak English, different accents and dialects may still leave you baffled. One thing you should bear in mind is that Scottish people like to abbreviate… a lot. Below are some common phrases and words you will undoubtedly come across regularly. This list is by no means exhaustive but gives you a taste of what to expect.

auld: old, as in "Auld Reekie," a nickname for Edinburgh

aye: yes

blether: what the English might call "small talk," to blether is simply to chat about not very much; you'll always find someone happy to blether with you

boggin': something that's horrible, often used to describe wet and miserable weather

bonnie: beautiful—the "bonnie" shores of Loch Ness

braw: something good or pleasing; it can also mean finely dressed

dae: do

dinnae: slang for "I don't"

dreich: dreary or bleak—usually used in reference to the weather

guid: pronounced "gid," it quite simply means "good"

havenae: have not

ken: know, as in "Ah dinnae ken," or "I don't know"

laddie: a young man or boy

lassie: a young woman or girl

mingin': really unpleasant—again, it is often used to describe the weather

muckle: a lot, or big

nae bother: not a problem

nay: no

reek: bad smell as in "Auld Reekie"

roastin': really, really hot, as in "it's roastin'" on a sunny day

scran: food, usually something tasty

wee: little—a much-used adjective to describe pretty much anything

yer: your

Suggested Reading

There are many, many books dedicated to Scotland, its landscape, and its history—believe me, my shelves are buckling at present and still there are so many more I'd like to buy.

There are also many books written by Scottish authors that in some way were inspired by the land of their home, from the brooding, gloomy graveyards, alleyways, and Gothic buildings of Edinburgh and Glasgow that helped shape J. K. Rowling's hugely popular *Harry Potter* books, to the childhood imaginings of J. M. Barrie, creator of the magical *Peter Pan.*

"Tartan Noir" has become a popular label for crime fiction from these shores, used to cover a huge variety of the books, from the psychological prowess of Val McDermid, to Ian Rankin's barely cloaked critique of Scottish society by way of his working-class protagonist Inspector Rebus, to the brooding atmosphere and sinister turns of Ann Cleeves's "Shetland" novels. Maybe it's the dark underbelly of its cities, the empty, desolate landscapes where you get the sense that anything could happen to you and no one would ever know, or the torrential rain,

threatening clouds, and ominous mountains that cast long shadows, but Scotland seems to fire the darkest of imaginations.

Below is a list of books, poems, and songs that I believe will enrich your travels in Scotland and give you a deeper understanding of its geography, history, culture, nature, people, and perhaps most importantly, its humor.

HISTORY AND BACKGROUND

The History of Scotland, Neil Oliver, 2010. From its geological origins through its early settlers, colonists, and bloody power battles, Scotland is revealed by archaeologist Oliver, who weaves the story together in a way that is both digestible and utterly enthralling.

Waverley, Sir Walter Scott, 1814. Scott's first foray into prose fiction, which tells the story of an English gentleman in the lead up to the Jacobite Rebellion of 1745, proved hugely successful. Other books followed, including *Rob Roy* in 1817, and so the romantic depiction of the Highlanders had begun.

A Journey to the Western Isles of Scotland, Samuel Johnson, 1775. This travelogue, written from the point of view of lexicographer Johnson (often called Dr. Johnson), depicts an 83-day journey that Johnson and his good friend, Scotsman James Boswell, took in 1773. The book is often published in one volume with Boswell's account, *A Journal of a Tour to the Hebrides,* to show the differing perspectives of the same trip.

Orkneyinga Saga: the History of the Earls of Orkney. The only real written record of life on the North Isles from the time of the Vikings, this book, written by an unknown writer or writers probably of Icelandic origin, tells the story of successive Earls of Orkney and how they claimed and held onto or lost power. Much of what we know of Orkney from this time comes from this book.

The Jacobites: Britain & Europe 1688-1788, Daniel Szechi, 2019 (2nd edition). There are innumerable books about the cause of the Jacobites, the various risings, and their crushing defeat at Culloden, but I've chosen this one as it is both accessible and comprehensive and it includes a complete revision of Szechi's 1994 work.

An Illustrated Treasury of Scottish Folk and Fairy Tales, Theresa Breslin and Kae Leiper, 2012. For me, a large part of the magic of Scotland is in its folktales, a love of which was implanted in me as a young child when my Irish granny told me how she'd once been taken away by the faeries. This beautifully illustrated collection of stories, retold with sparkling wit and energy, is a great way of enchanting the youngest members of your family or the child in you.

HUMOR

Made in Scotland: My Grand Adventures in a Wee Country, Billy Connolly, 2018. Born and bred in Glasgow, Billy Connolly is one of the city's most famous exports. His unique, self-deprecating humor and art of storytelling have led to international recognition. In this book he tells of his travels in Scotland and why he is so proud to hail from here, even though he now lives in America.

Whisky Galore, Compton Mackenzie, 1947. This comic novel, turned into an Ealing comedy and remade in 2017, imagines what would happen if a small Hebridean isle were to run out of whisky. The island's menfolk go into a type of mourning until a government ship with thousands of cases of whisky runs aground off its shores. Cue lots of japes as the islanders plot to replenish their stores, and then some.

44 Scotland Street, Alexander McCall Smith, 2004. For some gentle satire and a little leg-pulling of some of the snobbery and whims found in the residents of an upmarket urban street (it's set in Edinburgh's New Town), this, the first in a series of books, is a lovely, warm introduction to the capital.

To Be Continued, James Robertson, 2016. Set just a few weeks after the Scottish Referendum of 2014, this book follows the escapades of a freelance writer as he journeys from Edinburgh to the Highlands to interview a centenarian for a newspaper story, except things don't go quite as smoothly as that. There is a touch of the surreal in the main character's travel companion—a talking toad—and there are a few tongue-in-cheek nods to the "othering" of Scotland by visitors, which should give you a little understanding of some of the gentle ribbing you could experience here.

LANDSCAPE AND WILDLIFE

Findings, Kathleen Jamie, 2005. If you want to tap into the natural world of Scotland, then there really is no better book to encourage you to take your time and look, listen, and appreciate all that is going on around you.

Recommended Listening

Folk music is part of the fabric of Scotland. From the Celts to the Vikings, folktales, songs, and verses have been passed down through generations as a way of understanding and connecting with the land and remembering significant people and events. Many a Scottish pub hosts folk music sessions—some informal where the crowd can join in, others more organized with paid musicians. If you'd like to listen to some Scottish music before you come, then there are lots of artists who have recorded some of the country's most loved songs—from party-pleaser "The Bonnie Banks O' Loch Lomond" to the rousing "Wild Mountain Thyme (Will Ye Go Lassie Go)." Here are some other favorites to brush up on before your visit:

- **"The Skye Boat Song"** stirs a sense of patriotism among listeners whenever it is played. It tells the story of Bonnie Prince Charlie's escape, aided by Flora Macdonald, from Uist to the Isle of Skye. The song only entered the folklore cannon in the late 19th century when Anne Campbelle MacLeod supposedly first heard the Gaelic air being sung by boatmen who ferried her across Loch Coruisk on Skye, with lyrics added by songwriter Sir Harold Boulton.

- **"Flower of Scotland"** is one of the unofficial national anthems of Scotland (the others being "Scotland the Brave" and "Scots Wha Hae"). Sung with gusto at weddings and sporting celebrations, it was written in the 1960s by Roy Williamson of the band The Corries (a popular band who led the folk revival of the 1960s) and remembers Robert the Bruce's unexpected defeat of King Edward II of England at the Battle of Bannockburn in 1314.

- Eddi Reader is one of the best contemporary artists who performs folk songs. Among her repertoire, she does great versions of some Burns songs—her 2003 *Sings the Songs of Burns* album is excellent— including **"Red Red Rose,"** a beautiful ballad.

In the Cairngorms, Nan Shepherd, 1934. Shepherd's only book of poetry, this book could be put in the poetry section, but it has nature at its heart.

Ring of Bright Water, Gavin Maxwell, 1960. A classic, no doubt about it: Maxwell's book about the highs and lows of living in a remote cottage, just off the coast of Skye, with several otters, is one of the most successful nature books ever written.

A Last Wild Place, Mike Tomkies, 1984. This is part memoir part journal, telling of Tomkies life in a remote Highlands cottage on the shores of Loch Shiel with no phone, electricity, or gas over a period of 20 years, and the wildlife he observed there. He wrote 10 books from his time here, but this is his most famous.

POETRY

Robert Burns: The Scottish Bard, O. B. Duane, 1997. Scotland's national bard understood

the character of Scotland more than most and wrote of it so brilliantly in the language of Scots. This anthology, which includes some of his finest poems, is a great introduction to his work.

Hallaig and Other Poems: Selected Poems of Sorley MacLean, Angus Peter Campbell and Aonghas MacNeacail, 2014. This book's namesake poem, which hauntingly tells the story of the cleared village of Hallaig, invokes a sense of loss and longing that is so prevalent in MacLean's poetry.

Minstrelsy of the Scottish Borders, edited by Walter Scott, 1802. Sir Walter Scott grew up hearing Border ballads and even collected broadsheet ballads from sellers on the street, an interest that deepened as he got older. In the late 18th century, he began visiting Borders towns and villages to write down the traditional songs and ballads that people remembered, and this collection, which was added to right up until 1830, is the result of this dedicated toil.

Adoption Papers, Jackie Kay, 1991. It's hard to know where to begin with the works of Scotland's makar (national poet 2016-2021), so perhaps there is no better place than at the beginning. Renowned for her compassionate verses, honesty, and tackling of complex subjects—cultural identity and social injustices to name a couple—in her first collection of poetry, she broached the adoption system, which she understood from personal experience.

Finding Sea Glass, Poems from the Drift, Hannah Lavery, 2019. This thin pamphlet, published to accompany Lavery's spoken-word show that toured with the National Theatre of Scotland in 2019, asks some difficult questions, not least about Scotland and how it views race and national identity.

Internet Resources

ACCOMMODATIONS
AGRITOURISM
www.goruralscotland.com
Lots of farms are now offering places to stay, with other experiences such as farm tours, fruit-picking, and farm-to-fork cooking available. It's sustainable tourism in action as more of your money goes into supporting local communities.

BOOKING.COM
www.booking.com
This resource is a good place to compare prices and availability. It's easy to navigate, with options for all budgets, and it allows you to book directly with small B&Bs, often at slightly lower rates than you would otherwise pay.

AIRBNB
www.airbnb.co.uk
A lot of self-catering apartments and houses for hire are now only bookable through Airbnb. Prices have crept up as a result of COVID-19, but booking through a reputable site offers a degree of security.

SYKES COTTAGES
www.sykescottages.co.uk
These good standard cottages and houses can be hired across Scotland and are fairly priced.

COOL PLACES
www.coolplaces.co.uk/places-to-stay/uk/scotland
For something a little different, try trawling through this collection of places a little out of the ordinary.

HIKING
WALK HIGHLANDS
www.walkhighlands.co.uk
Walk Highlands is an incomparable resource for hiking routes and trekking advice across Scotland.

THE SCOTTISH OUTDOOR ACCESS CODE
www.outdooraccess-scotland.scot
Whether you are looking to hike, camp, or generally spend a lot of time outdoors, make sure you familiarize yourself with this.

TRANSPORTATION
SCOTRAIL
www.scotrail.co.uk
Visit ScotRail for details on train routes and connections across Scotland, as well as online tickets.

CALEDONIAN MACBRAYNE
www.calmac.co.uk
CalMac is the main ferry operator for trips to the islands.

CALEDONIAN SLEEPER

www.sleeper.scot

Take the Caledonian Sleeper for overnight train travel from London to Scotland.

STAGECOACH

www.stagecoachbus.com

Stagecoach provides the majority of local bus services throughout Scotland.

CITYLINK

www.citylink.co.uk

Use Citylink for buses between the main cities in Scotland.

TRAFFIC SCOTLAND

https://trafficscotland.org

Traffic Scotland provides up-to-date travel news for drivers.

MEDIA
THE HERALD

www.heraldscotland.com

This broadsheet newspaper is actually the longest-running national newspaper in the world.

SCOTSMAN

www.scotsman.com

The Scotsman is another reliable national newspaper that you will often find in hotels.

LGBT SCOTLAND

www.lgbt.scot

LGBT Scotland is a brilliant resource for lesbian, gay, bisexual, and transgender travelers in Scotland.

ANCESTRY
SCOTLANDSPEOPLE

www.scotlandspeople.gov.uk

Use this invaluable resource to research family connections to Scotland. Registration required to view records.

BLOGS
TRAVELS WITH A KILT

www.travelswithakilt.com

An excellent blog by Scotsman and eternal traveler Neil Robertson, this site is full of local insight and inspiring travel tales across the whole of Scotland.

THE WEE WHITE DUG

https://theweewhitedug.com

The premise here is simple but effective. Blogger Sam entices you with pictures of her absurdly cute Westie, Casper, set against beautiful backdrops, but then keeps you interested with informed and up-to-date travel content. If you're on Instagram you must follow them, if only for photos to cheer you on a miserable day.

THE CHAOTIC SCOT

www.thechaoticscot.com

Traveling Scotland without a car is possible, and nondriver Chaotic Scot will show you how. From transport links to local tour guides, lifts from hosts to pedaling around, it's refreshing to hear from someone who has done it all.

Index

List of Maps

Photo Credits

All photos © Sally Coffey except: Title page photo: Godrick | Dreamstime.com; page 4 © Stephen Bennett; page 5 © Wqsomeone | Dreamstime.com; page 6 © (top left) jim Divine | Unsplash.com; (top right) Stephen Bennett; (bottom) Stephen Bennett; page 7 © (top) Stephen Bennett; (bottom right) Paulina B | Unsplash.com; page 9 © (top) Stephen Bennett; page 10-11 © Drimafilm | Dreamstime.com; page 12 © (middle) Barmalini | Dreamstime.com; (bottom) Between11 | Dreamstime.com; page 13 © Jewhyte | Dreamstime.com; page 14 © (top) Swenstroop | Dreamstime.com; (middle) Photos841 | Dreamstime.com; (bottom) georgeclerk | istockphoto.com; page 15 (top) Courtesy Loch Bay Restaurant; (middle) PGregoryB | Dreamstime.com; (bottom) Migle Siauciulyte | Unsplash.com; page 16 © Pinkcandy | Dreamstime.com; page 19 © (bottom left) Stephen Bennett; page 20 © Stephen Bennett; page 23 © (bottom) Stephen Bennett; page 25 © (bottom) Jarino47 | Dreamstime.com; page 26 © (top) Mirco1 | Dreamstime.com; page 27 © (bottom) Mrcolobus | Dreamstime.com; page 28 © (top right) Stephen Bennett; page 30 © (bottom left) Julia Solonina | Unsplash.com; (bottom right) Peewam | Dreamstime.com; page 31 © (top left) Andrewsproule | Dreamstime.com; (top right) Donogl | Dreamstime.com; page 33 © Denisav | Dreamstime.com; page 34 © Shaiith | Dreamstime.com; page 35 (top left) courtesy Pickering's Gin / Peter Dibdin; page 46 © (top) Elxeneize | Dreamstime.com; (bottom) Matthi | Dreamstime.com; page 52 © (top) Stephen Bennett; (left middle) Chrisdorney | Dreamstime.com; page 54 © Elifranssens | Dreamstime. com; page 61 © (top right) Jewhyte | Dreamstime.com; (bottom) Between11 | Dreamstime.com; page 65 © (top left) Claudiodivizia | Dreamstime.com; page 66 courtesy Pickering's Gin / Peter Dibdin; page 87 © (top) Jewhyte | Dreamstime.com; (bottom) Stephen Bennett; page 97 © Onefivenine | Dreamstime. com; page 101 © (top left) Billybrant310 - Dreamstime.com; (bottom) Creativehearts | Dreamstime.com; page 104 © Silviaanestikova | Dreamstime.com; page 105 © (top left) Broker | Dreamstime.com; page 107 © (top left) Mikaelmales | Dreamstime.com; page 116 © Catalinapanait | Dreamstime.com; page 120 © Hayby | Dreamstime.com; page 137 © Maui01 | Dreamstime.com; page 141 © (top left) Mikaelmales | Dreamstime.com; (top right) Mino21 | Dreamstime.com; (bottom) Douglasmack | Dreamstime.com; page 143 © Numskyman | Dreamstime.com; page 144 © (top right) Douglasmack | Dreamstime.com; page 154 © (top) Anastasstyles | Dreamstime.com; page 160 © (bottom) Mlechanteur | Dreamstime. com; page 167 © (top left) Atlasphotoarchive | Dreamstime.com; (top right) Jack Skinner | Unsplash.com; (bottom) Joe Green | unsplash.com; page 175 © (top) Jewhyte | Dreamstime.com; (bottom) Bobbrooky | Dreamstime.com; page 184 © (top) Portadown | Dreamstime.com; (left middle) Frankwintermeyer | Dreamstime.com; (right middle)Donogl | Dreamstime.com; (bottom) Dalesd | Dreamstime.com; page 190 © Wqsomeone | Dreamstime.com; page 191 © (top left) Coleong | Dreamstime.com; (top right) Georgesixth | Dreamstime.com; page 202 © (top left) Douglasmack | Dreamstime.com; page 215 © left middle) Robertflynn | Dreamstime.com; page 223 © page 231 © Slidewarrior | Dreamstime. com; page 242 © (top) Magsellen | Dreamstime.com; (bottom) Ctollan | Dreamstime.com; page 244 © Epmiali | Dreamstime.com; page 245 © (top left) Hipproductions | Dreamstime.com; (top right) Juleberlin | Dreamstime.com; page 255 © (top) Juleberlin | Dreamstime.com; (bottom) Catuncia | Dreamstime.com; page 258 © Mango2friendly | Dreamstime.com; page 267 © (top) Jim6634 | Dreamstime.com; page 272 © (left middle) SnapTPhotography | Dreamstime.com; page 279 © (top) Chris148 | Dreamstime.com; (bottom) Matt6t6 | Dreamstime.com; page 280 © Holm610 | Dreamstime. com; page 283 © Arijeetbannerjee | Dreamstime.com; page 284 © (top left) Maisna | Dreamstime.com; page 294 © (top) Sa83lim | Dreamstime.com; (right middle) Anastasstyles | Dreamstime.com; page 300 © (top) Richardjohnsonuk | Dreamstime.com; (bottom) Stephen Bennett; page 305 © (bottom) Stephen Bennett; page 309 © (top) Julietphotography | Dreamstime.com; (bottom) Mrallen | Dreamstime.com; page 315 © (top) Spumador | Dreamstime.com; (bottom) Fintastique | Dreamstime.com; page 321 © (top) Stephen Bennett; (left middle)Stephen Bennett; (right middle)Stephen Bennett; (bottom) Martinmolcan | Dreamstime.com; page 325 © Giontzis | Dreamstime.com; page 326 © (top left) Pmstock | Dreamstime. com; (top right) Richie0703 | Dreamstime.com; page 334 © Lukassek | Dreamstime.com; page 337 © Josefkubes | Dreamstime.com; page 343 © (top right) Stevanzz | Dreamstime.com; (bottom) Lindamore | Dreamstime.com; page 344 © Rixie | Dreamstime.com; page 349 © David Dennis | Dreamstime.com; page 353 © Bnoragitt | Dreamstime.com; page 355 Courtesy Loch Bay Restaurant; page 359 © (top) Adrianpluskota | Dreamstime.com; (bottom) Hobbess4 | Dreamstime.com; page 363 © (top) Catuncia

Acknowledgments

Thanks to the many people who have provided useful hints and tips, and guided me on my travels. From old friends who shared their favorite places, to chance meetings with locals, and more thorough discussions with tourism businesses and operators. I've lost count of the number of tours I took with people who went out of their way to walk me through unfamiliar areas (sometimes literally) and explain local issues, geology, history, and environmental concerns.

Neil MacLeod of Caledonian Discovery (and general font of all knowledge), Alistair Danter of SkyeConnect and Alistair MacKay, a Skye-based filmmaker and Gaelic enthusiast, offered many insights.

Local tourism providers Alistair McQueen, David Malcolm, and Rebecca Hutton were infinitely helpful.

David Whiteford, former chairman of the North Highlands Initiative, was my go-to for so many questions, while Robert and Sally-Ann James of North Coast Explorer proved their knowledge of the North Coast 500 went far beyond the obvious.

Katie Strang of the Scottish Geology Trust, ecologist David Lambie, landowner Paul Lister, and the Scottish Rewilding Alliance helped me get my head around subjects that were relatively new to me, while Walk Highlands provided essential guidance.

VisitScotland was, of course, a useful resource, but more localized tourism organizations also proved invaluable assistance. The team at Glasgow Life was super helpful, as were staff at Loch Lomond and The Trossachs National Park, Explore Islay and Jura, VisitAberdeenshire, Visit Dundee, Visit Arran, The Coig and Outer Hebrides Tourism, among others.

My editor at Moon Travel, Megan Anderluh, was a voice of reason and stopped me from deviating from the schedule too often, while Hannah Brezack, my associate managing editor helped get me past the finish line. Thanks too, to all the staff behind the scenes at Moon Travel that helped bring this book to publication in trying times.

My occasional travel companions Cheryl Carroll, Michelle Dowd, Siobhan Murray, and Anna Garrod provided support and many, many laughs on various trips, breaking up the loneliness of solo travel, and also acting as useful soundboards.

And lastly, a big thanks to my husband Stephen, who kept the home fires burning while I nipped off on yet another research trip, and our two sons, Arthur and Stanley, who took our numerous Scottish road trips in their stride. I couldn't have done this without them.

Embark on an epic journey along the historic Camino de Santiago, stroll the top European cities, or chase Norway's northern lights with Moon Travel Guides!

FULLY REVISED AND UPDATED

MOON

CAMINO DE SANTIAGO

SACRED SITES, HISTORIC VILLAGES, LOCAL FOOD & WINE

BEEBE BAHRAMI

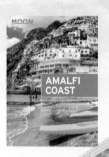

MOON

AMALFI COAST

LAURA THAYER

MOON

AMSTERDAM
BRUSSELS & BRUGES

MOON

CROATIA & SLOVENIA

SHANN FOUNTAIN ALIPOUR

MOON

FRENCH RIVIERA:
NICE, CANNES, MONACO & ST-TROPEZ

JON BRYANT

MOON

ICELAND

JENNA GOTTLIEB

WITH A ROAD TRIP ON THE RING ROAD

MOON

IRELAND

CAMILLE DeANGELIS

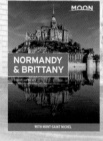

MOON

NORMANDY & BRITTANY

JAMIE HERBERG

WITH MONT-SAINT MICHEL

MOON

NORWAY

DAVID NIKEL

MOON

PORTUGAL

MOON

PRAGUE, VIENNA & BUDAPEST

JENNIFER D. WALKER & AURUUN BLAUVELT

MOON

PROVENCE

JAMIE IVEY

MOON

ROME,
FLORENCE & VENICE

MEREDITH TENNANT

MOON

SOUTHERN ITALY

LINDA SARRIS & LAURA THAYER

SICILY, PUGLIA, NAPLES & THE AMALFI COAST

WANDERLUST

WANDERLUST
Road Trips

40 BEAUTIFUL DRIVES AROUND THE WORLD

MOON

WANDERLUST
a traveler's guide to the globe

MOON

CREATE YOUR BUCKET LIST

LONDON WALKS

See the City Like a Local

MOON

NEW YORK CITY WALKS

See the City Like a Local

MOON

PARIS WALKS

See the City Like a Local

MOON

ROME WALKS

See the City Like a Local

MOON

Trips to Remember

CHILE
STEPH DYSON

ECUADOR
& THE GALÁPAGOS ISLANDS
BETHANY PITTS

EGYPT
SARAH SMIERCIAK

GREEK ISLANDS & ATHENS
SARAH SOULI

ISLAND ESCAPES WITH TIMELESS VILLAGES, SCENIC HIKES, AND LOCAL FLAVORS

ICELAND
JENNA GOTTLIEB

WITH A ROAD TRIP ON THE RING ROAD

Japan

PLAN YOUR TRIP   AVOID THE CROWDS   EXPERIENCE THE REAL JAPAN

TRIP OF A LIFETIME

MACHU PICCHU
RYAN DUBE

MOROCCO

PORTUGAL

PRAGUE, VIENNA & BUDAPEST
JENNIFER D. & AUBURN SCALLONI

ROME, FLORENCE & VENICE

Epic Treks

FULLY REVISED AND UPDATED

CAMINO DE SANTIAGO

SACRED SITES, HISTORIC VILLAGES, LOCAL FOOD & WINE

BEEBE BAHRAMI

Drive & Hike

APPALACHIAN TRAIL

THE BEST TRAIL TOWNS, DAY HIKES, AND ROAD TRIPS IN BETWEEN

TIMOTHY MALCOLM

Drive & Hike

PACIFIC CREST TRAIL

THE BEST TRAIL TOWNS, DAY HIKES, AND ROAD TRIPS IN BETWEEN

CAROLINE HINCHLIFF

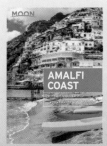

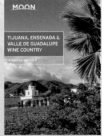

Get inspired for your next adventure

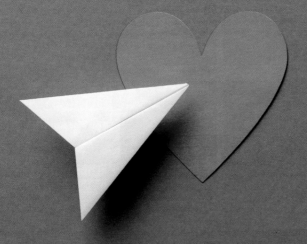

MAP SYMBOLS

≡≡≡	Expressway	○	City/Town	ⓘ	Information Center	
≡≡≡	Primary Road	⊙	State Capital	Ⓟ	Parking Area	
——	Secondary Road	✹	National Capital	♦	Church	
------	Unpaved Road	✪	Highlight	♣	Winery	
....	Trail	★	Point of Interest	⛨	Trailhead	
....	Ferry	•	Accommodation	Ⓣ	Train Station	
⊷⊷⊷	Railroad	▼	Restaurant/Bar	✈	Airport	
≡≡≡	Pedestrian Walkway	■	Other Location	✈	Airfield	
⊞⊞⊞	Stairs					

🛢	Whisky Distillery
⚑	Park
⚐	Golf Course
✛	Unique Feature
🗻	Waterfall
Λ	Camping
▲	Mountain
⛷	Ski Area

CONVERSION TABLES

°C = (°F − 32) / 1.8
°F = (°C × 1.8) + 32
1 inch = 2.54 centimeters (cm)
1 foot = 0.304 meters (m)
1 yard = 0.914 meters
1 mile = 1.6093 kilometers (km)
1 km = 0.6214 miles
1 fathom = 1.8288 m
1 chain = 20.1168 m
1 furlong = 201.168 m
1 acre = 0.4047 hectares
1 sq km = 100 hectares
1 sq mile = 2.59 square km
1 ounce = 28.35 grams
1 pound = 0.4536 kilograms
1 short ton = 0.90718 metric ton
1 short ton = 2,000 pounds
1 long ton = 1.016 metric tons
1 long ton = 2,240 pounds
1 metric ton = 1,000 kilograms
1 quart = 0.94635 liters
1 US gallon = 3.7854 liters
1 Imperial gallon = 4.5459 liters
1 nautical mile = 1.852 km

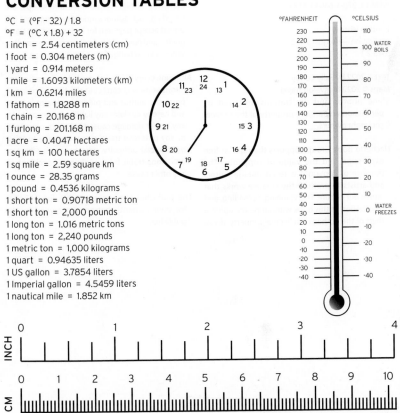

MOON SCOTLAND

Avalon Travel
Hachette Book Group
1700 Fourth Street
Berkeley, CA 94710, USA
www.moon.com

Editor: Megan Anderluh
Managing Editor: Hannah Brezack
Copy Editor: Barbara Schultz
Graphics Coordinator: Ravina Schneider
Production Coordinator: Ravina Schneider
Cover Design: Toni Tajima
Interior Design: Domini Dragoone
Map Editor: Kat Bennett
Cartographers: Brian Shotwell, Erin Greb, Karin Dahl, Kat Bennett
Proofreader: Lina Carmona

ISBN-13: 978-1-64049-417-6

Printing History
1st Edition — August 2022
5 4 3 2 1

Text © 2022 by Sally Coffey.
Maps © 2022 by Avalon Travel.

Front cover photo: Old Man of Storr, Isle of Skye. 1111IESPDJ | Gettyimages.com
Back cover photo: University of Glasgow cloisters. Perseo8888 | Dreamstime.com

Printed in Malaysia for Imago.